ISBN 978-1-4400-3504-3
PIBN 10181978

Similar Books Are Available from
www.forgottenbooks.com

APPEARANCE AND REALITY

SOME OPINIONS OF THE PRESS

"One of the most important books that have been published during the last twenty-five years."—J. H. Muirhead in *Literary Guide*.

"This is a truly great book. It is one of supreme interest and importance to the student of Ethics, as well as to the student of Metaphysics. Every particular thing in it is delightful. The style, though often paradoxical, is singularly bright and attractive. It is hardly too much to say that the book is altogether the most important independent work on Metaphysics that has ever been written in English."—*International Journal of Ethics*.

"This book must be studied and reckoned with by all students of Metaphysics."—*Guardian*.

APPEARANCE AND REALITY

A Metaphysical Essay

BY

F. H. BRADLEY, LL.D. Glasgow

Fellow of Merton College, Oxford

SIXTH IMPRESSION (CORRECTED)

LONDON: GEORGE ALLEN & UNWIN LTD.
RUSKIN HOUSE   40 MUSEUM STREET, W.C.

First Edition, *June*, 1893;
Second Edition (with an Appendix), *February*, 1897;
Third Impression, *June*, 1899;
Fourth Impression, *February*, 1906;
Fifth Impression (corrected), *November*, 1908;
Sixth Impression (corrected), *June*, 1916.

TO MY FRIEND

E—— R——

THIS UNWORTHY VOLUME

IS RESPECTFULLY

DEDICATED.

A.R.

PREFACE.

I HAVE described the following work as an essay in metaphysics. Neither in form nor extent does it carry out the idea of a system. Its subject indeed is central enough to justify the exhaustive treatment of every problem. But what I have done is incomplete, and what has been left undone has often been omitted arbitrarily. The book is a more or less desultory handling of perhaps the chief questions in metaphysics.

There were several reasons why I did not attempt a more systematic treatise, and to carry out even what I proposed has proved enough for my powers. I began this book in the autumn of 1887, and, after writing the first two fifths of it in twelve months, then took three years with the remainder. My work has been suspended several times through long intervals of compulsory idleness, and I have been glad to finish it when and how I could. I do not say this to obviate criticism on a book now deliberately published. But, if I had attempted more, I should probably have completed nothing.

And in the main I have accomplished all that lay within my compass. This volume is meant to be a critical discussion of first principles, and its object is to stimulate enquiry and doubt. To originality in any other sense it makes no claim. If the reader finds that on any points he has been led once more to reflect, I shall not have failed, so far as I can, to be original. But I should add that my book is not intended for the beginner. Its language in general I hope is not over-technical, but I have sometimes used terms intelligible only to the student. The index supplied is not an index but a mere collection of certain references.

My book does not design to be permanent, and will be satisfied to be negative, so long as that word implies an attitude of active questioning. The chief need of English philosophy is, I think, a sceptical study of first principles, and I do not know of any work which seems to meet this need sufficiently. By scepticism is not meant doubt about or disbelief in some tenet or tenets. I understand by it an attempt to become aware of and to doubt all preconceptions. Such scepticism is the result only of labour and education, but it is a training which cannot with impunity be neglected. And I know no reason why the English mind, if it would but subject itself to this discipline, should not in our day produce a rational system of first principles. If I have helped to forward this result, then, whatever form it may take, my ambition will be satisfied.

The reason why I have so much abstained from historical criticism and direct polemics may be briefly stated. I have written for English readers, and it would not help them much to learn my relation to German writers. Besides, to tell the truth, I do not know precisely that relation myself. And, though I have a high opinion of the metaphysical powers of the English mind, I have not seen any serious attempt in English to deal systematically with first principles. But things among us are not as they were some few years back. There is no established reputation which now does much harm to philosophy. And one is not led to feel in writing that one is face to face with the same dense body of stupid tradition and ancestral prejudice. Dogmatic Individualism is far from having ceased to flourish, but it no longer occupies the ground as the one accredited way of "advanced thinking." The present generation is learning that to gain education a man must study in more than one school. And to criticise a writer of whom you know nothing is now, even in philosophy, considered to be the thing that it is. We owe this improvement mostly to men of a time shortly before my own, and who insisted well, if perhaps incautiously, on the great claims of Kant and Hegel. But whatever other influences have helped, the result seems secured. There is a fair field for any one now, I believe, who has anything to say. And I feel no desire for mere polemics, which can seldom benefit oneself, and which seem no longer required by the state of our philosophy. I would rather keep my natural place as a learner among learners.

If anything in these pages suggests a more dogmatic frame of mind, I would ask the reader not hastily to adopt that suggestion. I offer him a set of opinions and ideas in part certainly wrong, but where and how much I am unable to tell him. That is for him to find out, if he cares to and if he can. Would it be better if I hinted in effect that he is in danger of expecting more, and that I, if I chose, perhaps might supply it? I have everywhere done my best, such as it is, to lay bare the course of ideas, and to help the reader to arrive at a judgment on each question. And, as I cannot suppose a necessity on my part to disclaim infallibility, I have not used set phrases which, if they mean anything, imply it. I have stated my opinions as truths whatever authority there may be against them, and however hard I may have found it to come to an opinion at all. And, if this is to be dogmatic, I certainly have not tried to escape dogmatism.

It is difficult again for a man not to think too much of his own pursuit. The metaphysician cannot perhaps be too much in earnest with metaphysics, and he cannot, as the phrase runs, take himself too seriously. But the same thing holds good with every other positive function of the universe. And the metaphysician, like other men, is prone to forget this truth. He forgets the narrow limitation of his special province, and, filled by his own poor inspiration, he ascribes to it an importance not its due. I do not know if anywhere in my work I may seem to have erred thus, but I am sure that such excess is not my conviction or my habitual mood. And to restore the balance, and as a confession possibly of equal defect, I will venture to transcribe some sentences from my note-book. I see written there that " Metaphysics is the finding of bad reasons for what we believe upon instinct, but to find these reasons is no less an instinct." Of Optimism I have said that " The world is the best of all possible worlds, and everything in it is a necessary evil." Eclecticism I have found preach that " Every truth is so true that any truth must be false," and Pessimism that " Where everything is bad it must be good to know the worst," or " Where all is rotten it is a man's work to cry stinking fish." About the Unity of Science I have set down that " Whatever you know it is all one," and of Introspection that " The one self-knowledge worth having is to know one's mind." The reader may judge how far these sentences form a *Credo*, and he must please himself again as to how seriously he takes a further extract : " To love unsatisfied the world is mystery, a mystery which love satisfied seems to comprehend. The latter is wrong only because it cannot be content without thinking itself right."

But for some general remarks in justification of metaphysics I may refer to the Introduction.

PREFACE

TO THE SECOND EDITION

IT is a pleasure to me to find that a new edition of this book is wanted. I am encouraged to hope that with all its defects it has helped to stimulate thought on first principles. And it has been a further pleasure to me to find that my critics have in general taken this work in the spirit in which it was offered, whether they have or have not found themselves in agreement with its matter. And perhaps in some cases sympathy with its endeavour may have led them to regard its shortcomings too leniently. I on my side have tried to profit by every comment, though I have made no attempt to acknowledge each, or to reply to it in detail. But I fear that some criticisms must have escaped my notice, since I have discovered others by mere chance.

For this edition I have thought it best not to make many alterations; but I have added in an Appendix, beside some replies to objections, a further explanation and discussion of certain difficulties.

TABLE OF CONTENTS.

Book I. Appearance.

Book II.—Reality.

INTRODUCTION.

THE writer on metaphysics has a great deal against him. Engaged on a subject which more than others demands peace of spirit, even before he enters on the controversies of his own field, he finds himself involved in a sort of warfare. He is confronted by prejudices hostile to his study, and he is tempted to lean upon those prejudices, within him and around him, which seem contrary to the first. It is on the preconceptions adverse to metaphysics in general that I am going to make some remarks by way of introduction. We may agree, perhaps, to understand by metaphysics an attempt to know reality as against mere appearance, or the study of first principles or ultimate truths, or again the effort to comprehend the universe, not simply piecemeal or by fragments, but somehow as a whole. Any such pursuit will encounter a number of objections. It will have to hear that the knowledge which it desires to obtain is impossible altogether; or, if possible in some degree, is yet practically useless; or that, at all events, we can want nothing beyond the old philosophies. And I will say a few words on these arguments in their order.

(a) The man who is ready to prove that metaphysical knowledge is wholly impossible has no right here to any answer. He must be referred for conviction to the body of this treatise. And he can hardly refuse to go there, since he himself has, perhaps unknowingly, entered the arena. He is a brother metaphysician with a rival theory of first principles. And this is so plain that I must excuse myself from dwelling on the point. To say the reality is such that our knowledge cannot reach it, is a claim to know reality ; to urge that our knowledge is of a kind which must fail to transcend appearance, itself implies that transcendence. For, if we had no idea of a beyond, we should assuredly not know how to talk about failure or success. And the test, by which we distinguish them, must obviously be some acquaintance with the nature of the goal. Nay, the would-be sceptic, who presses on us the contradictions of our thoughts, himself asserts dogmatically. For these contradictions might be ultimate and absolute truth, if the nature of the reality were not known to be otherwise. But this introduction is not the place to discuss a class of objections which are themselves, however unwillingly, metaphysical views, and which a little acquaintance with the subject commonly serves to dispel. So far as is necessary, they will be dealt with in their proper place ; and I will therefore pass to the second main argument against metaphysics.

(*b*) It would be idle to deny that this possesses great force. " Metaphysical knowledge," it insists, " may be possible theoretically, and even actual, if you please, to a certain degree ; but, for all that, it is practically no knowledge worth the name." And this objection may be rested on various grounds. I will state some of these, and will make the answers which appear to me to be sufficient.

The first reason for refusing to enter on our field is an appeal to the confusion and barrenness which prevail there. " The same problems," we hear it often, " the same disputes, the same sheer failure. Why not abandon it and come out ? Is there nothing else more worth your labour ?" To this I shall reply more fully soon, but will at present deny entirely that the problems have not altered. The assertion is about as true and about as false as would be a statement that human nature has not changed. And it seems indefensible when we consider that in history metaphysics has not only been acted on by the general development, but has also reacted. But, apart from historical questions, which are here not in place, I am inclined to take my stand on the admitted possibility. If the object is not impossible, and the adventure suits us—what then? Others far better than ourselves have wholly failed—so you say. But the man who succeeds is not apparently always the man of most merit, and even in philosophy's cold world perhaps some fortunes go by favour. One never knows until one tries.

But to the question, if seriously I expect to succeed, I must, of course, answer, No. I do not suppose, that is, that satisfactory knowledge is possible. How much we can ascertain about reality will be discussed in this book; but I may say at once that I expect a very partial satisfaction. I am so bold as to believe that we have a knowledge of the Absolute, certain and real, though I am sure that our comprehension is miserably incomplete. But I dissent emphatically from the conclusion that, because imperfect, it is worthless. And I must suggest to the objector that he should open his eyes and should consider human nature. Is it possible to abstain from thought about the universe? I do not mean merely that to every one the whole body of things must come in the gross, whether consciously or unconsciously, in a certain way. I mean that, by various causes, even the average man is compelled to wonder and to reflect. To him the world, and his share in it, is a natural object of thought, and seems likely to remain one. And so, when poetry, art, and religion have ceased wholly to interest, or when they show no longer any tendency to struggle with ultimate problems and to come to an understanding with them; when the sense of mystery and enchantment no longer draws the mind to wander aimlessly and to love it knows not what; when, in short, twilight has no charm—then metaphysics will be worthless. For the question (as things are now) is not whether we are to reflect and ponder on ultimate truth—for perhaps most of us do that, and are not likely to cease. The question is merely as to the way in which this should be done. And the claim of metaphysics is surely not unreasonable. Metaphysics takes its stand on this side of human nature, this desire to think about and comprehend reality. And it merely asserts that, if the attempt is to be made, it should be done as thoroughly as our nature permits. There is no claim on its part to supersede other functions of the human mind; but it protests that, if we are to think, we should sometimes try to think properly. And the opponent of metaphysics, it appears to me, is driven to a dilemma. He must either condemn all reflection on the essence of things,—and, if so, he breaks, or, rather, tries to break, with part of the highest side of human nature,—or else he allows us to think, but not to think strictly. He permits, that is to say, the exercise of thought so long as it is entangled with other functions of our being; but as soon as it attempts a pure development of its own, guided by the principles of its own distinctive working, he prohibits it forthwith. And this appears to be a paradox, since it seems equivalent to saying, You may satisfy your instinctive longing to reflect, so long as you do it in a way which is unsatisfactory. If your character is such that in your thought is satisfied by what does not, and cannot, pretend to be thought proper, that is quite legitimate. But if you are constituted otherwise, and if in you a more strict thinking is a want of your nature, that is by all means to be crushed out. And, speaking for myself, I must regard this as at once dogmatic and absurd.

But the reader, perhaps, may press me with a

different objection. Admitting, he may say, that thought about reality is lawful, I still do not understand why, the results being what they are, you should judge it to be desirable. And I will try to answer this frankly. I certainly do not suppose that it would be good for every one to study metaphysics, and I cannot express any opinion as to the number of persons who should do so. But I think it quite necessary, even on the view that this study can produce no positive results, that it should still be pursued. There is, so far as I can see, no other certain way of protecting ourselves against dogmatic superstition. Our orthodox theology on the one side, and our common-place materialism on the other side (it is natural to take these as prominent instances), vanish like ghosts before the daylight of free sceptical enquiry. I do not mean, of course, to condemn wholly either of these beliefs; but I am sure that either, when taken seriously, is the mutilation of our nature. Neither, as experience has amply shown, can now survive in the mind which has thought sincerely on first principles; and it seems desirable that there should be such a refuge for the man who burns to think consistently, and yet is too good to become a slave, either to stupid fanaticism or dishonest sophistry. That is one reason why I think that metaphysics, even if it end in total scepticism, should be studied by a certain number of persons.

And there is a further reason which, with myself perhaps, has even more weight. All of us, I presume, more or less, are led beyond the region of ordinary facts. Some in one way and some in others, we seem to touch and have communion with what is beyond the visible world. In various manners we find something higher, which both supports and humbles, both chastens and transports us. And, with certain persons, the intellectual effort to understand the universe is a principal way of thus experiencing the Deity. No one, probably, who has not felt this, however differently he might describe it, has ever cared much for metaphysics. And, where-ever it has been felt strongly, it has been its own justification. The man whose nature is such that by one path alone his chief desire will reach con-summation, will try to find it on that path, whatever it may be, and whatever the world thinks of it; and, if he does not, he is contemptible. Self-sacrifice is too often the "great sacrifice" of trade, the giving cheap what is worth nothing. To know what one wants, and to scruple at no means that will get it, may be a harder self-surrender. And this appears to be another reason for some persons pursuing the study of ultimate truth.

(c) And that is why, lastly, existing philosophies cannot answer the purpose. For whether there is progress or not, at all events there is change; and the changed minds of each generation will require a difference in what has to satisfy their intellect. Hence there seems as much reason for new philo-sophy as there is for new poetry. In each case the fresh production is usually much inferior to something already in existence; and yet it answers a purpose if it appeals more personally to the reader. What is really worse may serve better to promote, in cer-tain respects and in a certain generation, the exercise of our best functions. And that is why, so long as we alter, we shall always want, and shall always have, new metaphysics.

I will end this introduction with a word of warn-ing. I have been obliged to speak of philosophy as a satisfaction of what may be called the mystical side of our nature—a satisfaction which, by certain per-sons, cannot be as well procured otherwise. And I may have given the impression that I take the metaphysician to be initiated into something far higher than what the common herd possesses. Such a doctrine would rest on a most deplorable error, the superstition that the mere intellect is the highest side of our nature, and the false idea that in the intellectual world work done on higher subjects is for that reason higher work. Certainly the life of one man, in comparison with that of another, may be fuller of the Divine, or, again, may realize it with an intenser consciousness; but there is no calling or pursuit which is a private road to the Deity. And assuredly the way through speculation upon ultimate truths, though distinct and legitimate, is not superior to others. There is no sin, however prone to it the philosopher may be, which philosophy can justify so little as spiritual pride.

BOOK I.

APPEARANCE

CHAPTER I.

PRIMARY AND SECONDARY QUALITIES.

THE fact of illusion and error is in various ways forced early upon the mind; and the ideas by which we try to understand the universe, may be considered as attempts to set right our failure. In this division of my work I shall criticize some of these, and shall endeavour to show that they have not reached their object. I shall point out that the world, as so understood, contradicts itself; and is therefore appearance, and not reality.

In this chapter I will begin with the proposal to make things intelligible by the distinction between primary and secondary qualities. This view is old, but, I need hardly say, is far from obsolete, nor can it ever disappear. From time to time, without doubt, so long as there are human beings, it will reappear as the most advanced and as the one scientific theory of first principles. And I begin with it, because it is so simple, and in the main so easily disposed of. The primary qualities are those aspects of what we perceive or feel, which, in a word, are spatial; and the residue is secondary. The solution of the world's enigma lies in taking the former as reality, and everything else somehow as derivative, and as more or less justifiable appearance.

The foundation of this view will be known to the reader, but for the sake of clearness I must trace it in outline. We assume that a thing must be self-consistent and self-dependent. It either has a quality or has not got it. And, if it has it, it can not have it only sometimes, and merely in this or that relation. But such a principle is the condemnation of secondary qualities.

It matters very little how in detail we work with it. A thing is coloured, but not coloured in the same way to every eye ; and, except to some eye, it seems not coloured at all. Is it then coloured or not? And the eye—relation to which appears somehow to make the quality—does that itself possess colour? Clearly not so, unless there is another eye which sees it. Nothing therefore is really coloured; colour seems only to belong to what itself is colourless. And the same result holds, again, with cold and heat. A thing may be cold or hot according to different parts of my skin ; and, without some relation to a skin, it seems without any such quality. And, by a like argument, the skin is proved not itself to own the quality, which is hence possessed by nothing. And sounds, not heard, are hardly real ; while what hears them is the ear, itself not audible, nor even always in the enjoyment of sound. With smell and with taste the case seems almost worse ; for they are more obviously mixed up with our pleasure and pain. If a thing tastes only in the mouth, is taste its quality? Has it smell where there is no nose? But nose and tongue are smelt or tasted only by another nose or tongue ; nor can either again be said to have as a quality what they sometimes enjoy. And the pleasant and disgusting, which we boldly locate in the object, how can they be there? Is a thing delightful or sickening really and in itself? Am even I the constant owner of these wandering adjectives ?—But I will not weary the reader by insistence on detail. The argument shows everywhere that things have secondary qualities only for an organ; and that the organ itself has these

qualities in no other way.   They are found to be
adjectives, somehow supervening on relations of the
extended.   The extended only is real.   And the
facts of what is called subjective sensation, under
which we may include dream and delusion of all
kinds, may be adduced in support.   They go to
show that, as we can have the sensation without the
object, and the object without the sensation, the
one cannot possibly be a quality of the other.   The
secondary   qualities,   therefore,   are   appearance,
coming from the reality, which itself has no quality
but extension.

This argument has two sides, a negative and a
positive.   The first denies that secondary qualities
are the actual nature of things, the second goes on
to make an affirmation about the primary.   I will
enquire first if the negative assertion is justified.   I
will not dispute the truth of the principle that, if a
thing has a quality, it must have it ; but I will ask
whether on this basis some defence may not be
made.   And we may attempt it in this way.   All the
arguments, we may protest, do but show defect in, or
interference with, the organ of perception.   The
fact that I cannot receive the secondary qualities
except under certain conditions, fails to prove that
they are not there and existing in the thing.   And,
supposing that they are there, still the argument
proves their absence, and is hence unsound.   And
sheer delusion and dreams do not overthrow this
defence.   The qualities are constant in the things
themselves ; and, if they fail to impart themselves,
or impart themselves wrongly, that is always due to
something outside their nature.   If we could perceive them, they are there.

But this way of defence seems hardly tenable.
For, if the qualities impart themselves never except
under conditions, how in the end are we to say
what they are when unconditioned ? Having once
begun, and having been compelled, to take their

appearance into the account, we cannot afterwards
strike it out. It being admitted that the qualities
come to us always in a relation, and always as
appearing, then certainly we know them only as
appearance. And the mere supposition that in
themselves they may really be what they are, seems
quite meaningless or self-destructive. Further, we
may enforce this conclusion by a palpable instance.
To hold that one's mistress is charming, ever and in
herself, is an article of faith, and beyond reach of
question. But, if we turn to common things, the
result will be otherwise. We observed that the
disgusting and the pleasant may make part of the
character of a taste or a smell, while to take these
aspects as a constant quality, either of the thing or
of the organ, seems more than unjustifiable, and
even almost ridiculous. And on the whole we
must admit that the defence has broken down. The
secondary qualities must be judged to be merely
appearance.

But are they the appearance of the primary, and
are these the reality? The positive side of the
contention was that in the extended we have the
essence of the thing; and it is necessary to ask if
this conclusion is true. The doctrine is, of course,
materialism, and is a very simple creed. What is
extended, together with its spatial relations, is substantive fact, and the rest is adjectival. We have
not to ask here if this view is scientific, in the sense
of being necessarily used for work in some sciences.
That has, of course, nothing to do with the question now before us, since we are enquiring solely
whether the doctrine is true. And, regarded in this
way, perhaps no student would call materialism
scientific.

I will indicate briefly the arguments against the
sole reality of primary qualities. (a) In the first pᵉ,
we may ask how, in the nature of the extended,labe
terms stand to the relations which have to hold

between them.   This is a problem to be handled later (Chapter iv.), and I will only remark here that its result is fatal to materialism.   And, (*b*) in the second place, the relation of the primary qualities to the secondary—in which class feeling and thought have presumably to be placed — seems wholly unintelligible.   For nothing is actually removed from existence by being labelled "appearance."   What appears is there, and must be dealt with ; but materialism has no rational way of dealing with appearance.   Appearance must belong, and yet cannot belong, to the extended.   It neither is able to fall somewhere apart, since there is no other real place ; nor ought it, since, if so, the relation would vanish and appearance would cease to be derivative. But, on the other side, if it belongs in any sense to the reality, how can it be shown not to infect that with its own unreal character ?   Or we may urge that matter must cease to be itself, if qualified essentially by all that is secondary.   But, taken otherwise, it has become itself but one out of two elements, and is not the reality.

And, (*c*) thirdly, the line of reasoning which showed that secondary qualities are not real, has equal force as applied to primary.   The extended comes to us only by relation to an organ ; and, whether the organ is touch or is sight or muscle-feeling — or whatever else it may be — makes no difference to the argument.   For, in any case, the thing is perceived by us through an affection of our body, and never without that.   And our body itself is no exception, for we perceive that, as extended, solely by the action of one part upon another percipient part.   That we have no miraculous intuition of our body as spatial reality is perfectly certain. But, if so, the extended thing will have its quality only when perceived by something else ; and the percipient something else is again in the same case. Nothing, in short, proves extended except in relation to another thing, which itself does not possess the quality, if you try to take it by itself. And, further, the objection from dream and delusion holds again. That objection urges that error points to a necessary relation of the object to our knowledge, even where error is not admitted. But such a relation would reduce every quality to appearance. We might, indeed, attempt once more here to hold the former line of defence. We might reply that the extended thing is a fact real by itself, and that only its relation to our percipience is variable. But the inevitable conclusion is not so to be averted. If a thing is known to have a quality only under a certain condition, there is no process of reasoning from this which will justify the conclusion that the thing, if unconditioned, is yet the same. This seems quite certain; and, to go further, if we have no other source of information, if the quality in question is non-existent for us except in one relation, then for us to assert its reality away from that relation is more than unwarranted. It is, to speak plainly, an attempt in the end without meaning. And it would seem that, if materialism is to stand, it must somehow get to the existence of primary qualities in a way which avoids their relation to an organ. But since, as we shall hereafter see (Chapter iv.), their very essence is relative, even this refuge is closed.

(d) But there is a more obvious argument against the sole reality of spatial qualities; and, if I were writing for the people an attack upon materialism, I should rest great weight on this point. Without secondary quality extension is not conceivable, and no one can bring it, as existing, before his mind if he keeps it quite pure. In short, it is the violent abstraction of one aspect from the rest, and the mere confinement of our attention to a single side of things, a fiction which, forgetting itself, takes a ghost for solid reality. And I will say a few words on this obvious answer to materialism.

That doctrine, of course, holds that the extended can be actual, entirely apart from every other quality. But extension is never so given. If it is visual, it must be coloured; and if it is tactual, or acquired in the various other ways which may fall under the head of the " muscular sense,"—then it is never free from sensations, coming from the skin, or the joints, or the muscles, or, as some would like tc add, from a central source. And a man may say what he likes, but he cannot think of extensior. without thinking at the same time of a " what " that is extended. And not only is this so, but particular differences, such as " up and down," " right and left," are necessary to the terms of the spatial re- lation. But these differences clearly are not merely spatial. Like the general " what," they will consist in all cases of secondary quality from a sensation of the kinds I have mentioned above. Some psycho- logists, indeed, could go further, and could urge that the secondary qualities are original, and the primary derivative; since extension (in their view) is a con- struction or growth from the wholly non-extended. I could not endorse that, but I can appeal to what is indisputable. Extension cannot be presented, or thought of, except as one with quality that is secondary. It is by itself a mere abstraction, for some purposes necessary, but ridiculous when taken as an existing thing. Yet the materialist, from defect of nature or of education, or probably both, worships without justification this thin product of his untutored fancy.

" Not without justification," he may reply, " since in the procedure of science the secondary qualities are explained as results from the primary. Obviously, therefore, these latter are independent and prior." But this is a very simple error. For suppose that you have shown that, given one element, A, an- other, b, does in fact follow on it; suppose that you can prove that b comes just the same, whether A is

A R.   C

attended by *c*, or *d*, or *e*, or any one of a number
of other qualities, you cannot go from this to the result that *A* exists and works naked. The secondary
b can be explained, you urge, as issuing from the
primary *A*, without consideration of aught else. Let
it be so ; but all that could follow is, that the *special*
natures of *A*'s accompaniments are not concerned
in the process. There is not only no proof, but there
is not even the very smallest presumption, that *A*
could act by itself, or could be a real fact if alone.
It is doubtless scientific to disregard certain aspects
when we work ; but to urge that therefore such aspects are not fact, and that what we use without
regard to them is an independent real thing,—this
is barbarous metaphysics.

We have found then that, if the secondary qualities are appearance, the primary are certainly not
able to stand by themselves. This distinction, from
which materialism is blindly developed, has been
seen to bring us no nearer to the true nature of
reality.

CHAPTER II.

SUBSTANTIVE AND ADJECTIVE.

WE have seen that the distinction of primary from secondary qualities has not taken us far. Let us, without regard to it, and once more directly turning to what meets us, examine another way of making that intelligible. We find the world's contents grouped into things and their qualities. The substantive and adjective is a time-honoured distinction and arrangement of facts, with a view to understand them and to arrive at reality. I must briefly point out the failure of this method, if regarded as a serious attempt at theory.

We may take the familiar instance of a lump of sugar. This is a thing, and it has properties, adjectives which qualify it. It is, for example, white, and hard, and sweet. The sugar, we say, *is* all that ; but what the *is* can really mean seems doubtful. A thing is not any one of its qualities, if you take that quality by itself ; if "sweet" were the same as "simply sweet," the thing would clearly be not sweet. And, again, in so far as sugar is sweet it is not white or hard ; for these properties are all distinct. Nor, again, can the thing be all its properties, if you take them each severally. Sugar is obviously not mere whiteness, mere hardness, and mere sweetness ; for its reality lies somehow in its unity. But if, on the other hand, we inquire what there can be in the thing beside its several qualities, we are baffled once more. We can discover no real unity existing outside these qualities, or, again, existing within them.

But it is our emphasis, perhaps, on the aspect of unity which has caused this confusion. Sugar is, of course, not the mere plurality of its different adjectives; but why should it be more than its properties in relation? When " white," " hard," "sweet," and the rest co-exist in a certain way, that is surely the secret of the thing. The qualities are, and are in relation. But here, as before, when we leave phrases we wander among puzzles. " Sweet," " white," and " hard" seem now the subjects about which we are saying something. We certainly do not predicate one of the other; for, if we attempt to identify them, they at once resist. They are in this wholly incompatible, and, so far, quite contrary. Apparently, then, a relation is to be asserted of each. One quality, A, is in relation with another quality, B. But what are we to understand here by is? We do not mean that " in relation with B " is A, and yet we assert that A is " in relation with B." In the same way C is called " before D," and E is spoken of as $being$ " to the right of F." We say all this, but from the interpretation, then " before D " is C, and " to the right of F" is E, we recoil in horror. No, we should reply, the relation is not identical with the thing. It is only a sort of attribute which inheres or belongs. The word to use, when we are pressed, should not be is, but only has. But this reply comes to very little. The whole question is evidently as to the meaning of has; and, apart from metaphors not taken seriously, there appears really to be no answer. And we seem unable to clear ourselves from the old dilemma, If you predicate what is different, you ascribe to the subject what it is not; and if you predicate what is not different, you say nothing at all.

Driven forward, we must attempt to modify our statement. We must assert the relation now, not of one term, but of both. A and B are identical in such a point, and in such another point they differ; or, again, they are so situated in space or in time. And thus we avoid *is*, and keep to *are*.   But, seriously, that does not look like the explanation of a difficulty ; it looks more like trifling with phrases.   For, if you mean that *A* and *B*, taken each severally, even " have " this relation, you are asserting what is false. But if you mean that *A* and *B* in such a relation are so related, you appear to mean nothing.   For here, as before, if the predicate makes no difference, it is idle ; but, if it makes the subject other than it is, it is false.

But let us attempt another exit from this bewildering circle.   Let us abstain from making the relation an attribute of the related, and let us make it more or less independent.   " There is a relation *C*, in which *A* and *B* stand ; and it appears with both of them."   But here again we have made no progress.   The relation *C* has been admitted different from *A* and *B*, and no longer is predicated of them. Something, however, seems to be said of this relation *C*, and said, again, of *A* and *B*.   And this something is not to be the ascription of one to the other.   If so, it would appear to be another relation, *D*, in which *C*, on one side, and, on the other side, *A* and *B*, stand.   But such a makeshift leads at once to the infinite process.   The new relation *D* can be predicated in no way of *C*, or of *A* and *B* ; and hence we must have recourse to a fresh relation, *E*, which comes between *D* and whatever we had before.   But this must lead to another, *F* ; and so on, indefinitely. Thus the problem is not solved by taking relations as independently real.   For, if so, the qualities and their relation fall entirely apart, and then we have said nothing.   Or we have to make a new relation between the old relation and the terms ; which, when it is made, does not help us.   It either itself demands a new relation, and so on without end, or it leaves us where we were, entangled in difficulties.

The attempt to resolve the thing into properties, each a real thing, taken somehow together with in-

dependent relations, has proved an obvious failure.
And we are forced to see, when we reflect, that a
relation standing alongside of its terms is a delusion.   If it is to be real, it must be so somehow at
the expense of the terms, or, at least, must be something which appears in them or to which they belong.
A relation between A and B implies really a substantial foundation within them.   This foundation, if we
say that A is like to B, is the identity X which holds
these differences together.   And so with space and
time—everywhere there must be a whole embracing
what is related, or there would be no differences and
no relation.   It seems as if a reality possessed differences, A and B, incompatible with one another and
also with itself.   And so in order, without contradiction, to retain its various properties, this whole
consents to wear the form of relations between them.
And this is why qualities are found to be some incompatible and some compatible.   They are all
different, and, on the other hand, because belonging
to one whole, are all forced to come together.   And
it is only where they come together distantly by the
help of a relation, that they cease to conflict.   On the
other hand, where a thing fails to set up a relation
between its properties, they are contrary at once.
Thus colours and smells live together at peace in the
reality; for the thing divides itself, and so leaves
them merely side by side within itself.   But colour
collides with colour, because their special identity
drives them together.   And here again, if the identity becomes relational by help of space, they are
outside one another, and are peaceful once more.
The "contrary," in short, consists of differences possessed by that which cannot find the relation which
serves to couple them apart.   It is marriage attempted without a *modus vivendi*.   But where the
whole, relaxing its unity, takes the form of an arrangement, there is co-existence with concord.
   I have set out the above mainly because of the

light which it throws upon the nature of the " contrary." It affords no solution of our problem of inherence. It tells us how we are forced to arrange things in a certain manner, but it does not justify that arrangement. The thing avoids contradiction by its disappearance into relations, and by its admission of the adjectives to a standing of their own. But it avoids contradiction by a kind of suicide. It can give no rational account of the relations and the terms which it adopts, and it cannot recover the real unity, without which it is nothing. The whole device is a clear makeshift. It consists in saying to the outside world, " I am the owner of these my adjectives," and to the properties, " I am but a relation, which leaves you your liberty." And to itself and for itself it is the futile pretence to have both characters at once. Such an arrangement may work, but the theoretical problem is not solved.

The immediate unity, in which facts come to us, has been broken up by experience, and later by reflection. The thing with its adjectives is a device for enjoying at once both variety and concord. But the distinctions, once made, fall apart from the thing, and away from one another. And our attempt to understand their relations brought us round merely to a unity, which confesses itself a pretence, or else falls back upon the old undivided substance, which admits of no relations. We shall see the hopelessness of its dilemma more clearly when we have examined how relation stands to quality. But this demands another chapter.

I will, in conclusion, dispose very briefly of a possible suggestion. The distinctions taken in the thing are to be held only, it may be urged, as the ways in which *we* regard it. The thing itself maintains its unity, and the aspects of adjective and substantive are only *our* points of view. Hence they do no injury to the real. But this defence is futile, since the question is how without

error we may think of reality. If then your collection of points of view is a defensible way of so
thinking, by all means apply it to the thing, and
make an end of our puzzle. Otherwise the thing,
without the points of view, appears to have no
character at all, and they, without the thing, to
possess no reality—even if they could be made
compatible among themselves, the one with the
other. In short, this distinction, drawn between
the fact and our manner of regarding it, only serves
to double the original confusion. There will now
be an inconsistency in my mind as well as in the
thing; and, far from helping, the one will but
aggravate the other.

CHAPTER III.

RELATION AND QUALITY.

It must have become evident that the problem, discussed in the last chapter, really turns on the respective natures of quality and relation. And the reader may have anticipated the conclusion we are now to reach. The arrangement of given facts into relations and qualities may be necessary in practice, but it is theoretically unintelligible. The reality, so characterized, is not true reality, but is appearance.

And it can hardly be maintained that this character calls for no understanding—that it is a unique way of being which the reality possesses, and which we have got merely to receive. For it most evidently has ceased to be something quite immediate. It contains aspects now distinguished and taken as differences, and which tend, so far as we see, to a further separation. And, if the reality really has a way of uniting these in harmony, that way assuredly is not manifest at first sight. On our own side those distinctions which even consciously we make may possibly in some way give the truth about reality. But, so long as we fail to justify them and to make them intelligible to ourselves, we are bound, so far, to set them down as mere appearance.

The object of this chapter is to show that the very essence of these ideas is infected and contradicts itself. Our conclusion briefly will be this. Relation presupposes quality, and quality relation. Each can be something neither together

with, nor apart from, the other; and the vicious
circle in which they turn is not the truth about
reality.

1. Qualities are nothing without relations. In
trying to exhibit the truth of this statement, I will
lay no weight on a considerable mass of evidence.
This, furnished by psychology, would attempt to
show how qualities are variable by changes of relation. The differences we perceive in many cases
seem to have been so created. But I will not
appeal to such an argument, since I do not see that
it could prove wholly the non-existence of original
and independent qualities. And the line of proof
through the necessity of contrast for perception
has, in my opinion, been carried beyond logical
limits. Hence, though these considerations have
without doubt an important bearing on our problem,
I prefer here to disregard them. And I do not
think that they are necessary.

We may proceed better to our conclusion in the
following way. You can never, we may argue, find
qualities without relations. Whenever you take
them so, they are made so, and continue so, by
an operation which itself implies relation. Their
plurality gets for us all its meaning through relations; and to suppose it otherwise in reality is
wholly indefensible. I will draw this out in greater
detail.

To find qualities without relations is surely impossible. In the field of consciousness, even when
we abstract from the relations of identity and difference, they are never independent. One is together with, and related to, one other, at the least,
—in fact, always to more than one. Nor will an
appeal to a lower and undistinguished state of mind,
where in one feeling are many aspects, assist us in
any way. I admit the existence of such states without any relation, but I wholly deny there the
presence of qualities. For if these felt aspects,

while merely felt, are to be called qualities proper, they are so only for the observation of an outside observer. And then for him they are given *as* aspects—that is, together with relations. In short, if you go back to mere unbroken feeling, you have no relations and no qualities. But if you come to what is distinct, you get relations at once.

I presume we shall be answered in this way. Even though, we shall be told, qualities proper can not be discovered apart from relations, that is no real disproof of their separate existence. For we are well able to distinguish them and to consider them by themselves. And for this perception certainly an operation of our minds is required. So far, therefore, as you say, what is different must be distinct, and, in consequence, related. But this relation does not really belong to the reality. The relation has existence only for us, and as a way of our getting to know. But the distinction, for all that, is based upon differences in the actual ; and these remain when our relations have fallen away or have been removed.

But such an answer depends on the separation of product from process, and this separation seems indefensible. The qualities, as distinct, are always made so by an action which is admitted to imply relation. They are made so, and, what is more, they are emphatically kept so. And you cannot ever get your product standing apart from its process. Will you say, the process is not essential ? But that is a conclusion to be proved, and it is monstrous to assume it. Will you try to prove it by analogy ? It is possible for many purposes to accept and employ the existence of processes and relations which do not affect specially the inner nature of objects. But the very possibility of so distinguishing in the end between inner and outer, and of setting up the inner as absolutely independent of all relation, is here in question. Mental

operations such as comparison, which presuppose in
the compared qualities already existing, could in no
case prove that these qualities depend on no relations
at all.   But I cannot believe that this is a matter to
be decided by analogy, for the whole case is briefly
this.   There is an operation which, removing one
part of what is given, presents the other part in
abstraction.   This result is never to be found anywhere apart from a persisting abstraction.   And, if
we have no further information, I can find no excuse
for setting up the result as being fact without the
process.   The burden lies wholly on the assertor,
and he fails entirely to support it.   The argument
that in perception one quality must be given first
and before others, and therefore cannot be relative,
is hardly worth mentioning.   What is more natural
than for qualities always to have come to us in
some conjunction, and never alone?

  We may go further.   Not only is the ignoring of
the process a thing quite indefensible—even if it
blundered into truth—but there is evidence that it
gives falsehood.   For the result bears internally
the character of the process.   The manyness of the
qualities cannot, in short, be reconciled with their
simplicity.   Their plurality depends on relation,
and, without that relation, they are not distinct.
But, if not distinct, then not different, and therefore
not qualities.

  I am not urging that quality without difference is
in every sense impossible.   For all I know, creatures
may exist whose life consists, for themselves, in one
unbroken simple feeling; and the arguments urged
against such a possibility in my judgment come
short.   And, if you want to call this feeling a
quality, by all means gratify your desire.   But then
remember that the whole point is quite irrelevant.
For no one is contending whether the universe is
or is not a quality in this sense; but the question
is entirely as to qualities.   And a universe con-

fined to one feeling would not only not be qualities, but it would fail even to be one quality, as different from others and as distinct from relations. Our question is really whether relation is essential to differences.

We have seen that in fact the two are never found apart. We have seen that the separation by abstraction is no proof of real separateness. And now we have to urge, in short, that any separateness implies separation, and so relation, and is therefore, when made absolute, a self-discrepancy. For consider, the qualities *A* and *B* are to be different from each other; and, if so, that difference must fall somewhere. If it falls, in any degree or to any extent, outside *A* or *B*, we have relation at once. But, on the other hand, how can difference and otherness fall inside? If we have in *A* any such otherness, then inside *A* we must distinguish its own quality and its otherness. And, if so, then the unsolved problem breaks out inside each quality, and separates each into two qualities in relation. In brief, diversity without relation seems a word without meaning. And it is no answer to urge that plurality proper is not in question here. I am convinced of the opposite, but by all means, if you will, let us confine ourselves to distinctness and difference. I rest my argument upon this, that if there are no differences, there are no qualities, since all must fall into one. But, if there is any difference, then that implies a relation. Without a relation it has no meaning; it is a mere word, and not a thought; and no one would take it for a thought if he did not, in spite of his protests, import relation into it. And this is the point on which all seems to turn, Is it possible to think of qualities without thinking of distinct characters? Is it possible to think of these without some relation between them, either explicit, or else unconsciously supplied by the mind that tries only to apprehend? Have qualities without relation any meaning for thought? For myself, I am sure that they have none.

And I find a confirmation in the issue of the most thorough attempt to build a system on this ground. There it is not too much to say that all the content of the universe becomes something very like an impossible illusion. The Reals are secluded and simple, simple beyond belief if they never suspect that they are not so. But our fruitful life, on the other hand, seems due to their persistence in imaginary recovery from unimaginable perversion. And they remain guiltless of all real share in these ambiguous connections, which seem to make the world. They are above it, and fixed like stars in the firmament—if there only were a firmament.

2. We have found that qualities, taken without relations, have no intelligible meaning. Unfortunately, taken together with them, they are equally unintelligible. They cannot, in the first place, be wholly resolved into the relations. You may urge, indeed, that without distinction no difference is left; but, for all that, the differences will not disappear into the distinction. They must come to it, more or less, and they cannot wholly be made by it. I still insist that for thought what is not relative is nothing. But I urge, on the other hand, that nothings cannot be related, and that to turn qualities in relation into mere relations is impossible. Since the fact seems constituted by both, you may urge, if you please, that either one of them constitutes it. But if you mean that the other is not wanted, and that relations can somehow make the terms upon which they seem to stand, then, for my mind, your meaning is quite unintelligible. So far as I can see, relations must depend upon terms, just as much as terms upon relations. And the partial failure, now manifest, of the Dialectic Method seems connected with some misapprehension on this point.

Hence the qualities must be, and must *also* be related. But there is hence a diversity which falls inside each quality. Each has a double character, as both supporting and as being made by the relation. It may be taken as at once condition and result, and the question is as to how it can combine this variety. For it must combine the diversity, and yet it fails to do so. *A* is both made, and is not made, what it is by relation; and these different aspects are not each the other, nor again is either *A*. If we call its diverse aspects *a* and *α*, then *A* is partly each of these. As *a* it is the difference on which distinction is based, while as *α* it is the distinctness that results from connection. *A* is really both somehow together as *A* (*a*—*α*). But (as we saw in Chapter ii.) *without* the use of a relation it is impossible to predicate this variety of *A*. And, on the other hand, *with* an internal relation *A*'s unity disappears, and its contents are dissipated in an endless process of distinction. *A* at first becomes *a* in relation with *α*, but these terms themselves fall hopelessly asunder. We have got, against our will, not a mere aspect, but a new quality *a*, which itself stands in a relation; and hence (as we saw before with *A*) its content must be manifold. As going into the relation it itself is a^2, and as resulting from the relation it itself is a^2. And it combines, and yet cannot combine, these adjectives. We, in brief, are led by a principle of fission which conducts us to no end. Every quality in relation has, in consequence, a diversity within its own nature, and this diversity cannot immediately be asserted of the quality. Hence the quality must exchange its unity for an internal relation. But, thus set free, the diverse aspects, because each something in relation, must each be something also beyond. This diversity is fatal to the internal unity of each; and it demands a new relation, and so on without limit. In short, qualities in a relation have turned out as unintelligible as were qualities without one.   The problem from both sides has baffled us.

3. We may briefly reach the same dilemma from the side of relations.   They are nothing intelligible, either with or without their qualities.   In the first place, a relation without terms seems mere verbiage; and terms appear, therefore, to be something beyond their relation.   At least, for myself, a relation which somehow precipitates terms which were not there before, or a relation which can get on somehow without terms, and with no differences beyond the mere ends of a line of connection, is really a phrase without meaning.   It is, to my mind, a false abstraction, and a thing which loudly contradicts itself ; and I fear that I am obliged to leave the matter so. As I am left without information, and can discover with my own ears no trace of harmony, I am forced to conclude to a partial deafness in others.   And hence a relation, we must say, without qualities is nothing.

But how the relation can stand to the qualities is, on the other side, unintelligible.   If it is nothing to the qualities, then they are not related at all ; and, if so, as we saw, they have ceased to be qualities, and their relation is a nonentity.   But if it is to be something to them, then clearly we now shall require a *new* connecting relation.   For the relation hardly can be the mere adjective of one or both of its terms ; or, at least, as such it seems indefensible.[1] And, being something itself, if it does not itself bear a relation to the terms, in what intelligible way will it succeed in being anything to them ?   But here

---

[1] The relation is not the adjective of one term, for, if so, it does not relate.   Nor for the same reason is it the adjective of each term taken apart, for then again there is no relation between them.   Nor is the relation their common property, for then what keeps them apart ?   They are now not two terms at all, because not separate.   And within this new whole, in any case, the problem of inherence would break out in an aggravated form.   But it seems unnecessary to work this all out in detail.

again we are hurried off into the eddy of a hopeless process, since we are forced to go on finding new relations without end. The links are united by a link, and this bond of union is a link which also has two ends; and these require each a fresh link to connect them with the old. The problem is to find how the relation can stand to its qualities; and this problem is insoluble. If you take the connection as a solid thing, you have got to show, and you cannot show, how the other solids are joined to it. And, if you take it as a kind of medium or unsubstantial atmosphere, it is a connection no longer. You find, in this case, that the whole question of the relation of the qualities (for they certainly in some way *are* related) arises now outside it, in precisely the same form as before. The original relation, in short, has become a nonentity, but, in becoming this, it has removed no element of the problem.

I will bring this chapter to an end. It would be easy, and yet profitless, to spin out its argument with ramifications and refinements. And for me to attempt to anticipate the reader's objections would probably be useless. I have stated the case, and I must leave it. The conclusion to which I am brought is that a relational way of thought—any one that moves by the machinery of terms and relations—must give appearance, and not truth. It is a makeshift, a device, a mere practical compromise, most necessary, but in the end most indefensible. We have to take reality as many, and to take it as one, and to avoid contradiction. We want to divide it, or to take it, when we please, as indivisible; to go as far as we desire in either of these directions, and to stop when that suits us. And we succeed, but succeed merely by shutting the eye, which if left open would condemn us; or by a perpetual oscillation and a shifting of the ground, so as to turn our back upon the aspect we desire to ignore. But when these inconsistencies are forced together, as in metaphysics they must be, the result is an open and staring discrepancy. And we cannot attribute this to reality; while, if we try to take it on ourselves, we have changed one evil for two. Our intellect, then, has been condemned to confusion and bankruptcy, and the reality has been left outside uncomprehended. Or rather, what is worse, it has been stripped bare of all distinction and quality. It is left naked and without a character, and we are covered with confusion.

The reader who has followed and has grasped the principle of this chapter, will have little need to spend his time upon those which succeed it. He will have seen that our experience, where relational, is not true; and he will have condemned, almost without a hearing, the great mass of phenomena. I feel, however, called on next to deal very briefly with Space and Time.

CHAPTER IV.

SPACE AND TIME.

THE object of this chapter is far from being an attempt to discuss fully the nature of space or of time. It will content itself with stating our main justification for regarding them as appearance. It will explain why we deny that, in the character which they exhibit, they either have or belong to reality. I will first show this of space.

We have nothing to do here with the psychological origin of the perception. Space may be a product developed from non-spatial elements; and, if so, its production may have great bearing on the question of its true reality. But it is impossible for us to consider this here. For, in the first place, every attempt so to explain its origin has turned out a clear failure.[1] And, in the second place, its reality would not be necessarily affected by the proof of its development. Nothing can be taken as real because, for psychology, it is original; or, again, as unreal, because it is secondary. If it were a legiti-

---

[1] I do not mean to say that I consider it to be original. On the contrary, one may have reason to believe something to be secondary, even though one cannot point out its foundation and origin. What has been called "extensity" appears to me (as offered) to involve a confusion. When you know what you mean by it, it seems to turn out to be either spatial at once and downright, or else not spatial at all. It seems useful, in part, only as long as you allow it to be obscure. Does *all* perception of more and less (or all which does not involve degree in the strict sense) imply space, or not? *Any* answer to this question would, I think, dispose of "extensity" as offered. But see *Mind*, iv. pp. 232–5.

mate construction from elements that were true, then it might be derived only for our knowledge, and be original in fact.   But so long as its attempted derivation is in part obscure and in part illusory, it is better to regard this whole question as irrelevant.

Let us then, taking space or extension simply as it is, enquire whether it contradicts itself.   The reader will be acquainted with the difficulties that have arisen from the continuity and the discreteness of space.   These necessitate the conclusion that space is endless, while an end is essential to its being.   Space cannot come to a final limit, either within itself or on the outside.   And yet, so long as it remains something always passing away, internally or beyond itself, it is not space at all.   This dilemma has been met often by the ignoring of one aspect, but it has never been, and it will never be, confronted and resolved.   And naturally, while it stands, it is the condemnation of space.

I am going to state it here in the form which exhibits, I think, most plainly the root of the contradiction, and also its insolubility.   Space is a relation—which it cannot be ; and it is a quality or substance — which again it cannot be.   It is a peculiar form of the problem which we discussed in the last chapter, and is a special attempt to combine the irreconcilable.   I will set out this puzzle antithetically.

1. Space is not a mere relation.   For any space must consist of extended parts, and these parts clearly are spaces.   So that, even if we could take our space as a collection, it would be a collection of solids.   The relation would join spaces which would not be mere relations.   And hence the collection, if taken as a *mere* inter-relation, would not be space.   We should be brought to the proposition that space is nothing but a relation of spaces.   And this proposition contradicts itself.

Again, from the other side, if any space is taken

as a whole, it is evidently more than a relation. It is a thing, or substance, or quality (call it what you please), which is clearly as solid as the parts which it unites. From without, or from within, it is quite as repulsive and as simple as any of its contents. The mere fact that we are driven always to speak of its *parts* should be evidence enough. What could be the *parts* of a relation?

2. But space is nothing but a relation. For, in the first place, any space must consist of parts; and, if the parts are not spaces, the whole is not space. Take then in a space any parts. These, it is assumed, must be solid, but they are obviously extended. If extended, however, they will themselves consist of parts, and these again of further parts, and so on without end. A space, or a part of space, that really means to be solid, is a self-contradiction. Anything extended is a collection, a relation of extendeds, which again are relations of extendeds, and so on indefinitely. The terms are essential to the relation, and the terms do not exist. Searching without end, we never find anything more than relations; and we see that we cannot. Space is essentially a relation of what vanishes into relations, which seek in vain for their terms. It is lengths of lengths of—nothing that we can find.

And, from the outside again, a like conclusion is forced on us. We have seen that space vanishes internally into relations between units which never can exist. But, on the other side, when taken itself as a unit, it passes away into the search for an illusory whole. It is essentially the reference of itself to something else, a process of endless passing beyond actuality. As a whole it *is*, briefly, the relation of itself to a non-existent other. For take space as large and as complete as you possibly can. Still, if it has not definite boundaries, it is not space; and to make it end in a cloud, or in nothing,

is mere blindness and *our* mere failure to perceive.
A space limited, and yet without space that is outside, is a self-contradiction. But the outside, unfortunately, is compelled likewise to pass beyond
itself; and the end cannot be reached. And it is
not merely that we fail to perceive, or fail to understand, how this can be otherwise. We perceive
and we understand that it cannot be otherwise, at
least if space is to be space. [We either do not know
what space means ; and, if so, certainly we cannot
say that it is more than appearance. Or else, knowing what we mean by it, we see inherent in that
meaning the puzzle we are describing. Space, to
be space, must have space outside itself. It for
ever disappears into a whole, which proves never
to be more than one side of a relation to something
beyond. And thus space has neither any solid
parts, nor, when taken as one, is it more than the
relation of itself to a new self. As it stands, it is
not space ; and, in trying to find space beyond it,
we can find only that which passes away into a
relation. Space is a relation between terms, which
can never be found.

It would not repay us to dwell further on the
contradiction which we have exhibited. The reader
who has once grasped the principle can deal himself with the details.   I will refer merely in passing
to a supplementary difficulty. Empty space—space
without some quality (visual or muscular) which in itself is more than spatial—is an unreal abstraction. It
cannot be said to exist, for the reason that it cannot
by itself have any meaning. When a man realizes
what he has got in it, he finds that always he has a
quality which is more than extension (cp. Chapter
i.).   But, if so, how this quality is to stand to the
extension is an insoluble problem.   It is a case of
"inherence," which we saw (Chapter ii.) was in
principle unintelligible. And, without further delay,
I will proceed to consider time.   I shall in this

chapter confine myself almost entirely to the difficulties caused by the discretion and the continuity
of time. With regard to change, I will say something further in the chapter which follows.

Efforts have been made to explain time psychologically—to exhibit, that is to say, its origin from
what comes to the mind as timeless. But, for the
same reason which seemed conclusive in the case of
space, and which here has even greater weight, I
shall not consider these attempts. I shall inquire
simply as to time's character, and whether, that
being as it is, it can belong to reality.

It is usual to consider time under a spatial form.
It is taken as a stream, and past and future are regarded as parts of it, which presumably do not co-
exist, but are often talked of as if they did. Time,
apprehended in this way, is open to the objection
we have just urged against space. It is a relation
—and, on the other side, it is not a relation; and it
is, again, incapable of being anything beyond a relation. And the reader who has followed the
dilemma which was fatal to space, will not require
much explanation. If you take time as a relation
between units without duration, then the whole time
has no duration, and is not time at all. But, if
you give duration to the whole time, then at once
the units themselves are found to possess it; and
they thus cease to be units. Time in fact is " before" and " after" in one; and without this diversity
it is not time. But these differences cannot be
asserted of the unity; and, on the other hand and
failing that, time is helplessly dissolved. Hence
they are asserted under a relation. " Before in relation to after" is the character of time; and here
the old difficulties about relation and quality recom-
mence. The relation is not a unity, and yet the
terms are nonentities, if left apart. Again, to import
an independent character into the terms is to make

each somehow in itself both before and after. But this brings on a process which dissipates the terms into relations, which, in the end, end in nothing. And to make the relation of time an unit is, first of all, to make it stationary, by destroying within it the diversity of before and after. And, in the second place, this solid unit, existing only by virtue of external relations, is forced to expand. It perishes in ceaseless oscillation, between an empty solidity and a transition beyond itself towards illusory completeness.

And, as with space, the qualitative content—which is not merely temporal, and apart from which the terms related in time would have no character—presents an insoluble problem. How to combine this in unity with the time which it fills, and again how to establish each aspect apart, are both beyond our resources. And time so far, like space, has turned out to be appearance.

But we shall be rightly told that a spatial form is not essential to time, and that, to examine it fairly, we should not force our errors upon it. Let us then attempt to regard time as it stands, and without extraneous additions. We shall only convince ourselves that the root of the old dilemma is not torn up.

If we are to keep to time as it comes, and are to abstain at first from inference and construction, we must confine ourselves, I presume, to time as presented. But presented time must be time present, and we must agree, at least provisionally, not to go beyond the " now." And the question at once before us will be as to the "now's" temporal contents. First, let us ask if they exist. Is the "now" simple and indivisible? We can at once reply in the negative. For time implies before and after, and by consequence diversity; and hence the simple is not time. We are compelled then, so far, to take the present as comprehending diverse aspects.

How many aspects it contains is an interesting

question. According to one opinion, in the " now " we can observe both past and future; and, whether these are divided by the present, and, if so, precisely in what sense, admits of further doubt. In another opinion, which I prefer, the future is not presented, but is a product of construction; and the " now " contains merely the process of present turning into past. But here these differences, if indeed they are such, are fortunately irrelevant. All that we require is the admission of some process within the " now." [1]

For any process admitted destroys the " now " from within. Before and after are diverse, and their incompatibility compels us to use a relation between them. Then at once the old wearisome game is played again. The aspects become parts, the "now" consists of " nows," and in the end these " nows " prove undiscoverable. For, as a solid part of time, the " now " does not exist. Pieces of duration may to us appear not to be composite; but a very little reflection lays bare their inherent fraudulence. If they are not duration, they do not contain an after and before, and they have, by themselves, no beginning or end, and are by themselves outside of time. But, if so, time becomes merely the relation between them; and duration is a number of relations of the timeless, themselves also, I suppose, related somehow so as to make one duration. But how a relation is to be a unity, of which these differences are predicable, we have seen is incomprehensible. And, if it fails to be a unity, time is forthwith dissolved. But why should I weary the reader by developing in detail the impossible consequences of either alternative? If he has understood the principle, he is with us; and, otherwise, the uncertain *argumentum ad hominem* would too certainly pass into *argumentum ad nauseam.*

---

[1] On the different meanings of the " present " I have said something in my *Principles of Logic,* pp. 51, foll.

I will, however, instance one result which follows
from a denial of time's continuity. Time will in
this case fall somehow between the timeless, as
A—C—E. But the rate of change is not uniform
for all events; and, I presume, no one will assert
that, when *we* have arrived at *our* apparent units,
that sets a limit to actual and possible velocity. Let
us suppose then another series of events, which,
taken as a whole, coincides in time with A—C—E,
but contains the six units a—b—c—d—e—f. Either
then these other relations (those, for example, between a and b, c and d) will fall between A and C,
C and E, and what that can mean I do not know;
or else the transition a—b will coincide with A,
which is timeless and contains no possible lapse.
And that, so far as I can perceive, contradicts itself
outright. But I feel inclined to add that this whole
question is less a matter for detailed argument than
for understanding in its principle. I doubt if there
is any one who has ever grasped this, and then has
failed to reach one main result. But there are too
many respectable writers whom here one can hardly
criticise. They have simply never got to understand.

Thus, if in the time, which we call presented,
there exists any lapse, that time is torn by a dilemma, and is condemned to be appearance. But, if
the presented is timeless, another destruction awaits
us. Time will be the relation of the present to a
future and past; and the relation, as we have seen,
is not compatible with diversity or unity. Further,
the existence, not presented, of future and of past
seems ambiguous. But, apart from that, time
perishes in the endless process beyond itself. The
unit will be for ever its own relation to something
beyond, something in the end not discoverable. And
this process is forced on it, both by its temporal
form, and again by the continuity of its content,
which transcends what is given.

Time, like space, has most evidently proved not to be real, but to be a contradictory appearance. I will, in the next chapter, reinforce and repeat this conclusion by some remarks upon change.

CHAPTER V

I AM sensible that this chapter will repeat much of the former discussion. It is not for my own pleasure that I write it, but as an attempt to strengthen the reader. Whoever is convinced that change is a self-contradictory appearance, will do well perhaps to pass on towards something which interests him.

Motion has from an early time been criticised severely, and it has never been defended with much success. I will briefly point to the principle on which these criticisms are founded. Motion implies that what is moved is in two places in one time ; and this seems not possible. That motion implies two places is obvious ; that these places are successive is no less obvious. But, on the other hand, it is clear that the process must have unity. The thing moved must be one ; and, again, the time must be one. If the time were only many times, out of relation, and not parts of a single temporal whole, then no motion would be found. But if the time is one, then, as we have seen, it cannot also be many.

A common " explanation " is to divide both the space and the time into discrete corresponding units, taken literally *ad libitum*. The lapse in this case is supposed to fall somehow between them. But, as a theoretical solution, the device is childish. Greater velocity would in this case be quite impossible ; and a lapse, falling between timeless units, has really, as we have seen, no meaning. And where the unity of these lapses, which makes the

one duration, is to be situated, we, of course, are
not, and could not be, informed.   And how this
inconsistent mass is related to the identity of the
body moved is again unintelligible.   What becomes
clear is merely this, that motion in space gives no
solution of the problem of change.   It adds, in
space, a further detail which throws no light on the
principle.   But, on the other side, it makes the discrepancies of change more palpable ; and it forces
on all but the thoughtless the problem of the identity
of a thing which has changed.   But change in time,
with all its inconsistencies, lies below motion in
space ; and, if this cannot be defended, motion at
once is condemned.

The problem of change underlies that of motion,
but the former itself is not fundamental.   It points
back to the dilemma of the one and the many, the
differences and the identity, the adjectives and the
thing, the qualities and the relations.   How anything can possibly be anything else was a question
which defied our efforts.   Change is little beyond
an instance of this dilemma in principle.   It either
adds an irrelevant complication, or confuses itself in
a blind attempt at compromise.   Let us, at the cost
of repetition, try to get clear on this head.

Change, it is evident, must be change of something, and it is obvious, further, that it contains
diversity.   Hence it asserts two of one, and so falls
at once under the condemnation of our previous
chapters.   But it tries to defend itself by this distinction : " Yes, both are asserted, but not both in
one ; there is a relation, and so the unity and plurality are combined."   But our criticism of relations
has destroyed this subterfuge beforehand.   We
have seen that, when a whole has been thus broken
up into relations and terms, it has become utterly
self-discrepant.   You can truly predicate neither
one part of the other part, nor any, nor all, of the
whole.   And, in its attempt to contain these ele-

ments, the whole commits suicide, and destroys them in its death. It would serve no purpose to repeat these inexorable laws. Let us see merely how change condemns itself by entering their sphere.

Something, A, changes, and therefore it cannot be permanent. On the other hand, if A is not permanent, what is it that changes? It will no longer be A, but something else. In other words, let A be free from change in time, and it does not change. But let it contain change, and at once it becomes A^1, A^2, A^3. Then what becomes of A, and of its change, for we are left with something else? Again, we may put the problem thus. The diverse states of A must exist within one time ; and yet they cannot, because they are successive.

Let us first take A as timeless, in the sense of out of time. Here the succession of the change must belong to it, or not. In the former case, what is the relation between the succession and A ? If there is none, A does not change. If there is any, it forces unintelligibly a diversity onto A, which is foreign to its nature and incomprehensible. And then this diversity, by itself, will be merely the unsolved problem. If we are not to remove change altogether, then we have, standing in unintelligible relation with the timeless A, a temporal change which offers us all our old difficulties unreduced.

A must be taken as falling within the time-series ; and, if so, the question will be whether it has or has not got duration. Either alternative is fatal. If the one time, necessary for change, means a single duration, that is self-contradictory, for no duration is single. The would-be unit falls asunder into endless plurality, in which it disappears. The pieces of duration, each containing a before and an after, are divided against themselves, and become mere relations of the illusory. And the attempt to locate the lapse within relations of the discrete leads to hopeless absurdities. Nor, in any case, could we unite intelligibly the plurality of these relations so as to make one duration. In short, therefore, if the one time required for change means one duration, that is not one, and there is no change.

On the other hand, if the change actually took place merely in *one* time, then it could be no change at all. *A* is to have a plurality in succession, and yet simultaneously. This is surely a flat contradiction. If there is no duration, and the time is simple, it is not time at all. And to speak of diversity, and of a succession of before and after, in this abstract point, is not possible when we think. Indeed, the best excuse for such a statement would be the plea that it is meaningless. But, if so, change, upon any hypothesis, is impossible. It can be no more than appearance.

And we may perceive its main character. It contains both the necessity and the impossibility of uniting diverse aspects. These differences have broken out in the whole which at first was immediate. But, if they entirely break out of it, they are dissipated and destroyed; and yet, by their presence within the whole, that already is broken, and they scattered into nothings. The relational form in general, and here in particular this form of time, is a natural way of compromise. It is no solution of the discrepancies, and we might call it rather a method of holding them in suspension. It is an artifice by which we become blind on either side, to suit the occasion; and the whole secret consists in ignoring that aspect which we are unable to use. Thus it is required that *A* should change; and, for this, two characters, not compatible, must be present at once. There must be a successive diversity, and yet the time must be one. The succession, in other words, is not really successive unless it is present. And our compromise consists in regarding the process mainly from whichever of its aspects answers to our need, and in ignoring—that is, in failing or in

refusing to perceive—the hostility of the other side.
If you want to take a piece of duration as present
and as one, you shut your eyes, or in some way are
blind to the discretion, and, attending merely to the
content, take that as a unity. And, on the other
hand, it is as easy to forget every aspect but that of
discreteness. But change, as a whole, consists in
the union of these two aspects. It is the holding
both at once, while laying stress upon the one which
for the time is prominent, and while the difficulties
are kept out of sight by rapid shuffling. Thus, in
asserting that A alters, we mean that the one thing
is different at different times. We bring this diversity into relation with A's qualitative identity,
and all seems harmonious. Of course, as *we* know,
even so far, there is a mass of inconsistency, but
that is not the main point here. The main point is
that, so far, we have not reached a change of A.
The identity of a content A, in *some sort of* relation
with diverse moments and with varying states—if it
means anything at all—is still not what we understand by change. That the mere oneness of a
quality can be the unity of a duration will hardly
be contended. For change to exist at all, this oneness must be in *temporal* relation with the diversity.
In other words, if the *process itself* is not one state,
the moments are not parts of it ; and, if so, they
cannot be related in time to one another. On the
one hand, A remains A through a period of any
length, and is not changed *so far as A*. Considered
thus, we may say that its duration is mere presence
and contains no lapse. But the same duration, if
regarded as the succession of A's altered states, consists of many pieces. On the other hand, thirdly,
this whole succession, regarded as one sequence or
period, becomes a unity, and is again present.
"Through the present period," we should boldly
say, "A's processes have been regular. His rate
of growth is normal, and his condition is for the

present identical. But, during the lapse of this one period, there have been present countless successive differences in the state of B; and the coincidence in time, of B's unchanging excitement with the healthy succession of A's changes, shows that in the same interval we may have present either motion or rest." There is hardly exaggeration here; but the statement exhibits a palpable oscillation. We have the dwelling, with emphasis and without principle, upon separate aspects, and the whole idea consists essentially in this oscillation. There is total failure to unite the differences by any consistent principle, and the one discoverable system is the systematic avoidance of consistency. The single fact is viewed alternately from either side, but the sides are not combined into an intelligible whole. And I trust the reader may agree that their consistent union is impossible. The problem of change defies solution, so long as change is not degraded to the rank of mere appearance.

I will end this chapter by some remarks on the perception of succession, or, rather, one of its main features. And I will touch upon this merely in the interest of metaphysics, reserving what psychological opinions I may have formed for another occasion. The best psychologists, so far as I know, are becoming agreed that for this perception some kind of unity is wanted. They see that without an identity, to which all its members are related, a series is not one, and is therefore not a series. In fact, the person who denies this unity is able to do so merely because he covertly supplies it from his own unreflecting mind. And I shall venture to regard this general doctrine as established, and shall pass to the point where I think metaphysics is further interested.

It being assumed that succession, or rather, here, *perceived* succession, is relative to a unity, a ques-

tion arises as to the nature of this unity, generally
and in each case   The question is both difficult
and interesting psychologically; but I must confine
myself to the brief remarks which seem called for in
this place.   It is not uncommon to meet the view
that the unity is timeless, or that it has at any rate
no duration.   On the other hand, presumably, it
has a date, if not a place, in the general series of
phenomena, and is, in this sense, an event.   The
succession I understand to be apprehended somehow in an indivisible moment,—that is, without any
lapse of time,—and to be so far literally simultaneous.
Any such doctrine seems to me open to fatal objections, some of which I will state.

1. The first objection holds good only against
certain persons.   If the timeless act contains a relation, and if the latter must be relative to a real
unity, the problem of succession appears again to
break out without limit inside this timeless unit.

2. But those who would deny. the premises of
this first objection, may be invited to explain themselves on other points.   The act has no duration,
and yet it is a psychical event.   It has, that is, an
assignable place in history.   If it does *not* possess
the latter, how is it related to my perception?   But,
if it *is* an event with a before and an after in time,
how can it have no duration?   It occurs in time,
and yet it occupies no time; or it does not occur in
time, though it happens at a given date.   This does
not look like the account of anything real, but it is
a manufactured abstraction, like length without
breadth.   And if it is a mere way of stating the
problem in hand—viz., that from one point of view
succession has no duration—it seems a bad way
of stating it.   But if it means more, its meaning
seems quite unintelligible.

3. And it is the more plainly so since its content
is certainly successive, as possessing the distinction
of after and before.   This distinction is a fact; and,

if so, the psychical lapse is a fact; and, if so, this fact is left in flat contradiction with the timeless unity. And to urge that the succession, as used, is ideal—is merely content, and is not psychical fact—would be a futile attempt to misapply a great principle. It is not wholly true that "ideas are not what they mean," for if their meaning is *not* psychical fact, I should like to know how and where it exists. And the question is whether succession can, in any sense, come before the mind without some actual succession entering into the very apprehension. If you do not *mean* a lapse, then you have given up your contention. But, if you do mean it, then how, except in the form of some actual mental transition, is it to come ideally before your mind? I know of no intelligible answer; and I conclude that, in this perception, what is perceived *is* an actual succession; and hence the perception itself must have *some* duration.

4. And, if it has no duration, then I do not see how it is related to the before and after of the time perceived; and the succession of this, with all its unsolved problems, seems to me to fall outside it (cp. No. 1).

5. And, lastly, if we may have one of these occurrences without duration, apparently we may also have many in succession, all again without duration. And I do not know how the absurd consequences which follow can be avoided or met.

In short, this creation is a monster. It is not a working fiction, entertained for the sake of its work. For, like most other monsters, it really is impotent. It is both idle and injurious, since it has diverted attention from the answer to its problem.

And that, to the reader who has followed our metaphysical discussion, will, I think, be apparent. We found that succession required both diversity and unity. These could not intelligibly be combined, and their union was a mere junction, with oscillation of emphasis from one aspect to the other. And so, psychically also, the timeless unity is a piece of duration, not experienced *as* successive. Assuredly everything psychical is an event, and it really contains a lapse; but so far as you do not use, or notice, that lapse, it is not there for you and for the purpose in hand. In other words, there is a permanent in the perception of change, which goes right through the succession and holds it together. The permanent can do this, on the one hand, because it occupies duration and is, in its essence, divisible indefinitely. On the other hand, it is one and unchanging, so far as it is regarded or felt, and is used, from that aspect. And the special concrete identities, which thus change, and again do not change, are the key to the particular successions that are perceived. Presence is not absolute timelessness; it is any piece of duration, so far as that is considered from or felt in an identical aspect. And this mere relative absence of lapse has been perverted into the absolute timeless monstrosity which we have ventured to condemn.

But it is one thing to see how a certain feature of our time-perception is possible. It is quite another thing to admit that this feature, as it stands, gives the truth about reality. And that, as we have learnt, is impossible. We are forced to assert that *A* is both continuous and discrete, both successive and present. And our practice of taking it, now as one in a certain respect, and now again as many in another respect, shows only how we practise. The problem calls upon us to answer how these aspects and respects are consistently united in the one thing, either outside of our minds or inside—that makes no difference. And if we fail, as we shall, to bring these features together, we have left the problem unsolved. And, if it is unsolved, then change and motion are incompatible internally, and are set down to be appearance. And if, as a last resource, we use the phrases " potential " and " actual," and attempt by their aid to reach harmony, we shall have left the case as it stands. We shall mean by these phrases that the thing is, and yet that it is not, and that we choose for our own purpose to treat these irreconcilables as united. But that is only another, though perhaps a more polite, way of saying that the problem is insoluble.

In the chapter which comes next, we must follow the same difficulties a little further into other applications.

CHAPTER VI.

CAUSATION.

THE object of this chapter is merely to point out, first, the main discrepancy in causation, and, in the second place, to exhibit an obstacle coming from time's continuity. Some other aspects of the general question will be considered in later chapters.[1]

We may regard cause as an attempt to account rationally for change. A becomes B, and this alteration is felt to be not compatible with A. Mere A would still be mere A, and, if it turns to something different, then something else is concerned. There must, in other words, be a reason for the change. But the endeavour to find a satisfactory reason is fruitless.

We have seen that A *is* not B, nor, again, a relation to B. "Followed by B," "changing into $A B$," are not the same as A ; and we were able to discover no way of combining these with A which could be more than mere appearance. In causation we must now consider a fresh effort at combination, and its essence is very simple. If "A becomes B" is a self-contradiction, then add something to A which will divide the burden. In "$A + C$ becomes B" we may perhaps find relief. But this relief, considered theoretically, is a mass of contradictions.

It would be a thankless task to work these out into detail, for the root of the matter may be stated at once. If the sequence of the effect is different

---

[1] I have touched on the Law of Causation in Chapter xxiii.

from the cause, how is the ascription of this difference to be rationally defended? If, on the other
hand, it is not different, then causation does not
exist, and its assertion is a farce. There is no
escape from this fundamental dilemma.

We have in the cause merely a fresh instance of
compromise without principle, another case of pure
makeshift. And it soon exhibits its nature. The
cause was not mere A; that would be found too
intolerable. The cause was $A + C$; but this combination seems meaningless. It is offered in the
face of our result as to the nature of relations
(Chapter iii.); and by that result it has already been
undermined and ruined. But let us see how it pro-
poses to go about its business. In "$A + C$ followed
by B" the addition of C makes a difference to A,
or it makes no difference. Let us suppose, first, that
it does make a difference to A. But, if so, then A
has already been altered; and hence the problem of
causation breaks out within the very cause. A and
C become $A + C$, and the old puzzle begins about
the way in which A and C become other than they
are. We are concerned here with A, but, of course,
with C there is the same difficulty. We are, therefore, driven to correct ourselves, and to say that,
not A and C merely, but A and $C + D$ become
$A + C$, and so B. But here we perceive at once
that we have fallen into endless regress within the
cause. If the cause is to be the cause, there is some
reason for its being thus, and so on indefinitely.

Or let us accept the other alternative. Let us
assert boldly that in $A + C$, which is the cause of B,
their relation makes no difference either to A or to
C, and yet accounts for the effect. Although the
conjunction makes no difference, it justifies apparently our attribution to the cause of the difference
expressed by the effect. But (to deal first with the
cause) such a conjunction of elements has been
shown (Chapter iii.) to be quite unintelligible. And

to the defence that it is only our own way of going
on, the answer is twofold. If it is only our way,
then, either it does not concern the thing at all, or
else is admitted to be a mere practical makeshift.
If, on the other hand, it is a way of ours with the
thing which we are prepared to justify, let the justification be produced. But it cannot be produced
in any form but in the proof that our thinking is
consistent. On the other hand, the only reason for
our hesitation above to attribute our view to reality
seemed to lie in the fact that our view was not consistent. But, if so, it surely should not be our view.
And, to pass now to the effect, the same reasoning
there holds good. The sequence of a difference
still remains entirely irrational. And, if we attempt
here to take this difference upon ourselves, and to
urge that it does not attach to the thing, but only to
our view, the same result follows. For what is
this but a manner of admitting politely that in reality there is no difference and is no causation, and
that, in short, we are all agreed in finding causation
to be makeshift and merely appearance? We are
so far agreed, but we differ in our further conclusions. For I can discover no merit in an attitude
which combines every vice of theory. It is forced
to admit that the real world is left naked and
empty; while it cannot pretend itself to support
and to own the wealth of existence. Each party is
robbed, and both parties are beggared.

The only positive result which has appeared from
our effort to justify causation, seems to be the impossibility of isolating the cause or the effect. In
endeavouring to make a defensible assertion, we
have had to go beyond the connection as first we
stated it. The cause A not only recedes backwards
in time, but it attempts laterally to take in more and
more of existence. And we are tending to the
doctrine that, to find a real cause, we must take the
complete state of the world at one moment as this

passes into another state also complete. The several threads of causation seem, that is, always to imply the action of a background. And this background may, if we are judicious, be irrelevant practically. It may be practically irrelevant, not because it is ever idle, but because often it is identical, and so makes no *special* difference. The separate causes are, therefore, legitimate abstractions, and they contain enough truth to be practically admissible. But it will be added that, if we require truth in any strict sense, we must confine ourselves to one entire state of the world. This will be the cause, and the next entire state will be the effect.

There is much truth in this conclusion, but it remains indefensible. This tendency of the separate cause to pass beyond itself cannot be satisfied, while we retain the relational form essential to causation. And we may easily, I think, convince ourselves of this. For, in the first place, a complete state of existence, as a whole, is at any one moment utterly impossible. Any state is forced by its content to transcend itself backwards in a regress without limit. And the relations and qualities of which it is composed will refer themselves, even if you keep to the moment, for ever away from themselves into endless dissipation. Thus the complete state, which is necessary, cannot be reached. And, in the second place, there is an objection which is equally fatal. Even if we could have one self-comprised condition of the world preceding another, the relation between them would still be irrational. We assert something of something else ; we have to predicate *B* of *A*, or else its sequence of *A*, or else the one relation of both. But in these cases, or in any other case, can we defend our assertion ? It is the old puzzle, how to justify the attributing to a subject something other than itself, and which the subject is not. If "followed by *B*" is not the nature of *A*, then justify your predication. If it is essen-

tial to *A*, then justify, first, your taking *A* without
it; and in the next place show how, with such an
incongruous nature, *A* can succeed in being more
than unreal appearance.

And we may perhaps fancy at this point that a
door of exit is opened. How will it be, since the
difference is the source of our trouble, if we fall
back upon the identity of cause and effect? The
same essence of the world, persisting in unchanged
self-conservation from moment to moment, and
superior to diversity—this is perhaps the solution.
Perhaps; but, if so, what has been done with causation? So far as I am able to understand, *that* consists in the differences and in their sequence in time.
Mere identity, however excellent, is emphatically
not the relation of cause and effect. Either then
once more you must take up the problem of reconciling intelligibly the diversity with the unity, and
this problem so far has shown itself intractable. Or
you yourself have arrived at the same conclusion
with ourselves. You have admitted that cause and
effect is irrational appearance, and cannot be reality.

I will add here a difficulty, in itself superfluous,
which comes from the continuity of causal change.
Its succession, on the one hand, must be absolutely
without pause; while, on the other hand, it cannot be
so. This dilemma is based upon no new principle,
but is a mere application of the insoluble problem of
duration. The reader who is not attracted may
pass on.

For our perception change is not properly continuous. It cannot be so, since there are durations
which do not come to us as such; and however our
faculties were improved, there must always be a
point at which they would be transcended. On the
other hand, to speak of our succession as being properly discrete seems quite as indefensible. It is in
fact neither the one nor the other. I presume that

what we notice is events with time between them, whatever that may mean. But, on the other hand, when we deal with pieces of duration, as wholes containing parts and even a variable diversity of parts, the other aspect comes up. And, in the end, reflection compels us to perceive that, however else it may appear, all change must really be continuous. This conclusion cannot imply that no state is ever able to endure for a moment. For, without some duration of the identical, we should have meaningless chaos, or, rather, should not have even that. States may endure, we have seen, so long as we abstract. We take some partial state, or aspect of a state, which in itself does not alter. We fix one eye upon this, while we cast, in fear of no principle, our other eye upon the succession that goes with it, and so is called simultaneous. And we solve practically in this way the problem of duration. We have enduring aspects, A, B, C, one after the other. Alongside of these there runs on a current of changes minutely subdivided. This goes on altering, and in a sense it alters A, B, C, while in another sense they are unchanged pieces of duration. They do not alter in themselves, but in relation to other changes they are in constant internal lapse. And, when these other changes have reached a certain point of alteration, then A passes into B, and so later B into C. This is, I presume, the proper way of taking causation as continuous. We may perhaps use the following figure :—

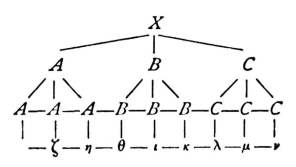

Here *A*, *B*, *C*, is the causal succession of enduring
states. The Greek letters represent a flow of other
events which are really a determining element in
the succession of *A*, *B*, *C*. And we understand at
once how *A*, *B*, and C both alter and do not alter.
But the Greek letters represent much more, which
cannot be depicted. In the first place, at any
given moment, there are an indefinite number of
them ; and, in the second place, they themselves are
pieces of duration, placed in the same difficulty
as were *A*, *B*, *C*. Coincident with each must be a
succession of events, which the reader may try to
represent in any character that he prefers. Only
let him remember that these events must be divided
indefinitely by the help of smaller ones. He must
go on until he reaches parts that have no divisibility.
And if we may suppose that he could reach them,
he would find that causation had vanished with his
success.

The dilemma, I think, can now be made plain.
(*a*) *Causation must be continuous.* For suppose that
it is not so. You would then be able to take a solid
section from the flow of events, solid in the sense of
containing no change. I do not merely mean that
you could draw a line without breadth across the
flow, and could find that this abstraction cut no
alteration. I mean that you could take a slice off,
and that this slice would have no change in it. But
any such slice, being divisible, must have duration.
If so, however, you would have your cause, enduring unchanged through a certain number of
moments, and then suddenly changing. And this
is clearly impossible, for what could have altered it?
Not any other thing, for you have taken the whole
course of events. And, again, not itself, for you
have got itself already without any change. In
short, if the cause can endure unchanged for any
the very smallest piece of duration, then it must
endure for ever. It cannot pass into the effect,

and it therefore is not a cause at all. On the other hand, (*b*) *Causation cannot be continuous.* For this would mean that the cause was entirely without duration. It would never be itself except in the time occupied by a line drawn across the succession. And since this time is not a time, but a mere abstraction, the cause itself will be no better. It is unreal, a nonentity, and the whole succession of the world will consist of these nonentities. But this is much the same as to suppose that solid things are made of points and lines and surfaces. These may be fictions useful for some purposes, but still fictions they, remain. The cause must be a real event, and yet there is no fragment of time in which it can be real. Causation is therefore not continuous; and so, unfortunately, it is not causation, but mere appearance.

The reader will understand at once that we have repeated here the old puzzle about time. Time, as we saw, must be made, and yet cannot be made, of pieces. And he perhaps will not be sorry to have reached an end of these pages through which I have been forced to weary him with continuity and discreteness. In the next chapter we shall arrive at somewhat different matter.

CHAPTER VII.

ACTIVITY.

In raising the question if activity is real **or** is only appearance, I may be met by the assertion that it is original, ultimate, and simple. I am satisfied myself that this assertion is incorrect, and is even quite groundless; but I prefer to treat it here as merely irrelevant. If the meaning of activity will not bear examination, and if it fails to exhibit itself intelligibly, then that meaning cannot, as such, be true of reality. There can be no origin, or want of origin, which warrants our predicating nonsense. And if I am told that, being simple, activity can have no meaning, then it seems a quality like one of our sensations or pleasures, and we have dealt with it already. Or I may possibly be answered, No, it is not simple in that sense, nor yet exactly composite. It somehow holds a variety, and is given in that character. Hence its idea may be indefensible, while itself is real. But the business of metaphysics is surely to understand; and if anything is such that, when thought of and not simply felt, it goes to pieces in our hands, we can find but one verdict. Either its nature is nonsensical, or we have got wrong ideas about it. The assertor of the latter alternative should then present us with the right ideas—a thing which, I need not add, he is not forward to perform. But let us leave these poor excuses to take care of themselves, and let us turn to the facts. There, if we examine the way in which the term activity is employed, the result is not doubtful. Force, energy, power, activity, these phrases certainly are used too often without clear understanding. But no rational man employs them except to convey some kind of meaning, which is capable of being discovered and subjected to analysis. And if it will not bear scrutiny, then it clearly does not represent reality.

There is a sense in which words like power, force, or energy, are distinguished from activity. They may be used to stand for something that does not happen at all, but somehow remains in a state of suspended animation, or in a region between non-existence and existence. I do not think it worth while to discuss this at present, and shall pass at once to the signification in which force means force in exercise—in other words, activity.

The element in its meaning, which comes to light at once, is succession and change. In all activity something clearly becomes something else. Activity implies a happening and a sequence in time. And, when I spoke of this meaning as coming to the light, I might have added that it positively stares us in the face, and it is not to be hidden. To deal frankly, I do not know how to argue this question. I have never seen a use of the term which to my mind retained its sense if time-sequence is removed. We can, of course, *talk* of a power sustaining or producing effects, which are subordinate and yet not subsequent; but to talk thus is not to think. And unless the sequence of our thought, from the power to its manifestation, is transferred to the fact as a succession there, the meaning is gone. We are left with mere co-existence, and the dependence, either of adjective on substantive, or of two adjectives on one another and on the substance which owns them. And I do not believe that any one, unless influenced by, and in the service of, some theory, would attempt to view the matter otherwise. And I fear that I must so leave it.

Activity implies the change of something into something different. So much, I think, is clear; but activity is not a mere uncaused alteration. And in fact, as we have seen, that is really not conceivable. For Ab to become Ac, something else beside Ab is felt to be necessary; or else we are left with a flat self-contradiction. Thus the transition of activity implies always a cause.

Activity is caused change, but it also must be more. For one· thing, altered by another, is not usually thought active, but, on the contrary, passive. Activity seems rather to be self-caused change. A transition that begins with, and comes out of, the thing itself is the process where we feel that it is active. The issue must, of course, be attributed to the thing as its adjective; it must be regarded, not only as belonging to the thing, but as beginning in it and coming out of it. If a thing carries out its own nature we call the thing active.

But we are aware, or may become aware, that we are here resting on metaphors. These cannot quite mean what they say, and what they intimate is still doubtful. It appears to be something of this kind: the end of the process, the result or the effect, seems part of the nature of the thing which we had at the beginning. Not only has it *not* been added by something outside, but it is hardly to be taken as an addition at all. So far, at least, as the end is considered as the thing's activity, it is regarded as the thing's character from the first to the last. Thus it somehow *was* before it happened. It did not exist, and yet, for all that, in a manner it was there, and so it became. We should like to say that the nature of the thing, which was ideal, realized itself, and that this process is what we mean by activity. And the idea need not be an idea in the mind of the thing; for the thing, perhaps, has no mind, and so cannot have that which would amount to volition. On the other hand, the idea in the thing is not a

mere idea in *our* minds which *we* have merely about
the thing. We are sure of this, and our meaning
falls between these extremes. But where precisely
it falls, and in what exactly it consists, seems at
present far from clear. Let us, however, try to go
forwards.

Passivity seems to imply activity. It is the alteration of the thing, in which, of course, the thing
survives, and acquires a fresh adjective. This
adjective was not possessed by the thing before the
change. It therefore does not belong to its nature,
but is a foreign importation. It proceeds from, and
is the adjective of, another thing which is active
—at the expense of the first Thus passivity is
not possible without activity; and its meaning is
obviously still left unexplained.

It is natural to ask next if activity can exist by
itself and apart from passivity. And here we begin
to involve ourselves in further obscurity. We have
spoken so far as if a thing almost began to be active
without any reason; as if it exploded, so to speak,
and produced its contents entirely on its own motion,
and quite spontaneously. But this we never really
meant to say, for this would mean a happening and
a change without any cause at all; and this, we
agreed long ago, is a self-contradiction and impossible. The thing, therefore, is not active without
an *occasion*. This, call it what you please, is something outside the standing nature of the thing, and is
accidental in the sense of happening to that essential
disposition. But if the thing cannot act unless the
act is occasioned, then the transition, so far, is imported into it by the act of something outside. But
this, as we saw, was passivity. Whatever acts then
must be passive, so far as its change is occasioned.
If we look at the process as the coming out of *its*
nature, the process is its activity. If we regard the
same process, on the other hand, as due to the
occasion, and, as we say, coming from that, we

A. R. F

still have activity.   But the activity now belongs to
the occasion, and the thing is passive.   We seem to
have diverse aspects, of which the special existence
in each case will depend on our own minds.

We find this ambiguity in the common distinction
between cause and condition, and it is worth our
while to examine this more closely.   Both of these
elements are taken to be wanted for the production
of the effect; but in any given case we seem able to
apply the names almost, or quite, at discretion.   It
is not unusual to call the last thing which happens
the cause of the process which ensues.   But this is
really just as we please.   The body fell because the
support was taken away ;   but probably most men
would prefer to call this " cause" a condition of a
certain kind.   But apparently we may gratify whatever preference we feel.   And the well-meant
attempt to get clear by defining the cause as the
" sum of the conditions " does not much enlighten
us.   As to the word " sum," it is, I presume,
intended to carry a meaning, but this meaning is
not stated, and I doubt if it is known.   And, further,
if the cause is taken as including every single condition, we are met by a former difficulty.   Either
this cause, not existing through any part of duration,
is really non-existent ; or else a condition will be
wanted for its change and its passing into
activity.   But if the cause already includes all, then,
of course, none is available (Chapter vi.).   But, to
pass this point by, what do you mean by these conditions, that all fall within the cause, so as to leave none
outside ?   Do you mean that what we commonly
call the " conditions " of an event are really complete ?   In practice certainly we leave out of the
account the whole background of existence ; we
isolate a group of elements, and we say that,
whenever these occur, then something else always
happens ; and in this group we consider ourselves
to possess the " sum of the conditions."   And this

assumption may be practically defensible, since the
rest of existence may, on sufficient ground, be taken
as irrelevant. We can therefore treat this whole
mass as if it were inactive. Yes, but that is one
thing, and it is quite another thing to assert that
really this mass does nothing. Certainly there is no
logic which can warrant such a misuse of abstraction.
The background of the whole world can be elimin-
ated by no sound process, and the furthest conclusion
which can be logical is that we need not consider it
practically. As in a number of diverse cases it
seems to add nothing special, we may for each
purpose consider that it adds nothing at all. But
to give out this working doctrine as theoretically
true is quite illegitimate.

The immediate result of this is that the true "sum
of conditions" must completely include all the
contents of the world at a given time And here
we run against a theoretical obstacle. The nature
of these contents seems such as to be essentially
incomplete, and so the "sum" to be nothing attainable. This appears fatal so far, and, having stated
it, I pass on. Suppose that you *have* got a complete
sum of the facts at one moment, are you any nearer
a result ? This entire mass will be the "sum of
conditions," and the cause of each following event.
For there is no process which will warrant your
taking the cause as *less*. Here there is at once
another theoretical trouble, for the same cause
produces a number of different effects ; and how will
you deal with that consequence? But, leaving this,
we are practically in an equal dilemma. For the
cause, taken so widely, is the cause of everything
alike, and hence it can tell us nothing about anything special ; and, taken less widely, it is not the
sum, and therefore not the cause. And by this
time it is obvious that our doctrine must be given
up. If we want to discover a particular cause (and
nothing else *is* a discovery), we must make a dis-

tinction in the "sum." Then, as before, in every
case we have conditions beside the cause; and, as
before, we are asked for a principle by which to
effect the distinction between them. And, for myself,
I return to the statement that I know of none which
is sound. We seem to effect this distinction always
to suit a certain purpose; and it appears to consist
in *our* mere adoption of a special point of view.

But let us return to the consideration of passivity
and activity. It is certain that nothing can be active
without an occasion, and that what is active, being
made thus by the occasion, is so far passive. The
occasion, again, since it enters into the causal process
—a thing it never would have done if left to itself—
suffers a change from the cause; and it therefore
itself is passive in its activity. If the cause is A,
and the occasion B, then each is active or passive,
according as you view the result as the expression
of its nature, or as an adjective imported from outside.

And we are naturally brought here to a case
where both these aspects seem to vanish. For
suppose, as before, that we have A and B, which
enter into one process, and let us call the result
ACB. Here A will suffer a change, and so also will
B; and each again may be said to produce change
in the other. But if the nature of A was, before,
Acb, and the nature of B was, before, Bca, we are
brought to a pause. The ideas which we are
applying are now plainly inadequate and likely to
confuse us. To A and B themselves they might
even appear to be ridiculous. How do I *suffer* a
change, each would answer, if it is nothing else but
what I will? We cannot adopt your points of
view, since they seem at best quite irrelevant.

To pass to another head, the conclusion, which so
far we have reached, seems to exclude the possibility
of one thing by itself being active. Here we must

make a distinction. If this supposed thing had no variety in its nature, or, again, if its variety did not change in time within it, then it is impossible that it should be active. The idea, indeed, is self-contradictory. Nor could one thing again be said to be active as a whole ; for that part of its nature which, changing, served as the occasion could not be included. I do not propose to argue these points, for I do not perceive anything on the other side beyond confusion or prejudice. And hence it is certain that activity implies finitude, and otherwise possesses no meaning. But, on the other hand, naturally where there are a variety of elements, changing in time, we may have activity. For part of these elements may suffer change from, and may produce it in, others. Indeed, the question whether this is to go on inside one thing by itself, appears totally irrelevant, until at least we have some idea of what we mean by one thing. And our enquiries, so far, have not tended to establish any meaning. It is as if we enquired about hermaphroditism, where we do not know what we understand by a single animal. Indeed, if we returned at this point to our A and B connected in one single process, and enquired of them if they both were parts of one thing, or were each one thing containing a whole process of change, we should probably get no answer. They would once more recommend us to improve our own ideas before we went about applying them.

Our result up to this point appears to be much as follows. Activity, under any of the phrases used to carry that idea, is a mass of inconsistency. It is, in the first place, riddled by the contradictions of the preceding chapters, and if it cannot be freed from these, it must be condemned as appearance. And its own special nature, so far as we have discovered that, seems certainly no better. The activity of anything seems to consist in the way in which *we* choose to look at that which it is and becomes. For, apart from the inner nature which comes out in the result, activity has no meaning. If this nature was not there, and was not real in the thing, is the thing really active? But when we press this question home, and insist on having something more than insincere metaphors, we find either nothing, or else the idea which *we* are pleased to entertain. And this, as an idea, we dare not attribute to the thing, and we do not know how to attribute it as anything else. But a confusion of this kind cannot belong to reality.

Throughout this chapter I have ignored a certain view about activity. This view would admit that activity, as we have discussed it, is untenable; but it would add that we have not even touched the real fact. And this fact, it would urge, is the activity of a self, while outside self the application of the term is metaphorical. And, with this question in prospect, we may turn to another series of considerations about reality.

CHAPTER VIII.

THINGS.

BEFORE proceeding further we may conveniently pause at this point. The reader may be asked to reflect whether anything of what is understood by a thing is left to us. It is hard to say what, as a matter of fact, *is* generally understood when we use the word "thing." But, whatever that may be, it seems now undermined and ruined. I suppose we generally take a thing as possessing some kind of independence, and a sort of title to exist in its own right, and not as a mere adjective. But our ideas are usually not clear. A rainbow probably is not a thing, while a waterfall might get the name, and a flash of lightning be left in a doubtful position. Further, while many of us would assert stoutly that a thing must exist, if at all, in space, others would question this and fail to perceive its conclusiveness.

We have seen how the attempt to reconstitute our ideas by the help of primary qualities broke down. And, since then, the results, which we have reached, really seem to have destroyed things from without and from within. If the connections of substantive and adjective, and of quality and relation, have been shown not to be defensible; if the forms of space and of time have turned out to be full of contradictions; if, lastly, causation and activity have succeeded merely in adding inconsistency to inconsistency,—if, in a word, nothing of all this can, as such, be predicated of reality,—what is it that is left? If things are to exist, then where and how?

But if these two questions are unanswerable, then we seem driven to the conclusion that things are but appearances. And I will add a few remarks, not so much in support of this conclusion as in order to make it possibly more plain.

I will come to the point at once. For a thing to exist it must possess identity; and identity seems a possession with a character at best doubtful. If it is merely ideal, the thing itself can hardly be real. First, then, let us inquire if a thing can exist without identity. To ask this question is at once to answer it; unless, indeed, a thing is to exist, and is to hold its diversity combined in an unity, somehow quite outside of time. And this seems untenable. A thing, if it is to be called such, must occupy some duration beyond the present moment, and hence succession is essential. The thing, to be at all, must be the same after a change, and the change must, to some extent, be predicated of the thing. If you suppose a case so simple as the movement of an atom, that is enough for our purpose. For, if this "thing" does not move, there is no motion. But, if it moves, then succession is predicated of it, and the thing is a bond of identity in differences. And, further, this identity is ideal, since it consists in the content, or in the "what we are able to say of the thing." For raise the doubt at the end of our atom's process, if the atom is the same. The question raised cannot be answered without an appeal to its character. It is different in one respect—namely, the change of place; but in another respect—that of its own character—it remains the same. And this respect is obviously identical content. Or, if any one objects that an atom has no content, let him throughout substitute the word "body," and settle with himself how, without any qualitative difference (such as right and left), he distinguishes atoms. And this identical content is called ideal because it transcends given existence. Existence is given only in presentation; and, on the other hand, the thing is a thing only if its existence goes beyond the now, and extends into the past. I will not here discuss the question as to the identity of a thing during a presented lapse, for I doubt if any one would wish to except to our conclusion on that ground.

Now I am not here raising the whole question of the Identity of Indiscernibles. I am urging rather that the continuity, which is necessary to a thing, seems to depend on its keeping an identity of character. A thing *is* a thing, in short, by being what it *was.* And it does not appear how this relation of sameness can be real. It is a relation connecting the past with the present, and this connection is evidently vital to the thing. But, if so, the thing has become, in more senses than one, the *relation* of passages in its own history. And if we assert that the thing is this inclusive relation, which transcends any given time, surely we have allowed that the thing, though not wholly an idea, is an idea essentially. And it is an idea which at no actual time is ever real.

And this problem is no mere abstract invented subtlety, but shows itself in practice. It is often impossible to reply when we are asked if an object is really the same. If a manufactured article has been worked upon and partly remade, such a question may have no sense until it has been specified. You must go on to mention the point or the particular respect of which you are thinking. For questions of identity turn always upon sameness in character, and the reason why here you cannot reply generally, is that you do not know this general character which is taken to make the thing's essence. It is not always material substance, for we might call an organism identical, though its particles were all different. It is not always shape, or size, or colour, or, again, always the purpose which the thing fulfils. The general nature, in fact, of a

thing's identity seems to lie, first, in the avoidance
of any absolute break in its existence, and, beyond
that, to consist in some qualitative sameness which
differs with different things.   And with some things
—because literally we do not know in what character their sameness lies—we are helpless when asked
if identity has been preserved.   If any one wants
an instance of the value of our ordinary notions,
he may find it, perhaps, in Sir John Cutler's silk
stockings.   These were darned with worsted until
no particle of the silk was left in them, and no one
could agree whether they were the same old stockings or were new ones.   In brief, the identity of
a thing lies in the view which you take of it.   That
view seems often a mere chance idea, and, where
it seems necessary, it still remains an idea.   Or, if
you prefer it, it is a character, which exists outside
of and beyond any fact which you can take.   But
it is not easy to see how, if so, any thing can be
real.   And things have, so far, turned out to be
merely appearances.

CHAPTER IX.

THE MEANINGS OF SELF.

OUR facts, up to the present, have proved to be illusory. We have seen our things go to pieces, crumbled away into relations that can find no terms. And we have begun, perhaps, to feel some doubt whether, since the plague is so deep-rooted, it can be stayed at any point. At the close of our seventh chapter we were naturally led beyond the inanimate, and up to the self. And here, in the opinion of many, is the end of our troubles. The self, they will assure us, is not apparent, but quite real. And it is not only real in itself, but its reality, if I may say so, spreads beyond its own limits and rehabilitates the selfless. It provides a fixed nucleus round which the facts can group themselves securely. Or it, in some way, at least provides us with a type, by the aid of which we may go on to comprehend the world. And we must now proceed to a serious examination of this claim. Is the self real, is it anything which we can predicate of reality ? Or is it, on the other hand, like all the preceding, a mere appearance—something which is given, and, in a sense, most certainly exists, but which is too full of contradictions to be the genuine fact ? I have been forced to embrace the latter conclusion.

There is a great obstacle in the path of the proposed inquiry. A man commonly thinks that he knows what he means by his self. He may be in doubt about other things, but here he seems to be at home. He fancies that with the self he at once

comprehends both that it is and what it is. And
of course the fact of one's own existence, *in some
sense*, is quite beyond doubt. But as to the sense
in which this existence is so certain, there the case
is far otherwise. And I should have thought that
no one who gives his attention to this question
could fail to come to one preliminary result. We
are all sure that we exist, but in what sense and
what character—as to that we are most of us in helpless uncertainty and in blind confusion. And so
far is the self from being clearer than things outside us that, to speak generally, we never know
what we mean when we talk of it. But the meaning and the sense is surely for metaphysics the vital
point. For, if none defensible can be found, such
a failure, I must insist, ought to end the question.
Anything the meaning of which is inconsistent and
unintelligible is appearance, and not reality.

I must use nearly the whole of this chapter in
trying to fix some of the meanings in which self is
used. And I am forced to trespass inside the limits
of psychology ; as, indeed, I think is quite necessary
in several parts of metaphysics. I do not mean that
metaphysics is based upon psychology. I am quite
convinced that such a foundation is impossible, and
that, if attempted, it produces a disastrous hybrid
which possesses the merits of neither science. The
metaphysics will come in to check a resolute analysis,
and the psychology will furnish excuses for half-
hearted metaphysics. And there can be really no
such science as the theory of cognition. But, on the
other hand, the metaphysician who is no psychologist runs great dangers. For he must take up, and
must work upon, the facts about the soul ; and, if he
has not tried to learn what they are, the risk is very
serious. The psychological monster he may adopt
is certain also, no doubt, to be monstrous metaphysically ; and the supposed fact of its existence does
not prove it less monstrous. But experience shows

that human beings, even when metaphysical, lack courage at some point. And we cannot afford to deal with monsters, who in the end may seduce us, and who are certain sometimes, at any rate, to be much in our way. But I am only too sensible that, with all our care, the danger nearest each is least seen.

I will merely mention that use of self which identifies it with the body. As to our perception of our own bodies, there, of course, exists some psychological error. And this may take a metaphysical form if it tries to warrant, through some immediate revelation, the existence of the organism as somehow the real expression of the self. But I intend to pass all this by. For, at the point which we have reached, there seems no exit by such a road from familiar difficulties.

1. Let us then, excluding the body as an outward thing, go on to inquire into the meanings of self. And the first of these is pretty clear. By asking what is the self of this or that individual man, I may be enquiring as to the present contents of his experience. Take a section through the man at any given moment. You will then find a mass of feelings, and thoughts, and sensations, which come to him as the world of things and other persons, and again as himself; and this contains, of course, his views and his wishes about everything. Everything, self and not-self, and what is not distinguished as either, in short the total filling of the man's soul at this or that moment—we may understand this when we ask what is the individual at a given time There is no difficulty here in principle, though the detail would naturally (as detail) be unmanageable. But, for our present purpose, such a sense is obviously not promising.

2. The congeries inside a man at one given moment does not satisfy as an answer to the question what is self. The self, to go no further, must be something beyond present time, and it

cannot contain a sequence of contradictory varia
tions. Let us then modify our answer, and say,
Not the mass of any one moment, but the constant
average mass, is the meaning of self. Take, as
before, a section completely through the man, and
expose his total psychical contents ; only now take
this section at different times, and remove what
seems exceptional. The residue will be the normal
and ordinary matter, which fills his experience; and
this is the self of the individual. This self will
contain, as before, the perceived environment—in
short, the not-self so far as that is for the self—
but it will contain now only the usual or average
not-self. And it must embrace the habits of the
individual and the laws of his character—whatever
we mean by these. His self will be the usual
manner in which he behaves, and the usual matter
to which he behaves, that is, so far as he behaves
to it.

We are tending here towards the distinction of
the essential self from its accidents, but we have
not yet reached that point. We have, however, left
the self as the whole individual of one moment, or
of succeeding moments, and are trying to find it as
the individual's *normal* constituents. What is that
which 'makes the man his usual self? We have
answered, It is his habitual disposition and contents, and it is not his changes from day to day and
from hour to hour. These contents are not merely
the man's internal feelings, or merely that which he
reflects on as his self. They consist quite as essentially in the outward environment, so far as relation
to that makes the man what he is. For, if we try
to take the man apart from certain places and
persons, we have altered his life so much that he is
not his usual self. Again, some of this habitual
not-self, to use that expression, enters into the
man's life in its individual form. His wife possibly,
or his child, or, again, some part or feature of his

inanimate environment, could not, if destroyed, be so made good by anything else that the man's self would fail to be seriously modified. Hence we may call these the constituents which are *individually* necessary; requisite for the man, that is, not in their vague, broad character, but in their specialty as this or that particular thing. But other tracts of his normal self are filled by constituents necessary, we may say, no more than *generically*. His usual life gets its character, that is, from a large number of details which are variable within limits. His habits and his environment have main outlines which may still remain the same, though within these the special features have been greatly modified. This portion of the man's life is necessary to make him his average self, but, if the generic type is preserved, the special details are accidental.

This is, perhaps, a fair account of the man's usual self, but it is obviously no solution of theoretical difficulties. A man's true self, we should be told, cannot depend on his relations to that which fluctuates. And fluctuation is not the word; for in the lifetime of a man there are irreparable changes. Is he literally *not* the same man if loss, or death, or love, or banishment has turned the current of his life? And yet, when we look at the facts, and survey the man's self from the cradle to the coffin, we may be able to find no one average. The usual self of one period is not the usual self of another, and it is impossible to unite in one mass these conflicting psychical contents. Either then we accept the man's mere history as his self, and, if so, why call it one ? Or we confine ourselves to periods, and there is no longer any single self. Or, finally, we must distinguish the self from the usual constituents of the man's psychical being. We must try to reach the self which is individual by finding the self which is *essential*.

3. Let us then take, as before, a man's mind, and inspect its furniture and contents. We must try to find that part of them in which the self really consists, and which makes it one and not another. And here, so far as I am aware, we can get no assistance from popular ideas. There seems, however, no doubt that the inner core of feeling, resting mainly on what is called Cœnesthesia, is the foundation of the self.[1]

But this inner nucleus, in the first place, is not separated from the average self of the man by any line that can be drawn; and, in the second place, its elements come from a variety of sources. In some cases it will contain, indivisibly from the rest, relation to a not-self of a certain character. Where an individual is such that alteration in what comes from the environment completely unsettles him, where this change may produce a feeling of self-estrangement so severe as to cause sickness and even death, we must admit that the self is not enclosed by a wall. And where the essential self is to end, and the accidental self to begin, seems a riddle without an answer.

For an attempt to answer it is baffled by a fatal dilemma. If you take an essence which can change, it is not an essence at all; while, if you stand on anything more narrow, the self has disappeared. What is this essence of the self which never is altered? Infancy and old age, disease and madness, bring new features, while others are borne away. It is hard indeed to fix any limit to the self's mutability. One self, doubtless, can suffer change in which another would perish. But, on the other hand, there comes a point in each where we should agree that the man is no longer himself. This

---

[1] I may refer here to a few further remarks in *Mind*, 12, p. 368 and foll. I am not suggesting that ideas may not form part of the innermost self. One thinks here naturally of the strange selves suggested in hypnotism.

creature lost in illusions, bereft of memory, transformed in mood, with diseased feelings enthroned
in the very heart of his being—is this still one self
with what we knew? Well, be it so; assert, what
you are unable to show, that there is still a point
untouched, a spot which never has been invaded.
I will not ask you to point this out, for I am sure
that is impossible. But I urge upon you the
opposite side of the dilemma. This narrow persisting element of feeling or idea, this fixed essence
not " servile to all the skyey influences," this
wretched fraction and poor atom, too mean to be in
danger—do you mean to tell me that this bare
remnant is really the self? The supposition is preposterous, and the question wants no answer. If
the self has been narrowed to a point which does
not change, that point is less than the real self.
But anything wider has a " complexion" which
"shifts to strange effects," and therefore cannot be
one self. The riddle has proved too hard for
us.

We have been led up to the problem of
personal identity, and any one who thinks that he
knows what he means by his self, may be invited
to solve this. To my mind it seems insoluble,
but not because all the questions asked are essentially such questions as cannot be answered. The
true cause of failure lies in this—that we will persist
in asking questions when we do not know what
they mean, and when their meaning perhaps presupposes what is false. In inquiries about identity,
as we saw before in Chapter viii., it is all-important
to be sure of the aspect about which you ask. A
thing may be identical or different, according as
you look at it. Hence in personal identity the
main point is to fix the meaning of person ; and it
is chiefly because our ideas as to this are confused,
that we are unable to come to a further result.

In the popular view a man's identity resides

mainly in his body.[1] There, before we reflect much,
lies the crucial point. Is the body the same? Has
it existed continuously? If there is no doubt about
this, then the man is the same, and presumably he
has preserved his personal identity, whatever else
we like to say has invaded or infected it. But, of
course, as we have seen, this identity of the body
is itself a doubtful problem (p. 73). And even
apart from that, the mere oneness of the organism
must be allowed to be a very crude way of settling
personal sameness. Few of us would venture to
maintain that the self *is* the body.

Now, if we add the requirement of *psychical*
continuity, have we advanced much further? For
obviously it is not known, and there seems hardly
any way of deciding, whether the psychical current
is without any break. Apparently, during sleep or
otherwise, such intervals are at least possible ; and,
if so, continuity, being doubtful, cannot be used to
prove identity. And further, if our psychical contents can be more or less transformed, the mere
absence of an interval will hardly be thought enough
to guarantee sameness. So far as I can judge, it is
usual, for personal identity, to require both continuity and qualitative sameness. But how much of
each is wanted, and how the two stand to one
another,—as to this I can find little else but sheer
confusion. Let us examine it more closely.

We should perhaps say that by one self we understand one experience. And this may either mean
one for a supposed outside observer, or one for the
consciousness of the self in question, the latter kind
of unity being added to or apart from the first kind.
And the self is not one unless within limits its
quality is the same. But we have already seen that
if the individual is simply viewed from outside, it is
quite impossible to find a limit within which change

---

[1] In the *Fortnightly Review*, ccxxviii., p. 820, I have further
discussed this question.

may not come, and which yet is wide enough to embrace a real self. Hence, if the test is only same-ness for an outside observer, it seems clear that sometimes a man's life must have a series of selves. But at what point of difference, and on what precise principle, that succession takes place seems not de-finable. The question is important, but the decision, if there is one, appears quite arbitrary. But per-haps, if we quit the view of the outside observer, we may discover some principle. Let us make the attempt.

We may take *memory* as the criterion. The self, we may hold, which remembers itself is so far one ; and in this lies personal identity. We perhaps may wish also to strengthen our case by regarding memory as something entirely by itself, and as, so to speak, capable of anything whatever. But this is, of course, quite erroneous. Memory, as a special application of reproduction, displays no exceptional wonders to a sane psychology, nor does it really offer greater diffi-culties than we find in several other functions. And the point I would emphasize here is its limits and defects. Whether you take it across its breadth, or down its length, you discover a great want of singleness. This one memory of which we talk is very weak for many aspects of our varied life, and is again disproportionately strong for other aspects. Hence it seems more like a bundle of memories run-ning side by side and in part unconnected. It is certain that at any one time what we can recall is most fragmentary. There are whole sides of our life which may be wanting altogether, and others which will come up only in various degrees of feebleness. This is when memory is at its best ; and at other times there hardly seems any limit to its failure. Not only may some threads of our bundle be want-ing or weak, but, out of those that remain, certain lengths may be missing. Pieces of our life, when we were asleep, or drugged, or otherwise distempered, are not represented. Doubtless the current, for all that, comes to us as continuous. But so it does when things go further, and when in present disease our recollection becomes partial and distorted. Nay, when in one single man there are periodic returns of two disconnected memories, the faculty still keeps its nature and proclaims its identity. And psychology explains how this is so. Memory depends on reproduction from a basis that is present—a basis that may be said to consist in self-feeling. Hence, so far as this basis remains the same through life, it may, to speak in general, recall anything once associated with it. And, as this basis changes, we can understand how its connections with past events will vary indefinitely, both in fulness and in strength. Hence, for the same reason, when self-feeling has been altered beyond a limit not in general to be defined, the base required for reproduction of our past is removed. And, as these different bases alternate, our past life will come to us differently, not as one self, but as diverse selves alternately. And of course these "reproduced" selves may, to a very considerable extent, have never existed in the past.[1]

Now I would invite the person who takes his sameness to consist in bare memory, to confront his view with these facts, and to show us how he understands them. For apparently, though he may not admit that personal identity has degrees, he at least cannot deny that in one life we are able to have more than one self. And, further, he may be compelled to embrace self-sameness with a past which exists, for him only sometimes, and for others not at all. And under these conditions it is not easy to see what becomes of the self. I will, however, go further. It is well known that after an injury followed by unconsciousness which is removed by an operation, our mental life may begin again from the

[1] Compare here once again the suggested selves of hypnotism.

moment of the injury. Now if the self remembers because and according as it is *now*, might not another self be made of a quality the same, and hence possessing the same past in present recollection? And if *one* could be made thus, why not also two or three? These might be made distinct at the present time, through their differing quality, and again through outward relations, and yet be like enough for each to remember the same past, and so, of course, to *be* the same. Nor do I see how this supposition is to be rejected as theoretically impossible. And it may help us to perceive, what was evident before, that a self is not thought to be the same because of bare memory, but only so when that memory is considered not to be deceptive. But this admits that identity must depend in the end upon past existence, and not solely upon mere present thinking. And continuity in some degree, and in some unintelligible sense, is by the popular view required for personal identity. He who is risen from the dead may really be the same, though we can say nothing intelligible of his ambiguous eclipse or his phase of half-existence. But a man wholly like the first, but created fresh after the same lapse of time, we might feel was too much to be one, if not quite enough to make two. Thus it is evident that, for personal identity, some continuity is requisite, but how much no one seems to know. In fact, if we are not satisfied with vague phrases and meaningless generalities, we soon discover that the best way is not to ask questions. But if we persist, we are likely to be left with this result. Personal identity is mainly a matter of degree. The question has a meaning, if confined to certain aspects of the self, though even here it can be made definite in each case only by the arbitrary selection of points of view. And in each case there will be a limit fixed in the end by no clear principle. But in what the *general* sameness of one self consists is a problem insoluble because it is meaningless. This question, I repeat it, is sheer nonsense until we have got some clear idea as to what the self is to stand for. If you ask me whether a man is identical in this or that respect, and for one purpose or another purpose, then, if we do not understand one another, we are on the road to an understanding. In my opinion, even then we shall reach our end only by more or less of convention and arrangement. But to seek an answer in general to the question asked at large is to pursue a chimera.

· We have seen, so far, that the self has no definite meaning. It was hardly one section of the individual's contents ; nor was it even such a section, if reduced to what is usual and taken somehow at an average. The self appeared to be the essential portion or function, but in what that essence lies no one really seemed to know. We could find nothing but opinions inconsistent with each other, not one of which would presumably be held by any one man, if he were forced to realize its meaning.

(4) By selecting from the individual's contents, or by accepting them in the gross, we have failed to find the self. We may hence be induced to locate it in some kind of monad, or supposed simple being. By this device awkward questions, as to diversity and sameness, seem fairly to be shelved. The unity exists as a unit, and in some sphere presumably secure from chance and from change. I will here first recall our result which turned out adverse to the possibility of any such being (Chapters iii. and v.). And secondly I will point out in a few words that its nature is most ambiguous. Is it the self at all, and, if so, to what extent and in what sense ?

If we make this unit something moving parallel with the life of a man, or, rather, something not moving, but literally *standing* in relation to his successive

variety, this will not give us much help. It will be
the man's self about as much as is his star (if he has
one), which looks down from above and cares not
when *he* perishes. And if the unit is brought down
into the life of the person, and so in any sense suffers
his fortunes, then in what sense does it remain any
longer a unit? And if we will but look at the question, we are forced to this conclusion. If we knew
already what we meant by the self, and could point
out its existence, then our monad might be offered
as a theory to account for that self. It would be an
indefensible theory, but at least respectable as being
an attempt to explain *something*. But, so long as
we have no clear view as to the limits in actual fact
of the self's existence, our monad leaves us with all
our old confusion and obscurity. But it further
loads us with the problem of its connection with
these facts about which we are so ignorant. What
I mean is simply this. Suppose you have accepted
the view that self consists in recollection, and then
offer me one monad, or two or three, or as many as
you think the facts call for, in order to account for
recollection. I think your theory worthless, but, to
some extent, I respect it, because at least it has
taken up some fact, and is trying to account for it.
But if you offer me a vague mass, and then a unit
alongside, and tell me that the second is the self of
the first, I do not think that you are saying *anything*. All I see is that you are drifting towards
this dilemma. If the monad owns the whole diversity, or any selected part of the diversity, which we
find in the individual, then, even if you had found
in this the identity of the self, you would have to
reconcile it all with the simplicity of the monad.
But if the monad stands aloof, either with no
character at all or a private character apart, then it
may be a fine thing in itself, but it is mere mockery
to call it the self of a man. And, with so much for
the present, I will pass away from this point

(5) It may be suggested that the self is the matter in which I take personal interest. The elements felt as mine may be regarded as the self, or, at all events, as all the self which exists. And interest consists mainly, though not wholly, in pain and pleasure. The self will be therefore that group of feelings which, to a greater or less extent, is constantly present, and which is always attended by pleasure or pain. And whatever from time to time is united with this group, is a personal affair and becomes part of self. This general view may serve to lead us to a fresh way of taking self; but it obviously promises very little result for metaphysics. For the contents of self are most variable from one time to another, and are largely conflicting; and they are drawn from many heterogeneous sources. In fact, if the self means merely what interests us personally, then at any one time it is likely to be too wide, and perhaps also to be too narrow; and at different times it seems quite at variance with itself.

(6) We are now brought naturally to a most important way of understanding the self. We have, up to the present, ignored the distinction of subject and object. We have made a start from the whole psychical individual, and have tried to find the self there or in connection with that. But this individual, we saw, contained both object and subject, both not-self and self. At least, the not-self must clearly be allowed to be in it, so far as that enters into relation with the self and appears as an object. The reader may prefer another form of expression, but he must, I think, agree as to the fact. If you take what in the widest sense is inside a man's mind, you will find there both subject and object and their relation. This will, at all events, be the case both in perception and thought, and again in desire and volition. And this self, which is opposed to the not-self, will most emphatically *not* coincide with the self, if that

is taken as the individual or the essential individual. The deplorable confusion, which is too prevalent on this head, compels me to invite the reader's special attention.

The psychical division of the soul into subject and object has, as is well known, two main forms. The relation of the self to the not-self is theoretical and practical. In the first we have, generally, perception or intelligence ; in the second we have desire and will. It is impossible for me here to point out the distinct nature of each; and still less can I say anything on their development from one root. What seems to me certain is that both these forms of relation are secondary products. Every soul either exists or has existed at a stage where there was no self and no not-self, neither Ego nor object in any sense whatever. But in what way thought and will have emerged from this basis—this whole of feeling given without relation—I cannot here discuss.[1] Nor is the discussion necessary to an understanding of the crucial point here. That point turns upon the contents of the self and the not-self; and we may consider these apart from the question of origin.

Now that subject and object have contents and are actual psychical groups appears to me evident. I am aware that too often writers speak of the Ego as of something not essentially qualified by this or that psychical matter. And I do not deny that in a certain use that language might be defended. But if we consider, as we are considering here, what we are to understand by that object and subject in relation, which at a given time we find existing in a soul, the case is quite altered. The Ego that pretends to be anything either before or beyond its concrete psychical filling, is a gross fiction and mere monster, and for no purpose admissible. And the question surely

---

[1] On this and other kindred points, compare my articles in *Mind*, Nos. 47 and 49. And see below (Chapters xix., xxvi., xxvii.).

may be settled by observation. Take any case of
perception, or whatever you please, where this relation of object to subject is found as a fact. There,
I presume, no one will deny that the object, at all
events, is a concrete phenomenon. It has a character which exists as, or in, a mental fact. And, if
we turn from this to the subject, is there any more
cause for doubt? Surely in every case that contains a mass of feeling, if not also of other psychical
existence. When I see, or perceive, or understand,
I (*my* term of the relation) am palpably, and perhaps
even painfully, concrete. And when I will or desire,
it surely is ridiculous to take the self as not qualified
by particular psychical fact. Evidently any self
which we can find is some concrete form of unity of ·
psychical existence. And whoever wishes to introduce it as something (now or at any time) apart or
beyond, clearly does not rest his case upon observation. He is importing into the facts a metaphysical
chimera, which, in no sense existing, can do no work ;
and which, even if it existed, would be worse than
useless.

　　The self and not-self, as discoverable, are concrete
groups,[1] and the question is as to the content of these.
What is that content, if any, which is essentially not-
self or self? Perhaps the best way of beginning this
inquiry is to ask whether there is *anything* which
may not become an object and, in that sense, a not-
self. We certainly seem able to set everything over
against ourselves. We begin from the outside, but
the distinguishing process becomes more inward,
until it ends with deliberate and conscious intro-
spection. Here we attempt to set before, and so
opposite to, self our most intimate features. We
cannot do this with all at any one time, but with
practice and labour one detail after another is detached from the felt background and brought before

　　[1] I am not saying that the whole soul is divided into two groups.
That is really not possible. See more below.

our view. It is far from certain that at some one time *every* feature of the self has, sooner or later, taken its place in the not-self; but it is quite certain that this holds of by far the larger part. And we are hence compelled to admit that very little of the self can belong to it essentially. Let us now turn from the theoretical to the practical relation. Is there here anything, let us ask, which is incapable of becoming an object to my will or desire ? But what becomes such an object is clearly a not-self and opposed to the self. Let us go at once to the region that seems most internal and inalienable. As intro-spection discloses this or that feature in ourselves, can we not wish that it were otherwise ? May not everything that we find within us be felt as a limit and as a not-self, against which we either do, or con-ceivably might, react. Take, for instance, some slight pain. We may have been feeling, in our dimmest and most inward recesses, uneasy and dis-composed ; and, so soon as this disturbing feature is able to be noticed, we at once react against it. The disquieting sensation becomes clearly a not-self, which we desire to remove. And, I think, we must accept the result that, if not everything may become at times a practical not-self, it is at least hard to find exceptions.

Let us now, passing to the other side of both these relations, ask if the not-self contains anything which belongs to it exclusively. It will not be easy to dis-cover many such elements. In the theoretical rela-tion it is quite clear that not everything can be an object, all together and at once. At any one moment that which is in any sense before me must be limited. What are we to say then becomes of that remainder of the not-self which clearly has not, even for the time, passed wholly from my mind ? I do not mean those features of the environment to which I fail to attend specially, but which I still go on perceiving as something before me. I refer to the features which have now sunk below this level. These are not even a setting or a fringe to the object of my mind. They have passed lower into the general background of feeling, from which that distinct object with its indistinct setting is detached. But this means that for the time they have passed into the self. A constant sound will afford us a very good instance.[1] That may be made into the principal object of my mind, or it may be an accompaniment of that object more or less definite. But there is a further stage, where you cannot say that the sensation has ceased, and where yet it is no feature in what comes as the not-self. It has become now one among the many elements of my feeling, and it has passed into that self for which the not-self exists. I will not ask if with any, or with what, portions of the not-self this relapse may be impossible, for it is enough that it should be possible with a very great deal. Let us go on to look at the same thing from the practical side. There it will surely be very difficult to fix on elements which essentially must confront and limit me. There are some to which in fact I seem never to be practically related; and there are others which are the object of my will or desire only from occasion to occasion. And if we cannot find anything which is essential to the not-self, then everything, it would appear, so far as it enters my mind, may form part of the felt mass. But if so, it would seem for the time to be connected with that group against which the object of will comes. And thus once again the not-self has become self.

The reader may have observed one point on which my language has been guarded. That point is the extreme limit of this interchange of content between the not-self and the self. I do not for one moment deny the existence of that limit. In my opinion it

___

[1] Another instance would be the sensations from my own clothes.

is not only possible, but most probable, that in every man there are elements in the internal felt core which are never made objects, and which practically cannot be. There may well be features in our Cœnesthesia which lie so deep that we never succeed in detaching them ; and these cannot properly be said to be ever our not-self. Even in the past we cannot distinguish their speciality. But I presume that even here the obstacle may be said to be practical, and to consist in the obscurity, and not otherwise in the essence, of these sensations.[1] And I will barely notice the assertion that pleasure and pain are essentially not capable of being objects. This assertion seems produced by the straits of theory, is devoid of all basis in fact, and may be ignored. But our reason for believing in elements which never are a not-self is the fact of a felt surplus in our undistinguished core. What I mean is this : we are able in our internal mass of feeling to distinguish and to recognise a number of elements ; and we are able, on the other side, to decide that our feeling contains beyond these an unexhausted margin.[2] It contains a margin which, in its general idea of margin, can be made an object, but which, in its particularity, cannot be. But from time to time this margin has been encroached upon ; and we have not the smallest reason to suppose that at some point in its nature lies a hard and fast limit to the invasion of the not-self.

[1] Notice that our emotional moods, where we hardly could analyse them, may qualify objects æsthetically.

[2] How the existence of this margin is observed is a question I cannot discuss here. The main point lies in our ability to feel a discrepancy between our felt self and any object before it. This, reflected on and made an object—as, of course, in its main vague type is always possible with past feeling—gives us the idea of an unreduced residue. The same ability to feel discrepancy is the ground of our belief as to difference or identity between past and present feeling. But the detail of this discussion does not belong to metaphysics.

On the side of the not-self, once more, I would
not assert that *every* feature of content may lapse
into mere feeling, and so fuse itself with the background.   There may be features which practically
manage never to do this.   And, again, it may be
urged that there are thought-products not capable of
existence, save when noticed in such a way as must
imply opposition to self.   I will not controvert this;
but will suggest only that it might open a question,
as to the existence in general of thought-products
within the feeling self, which might further bewilder
us.   I will come to the conclusion, and content
myself with urging the general result.   Both on the
side of the self and on the side of the not-self, there
are, if you please, admitted to be features not capable
of translocation.   But the amount of these will be so
small as to be incapable of characterizing and con-
stituting the self or the not-self.   The main bulk of
the elements on each side is interchangeable.

If at this point we inquire whether the present
meaning of self will coincide with those we had before, the answer is not doubtful.   For clearly well-
nigh everything contained in the psychical individual
may be at one time part of self and at another time
part of not-self.   Nor would it be possible to find
an essence of the man which was incapable of being
opposed to the self, as an object for thought and for
will.   At least, if found, that essence would consist
in a residue so narrow as assuredly to be insufficient
for making an individual.   And it could gain con-
creteness only by receiving into its character a
mortal inconsistency.   The mere instance of internal volition should by itself be enough to compel
reflection.   There you may take your self as deep-
lying and as inward as you please, and may narrow
it to the centre; yet these contents may be placed
in opposition to your self, and you may desire their
alteration.   And here surely there is an end of any
absolute confinement or exclusive location of the self.

For the self is at one moment the whole individual, inside which the opposites and their tension is contained ; and, again, it is one opposite, limited by and struggling against an opponent.

And the fact of the matter seems this. The whole psychical mass, which fills the soul at any moment, is the self so far as this mass is only felt. So far, that is, as the mass is given together in one whole, and not divisible from the group which is especially connected with pleasure and pain, this entire whole is felt as self. But, on the other side, elements of content are distinguished from the mass, which therefore is, so far, the background against which perception takes place. But this relation of not-self to self does not destroy the old entire self. This is still the whole mass inside which the distinction and the relation falls. And self in these two meanings coexists with itself, though it certainly does not coincide. Further, in the practical relation a new feature becomes visible. There we have, first of all, self as the whole felt condition. We have, next, the not-self which is felt as opposing the self. We have, further, the group, which is limited and struggles to expand, so causing the tension. This is, of course, felt specially as the self, and within this there falls a new feature worth noticing. In desire and volition we have an idea held against the existing not-self, the idea being that of a change in that not-self. This idea not only is felt to be a part of that self which is opposed to the not-self,— it is felt also to be the main feature and the prominent element there. Thus we say of a man that his whole self was centred in a certain particular end. This means, to speak psychologically, that the idea is one whole with the inner group which is repressed by the not-self, and that the tension is felt emphatically in the region of the idea. The idea becomes thus the prominent feature in the content of self. And hence its expansion against, or contraction by, the actual group of the not-self is felt as the enlargement or the restraint of myself. Here, if the reader will call to mind that the existing not-self may be an internal state, whose alteration is desired,—and, again, if he will reflect that the idea, viewed theoretically, itself is a not-self,—he may realize the entire absence of a qualification attached to, and indivisible from, one special content.

We have yet to notice even another meaning which is given to "self." But I must first attempt at this point to throw further light on the subject of our seventh chapter. The perception by the self of its own activity is a corner of psychology which is dangerous if left in darkness. We shall realize this danger in our next chapter; and I will attempt here to cut the ground from beneath some blind prejudices. My failure, if I fail, will not logically justify their existence. It may doubtless be used in their excuse, but I am forced to run that risk for the sake of the result.

The perception of activity comes from the expansion of the self against the not-self, this expansion arising from the self.[1] And by the self is not meant the whole contents of the individual, but one term of the practical relation described above. We saw there how an idea, over against the not-self, was the feature with which the self-group was most identified. And by the realization of this idea the self therefore is expanded; and the expansion, *as such*,[2] is always a cause of pleasure. The mere expansion, of course, would not be felt as activity, and its origi-

---

[1] I may refer the reader here to *Mind*, 43, pp. 319–320; 47, pp. 371–372; and 49, p. 33. I have not answered Mr. Ward's criticisms (*Mind* 48, pp. 572–575) in detail, because in my opinion they are mere misunderstandings, the removal of which is not properly my concern.

[2] For a further distinction on this point see *Mind*, 49, pp. 6 and foll.

nation from within the self is of the essence of the matter.

But there are several points necessary for the comprehension of this view. 1. The reader must understand, first of all, that the expansion is not necessarily the enlargement of the self in the sense of the whole individual. Nor is it even the enlargement of the self as against the not-self, in every meaning of those terms. It is the expansion of the self so far as that is identified with the idea of the change. If, for example, I wished to produce self-contraction, then that also would be enlargement, because in it the idea, before limited by the fact of a greater area, would transcend that limit. Thus even self-destruction is relative expansion, so long as the activity lasts. And we may say, generally, the self here *is* that in which it feels its chief interest. For this is both indivisible from and prominent in its inmost being. No one who misses this point can understand what activity means.

2. This leads us to a difficulty. For sometimes clearly I am active, where there is no idea proper, and, it might be added, even no limiting not-self. I will take the last point first. (*a*) Let us, for argument's sake, imagine a case where, with no outside Other, and no consciousness of an empty environment, the self feels expansion. In what sense can we discover any not-self here? The answer is simple. The self, as existing, is that limit to itself which it transcends by activity. Let us call the self, as it is before the activity, A, and, while active, AB. But we have a third feature, the inner nature of A, which emerges in AB. This, as we saw, is the idea of the change, and we may hence write it b. We have, therefore, at the beginning not merely A, but in addition A qualified by b; and these are opposite to one another. The unqualified A is the not-self of A as identified with b; and the tension between Ab and A is the inner source of the change,

which, of course, expands b to B, and by consequence, so far, A. We may, if we like these phrases, call activity the ideality of a thing carrying the thing beyond its actual limit. But what is really important is the recognition that activity has no meaning, unless in some sense we suppose an idea of the change · and that, as against this idea In which the self feels its interest, the actual condition of the self is a not-self. (*b*) And this, of course, opens a problem. For in some cases where the self apprehends itself as active, there seems at first sight to be no idea. But the problem is solved by the distinction between an idea which is explicit and an idea not explicit. The latter is ideal solely in the sense that its content is used beyond its existence.[1] It might indeed be argued that, when we predicate activity, the end is always transferred in idea to the beginning. That is doubtless true; but, when activity is merely felt, there will never be there an explicit idea. And, in the absence of this, I will try to explain what takes place. We have first a self which, as it exists, may be called Ac. This self becomes Acd, and is therefore expanded. But bare expandedness is, of course, by itself not activity, and could not be so felt. And the mere alteration consequently, of Ac to Acd, would be felt only as a change, and as an addition made to the identical A. When these differences, c and d, are connected before the mind by the identical A—and for the perception of change they must be connected—there is, so far, no action or passivity, but a mere change which happens. This is not enough for activity, since we require also δ, the idea of d, in Ac; and this idea we do not have in an explicit form. But what, I think, suffices is this. Ac, which as a fact passes into Acd, and is felt so to pass by the perception of a relation of sequence, is also previously felt as $Ac\delta$. That is, in the A,

---

[1] *Mind*, 49, p. 23. And see below, Chapter xv., p. 163.

apart from and before its actual change to d, we have the qualification $Ac\delta$ wavering and struggling against Ac. Ac suggests $Ac\delta$, which is felt as one with it, and not as given to it by anything else. But this suggestion $Ac\delta$, as soon as it arises, is checked by the negative, mere Ac, which maintains its position. A is therefore the site of a struggle of $Ac\delta$ against Ac. Each is felt in A as belonging to it and therefore as one; and there is no relation yet which serves as the solution of this discrepancy. Hence comes the feeling that A is, and yet is not, Acd. But when the relation of sequence seems to solve this contradiction, then the ensuing result is not felt as *mere* addition to Ac. It is felt as the success of Acd, which before was kept back by the stronger Ac. And thus, without any *explicit* idea, an idea is actually applied; for there is a content which is used beyond and against existence. And this, I think, is the explanation of the earliest felt activity.

This brief account is naturally open to objections, but all that are not mere misunderstanding can, I believe, be fully met. The subject, however, belongs to psychology, and I must not here pursue it. The reader will have seen that I assume, for the perception of change, the necessity of connecting the end with the beginning. This is effected by redintegration from the identical A, and it is probably assisted at first by the after-sensation of the starting-place, persisting together with the result. And this I am obliged here to assume. Further, the realization of Acd must not be attached as an adjective to anything *outside* A, such as E. This would be fatal to the appearance of a feeling of activity. A must, for our feeling, be Acd; and, again, that must be checked by the more dominant Ac. It must be unable to establish itself, and yet must struggle,— that is, oscillate and waver. Hence a wavering $Ac\delta$, causing pleasure at each partial success, and resisted by Ac, which you may take, as you prefer,

for its negative or its privation—this is what afterwards turns into that strange scandalous hybrid,
potential existence. And δ, as a content that is rejected by existence, is on the highway to become
an explicit idea. And with these too scanty explanations I must return from the excursion we
have made into psychology.

(7) There is still another meaning of self which
we can hardly pass by, though we need say very
little about it at present.[1] I refer to that use in
which self is the same as the " mere self " or the
" simply subjective." This meaning is not difficult
to fix in general. Everything which is part of the
individual's psychical contents, and which is not relevant to a certain function, is mere self to that
function. Thus, in thinking, everything in my
mind—all sensations, feelings, ideas which do not
subserve the thought in question—is unessential ;
and, because it is self, it is therefore *mere* self. So,
again, in morality or in æsthetic perception, what
stands outside these processes (if they are what they
should be) is simply " subjective," because it is not
concerned in the " object " of the process. Mere
self is whatever part of the psychical individual is,
for the purpose in hand, negative. It, at least, is
irrelevant, and it may be even worse.

This in general is clearly the meaning, and it
surely will give us no help in our present difficulties.
The point which should be noticed is that it has no
fixed application. For that which is " objective "
and essential to one kind of purpose, may be irrelevant and " subjective " to every other kind of purpose. And this distinction holds even among cases
of the same kind. That feature, for example, which
is essential to one moral act may be without significance for another, and may therefore be merely

---

[1] See Chapter xix.

myself. In brief, there is nothing in a man which is not thus " objective " or " subjective," as the end which we are considering is from time to time changed. The self here stands for that which, for a present purpose, is the *chance* self. And it is obvious, if we compare this meaning with those which have preceded, that it does not coincide with them. It is at once too wide and too narrow. It is too wide, because nothing falls essentially outside it ; and yet it is too narrow, because anything, so soon as you have taken that in reference to any kind of system, is at once excluded from the mere self. It is not the simply felt ; for it is essentially qualified by negation. · It is that which, as against anything transcending mere feeling, remains outside as a residue. We might, if we pleased, call it what, by contrast, is *only* the felt. But then we must include under feeling every psychical fact, if considered merely as such and as existing immediately. There is, however, here no need to dwell any further on this point.

I will briefly resume the results of this chapter We had found that our ideas as to the nature of things—as to substance and adjective, relation and quality, space and time, motion and activity—were in their essence indefensible But we had heard somewhere a rumour that the self was to bring order into chaos. And we were curious first to know what this term might stand for. The present chapter has supplied us with an answer too plentiful. Self has turned out to mean so many things, to mean them so ambiguously, and to be so wavering in its applications, that we do not feel encouraged. We found, first, that a man's self might be his total present contents, discoverable on making an imaginary cross section. Or it might be the average contents we should presume ourselves likely to find, together with something else which we call dis-

positions.   From this we drifted into a search for
the self as the essential point or area within the self;
and we discovered that we really did not know what
this was.   Then we went on to perceive that, under
personal identity, we entertained a confused bundle
of conflicting ideas.   Again the self, as merely that
which for the time being interests, proved not satisfactory; and from this we passed to the distinction
and the division of self as against the not-self.   Here,
in both the theoretical and again in the practical
relation, we found that the self had no contents that
were fixed; or it had, at least, none sufficient to
make it a self.   And in that connection we perceived the origin of our perception of activity.
Finally, we dragged to the light another meaning of
self, not coinciding with the others; and we saw
that this designates any psychical fact which remains
outside any purpose to which at any time psychical
fact is being applied.   In this sense self is the
unused residue, defined negatively by want of use,
and positively by feeling in the sense of mere
psychical existence.   And there was no matter
which essentially fell, or did not fall, under this
heading.

CHAPTER **X.**

THE REALITY OF SELF.

In the present chapter we must briefly inquire into the self's reality. Naturally the self is a fact, to some extent and in some sense; and this, of course, is not the issue. The question is whether the self in any of its meanings can, as such, be real. We have found above that things seem essentially made of inconsistencies. And there is understood now to be a claim on the part of the self, not only to maintain and to justify its own proper being, but, in addition, to rescue things from the condemnation we have passed on them. But the latter part of the claim may be left undiscussed. We shall find that the self has no power to defend its own reality from mortal objections.

It is the old puzzle as to the connection of diversity with unity. As the diversity becomes more complex and the unity grows more concrete, we have, so far, found that our difficulties steadily increase. And the expectation of a sudden change and a happy solution, when we arrive at the self, seems hence little warranted. And if we glance at the individual self, as we find it at one time, there seems at first sight no clear harmony which orders and unites its entangled confusion. At least, popular ideas are on this point visibly unavailing. The complexity of the phenomena, exhibited by a cross section, must be admitted to exist. But how in any sense they can be one, even apart from alteration, is a problem not attempted. And when the self changes in time, are we able to justify the inconsistency which most palpably appears, or, rather, stares us in the face? You may say that we are each assured of our personal identity in a way in which we are not assured of the sameness of things. But this is, unfortunately, quite irrelevant to the question. That selves exist, and are identical in some sense, is indubitable. But the doubt is whether their sameness, as we apprehend it, is really intelligible, and whether it can be true in the character in which it comes to us. Because otherwise, while it will be certain that the self and its identity *somehow* belong to reality, it will be equally certain that this fact has *somehow* been essentially misapprehended. And our conclusion must be that, since, as such, it contradicts itself, this fact must, as such, be unreal. The self also will in the end be no more than appearance.

This question turns, I presume, on the possibility of finding some special experience which will furnish a new point of view. It is, of course, admitted that the self presents us with fresh matter, and with an increased complication. The point in debate is whether at the same time it supplies us with any key to the whole puzzle about reality. Does it give an experience by the help of which we can *understand* the way in which diversity is harmonized? Or, failing that, does it remove all necessity for such an understanding? I am convinced that both these questions must be answered in the negative.

(*a*) For mere feeling, to begin the inquiry with this, gives no answer to our riddle. It may be said truly that in feeling, if you take it low enough down, there is plurality with unity and without contradiction. There being no relations and no terms, and yet, on the other side, more than bare simplicity, we experience a concrete whole as actual fact. And this fact, it may be alleged, is the understanding of our self, or is, at least, that which is superior to and over-rides any mere intellectual criticism. It must be accepted for what it is, and its reality must be admitted by the intelligence as a unique revelation.

But no such claim can be maintained. I will begin by pointing out that feeling, if a revelation, is not exclusively or even specially a revelation of the self. For you must choose one of two things. Either you do not descend low enough to get rid of relations with all their inconsistency, or else you have reached a level where subject and object are in no sense distinguished, and where, therefore, neither self nor its opposite exists. Feeling, if taken as immediate presentation, most obviously gives features of what later becomes the environment. And these are indivisibly one thing with what later becomes the self. Feeling, therefore, can be no unique or special revelation of the self, in distinction from any other element of the universe. Nor, even if feeling be used wrongly as equivalent to the aspect of pleasure or pain,[1] need we much modify our conclusion. This is a point on which naturally I have seen a good many dogmatic asser tions, but no argument that would bear a serious examination. Why in the case of a pleasant feeling —for example, that of warmth—the side of pleasure should belong to the self, and the side of sensation to the not-self (psychologically or logically), I really do not know. If we keep to facts, it seems clear that at the beginning no such distinction exists at all ; and it is clear too that at the latest stage there are some elements within the not-self which retain their original aspect of pleasure or pain. And hence we must come to this result. We could

[1] I think this confined use wrong, but it is, of course, legitimate. To ignore the existence of other uses is, on the other hand, inexcusable.

make little metaphysical use of the doctrine that pleasure and pain belong solely to the self as distinct from the not-self. And the doctrine itself is quite without foundation. It is not even true that at first self and not-self exist. And though it is true that pleasure and pain are the main feature on which later this distinction is based, yet it is even then false that they may not belong to the object.

But, if we leave this error and return once more to feeling, in the sense of that which comes undifferentiated, we are forced to see that it cannot give the knowledge which we seek. It is an apprehension too defective to lay hold on reality. In the first place, its content and its form are not in agreement; and this is manifest when feeling changes from moment to moment. Then the matter, which ought to come to us harmoniously and as one whole, becomes plainly discrepant within itself. The content exhibits its essential relativity. It depends, that is to say—in order to be what it is—upon something not itself. Feeling ought to be something all in one and self-contained, if not simple. Its essence ought not to include matter the adjective of, and with a reference to, a foreign existence. It should be real, and should not be, in this sense, partly ideal. And the form of immediacy, in which it offers itself, implies this self-subsistent character. But in change the content slips away, and becomes something else; while, again, change appears necessary and implied in its being. Mutability is a fact in the actual feeling which we experience, for that never continues at rest. And, if we examine the content at any one given moment, we perceive that, though it presents itself as self-subsistent, it is infected by a deep-seated relativity. And this will force itself into view, first in the experience of change, and later, for reflection. Again, in the second place, apart from this objection, and even if feeling were self-consistent, it would not suffice for a knowledge of reality. Reality, as it commonly appears, contains terms and relations, and indeed may be said to consist in these mainly. But the form of feeling (on the other side) is not above, but is below, the level of relations ; and it therefore cannot possibly express them or explain them. Hence it is idle to suppose, given relational matter as the object to be understood, that feeling will supply any way of understanding it. And this objection seems quite fatal. Thus we are forced beyond feeling, first by change, and then further by the relational form which remains obstinately outstanding. But, when once more we betake ourselves to reflection, we seem to have made no advance. For the incompleteness and relativity in the matter given by feeling become, when we reflect on them, open contradiction. The limitation is seen to be a reference to something beyond, and the self-subsistent fact shows ideality, and turns round into mere adjectives whose support we cannot find. Feeling can be, therefore, no solution of the puzzles which, so far, have proved to be insoluble. Its content is vitiated throughout by the old inconsistencies. It may be said even to thrust upon us, in a still more apparent form, the discrepancy that lies between identity and diversity, immediate oneness and relation.

(b) Thus mere feeling has no power to justify the self's reality, and naturally none to solve the problems of the universe at large. But we may perhaps be more fortunate with some form of self-consciousness. That possibly may furnish us with a key to the self, and so also to the world ; and let us briefly make an attempt. The prospect is certainly at first sight not very encouraging. For (i.) if we take the actual matter revealed by self-consciousness, that (in any sense in which it pleases us to understand self) seems quite inconsistent internally. If the reader will recall the discussions of the preceding chapter,

he may, I think, convince himself on this point.
Take the self, either at one time or throughout any
duration, and its contents do not seem to arrange
themselves as a harmony. Nor have we, so far,
found a principle by the application of which we are
enabled to arrange them without contradiction.
(ii.) But self-consciousness, we may be told, is a
special way of intuition, or perception, or what you
will. And this experience of both subject and object
in one self, or of the identity of the Ego through and
in the opposition of itself to itself, or generally the
self-apprehension of the self as one and many, is at
last the full answer to our whole series of riddles.
But to my mind such an answer brings no satisfaction. For it seems liable to the objections which
proved fatal to mere feeling. Suppose, for argument's sake, that the intuition (as you describe it)
actually exists; suppose that in this intuition, while
you keep to it, you possess a diversity without discrepancy. This is one thing, but it is quite another
thing to possess a principle which can serve for the
understanding of reality. For how does this way of
apprehension suffice to take in a long series of
events? How again does it embrace, and transcend,
and go beyond, the relational form of discursive intelligence? The world is surely not understood if
understanding is left out. And in what manner
can your intuition satisfy the claims of understanding? This, to my mind, forms a wholly insuperable
obstacle. For the contents of the intuition (this
many in one), if you try to reconstruct them relationally, fall asunder forthwith. And the attempt to
find in self-consciousness an apprehension at a level,
not below, but above relations—a way of apprehension superior to discursive thought, and including its
mere process in a higher harmony—appears to me
not successful. I am, in short, compelled to this
conclusion: even if your intuition is a fact, it is not
an *understanding* of the self or of the world. It is a

mere experience, and it furnishes no consistent view about itself or about reality in general. An experience, I suppose, can override understanding only in one way, by including it, that is, as a subordinate element somehow within itself. And such an experience is a thing which seems not discoverable in self-consciousness.

And (iii.) I am forced to urge this last objection against the whole form of self-consciousness, as it was described above. There does not really exist any perception, either in which the object and the subject are quite the same, or in which their sameness amid difference is an object for perception. Any such consciousness would seem to be impossible psychologically. And, as it is almost useless for me to try to anticipate the reader's views on this point, I must content myself with a very brief statement. Self-consciousness, as distinct from self-feeling, implies a relation. It is the state where the self has become an object that stands before the mind. This means that an element is in opposition to the felt mass, and is distinguished from it as a not-self. And there is no doubt that the self, in its various meanings, can become such a not-self. But, in whichever of its meanings we intend to consider it, the result is the same. The object is never wholly identical with the subject, and the background of feeling must contain a great deal more than what we at any time can perceive as the self. And I confess that I scarcely know how to argue this point. To me the idea that the whole self can be observed in one perception would be merely chimerical. I find, first, that in the felt background there remains an obscure residue of internal sensation, which I perhaps at no time can distinguish as an object. And this felt background at any moment will almost certainly contain also elements from outer sensation. On the other hand, the self, as an object, will at any one time embrace but a poor extent of detail. It is palpably and flagrantly much more narrow than the background felt as self. And in order to exhaust this felt mass (if indeed exhaustion is possible) we require a series of patient observations, in none of which will the object be as full as the subject.[1] To have the felt self in its totality as an object for consciousness seems out of the question. And I would further ask the reader to bear in mind that, where the self is observed as in opposition to the not-self, this whole relation is included within that felt background, against which, on the other hand, the distinction takes place.

And this suggests an objection. How, I may be asked, if self-consciousness is no more than you say, do we take one object as self and another as not-self? Why is the observed object perceived at all in the character of self? This is a question, I think, not difficult to answer, so far at least as is required for our purpose here. The all-important point is this, that the unity of feeling never disappears. The mass, at first undifferentiated, groups itself into objects in relation to me; and then again further the " me " becomes explicit, and itself is an object in relation to the background of feeling. But, none the less, the object not-self is still a part of the individual soul, and the object self likewise keeps its place in this felt unity. The distinctions have supervened upon, but they have not divided, the original whole; and, if they had done so, the result would have been mere destruction. Hence, in self-consciousness, those contents perceived as the self belong still to the whole individual mass. They, in the first place, are features in the felt totality; then again they are elements in that inner group from which the not-self is distinguished; and finally they become an object opposed to the internal back-

---

[1] The possibility of this series rests on the fact that sameness and alteration can be *felt* where they are not *perceived*. Cp. p. 93.

ground. And these contents exist thus in several forms all at once. And so, just as the not-self is felt as still psychically my state, the self, when made an object, is still felt as individually one with me. Nay, we may reflect upon this unity of feeling, and may say that the self, as self and as not-self all in one, is our object. And this is true if we mean that it is an object *for reflection*. But in that reflection once more there is an actual subject; and that actual sub-ject is a mass of feeling much fuller than the object; and it is a subject which in no sense is an object *for* the reflection. The feature, of being not-self and self in one self, can indeed be brought before the present subject, and can be felt to be its own. The unity of feeling can become an object for perception and thought, and can also be felt to belong to the self which is present, and which is the subject that perceives. But, without entering into psychological refinements and difficulties, we may be sure of this main result. The actual subject is never, in any state of mind, brought before itself as an object. It has that before it which it feels to be itself, so far at least as to fall within its own area, and to be one thing with its felt unity. But the actual subject never feels that it is all out there in its object, that there is nothing more left within, and that the difference has disappeared. And of this we can surely convince ourselves by observation. The subject in the end must be felt, and it can never (as it is) be perceived.

But, if so, then self-consciousness will not solve our former difficulties. For these distinctions, of self and of not-self in one whole, are *not* presented as the reality even of my self. They are given as found within it, but not as exhausting it. But even if the self did, what it cannot do, and guaranteed this arrangement as its proper reality, that would still leave us at a loss. For unless we could think the arrangement so as to be consistent with itself we could not admit it as being the truth about reality. It would merely be an experience, unintelligible or deceptive. And it is an experience which, we have now seen, has no existence in fact.

(c) We found the self, as mere feeling, gave us no key to our puzzles, and we have not had more success in our attempt with self-consciousness. So far as that transcends mere feeling, it is caught in, and is dissipated by, the old illusory play of relations and qualities. It repeats this illusion, without doubt, at a higher level than before; the endeavour is more ambitious, but the result is still the same. For we have not been taught how to understand diversity in unity. And though, in my judgment, the further task should now be superfluous, I will briefly touch upon some other claims made for the self. The first rests on the consciousness of personal identity. This may be supposed to have some bearing on the reality of the self, but to my mind it appears to be almost irrelevant. Of course the self, within limits and up to a certain point, is the same; and I will leave to others the attempt to fix those limits by a principle. For, in my opinion, there is none which at bottom is not arbitrary. But what I fail to perceive is the metaphysical conclusion which comes from a consciousness of self-sameness. I quite understand that this fact disproves any doctrine of the self's mere discreteness. Or, more correctly, it is an obvious instance against a doctrine which evidently contradicts itself in principle. The self is *not* merely discrete; and therefore (doubtless by some wonderful alternative) we are carried to a positive result about its reality. But the facts of the case seem merely to be thus. As long as there remains in the self a certain basis of content, ideally the same, so long may the self recall anything once associated with that basis. And this identity of content, working by redintegration and so bringing

up the past as the history of one self—really this is
all which we have to build upon. Now this, of
course, shows that self-sameness exists as a fact,
and that hence *somehow* an identical self must be
real. But then the question is *how ?* The question
is whether we can state the existence and the continuity of a real self in a way which is intelligible,
and which is not ruined by the difficulties of previous
discussions. Because, otherwise, we may have found
an interesting fact, but most assuredly we have not
found a tenable view about reality. That tenable
view, if we got sight of it, might show us that our
fact had been vitally misapprehended. At all
events, so long as we can offer only a bundle of
inconsistencies, it is absurd to try to believe that
these are the true reality. And, if any one likes to
fall back upon a miraculous faculty which he dis-
covers in memory, the case is not altered. For the
issue is as to the truth either of the message conveyed, or of our conclusion from that message.
And, for myself, I stand on this. Present your
doctrine (whatever it is) in a form which will bear
criticism, and which will enable me to understand
this confused mass of facts which I encounter on all
sides. Do this, and I will follow you, and I will
worship the source of such a true revelation. But I
will not accept nonsense for reality, though it be
vouched for by miracle, or proceed from the mouth
of a psychological monster.

And I am compelled to adopt the same attitude
towards another supposed fact. I refer to the unity
in such a function as, for instance, Comparison.
This has been assumed to be timeless, and to serve
as a foundation for metaphysical views about the self.
But I am forced to reject alike both basis and result,
if that result be offered as a positive view. It is in
the first place (as we have seen in Chapter v.)
psychologically untenable to take any mental fact
as free from duration. And, apart from that, what

works in any function must be something concrete
and specially relevant to that function. In comparison it must be, for instance, a special basis of
identity in the terms to be compared.[1]   A timeless
self, acting in a particular way from its general timeless nature, is to me, in the first place, a psychological monster.   And, in the second place, if this
extraordinary fact did exist, it would indeed serve to
show that certain views were not true ; but, beyond
that, it would remain a mere extraordinary fact.   At
least for myself I do not perceive how it supplies
us with a conclusion about the self or the world,
which is consistent and defensible.   And here once
again we have the same issue.   We have found
puzzles in reality, besetting every way in which we
have taken it.   Now give me a view not obnoxious
to these mortal attacks, and combining differences
in one so as to turn the edge of criticism—and then
I will thank you.   But I cannot be grateful for an
assertion which seems to serve merely as an object-
tion to another doctrine, otherwise known to be
false; an assertion, which, if we accepted it as we
cannot, would leave us simply with a very strange
fact on our hands.   Such a fact is certainly no
principle by which we could solve the riddle of the
universe.

(*d*) I must next venture a few words on an
embarrassing topic, the supposed revelation of
reality within the self as force or will.   And the
difficulty comes, not so much from the nature of the
subject, as from the manner of its treatment.   If we
could get a clear statement as to the matter revealed,
we could at this stage of our discussion dispose of it
in a few words, or rather point out that it has been
already disposed of.   But a clear statement is precisely that which (so far as my experience goes) is
not to be had.

[1] There are some further remarks in *Mind*, Nos. 41 and 43.

The reader who recalls our discussions on activity, will remember how it literally was riddled by contradictions. All the puzzles as to adjectives and relations and terms, every dilemma as to time and causation, seemed to meet in it and there even to find an addition. Far from reducing these to harmony, activity, when we tried to think it, fell helplessly asunder or jarred with itself. And to suppose that the self is to bring order into this chaos, after our experience hitherto of the self's total impotence, seems more sanguine than rational.

If now we take force or cause, as it is revealed in the self, to be the same as volition proper, that clearly will not help us. For in volition we have an idea, determining change in the self, and so producing its own realization.[1] Volition perhaps at first sight may seem to promise a solution of our metaphysical puzzles. For we seem to find at last something like a self-contained cause with an effect within itself. But this surely is illusory. The old difficulties about the beginning of change and its process in time, the old troubles as to diversity in union with sameness—how is any one of these got rid of, or made more tractable? It is bootless to enquire whether we have found a principle which is to explain the universe. For we have not even found anything which can bear its own weight, or can endure for one moment the most superficial scrutiny. Volition gives us, of course, an intense feeling of reality; and we may conclude, if we please, that in this lies the heart of the mystery of things. Yes, perhaps; here lies the answer—for those who may have understood; and the whole question turns on whether we *have* reached an understanding. But what you offer me appears much more like an experience, not understood but interpreted into hopeless confusion. It is with you as with the man who, transported by his

[1] I have discussed the nature of will psychologically in *Mind*, No. 49.

passion, feels and knows that only love gives the
secret of the universe.   In each case the result is
perfectly in order, but one hardly sees why it should
be called metaphysics.

And we shall make no advance, if we pass from
will proper where an idea is realized, and fall back
on an obscurer revelation of energy.   In the experience of activity, or. resistance, or will, or force
(or whatever other phrase seems most oracular), we
are said to come at last down to the rock of reality.
And I am not so ill-advised as to offer a disproof
of the message revealed.   It is doubtless a mystery,
and hence those who could inform the outer world
of its meaning, are for that very reason compelled
to be silent and to seem even ignorant.   What I can
do is to set down briefly the external remarks of one
not initiated.

In the first place, taken psychologically, the revelation is fraudulent.   There is no original experience
of anything like activity, to say nothing of resistance.
This is quite a secondary product, the origin of
which is far from mysterious, and on which I have
said something in the preceding chapter.[1]   You
may, doubtless, point to an outstanding margin of
undetermined sensations, but these will not contain
the essence of the matter.   And I do not hesitate
to say this : Where you meet a psychologist who
takes this experience as elementary, you will find a
man who has not ever made a serious attempt to
decompose it, or ever resolutely faced the question
as to what it contains.   And. in the second place,
taken metaphysically, these tidings, given from
whatever source, are either meaningless or false.
And here once again we have the all-important
point.   I do not care what your oracle is, and your

---

[1] I have touched the question only in its general form.   As to
the special source from which come the elements of this or that
perception of activity, I have not said anything.   This is a matter
for psychology.

preposterous psychology may here be gospel if you
please ; the real question is whether your response
(so far as it means anything) is not appearance and
illusion. If it means nothing, that is to say, if it
is merely a datum, which has no complex content
that can be taken as a principle—then it will be
much what we have in, say, pleasure or pain. But
if you offered me one of these as a theoretical
account of the universe, you would not be even
mistaken, but simply nonsensical. And it is the
same with activity or force, if these also merely are,
and say nothing. But if, on the other hand, the
revelation does contain a meaning, I will commit
myself to this : either the oracle is so confused that
its signification is not discoverable, or, upon the
other hand, if it can be pinned down to any definite
statement, then that statement will be false. When
we drag it out into the light, and expose it to the
criticism of our foregoing discussions, it will exhibit
its helplessness. It will be proved to contain mere
unsolved discrepancies, and will give us therefore,
not truth, but in the end appearance. And I intend
to leave this matter so without further remark.

(*e*) I will in conclusion touch briefly on the theory
of Monads. A tenable view of reality has been
sought in the doctrine that each self is an independent reality, substantial if not simple. But this
attempt does not call for a lengthy discussion. In
the first place, if there is more than one self in the
universe, we are met by the problem of their relation to each other. And the reply, " Why there is
none," we have already seen in Chapter iii., is no
sufficient defence. For plurality and separateness
without a relation of separation seem really to have
no meaning. And, from the other side, without
relations these poor monads would have no process
and would serve no purpose. But relations admitted,
again, are fatal to the monads' independence. The
substances clearly become adjectival, and mere

elements within an all-comprehending whole. And
hence there is left remaining for their internal contents no solid principle of stability.[1]   And in the
second place, even if this remained, it would be no
solution of our difficulties.   For consider : we have
found, so far, that diversity and unity can not be
reconciled.   Both in the existence of the whole self
in relation with its contents, and in the various
special forms which that existence takes, we have
encountered everywhere the same trouble.   We
have had features which *must* come together, and
yet were willing to do so in no way that we could
find.   In the self there is a variety, and in the self
there is a unity ; but, in attempting to understand
how, we fall into inconsistencies which, therefore, cannot be truth.   And now in what way is the monadic
character of the self—with whatever precise meaning (if with any) we take this up—about to assist
us ?   Will it in the least show us *how* the diversity
can exist in harmony with the oneness?   If it
can do this, then I would respectfully suggest that
it should do it.   Because, otherwise, the unity
seems merely stated and emphasized ; and the
problem of its diverse content is either wholly
neglected or hidden under a confusion of fictions
and metaphors.   But if more than an emphasis
on the unity is meant, that more is even positively
objectionable.   For while the diversity is slurred
over, instead of being explained, there will be a
negative assertion as to the limits within which
the self's true unity falls.   And this assertion cannot stand criticism.   And lastly the relation of
the self to its contents in time will tend to become
a new insoluble enigma.   Monadism, on the whole,

---

[1] The attentive reader of Lotze must, I think, have found it
hard to discover why individual selves with him are more than
phenomenal adjectives.   For myself I discern plainly his resolve
that somehow they have *got* to be more.   But I do not find that
he is ever willing to face this question fairly.

will increase and will add to the difficulties which already exist, and it will not supply us with a solution of any single one of them. It would be strange indeed if an explanation of all sides of our puzzle were found in mere obstinate emphasis upon one of those sides.

And with this result I will bring the present chapter to a close. The reader who has followed our discussions up to this point, can, if he pleases, pursue the detail of the subject, and can further criticise the claims made for the self's reality. But if he will drive home the objections which we have come to know in principle, the conclusion he will reach is assured already. In whatever way the self is taken, it will prove to be appearance. It cannot, if finite, maintain itself against external relations. For these will enter its essence, and so ruin its independency. And, apart from this objection in the case of its finitude, the self is in any case unintelligible. For, in considering it, we are forced to transcend mere feeling, itself not satisfactory ; and yet we cannot reach any defensible thought, any intellectual principle, by which it is possible to understand how diversity can be comprehended in unity. But, if we cannot understand this, and if whatever way we have of thinking about the self proves full of inconsistency, we should then accept what must follow. The self is no doubt the highest form of experience which we have, but, for all that, is not a true form. It does not give us the facts as they are in reality ; and, as it gives them, they are appearance, appearance and error.

And one of the reasons why this result is not admitted on all sides, seems to lie in that great ambiguity of the self which our previous chapter detailed. Apparently distinct, this phrase wavers from one meaning to another, is applied to various objects, and in argument is used too seldom in a

well-defined sense.   But there is a still more fundamental aid to obscurity.   The end of metaphysics
is to understand the universe, to find a way of
thinking about facts in general which is free from
contradiction.   But how few writers seem to trouble
themselves much about this vital issue. Of those who
take their principle of understanding from the self,
how few subject that principle to an impartial
scrutiny.   But it is easy to argue from a foregone
alternative, to disprove any theory which loses sight
of the self, and then to offer what remains as the
secret of the universe—whether what remains is
thinkable or is a complex which refuses to be understood.   And it is easy to survey the world which is
selfless, to find there vanity and illusion, and then
to return to one's self into congenial darkness and
the equivocal consolation of some psychological
monster.   But, if the object is to understand, there
can be only one thing which we have to consider.
It does not matter from what source our principle is
derived.   It may be the refutation of something
else—it is no worse for that.   Or it may be a response emitted by some kind of internal oracle, and
it is no worse for that.   But for metaphysics a
principle, if it is to stand at all, must stand absolutely
by itself.   While wide enough to cover the facts, it
must be able to be thought without jarring internally.
It is this, to repeat it once more, on which everything turns.   The diversity and the unity must be
brought to the light, and the principle must be seen
to comprehend these.   It must not carry us away
into a maze of relations, relations that lead to
illusory terms, and terms disappearing into endless
relations.   But the self is so far from supplying
such a principle, that it seems, where not hiding
itself in obscurity, a mere bundle of discrepancies.
Our search has conducted us again not to reality but
mere appearance.

CHAPTER XI.

PHENOMENALISM.

OUR attempts, so far, to reduce the world's diverse contents to unity have ended in failure. Any sort of group which we could find, whether a thing or a self, proved unable to stand criticism. And, since it seems that what appears must somewhere certainly be one, and since this unity is not to be discovered in phenomena, the reality threatens to migrate to another world than ours. We have been driven near to the separation of appearance and reality; we already perhaps contemplate their localization in two different hemispheres—the one unknown to us and real, and the other known and mere appearance. But, before we take this step, I will say a few words on a proposed alternative, stating this entirely in my own way and so as to suit my own convenience.

"Why," it may be said, "should we trouble ourselves to seek for a unity? Why do things not go on very well as they are? We really want no substance or activity, or anything else of the kind. For phenomena and their laws are all that science requires." Such a view may be called Phenomenalism. It is superficial at its best, and it is held of course with varying degrees of intelligence. In its most consistent form, I suppose, it takes its phenomena as feelings or sensations. These with their relations are the elements; and the laws somewhere and somehow come into this view. And against its opponents Phenomenalism would urge, What else exists? "Show me anything real," it would argue,

" and I will show you mere presentation; more is not to be discovered, and really more is meaningless. Things and selves are not unities in any sense whatever, except as given collections or arrangements of such presented elements. What appears is, as a matter of fact, grouped in such and such manners. And then, of course, there are the laws. When we have certain things given, then certain other things are given too; or we know that certain other occurrences will or may take place. There is hence nothing but events, appearances which happen, and the ways which these appearances have of happening. And how, in the name of science, can any one want any more ? "

The last question suggests a very obvious criticism. The view either makes a claim to take account of all the facts, or it makes no such claim. In the latter case there is at once an end of its pretensions. But in the former case it has to meet this fatal objection. All the ways of thinking which introduce an unity into things, into the world or the self—and there clearly is a good deal of such thinking on hand—are of course illusory. But, none the less, they are facts entirely undeniable. And Phenomenalism is invited to take some account of these facts, and to explain how on its principles their existence is possible. How, for example, with only such elements and their laws, is the theory of Phenomenalism itself a possible fact ? The theory seems a unity which, if it were true, would be impossible. And an objection of this sort has a very wide range, and applies to a considerable area of appearance. But I am not going to ask how Phenomenalism is prepared to reply. I will simply say that this one objection, to those who understand, makes an end of the business. And if there ever has been so much as an attempt to meet this fairly, it has escaped my notice. We may be sure beforehand that such an effort must be wholly futile.

Thus, without our entering into any criticism on the positive doctrine, a mere reference to what it must admit, and yet blindly ignores, is a sufficient refutation. But I will add a few remarks on the inconsistencies of that which it offers us.

What it states, in the first place, as to its elements and their relations, is unintelligible. In actual fact, wherever you get it, these distinctions appear and seem even to be necessary. At least I have no notion of the way in which they could be dispensed with. But if so, there is here at once a diversity in unity; we have somehow together, perhaps, several elements and some relations; and what is the meaning of "together," when once distinctions have been separated? And then what sort of things are relations? Can you have elements which are free from them even internally? And are relations themselves not given elements, another kind of phenomena? But, if so, what is the relation between the first kind and the second (Cf. Chapter iii.)? Or, if that question ends in sheer nonsense, who is responsible for the nonsense? Consider, for instance, any fact of sense, it does not matter what; and let Phenomenalism attempt to state clearly what it means by its elements and relations; let it tell us whether these two sides are in relation with one another, or, if not that, what else is the case. But I will pass to another point.

An obvious question arises as to events past and future. If these, and their relations to the present, are not to be real and in some sense to exist—then difficulties arise into which I will not enter. But, if past and future (or either of them) are in any sense real, then, in the first place, the unity of this series will be something inexplicable. And, in the second place, a reality, not presented and not given (and even the past is surely not given), was precisely that against which Phenomenalism set its face. This is another inconsistency.

Let us go on to consider the question as to identity. This Phenomenalism should deny, because identity is a real union of the diverse. But change is not to be denied, for obviously it must be there when something happens. Now, if there is change, there is by consequence something which changes. But if *it* changes, it is the same throughout a diversity. It is, in other words, a real unity, a concrete universal. Take, for example, the fact of motion; evidently here something alters its place. Hence a variety of places, whatever that means—in any case a variety—must be predicated of one something. If so, we have at once on our hands the One and the Many, and otherwise our theory declines to deal with ordinary fact.

In brief, identity—being that which the doctrine excluded—is essential to its being. And now how far is this to go? Is the series of phenomena, with its differences, one series? If it is not one, why treat it as if it were so? If it is one, then here indeed is a unity which gives us pause. Again, are the elements ever permanent and remaining identical from one time to another? But, whether they are or are not identical, how are facts to be explained? Suppose, in the first place, that we do have identical elements, surviving amid change and the play of variety. Here are metaphysical reals, raising the old questions we have been discussing through this Book. But perhaps nothing is really permanent except the laws. The problem of change is given up, and we fall back upon our laws, persisting and appearing in successions of fleeting elements. If so, phenomena seem now to have become temporal illustrations of laws.

And it is perhaps time to ask a question concerning the nature of these last-mentioned creatures. Are they permanent real essences, visible from time to time in their fleeting illustrations? If so, once more Phenomenalism has adored blindly what it rejected. And, of course, the relations of these essences—the one to the other, and each to the phenomena which in some way seem its adject-ives—take us back to those difficulties which proved too hard for us. But I presume that the reality of the laws must be denied, or denied, that is, not quite, but with a reservation. The laws are hypothetical ; they are in themselves but possibilities, and actual only when found in real presentation. Apart from this, and as mere laws, they are con-nections between terms which do not exist ; and, if so, as connections, they are not strictly anything actual. In short, just as the elements were nothing outside of presentation, so again, outside of presen-tation, the laws really are nothing. And *in* pre-sentation then—what is either side, the elements or the laws, but an unreal and quite indefensible thought? It seems that we can say of them only that we do not know what they are ; and all that we can be certain of is this, that they are *not* what we know, namely, given phenomena.

And here we may end. The view has started with mere presentation. It, of course, is forced to transcend this, and it has done so ignorantly and blindly. A little criticism has driven it back, and has left it with a universe, which must either be distinctions within one presentation, or else mere nonsense. And then these distinctions them-selves are quite indefensible. If you admit them, you have to deal with the metaphysical problem of the Many in One; and you cannot admit them, be-cause clearly they are not given and presented, but at least more or less made. And what it must come to is that Phenomenalism ends in this dilemma. It must either keep to the moment's presentation, and must leave there the presented entirely as it is given—and, if so, then surely there could be no more science; or it must "become transcendent" (as the phrase goes), and launch out into a sea of more preposterous inconsistencies than are perhaps to be found in any other attempt at metaphysics. As a working point of view, directed and confined to the ascertainment of some special branch of truth, Phenomenalism is of course useful and is indeed quite necessary. And the metaphysician who attacks it when following its own business, is likely to fare badly. But when Phenomenalism loses its head and, becoming blatant, steps forward as a theory of first principles, then it is really not respectable. The best that can be said of its pretensions is that they are ridiculous.

CHAPTER XII.

THINGS IN THEMSELVES.

WE have found, so far, that we have not been able to arrive at reality. The various ways, in which things have been taken up, have all failed to give more than mere appearance. Whatever we have tried has turned out something which, on investigation, has been proved to contradict itself. But that which does not attain to internal unity, has clearly stopped short of genuine reality. And, on the other hand, to sit down contented is impossible, unless, that is, we are resolved to put up with mere confusion. For to transcend what is given is clearly obligatory, if we are to think at all and to have any views whatever. But, the deliverance of the moment once left behind, we have succeeded in meeting with nothing that holds together. Every view has been seen only to furnish appearance, and the reality has escaped. It has baffled us so constantly, so persistently retreated, that in the end we are forced to set it down as unattainable. It seems to have been discovered to reside in another world than ours.

We have here reached a familiar way of regarding the universe, a doctrine held with very different degrees of comprehension. The universe, upon this view (whether it understands itself or not), falls apart into two regions, we may call them two hemispheres. One of these is the world of experience and knowledge — in every sense without reality. The other is the kingdom of reality—without either knowledge or experience. Or we have on one side phenomena, in other words, things as they are to us, and ourselves so far as we are anything to ourselves; while on the other side are Things as they are in themselves and as they do not appear; or, if we please, we may call this side the Unknowable. And our attitude towards such a divided universe varies a good deal. We may be thankful to be rid of that which is not relative to our affairs, and which cannot in any way concern us; and we may be glad that the worthless is thrown over the wall. Or we may regret that Reality is too good to be known, and from the midst of our own confusion may revere the other side in its inaccessible grandeur. We may even naively felicitate ourselves on total estrangement, and rejoice that at last utter ignorance has removed every scruple which impeded religion. Where we know nothing we can have no possible objection to worship.[1]

This view is popular, and to some extent is even plausible. It is natural to feel that the best and the highest is unknowable, in the sense of being something which our knowledge cannot master. And this is probably all that for most minds the doctrine signifies. But of course this is *not* what it says, nor what it means, when it has any definite meaning. For it does not teach that our knowledge of reality is imperfect; it asserts that it does not exist, and that we have no knowledge at all, however imperfect. There is a hard and fast line, with our apprehension on the one side and the Thing on the other side, and the two hopelessly apart. This is the doctrine, and its plausibility vanishes before criticism.

[1] I do not wish to be irreverent, but Mr. Spencer's attitude towards his Unknowable strikes me as a pleasantry, the point of which lies in its unconsciousness. It seems a proposal to take something for God simply and solely because we do not know what the devil it can be. But I am far from attributing to Mr. Spencer any one consistent view.

Its absurdity may be shown in several ways. The Unknowable must, of course, be prepared either to deserve its name or not. But, if it actually were not knowable, we could not know that such a thing even existed. It would be much as if we said, "Since all my faculties are totally confined to my garden, I cannot tell if the roses next door are in flower." And this seems inconsistent. And we may push the line of attack which we mentioned in the last chapter. If the theory really were true, then it must be impossible. There is no reconciling our knowledge of its truth with that general condition which exists if it is true. But I propose to adopt another way of criticism, which perhaps may be plainer.

I will first make a remark as to the plurality involved in Things in themselves. If this is *meant*, then within their secluded world we have a long series of problems. Their diversity and their relations bring us back to those very difficulties which we were endeavouring to avoid. And it seems clear that, if we wish to be consistent, the plural must be dropped. Hence in future we shall confine ourselves to the Thing in itself.

We have got this reality on one side and our appearances on the other, and we are naturally led to enquire about their connection. Are they related, the one to the other, or not? If they are related, and if in any way the appearances are made the adjectives of reality, then the Thing has become qualified by them. It is qualified, but on what principle? That is what we do not know. We have in effect every unsolved problem which vexed us before; and we have, besides, this whole confusion now predicated of the Thing, no longer, therefore, something by itself. But this perplexed attribution was precisely that which the doctrine intended to avoid. We must therefore deny any relation of our appearances to the Thing. But, if

so, other troubles vex us.   Either our Thing has
qualities, or it has not.   If it has them, then within
itself the same puzzles break out which we intended
to leave behind,—to make a prey of phenomena and
to rest contented with *their* ruin.   So we must
correct ourselves and assert that the Thing is
unqualified.   But, if so, we are destroyed with no
less certainty.   For a Thing without qualities is
clearly not real.   It is mere Being, or mere Nothing, according as you take it simply for what it is,
or consider also that which it *means* to be.   Such
an abstraction is palpably of no use to us.

And, if we regard the situation from the side of
phenomena, it is not more encouraging.   We must
take appearances in connection with reality, or not.
In the former case, they are not rendered one whit
less confused.   They offer precisely the old jungle
in which no way could be found, and which is not
cleared by mere attribution to a Thing in itself.
But, if we deny the connection of phenomena with
the Real, our condition is not improved.   Either
we possess now two realms of confusion and disorder, existing side by side, or the one above the
other.   And, in this case, the "other world" of the
Thing in itself only serves to reduplicate all that
troubles us here.   Or, on the other hand, if we
suppose the Thing to be unqualified, it still gives us
no assistance.   Everything in our concrete world
remains the same, and the separate existence somewhere of this wretched abstraction serves us only
as a poor and irrelevant excuse for neglecting our
own concerns.

And I will allow myself to dwell on this last
feature of the case.   The appearances after all,
being what we experience, must be what matters for
us.   They are surely the one thing which, from the
nature of the case, can possess human value.
Surely, the moment we understand what we mean
by our words, the Thing in itself becomes utterly

worthless and devoid of all interest. And we discover a state of mind which would be ridiculous to
a degree, if it had not unfortunately a serious side.
It is contended that contradictions in phenomena
are something quite in order, so long as the Thing
in itself is not touched. That is to say that everything, which we know and can experience, does not
matter, however distracted its case, and that this
purely irrelevant ghost is the ark of salvation to be
preserved at all costs. But how it can be anything
to us whether something outside our knowledge
contradicts itself or not—is simply unintelligible.
What is too visible is our own readiness to sacrifice
everything which possesses any possible claim on
us. And what is to be inferred is our confusion,
and our domination by a theory which lives only in
the world of misunderstanding.

We have seen that the doctrine of a Thing in
itself is absurd. A reality of this sort is assuredly
not something unverifiable. It has on the contrary
a nature which is fully transparent, as a false and
empty abstraction, whose generation is plain. We
found that reality was not the appearances, and
that result must hold good ; but, on the other hand,
reality is certainly not something else which is
unable to appear. For that is sheer self-contradiction, which is plausible only so long as we do not
realize its meaning. The assertion of a reality
falling outside knowledge, is quite nonsensical.

And so this attempt to shelve our problems, this
proposal to take no pains about what are *only*
phenomena, has broken down. It was a vain
notion to set up an idol apart, to dream that facts
for that reason had ceased to be facts, and had
somehow become *only* something else. And this
false idea is an illusion which we should attempt to
clear out of our minds once for all. We shall have
hereafter to enquire into the nature of appearance ;
but for the present we may keep a fast hold upon

this, that appearances exist. That is absolutely certain, and to deny it is nonsense. And whatever exists must belong to reality. That is also quite certain, and its denial once more is self-contradictory. Our appearances no doubt may be a beggarly show, and their nature to an unknown extent may be something which, as it is, is not true of reality. That is one thing, and it is quite another thing to speak as if these facts had no actual existence, or as if there could be anything but reality to which they might belong. And I must venture to repeat that such an idea would be sheer nonsense. What appears, for that sole reason, most indubitably *is*; and there is no possibility of conjuring its being away from it. And, though we ask no question at present as to the exact nature of reality, we may be certain that it cannot be less than appearances; we may be sure that the least of these in some way contributes to make it what it is. And the whole result of this Book may be summed up in a few words. Everything so far, which we have seen, has turned out to be appearance. It is that which, taken as it stands, proves inconsistent with itself, and for this reason cannot be true of the real. But to deny its existence or to divorce it from reality is out of the question. For it has a positive character which is indubitable fact, and, however much this fact may be pronounced appearance, it can have no place in which to live except reality. And reality, set on one side and apart from all appearance, would assuredly be nothing. Hence what is certain is that, in some way, these inseparables are joined. This is the positive result which has emerged from our discussion. Our failure so far lies in this, that we have not found the way in which appearances can belong to reality. And to this further task we must now address ourselves, with however little hope of more than partial satisfaction.

BOOK II.

REALITY

CHAPTER XIII.

THE GENERAL NATURE OF REALITY.

THE result of our First Book has been mainly negative.   We have taken up a number of ways of regarding reality, and we have found that they all
are vitiated by self-discrepancy.   The reality can
accept not one of these predicates, at least in the
character in which so far they have come.   We certainly ended with a reflection which promised something positive.   Whatever is rejected as appearance
is, for that very reason, no mere nonentity.   It
cannot bodily be shelved and merely got rid of, and,
therefore, since it must fall. somewhere, it must
belong to reality.   To take it as existing somehow
and somewhere in the unreal, would surely be quite
meaningless.   For reality must own and cannot be
less than appearance, and that is the one positive
result which, so far, we have reached.   But as to
the character which, otherwise, the real possesses,
we at present know nothing ; and a further knowledge is what we must aim at through the remainder
of our search.   The present Book, to some extent,
falls into two divisions.   The first of these deals
mainly with the general character of reality, and
with the defence of this against a number of objections.   Then from this basis, in the second place,
I shall go on to consider mainly some special features.   But I must admit that I have kept to no
strict principle of division.   I have really observed
no rule of progress, except to get forward in the
best way that I can.

At the beginning of our inquiry into the nature of the real we encounter, of course, a general doubt or denial.[1] To know the truth, we shall be told, is impossible, or is, at all events, wholly impracticable. We cannot have positive knowledge about first principles; and, if we could possess it, we should not know when actually we had got it. What is denied is, in short, the existence of a criterion. I shall, later on, in Chapter xxvii., have to deal more fully with the objections of a thorough-going scepticism, and I will here confine myself to what seems requisite for the present.

Is there an absolute criterion? This question, to my mind, is answered by a second question: How otherwise should we be able to say anything at all about appearance? For through the last Book, the reader will remember, we were for the most part criticising. We were judging phenomena and were condemning them, and throughout we proceeded as if the self-contradictory could not be real. But this was surely to have and to apply an absolute criterion. For consider: you can scarcely propose to be quite passive when presented with statements about reality. You can hardly take the position of admitting any and every nonsense to be truth, truth absolute and entire, at least so far as you know. For, if you think at all so as to discriminate between truth and falsehood, you will find that you cannot accept open self-contradiction. Hence to think is to judge, and to judge is to criticise, and to criticise is to use a criterion of reality. And surely to doubt this would be mere blindness or confused self-deception.. But, if so, it is clear that, in rejecting the inconsistent as appearance, we are applying a positive knowledge of the ultimate nature of things. Ultimate reality is such that it does not contradict itself; here is an absolute criterion. And it is proved absolute by the

[1] See the Introduction, p. 2.

fact that, either in endeavouring to deny it, or even
in attempting to doubt it, we tacitly assume its
validity.

One of these essays in delusion may be noticed
briefly in passing. We may be told that our criterion has been developed by experience, and that
therefore at least it may not be absolute. But why
anything should be weaker for having been developed is, in the first place, not obvious. And,
in the second place, the whole doubt, when understood, destroys itself. For the alleged origin of our
criterion is delivered to us by knowledge which
rests throughout on its application as an absolute
test. And what can be more irrational than to try
to prove that a principle is doubtful, when the proof
through every step rests on its unconditional truth?
It would, of course, not be irrational to take one's
stand on this criterion, to use it to produce a conclusion hostile to itself, and to urge that therefore
our whole knowledge is self-destructive, since it
essentially drives us to what we cannot accept. But
this is not the result which our supposed objector
has in view, or would welcome. He makes no
attempt to show in general that a psychological
growth is in any way hostile to metaphysical validity.
And he is not prepared to give up his own psychological knowledge, which knowledge plainly is ruined
if the criterion is *not* absolute. The doubt is seen,
when we reflect, to be founded on that which it
endeavours to question. And it has but blindly
borne witness to the absolute certainty of our knowledge about reality.

Thus we possess a criterion, and our criterion is
supreme. I do not mean to deny that we might
have several standards, giving us sundry pieces of
information about the nature of things. But, be
that as it may, we still have an over-ruling test of
truth, and the various standards (if they exist) are
certainly subordinate. This at once becomes evid-

ent, for we cannot refuse to bring such standards together, and to ask if they agree. Or, at least, if a doubt is suggested as to their consistency, each with itself and with the rest, we are compelled, so to speak, to assume jurisdiction. And if they were guilty of self-contradiction, when examined or compared, we should condemn them as appearance. But we could not do that if they were not subject all to one tribunal. And hence, as we find nothing not subordinate to the test of self-consistency, we are forced to set that down as supreme and absolute.

But it may be said that this supplies us with no real information. If we think, then certainly we are not allowed to be inconsistent, and it is admitted that this test is unconditional and absolute. But it will be urged that, for knowledge about any matter, we require something more than a bare negation. The ultimate reality (we are agreed) does not permit self-contradiction, but a prohibition or an absence (we shall be told) by itself does not amount to positive knowledge. The denial of inconsistency, therefore, does not predicate any positive quality. But such an objection is untenable. It may go so far as to assert that a bare denial is possible, that we may reject a predicate though we stand on no positive basis, and though there is nothing special which serves to reject. This error has been refuted in my *Principles of Logic* (Book I., Chapter iii.),[1] and I do not propose to discuss it here. I will pass to another sense in which the objection may seem more plausible. The criterion, it may be urged, in itself is doubtless positive; but, for our knowledge and in effect, is merely negative. And it gives us therefore no information at all about reality, for, although knowledge is there, it cannot be brought out. The criterion is a basis, which serves as the

[1] The word "not" here, on p. 120, line 12, is an error, and should be struck out.

foundation of denial ; but, since this basis cannot be exposed, we are but able to stand on it and unable to see it. And it hence, in effect, tells us nothing, though there are assertions which it does not allow us to venture on. This objection, when stated in such a form, may seem plausible, and there is a sense in which I am prepared to admit that it is valid. If by the nature of reality we understand its full nature, I am not contending that this in a complete form is knowable. But that is very far from being the point here at issue. For the objection denies that we have a standard which gives *any* positive knowledge, *any* information, complete or incomplete, about the genuine reality. And this denial assuredly is mistaken.

The objection admits that we know what reality *does*, but it refuses to allow us any understanding of what reality *is*. The standard (it is agreed) both exists and possesses a positive character, and it is agreed that this character rejects inconsistency. It is admitted that we know this, and the point at issue is whether such knowledge supplies any positive information. And to my mind this question seems not hard to answer. For I cannot see how, when I observe a thing at work, I am to stand there and to insist that I know nothing of its nature. I fail to perceive how a function is nothing at all, or how it does not positively qualify that to which I attribute it. To know only so much, I admit, may very possibly be useless ; it may leave us without the information which we desire most to obtain ; but, for all that, it is not total ignorance.

Our standard denies inconsistency, and therefore asserts consistency. If we can be sure that the inconsistent is unreal, we must, logically, be just as sure that the reality is consistent. The question is solely as to the meaning to be given to consistency. We have now seen that it is not the bare exclusion of discord, for that is merely our abstraction, and is otherwise nothing. And our result, so far, is this. I Reality is known to possess a positive character, but this character is at present determined only as that which excludes contradiction.

But we may make a further advance. We saw (in the preceding chapter) that all appearance must belong to reality. For what appears is, and whatever is cannot fall outside the real. And we may now combine this result with the conclusion just reached. We may say that everything, which appears, is somehow real in such a way as to be self-consistent. The character of the real is to possess everything phenomenal in a harmonious form.

I will repeat the same truth in other words. Reality is one in this sense that it has a positive nature exclusive of discord, a nature which must hold throughout everything that is to be real. Its diversity can be diverse only so far as not to clash, and what seems otherwise anywhere cannot be real. And, from the other side, everything which appears must be real. Appearance must belong to reality, and it must therefore be concordant and other than it seems. The bewildering mass of phenomenal diversity must hence somehow be at unity and self-consistent; for it cannot be elsewhere than in reality, and reality excludes discord. Or again we may put it so : the real is individual. It is one in the sense that its positive character embraces all differences in an inclusive harmony. And this knowledge, poor as it may be, is certainly more than bare negation or simple ignorance. So far as it goes, it gives us positive news about absolute reality.

Let us try to carry this conclusion a step farther on. We know that the real is one ; but its oneness, so far, is ambiguous. Is it one system, possessing diversity as an adjective ; or is its consistency, on the other hand, an attribute of independent realities ?

We have to ask, in short, if a plurality of reals is possible, and if these can merely co-exist so as not to be discrepant? Such a plurality would mean a number of beings not dependent on each other. On the one hand they would possess somehow the phenomenal diversity, for that possession, we have seen, is essential. And, on the other hand, they would be free from external disturbance and from inner discrepancy. After the enquiries of our First Book the possibility of such reals hardly calls for discussion. For the internal states of each give rise to hopeless difficulties. And, in the second place, the plurality of the reals cannot be reconciled with their independence. I will briefly resume the arguments which force us to this latter result.

If the Many are supposed to be without internal quality, each would forthwith become nothing, and we must therefore take each as being internally somewhat. And, if they are to be plural, they must be a diversity somehow co-existing together. Any attempt again to take their togetherness as unessential seems to end in the unmeaning. We have no knowledge of a plural diversity, nor can we attach any sense to it, if we do not have it somehow as one. And, if we abstract from this unity, we have also therewith abstracted from the plurality, and are left with mere being.

Can we then have a plurality of independent reals which merely co-exist? No, for absolute independence and co-existence are incompatible. Absolute independence is an idea which consists merely in one-sided abstraction. It is made by an attempted division of the aspect of several existence from the aspect of relatedness; and these aspects, whether in fact or thought, are really indivisible.

If we take the diversity of our reals to be such as we discover in feeling and at a stage where relations do not exist, that diversity is never found except as one integral character of an undivided whole. And if we forcibly abstract from that unity, then together with feeling we have destroyed the diversity of feeling. We are left not with plurality, but with mere being, or, if you prefer it, with nothing. Co-existence in feeling is hence an instance and a proof not of self-sufficiency, but of dependence, and beside this it would add a further difficulty. If the nature of our reals is the diversity found at a stage below relations, how are we to dispose of the mass of relational appearance? For that exists, and existing it must somehow qualify the world, a world the reality of which is discovered only at a level other than its own. Such a position would seem not easy to justify.

Thus a mode of togetherness such as we can verify in feeling destroys the independence of our reals. And they will fare no better if we seek to find their co-existence elsewhere. For any other verifiable way of togetherness must involve relations, and they are fatal to self-sufficiency. Relations, we saw, are a development of and from the felt totality. They inadequately express, and they still imply in the background that unity apart from which the diversity is nothing. Relations are unmeaning except within and on the basis of a substantial whole, and related terms, if made absolute, are forthwith destroyed. Plurality and relatedness are but features and aspects of a unity.

If the relations in which the reals somehow stand are viewed as essential, that, as soon as we understand it, involves at once the internal relativity of the reals. And any attempt to maintain the relations as merely external must fail. For if, wrongly and for argument's sake, we admit processes and arrangements which do not qualify their terms, yet such arrangements, if admitted, are at any rate not ultimate. The terms would be prior and independent only with regard to *these* arrangements, and they would remain relative otherwise, and vitally

dependent on some whole.   And severed from this
unity, the terms perish by the very stroke which
aims to set them up as absolute.

The reals therefore cannot be self-existent, and,
if self-existent, yet taken as the world they would
end in inconsistency.   For the relations, because
they exist, must somehow qualify the world.   The
relations then must externally qualify the sole and
self-contained reality, and that seems self-contra·
dictory or meaningless.[1]   And if it is urged that a
plurality of independent beings may be unintelligible,
but that after all some unintelligible facts must be
affirmed—the answer is obvious.   An unintelligible
fact may be admitted so far as, first, it is a fact, and
so far as, secondly, it has a meaning which does not
contradict itself internally or make self-discrepant
our view of the world.   But the alleged indepen·
dence of the reals is no fact, but a theoretical construction ;   and, so far as it has a meaning, that
meaning contradicts itself, and issues in chaos.   A
reality of this kind may safely be taken as unreal.

We cannot therefore maintain a plurality save as
dependent on the relations in which it stands.   Or
if desiring to avoid relations we fall back on the
diversity given in feeling, the result is the same.
The plurality then sinks to become merely an
integral aspect in a single substantial unity, and
the reals have vanished.

[1] To this brief statement we might add other fatal objections.
There is the question of the reals' interaction and of the general order
of the world.   Here, whether we affirm or deny, we turn in a maze.
The fact of knowledge plunges us again in a dilemma.   If we do not
know that the Many are, we cannot affirm them.   But the knowledge
of the Many seems compatible with the self-existence neither of what
knows nor of what is known.   Finally, if the relations are admitted
to an existence somehow alongside of the reals, the sole reality of the
reals is given up.   The relations themselves have now become a
second kind of real thing.   But the connection between these new
reals and the old ones, whether we deny or affirm it, leads to insoluble
problems.

CHAPTER XIV.

THE GENERAL NATURE OF REALITY (*continued*)

OUR result so far is this. Everything phenomenal
is somehow real; and the absolute must at least be
as rich as the relative. And, further, the Absolute
is not many; there are no independent reals. The
universe is one in this sense that its differences exist
harmoniously within one whole, beyond which there
is nothing. Hence the Absolute is, so far, an individual and a system, but, if we stop here, it
remains but formal and abstract. Can we then,
the question is, say anything about the concrete
nature of the system ?

Certainly, I think, this is possible. When we
ask as to the matter which fills up the empty outline, we can reply in one word, that this matter is
experience. And experience means something much
the same as given and present fact. We perceive,
on reflection, that to be real, or even barely to exist,
must be to fall within sentience. Sentient experience, in short, is reality, and what is not this is
not real. We may say, in other words, that there
is no being or fact outside of that which is commonly
called psychical existence. Feeling, thought, and
volition (any groups under which we class psychical
phenomena) are all the material of existence, and
there is no other material, actual or even possible.
This result in its general form seems evident at
once; and, however serious a step we now seem to
have taken, there would be no advantage at this
point in discussing it at length. For the test in the
main lies ready to our hand, and the decision rests

on the manner in which it is applied. I will state the case briefly thus. Find any piece of existence, take up anything that any one could possibly call a fact, or could in any sense assert to have being, and then judge if it does not consist in sentient experience. Try to discover any sense in which you can still continue to speak of it, when all perception and feeling have been removed ; or point out any fragment of its matter, any aspect of its being, which is not derived from and is not still relative to this source. When the experiment is made strictly, I can myself conceive of nothing else than the experienced. Anything, in no sense felt or perceived, becomes to me quite unmeaning. And as I cannot try to think of it without realizing either that I am not thinking at all, or that I am thinking of it against my will as being experienced, I am driven to the conclusion that for me experience is the same as reality. The fact that falls elsewhere seems, in my mind, to be a mere word and a failure, or else an attempt at self-contradiction. It is a vicious abstraction whose existence is meaningless nonsense, and is therefore not possible.

This conclusion is open, of course, to grave objection, and must in its consequences give rise to serious difficulties. I will not attempt to anticipate the discussion of these, but before passing on, will try to obviate a dangerous mistake. For, in asserting that the real is nothing but experience, I may be understood to endorse a common error. I may be taken first to divide the percipient subject from the universe ; and then, resting on that subject, as on a thing actual by itself, I may be supposed to urge that it cannot transcend its own states. [1] Such an argument would lead to impossible results, and would stand on a foundation of faulty abstraction. To set up the subject as real independently of the whole, and to make the whole into experience in

---

[1] This matter is discussed in Chapter xxi.

A. R.   I

the sense of an adjective of that subject, seems to
me indefensible. And when I contend that reality
must be sentient, my conclusion almost consists in
the denial of this fundamental error. For if, seeking
for reality, we go to experience, what we cei tainly
do *not* find is a subject or an object, or indeed any
other thing whatever, standing separate and on its
own bottom. What we discover rather is a whole
in which distinctions can be made, but in which
divisions do not exist. And this is the point on
which I insist, and it is the very ground on which I
stand, when I urge that reality is sentient experience.
I mean that to be real is to be indissolubly one thing
with sentience. It is to be something which comes
as a feature and aspect within one whole of feeling,
something which, except as an integral element of
such sentience, has no meaning at all. And what I
repudiate is the separation of feeling from the felt,
or of the desired from desire, or of what is thought
from thinking, or the division—I might add—of
anything from anything else. Nothing is ever so
presented as real by itself, or can be argued so to
exist without demonstrable fallacy. And in asserting
that the reality is experience, I rest throughout on
this foundation. You cannot find fact unless in
unity with sentience, and one cannot in the end be
divided from the other, either actually or in idea.
But to be utterly indivisible from feeling or perception, to be an integral element in a whole which is
experienced, this surely is itself to *be* experience.
Being and reality are, in brief, one thing with
sentience ; they can neither be opposed to, nor even
in the end distinguished from it.

I am well aware that this statement stands in
need of explanation and defence. This will, I hope,
be supplied by succeeding chapters, and I think it
better for the present to attempt to go forward.
Our conclusion, so far, will be this, that the Absolute
is one system, and that its contents are nothing but

sentient experience. It will hence be a single and all-inclusive experience, which embraces every partial diversity in concord. For it cannot be less than appearance, and hence no feeling or thought, of any kind, can fall outside its limits. And if it is more than any feeling or thought which we know, it must still remain more of the same nature. It cannot pass into another region beyond what falls under the general head of sentience. For to assert that possibility would be in the end to use words without a meaning. We can entertain no such suggestion except as self-contradictory, and as therefore impossible.

This conclusion will, I trust, at the end of my work bring more conviction to the reader; for we shall find that it is the one view which will harmonize all facts. And the objections brought against it, when it and they are once properly defined, will prove untenable. But our general result is at present seriously defective; and we must now attempt to indicate and remedy its failure in principle.

What we have secured, up to this point, may be called mere theoretical consistency. The Absolute holds all possible content in an individual experience where no contradiction can remain. And it seems, at first sight, as if this theoretical perfection could exist together with practical defect and misery. For apparently, so far as we have gone, an experience might be harmonious, in such a way at least as not to contradict itself, and yet might result on the whole in a balance of suffering. Now no one can genuinely believe that sheer misery, however self-consistent, is good and desirable. And the question is whether in this way our conclusion is wrecked.

There may be those possibly who here would join issue at once. They might perhaps wish to contend that the objection is irrelevant, since pain is no evil.

I shall discuss the general question of good and evil in a subsequent chapter, and will merely say here that for myself I cannot stand upon the ground that pain is no evil. I admit, or rather I would assert, that a result, if it fails to satisfy our whole nature, comes short of perfection. And I could not rest tranquilly in a truth if I were compelled to regard it as hateful. While unable, that is, to deny it, I should, rightly or wrongly, insist that the enquiry was not yet closed, and that the result was but partial. And if metaphysics is to stand, it must, I think, take account of all sides of our being. I do not mean that every one of our desires must be met by a promise of particular satisfaction; for that would be absurd and utterly impossible. But if the main tendencies of our nature do not reach consummation in the Absolute, we cannot believe that we have attained to perfection and truth. And we shall have to consider later on what desires must be taken as radical and fundamental. But here we have seen that our conclusion, so far, has a serious defect, and the question is whether this defect can be directly remedied. We have been resting on the theoretical standard which guarantees that Reality is a self-consistent system. Have we a practical standard which now can assure us that this system will satisfy our desire for perfect good? An affirmative answer seems plausible, but I do not think it would be true. Without any doubt we possess a practical standard; but that does not seem to me to yield a conclusion about reality, or it will not give us at least directly the result we are seeking. I will attempt briefly to explain in what way it comes short.

That a practical end and criterion exists I shall assume, and I will deal with its nature more fully hereafter (Chapter xxv.). I may say for the present that, taken in the abstract, the practical standard seems to be the same as what is used for

theory. It is individuality, the harmonious or consistent existence of our contents ; an existence,
further, which cannot be limited, because, if so, it
would contradict itself internally (Chapters xx. and
xxiv.). Nor need I separate myself at this stage
from the intelligent Hedonist, since, in my judgment,
practical perfection will carry a balance of pleasure.
These points I shall have to discuss, and for the
present am content to assume them provisionally
and vaguely. Now taking the practical end as individuality, or as clear pleasure, or rather as both in
one, the question is whether this end is known to be
realized in the Absolute, and, if so, upon what
foundation such knowledge can rest. It apparently
cannot be drawn directly from the theoretical
criterion, and the question is whether the practical
standard can supply it. I will explain why I
believe that this cannot be the case.

I will first deal briefly with the " ontological "
argument. The essential nature of this will, I hope,
be more clear to us hereafter (Chapter xxiv.),
and I will here merely point out why it fails to give
us help. This argument might be stated in several
forms, but the main point is very simple. We have
the idea of perfection—there is no doubt as to that
—and the question is whether perfection also actually
exists. Now the ontological view urges that the fact
of the idea proves the fact of the reality ; or, to put
it otherwise, it argues that, unless perfection existed,
you could not have it in idea, which is agreed to be
the case. I shall not discuss at present the general
validity of this argument, but will confine myself to
denying its applicability. For, if an idea has been
manufactured and is composed of elements taken up
from more than one source, then the result of manufacture need not as a whole exist out of my thought,
however much that is the case with its separate
elements. Thus we might admit that, in one sense,
perfection or completeness would not be present in

idea unless also it were real. We might admit this, and yet we might deny the same conclusion with respect to *practical* perfection. For the perfection that is real might simply be theoretical. It might mean system so far as system is mere theoretical harmony and does *not* imply pleasure. And the element of pleasure, taken, up from elsewhere, may then have been added in our minds to this valid idea. But, if so, the addition may be incongruous, incompatible, and really, if we knew it, contradictory. Pleasure and system perhaps are in truth a false compound, an appearance which exists, as such, only in our heads; just as would be the case if we thought, for example, of a perfect finite being. Hence the ontological argument cannot prove the existence of practical perfection; [1] and let us go on to enquire if any other proof exists.

It is in some ways natural to suppose that the practical end somehow postulates its existence as a fact. But a more careful examination tends to dissipate this idea. The moral end, it is clear, is not pronounced by morality to have actual existence. This is quite plain, and it would be easier to contend that morality even postulates the opposite (Chapter xxv.). Certainly, as we shall perceive hereafter, the religious consciousness does imply the reality of that object, which also is its goal. But a religion whose object is perfect will be founded on inconsistency, even more than is the case with mere morality. For such a religion, if it implies the existence of its ideal, implies at the same time a feature which is quite incompatible. This we shall discuss in a later chapter, and all that I will urge here is that the religious consciousness cannot prove that perfection really exists. For it is not true that in all religions the object is perfection; nor, where it is so, does

[1] The objection that, after all, the compound is there, will be met in Chapter xxiv. Notice also that I do not distinguish as yet between "existence" and "reality." But see p. 317.

religion possess any right to dictate to or to dominate over thought.   It does not follow that a belief must be admitted to be true, because, given a certain influence, it is practically irresistible.   There is a tendency in religion to take the ideal as existing; and this tendency sways our minds and, under certain conditions, may amount to compulsion.   But it does not, therefore, and merely for this reason, give us truth, and we may recall other experience which forces us to doubt.   A man, for instance, may love a woman whom, when he soberly considers, he cannot think true, and yet, in the intoxication of her presence, may give up his whole mind to the suggestions of blind passion.   But in all cases, that alone is really valid for the intellect, which in a calm moment the mere intellect is incapable of doubting. It is only that which for thought is compulsory and irresistible—only that which thought must assert in attempting to deny it—which is a valid foundation for metaphysical truth.

" But how," I may be asked, " can you justify this superiority of the intellect, this predominance of thought ?   On what foundation, if on any, does such a despotism rest ?   For there seems no special force in the intellectual axiom if you regard it impartially. Nay, if you consider the question without bias, and if you reflect on the nature of axioms in general, you may be brought to a wholly different conclusion. For *all* axioms, as a matter of fact, are practical. They all depend upon the will.   They none of them in the end can amount to more than the impulse to behave in a certain way.   And they cannot express more than this impulse, together with the impossibility of satisfaction unless it is complied with. And hence, the intellect, far from possessing a right to predominate, is simply one instance and one symptom of practical compulsion.   Or (to put the case more psychologically) the intellect is merely one result of the general working of pleasure and pain.

It is even subordinate, and therefore its attempt at despotism is founded on baseless pretensions."

Now, apart from its dubious psychological setting, I can admit the general truth contained in this objection. The theoretical axiom is the statement of an impulse to act in a certain manner. When that impulse is not satisfied there ensues disquiet and movement in a certain direction, until such a character is given to the result as contents the impulse and produces rest. And the expression of this fundamental principle of action is what we call an axiom. Take, for example, the law of avoiding contradiction. When two elements will not remain quietly together but collide and struggle, we cannot rest satisfied with that state. Our impulse is to alter it, and, on the theoretical side, to bring the content to a shape where without collision the variety is thought as one. And this inability to rest otherwise, and this tendency·to alter in a certain way and direction, is, when reflected on and made explicit, our axiom and our intellectual standard.

" But is not this," I may be asked further, " a surrender of your position ? Does not this admit that the criterion used for theory is merely a practical impulse, a tendency to movement from one side of our being ? And, if so, how can the intellectual standard be predominant ? " But it is necessary here to distinguish. The whole question turns on the difference between the several impulses of our being.[1] You may call the intellect, if you like, a mere tendency to movement, but you must remember that it is a movement of a very special kind. I shall enter more fully into the nature of thinking hereafter, but the crucial point may be stated at once. In thought the standard, you may say, amounts merely to "act so "; but then "act so" means "think so," and " think so" means " it is." And the psychological origin and base of this movement, and of this inability

---

[1] Compare here Chapter xxvi.

to act otherwise, may be anything you please; for
that is all utterly irrelevant to the metaphysical issue.
Thinking is the attempt to satisfy a special impulse,
and the attempt implies an assumption about reality.
You may avoid the assumption so far as you decline
to think, but, if you sit down to the game, there is
only one way of playing.   In order to think at all
you must subject yourself to a standard, a standard
which implies an absolute knowledge of reality; and
while you doubt this, you accept it, and obey while
you rebel.   You may urge that thought, after all, is
inconsistent, because appearance is not got rid of
but merely shelved.   That is another question which
will engage us in a future chapter, and here may be
dismissed.   For in any case thinking means the
acceptance of a certain standard, and that standard,
in any case, is an assumption as to the character of
reality.

"But why," it may be objected, "is this assumption better than what holds for practice?   Why is
the theoretical to be superior to the practical end?"
I have never said that this is so.   Only here, that is
in metaphysics, I must be allowed to reply, we are
acting theoretically.   We are occupied specially, and
are therefore subject to special conditions; and the
theoretical standard within theory must surely be
absolute.   We have no right to listen to morality
when it rushes in blindly.   "Act so," urges morality,
that is "*be* so or be dissatisfied."   But if I am dissatisfied, still apparently I may be none the less real.
"Act so," replies speculation, that is, "*think* so or
be dissatisfied; and if you do not think so, what you
think is certainly not real."   And these two com-
mands do not seem to be directly connected.   If I
am theoretically not satisfied, then what appears
must in reality be otherwise; but, if I am dissatisfied practically, the same conclusion does not hold.
Thus the two satisfactions are not the same, nor does
there appear to be a straight way from the one to the

other. Or consider again the same question from a different side. Morality seemed anxious to dictate to metaphysics, but is it prepared to accept a corresponding dictation? If it were to hear that the real world is quite other than its ideal, and if it were unable theoretically to shake this result, would morality acquiesce? Would it not, on the other hand, regardless of this, still maintain its own ground? Facts may *be* as you say, but none the less they should not be so, and something else *ought* to be. Morality, I think, would take this line, and, if so, it should accept a like attitude in theory. It must not dictate as to what facts are, while it refuses to admit dictation as to what they should be.

Certainly, to any one who believes in the unity of our nature, a one-sided satisfaction will remain incredible. And such a consideration to my mind carries very great weight. But to stand on one side of our nature, and to argue from that directly to the other side, seems illegitimate. I will not here ask how far morality is consistent with itself in demanding complete harmony (Chapter xxv.). What seems clear is that, in wishing to dictate to mere theory, it is abandoning its own position and is courting foreign occupation. And it is misled mainly by a failure to observe essential distinctions. " Be so " does not mean always " think so," and " think so," in its main signification, certainly does not mean "be so." Their difference is the difference between "you ought" and " it is "—and I can see no direct road from the one to the other. If a theory could be made by the will, that would have to satisfy the will, and, if it did not, it would be false. But since metaphysics is mere theory, and since theory from its nature must be made by the intellect, it is here the intellect alone which has to be satisfied. Doubtless a conclusion which fails to content all the sides of my nature leaves *me* dissatisfied. But I see no direct way of passing from " this does not satisfy my nature" to "therefore it is false." For false is the same as theoretically untenable, and we are supposing a case where mere theory has been satisfied, and where the result has in consequence been taken as true. And, so far as I see, we must admit that, *if* the intellect is contented, the question is settled. For we may feel as we please about the intellectual conclusion, but we cannot, on such external ground, protest that it is false.

Hence if we understand by perfection a state of harmony with pleasure, there is no direct way of showing that reality is perfect. For, so far as the intellectual standard at present seems to go, we might have harmony with pain and with partial dissatisfaction. But I think the case is much altered when we consider it otherwise, and when we ask if on another ground such harmony is possible. The intellect is not to be dictated to ; that conclusion is irrefragable. But is it certain, on the other hand, that the mere intellect can be self-satisfied, if other elements of our nature remain not contented ? Or must we not think rather that indirectly any partial discontent will bring unrest and imperfection into the intellect itself ? If this is so, then to suppose any imperfection in the Absolute is inadmissible. To fail in any way would introduce a discord into perception itself. And hence, since we have found that, taken perceptively, reality is harmonious, it must be harmonious altogether, and must satisfy our whole nature. Let us see if on this line we can make an advance.

If the Absolute is to be theoretically harmonious, its elements must not collide. Idea must not disagree with sensation, nor must sensations clash. In every case, that is, the struggle must not be a mere struggle. There must be a unity which it subserves, and a whole, taken in which it is a struggle no longer. How this resolution is possible we may be

able to see partly in our subsequent chapters, but for
the present I would insist merely that somehow it
must exist. Since reality is harmonious, the struggle
of diverse elements, sensations or ideas, barely to
qualify the self-same point must be precluded. But,
if idea must not clash with sensation, then there
cannot in the Absolute be unsatisfied desire or any
practical unrest. For in these there is clearly an
ideal element not concordant with presentation but
struggling against it, and, if you remove this discordance, then with it all unsatisfied desire is gone.
In order for such a desire, in even its lowest form,
to persist, there must (so far as I can see) be an
idea qualifying diversely a sensation and fixed for
the moment in discord. And any such state is not
compatible with theoretical harmony.

But this result perhaps has ignored an outstanding
possibility. Unsatisfied desires might, as such, not
exist in the Absolute, and yet seemingly there might
remain a clear balance of pain. For, in the first
place, it is not proved that all pain must arise from
an unresolved struggle ; and it may be contended,
in the second place, that possibly the discord might
be resolved, and yet, so far as we know, the pain
might remain. In a painful struggle it may be urged
that the pain can be real, though the struggle is
apparent. For we shall see, when we discuss error
(Chapter xvi.), how discordant elements may be
neutralized in a wider complex. We shall find how,
in that system, they can take on a different arrangement, and so result in harmony. And the question
here as to unsatisfied desires will be this. Can they
not be merged in a whole, so as to lose their character of discordance, and thus cease to be desires,
while their pain none the less survives in reality ?
If so, that whole, after all, would be imperfect. For,
while possessor of harmony, it still might be sunk in
misery, or might suffer at least with a balance of
pain. This objection is serious, and it calls for

some discussion here.   I shall have to deal with it once more in our concluding chapter.

I feel at this point our want of knowledge with regard to the conditions of pleasure and pain.[1]   It is a tenable view, one at least which can hardly be refuted, that pain is caused, or conditioned, by an unresolved collision.   Now, if this really is the case, then, given harmony, a balance of pain is impossible.   Pain, of course, is a fact, and no fact can be conjured away from the universe; but the question here is entirely as to a *balance* of pain.   Now it is common experience that in mixed states pain may be neutralized by pleasure in such a way that the balance is decidedly pleasant.   And hence it is possible that in the universe as a whole we may have a balance of pleasure, and in the total result no residue of pain.   This is possible, and *if* an unresolved conflict and discord is essential to pain, it is much more than possible.   Since the reality is harmonious, and since harmony excludes the conditions which are requisite for a balance of pain, that balance is impossible.   I will urge this so far as to raise a very grave doubt.   I question our right even to suppose a state of pain in the Absolute.

And this doubt becomes more grave when we consider another point.   When we pass from the conditions to the effects of painful feeling, we are on surer ground.   For in our experience the result of pain is disquietude and unrest.   Its main action is to set up change, and to prevent stability.   There is authority, I am aware, for a different view, but, so far as I see, that view cannot be reconciled with facts.   This effect of pain has here a most important bearing.   Assume that in the Absolute there is a balance of pleasure, and all is consistent.   For the pains can condition those processes which, as processes, disappear in the life of the whole; and these pains can be neutralized by an overplus of

[1] Cf. *Mind*, xiii. pp. 3–14 (No. 49).

pleasure. But if you suppose, on the other hand, a balance of pain, the difficulty becomes at once insuperable. We have postulated a state of harmony, and, together with that, the very condition of instability and discord. We have in the Absolute, on one side, a state of things where the elements cannot jar, and where in particular idea does not conflict with presentation. But with pain on the other side we have introduced a main-spring of change and unrest, and we thus produce necessarily an idea not in harmony with existence. And this idea of a better and of a non-existing condition of things must directly destroy theoretical rest. But, if so, such an idea must be called impossible. There is no pain on the whole, and in the Absolute our whole nature must find satisfaction. For otherwise there is no theoretical harmony, and that harmony we saw must certainly exist. I shall ask in our last chapter if there is a way of avoiding this conclusion, but for the present we seem bound to accept it as true. We must not admit the possibility of an Absolute perfect in apprehension yet resting tranquilly in pain. The question as to actual evidence of defect in the universe will be discussed in Chapter xvii.; and our position so far is this. We cannot argue directly that all sides of our nature must be satisfied, but indirectly we are led to the same result. For we are forced to assume theoretical satisfaction; and to suppose that existing one-sidedly, and together with practical discomfort, appears inadmissible. Such a state is a possibility which seems to contradict itself. It is a supposition to which, if we cannot find any ground in its favour, we have no right. For the present at least it is better to set it down as inconceivable.[1]

And hence, for the present at least, we must be-

---

[1] In our last chapter this conclusion will be slightly modified. The supposition will appear there to be barely possible.

lieve that reality satisfies our whole being. Our main wants—for truth and life, and for beauty and goodness—must all find satisfaction. And we have seen that this consummation must somehow be experience, and be individual. Every element of the universe, sensation, feeling, thought and will, must be included within one comprehensive sentience. And the question which now occurs is whether really we have a positive idea of such sentience. Do we at all know what we mean when we say that it is actual?

Fully to realize the existence of the Absolute is for finite beings impossible. In order thus to know we should have to be, and then *we* should not exist. This result is certain, and all attempts to avoid it are illusory. But then the whole question turns on the sense in which we are to understand " knowing." What is impossible is to construct absolute life in its detail, to have the specific experience in which it consists. But to gain an idea of its main features—an idea true so far as it goes, though abstract and incomplete—is a different endeavour. And it is a task, so far as I see, in which we may succeed. For these main features, to some extent, are within our own experience; and again the idea of their combination is, in the abstract, quite intelligible. And surely no more than this is wanted for a knowledge of the Absolute. It is a knowledge which of course differs enormously from the fact. But it is true, for all that, while it respects its own limits ; and it seems fully attainable by the finite intellect.

I will end this chapter by briefly mentioning the sources of such knowledge. First, in mere feeling, or immediate presentation, we have the experience of a whole (Chapters ix., xix., xxvi., xxvii.). This whole contains diversity, and, on the other hand, is not parted by relations. Such an experience, we must admit, is most imperfect and unstable, and its inconsistencies lead us at once to transcend it. Indeed, we hardly possess it as more than that which we are in the act of losing. But it serves to suggest to us the general idea of a total experience, where will and thought and feeling may all once more be one. Further, this same unity, felt below distinctions, shows itself later in a kind of hostility against them. We find it in the efforts made both by theory and practice, each to complete itself and so to pass into the other. And, again, the relational form, as we saw, pointed everywhere to a unity. It implies a substantial totality beyond relations and above them, a whole endeavouring without success to realize itself in their detail. Further, the ideas of goodness, and of the beautiful, suggest in different ways the same result. They more or less involve the experience of a whole beyond relations though full of diversity. Now, if we gather (as we can) such considerations into one, they will assuredly supply us with a positive idea. We gain from them the knowledge of a unity which transcends and yet contains every manifold appearance. They supply not an experience but an abstract idea, an idea which we make by uniting given elements. And the mode of union, once more in the abstract, is actually given. Thus we know what is meant by an experience, which embraces all divisions, and yet somehow possesses the direct nature of feeling. We can form the general idea of an absolute experience in which phenomenal distinctions are merged, a whole become immediate at a higher stage without losing any richness. Our complete inability to understand this concrete unity in detail is no good ground for our declining to entertain it. Such a ground would be irrational, and its principle could hardly everywhere be adhered to. But if we can realize at all the general features of the Absolute, if we can see that somehow they come together in a way known vaguely

and in the abstract, our result is certain.   Our conclusion, so far as it goes, is real knowledge of the
Absolute, positive knowledge built on experience,
and inevitable when we try to think consistently.
We shall realize its nature more clearly when we
have confronted it with a series of objections and
difficulties.   If our result will hold against them all,
we shall be able to urge that in reason we are bound
to think it true.

CHAPTER XV.

THOUGHT AND REALITY

THERE is a natural objection which the reader will raise against our account of the Absolute. The difficulty lies, he may urge, not in making a statement which by itself seems defensible, but rather in reconciling any view with obvious inconsistencies. The real problem is to show how appearance and evil, and in general finite existence, are compatible with the Absolute. These questions, however, he will object, have been so far neglected. And it is these which in the next chapter must begin to engage our serious attention. Still it is better not to proceed at once; and before we deal with error we must gain some notion of what we mean by truth. In the present chapter I will try to state briefly the main essence of thought, and to justify its distinction from actual existence. It is only by misunderstanding that we find difficulty in taking thought to be something less than reality.

If we take up anything considered real, no matter what it is, we find in it two aspects. There are always two things we can say about it; and, if we cannot say both, we have not got reality. There is a " what " and a " that," an existence and a content, and the two are inseparable. That anything should be, and should yet be nothing in particular, or that a quality should not qualify and give a character to anything, is obviously impossible. If we try to get the " that " by itself, we do not get it, for either we have it qualified, or else we fail utterly. If we try to get the " what " by itself, we find at once that it is not all. It points to something beyond, and cannot exist by itself and as a bare adjective. Neither of these aspects, if you isolate it, can be taken as real, or indeed in that case is itself any longer. They are distinguishable only and are not divisible.

And yet thought seems essentially to consist in their division. For thought is clearly, to some extent at least, ideal. Without an idea there is no thinking, and an idea implies the separation of content from existence. It is a " what " which, so far as it is a mere idea, clearly *is* not, and if it also *were*, could, so far, not be called ideal. For ideality lies in the disjoining of quality from being. Hence the common view, which identifies image and idea, is fundamentally in error. For an image is a fact, just as real as any sensation ; it is merely a fact of another kind and it is not one whit more ideal. But an idea is any part of the content of a fact so far as that works out of immediate unity with its existence. And an idea's factual existence may consist in a sensation or perception, just as well as in an image. The main point and the essence is that some feature in the " what " of a given fact should be alienated from its " that " so far as to work beyond it, or at all events loose from it. Such a movement is ideality, and, where it is absent, there is nothing ideal.

We can understand this most clearly if we consider the nature of judgment, for there we find thought in its completed form. In judgment an idea is predicated of a reality. Now, in the first place, what is predicated is not a mental image. It is not a fact inside my head which the judgment wishes to attach to another fact outside. The predicate is a mere " what," a mere feature of content, which is used to qualify further the " that " of the subject. And this predicate is divorced from its psychical existence in my head, and is used without any

regard to its being there.   When I say "this horse
is a mammal," it is surely absurd to suppose that I
am harnessing my mental state to the beast between
the shafts.   Judgment adds an adjective to reality,
and this adjective is an idea, because it is a quality
made loose from its own existence, and is working
free from its implication with that.   And, even
when a fact is merely analysed,—when the predicate
appears not to go beyond its own subject, or to have
been imported divorced from another fact outside—
our account still holds good.   For here obviously
our synthesis is a re-union of the distinguished, and
it implies a separation, which, though it is over-
ridden, is never unmade.   The predicate is a content which has been made loose from its own
immediate existence and is used in divorce from
that first unity.   And, again, as predicated, it is
applied without regard to its own being as abstracted
and in my head.   If this were not so, there would be
no judgment; for neither distinction nor predication
would have taken place.   But again, if it is so, then
once more here we discover an idea.

And in the second place, when we turn to the
subject of the judgment, we clearly find the other
aspect, in other words, the "that."   Just as in "this
horse is a mammal" the predicate was *not* a fact, so
most assuredly the subject is an actual existence.
And the same thing holds good with every judgment.   No one ever *means* to assert about anything
but reality, or to do anything but qualify a "that" by
a "what."   And, without dwelling on a point which
I have worked out elsewhere,[1] I will notice a source
of possible mistake.   "The subject, at all events," I
may be told, "is in no case a *mere* 'that.'   It is
never bare reality, or existence without character."
And to this I fully assent.   I agree that the subject
which we *mean*—even before the judgment is com-

---

[1] *Principles of Logic*, Book I.

plete, and while still we are holding its elements apart—is more than a mere " that." But then this is not the point. The point is whether with every judgment we do not find an aspect of existence, absent from the predicate but present in the subject, and whether in the synthesis of these aspects we have not got the essence of judgment. And for myself I see no way of avoiding this conclusion. judgment is essentially the re-union of two sides, " what " and " that," provisionally estranged. But it is the alienation of these aspects in which thought's ideality consists.

Truth is the object of thinking, and the aim of truth is to qualify existence ideally. Its end, that is, is to give a character to reality in which it can rest. Truth is the predication of such content as, when predicated, is harmonious, and removes inconsistency and with it unrest. And because the given reality is never consistent, thought is compelled to take the road of indefinite expansion. If thought were successful, it would have a predicate consistent in itself and agreeing entirely with the subject. But, on the other hand, the predicate must be always ideal. It must, that is, be a " what " not in unity with its own " that," and therefore, in and by itself, devoid of existence. Hence, so far as in thought this alienation is not made good, thought can never be more than merely ideal.

I shall very soon proceed to dwell on this last consideration, but will first of all call attention to a most important point. There exists a notion that ideality is something outside of facts, something imported into them, or imposed as a sort of layer above them ; and we talk as if facts, when let alone, were in no sense ideal. But any such notion is illusory. For facts which are not ideal, and which show no looseness of content from existence, seem hardly actual. They would be found, if anywhere, in feelings without internal lapse, and with a content wholly single.

But if we keep to fact which is given, this changes
in our hands, and it compels us to perceive inconsistency of content.   And then this content cannot
be referred merely to its given "that," but is forced
beyond it, and is made to qualify something outside.
But, if so, in the simplest change we have at once
ideality—the use of content in separation from its
actual existence.   Indeed, in Chapters ix. and x. we
have already seen how this is necessary.   For the
content of the given is for ever relative to something
not given, and the nature of its "what" is hence essentially to transcend its "that."   This we may call
the ideality of the given finite.   It is not manufactured by thought, but thought itself is its development and product.   The essential nature of the finite
is that everywhere, as it presents itself, its character
should slide beyond the limits of its existence.

And truth, as we have seen, is the effort to heal
this disease, as it were, homœopathically.   Thought
has to accept, without reserve, the ideality of the
"given," its want of consistency and its self-transcendence.   And by pushing this self-transcendence to
the uttermost point, thought attempts to find there
consummation and rest.   The subject, on the one
hand, is expanded until it is no longer what is given.
It becomes the whole universe, which presents itself and which appears in each given moment with
but part of its reality.   It grows into an all-inclusive
whole, existing somewhere and somehow, if we only
could perceive it.   But on the other hand, in qualifying this reality, thought consents to a partial ab-
negation.   It has to recognise the division of the
"what" from the "that," and it cannot so join
these aspects as to get rid of mere ideas and arrive
at actual reality.   For it is in and by ideas only that
thought moves and has life.   The content it applies
to the reality has, as applied, no genuine existence.
It is an adjective divorced from its "that," and never
in judgment, even when the judgment is complete,

restored to solid unity. Thus the truth belongs to existence, but it does not as such exist. It is a character which indeed reality possesses, but a character which, as truth and as ideal, has been set loose from existence; and it is never rejoined to it in such a way as to come together singly and *make* fact. Hence, truth shows a dissection and never an actual life. Its predicate can never be equivalent to its subject. And if it became so, and if its adjectives could be at once self-consistent and re-welded to existence, it would not be truth any longer. It would have then passed into another and a higher reality.

And I will now deal with the misapprehension to which I referred, and the consideration of which may, I trust, help us forward.[1]

There is an erroneous idea that, if reality is more than thought, thought itself is, at least, quite unable to say so. To assert the existence of anything in any sense beyond thought suggests, to some minds, the doctrine of the Thing-in-itself. And of the Thing-in-itself we know (Chapter xii.) that if it existed we could not know of it; and, again, so far as we know of it, we know that it does not exist. The attempt to apprehend this Other in succeeding would be suicide, and in suicide could not reach anything beyond total failure. Now, though I have urged this result, I wish to keep it within rational limits, and I dissent wholly from the corollary that nothing more than thought exists. But to think of anything which can exist quite outside of thought I agree is impossible. If thought is one element in a whole, you cannot argue from this ground that the remainder of such a whole must stand apart and independent. From this ground, in short, you can make no inference to a Thing-in-itself. And there is no impossibility in thought's existing as an element, and no

---

[1] The remainder of this chapter has been reprinted, with some alterations and omissions, from *Mind*, No. 51.

self-contradiction in its own judgment that it is less
than the universe.

We have seen that anything real has two aspects,
existence and character, and that thought always
must work within this distinction.   Thought, in its
actual processes and results, cannot transcend the
dualism of the " that " and the " what."   I do not
mean that in no sense is thought beyond this dualism,
or that thought is satisfied with it and has no desire
for something better.   But taking judgment to be
completed thought, I mean that in no judgment are
the subject and predicate the same.   In every
judgment the genuine subject is reality, which goes
beyond the predicate and of which the predicate is
an adjective.   And I would urge first that, in desiring to transcend this distinction, thought is aiming at
suicide.   We have seen that in judgment we find
always the distinction of fact and truth, of idea and
reality.   Truth and thought are not the thing itself,
but are of it and about it.   Thought predicates an
ideal content of a subject, which idea is not the same
as fact, for in it existence and meaning are necessarily divorced.   And the subject, again, is neither
the mere " what " of the predicate, nor is it any other
mere " what."   Nor, even if it is proposed to take up
a whole with both its aspects, and to predicate the
ideal character of its own proper subject, will that
proposal assist us.   For if the subject is the same as
the predicate, why trouble oneself to judge ?   But if
it is not the same, then what is it, and how is it different ?   Either then there is no judgment at all, and
but a pretence of thinking without thought, or there
is a judgment, but its subject is more than the predicate, and is a " that " beyond a mere "what."   The
subject, I would repeat, is never *mere* reality, or bare
existence without character.   The subject, doubtless,
has unspecified content which is not stated in the
predicate.   For judgment is the differentiation of a
complex whole, and hence always is analysis and

synthesis in one. It separates an element from, and restores it to, the concrete basis; and this basis of necessity is richer than the mere element by itself. But then this is not the question which concerns us here. That question is whether, in any judgment which really says anything, there is not in the subject an aspect of existence which is absent from the bare predicate. And it seems clear that this question must be answered in the affirmative. And if it is urged that the subject itself, being in thought, can therefore not fall beyond, I must ask for more accuracy; for "partly beyond" appears compatible with "partly within." And, leaving prepositions to themselves, I must recall the real issue. For I do not deny that reality *is* an object of thought; I deny that it is barely and *merely* so. If you rest here on a distinction between thought and its object, that opens a further question to which I shall return (p. 174). But if you admit that in asserting reality to fall within thought, you meant that in reality there is nothing beyond what is made thought's object, your position is untenable. Reflect upon any judgment as long as you please, operate upon the subject of it to any extent which you desire, but then (when you have finished) make an actual judgment. And when that is made, see if you do not discover, beyond the content of your thought, a subject of which it is true, and which it does not comprehend. You will find that the object of thought in the end must be ideal, and that there is no idea which, as such, contains its own existence. The "that" of the actual subject will for ever give a something which is not a mere idea, something which is different from any truth, something which makes such a difference to your thinking, that without it you have not even thought completely.

"But," it may be answered, " the thought you speak of is thought that is not perfect. Where thought is perfect there is no discrepancy between

subject and predicate. A harmonious system of
content predicating itself, a subject self-conscious in
that system of content, this is what thought should
mean. And here the division of existence and character is quite healed up. If such completion is not
actual, it is possible, and the possibility is enough."
But it is not even possible, I must persist, if it really
is unmeaning. And once more I must urge the
former dilemma. If there is no judgment, there is
no thought ; and if there is no difference, there is no
judgment, nor any self-consciousness. But if, on the
other hand, there is a difference, then the subject is
beyond the predicated content.

Still a mere denial, I admit, is not quite satisfactory. Let us then suppose that the dualism inherent
in thought has been transcended. Let us assume
that existence is no longer different from truth, and
let us see where this takes us. It takes us straight
to thought's suicide. A system of content is going
to swallow up our reality ; but in our reality we
have the fact of sensible experience, immediate presentation with its colouring of pleasure and pain.
Now I presume there is no question of conjuring
this fact away ; but how it is to be exhibited as an
element in a system of thought-content, is a problem
not soluble. Thought is relational and discursive,
and, if it ceases to be this, it commits suicide ; and
yet, if it remains thus, how does it contain immediate
presentation ? Let us suppose the impossible accomplished ; let us imagine a harmonious system of
ideal contents united by relations, and reflecting itself in self-conscious harmony. This is to be reality,
all reality ; and there is nothing outside it. The
delights and pains of the flesh, the agonies and rap-
tures of the soul, these are fragmentary meteors
fallen from thought's harmonious system. But these
burning experiences—how in any sense can they be
mere pieces of thought's heaven ? For, if the fall

is real, there is a world outside thought's region, and, if the fall is apparent, then human error itself is not included there. Heaven, in brief, must either not be heaven, or else not all reality. Without a metaphor, feeling belongs to perfect 'thought, or it does not. If it does not, there is at once a side of existence beyond thought. But if it does belong, then thought is different from thought discursive and relational. To make it include immediate experience, its character must be transformed. It must cease to predicate, it must get beyond mere relations, it must reach something other than truth. Thought, in a word, must have been absorbed into a fuller experience. Now such an experience may be called thought, if you choose to use that word. But if any one else prefers another term, such as feeling or will, he would be equally justified. For the result is a whole state which both includes and goes beyond each element; and to speak of it as simply one of them seems playing with phrases. For (I must repeat it) when thought begins to be more than relational, it ceases to be mere thinking. A basis, from which the relation is thrown out and into which it returns, is something not exhausted by that relation. It will, in short, be an existence which is not mere truth. Thus, in reaching a whole which can contain every aspect within it, thought must absorb what divides it from feeling and will. But when these all have come together, then, since none of them can perish, they must be merged in a whole in which they are harmonious. But that whole assuredly is not simply *one* of its aspects. And the question is *not* whether the universe is in any sense intelligible. The question is whether, if you thought it and understood it, there would be no difference left between your thought and the thing. And, supposing that to have happened, the question is then whether thought has not changed its nature.

Let us try to realize more distinctly what this

supposed consummation would involve. Since both truth and fact are to be there, nothing must be lost, and in the Absolute we must keep every item of our experience. We cannot have less, but, on the other hand, we may have much more; and this more may so supplement the elements of our actual experience that in the whole they may become transformed. But to reach a mode of apprehension, which is quite identical with reality, surely predicate and subject, and subject and object, and in short the whole relational form, must be merged. The Absolute does not want, I presume, to make eyes at itself in a mirror, or, like a squirrel in a cage, to revolve the circle of its perfections. Such processes must be dissolved in something not poorer but richer than themselves. And feeling and will must also be transmuted in this whole, into which thought has entered. Such a whole state would possess in a superior form that immediacy which we find (more or less) in feeling; and in this whole all divisions would be healed up. It would be experience entire, containing all elements in harmony. Thought would be present as a higher intuition; will would be there where the ideal had become reality; and beauty and pleasure and feeling would live on in this total fulfilment. Every flame of passion, chaste or carnal, would still burn in the Absolute unquenched and unabridged, a note absorbed in the harmony of its higher bliss. We cannot imagine, I admit, how in detail this can be. But if truth and fact are to be one, then in some such way thought must reach its consummation. But in that consummation thought has certainly been so transformed, that to go on calling it thought seems indefensible.

I have tried to show first that, in the proper sense of thought, thought and fact are not the same. I have urged, in the second place, that, if their identity is worked out, thought ends in a reality which swallows up its character. I will ask next whether thought's advocates can find a barrier to their client's happy suicide.

They might urge, first, that our consummation is the Thing-in-itself, and that it makes thought know what essentially is not knowable. But this objection forgets that our whole is not anything but sentient experience. And it forgets that, even when we understand by " thought " its strict discursive form, our reality does not exist apart from this. Emphatically the Absolute is nothing if taken apart from any single one of its elements. But the Thing-inself, on the other hand, must exist apart.

Let us pass to another objection against our view. We may be told that the End, because it is that which thought aims at, is therefore itself (mere) thought. This assumes that thought cannot desire a consummation in which it is lost. But does not the river run into the sea, and the self lose itself in love ? And further, as good a claim for predominance might be made on behalf of will, and again on behalf of beauty and sensation and pleasure. Where all elements reach their end in the Absolute, that end can belong to no one severally. We may illustrate this principle by the case of morality. That essentially desires an end which is not merely moral because it is super-moral. Nay, even personality itself, our whole individual life and striving, tends to something beyond mere personality. Of course, the Absolute has personality, but it fortunately possesses so much more, that to call it personal would be as absurd as to ask if it is moral.[1]

But in self-consciousness, I may be told, we actually experience a state where truth and being are identical ; and here, at all events, thinking is not different from reality. But in our tenth chapter we have seen that no such state exists. There is no

[1] See further, Chapters xxv. and xxvii.

self-consciousness in which the object is the same as the subject, none in which what is perceived exhausts the whole self. In self-consciousness a part or element, or again a general aspect or character, becomes distinct from the whole mass and stands over against the felt background. But the background is never exhausted by this object, and it never could be so. An experiment should convince any man that in self-consciousness what he feels cannot wholly come before him. It can be exhausted, if at all, only by a long series of observations, and the summed result of these observations cannot be experienced as a fact. Such a result cannot ever be verified as quite true at any particular given moment. In short consciousness implies discrimination of an element from the felt mass, and a consciousness that should discriminate every element at once is psychologically impossible. And this impossibility, if it became actual, would still leave us held in a dilemma. For there is either no difference, and therefore no distinction, and no consciousness ; or there is a distinction, and therefore a difference between object and reality. But surely, if self-consciousness is appealed to, it is evident that at any moment I am more than the self which I can think of. How far everything in feeling may be called intelligible, is not the question here. But what is felt cannot be understood so that its truth and its existence become the same. And, if that were possible, yet such a process would certainly not be thinking.

In thinking the subject which thinks is more than thought. And that is why we can imagine that in thinking we find all reality. But in the same way the whole reality can as well be found in feeling or in volition. Each is one element in the whole, or the whole in one of its aspects ; and hence, when you get an aspect or element, you have the whole with it. But because, given one aspect (whichever it may be), we find the whole universe, to conclude that in the universe there is nothing beyond this single aspect, seems quite irrational.

But the reader may agree that no one really can believe that mere thought includes everything. The difficulty lies, he may urge, in *maintaining* the opposite. Since in philosophy we must think, how is it possible to transcend thought without a self-contradiction? For theory can reflect on, and pronounce about, all things, and in reflecting on them it therefore includes them. So that to maintain in thought an Other is by the same act to destroy its otherness, and to persist is to contradict oneself. While admitting that thought cannot satisfy us as to reality's falling wholly within its limits, we may be told that, so long as we think, we must ignore this admission. And the question is, therefore, whether philosophy does not end in sheer scepticism—in the necessity, that is, of asserting what it is no less induced to deny. The problem is serious, and I will now attempt to exhibit its solution.

We maintain an Other than mere thought. Now in what sense do we hold this? Thought being a judgment, we say that the predicate is never the same as the subject; for the subject is reality presented as "this" (we must not say as *mere* "this"). You can certainly abstract from presentation its character of "thisness," or its confused relatedness; and you can also abstract the feature of presentation. Of these you can make ideas,[1] for there is nothing which you cannot think of. But you find that these ideas are not the same as the subject of which you must predicate them. You can think of the subject, but you cannot get rid of it, or substitute mere thought-content for it. In other words, in practice thought always is found with, and appears to demand, an Other.

[1] *Principles of Logic*, pp. 64–69

Now the question is whether this leads to self-contradiction. If thought asserted the existence of any content which was not an actual or possible object of thought—certainly that assertion in my judgment would contradict itself. But the Other which I maintain, is not any such content, nor is it another separated "what," nor in any case do I suggest that it lies outside intelligence. Everything, all will and feeling, is an object for thought, and must be called intelligible.[1] This is certain; but, if so, what becomes of the Other? If we fall back on the mere "that," thatness itself seems a distinction made by thought. And we have to face this difficulty: If the Other exists, it must be something; and if it is nothing, it certainly does not exist.

Let us take an actual judgment and examine the subject there with a view to find our Other. In this we at once meet with a complication. We always have more content in the presented subject than in the predicate, and it is hence harder to realize what, beside this overplus of content, the subject possesses. However, passing this by, we can find in the subject two special characters. There is first (*a*) sensuous infinitude, and (*b*) in the second place there is immediacy.

(*a*) The presented subject has a detail which is unlimited. By this I do not mean that the actual plurality of its features exceeds a finite number. I mean that its detail always goes beyond itself, and is indefinitely relative to something outside.[2] In its given content it has relations which do not terminate within that content; and its existence therefore is not exhausted by itself, as we ever can have it. If I may use the metaphor, it has always edges which are ragged in such a way as to imply another existence from which it has been torn, and without which

---

[1] On this point see below, Chapters xix. and xxvi.
[2] This sensible "infinite" is the same as the finite, which we just saw was in its essence "ideal."

it really does not exist. Thus the content of the subject strives, we may say, unsuccessfully towards an all-inclusive whole. Now the predicate, on its side, is itself not free from endlessness. For its content, abstracted and finite, necessarily depends on relation to what is beyond. But it lacks the sensible and compulsory detail of the subject. It is not given as one thing with an actual but indefinite context. And thus, at least ostensibly, the predicate is hostile to endlessness.

(*b*) This is one difference, and the second consists in immediacy. The subject claims the character of a single self-subsistent being. In it the aspects of " what " and " that " are not taken as divorced, but it is given with its content as forming one integral whole. The " what " is not sundered from the " that," and turned from fact into truth. It is not predicated as the adjective of another " that," or even of its own. And this character of immediacy is plainly not consistent with endlessness. They are, in truth, each an imperfect appearance of individuality.[1] But the subject clearly possesses both these discrepant features, while the predicate no less clearly should be without them. For the predicate seeks also for individuality but by a different road.

Now, if we take the subject to have these two characters which are absent from the predicate, and if the desire of thought implies removal of that which makes predicate and subject differ—we begin to perceive the nature of our Other. And we may see at once what is required in order to extinguish its otherness. Subject and predicate alike must accept reformation. The ideal content of the predicate must be made consistent with immediate individuality ; and, on its side, the subject must be changed so as to become consistent with itself. It must become a self-subsistent, and that means an

---

[1] Compare here the doctrine of Chapters xix. and xxiv.

all-inclusive, individual.   But these reforms are impossible. The subject must pass into the judgment,
and it becomes infected with the relational form.
The self-dependence and immediacy, which it claims,
are not possessed by its content.   Hence in the
attempted self-assertion this content drives the subject beyond actual limits, and so begets a process
which is infinite and cannot be exhausted.   Thus
thought's attempt wholly to absorb the subject must
fail.   It fails because it cannot reform the subject
so as to include and exhaust its content.   And, in
the second place, thought fails because it cannot reform itself. For, if *per impossibile* the exhausted
content were comprised within a predicate, that
predicate still could not bear the character of immediacy.   I will dwell for a little on both points.

Let us consider first the subject that is presented.
It is a confused whole that, so far as we make it an
object, passes into a congeries of qualities and relations.   And thought desires to transform this congeries into a system. But, to understand the subject,
we have at once to pass outside it in time, and
again also in space.   On the other hand these
external relations do not end, and from their own
nature they cannot end.   Exhaustion is not merely
impracticable, it is essentially impossible.   And this
obstacle would be enough ; but this is not all.   Inside the qualities, which we took first as solid end-
points of the relations, an infinite process breaks
out.   In order to understand, we are forced to distinguish to the end, and we never get to that which
is itself apart from distinction.   Or we may put
the difficulty otherwise thus. We can neither take
the terms with their relations as a whole that is self-
evident, that stands by itself, and that calls for no
further account ; nor, on the other side, when we
distinguish, can we avoid the endless search for the
relation between the relation and its terms.[1]

[1] For this see above, Chapter iii.

Thus thought cannot get the content into a harmonious system. And in the next place, even if it did so, that system would not *be* the subject. It would either be a maze of relations, a maze with a plan, of which for ever we made the circuit ; or otherwise it would wholly lose the relational form. Our impossible process, in the first place, would assuredly have truth distinguished from its reality. For it could avoid this only by coming to us bodily and all at once, and, further, by suppressing entirely any distinction between subject and predicate. But, if in this way thought became immediate, it would lose its own character. It would be a system of relations no longer, but would have become an individual experience. And the Other would certainly have been absorbed, but thought itself no less would have been swallowed up and resolved into an Other.

Thought's relational content can never be the same as the subject, either as that subject appears or as it really is. The reality that is presented is taken up by thought in a form not adequate to its nature, and beyond which its nature must appear as an Other. But, to come at last in full view of the solution of our problem, this nature also is the nature which thought wants for itself. It is the character which even mere thinking desires to possess, and which in all its aspects exists within thought already, though in an incomplete form. And our main result is briefly this. The end, which would satisfy mere truth-seeking, would do so just because it had the features possessed by reality. It would have to be an immediate, self-dependent, all-inclusive individual. But, in reaching this perfection, and in the act of reaching it, thought would lose its own character. Thought does desire such individuality, that is precisely what it aims at. But individuality, on the other hand, cannot be gained while we are confined to relations.

Still we may be told that we are far from the solution of our problem. The fact of thought's desiring a foreign perfection, we may hear, is precisely the old difficulty. If thought desires this, then it is no Other, for we desire only what we know. The object of thought's desire cannot, hence, be a foreign object; for what is an object is, therefore, *not* foreign. But we reply that we have penetrated below the surface of any such dilemma. Thought desires for its content the character which makes reality. These features, if realized, would destroy mere thought; and hence they are an Other beyond thought. But thought, nevertheless, can desire them, because its content has them already in an incomplete form. And in desire for the completion of what one has there is no contradiction. Here is the solution of our difficulty.

The relational form is a compromise on which thought stands, and which it developes. It is an attempt to unite differences which have broken out of the felt totality.[1] Differences forced together by an underlying identity, and a compromise between the plurality and the unity—this is the essence of relation. But the differences remain independent, for they cannot be made to resolve themselves into their own relation. For, if so, they would perish, and their relation would perish with them. Or, otherwise, their outstanding plurality would still remain unreconciled with their unity, and so within the relation would beget the infinite process. The relation, on the other side, does not exist beyond the terms; for, in that case, itself would be a new term which would aggravate the distraction. But again, it cannot lose itself within the terms; for, if so, where is their common unity and their relation? They would in this case not be related, but would fall apart. Thus the whole relational perception

[1] On this point see Chapter iii.

joins various characters. It has the feature of immediacy and self-dependence; for the terms are given to it and not constituted by it. It possesses again the character of plurality. And as representing the primitive felt whole, it has once more the character of a comprehending unity—a unity, however, not constituted by the differences, but added from without. And, even against its wish, it has further a restless infinitude; for such infinitude is the very result of its practical compromise. And thought desires, retaining these features, to reduce them to harmony. It aims at an all-inclusive whole, not in conflict with its elements, and at elements subordinate to a self-dependent whole. Hence neither the aspect of unity, nor of plurality, nor of both these features in one, is really foreign to thought. There is nothing foreign that thought wants in desiring to be a whole, to comprehend everything, and yet to include and be superior to discord. But, on the other hand, such a completion, as we have seen, would prove destructive; such an end would emphatically make an end of mere thought. It would bring the ideal content into a form which would *be* reality itself, and where mere truth and mere thought would certainly perish. Thought seeks to possess in its object that whole character of which it already owns the separate features. These features it cannot combine satisfactorily, though it has the idea, and even the partial experience, of their complete combination. And, if the object were made perfect, it would forthwith *become* reality, but would cease forthwith to be an object. It is this completion of thought beyond thought which remains for ever an Other. Thought can form the idea of an apprehension, something like feeling in directness, which contains all the character sought by its relational efforts. Thought can understand that, to reach its goal, it must get beyond relations. Yet in its nature it can

find no other working means of progress.   Hence it
perceives that somehow this relational side of its
nature must be merged and must include somehow
the other side. Such a fusion would compel thought
to lose and to transcend its proper self.   And the
nature of this fusion thought can apprehend in
vague generality, but not in detail; and it can see
the reason why a detailed apprehension is impossible.   Such anticipated self-transcendence *is* an
Other; but to assert that Other is *not* a self-contradiction.

Hence in our Absolute thought can find its Other
without inconsistency.   The entire reality will be
merely the object thought out, but thought out in
such a way that mere thinking is absorbed.   This
same reality will be feeling that is satisfied completely.   In its direct experience we get restored
with interest every feature lost by the disruption of
our primitive felt whole. We possess the immediacy
and the strength of simple apprehension, no longer
forced by its own inconsistencies to pass into the
infinite process.   And again volition, if willed out,
becomes our Absolute. For we reach there the
identity of idea and reality, not too poor but too rich
for division of its elements.   Feeling, thought, and
volition have all defects which suggest something
higher.   But in that higher unity no fraction of anything is lost.   For each one-sided aspect, to gain
itself, blends with that which seemed opposite, and
the product of this fusion keeps the riches of all.
The one reality, we may say from our human point
of view, was present in each aspect in a form which
does not satisfy.   To work out its full nature it has
sunk itself into these differences.   But in each it
longs for that absolute self-fruition which comes
only when the self bursts its limits and blends with
another finite self.   This desire of each element for
a perfection which implies fusion with others, is not
self-contradictory.   It is rather an effort to remove

a present state of inconsistency, to remain in which would indeed be fixed self-contradiction.

Now, if it is objected that such an Absolute is the Thing-in-itself, I must doubt if the objector can understand. How a whole which comprehends everything can deserve that title is past my conjecture. And, if I am told that the differences are lost in this whole, and yet the differences *are*, and must therefore be left outside—I must reply to this charge by a counter-charge of thoughtless confusion. For the differences are not lost, but are all contained in the whole. The fact that *more* is included there than these several, isolated, differences hardly proves that these differences are not there at all. When an element is joined to another in a whole of experience, then, on the whole, and for the whole, their mere specialities need not exist; but, none the less, each element in its own partial experience may retain its own speciality. "Yes; but these partial experiences," I may be told, "will at all events fall outside the whole." Surely no such consequence follows. The self-consciousness of the part, its consciousness of itself even in opposition to the whole— all will be contained within the one absorbing experience. For this will embrace all self-consciousness harmonized, though, as such, transmuted and suppressed. We cannot possibly construe, I admit, such an experience to ourselves. We cannot imagine how in detail its outline is filled up. But to say that it is real, and that it unites certain general characters within the living system of one undivided apprehension, is within our power. The assertion of this Absolute's reality I hope in the sequel to justify. Here (if I have not failed) I have shown that, at least from the point of view of thinking, it is free from self-contradiction. The justification for thought of an Other may help both to explain and to bury the Thing-in-itself.

CHAPTER XVI.

ERROR.

WE have so far sketched in outline the Absolute which we have been forced to accept, and we have pointed out the general way in which thought may fall within it. We must address ourselves now to a series of formidable objections. If our Absolute is possible in itself, it seems hardly possible as things are. For there are undeniable facts with which it does not seem compatible. Error and evil, space, time, chance and mutability, and the unique particularity of the "this" and the "mine"—all these appear to fall outside an individual experience. To explain them away or to explain them, one of these courses seems necessary, and yet both seem impossible. And this is a point on which I am anxious to be clearly understood. I reject the offered dilemma, and deny the necessity of a choice between these two courses. I fully recognise the facts, I do not make the smallest attempt to explain their origin, and I emphatically deny the need for such an explanation. In the first place to show how and why the universe is so that finite existence belongs to it, is utterly impossible. That would imply an understanding of the whole not practicable for a mere part. It would mean a view by the finite from the Absolute's point of view, and in that consummation the finite would have been transmuted and destroyed. But, in the second place, such an understanding is wholly unnecessary. We have **not** to choose between accounting for everything on one side and on the other side admitting it as a disproof of our doctrine of the Absolute. Such an alternative is not logical. If you wish to refute a wide theory based on general grounds, it is idle merely to produce facts which upon it are not explained. For the inability to explain these may be simply our failure in particular information, and it need imply nothing worse than confirmation lacking to the theory. The facts become an objection to the doctrine when they are incompatible with some part of it; while, if they merely remain outside, that points to incompleteness in detail and not falsity in principle. A general doctrine is not destroyed by what we fail to understand. It is destroyed only by that which we actually do understand, and can show to be inconsistent and discrepant with the theory adopted.

And this is the real issue here. Error and evil are no disproof of our absolute experience so long as we merely fail to see how in detail it comprehends them. They are a disproof when their nature is understood in such a way as to collide with the Absolute. And the question is whether this understanding of them is correct. It is here that I confidently join issue. If on this subject there exists a false persuasion of knowledge, I urge that it lies on the side of the objector. I maintain that we know nothing of these various forms of the finite which shows them incompatible with that Absolute, for the accepting of which we have general ground. And I meet the denial of this position by pointing out assumed knowledge where really there is ignorance. It is the objector who, if any one, asserts omniscience. It is he who claims to understand both the infinite and the finite, so as to be aware and to be assured of their incompatibility. And I think that he much overestimates the extent of human power. We cannot know that the finite is in collision with the Absolute. And if we cannot, and if, for all we understand, the two are at one and harmonious—then our conclusion is proved fully. For we have a general assurance that reality has a certain nature, and, on the other side, against that assurance we have to set nothing, nothing other than our ignorance. But an assurance, against which there is nothing to be set, must surely be accepted. And I will begin first with Error.

Error is without any question a dangerous subject, and the chief difficulty is as follows. We cannot, on the one hand, accept anything between non-existence and reality, while, on the other hand, error obstinately refuses to be either. It persistently attempts to maintain a third position, which appears nowhere to exist, and yet somehow is occupied. In false appearance there is something attributed to the real which does not belong to it. But if the appearance is not real, then it is not false appearance, because it is nothing. On the other hand, if it is false, it must therefore be true reality, for it is something which is. And this dilemma at first sight seems insoluble. Or, to put it otherwise, an appearance, which is, must fall somewhere. But error, because it is false, cannot belong to the Absolute; and, again, it cannot appertain to the finite subject, because that, with all its contents, cannot fall outside the Absolute; at least, if it did, it would be nothing. And so error has no home, it has no place in existence; and yet, for all that, it exists. And for this reason it has occasioned much doubt and difficulty.

For Psychology and for Logic the problem is much easier. Error can be identified with wrong inference, and can be compared on one side with a typical model; while, on the other side, we can show by what steps it originates. But these enquiries, however interesting, would not much assist us, and we must endeavour here to face the problem more directly. We must take our stand on the distinction between idea and reality.

Error is the same as false appearance,[1] or (if the reader objects to this) it is at any rate one kind of false appearance. Now appearance is content not at one with its existence, a "what" loosened from its "that." And in this sense we have seen that every truth is appearance, since in it we have divorce of quality from being (p. 163). The idea which is true is the adjective of reality so far as its content goes. It, so far, is restored, and belongs, to existence. But an idea has also another side, its own private being as something which is and happens. And an idea, as content, is alienated from this its own existence as an event. Even where you take a presented whole, and predicate one or more features, our account still holds good. For the content predicated has now become alien to its existence. On the one side it has not been left in simple unity with the whole, nor again is it predicated so far as changed from a mere feature into another and separate fact. In "sugar is sweet" the sweetness asserted of the sugar is *not* the sweetness so far as divided from it and turned into a second thing in our minds. This thing has its own being there, and to predicate it, as such, of the sugar would clearly be absurd. In respect of its own existence the idea is therefore always a mere appearance. But this character of divorce from its private reality becomes usually still more patent, where the idea is not taken from presentation but supplied by reproduction. Wherever the predicate is seen to be supplied from an image, the existence of that image can be seen at once *not* to be the predicate. It is something clearly left outside of the judgment and quite disregarded.[2]

Appearance then will be the looseness of char-

---

[1] See more, Chapter xxvi.
[2] Compare p. 164.

acter from being, the distinction of immediate oneness
into two sides, a "that" and a "what." And this
looseness tends further to harden into fracture and
into the separation of two sundered existences.
Appearance will be truth when a content, made
alien to its own being, is related to some fact which
accepts its qualification. The true idea is appearance in respect of its own being as fact and event,
but is reality in connection with other being which
it qualifies. Error, on the other hand, is content
made loose from its own reality, and related to a
reality with which it is discrepant. It is the rejection of an idea by existence which is not the
existence of the idea as made loose. It is the
repulse by a substantive of a liberated adjective.[1]
Thus it is an appearance which not only appears,
but is false. It is in other words the collision of a
mere idea with reality.

There are serious problems with regard both to
error and truth, and the distinction between them,
which challenge our scrutiny. I think it better
however to defer these to later chapters. I will
therefore limit here the enquiry, so far as is possible,
and will consider two main questions. Error is
content neither at one with its own being, nor
otherwise allowed to be an adjective of the real.
If so, we must ask (1) why it cannot be accepted
by reality, and (2) how it still actually can belong
to reality ; for we have seen that this last conclusion
is necessary.

1. Error is rejected by reality because that is
harmonious, and is taken necessarily to be so, while
error, on the other hand, is self-contradictory. I do
not mean that it is a content merely not at one (if
that were possible) with its own mere being.[2] I

---

[1] Whether the adjective has been liberated from this substantive or from another makes no difference.

[2] In the end no finite predicate or subject can possibly be
harmonious.

mean that its inner character, as ideal, is itself discordant and self-discrepant. But I should prefer
not to call error a *predicate* which contradicts itself.
For that might be taken as a statement that the
contradiction already is present in the mere predicate, *before* judgment is attempted ; and this, if
defensible, would be misleading. Error is the
qualification of a reality in such a way that in
the result it has an inconsistent content, which for
that reason is rejected. Where existence has a
" what " colliding within itself, there the predication
of this "what" is an erroneous judgment. If a
reality is self-consistent, and its further determination has introduced discord, there the addition is
the mistake, and the reality is unaffected. It is
unaffected, however, solely on the assumption that
its own nature in no way suggested and called in the
discordant. For otherwise the whole result is infected with falseness, and the reality could never
have been pure from discrepancy.[1]

It will perhaps tend to make clearer this general
view of error if I defend it against some possible
objections. Error is supposed by some persons to
be a departure from experience, or from what is
given merely. It is again taken sometimes as the
confusion of internal image with outward sensation.
But any such views are of course most superficial.
Quite apart from the difficulty of finding anything
merely given, and the impossibility of always using
actual present sensation as a test of truth—without
noticing the strange prejudice that outward sensations are never false, and the dull blindness which
fails to realize that the " inward " is a fact just as
solid as the "outward "—we may dismiss the whole
objection. For, if the given has a content which is
not harmonious, then, no matter in what sense we

---

[1] The doctrine here is stated subject to correction in Chapter
xxiv. No finite predicate or subject can really be self-consistent.

like to take "given," that content is not real.   And
any attempt, either to deny this, or to maintain that
in the given there is never discrepancy, may be
left to itself.   But I will go on to consider the
same view as it wears a more plausible form.   "We
do not," I may be told, "add or take away predicates simply at our pleasure.   We do not, so long
as this arbitrary result does not visibly contradict
itself, consider it true."   And I have not said that
we should do this.

Outside known truth and error we may, of course,
have simple ignorance.[1]   An assertion, that is, must
in every case be right or be wrong ; but, for us and
for the present, it may not yet be either.   Still, on
the other hand, we do know that, *if* the statement
is an error, it will be so because its content collides
internally.   "But this" (an objector may reply)
"is really not the case.   Take the statement that
at a certain time an event did, or did not, happen.
This would be erroneous because of disagreement
with fact, and not always because it is inconsistent
with itself."   Still I must insist that we have some
further reason for condemning this want of correspondence with fact.   For why, apart from such a
reason, should either we or the fact make an objection to this defect ?   Suppose that when William
has been hung, I assert that it was John.   My
assertion will then be false, because the reality does
not admit of both events, and because William is
certain.   And if so, then after all my error surely
will consist in giving to the real a self-discrepant
content.   For otherwise, when John is suggested,
I could not reject the idea.   I could only say that
certainly it was William, and might also, for all that
I knew, be John too.   But in our actual practice we
proceed thus : since "both John *and* William"
forms a discordant content, that statement is in

---

[1] For further explanation, see Chapter xxvii.

error—here to the extent of John.[1] In the same way, if where no man is you insist on John's presence, then, without discussing here the nature of the privative judgment,[2] we can understand the mistake. You are trying to force on the reality something which would make it inconsistent, and which therefore is erroneous. But it would be alike easy and idle to pursue the subject further ; and I must trust that, to the reader who reflects, our main conclusion is already made good. Error is qualification by the self-discrepant. We must not, if we take the predicate in its usual sense, in all cases place the contradiction within that. But where discrepancy is found in the result of qualification, it is there that we have error. And I will now pass to the second main problem of this chapter.

2. The question is about the relation of error to the Absolute. How is it possible for false appearance to take its place within reality ? We have to some extent perceived in what error consists, but we still are confronted by our original problem. Qualification by the self-discrepant exists as a fact, and yet how can it be real ? The self-contradiction in the content both belongs, and is unable to belong, to reality. The elements related, and their synthesis, and their reference to existence—these are things not to be got rid of. You may condemn them, but your condemnation cannot act as a spell to abolish them wholly. If they were not there, you could not judge them, and then you judge them not to be; or you pronounce them apparently somehow to exist without really existing. What is the exit from this puzzle?

There is no way but in accepting the whole mass of fact, and in then attempting to correct it and

---

[1] I do not here touch the question why John is sacrificed rather than William (or both). On this, see Chapter xxiv.

[2] See Chapter xxvii

make it good. Error *is* truth, it is partial truth,
that is false only because partial and left incomplete.
The Absolute *has* without subtraction all those
qualities, and it has every arrangement which we
seem to confer upon it by our mere mistake. The
only mistake lies in our failure to give also the
complement. The reality owns the discordance and
the discrepancy of false appearance; but it possesses also much else in which this jarring character
is swallowed up and is dissolved in fuller harmony.
I do not mean that by a mere re-arrangement of
the matter which is given to *us, we* could remove
its contradictions. For, being limited, we cannot
apprehend all the details of the whole. And we
must remember that every old arrangement, condemned as erroneous, itself forms part of that
detail. To know all the elements of the universe,
with all the conjunctions of those elements, good
and bad, is impossible for finite minds. And hence
obviously we are unable throughout to reconstruct
our discrepancies. But we can comprehend in
general what we cannot see exhibited in detail.
We cannot understand how in the Absolute a rich
harmony embraces every special discord. But, on
the other hand, we may be sure that this result is
reached ; and we can even gain an imperfect view
of the effective principle. I will try to explain this
latter statement.

There is only one way to get rid of contradiction,
and that way is by dissolution. Instead of one subject
distracted, we get a larger subject with distinctions,
and so the tension is removed. We have at first
A, which possesses the qualities *c* and *b*, inconsistent adjectives which collide; and we go on to
produce harmony by making a distinction within
this subject. That was really not mere A, but
either a complex within A, or (rather here) a wider
whole in which A is included, The real subject
is $A + D$; and this subject contains the contradic-

tion made harmless by division, since A is *c* and D
is *b*. This is the general principle, and I will
attempt here to apply it in particular. Let us
suppose the reality to be X (*a b c d e f g* . . .),
and that we are able only to get partial views of
this reality. Let us first take such a view as
" X (*a b*) is *b*." This (rightly or wrongly) we should
probably call a true view. For the content *b* does
plainly belong to the subject ; and, further, the
appearance also—in other words, the separation of
b in the predicate—can partly be explained. For.
answering to this separation, we postulate now
another adjective in the subject ; let us call it *β*.
The "thatness," the psychical existence of the predicate, which at first was neglected, has now also
itself been included in the subject. We may hence
write the subject as X (*a b β*) ; and in this way we
seem to avoid contradiction. Let us go further on
the same line, and, having dealt with a truth, pass
next to an error. Take the subject once more as
X (*a b c d e* . . .), and let us now say " X (*a b*)
is *d*." This is false, because *d* is not present in the
subject, and so we have a collision. But the collision
is resolved if we take the subject, not as mere X
(*a b*), but more widely as X (*a b c d*). In this case
the predicate *d* becomes applicable. Thus the error
consisted in the reference of *d* to *a b* ; as it might
have consisted in like manner in the reference of
a b to *c*, or again of *c* to *d*. All of these exist in
the subject, and the reality possesses with each both
its "what" and its "that." But not content with a
provisional separation of these indissoluble aspects,
not satisfied (as in true appearance) to have *aα*, *bβ*,
and *dδ*—forms which may typify distinctions that
bring no discord into the qualities—we have gone
on further into error. We have not only loosened
"what" from "that," and so have made appearance ; but we have in each case then bestowed the
"what" on a wrong quality within the real subject.

A. R.   O

We have crossed the threads of the connection between our "whats" and our "thats," and have thus caused collision, a collision which disappears when things are taken as a whole.

I confess that I shrink from using metaphors, since they never can suit wholly. The writer tenders them unsuspiciously as a possible help in a common difficulty. And so he subjects himself, perhaps, to the captious ill-will or sheer negligence of his reader. Still to those who will take it for what it is, I will offer a fiction. Suppose a collection of beings whose souls in the night walk about without their bodies, and so make new relations. On their return in the morning we may imagine that the possessors feel the benefit of this divorce; and we may therefore call it truth. But, if the wrong soul with its experience came back to the wrong body, that might typify error. On the other hand, perhaps the ruler of this collection of beings may perceive very well the nature of the collision. And it may even be that he provokes it. For how instructive and how amusing to observe in each case the conflict of sensation with imported and foreign experience. Perhaps no truth after all could be half so rich and half so true as the result of this wild discord—to one who sees from the centre. And, if so, error will come merely from isolation and defect, from the limitation of each being to the "this" and the " mine."

But our account, it will fairly be objected, is antenable because incomplete. For error is *not* merely negative. The content, isolated and so discordant, is after all held together in a positive discord. And so the elements may exist, and their relations to their subjects may all be there in the Absolute, together with the complements which make them all true, and yet the problem is not solved. For the point of error, when all is said, lies in this very insistence on the partial and discrepant, and this discordant emphasis will fall outside of every possible rearrangement. I admit this objection, and I endorse it. The problem of error cannot be solved by an enlarged scheme of relations. Each misarrangement cannot be taken up wholly as an element in the compensations of a harmonious mechanism. For there is a positive sense and a specific character which marks each appearance, and this will still fall outside. Hence, while all that appears somehow is, all has not been accounted for by any rearrangement.

But on the other side the Absolute is not, and can not be thought as, any scheme of relations. If we keep to these, there is no harmonious unity in the whole. The Absolute is beyond a mere arrangement, however well compensated, though an arrangement is assuredly one aspect of its being. Reality, consists, as we saw, in a higher experience, superior to the distinctions which it includes and overrides. And, with this, the last objection to the transformation of error has lost its basis. The one-sided emphasis of error, its isolation as positive and as not dissoluble in a wider connection—this again will contribute, we know not how, to the harmony of the Absolute. It will be another detail, which, together with every "what" and "that" and their relations, will be absorbed into the whole and will subserve its perfection.

On this view there still are problems as to error and truth which we must deal with hereafter. But the main dilemma as to false appearance has, I think, been solved. That both exists and is, as such, not real. Its arrangement becomes true in a wider rearrangement of "what" and of "that." Error is truth when it is supplemented. And its positive isolation also is reducible, and exists as a mere element within the whole. Error is, but is not barely what it takes itself to be. And its mere onesidedness again is but a partial emphasis, a note of insistence which contributes, we know not how, to greater energy of life. And, if so, the whole problem has, so far, been disposed of.

Now that this solution cannot be verified, in the sense of being made out in detail, is not an admission on my part. It is rather a doctrine which I assert and desire to insist on. It is impossible for us to show, in the case of every error, how in the whole it is made good. It is impossible, even apart from detail, to realize how the relational form is in general absorbed. But, upon the other hand, I deny that our solution is either unintelligible or impossible. And possibility here is all that we want. For we have seen that the Absolute *must be* a harmonious system. We have first perceived this in general, and here specially, in the case of error, we have been engaged in a reply to an alleged negative instance. Our opponent's case has been this, that the nature of error makes our harmony impossible. And we have shown, on the other side, that he possesses no such knowledge. We have pointed out that it is at least possible for errors to correct themselves, and, as such, to disappear in a higher experience. But, if so, we *must* affirm that they are thus absorbed and made good. For what is *possible*, and what a general principle compels us to say *must be*, that certainly *is*.

CHAPTER XVII.

EVIL.

WE have seen that error is compatible with absolute perfection, and we now must try to reach the same result in the case of evil. Evil is a problem which of course presents serious difficulties, but the worst have been imported into it and rest on pure mistake. It is here, as it is also with what is called " Free Will." The trouble has come from the idea that the Absolute is a moral person. If you start from that basis, then the relation of evil to the Absolute presents at once an irreducible dilemma. The problem then becomes insoluble, but not because it is obscure or in any way mysterious. To any one who has sense and courage to see things as they are, and is resolved not to mystify others or himself, there is really no question to discuss. The dilemma is plainly insoluble because it is based on a clear self-contradiction, and the discussion of it here would be quite uninstructive. It would concern us only if we had reason to suppose that the Absolute is (properly) moral. But we have no such reason, and hereafter we may hope to convince ourselves (Chapter xxv.), that morality cannot (as such) be ascribed to the Absolute. And, with this, the problem becomes certainly no worse than many others. Hence I would invite the reader to dismiss all hesitation and misgiving. If the questions we ask prove unanswerable, that will certainly not be because they are quite obscure or unintelligible. It will be simply because the data we possess are

insufficient. But let us at all events try to understand what it is that we seek.

Evil has, we all know, several meanings. It may
be taken (I.) as pain, (II.) as failure to realize end,
and (III.), specially, as immorality. The fuller
consideration of the last point must be postponed to
a later chapter, where we can deal better with the
relation of the finite person to the Absolute.

I. No one of course can deny that pain actually
exists, and I at least should not dream of denying
that it is evil. But we failed to see, on the other
hand, how pain, as such, can possibly exist in the
Absolute.[1] Hence, it being admitted that pain has
actual existence, the question is whether its nature
can be transmuted. Can its painfulness disappear
in a higher unity? If so, it will exist, but will have
ceased to be pain when considered on the whole.

We can to some extent verify in our actual experience the neutralization of pain. It is quite
certain that small pains are often wholly swallowed
up in a larger composite pleasure. And the assertion that, in all these cases, they have been destroyed
and not merged, would most certainly be baseless.
To suppose that my condition is never pleasant on
the whole while I still have an actual local pain, is
directly opposed to fact. In a composite state the
pain doubtless will detract from the pleasure, but
still we may have a resultant which is pleasurable
wholly. Such a balance is all that we want in the
case of absolute perfection.

We shall certainly so far have done nothing to
confute the pessimist. " I accept," he will reply,
" your conclusion in general as to the existence of a
balance. I quite agree that in the resultant one

---

[1] Chapter xiv. This conclusion is somewhat modified in
Chapter xxvii., but, for the sake of clearness, I state it here
unconditionally. The reader can correct afterwards, so far as is
required, the results of the present chapter.

feature is submerged. But, unfortunately for your view, that feature really is not pain but pleasure. The universe, taken as a whole, suffers therefore sheer pain and is hence utterly evil." But I do not propose to undertake here an examination of pessimism. That would consist largely in the weighing of psychological arguments on either side, and the result of these is in my opinion fatal to pessimism. In the world, which we observe, an impartial scrutiny will discover more pleasure than pain, though it is difficult to estimate, and easy to exaggerate, the amount of the balance. Still I must confess that, apart from this, I should hold to my conclusion. I should still believe that in the universe there is preponderance of pleasure. The presumption in its favour is based on a principle from which I see no escape (Chapter xiv.), while the world we see is probably a very small part of the reality. Our general principle must therefore be allowed to weigh down a great deal of particular appearance; and, if it were necessary, I would without scruple rest my case on this argument. But, on the contrary, no such necessity exists. The observed facts are clearly, on the whole, in favour of some balance of pleasure. They, in the main, serve to support our conclusion from principle, and pessimism may, without hesitation, be dismissed.

We have found, so far, that there is a possibility of pain ceasing, as such, to exist in the Absolute. We have shown that this possibility can to some extent be verified in experience. And we have a general presumption in favour of an actual balance of pleasure. Hence once more here, as before with error, possibility is enough. For what *may* be, if it also *must* be, assuredly *is*.

There are readers, perhaps, who will desire to go farther. It might be urged that in the Absolute pain not merely is lost, but actually serves as a kind of stimulus to heighten the pleasure. And doubtless this possibly may be the case ; but I can see no good reason for taking it as fact. In the Absolute there probably is no pleasure outside of finite souls (Chapter xxvii.) ; and we have no reason to suppose that those we do not see are happier than those which we know. Hence, though this is possible, we are not justified in asserting it as more. For we have no right to go farther than our principle requires. But, if there is a balance of clear pleasure, that principle is satisfied, for nothing then stands in the way of the Absolute's perfection. It is a mistake to think that perfection is made more perfect by increase of quantity (Chapter xx.).

II. Let us go on to consider evil as waste, failure, and confusion. The whole world seems to a large extent the sport of mere accident. Nature and our life show a struggle in which one end perhaps is realized, and a hundred are frustrated. This is an old complaint, but it meets an answer in an opposing doubt. Is there really any such thing as an end in Nature at all ? For, if not, clearly there is no evil, in the sense in which at present we are taking the word. But we must postpone the discussion of this doubt until we have gained some understanding of what Nature is to mean.[1] I will for the present admit the point of view which first supposes ends in Nature, and then objects that they are failures. And I think that this objection is not hard to dispose of. The ends which fail, we may reply, are ends selected by ourselves and selected more or less erroneously. They are too partial, as we have taken them, and, if included in a larger end to which they are relative, they cease to be failures. They, in short, subserve a wider scheme, and in that they are realized. It is here with evil as it was before with error. That was lost in higher

---

[1] For the question of ends in Nature see Chapters xxii. and xxvi.

truth to which it was subordinate, and in which, as such, it vanished. And with partial ends, in Nature or in human lives, the same principle will hold. Idea and existence we find not to agree, and this discord we call evil. But, when these two sides are enlarged and each taken more widely, both may well come together. I do not mean, of course, that every finite end, as such, is realized. I mean that it is lost, and becomes an element, in a wider idea which is one with existence. And, as with error, even our onesidedness, our insistence and our disappointment, may somehow all subserve a harmony and go to perfect it. The aspects of idea and of existence may be united in one great whole, in which evil, and even ends, as such, disappear. To verify this consummation, or even to see how in detail it can be, is alike impossible. But, for all that, such perfection in its general idea is intelligible and possible. And, because the Absolute is perfect, this harmony must also exist. For that which is both possible and necessary we are bound to think real.

III. Moral evil presents us with further difficulties. Here it is not a question simply of defect, and of the failure in outward existence of that inner idea which we take as the end. We are concerned further with a positive strife and opposition. We have an idea in a subject, an end which strives to gain reality ; and on the other side, we have the existence of the same subject. This existence not merely fails to correspond, but struggles adversely, and the collision is felt as such. In our moral experience we find this whole fact given beyond question. We suffer within ourselves a contest of the good and bad wills and a certainty of evil. Nay, if we please, we may add that this discord is necessary, since without it morality must wholly perish.

And this necessity of discord shows the road into the centre of our problem. Moral evil exists only in moral experience, and that experience in its essence is full of inconsistency. For morality desires unconsciously, with the suppression of evil, to become wholly non-moral. It certainly would shrink from this end, but it thus unknowingly desires the existence and perpetuity of evil. I shall have to return later to this subject (Chapter xxv.), and for the present we need keep hold merely of this one point. Morality itself, which makes evil, desires in evil to remove a condition of its own being. It labours essentially to pass into a super-moral and therefore a non-moral sphere.

But, if we will follow it and will frankly adopt this tendency, we may dispose of our difficulty. For the content, willed as evil and in opposition to the good, can enter as an element into a wider arrangement. Evil, as we say (usually without meaning it), is over-ruled and subserves. It is enlisted and it plays a part in a higher good end, and in this sense, un-knowingly is good. Whether and how far it is as good as the will which is moral, is a question later to be discussed. All that we need understand here is that " Heaven's design," if we may speak so, can realize itself as effectively in " Catiline or Borgia" as in the scrupulous or innocent. For the higher end is super-moral, and our moral end here has been confined, and is therefore incomplete. As before with physical evil, the discord as such disappears, if the harmony is made wide enough.

But it will be said truly that in moral evil we have something additional. We have not the mere fact of incomplete ends and their isolation, but we have in addition a positive felt collision in the self. And this cannot be explained away, for it has to fall within the Absolute, and it makes there a discord which remains unresolved. But our old principle may still serve to remove this objection. The col-lision and the strife may be an element in some fuller realization. Just as in a machine the resist-

ance and pressure of the parts subserve an end
beyond any of them, if regarded by itself—so at a
much higher level it may be with the Absolute.
Not only the collision but that specific feeling, by
which it is accompanied and aggravated, can be
taken up into an all-inclusive perfection. We do
not know how this is done, and ingenious metaphors
(if we could find them) would not serve to explain
it. For the explanation would tend to wear the
form of qualities in relation, a form necessarily (as
we have seen) transcended in the Absolute. Such
a perfect way of existence would, however, reconcile
our jarring discords; and I do not see how we can
deny that such a harmony is possible. But, if possible, then, as before, it is indubitably real. For,
on the one side, we have an overpowering reason
for maintaining it; while upon the other side, so
far as I can see, we have nothing.

I will mention in passing another point, the
unique sense of personality which is felt strongly in
evil. But I must defer its consideration until we
attack the problem of the "mine" and the "this"
(Chapter xix.). And I will end here with some
words on another source of danger. There is a
warning which I may be allowed to impress on the
reader. We have used several times already with
diverse subject-matters the same form of argument.
All differences, we have urged repeatedly, come together in the Absolute. In this, how we do not
know, all distinctions are fused, and all relations
disappear. And there is an objection which may
probably at some point have seemed plausible.
"Yes," I may be told, "it is too true that all difference is gone. First with one real existence, and
then afterwards with another, the old argument is
brought out and the old formula applied. There is
no variety in the solution, and hence in each case
the variety is lost to the Absolute. Along with

these distinctions all character has wholly disappeared, and the Absolute stands outside, an empty
residue and bare Thing-in-itself." This would be
a serious misunderstanding. It is true that we do
not know how the Absolute overrides the relational
form. But it does not follow from this that, when
the relational form is gone, the result is really poorer.
It is true that with each problem we cannot say
how its special discords are harmonized. But is
this to deny the reality of diverse contents in the
Absolute ? Because in detail we cannot tell in what
each solution consists, are we therefore driven to
assert that all the detail is abolished, and that our
Absolute is a flat monotony of emptiness ? This
would indeed be illogical. For though we do not
know in each case what the solution can be, we know
that in every case it contains the whole of the
variety. We do not know how all these partial
unities come together in the Absolute, but we may
be sure that the content of not one is obliterated.
The Absolute is the richer for every discord, and
for all diversity which it embraces ; and it is our
ignorance only in which consists the poverty of our
object. Our knowledge must be poor because it is
abstract. We cannot specify the concrete nature
of the Absolute's riches, but with every region of
phenomenal existence we can say that it possesses
so much more treasure. Objections and problems,
one after the other, are not shelved merely, but each
is laid up as a positive increase of character in the
reality. Thus a man might be ignorant of the exact
shape in which his goods have been realized, and
yet he might be rationally assured that, with each
fresh alienation of visible property, he has somehow
corresponding wealth in a superior form.

CHAPTER XVIII.

TEMPORAL AND SPATIAL APPEARANCE.

BOTH time and space have been shown to be un-real as such. We found in both such contradictions that to predicate either of the reality was out of the question. Time and space are mere appear-ance, and that result is quite certain. Both, on the other hand, exist; and both must somehow in some way belong to our Absolute. Still a doubt may be raised as to this being possible.

To explain time and space, in the sense of showing how such appearances come to be, and again how without contradiction they can be real in the Absolute, is certainly not my object. Any-thing of the kind, I am sure, is impossible. And what I wish to insist on is this, that such knowledge is not necessary. What we require to know is only that these appearances are not incompatible with our Absolute. They have been urged as instances fatal to any view such as ours; and this objection, we must reply, is founded on mistake. Space and time give no ground for the assertion that our Absolute is not possible. And, in their case once more, we must urge the old argument. Since it is possible that these appearances can be resolved into a harmony which both contains and transcends them; since again it is necessary, on our main prin-ciple, that this should be so—it therefore truly is real. But let us examine these appearances more closely, and consider time first.

It is unnecessary to take up the question of time's

origin. To show it as produced psychologically from timeless elements is, I should say, not possible. Its perception generally may supervene at some stage of our development; and, at all events in its complete form, that perception is clearly a result. But, if we take the sense of time in its most simple and undeveloped shape, it would be difficult to show that it was not there from the first. Still this whole question, however answered, has little importance for Metaphysics. We might perhaps draw, if we could assume that time has been developed, some presumption in favour of its losing itself once more in a product which is higher. But it is hardly worth while to consider this presumption more closely.

Passing from this point I will reply to an objection from fact. If time is not unreal, I admit that our Absolute is a delusion; but, on the other side, it will be urged that time cannot be mere appearance. The change in the finite subject, we are told, is a matter of direct experience; it is a fact, and hence it cannot be explained away. And so much of course is indubitable. Change is a fact, and, further, this fact, as such, is not reconcilable with the Absolute. And, if we could not in any way perceive how the fact can be unreal, we should be placed, I admit, in a hopeless dilemma. For we should have a view as to reality which we could not give up, and should, on the other hand, have an existence in contradiction with that view. But our real position is very different from this. For time has been shown to contradict itself, and so to be appearance. With this, its discord, we see at once, may pass as an element into a wider harmony. And, with this, the appeal to fact at once becomes worthless.

It is mere superstition to suppose that an appeal to experience can prove reality. That I find something in existence in the world or in my self, shows that this something exists, and it cannot show more.

Any deliverance of consciousness—whether original or acquired—is but a deliverance of consciousness. It is in no case an oracle and a revelation which we have to accept. It is a fact, like other facts, to be dealt with; and there is no presumption anywhere that any fact is better than appearance. The "given" of course is given; it must be recognised, and it cannot be ignored. But between recognising a datum and receiving blindly its content as reality is a very wide interval. We may put it thus once for all—there is nothing given which is sacred. Metaphysics can respect no element of experience except on compulsion. It can reverence nothing but what by criticism and denial the more unmistakably asserts itself.

Time is so far from enduring the test of criticism, that at a touch it falls apart and proclaims itself illusory. I do not propose to repeat the detail of its self-contradiction; for that I take as exhibited once for all in our First Book. What I must attempt here first is to show how by its inconsistency time directs us beyond itself. It points to something higher in which it is included and transcended.

1. In the first place change, as we saw (Chapter v.), must be relative to a permanent. Doubtless here was a contradiction which we found was not soluble. But, for all that, the fact remains that change demands some permanence within which succession happens. I do not say that this demand is consistent, and, on the contrary, I wish to emphasize the point that it is not so. It is inconsistent, and yet it is none the less essential. And I urge that therefore change desires to pass beyond simple change. It seeks to become a change which is somehow consistent with permanence. Thus, in asserting itself, time tries to commit suicide as itself, to transcend its own character and to be taken up in what is higher.

2. And we may draw this same conclusion from another inconsistency. The relation of the present to the future and to the past shows once more time's attempt to transcend its own nature. Any lapse, that for any purpose you take as one period, becomes forthwith a present. And then this lapse is treated as if it existed all at once. For how otherwise could it be spoken of as one thing at all? Unless it *is*, I do not see how we have a right to regard it as possessing a character. And unless it is present, I am quite unable to understand with what meaning we can assert that it *is*. And, I think, the common behaviour of science might have been enough by itself to provoke reflection on this head. We may say that science, recognising on the one side, on the other side quite ignores the existence of time. For it habitually treats past and future as one thing with the present (Chapter viii.). The character of an existence is determined by what it has been and by what it is (potentially) about to be. But if these attributes, on the other hand, are not present, how can they be real? Again in establishing a Law, itself without special relation to time, science treats facts from various dates as all possessing the same value. Yet how, if we seriously mean to take time as real, can the past be reality? It would, I trust, be idle to expand here these obvious considerations. They should suffice to point out that for science reality at least *tries* to be timeless, and that succession, as such, can be treated as something without rights and as mere appearance.

3. This same tendency becomes visible in another application. The whole movement of our mind implies disregard of time. Not only does intellect accept what is true once for true always, and thus fearlessly take its stand on the Identity of Indiscernibles—not only is this so, but the whole mass of what is called "Association" implies the same principle. For such a connection does not hold except

between universals.[1] The associated elements are divorced from their temporal context; they are set free in union, and ready to form fresh unions without regard for time's reality. This is in effect to degrade time to the level of appearance. But our entire mental life, on the other hand, has its movement through this law. Our whole being practically implies it, and to suppose that we can rebel would be mere self-deception. Here again we have found the irresistible tendency to transcend time. We are forced once more to see in it the false appearance of a timeless reality.

It will be objected perhaps that in this manner we do not get rid of time. In those eternal connections which rule in darkness our lowest psychical nature, or are used consciously by science, succession may remain. A law is not always a law of what merely coexists, but it often gives the relation of antecedent and sequent. The remark is true, but certainly it could not show that time is self-consistent. And it is the inconsistency, and hence the self-transcendence of time which here we are urging. This temporal succession, which persists still in the causal relation, does but secure to the end the old discrepancy. It resists, but it cannot remove, time's inherent tendency to pass beyond itself. Time is an appearance which contradicts itself, and endeavours vainly to appear as an attribute of the timeless.

It might be instructive here to mention other spheres, where we more visibly treat mere existence in time as appearance. But we perhaps have already said enough to establish our conclusion; and our result, so far, will be this. Time is not real as such, and it proclaims its unreality by its inconsistent attempt to be an adjective of the timeless. It is an appearance which belongs to a higher character in

---

[1] On these points see my *Principles of Logic*, and, below, Chapter xxiii.

A. R.

which its special quality is merged. Its own temporal nature does not there cease wholly to exist but is thoroughly transmuted. It is counterbalanced and, as such, lost within an all-inclusive harmony. The Absolute is timeless, but it possesses time as an isolated aspect, an aspect which, in ceasing to be isolated, loses its special character. It is there, but blended into a whole which we cannot realize. But that we cannot realize it, and do not know how in particular it can exist, does not show it to be impossible. It is possible, and, as before, its possibility is enough. For that which can be, and upon a general ground must be—that surely is real.

And it would be better perhaps if I left the matter so. For, if I proceed and do my best to bring home to our minds time's unreality, I may expect misunderstanding. I shall be charged with attempting to explain, or to explain away, the nature of our fact; and no notice will be taken of my protests that I regard such an attempt as illusory. For (to repeat it) we can know neither how time comes to appear, nor in what particular way its appearance is transcended. However, for myself and for the reader who will accept them as what they are, I will add some remarks There are considerations which help to weaken our belief in time's solidity. It is no mass which stands out and declines to be engulfed. It is a loose image confusedly thrown together, and that, as we gaze, falls asunder.

1. The first point which will engage us is the *unity* of time. We have no reason, in my opinion, to regard time as *one* succession, and to take all phenomena as standing in one temporal connection. We have a tendency, of course, to consider all times as forming parts of a single series. Phenomena, it seems clear, are all alike events which happen;[1]

---

[1] On this point see Chapter xxiii.

and, since they happen, we go on to a further con
clusion.   We regard them as members in one temporal whole, and standing therefore throughout to
one another in relations of "before" and "after"
or "together."   But this conclusion has no warrant.
For there is no valid objection to the existence of
any number of independent time-series.   In these
the internal events would be interrelated tempor-
arily, but each series, as a series and as a whole,
would have no temporal connection with anything
outside.   I mean that in the universe we might
have a set of diverse phenomenal successions.   The
events in each of these would, of course, be related
in time, but the series themselves need not have
temporal relation to one another.   The events, that
is, in one need not be after, or before, or together
with, the events in any other.   In the Absolute they
would not have a *temporal* unity or connection;
and, for themselves, they would not possess any
relations to other series.

I will illustrate my meaning from our own human
experience.   When we dream, or when our minds
go wandering uncontrolled, when we pursue imaginary histories, or exercise our thoughts on some
mere supposed sequence—we give rise to a problem.
There is a grave question, if we can see it.   For
within these successions the events have temporal
connection, and yet, if you consider one series with
another, they have no unity in time.   And they are
not connected in time with what we call the course
of our "real" events.   Suppose that I am asked how
the occurrences in the tale of Imogen are related
in time to each adventure of Sindbad the Sailor,
and how these latter stand to my dream-events both
of last night and last year—such questions surely
have no meaning.   Apart from the chance of local
colour we see at once that between these temporal
occurrences there is no relation of time.   You cannot say that one comes before, or comes after, the

other. And again to date these events by their
appearance in *my* mental world would be surely
preposterous. It would be to arrange all events,
told of by books in a library, according to the various
dates of publication—the same story repeating itself
in fact with every edition, and to-day's newspaper
and history simultaneous throughout. And this
absurdity perhaps may help us to realize that the
successive need have no temporal connection.

"Yes, but," I may be told, "all these series,
imaginary as well as real, are surely dated as events
in my mental history. They have each their place
there, and so beyond it also in the one real time-
series. And, however often a story may be repeated
in my mind, each occasion has its own date and its
temporal relations." Indubitably so, but such an
answer is quite insufficient. For observe first that
it admits a great part of what we urge. It has to
allow plainly that the times within our "unreal"
series have no temporal interrelation. Otherwise,
for instance, the time-succession, when a story is
repeated, would infect the contents, and would so
make repetition impossible. I wish first to direct
notice to this serious and fatal admission.

But, when we consider it, the objection breaks
down altogether. It is true that, in a sense and
more or less, we arrange all phenomena as events
in one series. But it does not follow that in the
universe, as a whole, the same tendency holds
good. It does not follow that *all* phenomena are
related in time. What is true of *my* events need
not hold good of all other events; nor again is my
imperfect way of unity the pattern to which the
Absolute is confined.

What, to use common language, I call "real"
events are the phenomena which I arrange in a
continuous time-series. This has its oneness in the
identity of my personal existence. What is presented is "real," and from this basis I construct a

time-series, both backwards and forwards; and I use as binding links the identical points in any content suggested.[1]   This construction I call the "real" series, and whatever content declines to take its place in my arrangement, I condemn as unreal. And the process is justifiable within limits.   If we mean only that there is a certain group of phenomena, and that, for reality within this group, a certain time-relation is essential, that doubtless is true.   But it is another thing to assert that every possible phenomenon has a place in this series. And it is once more another thing to insist that all time-series have a temporal unity in the Absolute.

Let us consider the first point.   If no phenomenon is "real," except that which has a place in *my* temporal arrangement, we have, first, left on our hands the whole world of "Imagination."   The fact of succession there becomes "unreal," but it is not got rid of by the application of any mere label. And I will mention in passing another difficulty, the disruption of my "real" series in mental disease. But—to come to the principle—it is denied that phenomena can exist unless they are in temporal relation with *my* world.   And I am able to find no ground for this assumption.   When I ask why, and for what reason, there cannot be changes of event, imperceptible to me and apart from my time-series, I can discover no answer.   So far as I can see, there may be many time-series in the Absolute, not related at all for one another, and for the Absolute without any unity of time.

And this brings us to the second point.   For phenomena to exist without inter-connection and unity, I agree is impossible.   But I cannot perceive that this unity must either be temporal or else nothing.   That would be to take a way of regard-

[1] For this construction see p. 84, and *Principles of Logic*, Chapter ii.

ing things which even *we* find imperfect, and to set
it down as the one way which is possible for the
Absolute. But surely the Absolute is not shut
up within our human limits. Already we have seen
that its harmony is something beyond relations.
And, if so, surely a number of temporal series may,
without any relation in time to one another, find a
way of union within its all-inclusive perfection.
But, if so, time will not be one, in the sense of
forming a single series. There will be many times,
all of which are at one in the Eternal—the possessor of temporal events and yet timeless. We
have, at all events, found no shred of evidence for
any other unity of time.

2. I will pass now to another point, the *direction*
of time. Just as we tend to assume that all phenomena form one series, so we ascribe to every series
one single direction. But this assumption too is
baseless. It is natural to set up a point in the
future towards which all events run, or from which
they arrive, or which may seem to serve in some
other way to give direction to the stream. But
examination soon shows the imperfection of this
natural view. For the direction, and the distinction
between past and future, entirely depends upon *our*
experience.[1] That side, on which fresh sensations
come in, is what we mean by the future. In our
perception of change elements go out, and something new comes to us constantly; and we construct
the time-series entirely with reference to this experience. Thus, whether we regard events as
running forwards from the past, or as emerging
from the future, in any case we use one method of
taking our bearings. Our fixed direction is given
solely by the advent of new arrivals.

[1] See on this point *Mind*, xii. 579-82. We think forwards,
one may say, on the same principle on which fish feed with their
heads pointing up the stream.

But, if this is so, then direction is relative to *our*
world.   You may object that it is fixed in the very
nature of things, and so imparts its own order to
our special sphere.   Yet how this assumption can
be justified I do not understand.   Of course there
is something not ourselves which makes this difference exist in our beings, something too which
compels us to arrange other lives and all our facts
in one order.   But must this something, therefore,
in reality and in itself, be direction ?   I can find no
reason for thinking so.   No doubt we naturally
regard the whole world of phenomena as a single
time-series ; we assume that the successive contents
of every other finite being are arranged in this construction, and we take for granted that their streams
all flow in one direction.   But our assumption
clearly is not defensible.   For let us suppose, first,
that there are beings who can come in contact in
no way with that world which we experience.   Is
this supposition self-contradictory, or anything but
possible ?   And let us suppose, next, that in the
Absolute the direction of these lives runs opposite
to our own.   I ask again, is such an idea either
meaningless or untenable ?   Of course, *if* in any
way *I* could experience *their* world, I should fail to
understand it.   Death would come before birth, the
blow would follow the wound, and all must seem to
be irrational.   It would seem to me so, but its
inconsistency would not exist except for my partial
experience.   If I did not experience their order, to
me it would be nothing.   Or, if I could see it from
a point of view beyond the limits of my life, I might
find a reality which itself had, as such, no direction.
And I might there perceive characters, which for
the several finite beings give direction to their lives,
which, as such, do not fall within finite experience,
and which, if apprehended, show *both* directions
harmoniously combined in a consistent whole.

To transcend experience and to reach a world of

Things-in-themselves, I agree, is impossible. But does it follow that the whole universe in every sense is a possible object of *my* experience? Is the collection of things and persons, which makes *my* world, the sum total of existence? I know no ground for an affirmative answer to this question. That many material systems should exist, without a material central-point, and with no relation in space —where is the self-contradiction?[1] That various worlds of experience should be distinct, and, for themselves, fail to enter one into the other—where is the impossibility? That arises only when we endorse, and take our stand upon, a prejudice. That the unity in the Absolute is merely our kind of unity, that spaces there must have a spatial centre, and times a temporal point of meeting— these assumptions are based on nothing. The opposite is possible, and we have seen that it is also necessary.

It is not hard to conceive a variety of time-series existing in the Absolute. And the direction of each series, one can understand, may be relative to itself, and may have, as such, no meaning outside. And we might also imagine, if we pleased, that these directions run counter, the one to the other. Let us take, for example, a scheme like this:

$$a \quad b \quad c \quad d$$
$$b \quad a \quad d \quad c$$
$$c \quad d \quad a \quad b$$
$$d \quad c \quad b \quad a$$

Here, if you consider the contents, you may suppose the whole to be stationary. It contains partial views, but, as a whole, it may be regarded as free from change and succession. The change will fall in the perceptions of the different series. And the diverse directions of these series will, as such, not exist for

[1] See Chapter xxii.

the whole. The greater or less number of the various series, which we may imagine as present, the distinct experience which makes each, together with the direction in which it runs—this is all matter, we may say, of individual feeling. You may take, as one series and set of lives, a line going any way you please, up or down or transversely. And in each case the direction will be given to it by sensation peculiar to itself. Now without any question these perceptions must exist in the whole. They must all exist, and in some way they all must qualify the Absolute. But, for the Absolute, they can one counterbalance another, and so their characters be transmuted. They can, with their successions, come together in one whole in which their special natures are absorbed.

And, if we chose to be fanciful, we might imagine something more. We might suppose that, corresponding to each of our lives, there is another individual. There is a man who traverses the same history with ourselves, but in the opposite direction. We may thus imagine that the successive contents, which make my being, are the lives also of one or more other finite souls[1] The distinctions between us would remain, and would consist in an additional element, different in each case. And it would be these differences which would add to each its own way of succession, and make it a special personality. The differences, of course, would have existence ; but in the Absolute, once more, in some way they might lose exclusiveness. And, with this, diversity of direction, and all succession itself, would, as such, disappear. The believer in second sight and witchcraft might find in such a view a wide field for his vagaries. But I note this merely in passing, since to myself fancies of this sort are not inviting. My purpose here has been simple. I have tried to show

---

[1] On the possibility of this compare Chapter xxiii.

that neither for the temporal unity of all time-series, nor for the community of their direction, is there one shred of evidence. However great their variety, it may come together and be transformed in the Absolute. And here, as before, possibility is all we require in order to prove reality.

The Absolute is above relations, and therefore we cannot construct a relational scheme which could exhibit its unity. But that eternal unity is made sure by our general principle. And time itself, we have now seen, can afford no presumption that the universe is not timeless.[1]

There is a remaining difficulty on which perhaps I may add a few remarks. I may be told that in causation a succession is involved with a direction not reversible. It will be urged that many of the relations, by which the world is understood, involve in their essence time sequent or co-existent. And it may be added that for this reason time conflicts with the Absolute. But, at the point which we have reached, this objection has no weight.

Let us suppose, first, that the relation of cause and effect is in itself defensible. Yet we have no knowledge of a causal unity in all phenomena. Different worlds might very well run on together in the universe, side by side and not in one series of effects and causes. They would have a unity in the Absolute, but a unity not consisting in cause and effect. This must be considered possible until we find some good argument in favour of causal unity. And then, even in our own world, how unsatisfactory the succession laid down in causation! It is really never true that mere a produces mere b. It is true only when we bring in the unspecified background, and, apart from that, such a statement is made merely upon sufferance (Chapters vi.,

---

[1] I shall make some remarks on Progress in Chapter xxvi.

xxiii., xxiv.). And the whole succession itself, if defensible, may admit of transformation. We assert that $(X)b$ is the effect which follows on $(X)a$, but perhaps the two are identical. The succession and the difference are perhaps appearances, which exist only for a view which is isolated and defective. The successive relation may be a truth which, when filled out, is transmuted, and which, when supplemented, must lose its character in the Absolute. It may thus be the fragment of a higher truth not prejudicial to identity.

Such considerations will turn the edge of any objection directed against our Absolute from the ground of causation. But we have seen, in addition, in our sixth chapter that this ground is indefensible. By its own discrepancy causation points beyond itself to higher truth; and I will briefly, here once more, attempt to make this plain. Causation implies change, and it is difficult to know of what we may predicate change without contradiction. To say "a becomes b, and there is nothing which changes," is really unmeaning. For, if there is change, something changes; and it is able to change because something is permanent. But then how predicate the change? "Xa becomes Xb"; but, if X is a and afterwards b, then, since a has ceased to qualify it, a change has happened within X. But, if so, then apparently we require a *further* permanent. But if, on the other side, to avoid this danger, we take Xa not to change, we are otherwise ruined. For we have somehow to predicate of X *both* elements at once, and where is the succession? The successive elements co-exist unintelligibly within X, and succession somehow is degraded to mere appearance.

To put it otherwise, we have the statement "X is first Xa, and later also Xb." But how can "later also b" be the truth, if before *mere a* was true? Shall we answer "No, not mere a; it is not *mere*

Xa, but Xa (given c), which is later also b"? But
this reply leaves us still face to face with a like
obstacle; for, if Xa (c) *is* X later b, then how
separate these terms? If there is a difference
between them, or if there is none, our assertion in
either case is untenable. For we cannot justify the
difference if it exists, or our making it, if it does not
exist. Hence we are led to the conclusion that
subject and predicate are identical, and that the
separation and the change are only appearance.
They are a character assuredly to be added to the
whole, but added in a way beyond our comprehension. They somehow are lost except as
elements in a higher identity.

Or, again, say that the present state of the world
is the cause of that total state which follows next
on it. Here, again, is the same self-contradiction.
For how can one state a become a different state b?
It must either do this without a reason, and that
seems absurd; or else the reason, being additional,
forthwith constitutes a new a, and so on for ever.
We have the differences of cause and effect, with
their relation of time, and we have no way in which
it is possible to hold these together. Thus we are
drawn to the view that causation is but partial, and
that we have but changes of mere elements within
a complex whole. But this view gives no help until
we carry it still further, and deny that the whole
state of the world can change at all. So we glide
into the doctrine that partial changes are no change,
but counterbalance one another within a whole
which persists unaltered. And here certainly the
succession remains as an appearance, the special
value of which we are unable to explain. But the
causal sequence has drifted beyond itself and into
a reality which essentially is timeless. And hence,
in attempting an objection to the eternity of the
Absolute, causation would deny a principle implied
in its own nature

At the end of this chapter, I trust, we may have reached a conviction. We may be convinced, not merely as before, that time is unreal, but that its appearance also is compatible with a timeless universe. It is only when misunderstood that change precludes a belief in eternity. Rightly apprehended it affords no presumption against our doctrine. Our Absolute must be; and now, in another respect, again, it has turned out possible. Surely therefore it is real.

I shall conclude this chapter with a few remarks on the nature of space.[1] In passing to this from time, we meet with no difficulties that are new, and a very few words seem all that is wanted. I am not attempting here to explain the origin of space; and indeed to show how it comes to exist seems to me not possible. And we need not yet ask how, on our main view, we are to understand the physical world. That necessary question is one which it is better to defer. The point here at issue is this, Does the form of space make our reality impossible? Is its existence a thing incompatible with the Absolute? Such a question, in my judgment, requires little discussion.

If we could prove that the spatial form were a development, and so secondary, that would give us little help. The proof could in no degree lessen the reality of a thing which, in any case, does exist. It would at most serve as an indication that a further growth in development might merge the space-form in a higher mode of perception. But it is better not to found arguments upon that which, at most, is hardly certain.

What I would stand upon is the essential nature of space. For that, as we saw in our First Book, is entirely inconsistent. It attempts throughout to

---

[1] I must here refer back to Chapter iv.

reach something which transcends its powers. It
made an effort to find and to maintain a solid self-
existence, but that effort led it away into the infinite
process both on the inside and externally. And its
evident inability to rest within itself points to the
solution of its discords. Space seeks to lose itself
in a higher perception, where individuality is gained
without forfeit of variety.[1]

And against the possibility of space being in this
way absorbed in a non-spatial consummation, I
know of nothing to set. Of course how in particular
this can be, we are unable to lay down. But our
ignorance in detail is no objection against the
general possibility. And this possible absorption,
we have seen, is also necessary.

[1] The question as to whether, and in what sense, space
possesses a unity, may be deferred to Chapter xxii. A discussion on this point was required in the case of time. But
an objection to our Absolute would hardly be based on the unity
of space.

CHAPTER XIX.

THE THIS AND THE MINE.

WE have seen that the forms of space and time supply no good objection to the individuality of the Absolute. But we have not yet faced a difficulty which perhaps may prove more serious. There is the fact which is denoted by the title of the present chapter. The particularity of feeling, it may be contended, is an obstacle which declines to be engulfed. The "this" and the "mine" are undeniable ; and upon our theory, it may be said, they are both inexplicable.

The "this" and the "mine" are names which stand for the immediacy of feeling, and each serves to call attention to one side of that fact. There is no "mine" which is not "this," nor any "this" which fails, in a sense, to be "mine." The immediate fact must always come as something felt in an experience, and an experience always must be particular, and, in a sense, must be "unique." But I shall not enter on all the problems implied in the last word. I am not going to inquire here how we are able to transcend the "this-mine," for that question will engage us hereafter (Chapter xxi.), and the problem now before us is confined to a single point. We are to assume that there does exist an indefinite number of "this-mines," of immediate experiences of the felt. And, assuming this fact, we are to ask if it is compatible with our general view.

The difficulty of this inquiry arises in great part from vagueness. The "this" and "mine" are taken as both positive and negative. They are to possess a singular reality, and they are to own in some sense an exclusive character. And from this shifting basis a rash conclusion is hastily drawn. But the singular reality, after all, may not be single and self-existent. And the exclusive character, perhaps, may be included and taken up in the Whole. And it is these questions which we must endeavour to clear up and discuss. I will begin with what we have called the positive aspect.

The "this" and the "mine" express the immediate character of feeling, and the appearance of this character in a finite centre. Feeling may stand for a psychical stage before relations have been developed, or it may be used generally for an experience which is not indirect (Chapters ix., xxvi., and xxvii.). At any time all that we suffer, do, and are, forms one psychical totality. It is experienced all together as a co-existing mass, not perceived as parted and joined by relations even of co-existence. It contains all relations, and distinctions, and every ideal object that at the moment exists in the soul. It contains them, not specially as such and with exclusive stress on their content as predicated, but directly as they are and as they qualify the psychical "that." And again any part of this co-existence, to which we attend, can be viewed integrally as one feeling.

Now whatever is thus directly experienced—so far as it is not taken otherwise—is "this" and "mine." And all such presentation without doubt has peculiar reality. One might even contend that logically to transcend it is impossible, and that there is no rational way to a plurality of "this-mines." But such a plurality we have agreed for the present to assume. . The "this," it is however clear, brings a sense of superior reality, a sense which is far from being wholly deceptive and untrue. For all our knowledge, in the first place, arises from the "this."

It is the one source of our experience, and every element of the world must submit to pass through it. And the "this," secondly, has a genuine feature of ultimate reality. With however great imperfection and inconsistency it owns an individual character. The "this" is real for us in a sense in which nothing else is real.

Reality is being in which there is no division of content from existence, no loosening of "what" from "that." Reality, in short, means what it stands for, and stands for what it means. And the "this" possesses to some extent the same wholeness of character. Both the "this" and reality, we may say, are immediate. But reality is immediate because it includes and is superior to mediation. It developes, and it brings to unity, the distinctions it contains. The "this" is immediate, on the other side, because it is at a level below distinctions. Its elements are but conjoined, and are not connected. And its content, hence, is unstable, and essentially tends to disruption, and by its own nature must pass beyond the being of the "this." But every "this" still shows a passing aspect of undivided singleness. In the mental background specially such a fused unity remains a constant factor, and can never be dissipated (Chapters ix., x., xxvii.). And it is such an unbroken wholeness which gives the sense of individual reality. When we turn from mere ideas to sensation, we experience in the "this" a revelation of freshness and life. And that revelation, if misleading, is never quite untrue.[1]

We may, for the present, take "this" as the positive feeling of direct experience. In that sense it will be either general or special. It will be the

[1] It is mere thoughtlessness that finds in Resistance the one manifestation of reality. For resistance, in the first place, is full of unsolved contradictions, and is also fixed and consists in that very character. And in the second place, what experience can come as more actual than sensuous pain or pleasure?

A. R.   Q

character which we feel always, or again in union
with some particular content. And we have to ask
if, so understood, the "this" is incompatible with
our Absolute.

The question, thus asked, seems to call for but
little discussion. Since for us the Absolute is a
whole, the sense of immediate reality, we must suppose, may certainly qualify it. And, again, I find
no difficulty when we pass to the special meaning of
"this." With every presentation, with each chance
mixture of psychical elements, we have the feeling
of one particular *datum*. We have the felt existence of a peculiar sensible whole. And here we
find beyond question a positive content, and a fresh
element which has to be included within our Absolute. But in such a content there is, so far, nothing
which could repel or exclude. There is no feature
there which could resist embracement and absorption by the whole.

The fact of actual fragmentariness, I admit, we
cannot explain. That experience should take place
in finite centres, and should wear the form of finite
"thisness," is in the end inexplicable (Chapter
xxvi.). But to be inexplicable, and to be incompatible, are not the same thing. And in such fragmentariness, viewed as positive, I see no objection
to our view. The plurality of presentations is a
fact, and it, therefore, makes a difference to our
Absolute. It exists in, and it, therefore, must qualify
the whole. And the universe is richer, we may be
sure, for all dividedness and variety. Certainly in
detail we do not know how the separation is overcome, and we cannot point to the product which is
gained, in each case, by that resolution. But our
ignorance here is no ground for rational opposition.
Our principle assures us that the Absolute is superior
to partition, and in some way is perfected by it.
And we have found, as yet, no reason even to

doubt if this result is possible. We have discovered, as yet, nothing which seems able from any side to stand out. There is no element such as could hesitate to blend with the rest and to be dissolved in a higher unity.

If the whole could be an arrangement of mere ideas, if it were a system barely intellectual, the case would be altered. We might combine such ideas, it would not matter how ingeniously; but we could not frame, and we should not possess, a product containing what we feel to be imparted directly by the " this." I admit that inability, and I urge it, as yet another confirmation and support of our doctrine. For our Absolute was not a mere intellectual system. It was an experience overriding every species of one-sidedness, and throughout it was at once intuition and feeling and will. But, if so, the opposition of the " this " becomes at once unmeaning. For feelings, each possessing a nature of its own, may surely come together, and be fused in the Absolute. And, so far is such a resolution from appearing impossible, that I confess to me it seems most natural and easy. That partial experiences should run together, and should unite their deliverances to produce one richer whole—is there anything here incredible? It would indeed be strange if bare positive feelings proved recalcitrant and solid, and stood out against absorption. For their nature clearly is otherwise, and they must be blended in the one experience of the Absolute. This consummation evidently is real, because on our principle it is necessary, and because again we have no reason to doubt that it is possible. And with so much, we may pass from the positive aspect of the " this."

For the " this " and " mine," it is clear, are taken also as negative. They are set up as in some way opposed to the Absolute, and they are considered, in some sense, to own an exclusive character. And

that their character, in part, is exclusive cannot be
denied ; but the question is in what sense, and how
far, they possess it.   For, if the repulsion is relative
and holds merely within the one whole, it is compatible at once with our view of the universe.

An immediate experience, viewed as positive, is
so far not exclusive.   It is, so far, what it is, and it
does not repel anything.   But the " this " certainly
is used also with a negative bearing.   It may mean
" this one," in distinction from that one and the
other one.   And here it shows obviously an exclusive aspect, and it implies an external and negative
relation.   But every such relation, we have found,
is inconsistent with itself (Chapter iii.).   For it
exists within, and by virtue of an embracing unity,
and apart from that totality both itself and its terms
would be nothing.   And the relation also must
penetrate the inner being of its terms.   " This," in
other words, would *not* exclude "that," unless in
the exclusion "this," so far, passed out of itself.
Its repulsion of others is thus incompatible with self-
contained singleness, and involves subordination to
an including whole.   But to the ultimate whole
nothing can be opposed, or even related.

And the self-transcendent character of the " this "
is, on all sides, open and plain.   Appearing as immediate, it, on the other side, has contents which
are not consistent with themselves, and which refer
themselves beyond.   Hence the inner nature of the
" this " leads it to pass outside itself towards a
higher totality.   And its negative aspect is but one
appearance of this general tendency.   Its very exclusiveness involves the reference of itself beyond
itself, and is but a proof of its necessary absorption
in the Absolute.[1]

[1] The above conclusion applies emphatically to the "this" as
signifying the point in which I am said to encounter reality.   All
contact necessarily implies a unity, in and through which it takes
place, and my self and the reality are, here, but partial appear-

And if the "this" is asserted to be all-exclusive because it is "unique," the discussion of that point need not long detain us. The term may imply that nothing else but the "this-mine" is real, and, in that case, the question has been deferred to Chapter xxi. And, if "unique" means that what is felt once can never be felt again, such an assertion, taken broadly, seems even untrue. For if feelings, the same in character, do in fact not recur, we at least hardly can deny that their recurrence is possible. The "this" is unique really so far as it is a member in a series, and so far as that series is taken as distinct from all others.[1] And only in this sense can we call its recurrence impossible. But here with uniqueness once more we have negative relations, and these relations involve an inclusive unity. Uniqueness, in this sense, does not resist assimilation by the Absolute. It is, on the other hand, itself incompatible with exclusive singleness.

Into the nature of self-will I shall at present not enter. This is opposition attempted by a finite subject against its proper whole. And we may see at once that such discord and negation can subserve unity, and can contribute towards the perfection of the universe. It is connection with the central fire which produces in the element this burning sense of selfness. And the collision is resolved within that harmony where centre and circumference are one. But I shall return in another place to the discussion of this matter (Chapter xxv.).

We have found that the "this," taken as exclusive, proclaims itself relative, and in that relation forfeits its independence. And we have seen that,

---

ances. And the "mine" never, we may say, could strike me as "not-mine," unless, precisely so far as it does so, it is a mere factor in my experience. I have spoken above on the true meaning of that sense of reality which is given by the "this."

[1] On this point compare *Principles of Logic*, Chapter ii.

as positive, the " this " is not exclusive at all.   The
" this " is inconsistent always, but, so far as it
excludes, so far already has it begun internally to
suffer dissipation.   We may now, with advantage
perhaps, view the matter in a somewhat different
way.   There is, I think, a vague notion that some
content sticks irremovably within the " this," or
that in the " this," again, there is something which
is not content at all.   In either case an element is
offered, which, it is alleged, cannot be absorbed by
the Whole.   And an examination of these prejudices
may throw some light on our general view.

In the " this," it may appear first, there is something more than content.   For by combining qualities indefinitely we seem unable to arrive at the
" this."   The same difficulty may be stated perhaps
in a way which points to its solution.   The " this "
on one hand, we may say, is nothing at all beside
content, and, on the other hand, the " this " is not
content at all.   For in the term " content " there
lies an ambiguity.   It may mean a " what " that is,
or again, is not, distinct from its " that."   And the
" this," we have already seen, has inconsistent
aspects.   It offers, from one aspect, an immediate
undivided experience, a whole in which " that " and
" what " are felt as one.   And here content, as implying distinction, will be absent from the " this."   But
such an undivided feeling, we have also seen, is a
positive experience.   It does not even attempt to
resist assimilation by our Absolute.

If, on the other hand, we use content generally,
and if we employ it in the sense of " what " without
distinction from "that"—if we take it to mean something which is experienced, and which is nothing
but experience—then, most emphatically, the " this "
is not anything but content.   For there is nothing
in it or about it which can be more than experience.
And in it there is further no feature which cannot
be made a quality.   Its various aspects can all be

separated by distinction and analysis, and, one after another, can thus be brought forward as ideal predicates. This assertion holds of that immediate sense of a special reality, which we found above in the character of each felt complex. There is, in brief, no fragment of the " this " such that it cannot form the object of a distinction. And hence the " this," in the first place, is mere experience throughout ; and, in the second place, throughout it may be called intelligible. It owns no aspect which refuses to become a quality, and in its turn to play the part of an ideal predicate.[1]

But it is easy here to deceive ourselves and to fall into error. For taking a given whole, or more probably selecting one portion, we begin to distinguish and to break up its confused co-existence. And, having thus possessed ourselves of definite contents and of qualities in relation, we call on our " this " to identify itself with our discrete product. And, on the refusal of the " this," we charge it with stubborn exclusiveness. It is held to possess either in its nature a repellent content, or something else, at all events, which is intractable. But the whole conclusion is fallacious. For, if we have not mutilated our subject, we have at least added a feature which originally was not there—a feature, which, if introduced, must of necessity burst the " this," and destroy it from within. The " this," we have seen, is a unity below relations and ideas ; and a unity, able to develope and to harmonize all distinctions, is not found till we arrive at ultimate Reality. Hence the " this " repels our offered predicates, not because its nature goes beyond, but rather because that nature comes short. It is not more, we may say, but less than our distinctions.

And to our mistake in principle we add probably an error in practice. For we have failed probably

---

[1] Compare here p. 175, and *Principles of Logic*, chapter ii.

to exhaust the full deliverance of our "this," and the
residue, left there by our mere failure, is then assumed blindly to stand out as an irreducible aspect.
For, if we have confined our "this" to but one portion of the felt totality, we have omitted from our
analysis, perhaps, the positive aspect of its special
unity.   But our analysis, if so, is evidently incomplete and misleading.   And then, perhaps again,
qualifying our limited "this" by exclusive relations,
we do not see that in these we have added a factor
to its original content.   And what we have added,
and have also overlooked, is then charged to the
native repellence of the "this."   But if again, on
the other hand, our "this" is not taken as limited,
if it is to be the entire complex of one present,
viewed without relation even to its own future and
past—other errors await us.   For the detail here is
so great that complete exhaustion is hardly possible.
And so, setting down as performed that which is in
fact impracticable, we once more stumble against a
residue which is due wholly to our weakness.   And
we are helped, perhaps, further into mistake by another source of fallacy.   We may confuse the feeling
which we study with the feeling which we are.   Attempting, so far as we can, to make an object of
some (past) psychical whole, we may unawares seek
there every feature which we now are and feel.
And we may attribute our ill success to the positive
obstinacy of the resisting object.[1]

The total subject of all predicates, which we feel
in the background, can be exhausted, we may say in
general, by no predicate or predicates.   For the

---

[1] Success here is impossible because, apart from the difficulty
of analysis and exhaustion, our present observing attitude forms a
new and incompatible feature.   It is an element in our state now,
which (*ex hyp.*) was absent from our state then.   In this connection I may remark that to observe a feeling is, to some extent,
always to alter it.   For the purpose in hand that alteration may
not be material, but it will in all cases be there.   I have touched
on this subject in *Principles of Logic*, p. 65, note.

subject holds all in one, while predication involves severance, and so inflicts on its subject a partial loss of unity. And hence neither ultimate Reality, nor any "this," can *consist* of qualities. That is one side of the truth, but the truth also has another side. Reality owns no feature or aspect which cannot in its turn be distinguished, none which cannot in this way become a mere adjective and predicate. The same conclusion holds of the "this," in whatever sense you take it. There is nothing there which could form an intractable crudity, nothing which can refuse to qualify and to be merged in the ultimate Reality.

We have found that, in a sense, the "this" is not, and does not own, content. But, in another sense, we have seen that it contains, and is, nothing else. We may now pass to the examination of a second prejudice. Is there any content which is owned by and sticks in the "this," and which thus remains outstanding, and declines union with a higher system? We have perceived, on the contrary, that by its essence the "this" is self-transcendent. But it may repay us once more to dwell and to enlarge on this topic. And I shall not hesitate in part to repeat results which we have gained already.

If we are asked what content is appropriated by the "this," we may reply that there is none. There is no inalienable content which belongs to the "this" or the "mine." My immediate feeling, when I say "this," has a complex character, and it presents a confused detail which, we have seen, is content. But it has no "what" which belongs to it as a separate possession. It has no feature identified with its own private exclusivity. That is first a negative relation which, in principle, must qualify the internal from outside. And in practice we find that each element contained can refer itself elsewhere. Each tends naturally towards a wider whole outside of the

" this." Its content, we may say, has no rest till it has wandered to a home elsewhere. The mere " this " can appropriate nothing.

The " this " appears to retain content solely through our failure. I may express this otherwise by calling it the region of chance; for chance is something given and for us not yet comprehended.[1] So far as any element falls outside of some ideal whole, then, in relation with that whole, this element is chance. Contingent matter is matter regarded as that which, as yet, we cannot connect and include. It has not been taken up, as we know that it must be, within some ideal whole or system. Thus one and the same matter both is, and is not, contingent. It is chance for one system or end, while in relation with another it is necessary. All chance is relative ; and the content which falls in the mere " this " is relative chance. So far as it remains there, that is through our failure to refer it elsewhere. It is merely " this " so far as it is not yet comprehended ; and, so far as it is taken as a feature in any whole beyond itself, it has to change its character. It is, in that respect at least, forthwith not *of* the " this," but only in it, and appearing there. And such appearance, of course, is not always presentation to outer sense. All that in any way we experience, we must experience within one moment of presentation. However ideal anything may be, it still must appear in a " now." And everything present there, so far as in any respect it is not subordinated to an ideal whole—no matter what that whole is—in relation to that defect is but part of the given. It may be as ideal otherwise as you please, but to that extent it fails to pass beyond immediate fact. Such an element so far is still immersed in the " now," " mine," and " this." It remains there, but, as we have seen,

[1] For a further discussion of the meaning of Chance see Chapter xxiv.

it is not owned and appropriated. It lingers, we may say, precariously and provisionally.

But at this point we may seem to have encountered an obstacle. For in the given fact there is always a co-existence of elements; and with this co-existence we may seem to ascribe positive content to the "this." Property, we asserted, was lacking to it, and that assertion now seems questionable. For co-existence supplies us with actual knowledge, and none the less it seems given in the content of the "this." The objection, however, would rest on misunderstanding. It *is* positive knowledge when I judge that in a certain space or time certain features co-exist. But such knowledge, on the other hand, is never the content of the mere "this." It is already a synthesis, imperfect no doubt, but still plainly ideal. And, at the cost of repetition, I will point this out briefly.

(*a*) The place or time, first, may be characterised by inclusion within a series. We may mean that, in some sense, the place or time is "this one," and not another. But, if so, we have forthwith transcended the given. We are using a character which implies inclusion of an element within a whole, with a reference beyond itself to other like elements. And this of course goes far beyond immediate experience. To suppose that position in a series can belong to the mere "this," is a misunderstanding.[1]

(*b*) And more probably the objection had something else in view. It was not conjunction in one moment, as distinct from another moment, which it urged was positive and yet belonged to the "this." It meant mere coincidence within some "here" or some "now," a co-presentation immediately given without regard to any "there" or "then." Such a bare conjunction seems to be something possessed by the "this," and yet offering on the other side a

---

[1] See above, and compare also Chapter xxi.

positive character.   But again, and in this form, the
objection would rest on a mistake.

The bare coincidence of the content, if you take
it as merely given within a presentation, and if you
consider it entirely without any further reference
beyond, is *not* a co-existence of elements.   I do not
mean, of course, that a whole of feeling is not positive at all.   I mean that, as soon as you have made
assertions about what it contains, as soon as you
have begun to treat its content *as* content, you have
transcended its felt unity.   For consider a " here "
or " now," and observe anything of what is in it,
and you have instantly acquired an ideal synthesis
(Chapter xv.).   You have a relation which, however
impure, is at once set free from time.   You have
gained an universal which, so far as it goes, is true
always, and not merely at the present moment ; and
this universal is forthwith used to qualify reality beyond that moment.   And thus the co-existence of *a*
and *b*, we may say, does not belong to the mere
" this," but it is ideal, and *appears* there.   Within
mere feeling it has doubtless a positive character,
but, excluding distinctions, it is not, in one sense,
coincidence at all.   In observing, we are compelled
to observe in the form of relations.   But these internal relations properly do not belong to the " this "
itself.   For its character does not admit of separation and distinction.   Hence to distinguish elements
within this whole, and to predicate a relation of co-
existence, is self-contradictory.   Our operation, in
its result, has destroyed what it acted on ; and the
product which has come out, was, as such, never
there.   Thus, in claiming to own a relation of co-
existence and a distinction of content, the mere
" this " commits suicide.

From another point of view, doubtless, the observed is a mere coincidence, when compared, that
is, with a purer way of understanding.   The relation is true, subject to the condition of a confused

context, which is not comprehended. And hence the connection observed is, to this extent, bare conjunction and mere co-existence. Or it is chance, when you measure it by a higher necessity. It is a truth conditioned by our ignorance, and so contingent and belonging to the "this." But, upon the other side, we have seen that the "this" can hold nothing. As soon as a relation is made out, that is universal knowledge, and has at once transcended presentation. For within the merely "this" no relation, taken as such, is possible. The content, if you distinguish it, is to that extent set free from felt unity. And there is no "what" which essentially adheres to the bare moment. So far as any element remains involved in the confusion of feeling, that is but due to our defect and ignorance. Hence, to repeat, the "this," considered as mere feeling, is certainly positive. As the absence of universal relations, the "this" again is negative. But, as an attempt to make and to retain distinctions of content, the "this" is suicidal.

It is so too with the "mere mine." We hear in discussions on morality, or logic, or æsthetics, that a certain detail is "subjective," and hence irrelevant. Such a detail, in other words, belongs to the "mere mine." And a mistake may be made, and we may imagine that there is matter which, in itself, is contingent.[1] It may be supposed that an element, such perhaps as pleasure, is a fixed part of something called the "this-me." But there is no content which, as such, can belong to the "mine." The "mine" is my existence taken as immediate fact, as an integral whole of psychical elements which simply are. It is my content, so far as not freed from the feeling moment. And it is merely my content, because it is not subordinate to this or that ideal whole. If I regard a mental fact, say, from the side

[1] Or again, having no clear ideas, we may try to help ourselves with such phrases as "the individuality of the individuals."

of its morality, then whatever is, here and now, not relevant to this purpose, becomes bare existence. It is something which is not the appearance of the ideal matter in hand. And yet, because it exists somehow, it exists as a fact in the mere "mine." The same thing happens also, of course, with æsthetics, or science, or religion. The same detail which, in one respect, was essential and necessary, may, from another point of view, become immaterial. And then at once, so far, it falls back into the merely felt or given. It exists, but, for the end we are regarding, it is nothing.

This is still more evident, perhaps, from the side of psychology. No particle of my existence, on the one hand, falls outside that science; and yet, on the other hand, for psychology the mere "mine" remains. When I study my events so as to trace a particular connection, no matter of what kind, then at any moment the psychical "given" contains features which are irrelevant. They have no bearing on the point which I am endeavouring to make good. Hence the fact of their co-existence is contingent, and it is by chance that they accompany what is essential. They exist, in other words, for my present aim, in that self which is merely given, and which is not transcended. On the other hand, obviously, these same particulars are essential and necessary, since (at the least) somehow they are links in the causal sequence of my history. *Every* particular in the same way has some end beyond the moment. Each can be referred to an ideal whole whose appearance it is; and nothing whatever is left to belong merely to the "this-mine." The simplest observation of what co-exists removes it from that region, and chance has no positive content, except in relation to our failure and ignorance.

And any psychology, which is not blind or else biassed by false doctrine, forces on our notice this alienation of content. Our whole mental life moves by a transcendence of the " this," by sheer disregard of its claim to possess any property. The looseness of some feature of the " what " from its fusion with the " that "—its self-reference to, and its operation on, something beyond—if you leave out this, you have lost the mainspring of psychical movement. But this is the ideality of the given, its non-possession of that character with which it appears, but which only appears in it. And Association—who could use it as mere co-existence within the " this " ?. But, if anything more, it is at once the union of the ideal, the synthesis of the eternal. Thus the " mine " has no detail which is not the property of connections beyond. The merest coincidence, when you observe it, is a distinction which couples universal ideas. And, in brief, the " mine " has no content except that which is left there by our impotence. Its character in this respect is, in other words, merely negative.

Hence to urge such a character against our Absolute would be unmeaning. It would be to turn our ignorance of system into a positive objection, to make our failure a ground for the denial of possibility. We have no basis on which to doubt that all content comes together harmoniously in the Absolute. We have no reason to think that any feature adheres to the " this," and is unable to transcend it. What is true is that, for us, the incomplete diversity of various systems, the perplexing references of each same feature to many ideal wholes, and again that positive special feeling, which we have dealt with above—all this detail is not made one in any way which we can verify. That it all is reconciled we know, but how, in particular, is hid from us. But because this result must be, and because there is nothing against it, we believe that it is.

We have seen that in the " this," on one side, there

is no element but content, and we have found that
no content, on the other side, is the possession of
the "this." There is none that sticks within its
precincts, but all tends to refer itself beyond. What
remains there is chance, if chance is used in the sense
of our sheer ignorance. It is not opposition, but
blank failure in regard to the claim of an idea.[1] And
opposition and exclusiveness, in any sense, must
transcend the bare "this." For their essence
always implies relation to a something beyond self ;
and that relation makes an end of all attempt at
solid singleness. Thus, if chance is taken as involving an actual relation to an idea, the "this" already
has, so far, transcended itself. The refusal of something given to connect itself with an idea is a
positive fact. But that refusal, as a relation, is
evidently not included and contained in the "this."
On the other hand, entering into that relation, the
internal content has, so far, set itself free. It has
already transcended the "this" and become universal. And the exclusiveness of the "this" everywhere in the same way proves self-contradictory.

And we had agreed before that the mere "this"
in a sense is positive. It has a felt self-affirmation
peculiar and especial, and into the nature of that
positive being we entered at length. But we found
no reason why such feelings, considered in any
feature or aspect, should persist self-centred and
aloof. It seemed possible, to say the least, that
they all might blend with one another, and be
merged in the experience of the one Reality. And
with that possibility, given on all sides, we arrive at
our conclusion. The "this" and "mine" are now
absorbed as elements within our Absolute. For
their resolution must be, and it may be, and so
certainly it *is*.

---

[1] Chance, in this sense of mere unperceived failure and privation, can hardly, except by a licence, be called chance. It cannot, at all events, be taken as qualifying the "this."

CHAPTER XX.

RECAPITULATION.

It may be well at this point perhaps to look back on the ground which we have traversed. In our First Book we examined some ways of regarding reality, and we found that each of them contained fatal inconsistency. Upon this we forthwith denied that, as such, they could be real. But upon reflection we perceived that our denial must rest upon positive knowledge. It can only be because we know, that we venture to condemn. Reality therefore, we are sure, has a positive character, which rejects mere appearance and is incompatible with discord. On the other hand it cannot be a something apart, a position qualified in no way save as negative of phenomena. For that leaves phenomena still contradictory, while it contains in its essence the contradiction of a something which actually is nothing. The Reality, therefore, must be One, not as excluding diversity, but as somehow including it in such a way as to transform its character. There is plainly not anything which can fall outside of the Real. That must be qualified by every part of every predicate which it rejects ; but it has such qualities as counterbalance one another's failings. It has a superabundance in which all partial discrepancies are resolved and remain as higher concord.

And we found that this Absolute is experience, because that is really what we mean when we predicate or speak of anything. It is not one-sided experience, as mere volition or mere thought ; but it is a whole superior to and embracing all incomplete forms of life. This whole must be immediate like feeling, but not, like feeling, immediate at a level below distinction and relation. The Absolute is immediate as holding and transcending these differences. And because it cannot contradict itself, and does not suffer a division of idea from existence, it has therefore a balance of pleasure over pain. In every sense it is perfect.

Then we went on to enquire if various forms of the finite would take a place within this Absolute. We insisted that nothing can be lost, and yet that everything must be made good, so as to minister to harmony. And we laid stress on the fact that the *how* was inexplicable. To perceive the solution in detail is not possible for our knowledge. But, on the other hand, we urged that such an explanation is not necessary. We have a general principle which seems certain. The only question is whether any form of the finite is a negative instance which serves to overthrow this principle. Is there anything which tends to show that our Absolute is not possible? And, so far as we have gone, we have discovered as yet nothing. We have at present not any right to a doubt about the Absolute. We have got no shred of reason for denying that it is possible. But, if it is possible, that is all we need seek for. For already we have a principle upon which it is necessary ; and therefore it is certain.

In the following chapters I shall still pursue the same line of argument. I shall enquire if there is anything which declines to take its place within the system of our universe. And, if there is nothing that is found to stand out and to conflict, or to import discord when admitted, our conclusion will be attained. But I will first add a few remarks on the ideas of Individuality and Perfection.

We have seen that these characters imply a

negation of the discordant and discrepant, and a doubt, perhaps, may have arisen about their positive aspect. Are they positive at all? When we predicate them, do we assert or do we only deny? Can it be maintained that these ideas are negative simply? It might be urged against us that reality means barely non-appearance, and that unity is the naked denial of plurality. And in the same way individuality might be taken as the barren absence of discord and of dissipation. Perfection, again, would but deny that we are compelled to go further, or might signify merely the failure of unrest and of pain. Such a doubt has received, I think, a solution beforehand, but I will point out once more its cardinal mistake.

In the first place a mere negation is unmeaning (p. 138). To deny, except from a basis of positive assumption, is quite impossible. And a bare negative idea, if we could have it, would be a relation without a term. Hence some positive basis must underlie these negations which we have mentioned. And, in the second place, we must remember that what is denied is, none the less, somehow predicated of our Absolute. It is indeed because of this that we have called it individual and perfect.

1. It is, first, plain that at least the idea of affirmative being supports the denial of discrepancy and unrest. Being, if we use the term in a restricted sense, is not positively definable. It will be the same as the most general sense of experience. It is different from reality, if that, again, is strictly used. Reality (proper) implies a foregone distinction of content from existence, a separation which is overcome. Being (proper), on the other hand, is immediate, and at a level below distinctions[1]; though I have not thought it necessary always to

---

[1] Compare here p. 225, and for the stricter meaning of some other phrases see p. 317.

employ these terms in a confined meaning. However, in its general sense of experience, being underlies the ideas of individuality and perfection. And these, at least so far, must be positive.

2. And, in the second place, each of them is positively determined by what it excludes. The aspect of diversity belongs to the essence of the individual, and is affirmatively contained in it. The unity excludes what is diverse, so far only as that attempts to be anything by itself, and to maintain isolation. And the individual is the return of this apparent opposite with all its wealth into a richer whole. How in detail this is accomplished I repeat that we do not know; but we are capable, notwithstanding, of forming the idea of such a positive union (Chapters xiv. and xxvii.). Feeling supplies us with a low and imperfect example of an immediate whole. And, taking this together with the idea of qualification by the rejected, and together with the idea of unknown qualities which come in to help— we arrive at individuality. And, though depending on negation, such a synthesis is positive.

And, in a different way, the same account is valid of the Perfect. That does not mean a being which, in regard to unrest and painful struggle, is a simple blank. It means the identity of idea and existence, attended also by pleasure. Now, so far as pleasure goes, that certainly is not negative. But pleasure is far from being the only positive element in perfection. The unrest and striving, the opposition of fact to idea, and the movement towards an end—these features are not left outside of that Whole which is consummate. For all the content, which the struggle has generated, is brought home and is laid to rest undiminished in the perfect. The idea of a being qualified somehow, without any alienation of its "what" from its "that"—a being at the same time fully possessed of all hostile distinctions, and the richer for their strife—this is a positive idea. And it can be realised in its outline, though certainly not in detail.

I will advert in conclusion to an objection drawn from a common mistake. Quantity is often introduced into the idea of perfection. For the perfect seems to be that beyond which we cannot go, and this tends naturally to take the form of an infinite number. But, since any real number must be finite, we are at once involved here in a hopeless contradiction. And I think it necessary to say no more on this evident illusion ; but will pass on to the objection which may be urged against our view of the perfect. If the perfect is the concordant, then no growth of its area or increase of its pleasantness could make it more complete. We thus, apparently, might have the smallest being as perfect as the largest ; and this seems paradoxical. But the paradox really, I should say, exists only through misunderstanding. For we are accustomed to beings whose nature is always and essentially defective. And so we suppose in our smaller perfect a condition of want, or at least of defect ; and this condition is diminished by alteration in quantity. But, where a being is really perfect, our supposition would be absurd. Or, again, we imagine first a creature complete in itself, and by the side of it we place a larger completion. Then unconsciously we take the greater to be, in some way, apprehended by the smaller ; and, with this, naturally the lesser being becomes by contrast defective. But what we fail to observe is that such a being can no longer be perfect. For an idea which is not fact has been placed by us within it ; and that idea at once involves a collision of elements, and by consequence also a loss of perfection. And thus a paradox has been made by our misunderstanding. We assumed completion, and then surreptitiously added a condition which destroyed it. And this, so far, was a mere error.

But the error may direct our attention to a truth. It leads us to ask if two perfections, great and small, can possibly exist side by side. And we must answer in the negative. If we take perfection in its full sense, we cannot suppose two such perfect existences. And this is not because one surpasses the other in size; for that is wholly irrelevant. It is because finite existence and perfection are incompatible. A being, short of the Whole, but existing within it, is essentially related to that which is not-itself. Its inmost being is, and must be, infected by the external. Within its content there are relations which do not terminate inside. And it is clear at once that, in such a case, the ideal and the real can never be at one. But their disunion is precisely what we mean by imperfection. And thus incompleteness, and unrest, and unsatisfied ideality, are the lot of the finite. There is nothing which, to speak properly, is individual or perfect, except only the Absolute.

CHAPTER XXI.

SOLIPSISM.

In our First Book we examined various ways of taking facts, and we found that they all gave no more than appearance. In the present Book we have been engaged with the nature of Reality. We have been attempting, so far, to form a general idea of its character, and to defend it against more or less plausible objections. Through the remainder of our work we must pursue the same task. We must endeavour to perceive how the main aspects of the world are all able to take a place within our Absolute. And, if we find that none refuses to accept a position there, we may consider our result secure against attack. I will now enter on the question which gives its title to this chapter.

Have we any reason to believe in the existence of anything beyond our private selves? Have we the smallest right to such a belief, and is it more than literally a self-delusion? We, I think, may fairly say that some metaphysicians have shown unwillingness to look this problem in the face. And yet it cannot be avoided. Since we all believe in a world beyond us, and are not prepared to give this up, it would be a scandal if that were something which upon our theory was illusive. Any view which will not explain, and also justify, an attitude essential to human nature, must surely be condemned. But we shall soon see, upon the other hand, how the supposed difficulties of the question have been created by false doctrine.   Upon our general theory they lose their foundation and vanish.

The argument in favour of Solipsism, put most simply, is as follows.   " I cannot transcend experience, and experience must be *my* experience.   From this it follows that nothing beyond my self exists ; for what is experience is its states."

The argument derives its strength, in part, from false theory, but to a greater extent perhaps from thoughtless obscurity.   I will begin by pointing out the ambiguity which lends some colour to this appeal to experience.   Experience may mean experience only direct, or indirect also.   Direct experience I understand to be confined to the given simply, to the merely felt or presented.   But indirect experience includes all fact that is constructed from the basis of the " this " and the " mine."   It is all that is taken to exist beyond the felt moment.   This is a distinction the fatal result of which Solipsism has hardly realized ; for upon *neither* interpretation of experience can its argument be defended.

I. Let us first suppose that the experience, to which it appeals, is direct.   Then, we saw in our ninth chapter, the mere "given" fails doubly to support that appeal.   It supplies, on the one hand, not enough, and, on the other hand, too much.   It offers us a not-self with the self, and so ruins Solipsism by that excess.   But, upon the other side, it does not supply us with any self at all, if we mean by self a substantive the possessor of an object or even its own states.   And Solipsism is, on this side, destroyed by defect.   But, before I develope this, I will state an objection which by itself might suffice.

My self, as an existence to which phenomena belong as its adjectives, is supposed to be given by a direct experience.   But this gift plainly is an illusion.   Such an experience can supply us with no reality beyond that of the moment.   There is no faculty which can deliver the immediate revelation of a self beyond the present (Chapter x.). And so, if Solipsism finds its one real thing in experience, that thing is confined to the limits of the mere " this." But with such a reflection we have already, so far, destroyed Solipsism as positive, and as anything more than a sufficient reason for total scepticism. Let us pass from this objection to other points.

Direct experience is unable to transcend the mere " this." But even in what that gives we are, even so far, not supplied with the self upon which Solipsism is founded. We have always instead either too much or too little. For the distinction and separation of subject and object is not original at all, and is, in that sense, not a *datum*. And hence the self cannot, without qualification, be said to be given (*ibid.*). I will but mention this point, and will go on to another. Whatever we may think generally of our original mode of feeling, we have now verifiably some states in which there is no reference to a subject at all (*ibid.*). And if such feelings are the mere adjectives of a subject-reality, that character must be inferred, and is certainly not given. But it is not necessary to take our stand on this disputable ground. Let us admit that the distinction of object and subject is directly presented—and we have still hardly made a step in the direction of Solipsism. For the subject and the object will now appear in correlation ; they will be either two aspects of one fact, or (if you prefer it) two things with a relation between them. And it hardly follows straight from this that only one of these two things is real, and that all the rest of the given total is merely its attribute. That is the result of reflection and of inference, a process which first sets up one half of the fact as absolute, and then turns the other half into an adjective of this fragment. And whether the half is object or is subject, and whether we are led to Materialism, or to what is called sometimes " Idealism," the process essentially is the same. It equally consists, in each case, in a vicious inference. And the result is emphatically *not* something which experience presents. I will, in conclusion, perhaps needlessly, remark on another point. We found (Chapter ix.) that there prevailed great confusion as to the boundaries of self and not-self. There seemed to be features not exclusively assignable to either. And, if this is so, surely that is one more reason for rejecting an experience such as Solipsism would suppose. If the self is given as a reality, with all else as its adjectives, we can hardly then account for the supervening uncertainty about its limits, and explain our constant hesitation between too little and too much.

What we have seen so far is briefly this. We have no direct experience of reality as my self with its states. If we are to arrive at that conclusion, we must do so indirectly and through a process of inference. Experience gives the "this-mine." It gives neither the "mine" as an adjective of the "this," nor the "this" as dependent on and belonging to the "mine." Even if it did so for the moment, that would still not be enough as a support for Solipsism. But experience supplies the character required, not even as existing within one presentation, and, if not thus, then much less so as existing beyond. And the position, in which we now stand, may be stated as follows. If Solipsism is to be proved, it must transcend direct experience. Let us then ask, (*a*) first, if transcendence of this kind is possible, and, (*b*) next, if it is able to give assistance to Solipsism. The conclusion, which we shall reach, may be stated at once. It is both possible and necessary to transcend what is given. But this same transcendence at once carries us into the universe at large. Our private self is not a resting-place which logic can justify.

II. (*a*) We are to enquire, first, if it is possible

to remain within the limits of direct experience.
Now it would not be easy to point out what *is* given
to us immediately. It would be hard to show what is
not imported into the "this," or, at least, modified
there by transcendence. To fix with regard to the
past the precise limit of presentation, might at times
be very difficult. And to discount within the
present the result of ideal processes would, at least
often, be impossible. But I do not desire to base
any objection on this ground. I am content here to
admit the distinction between direct and indirect
experience. And the question is whether reality
can go beyond the former? Has a man a right to
say that something exists, beside that which at this
moment he actually feels? And is it possible,
on the other side, to identify reality with the immediate present?

This identification, we have seen, is impossible;
and the attempt to remain within the boundary
of the mere "this" is hopeless. The self-discrepancy of the content, and its continuity with a
"what" beyond its own limits, at once settle the
question. We need not fall back for conviction
upon the hard shock of change. The whole movement of the mind implies disengagement from the
mere "this"; and to assert the content of the latter
as reality at once involves us in contradictions. But
it would not be profitable further to dwell on this
point. To remain within the presented is neither
defensible nor possible. We are compelled alike by
necessity and by logic to transcend it (Chapters xv.
and xix).

But, before proceeding to ask whither this transcendence must take us, I will deal with a question
we noticed before (Chapter xix.). An objection may
be based on the *uniqueness* of the felt; and it may
be urged that the reality which appears in the "this-
mine" is unique and exclusive. Whatever, therefore,
its predicates may seem to demand, it is not possible

to extend the boundaries of the subject. That will, in short, stick hopelessly for ever within the confines of the presented. Let us examine this contention.

It will be more convenient, in the first place, to dismiss the word " unique." For that seems (as we saw) to introduce the idea of existence in a series, together with a negative relation towards other elements. And, if such a relation is placed within the essence of the " this," then the " this " has become part of a larger unity.

The objection may be stated better thus.[1] " All reality must fall within the limits of the given. For, however much the content may desire to go beyond, yet, when you come to make that content a predicate of the real, you are forced back to the 'this-mine,' or the 'now-felt,' for your subject. Reality appears to lie solely in what is presented, and seems not discoverable elsewhere. But the presented, on the other hand, must be the felt 'this.' And other cases of 'this,' if you mean to take them as real, seem also to fall within the 'now-mine.' If they are not indirect predicates of that, and so extend it adjectivally, then they directly will fall within its *datum*. But, if so, they themselves become distinctions and features there. Hence we have the 'this-mine' as before, but with an increase of special internal particulars. And so we still remain within the confines of one presentation, and to have two at once seems impossible."

Now in answer, I admit that, to find reality, we must betake ourselves to feeling. It is the real, which there appears, which is the subject of all predicates. And to make our way to another fact, quite outside of and away from the " this" which is " mine," seems out of the question. But, while admitting so much, I reject the further consequence. I deny that the felt reality is shut up and confined

[1] On this whole matter compare my *Principles of Logic*, Chapter ii.

within *my* feeling. For the latter may, by addition, be extended beyond its own proper limits. It may remain positively itself, and yet be absorbed in what is larger. Just as in change we have a "now," which contains also a "then"; just as, again, in what is mine there may be diverse features, so, from the opposite side, it may be with my direct experience. There is no opposition between that and a wider whole of presentation. The "mine" does not exclude inclusion in a fuller totality. There may be a further experience immediate and direct, something that *is* my private feeling, and *also* much more. Now the Reality, to which all content in the end must belong, is, we have seen, a direct all-embracing experience. This Reality is present in, and is my feeling; and hence, to that extent, what I feel *is* the all-inclusive universe. But, when I go on to deny that this universe is more, I turn truth into error. There is a "more" of feeling, the extension of that which is "now mine"; and this whole is both the assertion and negation of *my* "this." That extension maintains it together with additions, which merge and override it as exclusive. My "mine" becomes a feature in the great "mine," which includes all "mines."

Now, if within the "this" there were found anything which could stand out against absorption—anything which could refuse to be so lost by such support and maintenance—an objection might be tenable. But we saw, in our nineteenth chapter, that a character of this kind does not exist. My incapacity to extend the boundary of my "this," my inability to gain an immediate experience of that in which it is subordinated and reduced—is my mere imperfection. Because I cannot spread out my window until all is transparent, and all windows disappear, this does not justify me in insisting on my window-frame's rigidity. For that frame has, as such, no existence in reality, but only in our impo-

tence (Chapter xix.).   I am aware of the miserable
inaccuracy of the metaphor, and of the thoughtless
objection which it may call up ; but I will still
put the matter so.   The one Reality *is* what comes
directly to my feeling through this window of a
moment ; and this, also and again, *is* the only
Reality.   But we must not turn the first " is " into
" is nothing at all but," and the second " is " into " is
all of."   There is no objection against the disappearance of limited transparencies in an all-embracing
clearness.   We are not compelled merely, but we
are justified, when we follow the irresistible lead of
our content.

(*b*) We have seen, so far, that experience, if you
take that as direct, does not testify to the sole reality
of my self.   Direct experience would be confined to
a " this," which is not even pre-eminently a " mine,"
and still less is the same as what we mean by a
" self."   And, in the second place, we perceived that
reality extends beyond such experience.   And here,
once more, Solipsism may suppose that it finds its
opportunity.   It may urge that the reality, which
goes beyond the moment, stops short at the self.
The process of transcendence, it may admit, conducts us to a " me " which embraces all immediate
experiences.   But, Solipsism may argue, this process can not take us on further.   By this road,
it will object, there is no way to a plurality of selves,
or to any reality beyond my private personality.
We shall, however, find that this contention is both
dogmatic and absurd.   For, if you have a right to
believe in a self beyond the present, you have the
same right to maintain also the existence of other
selves.
I will not enquire how, precisely, we come by
the idea of other animates' existence.   Metaphysics
has no direct interest in the origin of ideas, and its
business is solely to examine their claim to be true.

But, if I am asked to justify my belief that other selves, beside my own, are in the world, the answer must be this. I arrive at other souls by means of other bodies, and the argument starts from the ground of my own body. My own body is one of the groups which are formed in my experience. And it is connected, immediately and specially, with pleasure and pain, and again with sensations and volitions, as no other group can be.[1] But, since there are other groups like my body, these must also be qualified by similar attendants.[2] With my feelings and my volitions these groups cannot correspond. For they are usually irrelevant and indifferent, and often even hostile ; and they enter into collision with one another and with my body. Therefore these foreign bodies have, each of them, a foreign self of its own. This is briefly the argument, and it seems to me to be practically valid. It falls short, indeed, of demonstration in the following way. The identity in the bodies is, in the first place, not exact, but in various degrees fails to reach completeness. And further, even so far as the identity is perfect, its consequence might be modified by additional conditions. And hence the other soul might so materially differ from my own, that I should hesitate, perhaps, to give it the name of soul.[3] But still the argument, though not strict proof, seems sufficiently good.

It is by the same kind of argument that we reach our own past and future. And here Solipsism, in objecting to the existence of other selves, is unawares attempting to commit suicide. For *my* past self, also, is arrived at only by a process of inference, and by a process which also itself is fallible.

[1] Compare *Mind*, XII. 370 foll. (No. 47). It is hardly necessary for present purposes to elaborate this argument.

[2] This step rests entirely on the principle of the Identity of Indiscernibles.

[3] Cf. Chapter xxvii.

We are so accustomed each to consider his past self as his own, that it is worth while to reflect how very largely it may be foreign. My own past is, in the first place, incompatible with my own present, quite as much as my present can be with another man's. Their difference in time could not permit them both to be wholly the same, even if their two characters are taken as otherwise identical. But this agreement in character is at least not always found. And my past not only may differ so as to be almost indifferent, but I may regard it even with a feeling of hostility and hatred. It may be mine mainly in the sense of a persisting incumbrance, a compulsory appendage, joined in continuity and fastened by an inference. And that inference, not being abstract, falls short of demonstration.

My past of yesterday is constructed by a redintegration from the present. Let us call the present $X(B\text{-}C)$, with an ideal association $x(a\text{-}b)$. The reproduction of this association, and its synthesis with the present, so as to form $X(a\text{-}B\text{-}C)$, is what we call memory. And the justification of the process consists in the identity of x with X.[1] But it is a serious step not simply to qualify my present self, but actually to set up another self at the distance of an interval. I so insist on the identity that I ride upon it to a difference, just as, before, the identity of our bodies carried me to the soul of a different man. And it is obvious, once more here, that the identity is incomplete. The association does not contain all that now qualifies X; x is different from X, and b is different from B. And again, the passage, through this defective identity to another concrete fact, may to some extent be vitiated by unknown interfering conditions. Hence I cannot *prove* that the yester-

---

[1] For the sake of simplicity I have omitted the process of correcting memory. This is of course effected by the attempt to get a coherent view of the past, and by the rejection of everything which cannot be included.

day's self, which I construct, did, as such, have an actual existence in the past. The concrete conditions, into which my ideal construction must be launched, may alter its character. They may, in fact, unite with it so that, if I knew this unknown fact, I should no longer care to call it my self. Thus my past self, assuredly, is not demonstrated. We can but say of it that, like other selves, it is practically certain. And in each case the result, and our way to it, is in principle the same. Both other selves and my own self are intellectual constructions, each as secure as we can expect special facts to be. But, if any one stands out for demonstration, then neither is demonstrated. And, if this demand is pressed, you must remain with a feeling about which you can say nothing, and which is, emphatically, not the self of any one at all. On the other hand, if you are willing to accept a result which is not strictly proved, *both* results must be accepted. For the process, which conducts you to other selves, is not weaker sensibly, if at all, than the construction by which your own self is gained. On either alternative the conclusion of Solipsism is ruined.

And if memory, or some other faculty, is appealed to, and is invoked to secure the pre-eminent reality of my self, I must decline to be persuaded. For I am convinced that such convenient wonders do not exist, and that no one has any sufficient excuse for accepting them. Memory is plainly a construction from the ground of the present. It is throughout inferential, and is certainly fallible ; and its gross mistakes as to past personal existence should be very well known (pp. 84, 213). I prefer, in passing, to notice that confusion as to the present limits of self, which is so familiar a feature in hypnotic experiments. The assumption of a suggested foreign personality is, I think, strong evidence for the secondary nature of our own. Both, in short, are

results of manufacture ; and to account otherwise
for the facts seems clearly impossible.[1]

We have seen, so far, that direct experience is
no foundation for Solipsism. We have seen further
that, if at all we may transcend that experience,
we are no nearer Solipsism. For we can go to
foreign selves by a process no worse than the
construction which establishes our own self. And,
before passing on, I will call attention to a minor
point. Even if I had secured a right to the possession of my past self, and no right to the acceptance
of other selves as real, yet, even with this, Solipsism
is not grounded. It would not follow from this that
the not-myself is nothing, and that all the world is
merely a state of my self. The only consequence,
so far, would be that the not-myself must be inanimate. But between that result and Solipsism
is an impassable gulf. You can not, starting from
the given, construct a self which will swallow up and
own every element from which it is distinguished.

I will briefly touch on another source of misunderstanding. It is the old mistake in a form
which is slightly different. All I know, I may be
told, is what I experience, and I can experience
nothing beyond my own states. And it is argued
that hence my own self is the one knowable reality.
But the truth in this objection, once more, has been
pressed into falsehood. It is true that all I experience is my state—so far as I experience it.
Even the Absolute, as my reality, is my state of
mind. But this hardly shows that my experience
possesses no other aspect. It hardly proves that
what is my state of mind is no more, and must be
taken as real barely from that one point of view.

[1] It is of course the intervention of the foreign body which
prevents my usually confusing foreign selves with my own.
Another's body is, in the first place, not immediately connected
throughout with my pleasure and pain. And, in the second
place, its states are often positively incompatible with mine.

The Reality certainly must appear within my psychical existence; but it is quite another thing to limit its whole nature to that field.

My thought, feeling, and will, are, of course, all phenomena; they all are events which happen. From time to time, as they happen, they exist in the felt "this," and they are elements within its chance congeries. And they can be taken, further, as states of that self-thing which I construct by an inference. But, if you look at them merely so, then, unconsciously or consciously, you mutilate their character. You use a point of view which is necessary, but still is partial and one-sided. And we shall see more clearly, hereafter, the nature of this view (Chapters xxiii. and xxvii.). I will here simply state that the import and content of these processes does not consist in their appearance in the pyschical series. In thought the important feature is not our mental state, as such; and the same truth, if less palpable, is as certain with volition. My will is mine, but, none the less, it is also much more. The content of the idea willed (to put the matter only on that ground) may be something beyond me; and, since this content is effective, the activity of the process cannot simply be my state. But I will not try to anticipate a point which will engage us later on. It is sufficient here to lay down generally, that, if experience is mine, that is no argument for what I experience being nothing but my state. And this whole objection rests entirely on false preconceptions. My private self is first set up, as a substantive which is real independent of the Whole; and then its palpable community with the universe, which in experience is forced on us, is degraded into the adjective of our miserable abstraction. But, when these preconceptions are exposed, Solipsism disappears.

Considered as the apotheosis of an abstraction,

Solipsism is quite false.   But from its errors we may
collect aspects of truth, to which we sometimes are
blind.   And, in the first place, though my experience
is not the whole world, yet that world appears in my
experience, and, so far as it exists there, it *is* my
state of mind   That the real Absolute, or God
himself, is also *my* state, is a truth often forgotten
and to which later we shall return.   And there is
a second truth to which Solipsism has blindly borne
witness.   My way of contact with Reality is through
a limited aperture.   For I cannot get at it directly
except through the felt " this," and our immediate
interchange and transfluence takes place through
one small opening.   Everything beyond, though not
less real, is an expansion of the common essence
which we feel burningly in this one focus.   And so,
in the end, to know the Universe, we must fall back
upon our personal experience and sensation.

But beside these two truths there is yet another
truth worth noticing.   My self is certainly not the
Absolute, but, without it, the Absolute would not be
itself.   You cannot anywhere abstract wholly from
my personal feelings ; you cannot say that, apart
even from the meanest of these, anything else in the
universe would be what it is.   And in asserting
this relation, this essential connection, of all reality
with my self, Solipsism has emphasized what should
not be forgotten.   But the consequences, which
properly follow from this truth, will be discussed
hereafter.[1]

[1] I shall deal in Chapter xxvii. with the question whether,
in refuting Solipsism, we have removed any ground for our conclusion that the Absolute is experience.

CHAPTER XXII.

NATURE.

THE word Nature has of course more meanings than one. I am going to use it here in the sense of the bare physical world, that region which forms the object of purely physical science, and appears to fall outside of all mind. Abstract from everything psychical, and then the remainder of existence will be Nature. It will be mere body or the extended, so far as that is not psychical, together with the properties immediately connected with or following from this extension. And we sometimes forget that this world, in the mental history of each of us, once had no existence. Whatever view we take with regard to the psychological origin of extension, the result will be the same. There was a time when the separation of the outer world, as a thing real apart from our feeling, had not even been begun. The physical world, whether it exists independently or not, is, for each of us, an abstraction from the entire reality. And the development of this reality, and of the division which we make in it, requires naturally some time. But I do not propose to discuss the subject further here.[1]

Then there comes a period when we all gain the idea of mere body. I do not mean that we always, or even habitually, regard the outer world as standing and persisting in divorce from all feeling. But, still, at least for certain purposes, we get the notion of such a world, consisting both of primary and also

[1] For some further remarks see *Mind*, No. 47 (Vol. XII).

of secondary qualities.   This world strikes us as not
dependent on the inner life of any one.   We view it
as standing there, the same for every soul with
which it comes into relation.   Our bodies with their
organs are taken as the instruments and media,
which should convey it as it is, and as it exists apart
from them.   And we find no difficulty in the idea
of a bodily reality remaining still and holding firm
when every self has been removed.   Such a supposition to the average man appears obviously
possible, however much, for other reasons, he might
decline to entertain it.   And the assurance that his
supposition is meaningless nonsense he rejects as
contrary to what he calls common sense.

And then, to the person who reflects, comes in the
old series of doubts and objections, and the useless
attempts at solution or compromise.   For Nature to
the common man is not the Nature of the physicist;
and the physicist himself, outside his science, still
habitually views the world as what he must believe
it cannot be.   But there should be no need to recall
the discussion of our First Book with regard to
secondary and primary qualities.   We endeavoured
to show there that it is difficult to take both on a
level, and impossible to make reality consist of one
class in separation from the other.   And the un-
fortunate upholder of a mere physical nature escapes
only by blindness from hopeless bewilderment.   He
is forced to the conclusion that all I know is an
affection of my organism, and then my organism
itself turns out to be nothing else but such an
affection.   There is in short no physical thing but
that which is a mere state of a physical thing, and
perhaps in the end even (it might be contended)
a mere state of itself.   It will be instructive to consider Nature from this point of view.

We may here use the form of what has been called
an Antinomy.   (a) Nature is only for my body; but,
on the other hand, (b) My body is only for Nature.

(*a*) I need say no more on the thesis that the outer world is known only as a state of my organism. Its proper consequence (according to the view generally received) appears to be that everything else is a state of my brain. For that (apparently) is all which can possibly be experienced. Into the further refinements, which would arise from the question of cerebral localization, I do not think it necessary to enter.

(*b*) And yet most emphatically, as we have seen at the beginning of this work, my organism is nothing but appearance to a body. It itself is only the bare state of a natural object. For my organism, like all else, is but what is experienced, and I can only experience my organism in relation to its own organs. Hence the whole body is a mere state of these; and they are states of one another in indefinite regress.

How can we deny this? If we appeal to an immediate experience, which presents me with my body as a something extended and solid, we are taking refuge in a world of exploded illusions. No such peculiar intuition can bear the light of a serious psychology. The internal feelings which I experience certainly give nothing of the sort; and again, even if they did, yet for natural science they are no direct reality, but themselves the states of a material nervous system. And to fall back on a supposed wholesale revelation of Resistance would be surely to seek aid from that which cannot help. For the revelation in the first place (as we have already perceived in Chapter x.), is a fiction. And, in the second place, Resistance could not present us with a body independently real. It could supply only the relation of one thing to another, where neither thing, as what resists, is a separate body, either apart from, or again in relation to, the other. Resistance could not conceivably tell us what anything is in itself. It gives us one thing as qualified

by the state of another thing, each within that known
relation being only for the other, and, apart from it,
being unknown and, so far, a nonentity.

｜   And that is the general conclusion with regard to
Nature to which we are driven.   The physical world
is the relation between physical things.   And the
relation, on the one side, presupposes them as
physical, while apart from it, on the other side, they
certainly are not so.   Nature is the phenomenal
relation of the unknown to the unknown ; and the
terms cannot, because unknown, even be said to be
related, since they cannot themselves be said to be
anything at all.   Let us develope this further.

That the outer world is only for my organs appears inevitable.   But what is an organ except so
far as it is known ?   And how can it be known but
as itself the state of an organ ?   If then you are
asked to find an organ which *is* a physical object,
you can no more find it than a body which itself *is* a
body.   Each is a state of something else, which is
never more than a state—and the *something* escapes
us.   The same consequence, again, is palpable if we
take refuge in the brain.   If the world is my brain-
state, then what is my own brain ?   That is nothing
but the state of some brain, I need not proceed to
ask whose.[1]   It is, in any case, not real as a physical
thing, unless you reduce it to the adjective of a
physical thing.   And this illusive quest goes on for
ever.   It can never lead you to what is more than
either an adjective of, or a relation between,—what
you cannot find.

There is no escaping from this circle.   Let us take
the instance of a double perception of touch, a and b.
Then a is only a state of the organ C, and b is only
a state of the organ D.   And if you wish to say that
either C or D is itself real as a body, you can only
do so on the witness of another organ E or F.   You

---

[1] For me my own brain in the end must be a state of my own
brain, p. 263.

can in no case arrive at a something material existing as a substantive ; you are compelled to
wander without end from one adjective to another
adjective. And in double perception the twofold
evidence does not show that each side is body. It
leads to the conclusion that neither side is more than
a dependant, on we do not know what.

And if we consult common experience, we gain no
support for *one* side of our antinomy. It is clear
that, for the existence of our organism, we find there
the same evidence as for the existence of outer
objects. We have a witness which, with our body,
gives us the environment as equally real. For we
never, under any circumstances, are without *some*
external sensation. If you receive, in the ordinary
sense, the testimony of our organs, then, if the outer
world is not real, our organs are not real. You have
both sides given as on a level, or you have neither
side at all. And to say that one side is the substantive, to which the other belongs, as an appendage
or appurtenance, seems quite against reason. We
are, in brief, confirmed in the conclusion we had
reached. Both Nature and my body exist necessarily with and for one another. And both, on
examination, turn out to be nothing apart from their
relation. We find in each no essence which is not
infected by appearance to the other.

And with this we are brought to an unavoidable
result.[1] The physical world is an appearance ; it is
phenomenal throughout. It is the relation of two
unknowns, which, because they are unknown, we
cannot have any right to regard as really two, or
as related at all. It is an imperfect way of apprehension, which gives us qualities and relations, each
the condition of and yet presupposing the other.

[1] This result (the reader must remember) rests, not merely on
the above, but on the discussions of our First Book. The titles
of some chapters there should be a sufficient reference.

And we have no means of knowing how this confusion and perplexity is resolved in the Absolute. The material world is an incorrect, a one-sided, and self-contradictory appearance of the Real. It is the reaction of two unknown things, things, which, to be related, must each be something by itself, and yet, apart from their relation, are nothing at all. In other words it is a diversity which, as we regard it, is not real, but which somehow, in all its fulness, enters into and perfects the life of the Universe. But, as to the manner in which it is included, we are unable to say anything.

But is this circular connexion, this baseless inter-relation between the organism and Nature, a mistake to be set aside? Most emphatically not so, for it seems a vital scheme, and a necessary way of happening among our appearances. It is an arrangement among phenomena by which the extended only comes to us in relation with another extended which we call an organism. You cannot have certain qualities, of touch, or sight, or hearing, unless there is with them a certain connection of other qualities. Nature has phenomenal reality as a grouping and as laws of sequence and co-existence, holding good within a certain section of that which appears to us. But, if you attempt to make it more, you will re-enter those mazes from which we found no exit. You are led to take the physical world as a mere adjective of my body, and you find that my body, on the other hand, is not one whit more substantival. It is itself for ever the state of something further and beyond. And, as we perceived in our First Book, you can neither take the qualities, that are called primary, as real without the secondary, nor again the latter as existing apart from my feeling. These are all distinctions which, as we saw, are reduced, and which come together in the one great totality of absolute experience. They are lost there for our vision, but survive most assuredly in that which absorbs them. Nature is but one part of the feeling whole, which we have separated by our abstraction, and enlarged by theoretical necessity and contrivance. And then we set up this fragment as self-existing; and what is sometimes called " science " goes out of its way to make a gross mistake. It takes an intellectual construction of the conditions of mere appearance for independent reality. And it would thrust this fiction on us as the one thing which has solid being. But thus it turns into sheer error a relative truth. It discredits that which, as a working point of view, is fully justified by success, and stands high above criticism.

We have seen, so far, that mere Nature is not real. Nature is but an appearance within the reality; it is a partial and imperfect manifestation of the Absolute. The physical world is an abstraction, which, for certain purposes is properly considered by itself, but which, if taken as standing in its own right, becomes at once self-contradictory. We must now develop this general view in some part of its detail.

But, before proceeding, I will deal with a point of some interest. We, so far, have treated the physical world as extended, and a doubt may be raised whether such an assumption can be justified. Extension, I may be told, is not essential to Nature; for the extended need not always be physical, nor again the physical always extended. And it is better at once to attempt to get clear on this point. It is, in the first place, quite true that not all of the extended forms part of Nature. For I may think of, and may imagine, things extended at my pleasure, and it is impossible to suppose that all these psychical facts take a place within our physical system. Yet, upon the other hand, I do not see how we can deny their extension. That which for my mind is

extended, must be so as a fact, whether it does, or
does not, belong to what we call Nature. Take, for
example, some common illusion of sense. In that
we actually may have a perception of extension, and
to call this false does not show that it is not somehow spatial. But, if so, Nature and extension will
not coincide. Hence we are forced to seek the distinctive essence of Nature elsewhere, and in some
non-spatial character.

   In its bare principle I am able to accept this conclusion. The essence of Nature is to appear as a
region standing outside the psychical, and as (in
some part) suffering and causing change independent
of that. Or, at the very least, Nature must not be
always directly dependent on soul. Nature presupposes the distinction of the not-self from the self. It
is that part of the world which is not inseparably
one thing in experience with those internal groups
which feel pleasure and pain. It is the attendant
medium by which selves are made manifest to one
another. But it shows an existence and laws not belonging to these selves ; and, to some extent at least,
it appears indifferent to their feelings, and thoughts,
and volitions. It is this independence which would
seem to be the distinctive mark of Nature.

   And, if so, it may be urged that Nature is perhaps not extended, and I think we must admit that
such a Nature is possible. We may imagine groups
of qualities, for example sounds or smells, arranged
in such a way as to appear independent of the psychical. These qualities might seem to go their own
ways without any, or much, regard to our ideas or
likings; and they might maintain such an order as to
form a stable and permanent not-self. These groups,
again, might serve as the means of communication
between souls, and, in short, might answer every
known purpose for which Nature exists. Even as
things are, when these secondary qualities are localized in outer space, we regard them as physical ;

and there is a doubt, therefore, whether any such localization is necessary. And, for myself, I am unable to perceive that it is so. Certainly, if I try to imagine an unextended world of this kind, I admit that, against my will, I give it a spatial character. But, so far as I see, this may arise from mere infirmity; and the idea of an unextended Nature seems, for my knowledge at least, not self-contradictory.

But, having gone as far as this, I am unable to go farther. A Nature without extension I admit to be possible, but I can discover no good reason for taking it as actual. For the physical world, which we encounter, is certainly spatial; and we have no interest in trying to seek out any other. If Nature on our view were reality, the case would be altered; and we should then be forced to entertain every doubt about its essence. But for us Nature is appearance, inconsistent and untrue; and hence the supposition of another Nature, free from extension, could furnish no help. This supposition does not remove the contradictions ·from actual extension, which in any case is still a fact. And, again, even within itself, the supposition cannot be made consistent with itself. We may, therefore, pass on without troubling ourselves with such a mere possibility. We cannot conclude that all Nature essentially must have extension. But, since at any rate *our* physical world is extended, and since the hypothesis of another kind of Nature has no interest, that idea may be dismissed. I shall henceforth take Nature as appearing always in the form of space.[1]

Let us return from this digression. We are to

---

[1] I may perhaps add that "resistance" is no sufficient answer to the question "What is Nature?" A persisting idea may in the fullest sense "resist"; but can we find in that the essence of what we mean by the physical world? The claims of "resistance" have, however, been disposed of already, pp. 116, 225, 263.

consider Nature as possessed of extension, and we
have seen that mere Nature has no reality.   We
may now proceed to a series of subordinate questions, and the first of these is about the world which
is called inorganic.   Is there in fact such a thing as
inorganic Nature?   Now, if by this we meant a
region or division of existence, not subserving and
entering into the one experience of the Whole, the
question already would have been settled.   There
cannot exist an arrangement which fails to perfect,
and to minister directly to, the feeling of the Absolute.   Nor again, since in the Absolute all comes
together, could there be anything inorganic in the
sense of standing apart from some essential relation
to finite organisms.   Any such mutilations as these
have long ago been condemned, and it is in another
sense that we must inquire about the inorganic.

By an organism we are to understand a more or
less permanent arrangement of qualities and relations, such as at once falls outside of, and yet immediately subserves, a distinct unity of feeling.   We
are to mean a phenomenal group with which a felt
particularity is connected in a way to be discussed
in the next chapter.   At least this is the sense in
which, however incorrectly, I am about to use the
word.   The question, therefore, here will be whether
there are elements in Nature, which fail to make a
part of some such finite arrangement.   The inquiry
is intelligible, but for metaphysics it seems to have
no importance.

The question in the first place, I think, cannot be
answered.   For, if we consider it in the abstract, I
find no good ground for either affirmation or denial.
I know no reason why in the Absolute there should
not be qualities, which fail to be connected, as a
body, with some finite soul.   And, upon the other
hand, I see no special cause for supposing that these
exist.   And when, leaving the abstract point of
view, we regard this problem from the side of con-

crete facts, then, so far as I perceive, we are able to
make no advance. For as to that which can, and
that which cannot, play the part of an organism, we
know very little. A sameness greater or less with
our own bodies is the basis from which we conclude
to other bodies and souls. And what this inference
loses in exactitude (Chapter xxi.), it gains on the
other hand in extent, by acquiring a greater range
of application. And it would seem almost impossible, from this ground, to produce a satisfactory
negative result. A certain likeness of outward form,
and again some amount of similarity in action, are
what we stand on when we argue to psychical life.
But our failure, on the other side, to discover these
symptoms is no sufficient warrant for positive denial.[1] There may surely beyond our knowledge be
strange arrangements of qualities, which serve as
the condition of unknown personal unities. Given
a certain degree of difference in the outward form,
and a certain divergence in the way of manifestation,
and we should fail at once to perceive the presence
of an organism. But would it, therefore, always not
exist ? Or can we assume, because we have found
out the nature of some organisms, that we have
exhausted that of all ? Have we an ascertained
essence, outside of which no variation is possible ?
Any such contention would seem to be indefensible.
Every fragment of visible Nature might, so far as is
known, serve as part in some organism not like our
bodies. And, if we consider further how much of
Nature may be hid from our view, we shall surely
be still less inclined to dogmatism. For that which
we see may be combined in an organic unity with
the invisible ; and, again, one and the same element
might have a position and function in any number
of organisms. But there is no advantage in trying
to fill the unknown with our fancies. It should be

[1] It is natural in this connection to refer to Fechner's vigorous
advocacy.

clear, when we reflect, that we are in no condition
on this point to fix a limit to the possible.[1] Arrangements, apparently quite different from our own,
and expressing themselves in what seems a wholly
unlike way, might be directly connected with finite
centres of feeling.　And our result here must be
this, that, except in relation to our ignorance, we cannot call the least portion of Nature inorganic.　For
some practical purposes, of course, the case is radically altered.　We of course there have a perfect
right to act upon ignorance.　We not only may, but
even must, often treat the unseen as non-existent.
But in metaphysics such an attitude cannot be
justified.[2] We, on one side, have positive knowledge that some parts of Nature are organisms ; but
whether, upon the other side, anything inorganic
exists or not, we have no means of judging.　Hence
to give an answer to our question is impossible.

　　But this inability seems a matter of no importance.
For finite organisms, as we have seen, are but phenomenal appearance, and both their division and their
unity is transcended in the Absolute.　And assuredly the inorganic, if it exists, will be still more unreal.
It will, in any case, not merely be bound in relation
with organisms, but will, together with them, be included in a single and all-absorbing experience,　It
will become a feature and an element in that Whole
where no diversity is lost, but where the oneness is
something much more than organic.　And with this
I will pass on to a further inquiry.

　　We have seen that beyond experience nothing
can exist, and hence no part of Nature can fall outside of the Absolute's perfection.　But the question
as to the necessity of experience may still be raised

　　[1] If we consider further the possibility of diverse material systems,
and of the compenetrability of bodies within each system, we shall
be even less disposed to dogmatize.　See below, pp. 287, 289.
　　[2] On the main principle see Chapter xxvii.

in a modified sense. Is there any Nature not experienced by a finite subject? Can we suppose in
the Absolute a margin of physical qualities, which,
so to speak, do not pass through some finite percipient? Of course, if this is so, we cannot perceive
them. But the question is whether, notwithstanding,
we may, or even must, suppose that such a margin
exists. (*a*) Is a physical fact, which is not *for* some
finite sentient being, a thing which is possible? And
(*b*), in the next place, have we sufficient ground to
take it also as real?

(*a*) In defence, first, of its possibility there is
something to be said. "Admitted," we shall be
told, "that relation to a finite soul is the condition
under which Nature appears to us, it does not follow
that this condition is indispensable. To assert that
those very qualities, which we meet under certain
conditions, can exist apart from them, is perhaps
going too far But, on the other side, some qualities of the sort we call sensible might not require (so
to speak) to be developed on or filtered through a
particular soul. These qualities in the end, like all
the rest, would certainly, as such, be absorbed in the
Absolute ; but they (so to speak) might find their
way to this end by themselves, and might not require the mediation of a finite sentience." But this
defence, it seems to me, is insufficient. We can
think, in a manner, of sensible quality apart from a
soul, but the doubt is whether such a manner is
really legitimate. The question is, when we have
abstracted from finite centres of feeling, whether we
have not removed all meaning from sensible quality
And again, if we admit that in the Absolute there
may be matter not contained in finite experience,
can we go on to make this matter a part of Nature,
and call it physical? These two questions appear
to be vitally distinct.

A margin of experience, not the experience of any
finite centre, we shall find (Chapter xxvii.) can-

A. R. T

not be called impossible. But it seems another thing to place such matter in Nature. For Nature is constituted and upheld by a division in experience. It is, in its essence, a product of distinction and opposition. And to take this product as existing outside finite centres seems indefensible. The Nature that falls outside, we must insist, may perhaps not be nothing, but it is not Nature. If it is fact, it is fact which we must not call physical.

But this whole enquiry, on the other hand, seems unimportant and almost idle. For, though unperceived by finite souls, all Nature would enter into one experience with the contents of these souls. And hence the want of apprehension by, and passage through, a particular focus would lose in the end its significance. Thus, even if we admit fact, not included in finite centres of sentience, our view of the Absolute, after all, will not be altered. But such fact, we have seen, could not be properly physical.

(b) A part of Nature, not apprehended by finite mind, we have found in some sense is barely possible. But we may be told now, on the other hand, that it is necessary to assume it. There are such difficulties in the way of any other conclusion that we may seem to have no choice. Nature is too wide, we may hear, to be taken in by any number of sentient beings. And again Nature is in part not perceptible at all. My own brain, while I am alive, is an obvious instance of this. And we may think further of the objects known only by the microscope, and of the bodies, intangible and invisible, assured to us by science. And the mountains, that endure always, must be more than the sensations of short-lived mortals, and indeed were there in the time before organic life was developed. In the face of these objections, it may be said, we are unable to persist. The necessity of finite souls for the existence of Nature cannot possibly be maintained. And hence a physical world, not apprehended by these perceiving centres, must somehow be postulated.

The objections at first may seem weighty, but I will endeavour to show that they cannot stand criticism. And I will begin by laying down a necessary distinction. The physical world exists, of course, independent of me, and does not depend on the accident of my sensations. A mountain *is*, whether I happen to perceive it or not. This truth is certain; but, on the other hand, its meaning is ambiguous, and it may be taken in two very different senses. We may call these senses, if we please, categorical and hypothetical. You may either assert that the mountain always actually is, as it is when it is perceived. Or you may mean only that it is always something apart from sensible perception; and that whenever it is perceived, it then developes its familiar character. And a confusion between the mountain, as it is in itself, and as it becomes for an observer, is perhaps our most usual state of mind. But such an obscurity would be fatal to the present enquiry.

(i.) I will take the objections, first, as applying to what we have called the categorical sense. Nature must be in itself, as we perceive it to be; and, if so, Nature must fall partly beyond finite minds—this is, so far, the argument urged against our view. But this argument surely would be based upon our mere ignorance. For we have seen that organisms unlike our own, arrangements pervading and absorbing the whole extent of Nature, may very well exist. And as to the modes of perception which are possible with these organisms, we can lay down no limit. But if so, there is no reason why all Nature should not be always in relation to finite sentience. Every part of it may be now actually, for some other mind, precisely what it would be for us, if we happened to perceive it. And objects invisible like my brain, or found only by the microscope, need not cause us to hesitate. For we cannot deny that there may be some faculty of sense to which at all times they are obvious. And the mountains that endure may, for all that we know, have been visible always. They may have been perceived through their past as we perceive them to-day. If we can set no bounds to the existence and the powers of sentient beings, the objection, so far, has been based on a false assumption of knowledge.[1]

(ii.) But this line of reply, perhaps, may be carried too far. It cannot be refuted, and yet we feel that it tends to become extravagant. It may be possible that Nature throughout is perceived always, and thus always is, as we should perceive it; but we need not rest our whole weight on this assumption. Our conclusion will be borne out by something less. For beyond the things perceived by sense there extends the world of thought. Nature will not merely be the region that is presented and *also* thought of, but it will, in addition, include matter which is *only* thought of. Nature will hence be limited solely by the range of our intellects. It will be the physical universe apprehended in any way whatever by finite souls.

Outside of this boundary there is no Nature. We may employ the idea of a pre-organic time, or of a physical world from which all sentience has disappeared. But, with the knowledge that we possess, we cannot, even in a relative sense, take this result as universal. It could hold only with respect to those organisms which we know, and, if carried further, it obviously becomes invalid. And again, such a truth, where it is true, can be merely phenomenal. For, in any case, there is no history or progress in the Absolute (Chapter xxvi). A Nature without sentience is, in short, a mere construction for science,

---

[1] " 'Tis ignorance that makes a barren waste
Of all beyond itself."

and it possesses a very partial reality.[1]   Nor are the imperceptibles of physics in any better case.   Apart from the plain contradictions which prove them to be barely phenomenal, their nature clearly exists but in relation to thought.   For, not being perceived by any finite, they are not, as such, perceived at all; and what reality they possess is not sensible, but merely abstract.

Our conclusion then, so far, will be this.   Nature may extend beyond the region actually perceived by the finite, but certainly not beyond the limits of finite thought.   In the Absolute possibly there is a margin not contained in finite experiences (Chapter xxvii.), but this possible margin cannot properly be taken as physical.   For, included in Nature, it would be qualified by a relation to finite mind.   But the existence of Nature, as mere thought, at once leads to a difficulty.   For a physical world, to be real, must clearly be sensible.   And to exist otherwise than for sense is but to exist hypothetically.   If so, Nature, at least in part, is not actually Nature, but merely is what becomes so under certain conditions.   It seems another fact, a something else, which indeed we think of, but which, merely in itself and merely as we think of it, is not physical reality.   Thus, on our view, Nature to this extent seems not to be fact; and we shall have been driven, in the end, to deny part of its physical existence.

This conclusion urged against us, I admit, is in one sense inevitable.   The Nature that is thought of, and that we assume not to be perceived by any mind, is, in the strict sense, not Nature.[2]   Yet such a result, rightly interpreted, need cause us no trouble.   We shall understand it better when we have discussed the meaning of conditional existence (Chapter xxiv.);   I will however attempt to deal

[1] See more below, p. 283.

[2] That is, of course, so long as Nature is confined to actual physical fact.

here with the present difficulty. And what that
comes to is briefly this.   Nature on the one side
must be actual, and if so, must be sensible ; but,
upon the other hand, it seems in part to be merely
intelligible.   This is the problem, and the solution
is that what for us is intelligible only, is more for
the Absolute.   There somehow, we do not know
how, what we think is perceived.   Everything there
is merged and re-absorbed in an experience intuitive,
at once and in itself, of both ideas and facts.

What we merely think is not real, because in
thinking there is a division of the " what " from the
" that."   But, none the less, every thought gives us
actual content ; and the presence of that content is
fact, quite as hard as any possible perception.   And
so the Nature, that is thought of, to that extent does
exist, and does possess a certain amount of positive
character.   Hence in the Absolute, where all content is re-blended with existence, the Nature thought
of will gain once more an intuitional form.   It will
come together with itself and with other sides of the
Universe, and will make its special contribution to
the riches of the Whole.   It *is* not as we think of it,
it *is* not as it becomes when in our experience
thought is succeeded by perception.   It *is* something
which, only under certain conditions, turns to physical fact revealed to our senses.   But because in
the Absolute it is an element of reality, though not
known, as there experienced, to any finite mind,—
because, again, we rightly judge it to be physical
fact, if it became perceived by sense—therefore already it *is* fact, hypothetical but still independent.
Nature in this sense is not dependent on the fancies
of the individual, and yet it has no content but what
is relative to particular minds.   We may assume that
without any addition there is enough matter in these
centres to furnish a harmonious experience in the
Absolute.   There is no element in that unknown
unity, which cannot be supplied by the fragmentary

life of its members.   Outside of finite experience
there is neither a natural world nor any other world
at all.[1]

But it may be objected that we have now been
brought into collision with common sense. The
whole of nature, for common sense, *is* ; and it is
what it is, whether any finite being apprehends it or
not. On our view, on the other hand, part of
the physical world does not, as such, exist. This
objection is well founded, but I would reply, first,
that common sense is hardly consistent with itself.
It would perhaps hesitate, for instance, to place
sweet and bitter tastes, as such, in the world outside
of sense. But only the man who will go thus far,
who believes in colours in the darkness, and sounds
without an ear, can stand upon this ground. If
there is any one who holds that flowers blush when
utterly unseen, and smell delightfully when no one
delights in their odour—he may object to our
doctrine and may be invited to state his own. But
I venture to think that, metaphysically, his view
would turn out not worth notice. Any serious
theory must in some points collide with common
sense ; and, if we are to look at the matter from
this side, our view surely is, in this way, superior to
others. For us Nature, through a great part, certainly is as it is perceived. Secondary qualities are
an actual part of the physical world, and the existing thing sugar we take to be, itself, actually sweet
and pleasant. Nay the very beauty of Nature, we
shall find hereafter (Chapter xxvi.), is, for us, fact as
good as the hardest of primary qualities. Everything physical, which is seen or felt, or in any way
experienced or enjoyed, is, on our view, an existing
part of the region of Nature ; and it is in Nature as
we experience it. It is only that portion which is

---

[1] The question whether any part of the contents of the Universe is not contained in finite centres, is discussed in Chaptr.
xxvii.

but thought of, only that, of which we assume that no creature perceives it—which, as such, is not fact. Thus, while admitting our collision with common sense, I would lay stress upon its narrow extent and degree.

We have now seen that inorganic Nature perhaps does not exist. Though it is possible, we are unable to say if it is real. But with regard to Nature falling outside all finite subjects our conclusion is different. We failed to discover any ground for taking that as real, and, if strictly understood, we found no right to call it even possible. The importance of these questions, on the other hand we urged, is overrated. For they all depend on distinctions which, though not lost, are transcended in the Absolute. Whether all perception and feeling must pass through finite souls, whether any physical qualities stand out and are not worked up into organisms—into arrangements which directly condition such souls—these enquiries are not vital. In part we cannot answer them, and in part our reply gives us little that possesses a positive value. The interrelation between organisms, and their division from the inorganic, and, again, the separation of finite experiences, from each other and from the whole—these are not anything which, as such, can hold good in the Absolute. That one reality, the richer for every variety, absorbs and dissolves these phenomenal limitations. Whether there is a margin of quality not directly making part of some particular experience, whether, again, there is any physical extension outside the arrangements which immediately subserve feeling centres—in the end these questions are but *our* questions. The answers must be given in a language without meaning for the Absolute, until translated into a way of expression beyond our powers. But, if so expressed, we can perceive,

they would lose that importance our hard distinctions confer on them. And, from our own point of
view, these problems have proved partly to be insoluble. The value of our answers consists mainly
in their denial of partial and one-sided doctrines.

There is an objection which, before we proceed,
may be dealt with. " Upon your view," I may be
told, " there is really after all no Nature. For
Nature is one solid body, the images of which are
many, and which itself remains single. But upon
your theory we have a number of similar reflections ; and, though these may agree among themselves, no real thing comes to light in them. Such
an appearance will not account for Nature." But
this objection rests on what must be called a
thoughtless prejudice. It is founded on the idea
that identity in the contents of various souls is
impossible. Separation into distinct centres of feeling and thought is assumed to preclude all sameness between what falls within such diverse centres.
But, we shall see more fully hereafter (Chapter
xxiii.), this assumption is groundless. It is merely
part of that blind prejudice against identity in
general which disappears before criticism. That
which is identical in quality must always, so far, be
one ; and its division, in time or space or in several
souls, does not take away its unity. The variety of
course does make a difference to the identity, and,
without that difference and these modifications, the
sameness is nothing. But, on the other hand, to
take sameness as destroyed by diversity, makes
impossible all thought and existence alike. It is a
doctrine, which, if carried out, quite abolishes the
Universe. Certainly, in the end, to know *how* the
one and many are united is beyond our powers.
But in the Absolute somehow, we are convinced, the
problem is solved.

This apparent parcelling out of Nature is but appar-

ent. On the one side a collection of what falls within
distinct souls, on the other side it possesses unity in
the Absolute. Where the contents of the several
centres all come together, there the appearances of
Nature of course will be one. And, if we consider
the question from the side of each separate soul, we
still can find no difficulty. Nature for each percipient mainly *is* what to the percipient it seems to
be, and it mainly is so without regard to that special
percipient. And, if this is so, I find it hard to see
what more is wanted.[1] Of course, so far as any one
soul has peculiar sensations, the qualities it finds
will not exist unless in its experience. But I do
not know why they should do so. And there remains, I admit, that uncertain extent, through which
Nature is perhaps not sensibly perceived by any
soul. This part of Nature exists beyond me, but it
does not exist *as* I should perceive it. And we
saw clearly that, so far, common sense cannot be
satisfied. But, if this were a valid objection, I do
not know in whose mouth it would hold good.[2]
And if any one, again, goes on to urge that Nature
works and acts on us, and that this aspect of force
is ignored by our theory, we need not answer at
length. For if ultimate reality is claimed for any
thing like force, we have disposed, in our First Book,
of that claim already. But, if all that is meant is a
certain behaviour of Nature, with certain consequences in souls, there is nothing here but a

---

[1] If Nature were more in itself, could it be more to us? And
is it for our sake, or for the sake of Nature, that the objector asks
for more? Clearness on these points is desirable.

[2] It is possible that some follower of Berkeley may urge that
the whole of Nature, precisely as it is perceived (and felt?), exists
actually in God. But this by itself is not a metaphysical view.
It is merely a delusive attempt to do without one. The un-
rationalized heaping up of such a congeries within the Deity, with
its (partial?) reduplication inside finite centres, and then the
relation between these aspects (or divisions?) of the whole—this
is an effort surely not to solve a problem but simply to shelve it.

phenomenal co-existence and sequence. It is an order and way in which events happen, and in our view of Nature I see nothing inconsistent with this arrangement. From the fact of such an orderly appearance you cannot infer the existence of something not contained in finite experiences.[1]

We may now consider a question which several times we have touched on. We have seen that in reality there can be no mere physical Nature The world of physical science is not something independent, but is a mere element in one total experience. And, apart from finite souls, this physical world, in the proper sense, does not exist. But, if so, we are led to ask, what becomes of natural science? Nature there is treated as a thing without soul and standing by its own strength. And we thus have been apparently forced into collision with something beyond criticism. But the collision is illusive, and exists only through misunderstanding. For the object of natural science is not at all the ascertainment of ultimate truth, and its province does not fall outside phenomena. The ideas, with which it works, are not intended to set out the true character of reality. And, therefore, to subject these ideas to metaphysical criticism, or, from the other side, to oppose them to metaphysics, is to mistake their end and bearing. The question is not whether the principles of physical science possess an absolute truth to which they make no claim. The question is whether the abstraction, employed by that science, is legitimate and useful. And with regard to that question there surely can be no doubt. In order to understand the co-existence and sequence of phenomena, natural science makes an intellectual con-

---

[1] I admit that I cannot explain how Nature comes to us as an order (Chapters xxiii. and xxvi.), but then I deny that any other view is in any better case. The subject of Ends in Nature will be considered later.

struction of their conditions. Its matter, motion, and force are but working ideas, used to understand the occurrence of certain events. To find and systematize the ways in which spatial phenomena are connected and happen—this is all the mark which these conceptions aim at. And for the metaphysician to urge that these ideas contradict themselves, is irrelevant and unfair. To object that in the end they are not true, is to mistake their pretensions.

And thus when matter is treated of as a thing standing in its own right, continuous and identical, metaphysics is not concerned. For, in order to study the laws of a class of phenomena, these phenomena are simply regarded by themselves. The implication of Nature, as a subordinate element, within souls has not been denied, but in practice, and for practice, ignored. And, when we hear of a time before organisms existed, that, in the first place, should mean organisms of the kind that we know; and it should be said merely with regard to one part of the Universe. Or, at all events, it is not a statement of the actual history of the ultimate Reality, but is a convenient method of considering certain facts apart from others. And thus, while metaphysics and natural science keep each to its own business, a collision is impossible. Neither needs defence against the other, except through misunderstanding. .

But that misunderstandings on both sides have been too often provoked I think no one can deny. Too often the science of mere Nature, forgetting its own limits and false to its true aims, attempts to speak about first principles. It becomes transscendant, and offers us a dogmatic and uncritical metaphysics. Thus to assert that, in the history of the Universe at large, matter came before mind, is to place development and succession within the Absolute (Chapter xxvi.), and is to make real outside the Whole a mere element in its being. And such a doctrine not only is *not* natural science, but, even if we suppose it otherwise to have any value, for that science, at least, it is worthless. For assume that force matter and motion are more than mere working ideas, inconsistent but useful—will they, on that assumption, work better? If you, after all, are going to use them solely for the interpretation of spatial events, then, if they *are* absolute truth, that is nothing to you. This absolute truth you must in any case *apply* as a mere system of the conditions of the occurrence of phenomena; and for that purpose anything, which you apply, is the same, if it does the same work. But I think the failure of natural science (so far as it does fail) to maintain its own position, is not hard to understand. It seems produced by more than one cause. There is first a vague notion that absolute truth must be pursued by every kind of special science. There is inability to perceive that, in such a science, something less is all that we can use, and therefore all that we should want. But this unfortunately is not all. For metaphysics itself, by its interference with physical science, has induced that to act, as it thinks, in self-defence, and has led it, in so doing, to become metaphysical. And this interference of metaphysics I would admit and deplore, as the result and the parent of most injurious misunderstanding. Not only have there been efforts at construction which have led to no positive result, but there have been attacks on the sciences which have pushed into abuse a legitimate function. For, as against natural science, the duty of metaphysics is limited. So long as that science keeps merely to the sphere of phenomena and the laws of their occurrence, metaphysics has no right to a single word of criticism. Criticism begins when what is relative—mere ways of appearance—is, unconsciously or consciously, offered as more. And I do not doubt that there are doctrines,

now made use of in science, which on this ground
invite metaphysical correction, and on which it
might here be instructive to dwell. But for want
of competence and want of space, and, more than
all perhaps from the fear of being misunderstood, I
think it better to pass on. There are further questions about Nature more important by far for our
general enquiry.

Is the extended world one, and, if so, in what
sense? We discussed, in Chapter xviii., the unity
of time, and it is needful to recall the conclusion we reached. We agreed that all times have
a unity in the Absolute, but, when we asked if that
unity itself must be temporal, our answer was negative. We found that the many time-series are not
related in time. They do not make parts of one
series and whole of succession; but, on the contrary,
their interrelation and unity falls outside of time.
And, in the case of extension, the like considerations
produce a like result. The physical world is not
one in the sense of possessing a physical unity.
There may be any number of material worlds, not
related in space, and by consequence not exclusive
of, and repellent to, each other.

It appears, at first, as if all the extended was part
of one space. For all spaces, and, if so, all material
objects, seem spatially related. And such an inter-
relation would, of course, make them members in
one extended whole. But this belief, when we reflect, begins instantly to vanish. Nature in my
dreams (for example) possesses extension, and yet
spatially it is not one with my physical world. And
in imagination and in thought we have countless
existences, material and extended, which stand in no
spatial connection with each other or with the world
which I perceive. And it is idle to reply that these
bodies and their arrangements are unreal, unless we
are sure of the sense which we give to reality. For

that these all exist is quite clear; and, if they have not got extension, they are all able, at least, to appear with it and to show it. Their extension and their materiality is, in short, a palpable fact, while, on the other hand, their several arrangements are not inter-related in space. And, since in the Absolute these, of course, possess a unity, we must conclude that the unity is not material. In coming together their extensional character is transmuted. There are a variety of spatial systems, independent of each other, and each changed beyond itself, when absorbed in the one non-spatial system. Thus, with regard to their unity, Space and Time have similar characters (pp. 210–214).

That which for ordinary purposes I call "real" Nature, is the extended world so far as related to my body. What forms a spatial system with that body has "real" extension. But even "my body" is ambiguous, for the body, which I imagine, may have no spatial relation to the body which I perceive. And perception too can be illusive, for my own body in dreams is not the same thing with my true "real" body, nor does it enter with it into any one spatial arrangement. And what in the end I mean by my "real" body, seems to be this. I make a spatial construction from my body, as it comes to me when awake. This and the extended which will form a single system of spatial relations together with this, I consider as real.[1] And whatever extension falls outside of this one system of interrelation,

[1] With regard to the past and future of my "real" body and its "real" world, it is hard to say whether, and in what sense, these are supposed to have spatial connection with the present. What we commonly think on this subject is, I should say, a mere mass of inconsistency. There is another point, on which it would be interesting to develope the doctrine of the text, by asking how we distinguish our waking state. But an answer to this question is, I think, not called for here. I have also not referred to insanity and other abnormal states. But their bearing here is obvious.

I set down as "imaginary." And, as a mere subordinate point of view, this may do very well. But it is quite another thing on such a ground to deny existence in the Absolute to every other spatial system. For we have the "imaginary" extension on our hands as a fact which remains, and which should cause us to hesitate. And, when we reflect, we see clearly that a variety of physical arrangements may exist without anything like spatial inter-relation. They will have their unity in the Whole, but no connections in space each outside its own proper system of matter. And Nature therefore cannot properly be called a single world, in the sense of possessing a spatial unity.

Thus we might have any number of physical systems, standing independent of spatial relations with each other. And we may go on from this to consider another point of interest. Such diverse worlds of matter might to any extent still act on and influence one another. But, to speak strictly, they could not inter-penetrate at any point. Their interaction, however intimate, could not be called penetration; though, in itself and in its effects, it might involve a closer unity. Their spaces always would remain apart, and spatial contact would be impossible. But inside each world the case, as to penetration, might be different. The penetration of one thing by another might there even be usual; and I will try to show briefly that this presents no difficulty.

The idea of a Nature made up of solid matter, interspaced with an absolute void, has been inherited, I presume, from Greek metaphysics. And, I think, for the most part we hardly realize how entirely this view lies at the mercy of criticism. I am speaking, not of physics and the principles employed by physics, but of what may be called the metaphysics of the literary market-place. And the notion common there, that one extended thing cannot penetrate another, rests mainly on prejudice. For whether matter, conceivably and possibly, can enter into matter or not, depends entirely on the sense in which matter is taken. Penetration means the abolition of spatial distinction, and we may hence define matter in such a way that, with loss of spatial distinction, itself would be abolished. If, that is to say, pieces of matter are so one thing with their extensions as, apart from these, to keep no individual difference—then these pieces obviously cannot penetrate; but, otherwise, they may. This seems to me clear, and I will go on to explain it shortly.

It is certain first of all that two parts of one space cannot penetrate each other. For, though these two parts must have some qualities beside their mere extension (Chapter iii.), such bare qualities are not enough. Even if you suppose that a change has forced both sets of qualities to belong to one single extension, you will after all have not got two extended things in one. For you will not have two extended things, since one will have vanished. And, hence, penetration, implying the existence of both, has become a word without meaning. But the case is altered, if we consider two pieces of some element more concrete than space. Let us assume with these, first, that their other qualities, which serve to divide and distinguish them, still depend on extension—then, so far, these things still cannot penetrate each other. For, as before, in the one space you would not have *two* things, since (by the assumption) one thing has lost separate existence. But now the whole question is whether with matter this assumption is true, whether in Nature, that is, qualities are actually so to be identified with extension. And, for myself, I find no reason to think that this is so. If in two parts of one extended there are distinctions sufficient to individualize, and to keep these two things still two, when their separate spaces are gone—then clearly these two things may be compenetrable. For penetration is the survival of distinct existence notwithstanding identification in space. And thus the whole question really turns on the possibility of such a survival. Cannot, in other words, two things still be two, though their extensions have become one?

We have no right then (until this possibility is got rid of) to take the parts of each physical world as essentially exclusive. We may without contradiction consider bodies as not resisting other bodies. We may take them as standing towards one another, under certain conditions, as relative vacua, and as freely compenetrable. And, if in this way we gain no positive advantage, we at least escape from the absurdity, and even the scandal, of an absolute vacuum.[1]

We have seen that, except in the Absolute in which Nature is merged, we have no right to assert that all Nature has unity. I will now add a few words on some other points which may call for explanation. We may be asked, for example, whether Nature is finite or infinite; and we may first endeavour to clear our ideas on this subject. There is of course, as we know, a great difficulty on either side. If Nature is infinite, we have the absurdity of a something which exists, and still does not exist. For actual existence is, obviously, all finite. But,

---

[1] I would repeat that in the above remarks I am not trying to say anything against the ideas used in physics, and against the apparent attempt there to compromise between something and nothing. In a phenomenal science it is obvious that no more than a relative vacuum is wanted. More could not possibly be *used*, supposing that in fact more *existed*. In any case for metaphysics an absolute vacuum is nonsense. Like a mere piece of empty Time, it is a sheer self-contradiction; for it presupposes certain internal distinctions, and then in the same breath denies them.

on the other hand, if Nature is finite, then Nature must have an end; and this again is impossible. For a limit of extension must be relative to extension beyond. And to fall back on empty space, will not help us at all. For this (itself a mere absurdity) repeats the dilemma in an aggravated form. It is itself both something and nothing, is essentially limited and yet, on the other side, without end.

But we cannot escape the conclusion that Nature is infinite. And this will be true not of *our* physical system alone, but of every other extended world which can possibly exist. None is limited but by an end over which it is constantly in the act of passing. Nor does this hold only with regard to present existence, for the past and future of these worlds has also no fixed boundary in space. Nor, once again, is this a character peculiar to the extended. Any finite whole, with its incomplete conjunction of qualities and relations, entails a process of indefinite transition beyond its limits as a consequence. But with the extended, more than anything, this self-transcendence is obvious. Every physical world is, essentially and necessarily, infinite.

But, in saying this, we do not mean that, at any given moment, such worlds possess more than a given amount of existence. Such an assertion once again would have no meaning. It would be once more the endeavour to be something and yet nothing, and to find an existence which does not exist. And thus we are forced to maintain that every Nature must be finite. The dilemma stares us in the face, and brings home to us the fact that all Nature, as such, is an untrue appearance. It is the way in which a mere part of the Reality shows itself, a way essential and true when taken up into and transmuted by a fuller totality, but, considered by itself, inconsistent and lapsing beyond its own being. The essence of the relative is to have and to come to an end, but, at the same time, to end always in a self-

contradiction.   Again the infinity of Nature, its
extension beyond all limits, we might call Nature's
effort to end itself as Nature.   It shows in this its
ideality, its instability and transitoriness, and its
constant passage of itself into that which transcends it.   In its isolation as a phenomenon Nature
is both finite and infinite, and so proclaims itself
untrue.   And, when this contradiction is solved,
both its characters disappear into something beyond
both.   And it is perhaps not necessary to dwell
further on the infinity of Nature.

And, passing next to the question of what is
called Uniformity, I shall dismiss this almost at
once.   For there is, in part, no necessity for metaphysics to deal with it, and, in part, we must return
to it in the following chapter.   But, however uniformity is understood, in the main we must be
sceptical, and stand aloof.   I do not see how it can
be shown that the amount of matter and motion,
whether in any one world or in all, remains always
the same.   Nor do I understand how we can know
that any world remains the same in its sensible
qualities.   As long as, on the one side, the Absolute
preserves its identity, and, on the other side, the
realms of phenomena remain in order, all our postulates are satisfied.   This order in the world need
not mean that, in each Nature, the same characters
remain.   It implies, in the first place, that all changes
are subject to the identity of the one Reality.   But
that by itself seems consistent with almost indefinite
variation in the several worlds.   And, in the second
place, order must involve the possibility of experience
in finite subjects.   Order, therefore, excludes all
change which would make each world unintelligible
through want of stability.   But this stability, in the
end, does not seem to require more than a limited
amount of identity, existing from time to time in
the sensations which happen.   And, thirdly, in

phenomenal sequence the law of Causation must remain unbroken. But this, again, comes to very little. For the law of Causation does not assert that in existence we have always the same causes and effects. It insists only that, given one, we must inevitably have the other. And thus the Uniformity of Nature cannot warrant the assumption that the world of sense is uniform. Its guarantee is in that respect partly non-existent, and partly hypothetical.[1]

There are other questions as to Nature which will engage us later on, and we may here bring the present chapter to a close. We have found that Nature by itself has no reality. It exists only as a form of appearance within the Absolute. In its isolation from that whole of feeling and experience it is an untrue abstraction ; and in life this narrow view of Nature (as we saw) is not consistently maintained. But, for physical science, the separation of one element from the whole is both justifiable and necessary. In order to understand the co-existence and sequence of phenomena in space, the conditions of these are made objects of independent study. But to take such conditions for hard realities standing by themselves, is to deviate into uncritical and barbarous metaphysics.

Nature apart from and outside of the Absolute is nothing. It has its being in that process of intestine division, through which the whole world of appearance consists. And in this realm, where aspects fall asunder, where being is distinguished from thought, and the self from the not-self, Nature marks one extreme. It is the aspect most opposed to self-dependence and unity. It is the world of those particulars which stand furthest from possessing individuality, and we may call it the region of externality and chance. Compulsion from the out-

---

[1] For a further consideration of these points see Chapter xxiii.

side, and a movement not their own, is the law of
its elements; and its events seem devoid of an internal meaning.   To exist and to happen, and yet
not to realize an end, or as a member to subserve
some ideal whole, we saw (Chapter xix.) was to be
contingent.   And in the mere physical world the
nearest approach to this character can be found.
But we can deal better with such questions in a
later context.   We shall have hereafter to discuss
the connection of soul with body, and the existence
of a system of ends in Nature.   The work of this
chapter has been done, if we have been able to show
the subordination of Nature as one element within
the Whole.

CHAPTER XXIII.

BODY AND SOUL.

WITH the subject of this chapter we seem to have arrived at a hopeless difficulty. The relation of body to soul presents a problem which experience seems to show is really not soluble. And I may say at once that I accept and endorse this result. It seems to me impossible to explain how precisely, in the end, these two forms of existence stand one to the other. But in this inability I find a confirmation of our general doctrine as to the nature of Reality. For body and soul are mere appearances, distinctions set up and held apart in the Whole. And fully to understand the relation between them would be, in the end, to grasp how they came together into one. And, since this is impossible for our knowledge, any view about their connection remains imperfect.

But this failure to comprehend gives no ground for an objection against our Absolute. It is no disproof of a theory (I must repeat this) that, before some questions as to " How," it is forced to remain dumb. For you do not throw doubt on a view till you find inconsistency. If the general account is such that it is bound to solve this or that problem, then such a problem, left outside, is a serious objection. And things are still worse where there are aspects which positively collide with the main conclusion. But neither of these grounds of objection holds good against ourselves. Upon the view which we have found to be true of the Absolute, we

can see how and why some questions cannot possibly
be answered. And in particular this relation of
body and soul offers nothing inconsistent with our
general doctrine. My principal object here will be
to make this last point good. And we shall find
that neither body nor soul, nor the connection
between them, can furnish any ground of objection
against our Absolute.

The difficulties, which have arisen, are due mainly
to one cause. Body and soul have been set up as
independent realities. They have been taken to be
things, whose kinds are different, and which have
existence each by itself, and each in its own right.
And then, of course, their connection becomes incomprehensible, and we strive in vain to see how
one can influence the other. And at last, disgusted
by our failure, we perhaps resolve to deny wholly
the existence of this influence. We may take refuge
in two series of indifferent events, which seem to
affect one another while, in fact, merely running
side by side. And, because their conjunction can
scarcely be bare coincidence, we are driven, after
all, to admit some kind of connection. The connection is now viewed as indirect, and as dependent on
something else to which both series belong. But,
w..ile each side retains its reality and self-subsist-
ence, they, of course, cannot come together ; and,
on the other hand, if they come together, it is because they have been transformed, and are not
things, but appearances. Still this last is a conclusion for which many of us are not prepared. If
soul and body are not two " things," the mistake,
we fancy, has lain wholly on the side of the soul.
For the body at all events seems a thing, while the
soul is unsubstantial. And so, dropping influence
altogether, we make the soul a kind of adjective
supported by the body. Or, since, after all, adjectives must qualify their substantives, we turn the
soul into a kind of immaterial secretion, ejected and,

because "out," making no difference to the organ. Nor do we always desert this view when " matter " has itself been discovered to be merely phenomenal. It is common first to admit that body is mere sensation and idea, and still to treat it as wholly independent of the soul, while the soul remains its non-physical and irrelevant secretion.

But I shall make no attempt to state the various theories as to the nature and relations of body and soul, and I shall not criticise in detail views, from most of which we could learn nothing. It will be clear at once, from the results of preceding chapters, that neither body nor soul can be more than appearance. And I will attempt forthwith to point out the peculiar nature of each, and the manner in which they are connected with, and influence, each other. It would be useless to touch the second question, until we have endeavoured to get our minds clear on the first.

What is a body ? In our last chapter we have anticipated the answer. A body is a part of the physical world, and we have seen that Nature by itself is wholly unreal. It was an aspect of the Whole, set apart by abstraction, and, for some purposes, taken as independent reality. So that, in saying that a body is one piece of Nature, we have at once pointed out that it is no more than appearance. It is an intellectual construction out of material which is not self-subsistent. This is its general character as physical; but, as to the special position given to the organic by natural science, I prefer to say nothing. It is, for us, an (undefined) arrangement possessing temporal continuity,[1] and a certain amount of identity in quality, the degree and nature of which last I cannot attempt to fix.

---

[1] I shall have to say something more on this point lower down. The bodies which we know have also continuity in space. Whether this is essential will be discussed hereafter.

And I think, for metaphysics, it is better also to make relation to a soul essential for a body (Chapter xxii.). But what concerns us at this moment is, rather, to insist on its phenomenal character. The materials, of which it is made, are inseparably implicated with sensation and feeling. They are divorced from this given whole by a process, which is necessary, but yet is full of contradictions. The physical world, taken as separate, involves the relation of unknown to unknown, and of these make-shift materials the particular body is built. It is a construction riddled by inconsistencies, a working point of view, which is of course quite indispensable, but which cannot justify a claim to be more than appearance.

And the soul is clearly no more self-subsistent than the body. It is, on its side also, a purely phenomenal existence, an appearance incomplete and inconsistent, and with no power to maintain itself as an independent " thing." The criticism of our First Book has destroyed every claim of the self to be, or to correspond to, true reality. And the only task here before us is, accepting this result, to attempt to fix clearly the meaning of a soul. I will first make a brief statement, and then endeavour to explain it and to defend it against objections. The soul[1] is a finite centre of immediate experience, possessed of a certain temporal continuity of exist-ence, and again of a certain identity in character. And the word "immediate" is emphatic. The soul is a particular group of psychical events, so far as these events are taken merely as happening in time. It excludes consideration of their content, so far as this content (whether in thought or volition or feeling) qualifies something beyond the serial exist-ence of these events. Take the whole experience of

---

[1] Cp. *Mind*, XII. 355 (No. 47).

any moment, one entire "this-now," as it comes,
regard that experience as changed and as continued
in time, consider its character solely as happening,
and, again, as further influencing the course of its
own changes—this is perhaps the readiest way of
defining a soul.[1] But I must endeavour to draw
this out, and briefly to explain it.

It is not enough to be clear that the soul is phenomenal, in the sense of being something which, as
such, fails to reach true reality. For, unless we
perceive to some extent how it stands towards other
sides of the Universe, we are likely to end in complete bewilderment. And a frequent error is to
define what is "psychical" so widely as to exclude
any chance of a rational result. For all objects and
aims, which come before me, are in one sense the
states of my soul. Hence, if this sense is not excluded, my body and the whole world become
"psychical" phenomena ; and amid this confusion
my soul itself seeks an unintelligible place as one
state of itself. What is most important is to distinguish the soul's existence from what fills it, and
yet there are few points, perhaps, on which neglect
is more common. And we may bring the question
home thus. If we were to assume (Chapter xxvii.)
that in the Universe there is nothing beyond souls,
still within these souls the same problem would call
for solution. We should still have to find a place
for the existence of soul, as distinct both from body
and from other aspects of the world.

It may assist us in perceiving both what the soul
is, and again what it is not, if we view the question
from two sides. Let us look at it, first, from the
experience of an individual person, and then, afterwards, let us consider the same thing from outside,

---

[1] I have for the moment excluded relation to a body. It is
better not to define the soul as "the facts immediately experienced within one organism" for several reasons. I shall return
to this point.

and from the ground of an admitted plurality of
souls.

If then, beginning from within, I take my whole
given experience at any one moment, and if I regard
a single "this-now," as it comes in feeling and is
"mine,"—may I suppose that in this I have found
my true soul ?   Clearly not so, for (to go no farther)
such existence is too fleeting. My soul (I should
reply) is not merely the something of one moment,
but it must endure for a time and must preserve its
self-sameness.   I do not mean that it must itself be
self-conscious of identity, for that assertion would
carry us too far on the other side.   And as to the
amount of continuity and of self-same character
which is wanted, I am saying nothing here.   I shall
touch later on both these questions, so far as is
necessary, and for the present will confine myself to
the general result.   The existence of a soul must
endure through more than one presentation ; and
hence experience, if immediate and given and not
transcending the moment, is less than my soul.

But if, still keeping to "experience," we take it
in another sense, we none the less are thwarted.
For experience now is as much too wide as before it
was too narrow.   The whole contents of my experience—it makes no difference here whether I
myself or another person considers them—cannot
possibly be my soul, unless my soul is to be as large
as the total Universe.   For other bodies and souls,
and God himself, are (so far as I know them) all
states of my mind, and in this sense make part of
my particular being.   And we are led at once to
the distinction, which we noticed before (Chapter
xxi.), between the diverse aspects of content and
of psychical existence.   Our experience in short is,
essentially and very largely, ideal.   It shows an ideal
process which, beginning from the unity of feeling,
produces the differences of self and not-self, and
separates the divisions of the world from themselves

and from me.[1] All this wealth, that is, subsists through a divorce between the sides of existence and character. What is *meant* by any one of the portions of my world is emphatically not a mere fact of experience. If you take it there, as it exists there, it always is something, but this something can never be the object in question. We may use as an example (if you please) my horse or my own body. Both of these must, for me at least, be nothing but " experience "; for, what I do not "experience," to me must be nothing. And, if you push home the question as to their given existence, you can find it nowhere except in a state of my soul. When I perceive them, or think of them, there is, so far, no discoverable "fact" outside of my psychical condition. But such a " fact " is for me not the " fact " of my horse or, again, of my body. Their true existence is not that which is present *in* my mind, but rather, as perhaps we should say, present *to* it. Their existence is a content which works apart from, and is irreconcilable with, its own psychical being ; it is a "what" discrepant with, and transcending its "that." We may put it shortly by saying that the true fact is fact, only so far as it is ideal. Hence the Universe and its objects must not be called states of my soul. Indeed it would be better to affirm that these objects exist, so far as the psychical states do *not* exist. For such experience of objects is possible, only so far as the meaning breaks loose from the given existence, and has, so regarded, broken this existence in pieces. And we may state the conclusion thus. If my psychical state does not exist, then the object is destroyed ; but, again, unless my state could, *as such*, perish, no object would exist. The two sides of fact, and of content working loose from that fact, are essential to each other. But the essence of the second is disruption of a " what " from a " that,"

---

[1] I have tried to sketch the main development in *Mind*, as referred to above.

while in the union of these aspects the former has its life.

The soul *is* not the contents which appear in its states, but, on the other hand, without them it would not be itself. For it is qualified essentially by the presence of these contents. Thus a man, we may say, is not what he thinks of; and yet he is the man he is, because of what he thinks of. And the ideal processes of the content have necessarily an aspect of psychical change. Those connections, which have nothing which is personal to myself, cause a sequence of my states when they happen within me. Thus a principle, of logic or morality, works in my mind. This principle is most certainly not a part of my soul, and yet it makes a great difference to the sequence of my states. I shall hereafter return to this point, but it would belong to psychology to develope the subject in detail. We should have there to point out, and to classify, the causes which affect the succession of psychical phenomena.[1] It is enough here to have laid stress on an essential distinction. Ideal contents appear in, and affect, my existence, but still, for all that, we cannot call them my soul.

We have now been led to two results. The soul is certainly not all that which is present in experience, nor, on the other hand, can it consist in mere experience itself. It cannot be actual feeling, or that immediate unity of quality and being which comes in the "this" (Chapter xix.). The soul is not these things, and we must now try to say what it is. It is one of these same personal centres, not taken at an instant, but regarded as a "thing." It is a feeling whole which is considered to continue in time, and to maintain a certain sameness. And the soul is, therefore, not presented fact, but is an ideal construction which transcends what is given. It is

---

[1] I have said something on this in *Mind*, XII. 362–3

emphatically the result of an ideal process; but this process, on the other hand, has been arbitrarily arrested at a very low point. Take a fleeting moment of your "given," and then, from the basis of a personal identity of feeling, enlarge this moment by other moments and build up a "thing." Idealize "experience," so as to make its past one reality with its present, and so as to give its history a place in the fixed temporal order. Resolve its contingency enough to view it as a series of events, which have causal connections both without and within. But, having gone so far, pause, and call a halt to your process, or, having got to a soul, you will be hurried beyond it. And, to keep your soul, you must remain fixed in a posture of inconsistency. For, like every other "thing" in time, the soul is essentially ideal. It has transcended the given moment, and has spread out its existence beyond that which is "actual" or could ever be experienced. And by its relations and connections of coexistence and sequence, and by its subjection to "laws," it has raised itself into the world of eternal verity. But to persist in this process of life would be suicide. Its advance would force you to lose hold altogether on "existence," and, with that loss, to forfeit individual selfness. And hence, on the other side, the soul clings to its being in time, and still reaches after the unbroken unity of content with reality. Its contents, therefore, are allowed only to qualify the series of temporal events. And this result is a mere compromise. Hence the soul persists through a contrivance, and through the application of matter to a particular purpose. And, because this application is founded on and limited by no principle, the soul in the end must be judged to be rooted in artifice. It is a series, which depends on ideal transcendence, and yet desires to be taken as sensible fact. And its inconsistency is now made manifest in its use of its contents. These (we have seen) are as wide as the Universe itself, and, on this account, they are unable to qualify the soul. And yet, on the other hand, they must do so, if the soul is to have the quality which makes it itself. Hence these contents must be taken from one side of their being, and the other side, for a particular end, is struck out. In order for the soul to exist, "experience" must be mutilated. It must be *regarded* so far as it makes a difference to that series of events which is taken as a soul; it must be *considered* just to that extent to which it serves as the adjective of a temporal series—serves to make the "thisness" of the series of a certain kind, and to modify its past and its future "thisness" But, beyond this, experience is taken merely to be present to the soul and operative within it. And the soul exists precisely so far as the abstraction is maintained. Its life endures only so long as a particular purpose holds. And thus it consists in a convenient but one-sided representation of facts, and has no claim to be more than a useful appearance.

In brief, because the existence of the soul is not experienced and not given, because it is made by, and consists in, transcendence of the "present," and because its content is obviously never one with its being, its "what" always in flagrant discrepancy with its "that"—therefore its whole position is throughout inconsistent and untenable. It is an arrangement natural and necessary, but for all that phenomenal and illusive, a makeshift, valuable but still not genuine reality. And, looked at by itself, the soul is an abstraction and mutilation. It is the arbitrary use of material for a particular purpose. And it persists only by refusing to see more in itself than subserves its own existence.

It may be instructive, before we go on, to regard the same question from the side of the Absolute. Let us, for the sake of argument, assume that in the Whole there is no material which is not a state of some soul (Chapter xxvii). From this we might be tempted to conclude that these souls are the Reality, or at least must be real. But that conclusion would be false, for the souls would fall within the realm of appearance and error. They would be, but, as such, they would not have reality. They would require a resolution and a re-composition, in which their individualities would be transmuted and absorbed (Chapter xvi.). For we have seen that the Absolute is the union of content and existence. It stands at a level above, and comprehending, those distinctions and relations in which the imperfect unity of feeling is dissipated. Let us then take the indefinite plurality of the " this-nows," or immediate experiences, as the basis and starting-point, and, on the other side, let us take the Absolute as the end, and let us view the region between as a process from the first to the second. It will be a field of struggle in which content is divorced from, and strives once more towards, unity with being. Our assumption in part will be false, since (as we have seen) the immediately given is already inconsistent.[1] But, in order to instruct ourselves, let us suppose here that the " fact " of experience is real, and that, above it once more, the Absolute gains higher reality—still where is the soul ? The soul is not immediate experience, for that comes given at one moment ; and the soul still less can be the perfected union of all being and content. This is obvious, and, if so, the soul must fall in the middle-space of error and appearance. It is the ideal manufacture of one extreme with a view to reach the other, a manufacture suspended at a very low stage, and suspended on no defensible ground. The plurality of souls in the Absolute is, therefore, appearance, and their existence is not genuine. But

---

[1] Compare Chapters xv., xix., xxi.

because the upward struggle of the content to ideal
perfection, having made these souls, still rises both
in them and above them, they, in themselves, are
nearer the level of the lower reality.   The first and
transitory union of existence and content is, with
souls, less profoundly broken up and destroyed.
And hence souls, taken as things with a place in
the time-series, are said to be facts and actually to
exist.   Nay on their existence, in a sense, all reality
depends.   For the higher process is carried on in a
special relation with these lower results; and thus,
while moving in *its* way, it affects the souls in *their*
way ; and thus everything happens *in* souls, and
everything *is* their states.   And this arrangement
seems necessary ; but on the other hand, if we view
it from the side of the Absolute, it is plainly self-
inconsistent.   To gain consistency and truth it must
be merged, and recomposed in a result in which
its specialty must vanish.   Souls, like their bodies,
are, as such, nothing more than appearance.

And, that we may realize this more clearly, we find
ourselves turning in a circular maze.   Just as the
body was for Nature, and upon the other hand
Nature merely through relation to a body, so in a
different fashion it is with the soul.   For thought is
a state of souls, and therefore is made by them,
while, upon its side, the soul is a product of thought.
The "thing," existing in time and possessor of
"states," is made what it is by ideal construction.
But this construction itself appears to depend on a
psychical centre, and to exist merely as its "state."
And such a circle seems vicious.   Again, the body
is dependent on the soul, for the whole of its
material comes by way of sensation, and its identity
is built up by ideal construction.   And yet this
manufacture takes place as an event in a soul, a soul
which, further, exists only in relation to a body.[1]

· [1] I am not denying here the *possibility* of soul without body.
See below, p. 340.

But, where we move in circles like these, and where, pushing home our enquiries, we can find nothing but the relation of unknown to unknown—the conclusion is certain. We are in the realm of appearance, of phenomena made by disruption of content from being, arrangements which may represent, but which *are* not, reality. Such ways of understanding are forced on us by the nature of the Universe, and assuredly they possess their own worth for the Absolute (Chapter xxiv.). But, as themselves and as they come to us, they are no less certainly appearance. So far as we know them, they are but inconsistent constructions; and, beyond our knowledge, they are forthwith beyond themselves. The underlying and superior reality in each case we have no right to call either a body or a soul. For, in becoming more, each loses its title to that name. The body and soul are, in brief, phenomenal arrangements, which take their proper place in the constructed series of events ; and, in that character, they are both alike defensible and necessary. But neither is real in the end, each is merely phenomenal, and one has no title to fact which is not owned by the other.

We have seen, so far, that soul and body are, each alike, phenomenal constructions, and we must next go on to point out the connection between them. But, in order to clear the ground, I will first attempt to dispose of several objections. (1) It will be urged against the phenomenal view of the soul that, upon this, the soul loses independent existence. If it is no more than a series of psychical events, it becomes an appendage to the permanent body. For a psychical series, we shall be told, has no inherent bond of continuity ; nor is it, even as a matter of fact, continuous ; nor, again, does it offer anything of which we can predicate " dispositions." Hence, if phenomenal, the soul sinks to be an adjective of the

body. (2) And, from another side, we shall hear it
argued that the psychical series demands, as its
condition, a transcendent soul or Ego, and indeed
without this is unintelligible. (3) And, in the third
place, we may be assured that some psychical fact
is given which contains more than phenomena, and
that hence the soul has by us been defined erroneously. I must endeavour to say something on
these objections in their order.

I. I shall have to show lower down that it is
impossible to treat soul as the bare adjective of body,
and I shall therefore say nothing on that point at
present. "But why," I may be asked, "not at least
assist yourself with the body? Why strain yourself to define the soul in mere psychical terms?
Would it not be better to call a soul those psychical
facts from time to time experienced within one
organism?" I am forced to reply in the negative.
Such a definition would, in psychology, perhaps not
take us wrong, but, for all that, it remains incorrect
and indefensible. For, with lower organisms especially, it is not so easy to fix the limits of a
single organism. And, again further, we might
perhaps wish to define the organism by its relation
to a single soul; and, if so, we should have fallen
into a vicious circle. Nor is it, once more, even
certain that the identities of soul and of body coincide. We, I presume, are not sure that one soul
might not have a succession of bodies. And, in any
case, we certainly do not know that one organism can
be organic to no more than one soul. There might
be more than one psychical centre at one time
within the same body, and several bodies might be
organs to a higher unknown soul. And, even if we
disregard these possibilities as merely theoretical, we
have still to deal with the facts of mental disease.
It seems at best doubtful if in some cases the soul
can be said to have continuous unity, or if it ought
strictly to be called single. And then, finally, there

remains the question, to which we shall return, whether an organism is necessary in all cases for the existence of a soul. We have perhaps with this justified our refusal to introduce body into our definition of soul.[1]

But without this introduction what becomes of the soul ? " What," we shall be asked, " at any time can you say that the soul *is*, more especially at those times when nothing psychical exists ? And where will you place the dispositions and acquired tendencies of the soul ? For, in the first place, the psychical series is not unbroken, and, in the second place, dispositions are not psychical events. Are you then not forced back to the body as the one continuous substrate ? " This is a serious objection, and, though our answer to it may prove sufficient, I think no answer can quite satisfy.

I must begin by denying a principle, or, as it seems to me, a prejudice with regard to continuity. Real existence (we must allow) either is or is not; and hence I agree also that, if in time, it cannot cease and reappear, and that it must, therefore, be continuous. But, on the other hand, we have proved that reality does not exist in time, but only appears there. What we find in time is mere appearance; and with regard to appearance I know no reason why *it* should not cease and reappear without for-

---

[1] I may be allowed to say here why I think such phrases as "individual," or "individualistic point of view," cannot serve to fix the definition of "soul." To regard a centre of experience from an individualistic point of view may *mean* to view it as a series of psychical events. But if so, the meaning is only meant, and is certainly not stated. And the term "individual" sins by excess as well as by defect. For it may stand for "Monad" or "Ego"; and in this case the soul is at once more than phenomenal, and we have on our hands the relation of its plurality to the one Monad—a difficulty which, as we have seen, is insuperable. On the other hand "individualistic" might imply that the soul's contents do not, in any sense, transcend its private existence. The term, in short, requires definition, quite as much as does the object which it is used to define.

feiting identity.   A phenomenon *A* is produced by
certain conditions, which then are modified.   Upon
this, *A*, wholly or partially, retires from existence,
but, on another change, shows itself partly or in full.
A disappears into conditions which, even as such,
need not persist ; but, when the proper circumstances
are re-created, *A* exists once again.   Shall we assert
that, if so, *A*'s identity is gone?   I do not know on
what principle.   Or shall we insist that, at least in
the meantime, *A* cannot be said to be?   But it
seems not clear on what ground.   If we take such
common examples as a rainbow, or a waterfall, or
the change of water into ice, we seek in vain for
any principle but that of working convenience.   We
feel sure that material atoms and their motion
continue unaltered, and that their existence, if
broken, would be utterly destroyed.   But, unless we
falsely take these atoms and their motion for ultimate reality, we are resting here on no basis beyond
practical utility.   And even here some of us are too
inclined to lapse into an easy-going belief in the
" potential."   But, as soon as these atoms are left
behind, can we even pretend to have any principle?
We call an organism identical, though we do not
suppose that its atoms have persisted.   It is identical because its quality is (more or less) the same, and
because that quality has been (more or less) all the
time there.   But why an interval must be fatal, is
surely far from evident.   And, in fact, we are driven
to the conclusion that we are arguing without any
rational ground.   As soon as an existence in time is
perceived to be appearance, we can find no reason
why it should not lapse, and again be created.   And
with an organism, where even the matter is not supposed to persist, we seem to have deserted every
show of principle.[1]

   There is a further point which, before proceeding,

---

[1] On the subject of Identity see more below.   And compare
Chapter ix.

we may do well to notice. We saw in the last chapter
that part of Nature could hardly be said to have
actual existence (p. 277). Some of it seemed (at least
at some times) to be only hypothetical or barely
potential ; and I would urge this consideration here
with regard to the organism. My body is to be
real because it exists continuously ; but, if, on the
other hand, that existence must be actual, can we
call it continuous ? The essential qualities of my
body (whatever these are) are certainly not, so far as
we know, perceived always. But, if so, and if they
exist sometimes not for perception but for thought,
then most assuredly sometimes they do not exist as
such, and hence their continuity is broken. Thus
we have been forced to another very serious
admission. We not only are ignorant why continuity in time should be essential, but, so far as the
organism goes, we do not know that it possesses
such continuity. It seems rather to exist at times
potentially and merely in its conditions. This is a
sort of existence which we shall discuss in the following chapter, but it is at all events *not* existence
actual and proper.

After these more general remarks we may proceed
to the difficulties urged against our view of the soul.
We have defined the soul as a series of psychical
events, and it has been objected that, if so, we cannot say what the soul is at any one time. But at
any one time, I reply, the soul is the present *datum*
of psychical fact, plus its actual past and its conditional future. Or, until the last phrase has been
explained, we may content ourselves with saying
that the soul *is* those psychical events, which it both
is now and has been. And this account, I admit,
qualifies something by adjectives which are not, and
to offer it as an expression of ultimate truth would
be wholly indefensible. But then the soul, I must
repeat, is itself not ultimate fact. It is appearance,

and any description of it must contain inconsistency.
And, if any one objects, he may be invited to define,
for example, a body moving at a certain rate, and to
define it without predicating of the present what is
either past or future.   And, if he will attempt this,
he will, I think, perhaps tend to lose confidence.

But we have, so far, not said what we mean by
" dispositions." A soul after all, we shall be reminded,
possesses a character, if not original, at least acquired.
And we certainly say that it *is*, because of that which
we expect of it.   The soul's habits and tendencies
are essential to its nature, and, on the other hand,
they cannot be psychical events.   Hence (the objection goes on to urge) they are not psychical at all, but
merely physical facts.   Now to this I reply first
that a disposition may be " physical," and may, for
all that, be still not an actual fact.   Until I see it
defined so as to exclude reference to any past or
future, and freed from every sort of implication with
the conditional and potential, I shall not allow that
it has been translated into physical fact.   But, even in
that case, I should not accept the translation, for I
consider that we have a right everywhere for the
sake of convenience to use the " conditional."   Into
the proper meaning of this term I shall enquire in the
next chapter, but I will try to state briefly here how
we apply it to the soul.   In saying that the soul has
a disposition of a certain kind, we take the present
and past psychical facts as the subject, and we predicate of this subject other psychical facts, which we
think it may become.   The soul at present is such
that it is part of those conditions which, given the
rest, would produce certain psychical events.   And
hence the soul is the real possibility of these events,
just as objects in the dark are the possibility of
colour.   Now this way of speaking is, of course, in
the end incorrect, and is defensible only on the
ground of convenience.   It is convenient, when facts
are and have been such and such, to have a short

way of saying what we infer that in the future they may be. But we have no right to speak of dispositions at all, if we turn them into actual qualities of the soul. The attempt to do this would force us to go on enlarging the subject by taking in more conditions, and in the end we should be asserting of the Universe at large.[1] I admit that it is arbitrary and inconsistent to predicate what you cannot say the soul is, but what you only judge about it. But everywhere, in dealing with phenomena, we can find no escape from inconsistency and arbitrariness. We should not lessen these evils, but should greatly increase them, if we took a disposition as meaning more than the probable course of psychical events.

But the soul, I shall be reminded, is not continuous in time, since there are intervals and breaks in the psychical series. I shall not attempt to deny this. We might certainly fall back upon unconscious sensations, and insist that these, in any case and always, are to some extent there. And such an assumption could hardly be shown to be untrue. But I do not see that we could justify it on any sufficient ground, and I will admit that the psychical series either is, or at all events may be broken.[2]

But, on the other side, this admitted breach seems quite unimportant. I can find no reason why a soul's existence, if interrupted and resumed, should not be identical. Even apart from memory, if these divided existences showed the same quality, we should call them the same, or, if we declined, we should find no reason that would justify our refusal. We might insist that, at any rate, in the interval the soul has lived elsewhere, or that this

---

[1] I shall endeavour to explain this in the following chapter.

[2] Unconscious states could also be used to explain " dispositions," in my opinion quite indefensibly. I may add that, within proper limits, I think psychology must make use of unconscious psychical facts.

interval must, at all events, not be too long; but, so far as I see, in both cases we should be asserting without a ground. On the other hand, the amount of qualitative sameness, wanted for psychical identity, seems fixed on no principle (Chapter ix.). And the sole conclusion we can draw is this, that breaks in the temporal series are no argument against our regarding it as a single soul.

"What then in the interim," I may be asked, "do you say that the soul *is*?" For myself, I reply, I should not say it *is* at all, when it does not appear. All that in strictness I could assert would be that actually the soul is *not*, though it has been, and again may be. And I have urged above, that we can find no valid objection to intervals of non-existence. But speaking not strictly, but with a view to practical convenience, we might affirm that in these intervals the soul still persists. We might say it is the conditions, into which it has disappeared, and which probably will reproduce it. And, since the body is a principal part of these conditions, we may find it convenient to identify the "potential" soul with the body. This may be convenient, but we must remember that really it is incorrect. For, firstly, conditions are one thing, and actual fact another thing. And, in the second place, the body (upon any hypothesis) is not all the conditions required for the soul. It is impossible wholly to exclude the action of the environment. And there is again, thirdly, a consideration on which I must lay emphasis. If the soul is resolved and disappears into that which may restore it, does not the same thing hold precisely with regard to the body? Is it not conceivable that, in that interval when the soul is "conditional," the body also should itself be dissolved into conditions which afterwards re-create it? But, if so, these ulterior conditions which now, I presume we are to say, the soul *is*, are assuredly in strictness not the body at all. As a matter of fact, doubtless, this event does not happen within our knowledge. We do not find that bodies disappear and once more are re-made ; but, merely on that ground, we are not entitled to deny that it is possible. And, if it is possible, then I would urge at once the following conclusions. You cannot, except as a matter of convenience, identify the conditions of the soul with the body. And you cannot assert that the continuous existence of the body is *essentially* necessary for the sameness and unity of the soul.[1]

We have now dealt with the subject of the soul's continuity, and have also said something on its "dispositions." And, before passing on to objections of another kind, I will here try to obviate a misunderstanding. The soul is an ideal construction, but a construction by whom ? Could we maintain that the soul exists only for Itself ? This would be certainly an error, for we can say that a soul is before memory exists, or when it does not remember The soul exists always for a soul, but not always for itself. And it is an ideal construction, not because it is psychical, but because (like my body) it is a series appearing in time. The same difficulty attaches to all phenomenal existence. Past and future, and the Nature which no one perceives (Chapter xxii.) exist, as such, only for some subject which thinks them. But this neither means that their ultimate reality consists in being thought, nor does it mean that they exist outside of finite souls. And it does not mean that the Real is made by merely adding thought to our actual presentations. Immediate experience in time, and thought, are each alike but false appearance, and, in coming together, each must forego its own distinctive character. In the Absolute there is neither mere existence at one moment

---

[1] How far the soul can be said to result from merely physical conditions I shall enquire lower down.

nor any ideal construction. Each is merged in a
higher and all-containing Reality (Chapter xxiv.).

2. We have seen, so far, that our phenomenal
view of the soul does not degrade it to an adjective
depending on the body.   Can we reply to objections
based on other grounds ?   The psychical series, we
may be told, demands as its condition a something
transcendent, a soul or Ego which stands above,
and gives unity to, the series.   But such a soul, I
reply, merely adds further difficulties to those we
had before.   No doubt the series, being phenomenal, is the appearance of Reality, but it hardly
follows from this that its reality is an Ego or soul.
We have seen (Chapter x.) that such a being, because finite, is infected with its own relations to
other finites.   And it is so far from giving unity to
the series of events, that their plurality refuses to
come together with its singleness.   Hence the oneness remains standing outside the many, as a further
finite unit.   You cannot show how the series becomes a system in the soul ; and, if you could, you
cannot free that soul from its perplexed position as
one finite related to other finites.   In short, metaphysically your soul or Ego is a mass of confusion,
and we have now long ago disposed of it.   And if
it is offered us merely as a working conception,
which does not claim truth, then this conception, as
we have seen, will not work in metaphysics.   Its
alleged function must be confined to psychology, an
empirical science, and the further consideration of it
here would be, therefore, irrelevant.[1]

3. But our account of the soul, as a series of

[1] In another place I should be ready to enter on this question.
It would, I think, not be difficult to show in psychology that the
idea of a soul, or an Ego, or a Will, or an activity beyond events
explains nothing at all.   It serves only to produce false appearances of explanation, and to throw a mist over what is really left
quite unexplained.

events, may be attacked perhaps from the ground of
psychology itself. There are psychical facts, it may
be urged, which are more than events, and these
facts, it may be argued, refute our definition. I
must briefly deal with this objection, and my reply
may be summed up thus. There *are* psychical
facts, which are more than events; but, if they are
not *also* events, they are not facts at all. I will take
these two propositions in their order.[1]

(*a*) We have seen that my psychical states, and
my private experience, can be at the same time
what they are, and yet something much more.[2]
Every distinction that is made in the fact of presentation, every content, or "what," that is loosened
from its "that," is at once more than a mere event.
Nay an event itself, as one member in a temporal
series, is only itself by transcending its own pre-

---

[1] There are some distinctions which we must keep in mind.
By *existence* (taken strictly) I mean a temporal series of events or
facts. And this series is not throughout directly experienced. It
is an ideal construction from the basis of what is presented. But,
though partly ideal, such a series is not wholly so. For it leaves
its contents in the form of particulars, and the immediate conjunction of being and quality is not throughout broken up. Thisness,
or the irrelevant context, is retained, in short, except so far as is
required to make a series of events. And, though the events of
the whole series are not actually perceived, they must be taken as
what is in its character perceptible.

Any part of a temporal series, no matter how long, can be
called an event or fact. For it is taken as a piece, or quantity,
made up of perceptible duration.

By *fact* I mean either an event, or else what is directly experienced. Any aspect of direct experience, or again of an event,
can itself be loosely styled a fact or event, so far as you consider
it as a qualifying adjective of one

I may notice, last, that an immediate experience, *e.g.* of succession, can contain that which, when distinguished, is more than
one event, and it can contain also an aspect which, as distinguished, is beyond events. But I should add that I have not
tried to use any of the above words everywhere strictly.

[2] See above, p. 300, and compare Chapters xix. and xxi. And
for the relation of existence to thought see, further, Chapter
xxiv.

sent existence. And this transcendence becomes more obvious, when an identical quality persists unaltered through a succession of changes. There is, to my mind, no question as to our being concerned here with more than mere events. And, far from contesting this, I have endeavoured to insist on the conclusion that *everything* in time has a quality which passes beyond itself.

(*b*) But then, if so, have we allowed the force of the objection? Have we admitted that there are facts which are not events in time? This would be a grave misunderstanding, and against it we must urge our second proposition. A fact, or event, is always more than itself; but, if less than itself, it is no longer properly a fact. It has now been taken as a content working loose from the "this," and has, so far, become a mere aspect and abstraction. And yet this abstraction, on the other hand, must have its existence. It must appear, somehow, as, or in a particular event, with a given place and duration in the temporal series. There are, in brief, aspects which, taken apart, are not events; and yet these aspects must appear in psychical existence.

The objection has failed to perceive this double nature of things, and it has hence fallen blindly into a vicious dilemma. Because in our life there is more than events, it has rashly argued that this "more" must be psychical fact. But, if it is psychical fact, and not able to be experienced, I do not know what it could mean, or in what wonderful way we could be supposed to get at it. And, on the other side, to be experienced without happening in the psychical series, or to occur there without taking place as an event among events, seem phrases without meaning. What we experience is a content, which is one with, and which occurs as, a particular mental state. The same content, again, as ideal, is used away from its state, and only appears there. By itself it is *not* a fact; and, if it were one, it would, so far, cease to be ideal, and would *therefore* become a mere event among events.

If you take the identity of a series, whether physical or psychical, this identity, considered as such, is not an event which happens.[1] But, on the other hand, can we call it a fact of experience? To speak strictly, we cannot, since all identity is ideal. It, as such, is not directly experienced, even as occurring in the facts, and, still less, as something which happens alongside of or between them. It is an adjective which, as separate, could not exist, and its essence, we may say, consists in distinction. But, on the other side, this distinction, and, again the construction of a series, is an event. And it must happen in a soul[2]; for where else could it exist? As a mental state, more than its mere content, it also must have a place, and duration, in the psychical series. And, otherwise, it could not be a part of experience. But the identity itself is but an aspect of the events, or event, and is certainly ideal.

"No," I shall be told, "the identity and continuity of the soul must be more than this. It cannot fall in what is given, for all the given is discrete. And it cannot consist in ideal content, for, in that case, it would not be real. It must therefore come somehow along with phenomena, in such a way that it does not happen as an event within the psychical series." But, as soon as we consider this claim, its inconsistency is obvious. If anything is experienced, now or always, along with what is given, then this (whatever it is) is surely a psychical event, with a place, or places, in the series. But, if, on the other hand, it has not, in any sense, position or duration in my history, you will hardly persuade me that it

---

[1] The whole series itself will, in a sense, be one event since it has a place and duration. But it will not be throughout an experienced fact.

[2] That the identity of a soul should be only so far as it exists for some soul, is one of the circles we have pointed out already.

makes part of my experience at all. I do not see,
in short, how anything can come there, unless it is
prepared, from some side, to enter and to take its
place there.   And, if it is not to be an element in
experience, it will be nothing.   And I doubt if any
one would urge a claim so suicidal and so absurd,
unless for the sake of, and in order to defend, a pre-
conceived doctrine.   Because phenomena in time
are not real, there must be something more than
temporal.   But because we wrongly assume that
nothing is real, unless it exists as a thing, therefore
the element, which transcends time, must be somehow and somewhere *beside* it.   This element is a
world, or a soul, or an Ego, which never descends
into our series.   It never comes down there itself,
though we are forced, I presume, to say that it works,
and that it makes itself felt.   But this irrational influence and position results merely from our false
assumption.   We are attempting to pass beyond the
series, while we, in effect, deny that anything is real,
unless it is a member there.   For our other world,
and our soul, and our Ego, which exist beside
temporal events, have been taken themselves as but
finite things.   They merely reduplicate phenomena,
they do but double the world of appearance.   They
leave on our hands unsolved the problem that vexed
us before, and they load us beside with an additional
puzzle.   We have now, not only another existence
no better than the first, but we have to explain also
how one of these stands to, or works on, the other.
And the result is open self-contradiction or thoughtless obscurity.   But the remedy is to purge ourselves of our groundless prejudice, and to seek
reality elsewhere than in the existence of things.
Continuity and identity, the other world and the
Ego, do not, as such, exist.   They are ideal, and, as
such, they are not facts.   But none the less they
have reality, at least not inferior to that of temporal
events.   We must admit that, in the full sense,

neither ideality nor existence is real. But you cannot pass, from the one-sided denial of one, to the one-sided assertion of the other. The attempt is based on a false alternative, and, in either case, must result in self-contradiction.

It is perhaps necessary, though wearisome, to add some remarks on the Ego. The failure to see that continuity and identity are ideal, has produced efforts to find the Ego existing, as such, as an actual fact. This Ego is, on the one hand, to be somehow experienced as a fact, and, on the other hand, it must not exist either as one or as a number of events. And the attempt naturally is futile. For most assuredly, as we find it, the self is determinate. It is always qualified by a content.[1] The Ego and Non-ego are at any time experienced, not in general, but with a particular character. But such an appearance is obviously a psychical event, with a given place in the series. And upon this I urge the following dilemma. If your Ego has no content, it is nothing, and it therefore is not experienced ; but, if on the other hand it is anything, it is a phenomenon in time. But " not at all," may be the answer, "since the Ego is outside the series, and is merely related to it, and perhaps acting on it." I do not see that this helps us. If, I repeat, your Ego has no content, then *anywhere* it is nothing; and the relation of something to this nothing, and again its action upon anything, are utterly unmeaning. But, if upon the other hand this Ego has a content, then, for the sake of argument, you may say, if you please, that it exists. But, in any case, it stands outside, and it does not come into, experience at all. " No, it does not come there itself ; it never, so to speak, appears in person ; but its relation to phenomena, or its action on them, is certainly somehow experienced,

---

[1] I should add that I am convinced that the Ego is a derivative product (*Mind*, No. 47). But the argument above is quite independent of this conclusion.
     A. R.

or at least known." In this answer the position
seems changed, but it is really the same, and it does
but lead back to our old dilemma. You cannot, in
any sense, know, or perceive, or experience, a term
as in relation, unless you have also the other term
to which it is related. And, if we will but ponder
this, surely it becomes self-evident. Well then,
either you have not got any relation of phenomena
to anything at all; or else the other term, your
thing the Ego, takes its place among the rest. It
becomes another event among psychical events.[1]

It would be useless to pursue into its ramifications a view false at the root, and based (as we have
seen) on a vicious alternative. That which is more
than an event must also, from another side, exist,
and must thus appear in, or as, one member of the
temporal series. But, so far as it transcends time,
it is ideal, and, as such, is *not* fact. The attempt to
take it as existing somehow and somewhere alongside, thrusts it back into the sphere of finite particulars. In this way, with all our struggles, we never
rise beyond some world of mere events, and we
revolve vainly in a circle which brings us round to
our starting-place. If it were possible for us to
apprehend the whole series at once, and to take in its
detail as one undivided totality, certainly then the
timeless would have been experienced as a fact.
But in that case ideality on the one side, and events
on the other, would have each come to an end in a
higher mode of being.

The objections, which we have discussed, have all
shown themselves ill-founded. There is certainly
nothing experienced which is *not* an event, though

[1] If action is attributed to the Ego things are made even worse,
for activity has been shown to imply a sequence in time (Chapter
vii.). I may perhaps remind the reader here that to speak of a
relation between phenomena and the Reality is quite incorrect.
There are no relations, properly, except between things finite. If
we speak otherwise, it should be by a licence.

we have seen that in events there is that which
transcends them. All continuity is ideal, and the
arguments brought against the oneness of a psychical series, we saw, were not valid. Nor could we
find that our phenomenal view of the soul brought it
down to be an adjective depending on the organism.
For the organism itself is also phenomenal. Soul
and body are alike in being only appearance, and
their connection is merely the relation of phenomena.
It is the special nature of this relation that we have
next to discuss.

I will begin by pointing out a view from which
we must dissent. The soul and body may be regarded as two sides of one reality, or as the same
thing taken twice and from two aspects of its being.
I intend to say nothing here on the reasons which
may lead to this conclusion, nor to discuss the various
objections which might be brought against them. I
will briefly state the ground on which I am forced
to reject the proposed identity. In the first place,
even if we confine our attention to phenomena, I do
not see that we are justified in thus separating each
soul with its body from the rest of the world (p. 358).
And there is a fatal objection to this doctrine, if
carried further. If in the end soul and body are to
be one thing, then, with whatever justification, you
have concluded to a plurality of finite reals within
the Absolute. But we have seen that such a conclusion is wholly indefensible. When soul and body
come together in Reality, I utterly fail to perceive
any reason why the special nature of each is, as such,
to be preserved. It is one thing to be convinced that
no element, or aspect of phenomena, can be lost in the
Absolute. But it is quite another thing to maintain
that every appearance, when there, continues to keep
its distinctive character. To be resolved rather and
to be merged, each as a factor in what is higher, is
the nature of such things as the body and the soul.

And with this we are brought to a well-known and much-debated question. Is there a causal connection between the physical and the psychical, and are we to say that one series influences the other? I will begin by stating the view which *prima facie* suggests itself, I will then briefly discuss some erroneous doctrines, and will end by trying to set out a defensible conclusion. And, first, the belief which occurs to the unbiassed observer is that soul acts upon body and body on soul. I do not mean by this that bare soul seems to work on bare body, for such a distinction is made only by a further reflection. I mean that, if without any theory you look at the facts, you will find that changes in one series (whichever it is) are often concerned in bringing on changes in the other. Psychical and physical, each alike, make a difference to one another. It is obvious that alterations of the soul come from movements in the organism, and it is no less obvious that the latter may be consequent on the former. We may be sure that no one, except to save a theory, would deny that in volition mind influences matter. And with pain and pleasure such a denial would be even less natural. To hold that now in the individual pleasure and pain do not move, but are mere idle accompaniments, to maintain that never in past development have they ever made a difference to anything— surely this strikes the common observer as a wilful paradox. And, for myself, I doubt if most of those, who have accepted the doctrine in general, have fully realized its meaning.

This natural view, that body and soul have influence on each other, we shall find in the end to be proof against attack. But we must pass on now to consider some opposing conclusions. The man who denies the inter-action in any sense of body and soul, must choose from amongst the possibilities which remain. He may take the two series as going on independently and side by side, or may make one the subordinate and adjective of the other. And I will begin by making some remarks on the parallel series. But I must ignore the historical development of this view, and must treat it barely as if it were an idea which is offered us to-day.

I would observe, first, that an assertion or a denial of causation can hardly be proved if you insist on demonstration. You may show that every detail we know points towards one result, and that we can find no special reason for taking this result as false. And, having done so much, you certainly have proved your conclusion. But, even after this, a doubt remains with regard to what is possible. And, unless all other possibilities can be disposed of, you have failed to demonstrate. In the particular doctrine before us we have, I think, a case in point. The mere coincidence of soul and body cannot be shown to be impossible; but this bare possibility is, on the other hand, no good reason for supposing the coincidence to be fact.

Appearance points to a causal connection between the physical and psychical series. And yet this appearance might possibly be a show, produced in the following way. There might on each side be other conditions, escaping our view, which would be enough to account for the changes in each series. And we may even carry our supposition a step further on. There might *on both sides* be, within each series, no causal connection between its events. A play of unknown conditions might, on either side, present the appearance of a series. The successive facts would in that case show a regular sequence, but they would not actually be members and links of any one connected series. I do not see how such a suggestion can be proved to be impossible; but that is surely no reason for regarding it as fact. And to this same result we are led, when we return to consider the idea of two coinciding series. The

idea seems baseless, and I do not think it necessary
to dwell further on this point.[1]

We seem, therefore, driven to regard soul and
body as causally connected, and the question will be
as to the nature of their connection. Can this be
all, so to speak, on one side ? Is the soul merely
an adjective depending on the body, and never more
than an effect? Or is, again, the body a mere accompaniment resulting from the soul? Both these questions must be met by an emphatic negative. The
suggested relation is, in each case, inconsistent and
impossible. And, since there is no plausibility in
the idea of physical changes always coming from,
and never reacting on, the soul, I will not stop to consider it. I will pass to the opposite one-sidedness,
a doctrine equally absurd, though, at first sight,
seeming more plausible.

Psychical changes, upon this view, are never
causes at all, but are solely effects. They are
adjectives depending upon the body, but which
at the same time make absolutely no difference to
it. They do not quite fall outside causation, for
they are events which certainly are produced by
physical changes. But they enter the causal series
in one character only. They are themselves produced, but on the other hand nothing ever results
from them. And this does not merely mean that,
for certain purposes, you may *take* primary qualities
as unaffected by secondary, and may *consider* second-

---

[1] Of course, even on these hypotheses, one link of a series will
be a cause of what follows, if you take that link in connection
with the rest of the universe. Hence with regard to "occa-
sionalism" we may say that, since every cause must be limited
more or less artificially, every cause therefore is able to be called
an "occasion." You may take in further and further conditions,
until your partial cause seems an item unimportant, and even
therefore ineffective. And here we are on the confines of absolute
error. If the "occasion" is divided from the whole entire cause,
and so held to be without an influence on the effect, that is at
once quite indefensible.

ary qualities as idle adjectives which issue from primary. It means that all psychical changes are effects, brought about by what is physical, while themselves absolutely without any influence on the succession of phenomena. I have been forced to state this view in my own terms as, though widely held, I do not find it anywhere precisely expressed. Its adherents satisfy themselves with metaphors, and rest on half worked out comparisons. And all that their exposition, to me, makes clear, is the confusion which it springs from.

The falseness of this doctrine can be exhibited from two points of view. It involves the contradiction of an adjective which makes no difference to its substantive,[1] and the contradiction of an event in time, which is an effect but not a cause. For the sake of brevity I shall here confine myself to the second line of criticism. I must first endeavour, in my own way, to give to the materialistic doctrine a reasonable form ; and I will then point out that its inconsistency is inherent and not removable.

If we agree to bring psychical events under the head of what is "secondary," we may state the proposed way of connection as follows ·

$$A\text{--}B\text{---}C.$$
$$\begin{array}{ccc} | & | & | \\ \alpha & \beta & \gamma. \end{array}$$

A, B, C is the succession of primary qualities, and it is taken to be a true causal series. Between the secondary products, α, β, γ, is no causal connection, nor do they make any difference to the sequence of C from B and of B from A. They are, each of them, adjectives which happen, but which

---

[1] The same false principle, which is employed in the materialistic view of the soul, appears in the equally materialistic doctrine of the Real Presence.

produce no consequence. But, though their succession is not really causal, it must none the less appear so, because it is regular. And it must be regular, since it depends on a series which is unalterably fixed by causation. And in this way (it may be urged) the alleged inconsistency is avoided, and all is made harmonious. We are not forced into the conclusion that the self-same cause can produce two different effects. A is not first followed by mere B, and then again by $\genfrac{}{}{0pt}{}{B}{\genfrac{}{}{0pt}{}{|}{\beta}}$, since a is, in fact, irremovable from A. Nor is it necessary to suppose that the sequence A—B must ever occur by itself. For a will, in fact, accompany A, and β will always occur with B. Still this inseparability will in no way affect our result, which is the outcome and expression of a general principle. A—B—C is the actual and sole thread of causation, while a, β, γ are the adjectives which idly adorn it. And hence these latter must seem to be that which really they are not. They are in fact decorative, but either always or usually so as to appear constructional.

This is the best statement that I can make in defence of my unwilling clients, and I have now to show that this statement will not bear criticism. But there is one point on which I, probably, have exceeded my instructions. To admit that the sequence A—B—C does not exist by itself, would seem contrary to that view which is more generally held. Yet, without this admission, the inconsistency can be exhibited more easily.

The Law of Causation is the principle of Identity, applied to the successive. Make a statement involving succession, and you have necessarily made a statement which, if true, is true always. Now, if it is true universally that B follows A, then that sequence is what we mean by a causal law. If, on the other hand, the sequence is *not* universally true, then it is not true at all. For B, in that case, must have followed something more or less than A ; and hence the judgment $A—B$ was certainly false. Thus a stated fact of succession is untrue, till it has been taken as a fact of causation. And a fact of causation is truth which is, and must be, universal.[1] It is an abstracted relation, which is either false always, or always true. And hence, if we are able to say ever that B follows mere A, then this proposition $A—B$ is eternal verity. But, further, a truth cannot be itself and at the same time something different. And therefore once affirm $A—B$, and you can not affirm also and as well $A—B\beta$, if (that is to say) in both cases you are keeping to the same A. For if the event β follows, while arising from no difference, you must assert of mere A both "$—B$" and "$—B\beta$." But these two assertions are incompatible. In the same way, if $A\alpha$ has, as a consequence, mere B, it is impossible that bare A should possess the same consequence. If it seems otherwise, then certainly A was *not* bare, or else α was *not* relevant. And any other conclusion would imply two incompatible assertions with regard to B.[2]

Hence we may come to a first conclusion about the view which makes an idle adjective of the soul. If it asserts that these adjectives both happen, and do not happen, for no reason at all, if it will say that the physical sequence is precisely the same, both without them and with them, then such a view flatly contradicts itself. For it not only supposes differences, which do not make any difference—a

---

[1] The addition of "unconditional" would be surplusage. Cp. *Principles of Logic*, p. 485.

[2] The judgments, "B follows from A" and "B follows from $A\alpha$," are, if pure, not reconcilable. The same effect cannot have two causes, unless "cause" is taken loosely. See Mr. Bosanquet's *Logic*, Book I, Chapter vi. I have remarked further on this subject below in Chapter xxiv.

supposition which is absurd; but it also believes in
a decoration, which at one time goes with, and at
another time stays away from its construction, and
which is an event which, equally in either case, is
without any reason.[1] And, with this, perhaps we
may pass on.

Let us return to that statement of the case which
appeared to us more plausible   There is a succession

$$A—B—C$$
$$|\quad|\quad|$$
$$\alpha\quad\beta\quad\gamma,$$

and in this the secondary qualities are inseparable
from the primary. $A—B—C$ is, in fact, never found
by itself, but it is, for all that, the true and the only
causal sequence. We shall, however, find that this
way of statement does but hide the same mistake
which before was apparent.   In the succession
above, unless there really is more than we are sup-
posed to take in, and unless α, β, γ are connected
with something outside, we have still the old inconsistency. If $A—B—C$ is the truth, then the succession, which we had, is in fact impossible; and, if
the sequence is modified, then $A—B—C$ can not
possibly be true. I will not urge that, *if* it were
true, it would at least be undiscoverable, since, by
the hypothesis, α is inseparable from A. I admit
that we may postulate sometimes where we cannot
prove or observe; and I prefer to show that such
a postulate is here self-contradictory.   It is assumed
that α is an adjective indivisible from A, but is an
adjective which at the same time makes no difference to its being. Or α, at any rate, makes no
difference to the action of A, but is perfectly inert.
But, if so, then, as before, A possesses two predicates incompatible with each other.   We cannot

[1] If there were a reason, then *mere* A would no longer be the
cause of both B and $B\beta$.   I shall return to this lower down.

indeed say, as before, that *in fact* it is followed first by mere B, and then again by $B\beta$. But we, none the less, are committed to assertions which clash. We hold that A produces B, and that A produces $B\beta$; and one of these judgments must be false. For, if A produces *mere B*, then it does not produce $B\beta$. Hence β is either an event which is a gratuitous accident, or else a must have somehow (indirectly or directly) *made* this difference in B. But, if so, a is not inert, but is a part-cause of B; and therefore the sequence of B from mere A is false.[1] The plausibility of our statement has proved illusory.

I am loath to perplex the question by subtleties, which would really carry us no further; but I will notice a possible evasion of the issue. The secondary qualities, I may be told, do not depend each on one primary, but are rather the adjectives of relations between these. They attend on certain relations, yet make no difference to what follows. But here the old and unresolved contradiction remains. It cannot be true that any relation (say of A to E), which produces another relation (say of B to F), should *both* produce this latter naked, *and* also attended by an adjective, β. One of these assertions *must* be false, and, with it, your conclusion. It is in short impossible to have differences which come without a difference, or which make no difference to what follows them. The attempt involves a contradiction, explicit or veiled, but in either case ruinous to the theory which adopts it.

We have now finished our discussion of erroneous views.[2] We have seen that to deny the active

---

[1] The reader will remember that β (by the hypothesis) cannot follow directly from a. It is taken as dependent solely on B.

[2] I may perhaps, in this connection, be expected to say something on the Conservation of Energy. I am most unwilling to do this. One who, like myself, stands outside the sciences which

connection of body and soul is either dangerous **or**
impossible.   It is impossible, unless we are pre-

use this idea, can hardly hope to succeed in apprehending it
rightly.   He constantly fails to distinguish between a mere
working conception and a statement of fact.   Thus, for example,
" energy of position " and " potential energy " are phrases which
in their actual employment, doubtless, are useful and accurate.
But, to speak strictly, they are nonsense.   If a thing disappears
into conditions, which will hereafter produce it, then most
assuredly in the interim *it* does *not* exist ; and it is surely only by
a licence that you can call the non-existent "in a state of conservation."   And hence, passing on, I will next take the Conservation of Energy to mean that at any moment actual matter and
actual motion are an unaltered quantity.   And this constancy
may hold good either in each of several physical systems, or again
in Nature as a whole (Chapter xxii).   Now, if the idea is put
forward as a hypothesis for working use only, I offer no criticism
of that which is altogether beyond me.   But, if it is presented,
on the other hand, as a statement of fact, I will say at once that
I see no reason to accept it as true ; and I am quite sure that it
is not provable.   If, for the sake of argument however, we accept
the quantitative constancy of matter and motion, I do not find
that this tells us anything as to the position of the soul.   For,
although mind influences body and body alters mind, the quantity
may throughout remain precisely the same.   The loss and gain,
on the psychical and physical side, may each, upon the whole,
exactly balance the other ; and thus the physical energy of the
system may be thoroughly preserved.   If, however, any one
insists that motion always must be taken as resulting from motion,
even then he may avoid the conclusion that psychical events are
not causes.   He may fall back on some form of the two parallel
series which only seem to be connected.   Or he may betake
himself to a hypothesis which still maintains their causal connection.   An arrangement is possible, by which soul and body
make a difference to each other, while the succession on each
side appears, and may be treated, as independent.   The losses
and gains upon each side amongst the different threads of causal
sequence might counterbalance one another.   They might
hinder and help each other, so that in the end all would *look*
as if they really did nothing, and as if each series was left alone
to pursue its own private course.   Such an arrangement seems
undeniably possible, but I am far from suggesting that it is fact.
For I reject the principle which would force us, without any
reason, to entertain such subtleties.
   I may be allowed to remark in conclusion that those who hold
to the doctrine of " Conservation," and who use this in any way

pared to contradict ourselves, to treat the soul as a
mere adjective not influencing the body. And to
accept, on the other hand, two coinciding and
parallel series is to adopt a conclusion opposed to
the main bulk of appearance. Nor for such a deser-
tion of probability can I find any warrant. The
common view, that soul and body make a difference
to one another, is in the end proof against objection.
And I will endeavour now to set it out in a defensible form.

Let me say at once that, by a causal connection
of mind with matter, I do *not* mean that one influences the other when bare. I do *not* mean that soul
by itself ever acts upon body, or that mere bodily
states have an action on bare soul. Whether anything of the kind is possible, I shall enquire lower
down ; but I certainly see no reason to regard it as
actual. I understand that, normally, we have an
event with two sides, and that these two sides, taken
together, are the inseparable cause of the event which
succeeds. What is the effect ? It is a state of soul
going along with a state of body, or rather with a
state of those parts of our organism which are considered to be in immediate relation with mind. And
what are we to say is the cause ? It is a double
event of the same kind, and the two sides of it, both
in union, produce the effect. The alteration of
mind, which results, is not the effect of mind or
body, acting singly or alone, but of both working
at once. And the state of body, which accompanies
it, is again the product of two influences. It is
brought about neither by bare body, nor yet again

as bearing on our views about the soul, may fairly be expected
to make some effort. It seems incumbent on them to try to
reconcile the succession of psychical events with the law of
Causation. No one is bound to be intelligible outside his own
science, I am quite convinced as to that. But such a plea is good
only in the mouths of those who are willing to remain inside.
And I must venture, respectfully but firmly, to insist on this
point.

by bare soul.   Hence a difference, made in one side,
must make a difference to the other side, and it
makes a difference also to both sides of what follows.
And, though this statement will receive later some
qualification (p. 337), the causal connection of the
soul's events, in general, is inseparably double.

In physiology and in psychology we, in practice,
disregard this complication.   We for convenience
sake regard as the cause, or as the effect, what is in
reality but a prominent condition or consequence.
And such a mutilation of phenomena is essential to
progress.   We speak of an intellectual sequence, in
which the conclusion, as a psychical event, is the
effect of the premises.   We talk as if the antecedent
mental state were truly the cause, and were not
merely one part of it.   Where, in short, we find that
on either side the succession is regular, we regard it
as independent.   And it is only where irregularity
is forced on our attention, that we perceive body
and mind to interfere with one another.   But, at
this point, practical convenience has unawares led
us into difficulty.   We are puzzled now to comprehend how that which *was* independent has been
induced to leave its path.   We begin to seek the
cause which forces it to exert and to suffer influence ;
and, with this, we are well on the road to false
theory and ruinous error.

But the truth is that no mere psychical sequence
is a fact, or in any way exists.   With each of its
members is conjoined always a physical event, and
these physical events enter into every link of causation.   The state of mind, or body, is here never more
than part-cause, or again more than part-effect.   We
may attend to either of the sides, which for our
purpose is prominent ; we may ignore the action of
the other side, where it is constant and regular ; but
we cannot deny that both really contribute to the
effect.   Thus we speak of feelings and of ideas as
influencing the body.   And so they do, since they

make a difference to the physical result, and since this result is *not* the consequence from a mere physical cause. But feelings and ideas, on the other hand, neither act nor exist independent of body. The altered physical state is the effect of conditions, which are, at once, both psychical and physical. We find the same duplicity when we consider alterations of the soul. An incoming sensation may be regarded as caused by the body; but this view is, taken generally, onesided and incorrect. The prominent condition has been singled out, and the residue ignored. And, if we deny the influence of the antecedent psychical state, we have pushed allowable. licence once more into mistake.

The soul and its organism are each a phenomenal series. Each, to speak in general, is implicated in the changes of the other. Their supposed independence is therefore imaginary, and to overcome it by invoking a faculty such as Will—is the effort to heal a delusion by means of a fiction. In every psychical state we have to do with two sides, though we disregard one. Thus in the "Association of Ideas" we have no right to forget that there is a physical sequence essentially concerned. And the law of Association must itself be extended, to take in connections formed between physical and psychical elements. The one of these phenomena, on its re-occurrence, may bring back the other. In this way a psychical state, once conjoined with a physical, may normally restore it; and hence this psychical state can be treated as the cause. It is not properly the cause, since it is not the whole cause; but it is most certainly an effective and differential condition. The physical event is not the result from a mere physical state. And if the idea or feeling had been absent, or if again it had not acted, this physical event would not have happened.

I am aware that such a statement is not an explanation, but I insist that in the end no explanation

is possible. There are many enquiries which are
legitimate. To ask about the "seat" of the soul,
and about the ultimate modes of sequence and co-
existence, both physical and psychical, is proper and
necessary. We may remain incapable, in part, of
resolving these problems; but at all events the
questions they put are essentially answerable, however little we are called upon to deal with them
here. But the connection of body and soul is in its
essence inexplicable, and the further enquiry as to the
"how" is irrational and hopeless. For soul and
body are not realities. Each is a series, artificially
abstracted from the whole, and each, as we have
seen, is self-contradictory. We cannot in the end
understand how either comes to exist, and we know
that both, if understood, would, as such, have been
transmuted. To comprehend them, while each is
fixed in its own untrue character, is utterly impossible. But, if so, their way of connection must
remain unintelligible.

And the same conclusion may be reached by considering the causal series. In this normally the
two sides are inseparable from each other, and it
was by a licence only that we were permitted ever to
disregard one side. But, with this result, still we
have not reached the true causal connection. It is
only by a licence that in the end both sides taken
together can be abstracted from the universe. The
cause is not the true cause unless it is the whole
cause; and it is not the whole cause unless in it you
include the environment, the entire mass of unspecified conditions in the background. Apart from
this you have regularities, but you have not attained
to intelligible necessity. But the entire mass of
conditions is not merely inexhaustible, but also it is
infinite; and thus a complete knowledge of causation
is theoretically impossible.[1] Our known causes and

---

[1] Cf. Chapter vi.

effects are held always by a licence and partly on sufferance. To observe regularities, to bring one under the other as far as possible, to remove everywhere what can be taken as in practice irrelevant, and thus to reduce the number of general facts— we cannot hope for more than this in explaining concrete phenomena. And to seek for more in the connection of body and soul is to pursue a chimera.

But, before we proceed, there are points which require consideration. A state of soul seems not always to follow, even in part, from a preceding state. And an arrangement of mere physical conditions seems to supply the whole origin of a psychical life. And again, when the soul is suspended and once more reappears, the sole cause of the reappearance seems to lie in the body. I will begin by dealing with the question about the soul's origin. We must remember, in the first place, that mere body is an artificial abstraction, and that its separation from mind disappears in the Whole. And, when the abstraction is admitted and when we are standing on this basis, it is not certain, even then, that any matter exists unconnected with soul (Chapter xxii.). Now, if we bear in mind these considerations, we need not seek to deny that physical conditions can be the origin of a psychical life. We might have at one moment a material arrangement and at the next moment we might find that this arrangement was modified, and was accompanied by a certain degree of soul. Even if this as a fact does not happen, I can find absolutely no reason to doubt that it is possible, nor does it seem to me to clash with our preceding view. But we must beware of misunderstandings. We can hardly believe, in the first place, that a soul, highly developed, arises thus all at once. And we must remember, in the second place, that a soul which is the result of mere matter, on the other hand at once qualifies and

A. R.   z reacts on that matter. Mere body will, even here, never act upon bare mind. The event is single at one moment, and is double at the next; but in this twofold result the sides will imply, and will make a difference to one another. They are a joint-effect, and in what follows, whether as passive or active, each is nothing by itself. The soul is never mere soul, and the body, as soon as ever the soul has emerged, is no longer bare body. And, when this is understood, we may assent to the physical origin of mind. But we must remember that the material cause of the soul will be never the whole cause. Matter is a phenomenal isolation of one aspect of reality. And the event which results from any material arrangement, really pre-supposes and depends on the entire background of conditions. It is only through a selection, and by a licence, that a mere physical cause can anywhere be supposed to exist.[1]

And the same conclusion holds when we consider the suspension of a soul. The psychical life of an organism seems more or less to disappear, and again to be restored, and we have to ask whether this restoration is effected by mere matter. We may distinguish here two questions, one of which concerns fact, and the other possibility. It is first, I think, impossible to be sure that anywhere psychical functions have ceased wholly. You certainly cannot conclude from the absence of familiar phenomena to the absence of everything, however different in degree or in kind. And whether, as a fact, anywhere in an organism its soul is quite suspended, I do not pretend to know. But assume for argument's sake that this is so, it does not lead to a new difficulty. We have a case once more here, where physical conditions are the origin of a psychical result, and there seems no need to add anything to

---

[1] Whether mere soul can act on or produce matter, I shall enquire lower down.

our discussion of this point. And what we are to say the soul *is* in the interval, during which it has ceased to exist, we have already enquired.

And under this head of suspension may fall all those cases, where a psychical association seems to have become merely physical. In psychology we have connections, which once certainly or possibly were conscious, but now, in part or altogether, and either always or at times, *appear* to happen without any psychical links. But, however interesting for psychology,[1] these cases have little metaphysical importance. And I will content myself here with repeating our former warnings. It is, in the first place, not easy to be sure of our ground, when we wholly exclude an unconscious process in the soul. But, even when this has been excluded, and we are left with bare body, the body will be no more than relatively bare. We shall have reached something where the soul in question is absent, but where we cannot say that soul is absent altogether. For there is no part of Nature, which we can say (Chapter xxii.) is not directly organic to a soul or souls. And the merely physical, we saw, is in any case a mere abstraction. It is set apart from, and still depends on, the whole of experience.

I will briefly notice another point. It may be objected that our view implies interference with, or suspension of, the laws of matter or of mind. And it will be urged that such interference is wholly untenable. This objection would rest on a misunderstanding. Every law which is true is true always and for ever; but, upon the other hand, every law is emphatically an abstraction. And hence obviously all laws are true only in the abstract. Modify the conditions, add some elements to make the connection more concrete, and the law is transcended. It

---

[1] Psychology, I should say, has a right to take the soul as suspended, or generally as absent so far as is convenient. I doubt if there is any other limit.

is not interfered with, and it holds, but it does not hold of this case. It remains perfectly true, but is inapplicable where the conditions which it supposes are absent.

I have dwelt at length on the connection of body and soul, but it presents a series of questions which we have, even yet, not discussed. I must endeavour to dispose of these briefly. Can we say that bare soul ever acts upon body, and can soul exist at all without matter, and if so, in what sense ? In our experience assuredly bare soul is not found. Its existence there, and its action, are inseparable from matter ; but a question obviously can be asked with regard to what is possible. As to this, I would begin by observing that, if bare soul exists, I hardly see how we could prove its existence. We have seen (Chapter xxii.) that we can set no bounds to the variety of bodies. An extended organism might, none the less, be widely scattered and discontinuous ; and again organisms might be shared wholly or partially between souls. Further, of whatever extended material a body is composed, there remains the question of its possible functions and properties. I cannot see how, on the one hand, we can fix the limits of these. But upon the other hand, if we fail to do so, I do not understand by what process we even begin to infer the existence of bare soul.[1] And our result so far must be this. We may agree that soul, acting or existing in separation from body, is a thing which is possible ; but we are still without the smallest reason, further, for regarding it as real.

But is such a soul indeed possible ? Or let us rather ask, first, what such a soul would mean. For, if disconnected from all extension, it might even then not be naked. One can imagine an arrange-

[1] See further *The Evidences of Spiritualism*, Fortnightly Review, No. ccxxviii.

ment of secondary qualities, not extended but constant; and this might accompany psychical life and serve as a body (p. 268). We have no reason for seriously entertaining this idea, but, on the other hand, is there any argument which would prove it impossible? And we may come to the same conclusion with regard to bare soul. This would mean a psychical series devoid of every quality that could serve as an organism. Of course if it were a "spirit," immaterial and at the same time localized and extended, it would be inconsistent with itself. But there is no necessity for our falling into such self-contradiction. A psychical series without extension or locality in space, I presume, is conceivable. And this bare series might, for all we know, normally, or on occasion, even influence body. Nay, for all that I can perceive, such a naked soul might do more. Just as we saw that soul can follow from material conditions, so, in the course of events, some matter might itself result from soul. All these things are "possible" in this sense, that, within our knowledge, they cannot any of them be proved to be unreal. But they are mere idle possibilities. We can find no further ground for entertaining them, and in an estimate of probability we could not give them an appreciable value. But surely that which we have no more reason for taking as true, is nothing which we need trouble ourselves to consider. We have in fact no choice but to treat it as wholly non-existent.[1]

We have now discussed the general connection of soul with body. We have seen that neither is reality. Each is a phenomenal series, and their members, as events in time, are causally related. The changes on one side in their sequence are in-

---

[1] These worthless fancies really possess no kind of interest at all. The continuance of the soul after death will be touched on hereafter. On the general nature of the Possible, see, further, Chapters xxiv. and xxvii.

separable from, and affected by, the changes on the
other side.   This, so far as body and soul are connected at all, is the normal course of things.   But
when we went on to investigate, we found a difference.   The existence and action of bare soul is a
mere possibility.   We have no further reason to
believe in it ; nor, if it were fact, do I see how we
should be able to discover it.   But the existence of
mere body, and the appearance of soul as its consequence, and again the partial absence or abeyance
of psychical links, we found much more than possible.   When properly interpreted, though we cannot
prove that these are facts, they have very great
probability.   Still there is not, after all, the smallest
ground to suppose that mere matter directly acts
upon psychical states.   To gain an accurate view
of this connection in all its features is exceedingly
difficult.   But what is important for metaphysics, is
to realize clearly that the interest of such details is
secondary.   Since the phenomenal series, in any
case, come together in the Absolute, since their
special characters must be lost there and be dissolved in what transcends them—the existence by
itself of either body or soul is illusory.   Their
separation may be used for particular purposes, but
it is, in the end, an untrue or a provisional abstraction.

It is necessary, before ending this chapter, to say
something on the relation of soul to soul.   The way
of communication between souls, and again their
sameness and difference, are points on which we
must be careful to guard against error.   It is cer-
tam, in the first place, that experiences are all
separate from each other.   However much their
contents are identical, they are on the other hand
made different by appearing as elements in distinct
centres of feeling.   The immediate experiences of
finite beings cannot, as such, come together ; and to

be possessed directly of what is personal to the mind of another, would in the end be unmeaning. Thus souls, in a sense at least, are separate; but, upon the other hand, they are able to act on one other. And I will begin by enquiring how, in fact, they exercise this influence.

The direct action of soul on soul is, for all we know, possible; but we have, at the same time, no reason for regarding it as more. That which influences, and that which acts, is, so far as we know, always the outside of our bodies. Nor, even if we admit abnormal perception and influence at a distance, need we modify this result. For here the natural inference would be to a medium extended in space, and of course, like "ether," quite material. And in this way the abnormal connection, if it exists, does not differ in kind from what is familiar. Again the inside of one organism might, I presume, act directly on the inside of another. But, if this is possible, we need not therefore consider it as actual. Nor do such enquiries possess genuine metaphysical interest. For the influence of the internal, whether body or soul, is not less effective because it operates through, and with, the outside; nor would it gain in reality by becoming direct. And with this we may dismiss an idea, misemployed by superstition, but from which no conclusion of the smallest importance could follow. A direct connection between souls we cannot say is impossible, but, on the other hand, we find no good reason for supposing it to exist. The possibility seems, in addition, to be devoid of all interest.

We may assume then that souls do not influence each other, except through their bodies. And hence it is only by this way that they are able to communicate. Alterations of the phenomenal group which I call my body, produce further changes in the physical environment. And thus, indirectly or directly, other organisms are altered, with consequent effects on the course of their accompanying souls. This account, which is true of my soul, holds good also with others. The world is such that we can make the same intellectual construction. We can, more or less, set up a scheme, in which every one has a place, a system constant and orderly, and in which the relations apprehended by each percipient coincide. Why and how this comes about we in the end cannot understand ; but it is such a Uniformity of Nature which makes communication possible.[1]

But this may suggest to us a doubt. If such alterations of bodies are the sole means which we possess for conveying what is in us, can we be sure in the end that we really have conveyed it? For suppose that the contents of our various souls differed radically, might we not still, on the same ground, be assured of their sameness ? The objection is serious, and must be admitted in part to hold good. I do not think we can be sure that the sensible qualities we perceive are for every one the same. We infer from the apparent identity of our structure that this is so ; and our conclusion, though not proved, possesses high probability. And, again, it may be impossible in fact that, while the relations are constant, the qualities should vary ; but to assert this would be to pass beyond the limits of our knowledge. What, however, we are convinced of, is briefly this, that we understand and, again, are ourselves understood. There is, indeed, a theoretical possibility that these other bodies are without any souls,[2] or that, while behaving as if they under-

---

[1] Cf. Chapter xxii. There may, so far as I see, be many systems of souls, each system without a way of communication with the others. On this point we seem to be without any means of judging.

[2] I do not mean that it is possible that my soul should contain all the experience which exists.

stood us, their souls really remain apart in worlds shut up from ours. But, when this bare possibility is excluded, the question stands thus. A common understanding being admitted, how much does that imply? What is the minimum of sameness that we need suppose to be involved in it?

It might be interesting elsewhere to pursue this question at length, but I must content myself here with an attempt briefly to indicate the answer. The fact is that, in the main, we behave as if our internal worlds were the same. But this fact means that, for each one, the inner systems coincide. Through all their detail these several orders must lead to the same result. But, if so, we may go further, and may conclude that each comes to the same thing. What is the amount of variety then which such coinciding orders will admit? We must, I presume, answer that, for all we know, the details may be different, but that the principles cannot vary. There seems to be a point beyond which, if laws and systems come to the same thing, they must be actually the same. And the higher we mount from facts of sense, and the wider our principles have become, the more nearly we have approached to this point of identity. Thus sensible qualities, we may suppose, at one end are largely divergent; while, if we rise high enough at the other end, we must postulate sameness. And, between these two extremes, as we advance, the probability increases that coincidence results from identical character. It is, for example, more likely that we share our general morality with another man, than that we both have the same tastes or odours in common. And with this I will pass from a subject which seems both difficult and interesting, but which for metaphysics possesses but secondary importance. Whatever variety there may be, cannot extend to first principles; and all variety comes together, and is transformed, in the Absolute.

But there is a natural mistake which, perhaps, I should briefly notice. Our inner worlds, I may be told, are divided from each other, but the outer world of experience is common to all; and it is by standing on this basis that we are able to communicate. Such a statement would be incorrect. My external sensations are no less private to myself than are my thoughts or my feelings. In either case my experience falls within my own circle, a circle closed on the outside; and, with all its elements alike, every sphere is opaque to the others which surround it. With regard to communicability, there is in fact not any difference of kind, but only of degree. In every case the communication must be made indirectly, and through the medium of our outsides. What is true is that, with certain elements, the ways of expression may be shorter and less mistakeable; and again the conditions, which secure a community of perception, are, with certain elements, more constant and more subject to our control. So much seems clear, but it is not true that our physical experiences have unity, in any sense which is inapplicable to the worlds we call internal. Nor again, even in practice, is it *always* more easy to communicate an outer than an inner experience. In brief, regarded as an existence which appears in a soul, the whole world for each is peculiar and private to that soul. But, if on the other hand, you are considering identity of content, and, on that basis, are transcending such particular existences, then there is at once, in principle, no difference between the inner and the outer.[1] No experience can lie open to inspection from outside; no direct guarantee of identity is possible. Both our knowledge of sameness, and

---

[1] It is of course true that outer experience to be properly outer, must already have passed beyond the stage of mere feeling, and that what is called inner experience, need not have done so. But this is, only in part, relevant to the issue.

our way of communication, are indirect and inferential. They must make the circuit, and must
use the symbol, of bodily change. If a common
ruler of souls could give to any one a message from
the inside, such a message could never be handed
on but by alterations of bodies. That real identity
of ideal content, by which all souls live and move,
cannot work in common save by the path of external appearance.

And, with this, we are led to the question of the
identity between souls. We have just seen that
immediate experiences are separate, and there is
probably no one who would desire to advocate
a contrary opinion. But there are those, I presume,
who will deny the possibility of two souls being, in
any respect, really the same. And we must endeavour very briefly to clear our ideas on this
matter.

It would be, of course, absurd to argue that two
persons are not two but only one, or that, in general,
differences are not different, but simply the same;
and any such contention would be, doubtless, a
wilful paradox. But the principle of what we may
call the Identity of Indiscernibles, has quite another
meaning. It implies that sameness can exist together with difference, or that what is the same is
still the same, however much in other ways it differs.
I shall soon attempt to define this principle more
clearly, but what I would insist on, first, is that to
deny it is to affront common sense. It is, in fact, to
use words which could have no meaning. For every
process of psychical Association is based on this
ground; and, to come to what is plainer, every
movement of our intellect rests wholly upon it. If
you will not assume that identity holds throughout
different contexts, you cannot advance one single
step in apprehending the world. There will be
neither change nor endurance, and still less, motion

through space of an identical body ; there will neither be selves nor things, nor, in brief, any intelligible fact, unless on the assumption that sameness in differents is real. Apart from this main principle of construction, we should be confined to the feeling of a single moment.

And to appeal to Similarity or Resemblance would be a futile attempt to escape in the darkness. For Similarity itself, when we view it in the daylight, is nothing in the world but more or less unspecified sameness. I will not dwell here on a point which elsewhere I have possibly pursued *ad nauseam.*[1] No one, perhaps, would ever have betaken himself to mere Resemblance, unless he had sought in it a refuge from the dangers of Identity. And these dangers are the product of misunderstanding.

There is a notion that sameness implies the denial of difference, while difference is, of course, a palpable fact. But really sameness, while in one respect exclusive of difference, in another respect most essentially implies it. And these two " respects " are indivisible, even in idea. There would be no meaning in sameness, unless it were the identity of differences, the unity of elements which it holds together, but must not confound. And in the same way difference, while it denies, presupposes identity. For difference must depend on a relation, and a relation is possible only on a basis of sameness. It is not common

[1] *Principles of Logic,* pp. 261–2. Cp. *Ethical Studies,* p. 151. I do not understand that there is any material difference on this head between myself and Mr. Bosanquet, *Knowledge and Reality,* pp. 97–108. I would add that in psychology the alternative, between Association by general resemblance and by (explicit) partial identity, is a false one. The feeling that two things are similar need not imply the perception of the identical point, but none the less this feeling is based always on partial sameness. For a confusion on this head see Stumpf, *Tonpsychologie,* I., 112–114. And now (while revising these words for the press) I regret to have to add to Stumpf's name that of Professor James. I have examined the above confusion, more in detail, in *Mind,* No. 5, N.S. For Professor James' reply, see No. 6.

sense that has any desire to reject such truths, and
blindly to stand upon difference to the exclusion of
identity. In ordinary science no one would question
the reality of motion, because it makes one thing the
same throughout diverse times and spaces. That
things to be the same must always be different, and
to be different must be, therefore, the same—this is
not a paradox, until it is paradoxically stated. It
does not seem absurd, unless, wrongly, it is taken to
imply that difference and sameness themselves are
actually not different.[1] And, apart from such misunderstanding, the ground and reason of the
antagonism to identity is furnished merely by one-
sided and uncritical metaphysics.

This mistaken opposition is based upon a truth, a
truth that has been misapprehended and perverted
into error. What has been perceived, or dimly felt,
is in fact a principle that, throughout this work, has
so often come before us. The Real in the end is
self-subsistent, and contained wholly in itself; and
its being is therefore not relative, nor does it admit
a division of content from existence. In short relativity and self-transcendence, or, as we may call it,
ideality, cannot as such be the character of ultimate
Reality. And, so far as this goes, we are at one
with the objectors to identity. But the question
really is about the conclusion which follows from this
premise. *Our* conclusion is that finite existence
must, in the end, not be real; it is an appearance
which, as such, is transformed in the Absolute. But
such a result obviously does not imply that, within
the world of phenomena, identity is unreal. And
hence the conclusion, which more or less explicitly
is drawn by our opponents, differs widely from ours.
From the self-subsistent nature of the Real they have

---

[1] So long as we avoid this mistake, we may, and even must,
affirm that things are different, so far as they are the same, and
the same, so far as they are different. To get difference, or
sameness, bare would be to destroy its character.

inferred the reality of diverse existences, beings in any case several and finite, and without community of essence.[1] But this conclusion, as we have seen, is wholly untenable. For plurality and separateness themselves exist only by means of relations (Chapter iii.). To be different from another is to have already transcended one's own being ; and all finite existence is thus incurably relative and ideal. . Its quality falls, more or less, outside its particular "thatness" ; and, whether as the same or again as diverse, it is equally made what it is by community with others. Finite elements are joined by what divides, and are divided by what joins them, and their division and their junction alike are ideal. But, if so, and unless some answer is found to this contention, it is impossible to deny that identity is a fact.[2] It is not real ultimately, we are agreed, but then facts themselves are not ultimate, and the question is confined to the realm of phenomenal existence. For difference itself is but phenomenal, and is itself assuredly not ultimate. And we may end, I think, with this reply. Show us (we may urge) a region of facts which are neither different nor yet the same ; show us how quality without relation, or how mere being, can differentiate ; point out how difference is to keep any meaning, as soon as sameness is wholly banished ; tell us the way in which sameness and difference can exist, if they may not be ideal ; explain how, if identity is not real, the world of experience in any part holds together—at least attempt this, or else admit that identity is ideal and is, at the same time, a fact, and that your objection, in

[1] The English writers who have objected to identity have left their principle of atomism and their principle of relativity simply standing side by side. Not one has (so far as I know) made the smallest attempt seriously to explain the position given to relations. Cp. *Principles of Logic*, p. 96.

[2] Fact in the sense of unseparated adjective of fact. See above, p. 317.

short, had no basis but confusion and traditional prejudice.

But the principle that sameness is real and is not destroyed by differences, demands, as we have seen, some explanation. It would be absurd, for instance, to suppose that two souls really are but one soul, since identity always implies and depends upon difference ; and we may now treat this point as sufficiently discussed. Sameness is real amid differences ; but we must neither deny that these differences, in one sense, affect it, nor may we assert that sameness is always a working connection. I will take these points in their order.

We may say that what is once true remains true always, or that what is the same in any one context, is still the same in any other context. But, in affirming this, we must be on our guard against a serious mistake. For a difference of conditions, it is obvious, will make a difference to sameness, and it is certain that contexts can modify their identical element. If, that is, rushing to the opposite extreme, you go on to immerse wholly your truths in their conditions, if you refuse in any respect to abstract from this total diversity, then the principle of identity becomes inapplicable. You then would not have the same thing under different circumstances, because you would have declined to see anything whatever but difference. But, if we avoid these errors on each side, the principle soon becomes clear. Identity obviously by its essence must be more or less abstract ; and, when we predicate it, we are disregarding other sides of the whole. We are asserting that, notwithstanding other aspects, this one aspect of sameness persists and is real. We do not say how far it extends, or what proportion it bears to the accompanying diversity ; but sameness, so far as it goes, is actually and genuinely the same. Given a fresh instance of a law, and the law still holds good, though in the whole result this one

factor may seem overborne.   The other conditions
here have joined to modify the general consequence,
but the law itself has worked fully, and has maintained its selfsame character.   And, given two individuals with any part of their content indiscernible,
then, while that is so, we are bound, so far, to consider them the same.   However much their diversity
may preponderate, however different may be the
whole effect of each separate compound, yet, for all
that, what is the same in them is one and identical.
And our principle, thus understood, is surely irrefragable, and wears the air, perhaps, more of triviality
than of paradox.   Its results indeed often would be
trivial, most empty and frivolous.   Its significance
varies with varying conditions.   To know that two
souls have an element of their contents in common,
may thus be quite unimportant.   Such knowledge
may, again, assure us of the very gravest and most
fundamental truths.   But of all this the principle
itself, being abstract, tells us nothing.

And as to any working connection our principle
is silent.   Whether an identical point in two things
affects them otherwise, so as to cause other changes
to happen, we are unable to learn from it.   For how
a thing works must depend on its special relations,
while the principle, as we have seen, remains perfectly general.   Two souls, for example, which live
together, may by their identity be drawn into active
community.   If the same were sundered in time,
this, for our knowledge, would be impossible.   But,
in the latter case, the identity exists actually as
much as it exists in the former.   The amount of
sameness, and the kind of sameness, and what the
sameness will bring forth—these points all fall outside of our abstract principle.   But if any one bases
an objection on this ground, he would seem to be
arguing in effect that, because, in fact, diverse identities exist, therefore identity, as a fact, has no actual
existence.   And such a position seems irrational.

Our result, so far, is that the sameness between souls is a fact. The identity of their content is just as real as is their separate existence. But this identity, on the other hand, need not imply a further relation between them. It need not, so far as we can see, act in any way ; and its action, where it acts, appears to be always indirect. Souls seem to influence one another only by means of their bodies.

But this limited view of identity, as a working force, must be modified when we consider the individual soul. In the course of its internal history we must admit that the sameness of its states is an actual mover. In other words the mechanical interpretation, if throughout applicable to Nature, must in dealing with souls be in part given up. And I will end the chapter by pointing out this important distinction.

I mean by Nature here the physical world, considered merely as physical and in abstraction from soul (Chapter xxii.). And in Nature sameness and difference may be said everywhere to exist, but never anywhere to work. This would, at least, appear to be the ideal of natural science, however incompletely that ideal has been carried into practice. No element, according to this principle, can be anything to any other, merely because it is the same, or because it is different. For these are but internal characters, while that which works is in every case an outward relation.[1] But then, if so, sameness and difference may appear at first sight to have no

---

[1] I have not thought it necessary in the text to say anything on the view which finds a solution of all puzzles in impact. For why, in the first place, the working of impact should be self-evident, seems, except by the influence of mere habit, not easy to perceive. And, in the second place, it is sheer thoughtlessness if we imagine that by impact we get rid of the universal. Complete relativity, and an ideal unity which transcends the particulars, are just as essential to impact as to everything else.

meaning at all. They may look like idle ornaments of which science, if consistent, should strip itself. Such a conclusion, however, would be premature, since, if these two characters are removed, science bodily disappears. It would be impossible without them ever to ask Why, or any longer to say Because. And the function of sameness and difference, if we consider it, is obvious. For the external relations, which work, are summed up in the laws; and, on the other hand, the internal characters of the separate elements serve to connect them with these universal strings or hinges. And thus, while inoperative, sameness and difference are still effective indirectly, and in fact are indispensable. This would appear to be the essence of the mechanical view. But I am unable to state how far at present, through the higher regions of Nature, it has been in practice applied; and again I do not know how properly to interpret, for example, the (apparent) effect of identity in the case of continued motion through space. To speak generally, the mechanical view is in principle nonsense, because the position of the laws is quite inconsistent and unintelligible. This is indeed a defect which belongs necessarily to every special science (Chapter xi.), but in the sphere of Nature it reaches its lowest extreme. The identity of physical elements may thus be said to fall outside their own being, their universality seems driven into banishment and forced to reside solely in laws. And, since these laws on the one hand are *not* physical, and since on the other hand they seem essential to Nature, the essence of Nature seems, therefore, made alien to itself, and to be on either side unnaturally sundered. However, compulsion from outside is the one working principle which is taken to hold in the physical world. And, at least if we are true to our ideal, neither identity nor difference can act in Nature.

When we come to psychology this is altered. I do not mean that there the mechanical view ceases wholly, nor do I mean that, where it is superseded, as in the working of pleasure and pain, that which operates must be ideal.[1] But, to a greater or less extent, all psychology, in its practice, is compelled to admit the working power of Identity. A psychologist may employ this force unwillingly, or may deny that he employs it; but without it he would be quite unable to make his way through the subject. I do not propose here to touch upon Coalescence or Blending, a principle much neglected by English psychologists. I will come at once to Redintegration, or what is more familiar to us as Association by Contiguity. Here we are forced to affirm that what happens now in the soul happens because of something else which took place there before. And it happens, further, because of a point of identity connecting the present with the past.[2] That is to say, the past conjunction in the soul has become a law of its being. It actually exists there again because it happened there once, and because, in the present and in the past, an element of content is identical. And thus in the soul we can have habits, while habits that are but physical exist, perhaps, only through a doubtful metaphor. Where present and past functions have not an inner basis of identity, the word habit, if used, has no longer its meaning.[3] Hence we may say that to a large extent the soul is itself its own laws, consists, itself, in the identity between its present and its past, and (unlike Nature) has its own ideal essence not quite external to itself. This seems, at all events, the view which, however erroneous, must be employed by every working psychologist.

[1] On this point, and on what follows, compare *Mind*, xii., pp. 360 and foll.

[2] I have shown, in my *Principles of Logic*, that Contiguity cannot be explained by mere Similarity. See the chapter there on the Association of Ideas.

[3] The question seems to turn on the amount of inward identity which we are prepared to attribute to a physical thing.

But I must hasten to add that this view remains
gravely imperfect. It is in the end impossible to
maintain that anything *is* because it *has been.* And
with regard to the soul, such an objection can be
pressed from two sides. Suppose, in the first place,
that another body like my own were manufactured,
can I deny that with this body would go everything
that I call my self? So long as the soul is not
placed in the position of an idle appendage, I have
already, in principle, accepted this result. I think
that in such a case there would be the same associations and of course the same memory. But we could
no longer repeat here that the soul is, because it
has been. We should be compelled rather to assert
that (in a sense) the soul has been, because it now
is. This imaginary case has led us back, in fact, to
that problem of " dispositions," which we found before was insoluble. Its solution (so far as we could
perceive) would dissolve each of the constructions
called body and soul.

And, in the second place, regarded from the inside, the psychological view of identity is no less a
compromise. We may perhaps apprehend this by
considering the double aspect of Memory. We remember, on the one hand, because of prior events in
our existence. But, on the other hand, memory is
most obviously a construction from the present, and
it depends absolutely upon that which at the moment
we are. And this latter movement, when developed,
carries us wholly outside the psychological view, and
altogether beyond memory. For the main object
of thought may be called the attempt to get rid of
mere conjunctions in the soul. A true connection,
in the end, we see cannot be true because once upon
a time its elements happened together. Mere associations, themselves always universal from the
first,[1] are hence by thought deliberately purified.

[1] I have endeavoured to prove this point in *Principles of Logic*,
pp. 36 and foll. ; 284 and foll.; cp. 460-1. I venture to think that

Starting from mere " facts "—from those relations which are perceived in confused union with an irrelevant context—thought endeavours to transform them. Its advance would end in an ideal world where nothing stands by itself, where, in other words, nothing is forced to stand in relation with what is foreign, but where, on the contrary, truth consists in an absolute relativity. Every element here would be because of something other which supports it, in which other, and in the whole, it finds its own identity. I certainly admit that this ideal can not be fully realized (Chapter xv.) ; but it furnishes the test by which we must judge whatever offers itself as truth. And, measured by this test, the psychological view is condemned.

The entire phenomenal world, as a connected series, and, in this world, the two constructions known as body and soul, are, all alike, imperfect ways of regarding Reality. And these ways at every point have proved unstable. They are arbitrary fixtures which tend throughout to transcend their limits, the limits which, for the sake of practice, we are forced to impose. And the result is everywhere inconsistency. We found that body, attempting to work without identity, became unintelligible. And we saw that the soul, admitting identity as a function in its life, ended also in mere compromise. These things are both appearances, and both are untrue ; but still untruth has got degrees. And, compared with the physical world, the soul is, by far, less unreal. It shows to a larger extent that self-dependence in which Reality consists.

But the discussion of degrees in Reality will engage us hereafter. We may now briefly recall the main results of this chapter. We have seen that body and soul are phenomenal constructions. They

psychology is suffering seriously from want of clearness on this head.

are each inconsistent abstractions, held apart for the
sake of theoretical convenience. And the superior
reality of the body we found was a superstition.
Passing thence to the relation which seems to couple
these two makeshifts, we endeavoured to define it.[1]
We rejected both the idea of mere concomitance,
and of the one-sided dependence of the soul; and
we urged that an adjective which makes no difference to anything, is nonsense. We then discussed
briefly the possibilities of bare soul and bare body,
and we went from this to the relations which actually
exist between souls. We concluded that souls affect
each other, in fact, only through their bodies, but we
insisted that, none the less, ideal identity between
souls is a genuine fact. We found, last of all, that,
in the psychical life of the individual, we had to recognise the active working of sameness. And we
ended this chapter with the reflection which throughout has been near us. We have here been handling
problems, the complete solution of which would involve the destruction of both body and soul. We
have found ourselves naturally carried forward to
the consideration of that which is beyond them.

[1] I would append a few words to explain further my attitude
towards the view which takes the soul as the *ideality* of its body.
If that view made soul and body together an ultimate reality, I
should reject it on this ground. Otherwise certainly I hold that
individuality is ideal, and that soul in general realizes individuality
at a stage beyond body. But I hesitate to assert that the particular soul and body correspond, so that the first is throughout
the fulfilment and inner reality of the second. And I doubt our
right generally to take soul and body together as always making
or belonging to but one finite individual. Further I cannot admit
that the connection of soul and body is really either intelligible
or explicable. My attitude towards this whole doctrine is thus
in the main sympathetically neutral.

CHAPTER XXIV.

DEGREES OF TRUTH AND REALITY.

In our last chapter we reached the question of degrees in Truth and Reality, and we must now endeavour to make clear what is contained in that idea.[1] An attempt to do this, thoroughly and in detail, would carry us too far. To show how the world, physical and spiritual, realizes by various stages and degrees the one absolute principle, would involve a system of metaphysics. And such a system I am not undertaking to construct. I am endeavouring merely to get a sound general view of Reality, and to defend it against a number of difficulties and objections. But, for this, it is essential to explain and to justify the predicates of higher and lower. While dealing with this point, I shall develope further the position which we have already assigned to Thought (Chapters xv. and xvi.).

The Absolute, considered as such, has of course no degrees; for it is perfect, and there can be no more or less in perfection (Chapter xx.). Such predicates belong to, and have a meaning only in the world of appearance. We may be reminded, indeed, that the same absoluteness seems also possessed by existence in time. For a thing either may have a place there, or may have none, but it cannot inhabit any interval between presence and absence. This view would assume that existence in time is Reality; and in practice, and for some purposes,

[1] I may mention that in this chapter I am, perhaps even more than elsewhere, indebted to Hegel.

that is admissible.   But, besides being false, the
assumption tends naturally to pass beyond itself.
For, if a thing may not exist less or more, it must
certainly more or less occupy existence.   It may
usurp ground by its direct presence, but again,
further, by its influence and relative importance.
Thus we should find it difficult, in the end, to say
exactly what we understand by "having" existence.
We should even find a paradox in the assertion, that
everything alike *has* existence to precisely the same
degree.

But here, in metaphysics, we have long ago
passed beyond this one-sided point of view.   On
one hand the series of temporal facts has been perceived to consist in ideal construction.   It is ideal,
not indeed wholly (Chapter xxiii.), but still essentially.   And such a series is but appearance; it is
not absolute, but relative; and, like all other appearance, it admits the distinction of more and less.   On
the other hand, we have seen that truth, which again
itself is appearance, both unconsciously and deliberately diverges from this rude essay.   And, without
considering further the exploded claim set up by
temporal fact, we may deal generally with the question of degrees in reality and truth.

We have already perceived the main nature of
the process of thinking.[1]   Thought essentially consists in the separation of the "what" from the
"that."   It may be said to accept this dissolution
as its effective principle.   Thus it renounces all
attempt to *make* fact, and it confines itself to content.   But by embracing this separation, and by
urging this independent development to its extreme,
thought indirectly endeavours to restore the broken
whole.   It seeks to find an arrangement of ideas,
self-consistent and complete; and by this predicate

[1] Chapters xv. and xvi.   Cp. *Mind*, No. 47.

it has to qualify and make good the Reality. And, as we have seen, its attempt would in the end be suicidal. Truth should mean what it stands for, and should stand for what it means; but these two aspects in the end prove incompatible. There is still a difference, unremoved, between the subject and the predicate, a difference which, while it persists, shows a failure in thought, but which, if removed, would wholly destroy the special essence of thinking.

We may put this otherwise by laying down that any categorical judgment must be false. The subject and the predicate, in the end, cannot either *be* the other. If however we stop short of this goal, our judgment has failed to reach truth; while, if we attained it, the terms and their relation would have ceased. And hence all our judgments, to be true, must become conditional. The predicate, that is, does not hold unless by the help of something else. And this "something else" cannot be stated, so as to fall inside even a new and conditional predicate.[1]

It is however better, I am now persuaded, not to say that every judgment is hypothetical.[2] The word, it is clear, may introduce irrelevant ideas. Judgments are conditional in this sense, that what they affirm is incomplete. It cannot be attributed to Reality, as such, and before its necessary complement is added. And, in addition, this complement in the end remains unknown. But, while it remains unknown, we obviously cannot tell how, if present, it would act upon and alter our predicate. For to suppose that its presence would make no difference is plainly absurd, while the precise nature of the

---

[1] I may, perhaps, refer here to my *Principles of Logic.* Even metaphysical statements about the Absolute, I would add, are not strictly categorical. See below Chapter xxvii.

[2] This term often implies the reality of temporal existence, and is also, apart from that, objectionable. See Mr. Bosanquet's admirable *Logic*, I., Chapter vi.

difference falls outside our knowledge. But, if so, this unknown modification of our predicate may, in various degrees, destroy its special character. The content in fact might so be altered, be so redistributed and blended, as utterly to be transformed. And, in brief, the predicate may, taken as such, be more or less completely untrue. Thus we really always have asserted subject to, and at the mercy of, the unknown.[1] And hence our judgment, always but to a varying extent, must in the end be called conditional.

But with this we have arrived at the meeting-ground of error and truth. There will be no truth which is entirely true, just as there will be no error which is totally false. With all alike, if taken strictly, it will be a question of amount, and will be a matter of more or less. Our thoughts certainly, for some purposes, may be taken as wholly false, or again as quite accurate ; but truth and error, measured by the Absolute, must each be subject always to degree. Our judgments, in a word, can never reach as far as perfect truth, and must be content merely to enjoy more or less of *Validity*. I do not simply mean by this term that, for working purposes, our judgments are admissible and will pass. I mean that less or more they actually possess the character and type of absolute truth and reality. They can take the place of the Real to various extents, because containing in themselves less or more of its nature. They are its representatives, worse

---

[1] Hence in the end we must be held to have asserted the unknown. It is however better *not* to call this the predication of an unknown quality (*Principles of Logic*, p. 87), since "quality" either adds nothing, or else adds what is false. The doctrine of the text seems seriously to affect the reciprocity of ground and consequence, of cause and effect. I certainly agree here that, if the judgments are pure, the relation holds both ways (Bosanquet. *Logic*, I., pp. 261-4). But, if in the end they remain impure, and must be qualified always by an unspecified background, that circumstance must be taken into consideration.

or better, in proportion as they present us with truth
affected by greater or less derangement. Our
judgments hold good, in short, just so far as they
agree with, and do not diverge from, the real standard. We may put it otherwise by saying that truths
are true, according as it would take less or more to
convert them into reality.

We have perceived, so far, that truth is relative
and always imperfect. We have next to see that,
though failing of perfection, all thought is to some
degree true. On the one hand it falls short of, and,
on the other hand at the same time, it realizes the
standard. But we must begin by enquiring what
this standard is.

Perfection of truth and of reality has in the end
the same character. It consists in positive, self-sub-
sisting individuality; and I have endeavoured to
show, in Chapter xx., what individuality means.
Assuming that the reader has recalled the main
points of that discussion, I will point out the two
ways in which individuality appears. Truth must
exhibit the mark of internal harmony, or, again, the
mark of expansion and all-inclusiveness. And these
two characteristics are diverse aspects of a single
principle. That which contradicts itself, in the first
place, jars, because the whole, immanent within it,
drives its parts into collision. And the way to find
harmony, as we have seen, is to re-distribute these
discrepancies in a wider arrangement. But, in the
second place, harmony is incompatible with restriction and finitude. For that which is not all-inclusive must by virtue of its essence internally disagree;
and, if we reflect, the reason of this becomes plain.
That which exists in a whole has external relations.
Whatever it fails to include within its own nature,
must be related to it by the whole, and related externally. Now these extrinsic relations, on the one
hand, fall outside of itself, but, upon the other hand,

cannot do so. For a relation must at both ends
affect, and pass into, the being of its terms. And
hence the inner essence of what is finite itself both
is, and is not, the relations which limit it. Its nature
is hence incurably relative, passing, that is, beyond
itself, and importing, again, into its own core a mass
of foreign connections. Thus to be defined from
without is, in principle, to be distracted within.
And, the smaller the element, the more wide is this
dissipation of its essence—a dissipation too thorough
to be deep, or to support the title of an intestine
division.[1] But, on the contrary, the expansion of
the element should increase harmony, for it should
bring these external relations within the inner substance. By growth the element becomes, more and
more, a consistent individual, containing in itself its
own nature; and it forms, more and more, a whole
inclusive of discrepancies and reducing them to system. The two aspects, of extension and harmony,
are thus in principle one, though (as we shall see
later) for our practice they in some degree fall apart.
And we must be content, for the present, to use them
independently.

Hence to be more or less true, and to be more or
less real, is to be separated by an interval, smaller
or greater, from all-inclusiveness or self-consistency.
Of two given appearances the one more wide, or
more harmonious, is more real. It approaches
nearer to a single, all-containing, individuality. To
remedy its imperfections, in other words, we should
have to make a smaller alteration. The truth and
the fact, which, to be converted into the Absolute,
would require less re-arrangement and addition, is
more real and truer. And this is what we mean by

---

[1] It may seem a paradox to speak of the distraction, say, of a
material particle. But try to state what that *is*, without bringing
into it what it is *not*. Its distraction, of course, is not felt. But
the point is that self-alienation is here too extreme for any feeling,
or any self, to exist.

degrees of reality and truth.   To possess more the
character of reality, and to contain within oneself a
greater amount of the real, are two expressions for
the same thing.

And the principle on which false appearance can
be converted into truth we have already set forth in
our chapter on Error.   The method consists, as we
saw, in supplementation and in re-arrangement; but
I will not repeat here our former discussion.   A
total error would mean the attribution of a content
to Reality, which, even when redistributed and dissolved, could still not be assimilated.   And no such
extreme case seems possible.   An error can be total
only in this sense that, when it is turned into truth,
its particular nature will have vanished, and its
actual self be destroyed.   But this we must allow,
again, to happen with the lower kinds of truth.
There cannot for metaphysics be, in short, any hard
and absolute distinction between truths and false-
hoods.   With each assertion the question is, how
much will be left of that assertion, if we suppose it
to have been converted into ultimate truth?   Out
of everything that makes its special nature as the
predication of this adjective, how much, if anything,
will survive?   And the amount of survival in each
case, as we have already seen, gives the degree of
reality and truth.

But it may perhaps be objected that there are
judgments without any real meaning, and that there
are mere thoughts, which do not even pretend to
attribute anything to Reality.   And, with these, it
will be urged that there can no longer remain the
least degree of truth.   They may, hence, be adjectives of the Real, but are not judgments about it.
The discussion of this objection falls, perhaps, outside the main scope of my work, but I should like
briefly to point out that it rests on a mistake.   In
the first place every judgment, whether positive or

negative, and however frivolous its character, makes an assertion about Reality.[1] And the content asserted cannot, as we have seen, be altogether an error, though its ultimate truth may quite transform its original meaning. And, in the second place, every kind of thought implies a judgment, in this sense that it ideally qualifies Reality. To question, or to doubt, or to suggest, or to entertain a mere idea, is not explicitly to judge. So much is certain and obvious. But, when we enquire further into what these states necessarily imply, our conclusion must be otherwise. If we use judgment for the reference, however unconscious and indefinite, of thought to reality, then without exception to think must be, in some sense, to judge. Thought in its earliest stage immediately modifies a direct sensible presentation; and, although, on one side, the qualification becomes conditional, and although the reality, on the other side, becomes partly non-sensuous, thought's main character is still preserved. The reference to reality may be, in various degrees, undefined and at large. The ideal content may be applied subject to more or less transformation; its struggling and conditional character may escape our notice, or may again be realized with less or more consciousness. But to hold a thought, so to speak, in the air, without a relation of any kind to the Real, in any of its aspects or spheres, we should find in the end to be impossible.[2]

This statement, I am aware, may seem largely paradoxical. The merely imaginary, I may be told, is not referred to reality. It may, on the contrary, be even with consciousness held apart. But, on

[1] I may refer the reader here to my *Principles of Logic*, or, rather, to Mr. Bosanquet's *Logic*, which is, in many points, a great advance on my own work. I have, to a slight extent, modified my views on Judgment. Cf. *Mind*, N.S., No. 60.

[2] See Mr. Bosanquet's *Logic*, Introduction, and the same author's *Knowledge and Reality*, pp. 148–155.

further reflection, we should find that our general account will hold good. The imaginary always is regarded as an adjective of the real. But, in referring it, (*a*) we distinguish, with more or less consciousness, the regions to which it is, and to which it is not, applicable. And (*b*) we are aware, in different degrees, of the amount of supplementation and re-arrangement, which our idea would require before it reached truth. These are two aspects of the same principle, and I will deal briefly with each.

(*a*) With regard to the first point we must recall the want of unity in the world, as it comes within each of us. The universe we certainly feel is one, but that does not prevent it from appearing divided, and in separate spheres and regions. And between these diverse provinces of our life there may be no visible connection. In art, in morality and religion, in trade or politics, or again in some theoretical pursuit, it is a commonplace that the individual may have a world of his own. Or he may rather have several worlds without rational unity, conjoined merely by co-existence in his one personality. And this separation and disconnectedness (we may fail to observe) is, in some degree, normal. It would be impossible that any man should have a world, the various provinces of which were quite rationally connected, or appeared always in system. But, if so, no one, in accepting or rejecting ideas, can always know the precise sense in which he affirms or denies. He means, from time to time, by reality some one region of the Real, which habitually he fails to distinguish and define. And the attempt at distinction would but lead him to total bewilderment. The real world, perhaps consciously, may be identified with the spatial system which we construct. This is "actual fact," and everything else may be set apart as mere thought, or as mere imagination or feeling, all equally unreal. But, if so,

against our wills these banished regions, nevertheless, present themselves as the *worlds* of feeling,
imagination, and thought.　However little we desire
it, these form, in effect, actual constituent factors in
our real universe.　And the ideas, belonging to
these several fields, certainly cannot be entertained
without an identification, however vague, of each
with its department of the Real.　We treat the
imaginary as existing somehow in some world, or in
some by-world, of the imagination.　And, in spite of
our denial, all such worlds are for us inevitably the
appearances of that whole which we feel to be a
single Reality.[1]

And, even when we consider the extreme cases of
command and of wish, our conclusion is unshaken.
A desire is not a judgment, but still in a sense it
implies one.　It might, indeed, appear that what is
ordered or desired is, by its essence, divorced from
all actual reality.　But this first impression would
be erroneous.　All negation, we must remember, is
relative.　The idea, rejected by reality, is none the
less predicable, when its subject is altered.　And it
is predicable again, when (what comes to the same
thing) itself is modified.　Neglecting this latter refinement, we may point out how our account will
hold good in the case of desire.　The content
wished for certainly in one sense is absent from
reality ; and the idea, we must be able to say, does
not exist.　But real existence, on the other hand,
has been taken here in a limited meaning.　And
hence, outside that region of fact which repels the
idea, it can, at the same time, be affirmatively
referred to reality.　It is this reference indeed
which, we may say, makes the contradiction of desire
intolerable.　That which I desire is not consciously

---

[1] The reader may compare here the discussion on the unity of
nature in Chapter xxii.　The want of unity in the self, a point
established by general psychology, has been thrown into promi-
nence by recent experiments in hypnotism.

assumed to exist, but still vaguely, somehow and in some strange region, it is felt to be there ; and, because it is there, its non-appearance excites painful tension. Pursuing this subject we should find that, in every case in the end, to be thought of is to be entertained as, and so judged to be, real.

(*b*) And this leads us to the second point. We have seen that every idea, however imaginary, is, in a sense, referred to reality. But we saw also that, with regard to the various meanings of the real subject, and the diverse provinces and regions in which it appears, we are all, more or less, unconscious. This same want of consciousness, in varying amounts, is visible also in our way of applying the predicate.[1] Every idea can be made the true adjective of reality, but, on the other hand (as we have seen), every idea must be altered. More or less, they all require a supplementation and re-arrangement. But of this necessity, and of the amount of it, we may be totally unaware. We commonly use ideas with no clear notion as to how far they are conditional, and are incapable of being predicated downright of reality. To the suppositions implied in our statements we usually are blind; or the precise extent of them is, at all events, not distinctly realized. This is a subject upon which it might be interesting to enlarge, but I have perhaps already said enough to make good our result. However little it may appear so, to think is always,

---

[1] As was before remarked, these two points, in the end, are the same. Since the various worlds, in which reality appears, cannot each stand alone, but must condition one the other, hence that which is predicated categorically of one world, will none the less be conditional, when applied to the whole. And, from the other side, a conditional predicate of the whole will become categorical, if made the adjective of a subject which is limited and therefore is conditional. These ways of regarding the matter, in the end, are but one way. And, in the end, there is no difference between conditional and conditioned. On this point see farther Chapter xxvii.

in effect, to judge. And all judgments we have
found to be more or less true, and in different
degrees to depart from, and to realize, the standard.
With this we may return from what has been,
perhaps, to some extent a digression.

Our single standard, as we saw above, wears
various aspects, and I will now proceed briefly to
exemplify its detail. (*a*) If we take, first, an appearance in time, and desire to estimate the amount
of its reality, we have, on one side, to consider its
harmoniousness. We have to ask, that is, how far,
before its contents can take their place as an adjective of the Real, they would require re-arrangement.
We have to enquire how far, in other words, these
contents are, or are not, self-consistent and systematic. And then, on the other side, we must have
regard to the extent of time, or space, or both,
which our appearance occupies.[1] Other things
being equal, whatever spreads more widely in space,
or again lasts longer in time, is therefore more
real. But (*b*), beside events, it is necessary to take
account of laws. These are more and less abstract
or concrete, and here our standard in its application
will once more diverge. The abstract truths, for
example, of mathematics on one side, and, on the
other side, the more concrete connections of life or
mind, will each set up a varying claim. The first are
more remote from fact, more empty and incapable
of self-existence, and they are therefore less true.
But the second, on the other hand, are narrower,
and on this account more false, since clearly they
pervade, and hold good over, a less extent of reality.
Or, from the other side, the law which is more
abstract contradicts itself more, because it is deter-

---

[1] The intensity of the appearance can be referred, I think, to
two heads, (i.) that of extent, and (ii.) that of effectiveness. But
the influence of a thing outside of its own limits will fall under an
aspect to be mentioned lower down (p. 376).

mined by exclusion from a wider area. Again the
generalization nearer sense, being fuller of irrelevancy, will, looked at from this point of view, be
more internally discordant. In brief, whether the
system and the true individual is sought in temporal
existence, or in the realm standing above events,
the standard still is the same. And it is applied
always under the double form of inclusiveness and
harmony. To be deficient in either of these aspects
is to fall short of perfection ; and, in the end, any
deficiency implies failure in both aspects alike.

And we shall find that our account still holds good
when we pass on to consider higher appearances of
the universe. It would be a poor world which consisted merely of phenomenal events, and of the laws
that somehow reign above them. And in our every-
day life we soon transcend this unnatural divorce
between principle and fact. (c) We reckon an event
to be important in proportion to its effectiveness, so
far as its being, that is, spreads in influence beyond
the area of its private limits. It is obvious that here
the two features, of self-sufficiency and self-transcendence, are already discrepant. We reach a
higher stage where some existence embodies, or in
any way presents in itself, a law and a principle.
However, in the mere example and instance of an
universal truth, the fact and the law are still essentially alien to each other, and the defective character
of their union is plainly visible. Our standard
moves us on towards an individual with laws of its
own, and to laws which form the vital substance of
a single existence. And an imperfect appearance
of this character we were compelled, in our last
chapter, to recognize in the individual habits of the
soul. Further in the beauty which presents us
with a realized type, we find another form of the
union of fact with principle. And, passing from this
to conscious life, we are called on still for further
uses and fresh applications of our standard. In the

will of the individual, or of the community, so far as
adequately carried out and expressing itself in outward fact, we have a new claim to harmonious and
self-included reality. And we have to consider
in each case the consistency, together with the range
and area, of the principle, and the degree up to
which it has mastered and passed into existence.
And we should find ourselves led on from this, by
partial defect, to higher levels of being. We should
arrive at the personal relation of the individual to
ends theoretical and practical, ends which call for
realization, but which from their nature cannot be
realized in a finite personality. And, once more
here, our standard must be called in when we endeavour, as we must, to form a comparative estimate.
For, apart from the success or failure of the individual's will, these ideas of ultimate goodness and
reality themselves possess, of course, very different
values. And we have to measure the amount of
discordancy and limitation, which fixes the place to
be assigned, in each case, to these various appearances of the Absolute.

To some of these provinces of life I shall have to
return in later chapters. But there are several
points to which, at present, I would draw attention.
I would repeat, first, that I am not undertaking to
set out completely the different aspects of the world ;
nor am I trying to arrange these according to their
comparative degrees of reality and truth. A serious
attempt to perform this would have to be made by
any rational system of first principles, but in this
work I am dealing solely with some main features
of things. However, in the second place, there is a
consideration which I would urge on the reader.
With any view of the world which confines known
reality to existence in time, and which limits truth
to the attempt to reproduce somehow the series of
events—with any view for which merely a thing

exists, or barely does not exist, and for which an idea is false, or else is true—how is it possible to be just to the various orders of appearance? For, if we are consistent, we shall send the mass of our chief human interests away to some unreal limbo of undistinguished degradation. And, if we are not consistent, yet how can we proceed rationally without an intellectual standard? And I think we are driven to this alternative. We must either be incapable of saying one word on the relative importance of things; we can tell nothing of the comparative meaning, and place in the world, owned by art, science, religion, social life or morality; we are wholly ignorant as to the degrees of truth and reality which these possess, and we cannot even say that for the universe any one of them has any significance, makes any degree of difference, or matters at all. Either this, or else our one-sided view must be revolutionized. But, so far as I see, it can be revolutionized only in one of two ways. We may accept a view of truth and reality such as I have been endeavouring to indicate, or we must boldly subordinate everything to the test of feeling. I do not mean that, beside our former inadequate ideal of truth, we should set up, also and alongside, an independent standard of worth. For this expedient, first, would leave no clear sense to " degrees of truth" or " of reality"; and, in the second place, practically our two standards would tend everywhere to clash. They would collide hopelessly without appeal to any unity above them. Of some religious belief, for example, or of some æsthetic representation, we might be compelled to exclaim, " How wholly false, and yet how superior to truth, and how much more to us than any possible reality!" And of some successful and wide-embracing theory we might remark that it was absolutely true and utterly despicable, or of some physical facts, perhaps, that they deserved no kind of attention. Such a separa-

tion of worth from reality and truth would mutilate
our nature, and could end only in irrational compromise or oscillation. But this shifting attitude, though
common in life, seems here inadmissible; and it was
not this that I meant by a subordination to feeling.
I pointed to something less possible, but very much
more consistent. It would imply the setting up of
feeling in some form as an absolute test, not only of
value but also of truth and reality. Here, if we
took feeling as our end, and identified it with pleasure, we might assert of some fact, no matter how
palpable, This is absolutely nothing; or, because
it makes for pain, it is even worse, and is therefore
even less than nothing. Or because some truth,
however obvious, seemed in our opinion not favourable to the increase of pleasure, we should have to
treat it at once as sheer falsehood and error. And
by such an attitude, however impracticable, we
should have at least *tried* to introduce some sort of
unity and meaning into our world.[1]

But if to make mere feeling our one standard is in
the end impossible, if we cannot rest in the intolerable confusion of a double test and control, nor can relapse into the narrowness, and the inconsistency,
of our old mutilated view—we must take courage to
accept the other revolution. We must reject wholly
the idea that known reality consists in a series of
events, external or inward, and that truth merely is
correspondence with such a form of existence. We
must allow to every appearance alike its own degree
of reality, if not also of truth,[2] and we must every-

[1] Such an attitude, beside being impracticable, would however
still be internally inconsistent. It breaks down in the position
which it gives to truth. The understanding, so far as used to
judge of the tendencies of things, is still partly independent. We
either then are forced back, as before, to a double standard, or we
have to make mere feeling the judge also with regard to these tendencies. And this is clearly to end in mere momentary caprice,
and in anarchy.

[2] Whether, and in what sense, every appearance of the Reality
has truth, is a point taken up later in Chapter xxvi.

where estimate this degree by the application of our single standard. I am not here attempting even (as I have said) to make this estimate in general ; and, in detail, I admit that we might find cases where rational comparison seems hopeless. But our failure in this respect would justify no doubt about our principle. It would be solely through our ignorance and our deficiency that the standard ever could be inapplicable. And, at the cost of repetition, I may be permitted to dwell briefly on this head.

Our standard is Reality in the form of self-existence ; and this, given plurality and relations, means an individual system. Now we have shown that no perfect system can possibly be finite, because any limitation from the outside infects the inner content with dependence on what is alien. And hence the marks of harmony and expansion are two aspects of one principle. With regard to harmony (other things remaining the same), that which has extended over and absorbed a greater area of the external, will internally be less divided.[1] And the more an element is consistent, the more ground, other things being equal, is it likely to cover. And if we forget this truth, in the case of what is either abstracted for thought or is isolated for sense, we can recall it by predicating these fragments, as such, of the Universe. We are then forced to perceive both the inconsistency of our predicates, and the large extent of outer supplement which we must add, if we wish to make them true. Hence the amount of either wideness or consistency gives the degree of reality and also of truth. Or, regarding the same thing from the other side, you may estimate by what is lacking. You may measure the reality of anything by the relative amount of transformation, which would follow if its defects were made good. The more an

---

[1] The reader must not forget here that the inconsistency and distraction, which cannot be felt, is *therefore* the greatest (p. 364). Feeling is itself a unity and a solution, however incomplete.

appearance, in being corrected, is transmuted and destroyed, the less reality can such an appearance contain ; or, to put it otherwise, the less genuinely does it represent the Real. And on this principle we succeeded in attaching a clear sense to that nebulous phrase " Validity. "

And this standard, in principle at least, is applicable to every kind of subject-matter. For everything, directly or indirectly, and with a greater or less preservation of its internal unity, has a relative space in Reality. For instance, the mere intensity of a pleasure or pain, beside its occupancy of consciousness, has also an outer sphere or halo of effects. And in some low sense these effects make a part of, or at least belong to, its being. And with facts of perception their extent both in time, and also in space, obviously gives us a point of comparison between them. If, again, we take an abstract truth, which, as such, nowhere has existence, we can consider the comparative area of its working influence. And, if we were inclined to feel a doubt as to the reality of such principles, we might correct ourselves thus. Imagine everything which they represent removed from the universe, and then attempt to maintain that this removal makes no real difference. And, as we proceed further, a social system, conscious in its personal members of a will carried out, submits itself naturally to our test. We must notice here the higher development of concrete internal unity. For we find an individuality, subordinating to itself outward fact, though not, as such, properly visible within it. This superiority to mere appearance in the temporal series is carried to a higher degree as we advance into the worlds of religion, speculation, and art. The inward principle may here become far wider, and have an intenser unity of its own ; but, on the side of temporal existence, it cannot possibly exhibit itself as such. The higher the principle, and

the more vitally it, so to speak, possesses the soul
of things, so much the wider in proportion must be
that sphere of events which in the end it controls.
But, just for this reason, such a principle cannot be
handled or seen, nor is it in any way given to outward or inward perception. It is only the meaner
realities which can ever be so revealed, and which
are able to be verified as sensible facts.

And it is only a standard such as ours which can
assign its proper rank to sense-presentation. It is
solely by accepting such a test that we are able to
avoid two gross and opposite mistakes. There is
a view which takes, or attempts to take, sense-perception as the one known reality. And there is
a view which endeavours, on the other side, to consider appearance in time as something indifferent.
It tries to find reality in the world of insensible
thought. Both mistakes lead, in the end, to a like
false result, and both imply, and are rooted in, the
same principle of error. In the end each would
force us to embrace as complete reality a meagre and
mutilated fraction, which is therefore also, and in
consequence, internally discrepant. And each is
based upon one and the same error about the nature
of things. We have seen that the separation of the
real into idea and existence is a division admissible only within the world of appearance. In the
Absolute every such distinction must be merged
and disappears. But the disappearance of each
aspect, we insisted also, meant the satisfaction of its
claims in full. And hence, though how in detail we
were unable to point out, either side must come
together with its opposite in the Whole. There
thought and sense alike find each its complement
in the other. The principle that reality can wholly
consist in one of these two sides of appearance, we
therefore reject as a fundamental error.

Let us consider more closely the two delusions

which have branched from this stem. The first of
these, perceiving that the series of events is essential, concludes from this ground that mere sense,
either outward or inward, is the one reality. Or, if
it stops short of this, it still argues that to be real is
to be, as such, perceptible. Because, that is, appearance in the temporal series is found necessary for
reality [1]—a premise which is true—an unconscious
passage is made, from this truth, to a vicious conclusion. To appear is construed to imply appearance
always, so to speak, in person. And nothing is
allowed to be real, unless it can be given bodily,
and can be revealed, within one piece of the series.
But this conclusion is radically erroneous. No perception ever, as we have seen clearly, has a character
contained within itself. In order to be fact at all,
each presentation must exhibit ideality, or in other
words transcendence of self; and that which appears at any one moment, is, as such, self-contradictory. And, from the other side, the less a
character is able, as such, to appear—the less its
necessary manifestation can be narrowed in time or
in space—so much the more is it capable of both
expansion and inner harmony. But these two
features, as we saw, are the marks of reality.

And the second of the mistakes is like the first.
Appearance, once more, is falsely identified with
presentation, as such, to sense ; and a wrong conclusion is, once more, drawn from this basis. But
the error now proceeds in an opposite direction.
Because the highest principles are, obviously and
plainly, not perceptible by sense, they are taken to
inhabit and to have their being in the world of pure
thought. And this other region, with more or less
consistency, is held to constitute the sole reality.
But here, if excluded wholly from the serial flow of
events, this world of thought is limited externally

---

[1] Compare here Chapters xix. and xxiii.

and is internally discordant; while, if, further, we attempt to qualify the universe by our mere ideal abstract, and to attach this content to the Reality which appears in perception, the confusion becomes more obvious. Since the sense-appearance has been given up, as alien to truth, it has been in couse-quence set free, and is entirely insubordinate. And its concrete character now evidently determines, and infects from the outside, whatever mere thought we are endeavouring to predicate of the Real. But the union in all perception of thought with sense, the co-presence everywhere in all appearances of fact with ideality—this is the one foundation of truth. And, when we add to this the saving distinction that to have existence need not mean to exist, and that to be realized in time is not always to be visible by any sense, we have made ourselves secure against the worst of errors. From this we are soon led to our principle of degrees in truth and reality. Our world and our life need then no longer be made up arbitrarily. They need not be compounded of the two hemispheres of fact and fancy. Nor need the Absolute reveal itself indiscriminately in a chaos where comparison and value are absent. We can assign a rational meaning to the distinctions of higher and lower.[1] And we have grown convinced that, while not to appear is to be unreal, and while the fuller appearance marks the fuller reality, our principle, with but so much, is only half stated. For comparative ability to exist, individually and as such, within the region of sense, is a sign everywhere, so far as it goes, of degradation in the scale of being.

Or, dealing with the question somewhat less abstractly, we may attempt otherwise to indicate the true position of temporal existence. This, as we have seen, is not reality, but it is, on the other hand, in our experience one essential factor. And to

[1] The position which, in estimating value, is to be assigned to pleasure and pain will be discussed in Chapter xxv.

suppose that mere thought without facts could either be real, or could reach to truth, is evidently absurd. The series of events is, without doubt, necessary for our knowledge,[1] since this series supplies the one source of all ideal content. We may say, roughly and with sufficient accuracy, that there is nothing in thought, whether it be matter or relations, except that which is derived from perception. And, in the second place, it is only by starting from the presented basis that we construct our system of phenomena in space and time. We certainly perceived (Chapter xviii.) that any such constructed unity was but relative, imperfect, and partial. But, none the less, a building up of the sense-world from the ground of actual presentation is a condition of all our knowledge. It is not true that everything, even if temporal, has a place in *our* one " real " order of space or time. But, indirectly or directly, every known element must be connected with its sequence of events, and, at least in some sense, must show itself even there. The test of truth after all, we may say, lies in presented fact.

We should here try to avoid a serious mistake. Without existence we have perceived that thought is incomplete; but this does not mean that, without existence, mere thought in itself is complete fully, and that existence to this super-adds an alien but necessary completion. For we have found in principle that, if anything were perfect, it would not gain by an addition made from the outside. And, here in particular, thought's first object, in its pursuit of actual fact, is precisely the enlarging and making harmonious of its own ideal content. And the reason for this, as soon as we consider it, is obvious. The dollar, merely thought of or imagined, is comparatively abstract and void of properties. But the dollar, verified in space, has got its place

---

[1] The series, in its proper character, is, of course, an ideal construction. But we may disregard that here.

in, and is determined by, an enormous construction
of things.   And to suppose that the concrete context of these relations in no sense qualifies its inner
content, or that this qualification is a matter of indifference to thought, is quite indefensible.

A mere thought would mean an ideal content
held apart from existence.   But (as we have learnt)
to hold a thought is always somehow, even against
our will, to refer it to the Real.   Hence our mere
idea, now standing in relation with the Real, is related also to the phenomenal system of events in time.
It is related to them, but without any connection
with the internal order and arrangements of their system.   But this means that our mere idea is determined
by that system entirely from the outside.   And it will
therefore itself be permeated internally, and so destroyed, by the contingency forced into its content
through these chaotic relations.   Considered from
this side, a thought, if it actually were bare, would
stand at a level lower than the, so-called, chance
facts of sense.   For in the latter we have, at least,
some internal connection with the context, and
already a fixed relation of universals, however
impure.

All reality must be revealed in the world of
events; and that is most real which, within such an
order or orders, finds least foreign to itself.   Hence,
if *other things remain equal*, a definite place in, and
connection with, the temporal system gives increase
of reality.   For thus the relations to other elements,
which must in any case determine, determine, at
least to some extent, internally.   And thus the
imaginary, so far, must be poorer than the perceptible fact; or, in other words, it is compulsorily
qualified by a wider area of alien and destructive
relations.   I have emphasized "if other things remain equal," for this restriction is important.   There
is imagination which is higher, and more true, and
most emphatically more real, than any single fact

of sense. And this brings us back to our old distinction. Every truth must appear, and must subordinate existence; but this appearance is not the same thing as to be present, properly and as such, within given limits of sense-perception. With the general principles of science we may perhaps see this at once. And again, with regard to the necessary appearances of art or religion, the same conclusion is evident. The eternal experience, in every case, fails to enter into the series of space or of time; or it enters that series improperly, and with a show which in various ways contradicts its essence. To be nearer the central heart of things is to dominate the extremities more widely; but it is not to appear there except incompletely and partially through a sign, an unsubstantial and a fugitive mode of expression. Nothing anywhere, not even the realized and solid moral will, can either be quite real, as it exists in time, or can quite appear in its own essential character. But still the ultimate Reality, where all appearance as such is merged, is in the end the actual identity of idea and existence. And, throughout our world, whatever is individual is more real and true; for it contains within its own limits a wider region of the Absolute, and it possesses more intensely the type of self-sufficiency. Or, to put it otherwise, the interval between such an element and the Absolute is smaller. We should require less alteration, less destruction of its own special nature, in order to make this higher element completely real.

We may now pass from this general principle to notice various points of interest, and, in the first place, to consider some difficulties handed on to this chapter. The problems of unperceived Nature, of dispositions in the soul, and the meaning in general of "potential" existence, require our attention. And I must begin by calling attention to an error.

We have seen that an idea is more true in proportion as it approaches Reality. And it approaches
Reality in proportion as it grows internally more
complete. And from this we possibly might conclude that thought, if completed as such, would
itself be real; or that the ideal conditions, if fully
there, would be the same as actual perfection. But
such a conclusion would not hold; for we have
found that mere thought could never, as such, be
completed; and it therefore remains internally inconsistent and defective. And we have perceived,
on the other side, that thought, completed, is forced
to transcend itself. It has then to become one
thing with sense and feeling. And, since these
conditions of its perfection are partly alien to itself,
we cannot say either that, by itself, it can arrive at
completion, or that, when perfected, it, as such, any
longer exists.

And, with this, we may advance to the consideration of several questions. We found (Chapter xxii.)
that parts of the physical world might exist, and
yet might exist, for us, only in the shape of thought.
But we realized also that in the Absolute, where the
contents of all finite selves are fused, these thought-
existences must, in some way, be re-combined with
sense. And the same conclusion held good also
with psychical dispositions (Chapter xxiii.). These,
in their proper character, have no being except in
the world of thought. For they, as we saw, are conditional; and the conditional, as such, has not actual
existence. But once more here the ideas—how in
detail we cannot say—must find their complement
in the Whole. With the addition of this other side
they will make part of the concrete Reality.

Our present chapter, perhaps, may have helped
us to see more clearly on these points. For we
have found that ideal conditions, to be complete
and in this way to become real, must transcend
themselves. They have to pass beyond the world

of mere thought. And we have seen, in the second place, that every idea must possess a certain amount both of truth and reality. The ideal content must appear in the region of existence; and we have found that we have no right ever to regard it as unreal, because it is unable, as such, to show itself and to occupy a place there. We may now apply this principle both to the capacities of the soul, and to the unseen part of Nature. The former cannot properly exist, and the latter (so far as we saw) certainly need not do so. We may consider them each to be, as such, incapable of appearance. But this admission (we now have learnt) does not weaken, by itself, their claim to be real. And the amount of their reality, when our standard is applied, will depend on their importance, on the influence and bearing which each of them possesses in the universe.

Each of them will fall under the head of " potential existence," and we may pass on to consider the meaning of this phrase. The words " potential," and " latent," and " nascent," and we may add " virtual " and " tendency," are employed too often. They are used in order to imply that a certain thing exists ; and this, although either we ought to know, or know, that the thing certainly does not exist. It would be hard to over-estimate the service rendered by these terms to some writers on philosophy. But that is not our business here. Potential existence means a set of conditions, one part of which is present at a certain point of space or time, while the other part remains ideal. It is used generally without any clear perception as to how much is wanted in order to make these conditions complete. And then the whole is spoken of, and is regarded, as existing at the point where actually but a portion of its factors are present. Such an abuse clearly is indefensible.

" Potential existence " is fairly applicable in the

following sense. We may mean by it that something somehow appears already in a given point of time, although it does not as yet appear fully or in its own proper character. I will try to show later the positive conditions required for this use, but it is better to begin by pointing out where it is quite inadmissible. We ought not to speak of potential existence where, if the existence were made actual, the fact given now would be quite gone. That part of the conditions which appears at present, must produce causally the rest; and, in order for this to happen, foreign matter must be added. But, if so much is added that the individuality of this first appearance is wholly destroyed, or is even overwhelmed and swamped—"potential existence" is inapplicable. Thus the death of a man may result from the lodgment of a cherry-stone; but to speak of every cherry-stone as, therefore, the potential death of a man, and to talk of such a death as appearing already in any and every stone, would surely be extravagant. For so large an amount of foreign conditions must contribute to the result, that, in the end, the condition and the consequence are joined externally by chance. We may perhaps apprehend this more clearly by a grosser instance of misuse. A piece of bread, eaten by a poet, may be a condition required for the production of a lyrical poem. But would any one place such a poem's existence already virtually in each piece of food, which may be considered likely by any chance to make its way into a poet?

These absurdities may serve to suggest the proper employment of our term. It is applicabl¹ wherever the factor present is considered capable o producing the rest; and it must effect this without the entire loss of its own existing character. The individuality, in other words, must throughout the process be continuous; and the end must very largely be due to the beginning. And these are two aspects of one principle. For clearly, if more than a certain amount of external conditions are brought in, the ideal identity of the beginning and of the end is destroyed. And, if so, obviously the result itself was not there at the first, and could in no rational sense have already appeared there. The ordinary example of the egg, which itself later becomes a fowl, is thus a legitimate application of potential existence. On the other hand to call every man, without distinction, a potential case of scarlet fever, would at least border on inaccuracy. While to assert that he now is already such products as can be produced only by his own disintegration, would be obviously absurd. Potential existence can, in brief, be used only where "development" or "evolution" retains its proper meaning. And by the meaning of evolution I do not understand that arbitrary misuse of the term, which has been advocated by a so-called "System of Philosophy."

Under certain conditions, then, the idea of potential being may be employed. But I must add at once that it can be employed nowhere with complete truth and accuracy. For, in order for anything to evolve itself, outer conditions must come in ; and it is impossible in the end to assign a limit to the extent of this foreign matter. The genuine cause always must be the whole cause, and the whole cause never could be complete until it had taken in the universe.[1] This is no mere speculative refinement, but a difficulty experienced in working ; and we met it lately while enquiring into the body and soul (Chapter xxiii.). In strictness you can never assert that a thing will be, because of that which it is ; but, where you cannot assert this, potential existence is partly inaccurate. It must be applied more or less vaguely, and more or less on sufferance. We are, in brief, placed between two dangers. If, with anything finite, you refuse wholly to pre-

[1] And this is impossible. See Chapters vi. and xviii.

dicate its relations—relations necessarily in part external, and in part, therefore, variable—then your account of this thing will fall short and be empty. But, otherwise, you will be affirming of the thing that which only it may be.

And, once driven to enter on this course, you are hurried away beyond all landmarks. You are forced indefinitely to go on expanding the subject of your predicates, until at last it has disappeared into something quite different. And hence, in employing potential existence, we are, so to speak, on an inclined plane. We start by saying, "A is such that, under probable conditions, its nature will develope into B; and therefore, because of this, I venture already to call it B." And we end by claiming that, because A may possibly be made to pass into another result C, C may, therefore, on this account, be predicated already. And we have to hold to this, although C, to but a very small extent, has been produced by A, and although, in the result, A itself may have totally vanished.

We must therefore admit that potential existence implies, to some extent, a compromise. Its use, in fact, cannot be defined upon a very strict principle. Still, by bearing in mind what the term endeavours to mean, and what it always must be taken more or less to involve, we may, in practice, succeed in employing it conveniently and safely. But it will remain, in the end, a wide-spread source of confusion and danger. The more a writer feels himself led naturally to have recourse to this phrase, the better cause he probably has for at least attempting to avoid it.

It may throw light on several problems, if we consider further the general nature of Possibility and Chance.[1] We touched on this subject above,

---

[1] On Possibility compare Chapter xxvii, and *Principles of Logic*, Book I., Chap. vii.

when we enquired if complete possibility is the same
as reality (p. 383). Our answer to that question
may be summed up thus : Possibility implies the
separation of thought from existence; but, on the
other hand, since these two extremes are essentially
one, each, while divided from the other, is internally
defective.　　Hence *if* the possible *could* be completed as such, it would have passed into the real.
But, in reaching this goal, it would have ceased
altogether to be mere thought, and it would in consequence, therefore, be no longer possibility.

The possible implies always the partial division
of idea from reality.　　It is, properly, the consequence in thought from an ideal antecedent.　　It
follows from a set of conditions, a system which is
never complete in itself, and which is not taken to
be real, as such, except through part of its area.
But this last qualification is necessary.　The possible, itself, is not real ; but its essence partly transcends ideas, and it has no meaning at all unless it
is possible really.　It must be developed from, and
be relative to, a real basis.　And, hence, there can
be no such thing as unconditional possibility.　The
possible, in other words, is always relative.　And,
if it attempts to be free, it ceases to be itself.

We shall understand this, perhaps, better, if we
recall the nature of relative chance (Chapter xix.).
Chance is the given fact which falls outside of some
ideal whole or system.　And any element, not included within such a universal, is, in relation to
that universal, bare fact, and so relative chance.
Chance, in other words, would not be actual chance,
if it were not also more.　It is viewed in negative.
relation to some idea, but it could not exist in
relation unless in itself it were ideal already.　And
with relative possibility, again, we find a counterpart
implication.　The possible itself would not be
possible, if it were not more, and if it were not
partially real.　There must be an actual basis in

which a part of its conditions is realized, though, by and in the possible, this actual basis need not be expressed, but may be merely understood. And, since the conditions are manifold, and since the part which is taken as real is largely variable, possibility varies accordingly. Its way of completing itself, and in particular the actual basis which it implies, are both capable of diversity. Thus the possibility of an element is different, according as it is understood in these diverse relations. Possibility and chance, we may say, stand to one another thus. An actual fact more or less ignores the ideal complement which, within its own being, it involves. And hence, if you view it merely in relation to some system which falls outside itself, the actual fact is, so far, chance The possible, on the other hand, explicitly isolates one part of the ideal complement, and, at the same time, implies, more or less vaguely, its real completion. It fluctuates, therefore, with the various conditions which are taken as necessary to complete it. But of these conditions part must have actual existence, or must, as such, be real.

And this account still holds good, when we pass to the lowest grade of possibility. I take an idea, which, in the first place, I cannot call unmeaning. And this idea, secondly, I do not see to contradict itself or the Reality. I therefore assume that it has not this defect. And, merely on the strength of this, I go on to call such an idea possible. It might seem as if here we had passed from relative to unconditional possibility; but that view would be erroneous. The possible here is still a consequence from conditions, part of which is actual. For, though of its special conditions we know nothing, we are not quite ignorant. We have assumed in it more or less of the general character, material and formal, which is owned by Reality. This character is its actual basis and real ground of possibility.

And, without this, the idea would cease altogether to be possible.

What are we to say then about the possibility, or about the chance, which is *bare*, and which is not relative, but absolute and unconditional ? We must say of either that it presents one aspect of the same fundamental error. Each expresses in a different way the same main self-contradiction ; and it may perhaps be worth while to exhibit this in detail. With mere possibility the given want of all connection with the Real is construed into a ground for positive predication. Bare chance, again, gives us as a fact, and gives us therefore in relation, an element which it still persists is unrelated. I will go on to explain this statement.

I have an idea, and, because in my opinion I know nothing about it, I am to call it possible. Now, if the idea has a meaning, and is taken not to contradict itself, this (as we have seen) is, at once, a positive character in the idea. And this gives a known reason for, at once so far, regarding it as actual. And such a possibility, because in relation with an attribute of the Real, we have seen, is still but a relative possibility. In absolute possibility we are supposed to be without this knowledge. There, merely because I do *not* find any relation between my idea and the Reality, I am to assert, upon this, that my idea is compatible. And the assertion clearly is inconsistent. Compatible means that which in part is perceived to be true ; it means that which internally is connected with the Real. And this implies assimilation, and it involves penetration of the element by some quality or qualities of the Real. If the element is compatible it will be preserved, though with a greater or less destruction of its particular character. But in bare possibility I have perverted the sense of compatible. Because I find absence of incompatibility, because, that is,

I am without a certain perception, I am to call my idea compatible. On the ground of my sheer ignorance, in other words, I am to know that my idea is assimilated, and that, to a greater or less extent, it will survive in Reality. But such a position is irrational.

That which is unconditionally possible is viewed apart from, and is supposed to remain undetermined by, relation to the Real. There are no seen relations, and therefore none, and therefore no alien relations which can penetrate and dissolve our supposed idea. And we hold to this, even when the idea is applied to the Real. But a relation to the Real implies essentially a relation to what the Real possesses, and hence to have no relations of one's own means to have them all from the outside. Bare possibility is therefore, against its will, one extreme of relatedness. For it is conjoined *de facto* with the Reality, as we have that in our minds ; and, since the conjunction is external, the relatedness is given by outer necessity. But necessary relation of an element to that which is outside means, as we know, the disruption of this element internally. The merely possible, if it could exist, would be, therefore, for all we know, sheer error. For it would, so far as we know, be an idea, which, in no way and to no extent, is accepted by Reality. But possibility, in this sense, has contradicted itself. Without an actual basis in, and without a positive connection with, Reality, the possible is, in short, not possible at all.[1]

[1] It may be worth while to notice that Possibility, if you try to make it unconditional, is the same thing as one sense of Inconceivability or Impossibility. The Impossible really is that which contradicts positive knowledge (Chapter xxvii.). It is never that which you merely fail to connect with Reality. But, if you wrongly took it in this sense, and if you based it on mere privation, it would unawares have turned round into the unconditionally possible. For that is actually incompatible with the Reality, as *de facto* we have the Reality in our minds. Each of these ideas,

There is a like self-contradiction in absolute chance. The absolutely contingent would mean a fact which is given free from all internal connection with its context. It would have to stand without relation, or rather with all its relations outside. But, since a thing must be determined by the relations in which it stands, the absolutely contingent would thus be utterly determined from the outside. And so, by consequence, chance would involve complete internal dissipation. It would hence implicitly preclude the given existence which explicitly it postulates. Unless chance is more than mere chance, and thus consents to be relative, it fails to be itself. Relative chance implies inclusion within some ideal whole, and, on that basis, asserts an external relation to some other whole. But chance, made absolute, has to affirm a positive existence in relation, while insisting that all relations fall outside this existence. And such an idea contradicts itself.

Or, again, we may bring out the same discrepancy thus. In the case of a given element we fail to see its connection with some system. We do not perceive in its content the internal relations to what is beyond it—relations which, because they are ideal, are necessary and eternal. Then, upon the ground of this failure, we go on to a denial, and we insist that no such internal relations are present. But every relation, as we have learnt, essentially penetrates the being of its terms, and, in this sense, is intrinsical; or, in other words, every relation must be a relation of content. And hence the element, deprived by bare chance of all ideal relations, is unrelated altogether. But, if unrelated and undetermined, it is no longer any separate element at all. It cannot have the existence ascribed to it by absolute chance.

Chance and possibility may be called two different in short, is viciously based on privation, and each is a different aspect of the same self-contradictory complex aspects of one complex. Relative chance stands for something which is, but is, in part, not connected and understood. It is therefore that which exists, but, in part, only somehow. The relatively possible is, on the other hand, what is understood incompletely, and yet is taken, more or less only somehow, to be real. Each is thus an imperfect way of representing reality. Or we may, if we please, repeat the distinction in another form. In bare chance something is to be given, and therefore given in a connection of outer relations ; and it yet is regarded as not intrinsically related. The abstractly possible, again, is the not-related ; but it is taken, at the same time, in relation with reality, and is, therefore, unawares given with external relations. Chance forgets, we may say, the essential connection ; and possibility forgets its *de facto* relation to the Real, that is, its given external conjunction with context. Chance belongs to the world of existence and possibility to thought ; but each contains at bottom the same defect, and each, against its will, when taken bare, becomes external necessity.[1] If the possible could be given, it would be indifferently chance or fate. If chance is thought of, it is at once but merely possible ; for what is contingent has no complete connection with Reality.

With this I will pass from a subject, on which I have dwelt perhaps too long. There is no such thing as absolute chance, or as mere external necessity, or as unconditional possibility. The possible must, in part, be really, and that means internally, necessary. And the same, again, is true of the

[1] The identity, in the end, of possibility with chance, and of chance with external or brute necessity, has instructive consequences. It would obviously give the proper ground for an estimate of that which vulgarly is termed Free Will. This doctrine may in philosophy be considered obsolete, though it will continue to flourish in popular Ethics. As soon as its meaning is apprehended, it loses all plausibility. But the popular moralist will always exist by not knowing what he means.

contingent. Each idea is relative, and each lays stress on an opposite aspect of the same complex. And hence each, forced to a one-sided extreme, disappears altogether.

We are led from this to ask whether there are degrees of possibility and contingency, and our answer to this question must be affirmative. To be more or less possible, and to be more or less true, and intrinsically necessary,—and, from the other side, to be less or more contingent—are, in the end, all the same. And we may verify here, in passing, the twofold application of our standard. That which is more possible is either internally more harmonious and inclusive ; it is, in other words, nearer to a complete totality of content, such as would involve passage into, and unity with, the Real. Or the more possible is, on the other hand, partly realized in a larger number of ideal groups. Every contact, even with a point in the temporal series, means ideal connection with a concrete group of relations. Hence the more widely possible is that which finds a smaller amount of content lying wholly outside its own area. It is, in other words, the more individual, the truer, and more real. And, since it contains more connections, it has in itself more internal necessity. For a like reason, on the other side, increase of contingency means growth in falseness. That which, so far as it exists, has more external necessity—more conjunction from the outside with intelligible systems—has, therefore, less connection with any. It is hence more empty, and, as we have seen, on that account less self-contained and harmonious. This brief account, however incorrect to the eye of common sense, may perhaps, as part of our main thesis, be found defensible.

It will throw a light on that thesis, if we end by briefly considering the " ontological " proof. In

Chapter xiv. we were forced to deal with this in
one of its bearings, and here we may attempt to
form an estimate of its general truth.   As an argument, it is a conclusion drawn from the presence
of some thought to the reality of that which the
thought contains.   Now of course any one at a
glance can see how futile this might be.   If you
identify reality with spatial or even temporal existence, and understand by thought the idea of some
distinct finite object, nothing seems more evident
than that the idea may be merely " in my head."
When, however, we turn from this to consider the
general nature of error, then what seemed so evident
becomes obscure and presents us with a puzzle.
For what is " in my head " must, after all, be surely
somewhere in the universe.   And when an idea
qualifies the universe, how can it be excluded from
reality?   The attempt to answer such a question
leads to a distinction between reality and finite existence.   And, upon this, the ontological proof may
perhaps seem better worth examining.

Now a thought only " in my head," or a bare idea
separated from all relation to the real world, is a
false abstraction.   For we have seen that to hold
a thought is, more or less vaguely, to refer it to
Reality.   And hence an idea, wholly un-referred,
would be a self-contradiction.   This general result
at once bears upon the ontological proof.   Evidently
the proof must start with an idea referred to and
qualifying Reality, and with Reality present also
and determined by the content of the idea.   And
the principle of the argument is simply this, that,
standing on one side of such a whole, you find yourself moved necessarily towards the other side.
Mere thought, because incomplete, suggests logically
the other element already implied in it; and that
element is the Reality which appears in existence.
On precisely the same principle, but beginning from
the other end, the " Cosmological " proof may be

said to argue to the character of the Real. Since Reality *is* qualified by thought, it therefore *must* possess whatever feature thought's essence involves. And the principle underlying these arguments— that, given one side of a connected whole, you can go from this to the other sides—is surely irrefragable.

The real failure of the ontological proof lies elsewhere. For that proof does not urge merely that its idea must certainly somehow be real. It goes beyond this statement, and qualifies it by " real as such." And here the argument seems likely to deviate into error. For a general principle that every predicate, as such, is true of Reality, is evidently false. We have learnt, on the contrary, that truth and reality are matter of degree. A predicate, we may say, in no case is, as such, really true. All will be subject to addition, to qualification and rearrangement. And its truth will be the degree up to which any predicate, when made real, preserves its own character. In Chapter xiv., when dealing with the idea of perfection, we partly saw how the ontological argument breaks down. And the general result of the present chapter should have cleared away difficulties. Any arrangement existing in my head must qualify the absolute Reality. But, when the false abstraction of my private view is supplemented and made good, that arrangement may, as such, have completely disappeared. The ontological proof then should be merely another way of insisting on this doctrine. Not every idea will, as such, be real, or, as such, have existence. But the greater the perfection of a thought, and the more its possibility and its internal necessity are increased, so much more reality it possesses. And so much the more necessarily must it show itself, and appear somehow in existence.

But the ontological argument, it will be rightly said, makes no pretence of being applicable to every finite matter. It is used of the Absolute, and, if confined to that, will be surely legitimate. We are, I think, bound to admit this claim. The idea of the Absolute, as an idea, is inconsistent with itself; and we find that, to complete itself, it is internally driven to take in existence. But even here we are still compelled to keep up some protest against the addition of "as such." No idea in the end can, strictly as such, reach reality; for, as an idea, it never includes the required totality of conditions. Reality is concrete, while the truest truth must still be more or less abstract. Or we may put the same thing otherwise by objecting to the form of the argument. The separation, postulated in the premise, is destroyed by the conclusion; and hence the premise itself could not have been true. This objection is valid, and it is not less valid because it holds, in the end, of every possible argument. But the objection disappears when we recognise the genuine character of the process. This consists in the correction by the Whole of an attempted isolation on the part of its members. And, whether you begin from the side of Existence or of Thought, the process will remain essentially the same. There is a subject and a predicate, and there is the internal necessity, on each side, of identity with the other side. But, since in this consummation the division as such is transcended, neither the predicate nor the subject is able to survive. They are each preserved, but transmuted.

There is another point on which, in conclusion, it is well to insist. If by reality we mean existence as a presented event, then to be real, in this sense, marks a low type of being. It needs no great advance in the scale of reality and truth, in order to make a thing too good for existence such as this. And I will illustrate my meaning by a kind of bastard use of the ontological proof.[1] Every idea,

---

[1] *Principles of Logic*, pp. 67-9.

it is certain, possesses a sensible side or aspect.
Beside being a content, it, in other words, must be
also an event. Now to describe the various existences of ideas, as psychical events, is for the most
part a task falling outside metaphysics.[1] But the
question possesses a certain bearing here. The
existence of an idea can be, to a greater or to a less
degree, incongruous with its content; and to predicate the second of the first would involve various
amounts of inconsistency. The thought of a past
idea, for example, is a present state of mind; the
idea of a virtue may be moral vice; and the horse,
as judged to exist, cannot live in the same field
with the actual horse-image.[2] On the other hand,
at least in most cases, to think of anger is, to however slight an extent, to be angry; and, usually,
ideas of pleasures and pains are, as events, themselves pleasures and pains in fact. Wherever the
idea can be merely one aspect of a single presentation, there we can say that the ideal content exists,
and is an actual event. And it is possible, in such
cases, to apply a semblance of the ontological proof.
Because, that is, the existence of the fact is necessary, as a basis and as a condition, for the idea, we
can go from the presence of the idea to the presence
of the fact. The most striking instance would be
supplied by the idea of " this " or " mine." Immediate contact with Reality can obviously, as a fact,
never fail us; and so, when we use the idea of this
contact, we take it always from the fact as, in some
form, that appears. It is therefore impossible that,
given the idea, its existence should be lacking.

But, when we consider such a case more closely,

---

[1] The question is one for psychology, and I may perhaps be
permitted to remark that, with regard to abstract ideas, it seems
still in a very unsatisfactory condition. To fall back on Language,
after all, will not tell us precisely how much passes through the
mind, when abstract ideas are made use of.

[2] Compare *Mind*, xxxiv., pp. 286–90, and xliii., pp. 313–14.

its spuriousness is manifest. For (*a*), in the first place, the ideal content is not moved from within. It does not of itself seek completion through existence, and so imply that by internal necessity.[1] There is no intrinsic connection, there is but a mere found conjunction, between the two sides of idea and existence. And hence the argument, to be valid here, must be based on the mediation of a third element, an element coexisting with, but of itself extraneous to, both sides. But with this the essence of the ontological argument is wanting. And (*b*), in the second place, the case we are considering exhibits another gross defect. The idea, which it predicates of the Real, possesses hardly any truth, and has not risen above the lowest level of worth and reality. I do not mean merely that the idea, as compared with its own existence, is abstract, and so false. For that objection, although valid, is relatively slight. I mean that, though the argument starting from the idea may exhibit existence, it is not able to show either truth or reality. It proves on the other hand, contrary to its wish, a vital failure in both. Neither the subject, nor again the predicate, possesses really the nature assigned to it. The subject is taken as being merely a sensible event, and the predicate is taken as one feature included in that fact. And in each of these assumptions the argument is grossly mistaken. For the genuine subject is Reality, while the genuine predicate asserts of this every character contained in the ostensible predicate and subject. The idea, qualified as existing in a certain sensible event, is the predicate, in other words, which is affirmed of the Absolute. And since such a predicate is a poor abstraction, and since its essence, therefore, is determined by what falls outside its own being, it is, hence, inconsistent with itself, and contradicts its proper subject.

[1] So far as it did this, it would have to expand itself to its own destruction.

We have in brief, by considering the spurious ontological proof, been led once more to the conclusion
that existence is not reality.

Existence is not reality, and reality must exist.
Each of these truths is essential to an understanding of the whole, and each of them, necessarily in
the end, is implied in the other. Existence is, in
other words, a form of the appearance of the Real.
And we have seen that to appear, as such, in one
or in many events, is to show therefore a limited
and low type of development. But, on the other
hand, not to appear at all in the series of time, not
to exhibit one's nature in the field of existence, is
to be false and unreal. And to be more true, and
to be more real, is, in some way or other, to be
more manifest outwardly. For the truer always is
wider. There is a fair presumption that any truth,
which cannot be exhibited at work, is for the most
part untrue. And, with this understanding, we may
take our leave of the ontological proof. Our inspection of it, perhaps, has served to confirm us in
the general doctrine arrived at in our chapter. It
is only a view which asserts degrees of reality and
truth, and which has a rational meaning for words
such as "higher" and "lower"—it is only such a
view which can do justice alike to the sides of idea
and existence.

CHAPTER XXV.

GOODNESS.

In a former chapter I tried to show, briefly, that the existence of evil affords no good ground for an objection against our Absolute. Evil and good are not illusions, but they are most certainly appearances. They are one-sided aspects, each over-ruled and transmuted in the Whole. And, after the discussions of our last chapter, we should be better able to appreciate their position and value. As with truth and error, so with good and bad, the opposition is not absolute. For, to some extent and in some manner, perfection is everywhere realized And yet, upon the other hand, the distinction of degrees is no less vital. The interval which exists between, and which separates, the lower and the higher, is measured by the idea of perfect Reality. The lower is that which, to be made complete, would have to undergo a more total transformation of its nature. And viewed from the ground of what is higher—of what they fail to reach or even oppose—the lower truth and lower goodness become sheer error and evil. The Absolute is perfect in all its detail, it is equally true and good throughout. But, upon the other side, each distinction of better and more true, every degree and each comparative stage of reality is essential. They are made and justified by the all-pervasive action of one immanent perfection.

And guided by this two-fold principle we might approach without misgiving the diverse worlds of appearance. But in this work I am endeavouring merely to defend a general view. And so, both on the whole and here in particular with regard to goodness, I, cannot attempt to deal fully with any aspect of the Absolute. It is mainly the common prejudice in favour of the ultimate truth of morality or religion, that has led me to give to them here a space which perhaps is undue. But, even with this, I can but touch on certain features of the subject; and I must deal chiefly with those which are likely to be urged as objections to our doctrine.[1]

We may speak of the good, generally, as that which satisfies desire. It is that which we approve of, and in which we can rest with a feeling of contentment. Or we may describe it again, if we please, as being the same as worth. It contains those elements which, also, we find in truth. Truth and goodness are each the correspondence, or rather each the identity, of idea and existence. In truth we start with existence, as being the appearance of perfection, and we go on to complete ideally what really must be there. In goodness, on the other hand, we begin with an idea of what is perfect, and we then make, or else find, this same idea in what exists. And the idea also I take to be desired. Goodness is the verification in existence of a desired ideal content, and it thus implies the measurement of fact by a suggested idea. Hence both goodness and truth contain the separation of idea and existence, and involve a process in time. And, there-

---

[1] My *Ethical Studies*, 1876, a book which in the main still expresses my opinions, contains a further discussion on many points. For my views on the nature of pleasure, desire, and volition, I must refer to *Mind*, No. 49. My former volume would have been reprinted, had I not desired to rewrite it. But I feel that the appearance of other books, as well as the decay of those superstitions against which largely it was directed, has left me free to consult my own pleasure in this matter.

fore, each is appearance, and but a one-sided aspect of the Real.[1]

But the good (it may be objected) need involve no idea. Is not the pleasant, as such, good? Is not at any rate any feeling in which we rest with satisfaction, at once good in itself? I answer these questions in the negative. Good, in the proper sense, implies the fulfilment of desire; at least, if you consider anything apart from the realization of a suggested idea, it is at a stage below goodness. Such an experience would *be*, but it would not, properly, have yet become either good or true. And on reflection, perhaps, we should not wish to make use of these terms. For, at our level of mental life, whatever satisfies and contents us can hardly fail to have some implication with desire. And, if we take it where as yet it suggests nothing, where we have no idea of what we feel, and where we do not realize, however dimly, that " it is this which is good "—then it is no paradox to refuse to such a stage the name of goodness. Such a feeling would *become* good, if for a moment I were so to regard it; for I then should possess the idea of what satisfies, and should find that idea given also in fact. But, where ideas are absent, we should not speak of anything as being actually good or true. Goodness and truth may be there potentially, but as yet neither of them *is* there.

And that an idea is required for goodness seems fairly clear, but with regard to desire there is more room for doubt. I may approve, in the sense of finding a pleasant idea realized, and yet, in some cases, desire appears to be absent. For, in some cases, existence does not oppose my idea, and there

[1] In the main, what is true is good, because the good has to satisfy desire, and, on the whole, we necessarily desire to find the more perfect. What is good is true, in the main, because the idea desired, being, in general, more perfect, is more real. But on the relation of these aspects further see the next chapter.

is, hence, no place open for the tension of desire. This assertion might be combated, but, for myself, I am prepared to admit it. And the inclusion of desire in the idea of good, to this extent I allow, may be called arbitrary. But it seems justifiable, because (as things are) desire must be developed. Approval without desire is but an extreme and a passing condition. There cannot fail to come a wavering, and so an opposition, in my state; and with this at once we have the tension required for desire. Desire, I thus admit, may, for the moment, be absent from approval; but, because it necessarily must ensue, I take it as essential. Still this point, in my opinion, has little importance. What is important is to insist that the presence of an idea is essential to goodness.

And for this reason we must not admit that the pleasant, as such, is good. The good is pleasant, and the better, also, is in proportion more pleasant. And we may add, again, that the pleasant is generally good, if we will leave out " as such." For the pleasant will naturally become desired, and will therefore on the whole be good. But we must not assert that everything pleasant is the satisfaction of a desire, or even always must imply desire or approval. And hence, since an idea may be absent, the pleasant sometimes may be not properly good.

And against the identification of bare pleasure, as such, with the good we may unhesitatingly pronounce. Such a view separates the aspect of pleasure, and then denies that anything else in the world is worth anything at all. If it merely asserted that the more pleasant and the better were one, its position would be altered. For, since pleasure goes with everything that is free from discord, or has merged discord in fuller harmony, naturally the higher degree of individuality will be therefore more pleasant.[1] And we have included pleasure as an

---

[1] I must refer here to *Mind*, No. 49.

essential element in our idea of perfection (Chapter xx.). But it will hardly follow from this that nothing in the universe except pleasure is good, and that, taking this one aspect as the end, we may regard all else as mere means. Where everything is connected in one whole, you may abstract and so may isolate any one factor. And you may prove at your ease that, without this, all the rest are imperfect and worthless ; and you may show how, this one being added, they all once more gain reality and worth. And hence of every one alike you may conclude that it is the end for the sake of which all the others exist. But from this to argue, absolutely and blindly, that some one single aspect of the world is the sole thing that is good, is most surely illogical. It is to narrow a point of view, which is permissible only so long as it is general, into a one-sided mistake. And thus, in its denial that anything else beside pleasure is good, Hedonism must be met by a decided rejection.

Is a thing desired always, because it is first pleasant, or is it ever pleasant rather, on the other hand, because we desire it ?[1] And we may ask the same question as to the relation of the desired to the good. But, again, is anything true because I am led to think it, or am I rather led to think it because of its truth? And, once more, is *it* right because *I* ought, or does the " because " only hold in the opposite direction ? And is an object beauti-

---

[1] The object of *any* idea has a tendency to become desired, if held over against fact, although, beforehand and otherwise, it has not been, and is not pleasant. *Every* idea, as the enlargement of self, is, in the abstract and so far, pleasant. And the pleasantness of an idea, as my psychical state, can be transferred to its object. We have to ask always what it is that fixes an idea against fact. Is it there because its object has been pleasant, or because it, or its object, is now pleasant? And can we not say sometimes that it is pleasant only because it is there ? The discussion of these matters would lead to psychological subtleties, which here we may neglect.

ful because it affects me, or is, on the other hand,
my emotion the result of its beauty ? In each of
these cases we first have made a separation which
is too rigid, and on this foundation are built questions which threaten us with a dilemma. We set
down upon each side, as a fact and as presupposed,
what apart from the other side, at least sometimes,
would have no existence. If good is the satisfaction
of desire, you may take desire as being its condition ; but, on the other hand, you would desire
hardly anything at all, unless in some sense it had
given satisfaction already. Certainly the pleasant,
as we have seen, may, for a time and at a low level,
be not approved of or desired. But it is another
thing to assert that goodness consists in, or is a
mere result from, pleasure.

That which consistent Hedonism would, at least
by implication, deny, is the direction of desire in the
end towards anything but pleasure. Something *is*
pleasant as a fact, and solely for that cause it is
desired ; and with this the whole question seems
forthwith settled. But pleasure itself, like every
other fact, cannot be something which just happens.
Upon its side also, assuredly, it is not without a
reason. And, when we ask, we find that pleasure
co-exists always with what we call perfection or
individuality. But, if so, then surely the "because"
holds as firmly in one way as in the other. And,
so far as I see, if we have a right to deny that a
certain character is necessary for pleasure, we should
have the same right to repudiate the connection between pleasure and desire. If the one co-existence
is mere accident and a conjunction which happens,
then why not also, and as much, the other ? But,
if we agree that the connection is two-sided, and
that a degree of relative perfection is essential to
pleasure, just as pleasure, on its side, is an element
in perfection, then Hedonism, at once, is in principle
refuted. The object of desire will never fail, as

such, to contain more than pleasure; and the idea that either pleasure, or any other aspect, is the single End in the universe must be allowed to be untenable (Chapter xxvi.). I may perhaps put this otherwise by urging that, even if Hedonism *were* true, there would be no possible way in which its truth could be shown.[1]

Passing from this mistake I will notice another doctrine from which we must dissent. There is a temptation to identify goodness with the realization of the Will; and, on the strength of a certain assumption, this conclusion would, taken broadly, be right. But we shall see that this assumption is not tenable (Chapter xxvi.), and, without it, the conclusion cannot stand. We have noticed that the satisfaction of desire can be *found* as well as *made* by the individual. And where experienced existence is both pleasant and satisfies desire, I am unable to see how we can refuse to call it good. Nor, again, can pleasure be limited so as to be the feeling of the satisfied will, since it clearly seems to exist in the absence of volition.[2]

I may perhaps express our general view by saying that the good is co-extensive with approbation. But I should add that approbation is to be taken in

---

[1] I have noticed above (p. 374) the want of thoroughness displayed by Hedonism in its attitude towards the intellect. See more below, p. 434. For further criticism of details I may refer to my *Ethical Studies*, and again to a pamphlet that was called *Mr. Sidgwick's Hedonism*. Cp. *Mind*, 49, p. 36.

[2] I may add that in time it precedes the development of will. Will and thought, proper, imply the distinction of subject from object, and pain and pleasure seem prior to this distinction, and indeed largely to effect it. I may emphasize my dissent from certain views as to the dependence of pleasure on the Will, or the Self, or the Ego, by stating that I consider these to be products and subsequent to pleasure. To say that they are made solely by pleasure and pain would be incorrect. But it would be much *more* correct than to take the latter always as being a reaction from them.

its widest sense. To approve is to have an idea in which we feel satisfaction, and to have or imagine the presence of this idea in existence. And against the existence which, actually or in imagination, fails to realize the idea, the idea becomes an " is to be," a "should" or an "ought." Nor is approbation in the least confined to the realm of morality proper, but is found just as much in the worlds of specula-tion or art. Wherever a result, external or inward, is measured by an idea which is pleasant, and is seen to correspond, we can, in a certain sense, be said to approve. And, where we approve, there certainly we can be said also to find the result good.[1]

The good, in general, is often identified with the desirable. This, I think, is misleading. For the desirable means that which is to be, or ought to be, desired. And it seems, hence, to imply that the good

---

[1] For the sake of convenience I assume that approval implies desire, but in certain cases the assumption would hardly be cor-rect (p. 404). But approval always must imply that the idea is pleasant. Apart from, or in abstraction from, that feature, we should have mere recognition. And, though recognition tends always to become approval, yet in idea they are not the same ; and again in fact recognition, I think, is possible where approval is absent.

We approve, of course, not always absolutely, but from some one point of view. Even where the result is most unwelcome we may still approve theoretically ; and to find what we are looking for, however bad, is an intellectual success, and may, so far, be approved of. It will then be good, so far as it is regarded solely from this one aspect. The real objection against making approval co-extensive with goodness is that approval implies usually a certain degree of reflection, and suggests the judging from an abstracted and impersonal point of view. In this way approba-tion may be found, for instance, to be, so far, incompatible with love, and so also with some goodness. But if approbation is taken at a low level of development, and is used to mean no more than the finding anything to be that which gives satisfaction, the objection disappears. The relation of practical to theo-retical approval will be touched on further in Chapter xxvi. Approval, of course, is practical where the idea is of something to be done.

might be good, and yet not be desired, or, again, that something might be desired which is not good. And, if good is taken generally, these assertions at least are disputable. The term "desirable" belongs to the world of relative goods, and has a clear meaning only where we can speak of better and worse. But to good in general it seems not strictly applicable. A thing is desirable, when to desire it is better. It is not desirable, properly, when you can say no more than that to desire it is good.[1]

The good might be called desirable in the sense that it essentially has to be desired. For desire is not an external means, but is contained and involved in goodness, or at least follows from it necessarily. Goodness without desire, we might say, would not be itself, and it is hence desirable (p. 404). This use of "desirable" would call attention to an important point, but, for the reason given above, would be misleading. At any rate it clearly separates for the moment desire from goodness.

We have attempted now to fix generally the meaning of goodness, and we may proceed from this to lay stress on its contradictory character. The good is not the perfect, but is merely a one-sided aspect of perfection. It tends to pass beyond itself, and, if it were completed, it would forthwith cease properly to be good. I will exhibit its incompleteness first by asking *what* it is that is good, and will then go on briefly to point out the self-contradiction in its essence.

---

[1] If pleasure were the only thing that could be desired, it would, hence, not follow straight from this that pleasure is desirable at all, or that, further, it is the sole desirable. These conclusions might follow, but in any case not directly; and the intermediate steps should be set out and discussed. The word "desirable" naturally lends itself to misuse, and has on this account been of service to some Hedonistic writers. It veils a covert transition from "is" to "is to be."

If we seek to know what is goodness, we find it always as the adjective of something not itself. Beauty, truth, pleasure, and sensation are all things that are good. We desire them all, and all can serve as types or "norms" by which to guide our approbation. And hence, in a sense, they all will fall under and be included in goodness. But when we ask, on the other hand, if goodness exhausts all that lies in these regions, the answer must be different. For we see at once that each possesses a character of its own ; and, in order to be good, the other aspects of the universe must also be themselves. The good then, as such, is obviously not so wide as the totality of things. And the same conclusion is at once forced on us, if we go on to examine the essence of goodness. For that is self-discrepant, and is therefore appearance and not Reality. The good implies a distinction of idea from existence, and a division which, in the lapse of time, is perpetually healed up and re-made.

And such a process is involved in the inmost being of the good. A satisfied desire is, in short, inconsistent with itself. For, so far as it is quite satisfied, it is not a desire ; and, so far as it is a desire, it must remain at least partly unsatisfied. And where we are said to want nothing but what we have, and where approbation precludes desire, we have, first, an ideal continuance of character in conflict with change. But in any case, apart from this, there is implied the suggestion of an idea, distinct from the fact while identified with it. Each of these features is necessary, and each is inconsistent with the other. And the resolution of this difference between idea and existence is both demanded by the good, and yet remains unattainable. Its accomplishment, indeed, would destroy the proper essence of goodness, and the good is therefore in itself incomplete and self-transcendent. It moves towards an other and a higher character, in which, becoming perfect, it would be merged.

Hence obviously the good is not the Whole, and the Whole, as such, is not good. And, viewed thus in relation to the Absolute, there is nothing either bad or good, there is not anything better or worse. For the Absolute is *not* its appearances. But (as we have seen throughout) such a truth is itself partial and false, since the Absolute appears in its phenomena and is real nowhere outside them. We indeed can only deny that it is any one, because it is all of them in unity. And so, regarded from this other side, the Absolute *is* good, and it manifests itself throughout in various degrees of goodness and badness. The destiny of goodness, in reaching which it must itself cease to be, is accomplished by the Whole. And, since in that consummation idea and existence are not lost but are brought into harmony, the Whole therefore is still good. And again, since reference to the perfect makes finite satisfactions all higher and lower, the Absolute is realized in all of them to different degrees. I will briefly deal with this latter point.

We saw, in our last chapter, the genuine meaning of degrees in reality and truth. That is more perfect which is separated from perfection by a smaller interval. And the interval is measured by the amount of re-arrangement and of addition required in order to 'turn an appearance into Reality. We found, again, that our one principle has a double aspect, as it meets two opposite defects in phenomena. For an element is lower as being either more narrow or less harmonious. And we perceived, further, how and why these two defects are essentially connected. Passing now to goodness, we must content ourselves by observing in general that the same principle holds. The satisfaction which is more true and more real, is better. And we measure, here again, by the double aspect of extension and harmony.[1] Only the perfect and complete would, in the end, content our desires. And a satisfaction more consistent with itself, or again wider and fuller, approaches more nearly to that consummation in which we could rest. Further the divergence of these two aspects is itself but apparent, and consists merely in a one-sided confinement of our view. For a satisfaction determined from the outside cannot internally be harmonious, while on the other hand, if it became all-inclusive, it would have become also concordant. In its application this single principle tends naturally to fall apart into two different standards. Still, for all that, it remains in essence and at bottom the same, and it is everywhere an estimation by the Absolute.

In a sense, therefore, the Absolute is actually good, and throughout the world of goodness it is truly realized in different degrees of satisfaction. Since in ultimate Reality all existence, and all thought and feeling, become one, we may even say that every feature in the universe is thus absolutely good.

I have now briefly laid down the general meaning and significance of goodness, and may go on to consider it in a more special and restricted sense. The good, we have seen, contains the sides of existence and idea. And the existence, so far, has been *found* to be in accordance with the idea, but the idea itself, so far, has not necessarily produced or realized itself in the fact. When, however, we take goodness in its narrower meaning, this last feature is essential. The good, in short, will become the realized end or completed will. It is now an idea which not only *has* an answering con-

---

[1] In estimating pains and pleasures we consider not merely their degree and extent, but also their effects, and generally all those qualities with which they are inseparably connected.

tent in fact, but, in addition also, has *made*, and has brought about, that correspondence. We may say that the idea has translated or has carried itself out into reality; for the content on both sides is the same, and the existence has become what it is through the action of the idea. Goodness thus will be confined to the realm of ends or of self-realization. It will be restricted, in other words, to what is commonly called the sphere of morality.

For we must here take self-realization to have no meaning except in finite souls; and of course every soul is finite, though certainly not all are human. Will, implying a process in time, cannot belong, as such, to the Absolute; and, on the other side, we cannot assume the existence of ends in the physical world. I shall return in the next chapter to this question of teleology in Nature, but, for the sake of convenience, we must here exclude it from our view. There is to be, in short, no self-realization except that of souls.

Goodness then, at present, is the realization of its idea by a finite soul. It is not perfection simply, but perfection as carried out by a will. We must forget, on the one hand, that, as we have seen, approbation goes beyond morality; and we must, as yet, be blind to that more restricted sense in which morality is inward. Goodness is, here, to be the carrying out by the individual of his idea of perfection. And we must go on to show briefly how, in this sense also, the good is inconsistent. It is a point of view which is compelled perpetually to pass beyond itself.

If we enquire, once more, " What is good ? " in the sense of asking for some element of content which is special, we must answer, as before, " There is nothing." Pleasure, we have seen, is by itself not the essence of goodness; and, on the other hand, no feature of the world falls outside of what is good. Beauty, truth, feeling, and sensation, every imaginable matter must go to constitute perfection. For perfection or individuality is a system, harmonious and thus inclusive of everything. And goodness we have now taken to be the willed reality of its perfection by a soul. And hence neither the form of system by itself, nor again, any one matter apart from the whole, is either perfect or good.[1]

But, as with truth and reality, so with goodness our one standard becomes double, and individuality falls apart into the aspects of harmony and extent. In principle, and actually in the end, these two features must coincide (Chapter xxiv.) ; but in judging of phenomena we are constantly forced to apply them separately. I propose to say nothing about the various concrete modes in which this two-fold perfection has been realized in fact. But, solely with a view to bring out the radical vice of all goodness, I will proceed to lay stress on this divergence in application. The aspects of extent and of harmony come together in the end, but no less certainly in that end goodness, as such, will have perished.

I am about, in other words, to invite attention to what is called self-sacrifice. Goodness is the realization by an individual of his own perfection, and that perfection consists, as we have seen, in both harmony and extent. And provisionally these two features will not quite coincide. To reduce the raw material of one's nature to the highest degree of system, and to use every element from whatever source as a subordinate means to this object, is certainly one genuine view of goodness. On the other hand to widen as far as possible the end to be pursued, and to realize this through the distraction or the dissipation of one's own individuality, is certainly also good. An individual system, aimed at in one's self, and again the subordination of one's own development to a wide-embracing end, are each

---

[1] This applies emphatically to any specific feeling of goodness or morality.

an aspect of the moral principle. So far as they
are discrepant, these two pursuits may be called,
the one, self-assertion, and the other, self-sacrifice.
And, however much these must diverge, each is
morally good; and, taken in the abstract, you cannot say that one is better than the other.

I am far from suggesting that in morality we are
forced throughout to make a choice between such
incompatible ideals. For this is not the case, and,
if it were so, life could hardly be lived. To a very
large extent by taking no thought about his individual perfection, and by aiming at that which seems
to promise no personal advantage, a man secures
his private welfare. We may, perhaps, even say
that in the main there is no collision between self-
sacrifice and self-assertion, and that on the whole
neither of these, in the proper sense, exists for
morality. But, while admitting or asserting to the
full the general identity of these aspects, I am here
insisting on the fact of their partial divergence.
And that, at least in some respects and with some
persons, these two ideals seem hostile no sane
observer can deny.

In other words we must admit that two great
divergent forms of moral goodness exist. In order
to realize the idea of a perfect self a man may have
to choose between two partially conflicting methods.
Morality, in short, may dictate either self-sacrifice
or self-assertion, and it is important to clear our
ideas as to the meaning of each. A common mistake is to identify the first with the living for others,
and the second with living for oneself. Virtue upon
this view is social, either directly or indirectly, either
visibly or invisibly. The development of the individual, that is, unless it reacts to increase the welfare
of society, can certainly not be moral. This doctrine
I am still forced to consider as a truth which has
been exaggerated and perverted into error.[1] There

[1] See *Ethical Studies*, pp. 200-203. And compare here below,
p. 431, and p. 529.

are intellectual and other accomplishments, to which I at least cannot refuse the title of virtue. But I cannot assume that, without exception, these must all somehow add to what is called social welfare; nor, again, do I see how to make a social organism the subject which directly possesses them. But, if so, it is impossible for me to admit that all virtue is essentially or primarily social. On the contrary, the neglect of social good, for the sake of pursuing other ends, may not only be moral self-assertion, but again, equally under other conditions, it *may* be moral self-sacrifice. We can even say that the living "for others," rather than living "for myself," *may* be immoral and selfish.

And you can hardly make the difference between self-sacrifice and self-assertion consist in this, that the idea pursued, in one case, falls beyond the individual and, in the other case, fails to do so. Or, rather, such a phrase, left undefined, can scarcely be said to have a meaning. Every permanent end of every kind will go beyond the individual, if the individual is taken in his lowest sense. And, passing that by, obviously the content realized in an individual's perfection must be also above him and beyond him. His perfection is not one thing apart from the rest of the universe, and he gains it only by appropriating, and by reducing to a special harmony, the common substance of all. It is obvious that his private welfare, so far as he is social, must include to some extent the welfare of others. And his intellectual, æsthetic, and moral development, in short the whole ideal side of his nature, is clearly built up out of elements which he shares with other souls. Hence the individual's end in self-advancement must always transcend his private being. In fact, the difference between self-assertion and self-sacrifice does not lie in the contents which are used, but in the diverse uses which are made of them; and I will attempt to explain this.

In moral self-assertion the materials used may be drawn from any source, and they may belong to any world. They may, and they must, largely realize ends which visibly transcend my life. But it is self-assertion when, in applying these elements, I am guided by the idea of the greatest system in myself. If the standard used in measuring and selecting my material is, in other words, the development of my individual perfection, then my conduct is palpably *not* self-sacrifice, and may be opposed to it. It is self-sacrifice when I pursue an end by which my individuality suffers loss. In the attainment of this object my self is distracted, or is diminished, or even dissipated. I may, for social purposes, give up my welfare for the sake of other persons; or again I may devote myself to some impersonal pursuit, by which the health and harmony of my self is injured. Wherever the moral end followed is followed to the loss of individual well-being, then that is self-sacrifice, whether I am living "for others" or not.[1] But self-sacrifice is also, and on the other hand, a form of self-realization. The wider end, which is aimed at, is, visibly or invisibly, reached; and in that pursuit and that attainment I find my personal good.

It is the essential nature of my self, as finite, equally to assert and, at the same time, to pass beyond itself; and hence the objects of self-sacrifice and of self-advancement are each equally mine. If we are willing to push a metaphor far beyond its true and natural limits, we may perhaps state the contrast thus. In self-assertion the organ considers first its own development, and for that purpose it draws material from the common life of all organs. But in self-sacrifice the organ aims at realizing some feature of the life larger than its own, and is ready to do this at the cost of injury to its own existence. It has foregone the idea of a perfection, individual,

[1] I am, for the present purpose, taking no account of immorality or of the self-sacrifice which seems failure.

A. R.   E E

rounded, and concrete. It is willing to see itself abstract and mutilated, over-specialized, or stunted, or even destroyed. But this actual defect it can make up ideally, by an expansion beyond its special limits, and by an identification of its will with a wider reality. Certainly the two pursuits, thus described, must in the main coincide and be one. The whole is furthered most by the self-seeking of its parts, for in these alone the whole can appear and be real. And the part again is individually bettered by its action for the whole, since thus it gains the supply of that common substance which is necessary to fill it. But, on the other hand, this general coincidence is only general, and assuredly there are points at which it ceases. And here self-assertion and self-sacrifice begin to diverge, and each to acquire its distinctive character.

Each of these modes of action realizes the self, and realizes that which is higher; and (I must repeat this) they are equally virtuous and right. To what then should the individual have any duty, if he has none to himself? Or is it, again, really supposed that in his perfection the whole is not perfected, and that he is somewhere enjoying his own advantage and holding it apart from the universe? But we have seen that such a separation between the Absolute and finite beings is meaningless. Or shall we be assured, upon the other side, that for a thing to sacrifice itself is contrary to reason? But we have found that the very essence of finite beings is self-contradictory, that their own nature includes relation to others, and that they *are* already each outside of its own existence. And, if so, surely it would be impossible, and most contrary to reason, that the finite, realizing itself, should not also transcend its own limits. If a finite individual really is not self-discrepant, then let that be argued and shown. But, otherwise, that he should be compelled to follow two ideals of perfection which diverge, appears natural and necessary. And each of these pursuits, in general and in the abstract, is equally good. It is only the particular conditions which in each case can decide between them.

Now that this divergence ceases, and is brought together in the end, is most certain. For nothing is outside the Absolute, and in the Absolute there is nothing imperfect. And an un-accomplished object, implying discrepancy between idea and existence, is most surely imperfection. In the Absolute everything finite attains the perfection which it seeks ; but, upon the other hand, it cannot gain perfection precisely as it seeks it. For, as we have seen throughout, the finite is more or less transmuted, and, as such, disappears in being accomplished. This common destiny is assuredly the end of the Good. The ends sought by self-assertion and self-sacrifice are, each alike, unattainable. The individual never can in himself become an harmonious system. And in the wider ideal to which he devotes himself, no matter how thoroughly, he never can find complete self-realization. For, even if we take that ideal to be perfect and to be somehow completely fulfilled, yet, after all, he himself is not totally absorbed in it. If his discordant element is for faith swallowed up, yet faith, no less, means that a jarring appearance remains. And, in the complete gift and dissipation of his personality, *he*, as such, must vanish ; and, with that, the good is, as such, transcended and submerged. This result is but the conclusion with which our chapter began. Goodness is an appearance, it is phenomenal, and therefore self-contradictory. And therefore, as was the case with degrees of truth and reality, it shows two forms of one standard which will not wholly coincide. In the end, where every discord is brought to harmony, every idea is also realized. But there, where nothing can be lost, everything, by addition and by re-arrangement, more or less changes its character. And most emphatically no self-assertion nor any self-sacrifice, nor any goodness or morality, has, as such, any reality in the Absolute. Goodness is a subordinate and, therefore, a self-contradictory aspect of the universe.

And, with this, it is full time that we went forward ; but, for the sake of some readers, I will dwell longer on the relative character of the Good. Too many English moralists assume blindly that goodness is ultimate and absolute. For as regards metaphysics they are incompetent, and that in the religion which probably they profess or at least esteem, morality, as such, is subordinate—such a fact suggests to them nothing. They are ignorant of the view for which all things finite in different degrees are real and true, and for which, at the same time, not one of them is ultimate. And they cannot understand that the Whole may be consistent, when the appearances which qualify it conflict with one another. For holding on to each separate appearance, as a thing absolute and not relative, they fix these each in that partial character which is unreal and untrue. And such one-sided abstractions, which in coming together are essentially transformed, they consider to be ultimate and fundamental facts. Thus in goodness the ends of self-assertion and of self-sacrifice are inconsistent, each with itself and each with the other. They are fragmentary truths, neither of which is, as such, ultimately true. But it is just these relative aspects which the popular moralist holds to, each as real by itself; and hence ensues a blind tangle of bewilderment and error. To follow this in detail is not my task, and still less my desire, but it may be instructive, perhaps, briefly to consider it further.

There is first one point which should be obvious, but which seems often forgotten. In asking whether goodness can, in the end, be self-consistent and be real, we are not concerned merely with the relation between virtue and selfishness. For suppose that there is no difference between these two, except merely for our blindness, yet, possessing this first crown of our wishes, we have still not solved the main problem. It will certainly now be worth my while to seek the good of my neighbour, since by no other course can I do any better for myself, and since what is called self-sacrifice, or benevolent action, is in fact the only possible way to secure my advantage. But then, upon the other hand, a mere balance of advantage, however satisfactory the means by which I come to possess it, is most assuredly *not* the fulfilment of my desire. For the desire of human beings (this is surely a commonplace) has no limit. Goodness, in other words, must imply an attempt to reach perfection, and it is the nature of the finite to seek for that which nothing finite can satisfy. But, if so, with a mere balance of advantage I have *not* realized my good. And, however much virtue may be nothing in the world but a refined form of self-seeking, yet, with this, virtue is not one whit the less a pursuit of what is inconsistent and therefore impossible. And goodness, or the attainment of such an impossible end, is still self-contradictory.

Further, since it seems necessary for me not to be ashamed of platitude, let me call the attention of the reader to some evident truths. No existing social organism secures to its individuals any more than an imperfect good, and in all of them self-sacrifice marks the fact of a failure in principle. But even in an imaginary society, such as is foretold to us in the New Jerusalem of Mr. Spencer, it is only for thoughtless credulity that evil has vanished. For it is not easy to forget that finite beings are physically subject to accident, or easy to believe that this their natural essence is somehow to be removed. And, even so and in any case, the members of an organism must of necessity be sacrificed more or less to the whole. For they must more or less be made special in their function, and that means rendered, to some extent, one-sided and narrow. And, if so, the harmony of their individual being must inevitably in some degree suffer. And it must suffer again, if the individual devotes himself to some æsthetic or intellectual pursuit. On the other side, even within the New Jerusalem, if a person aims merely at his own good, he, none the less, is fore-doomed to imperfection and failure. For on a defective and shifting natural basis he tries to build a harmonious system; and his task, hopeless for this reason, is for another reason more hopeless. He strives within finite limits to construct a concordant whole, when the materials which he is forced to use have no natural endings, but extend themselves indefinitely beyond himself into an endless world of relations. And, if so, once more we have been brought back to the familiar truth, that there is no such possibility as human perfection. But, if so, then goodness, since it must needs pursue the perfect, is in its essence self-discrepant, and in the end is unreal. It is an appearance one-sided and relative, and not an ultimate reality.

But to this idea of relativity, both in the case of goodness and every other order of phenomena, popular philosophy remains blind. Everything, for it, is either a delusion, and so nothing at all, or is on the other hand a fact, and, because it exists, therefore, as such, real. That reality can appear nowhere except in a system of relative unrealities; that, taken apart from this system, the several appearances are in contradiction with one another and each within itself; that, nevertheless, outside of this field of jarring elements there neither is nor can be anything; and that, if appearances were *not* irremediably self-discrepant, they could not possibly

be the appearances of the Real—all this to popular thought remains meaningless. Common sense openly revolts against the idea of a fact which is not a reality ; or again, as sober criticism, it plumes itself on suggesting cautious questions, doubts which dogmatically assume the truth of its coarsest prejudices. Nowhere are these infirmities illus-
.trated better than by popular Ethics, in the attitude it takes towards the necessary discrepancies of goodness. That these discrepancies exist because goodness is not absolute, and that their solution is not possible until goodness is degraded to an appearance—such a view is blindly ignored. Nor is it asked if these opposites, self-assertion and self-sacrifice, are not each internally inconsistent and so irrational. But the procedure is, first, tacitly to assume that each opposite is fixed, and will not pass beyond itself. And then, from this basis, one of the extremes is rejected as an illusion ; or else, both being absolute and solid, an attempt is made to combine them externally or to show that somehow they coincide. I will add a few words on these developments.

(i.) The good may be identified with self-sacrifice, and self-assertion may, therefore, be totally ex-cluded. But the good, as self-sacrifice, is clearly in collision with itself. For an act of self-denial is, no less, in some sense a self-realization, and it inevit-ably includes an aspect of self-assertion And hence the good, as the mere attainment of self-sacrifice, is really unmeaning. For it is in finite selves, after all, that the good *must* be realized. And, further, to say that perfection must be always the perfection of something else, appears quite in-consistent For it will mean either that on the whole the good is nothing whatever, or else that it consists in that which each does or may enjoy, yet not as good, but as a something extraneously added unto him. The good, in other words, in this case

will be not good ; and in the former case it will be
nothing positive, and therefore nothing.   That each
should pursue the general perfection, should act for
the advantage of a whole in which his self is included, or should add to a collection in which he may
share—is certainly *not* pure self-sacrifice.   And a
maxim that each should aim purely at his neighbour's welfare in separation from his own, we have
seen is self-inconsistent.   It can hardly be ultimate
or reasonable, when its meaning seems to end in
nonsense.[1]

(ii.) Or, rejecting all self-transcendence as an idle
word, popular Ethics may set up pure self-assertion
as all that is good.   It may perhaps desire to add
that by the self-seeking of each the advantage of all
is best secured, but this addition clearly is not
contained in self-assertion, and cannot properly be
included.   For by such an addition, if it were
necessary, the end at once would have been
essentially modified.   It was self-assertion pure,
and not qualified, which was adopted as goodness ;
and it is this alone which we must now consider.
And we perceive first (as we saw above) that such a
good is unattainable, since perfection cannot be
realized in a finite being.   Not only is the physical
basis too shifting, but the contents too essentially
belong to a world outside the self ; and hence it is
impossible that they should be brought to completion
and to harmony within it.   One may indeed seek
to approach nearer to the unattainable.   Aiming at
a system within oneself, one may forcibly abstract
from the necessary connections of the material used.
We may consider this and strive to apply it one-
sidedly, and in but a single portion of its essential
aspects.   But the other aspect inseparably against

[1] It may be as well perhaps to add that, neither in this sense
nor in any other, can the good be defined negatively.   At that
point, in any definition, where a negative term is introduced, the
reader should specially look for a defect.

our will is brought in, and it stamps our effort with inconsistency. Thus even to pursue imperfectly one's own advantage by itself is unreasonable, for by itself and purely it has no existence at all. It was a trait characteristic of critical Common Sense when it sought for the individual's moral end by first supposing him isolated. For a dogmatic assumption that the individual remains what he is when you have cut off his relations, is very much what the vulgar understand by criticism. But, when such a question is discussed, it must be answered quite otherwise. The contents, asserted in the individual's self-seeking, necessarily extend beyond his private limits. A maxim, therefore, merely to pursue one's own advantage is, taken strictly, inconsistent. And a principle which contradicts itself is, once more, not reasonable.[1]

(iii.) In the third place, admitting self-assertion and self-denial as equally good, popular thought attempts to bring them together from outside. Goodness will now consist in the coincidence of these independent goods. The two are not to be absorbed by and resolved into a third. Each, on the other hand, is to retain unaltered the character which it has, and the two, remaining two, are somehow to be conjoined. And this, as we have seen throughout our work, is quite impossible. If two conflicting finite elements are anywhere to be harmonized, the first condition is that each should forego and should transcend its private character. Each, in other words, working out the discrepancy

---

[1] The same conclusion holds if for "advantage" one writes "pleasure." For pleasure is necessarily connected with other content, and is not isolated, or again conjoined hap-hazard and accidentally. One may of course pursue "merely one's own" pleasure, in the sense that one tries to aim at and to consider this partial end by itself. But, if you assert that this end has not another aspect which contradicts "merely one's own," the assertion is false. And it is, I presume, a moral platitude that selfish action always *must* concern more than the actor.

already within itself, passes beyond itself and unites
with its opposite in a product higher than either.
But such a transcendence can have no meaning to
popular Ethics. That has assumed without examination that each finite end, taken by itself, is reasonable; and it therefore demands that each, as such,
should together be satisfied. And, blind to theory,
it is blind also to the practical refutation of its
dogmas by everyday life. There a man can seek
the general welfare in his own, and can find his own
end accomplished in the general; for goodness there
already is the transcendence and solution of one-
sided elements. The good is already there, not the
external conjunction, but the substantial identity of
these opposites. They are not coincident with, but
each is in, and makes one aspect of, the other. In
short, already within goodness that work is imperfectly begun, which, when completed, must take us
beyond goodness altogether. But for popular Ethics,
as we saw, not only goodness itself, but each of its
one-sided features is fixed as absolute. And, these
having been so fixed in irrational independence, an
effort is made to find the good in their external
conjunction.

Goodness is apparently now to be the coincidence
of two ultimate goods, but it is hard to see how
such an end can be ultimate or reasonable. That
two elements should necessarily come together, and,
at the same time, that neither should be qualified
by this relation, or again that a relation in the end
should not imply a whole, which subordinates and
qualifies the two terms—all this in the end seems
unintelligible. But, again, if the relation and the
whole *are* to qualify the terms, one does not understand how either by itself could ever have been
ultimate.[1] In short, the bare conjunction of inde-

---

[1] The same difficulty will appear if an attempt is made to state
the general maxim. Both ends are to remain and to be ultimate,
and hence neither is to be qualified by the other or the whole,

pendent reals is an idea which contradicts itself. But of this naturally Common Sense has no knowledge at all, and it therefore blindly proceeds with its impossible task.

That task is to defend the absolute character of goodness by showing that the discrepancies which it presents disappear in the end, and that these discrepant features, none the less, survive each in its own character. But by popular Ethics this task usually is not understood. It directs itself therefore to prove the coincidence of self-seeking and benevolence, or to show, in other words, that self-sacrifice, if moral, is impossible. And with this conclusion reached, in its opinion, the main problem would be solved. Now I will not ask how far in such a consummation its ultimate ends would, one or both, have been subordinated; for by its conclusion, in any case, the main problem is not touched. We have already seen that our desires, whether for ourselves or for others, do not stop short of perfection. But where each individual can say no more than this, that it has been made worth his while to regard others' interests, perfection surely may be absent. And where the good aimed at is absent, to affirm that we have got rid of the puzzle offered by goodness seems really thoughtless. It is, however, a thoughtlessness which, as we have perceived, is characteristic; and let us pass to the external means employed to produce moral harmony.

Little need here be said. We may find, thrust forward or indicated feebly, a well-worn contrivance. This is of course the *deus ex machina*, an idea which no serious student of first principles is called on to consider. A God which has to make things what otherwise, and by their own nature, they are *not*,

for to be so qualified is to be transcended. I may add that a negative form of statement, here as everywhere, serves no purpose but to obscure the problem. This is, however, a reason why it may be instinctively selected.

may summarily be dismissed as an exploded absurdity. And that perfection should exist in the
finite, as such, we have seen to be even directly
contrary to the nature of things. A supposition
that it may be made worth my while to be benevolent—especially when an indefinite prolongation of
my life is imagined—cannot, in itself and for our
knowledge, be called impossible. But then, upon
the other hand, we have remarked that such an
imagined improvement is not a solution of the
actual main problem. The belief may possibly add
much to our comfort by assuring us that virtue is
the best, and is the only true, selfishness. But such
a truth, if true, would not imply that both or either
of our genuine ends is, as such, realized. And,
failing this, the wider discrepancy has certainly not
been removed from goodness. We may say, in a
word, that the *deus ex machina* refuses to work.
Little can be brought in by this venerable artifice
except a fresh source of additional collision and
perplexity. And, giving up this embarrassing
agency, popular Ethics may prefer to make an
appeal to " Reason." For, if its two moral ends are
each reasonable, then, if somehow they do not
coincide, the nature of things must be unreasonable.
But we have shown, on the other hand, that neither
end by itself is reasonable ; and, if the nature of
things were to bring together elements discordant
within themselves and conflicting with one another,
and were to attempt, without transforming their
character, to make these coincide,—the nature of
things would have revealed itself as an apotheosis
of unreason or of popular Ethics. And, baffled by
its failure to find its dogmas realized in the universe,
this way of thinking at last may threaten us with
total scepticism. But here, once more, it is but
speaking of that of which it knows really nothing ;
for an honest scepticism is a thing outside its comprehension. An honest and truth-seeking sceptic-

ism pushes questions to the end, and knows that the end lies hid in that which is assumed at the beginning. But the scepticism (so-called) of Common Sense from first to last is dogmatic. It takes for granted, first, without examination that certain doctrines are true; it then demands that this collection of dogmas should come to an agreement; and, when its demand is rejected by the universe, it none the less persists in reiterating its old assumptions. And this dogmatism, simply because it is baffled and perplexed, gets the name of scepticism. But a sincere scepticism, attacking without fear each particular prejudice, finds that every finite view, when taken by itself, becomes inconsistent. And borne on this inconsistency, which in each case means a self-transcendence, such a scepticism is lifted to see a whole in which all finites blend and are resolved. But when each fact and end has foregone its claim, as such, to be ultimate or reasonable, then reason and harmony in the highest sense have begun to appear. And scepticism in the end survives as a mere aspect of constructive metaphysics. With this we may leave the irrational dogmas of popular Ethics.

The discussion of these has been wearisome, but perhaps not uninstructive. It should have confirmed us in our general conclusion as to the nature of the good. Goodness is not absolute or ultimate; it is but one side, one partial aspect, of the nature of things. And it manifests its relativity by inconsistency, by a self-contradiction in principle, and by a tendency shown towards separation in that principle's working, an attempted division, which again is inconsistent and cannot rest in itself. Goodness, as such, is but appearance which is transcended in the Absolute. But, upon the other hand, since in that Absolute no appearance is lost, the good is a main and essential factor in the universe. By accepting its transmutation it both realizes its own destiny and survives in the result.

We might reach the same conclusion briefly, perhaps, by considering the collision of ends. In the Whole every idea must be realized; but, on the other hand, the conflict of ends is such that to combine them mechanically is quite impossible. It will follow then that, in their attainment, their characters must be transmuted. We may say at once that none of them, and yet that each of them, is good. And among these ends must be included what we rightly condemn as Evil (Chapter xvii.). That positive object which is followed in opposition to the good, will unite with, and will conduce to, the ultimate goal. And the conduct which seems merely bad, which appears to pursue no positive content and to exhibit no system, will in the same way become good. Both by its assertion and its negation it will subserve an over-ruling end. Good and evil reproduce that main result which we found in our examination of truth and error. The opposition in the end is unreal, but it is, for all that, emphatically actual and valid. Error and evil are facts, and most assuredly there are degrees of each; and whether anything is better or worse, does without any doubt make a difference to the Absolute. And certainly the better anything is, the less totally in the end is its being over-ruled. But nothing, however good, can in the end be real precisely as it appears. Evil and good, in short, are not ultimate; they are relative factors which cannot retain their special characters in the Whole. And we may perhaps now venture to consider this position established.

But, bearing in mind the unsatisfactory state of current thought on these topics, I think it well to follow the enquiry into further detail. There is a more refined sense in which we have not yet dealt with goodness.[1]   The good, we may be informed, is morality, and morality is inward.   It does not consist in the attainment of a mere result, either outside the self or even within it.   For a result must depend on, and be conditioned by, what is naturally given, and for natural defects or advantages a man is not responsible.   And therefore, so far as regards true morality, any realized product is chance; for it must be infected and modified, less or more, by non-moral conditions.   It is, in short, only that which comes out of the man himself which can justify or condemn him, and his disposition and circumstances do not come from himself.   Morality is the identification of the individual's will with his own idea of perfection.   The moral man is the man who tries to do the best which he knows.   If the best he knows is *not* the best, that is, speaking morally,

---

[1] This view of morality is of course a late development, but I do not propose to say anything on its origin.   With regard to the origin of morality, in general, I will only say this, that one may lay too much stress on its directly social aspect.   Certainly to isolate the individual is quite indefensible.   But, upon the other hand, it is wrong to make the sole root of morality consist in the direct identification of the individual with the social will.   Morality, as we have remarked, is not confined to that in its end; and in the same way, we must add, it is not merely that in its beginning.   I am referring here to the facts of self-esteem and self-disapprobation, or the satisfaction or dissatisfaction of a creature with itself.   This feeling must begin when that creature is able to form an idea of itself, as doing or enjoying something desired, and can bring that idea into relation with its own actual success or failure.   The dissatisfied brooding of an animal that has, for example, missed its prey, is, we may be sure, not yet moral.   But it will none the less contain in rudiment that judgment of one's self which is a most important factor of morality.   And this feeling attaches itself indifferently to the idea of every sort of action or performance, success in which is desired.   If I feel or consider myself to correspond with such an idea, I am at once pleased with myself; and, even if it is only for luck at cards, I approve of and esteem myself.   For approbation, as we saw, is not all moral; nor is it, even in its origin, all directly social. But this subject deserves treatment at a length which here is impossible.

beside the question. If he fails to accomplish it, and ends in an attempt, that is once more morally irrelevant. And hence (we may add) it will be hard to find a proper sense in which different epochs can be morally compared, or in which the morality of one time or person stands above that of others. For the intensity of a volitional identification with whatever seems best appears to contain and to exhaust the strict essence of goodness. On this alone are based moral responsibility and desert, and on this, perhaps, we are enabled to build our one hope of immortality.

This is a view towards which morality seems driven irresistibly. That a man is to be judged solely by his inner will seems in the end undeniable. And, if such a doctrine contradicts itself and is inconsistent with the very notion of goodness, that will be another indication that the good is but appearance. We may even say that the present view takes a pride in its own discrepancies. It might, we must allow, contradict itself more openly. For it might make morality consist in the direct denial of that very element of existence, without which it actually is nothing.[1] But the same inconsistency, if more veiled, is still inherent in our doctrine. For a will, after all, must do something and must be characterized by what it does; while, on the other hand, this very character of what it does must depend on that which is "given" to it. And we shall have to choose between two fatal results; for either it will not matter what one does, or else something beyond and beside the bare "will" must be admitted to be good.

I will begin by saying a few words on what is called "moral desert." If this phrase implies that for either good or bad there is any reward beyond themselves, it is at once inconsistent. For, if be-

---

[1] *Ethical Studies*, Essay IV.

tween virtue and happiness there is an *essential* connection, then virtue must be re-defined so as to take in all its essence. But if, on the other hand, the connection is but external, then in what proper sense are we to call it moral ? We must either give up or alter the idea of desert, or else must seriously modify our extreme conception of moral goodness. And with this I will proceed to show how in its working that conception breaks down.

It is, first, in flat contradiction with ordinary morality. I am not referring to the fact that in common life we approve of all human qualities which to us seem desirable. Beauty, riches, strength, health and fortune—everything, and, perhaps, *more* than everything, which could be called a human excellence—we find admirable and approve of. But such approbations, together with their counterpart disapprovals, we should probably find ourselves unwilling to justify morally. And, passing this point by for the present, let us attend solely to those excellencies which would by all be called moral. These, the common virtues of life by which individuals are estimated, obviously depend to a large extent on disposition and bringing up. And to discard them utterly, because, or in so far as, you cannot attribute them to the individual's will, is a violent paradox. Even if that is correct, it is at least opposed to every-day morality.

And this doctrine, when we examine it further, is found to end in nothing. Its idea is to credit a man merely with what comes out of his will, and that in fine is not anything. For in the result from the will there is no material which is not derived from a " natural" source; and the whole result, whether in its origin, its actual happening, or its end, is throughout conditioned and qualified by " natural " factors. The moral man is allowed not to be omnipotent or omniscient. He is morally perfect, if only he will but do what he knows. But how

A. R.   F F

can he do it when weakness and disease, either bodily or mental, opposes his effort? And how can he even make the effort, except on the strength of some "natural" gift? Such an idea is psychologically absurd. And, if we take two different individuals, one dowered with advantages external and inward, and the other loaded with corresponding drawbacks, and if, in judging these, we refuse to make the very smallest allowance—in what have we ended? But to make an allowance would be to give up the essence of our doctrine, for the moral man no longer would be barely the man who wills what he knows. The result then is that we are unable to judge morally at all, for, otherwise, we shall be crediting morality with a foreign gift or allowance. Nor, again, do we find a less difficulty, when we turn to consider moral knowledge. For one man by education or nature will know better than another, and certainly no one can possibly know always the best.[1] But, once more, we cannot allow for this, and must insist that it is morally irrelevant. In short, it matters nothing what any one knows, and we have just seen that it matters as little what any one does. The distinction between evil and good has in fact disappeared. And to fall back on the intensity of the moral struggle will not help us.[2] For that intensity is determined, in the first place, by natural conditions, and, in the next place, goodness would be taken to consist in a struggle with itself. To make a man better you would in some cases have to add to his badness, in order to increase the division and the morality within him. Goodness, in short, meant at the beginning

[1] On the common Hedonistic view we may say that he *never* can hope to do this, or know when he has done it. What it would call "objective rightness" seems in the end to be not ascertainable humanly, or else to be the opinion of the subject, however wrong that may be. But an intelligent view of the connection between goodness and truth is not a thing which we need expect from common Hedonism (p. 407).

[2] Cp. *Ethical Studies*, pp. 213-217.

that one does what one can, and it has come now to mean merely that one does what one does. Or rather, whatever one does and whatever one wills, it is all alike infected by nature and morally indifferent. There is, in plain words, no difference left between goodness and badness.

But such a conclusion, we may possibly yet be told, is quite mistaken. For, though all the matter of goodness must be drawn from outside, yet the self, or the will, has a power of appropriation. By its formal act it works up and transforms that given matter, and it so makes its own, and makes moral, the crude natural stuff. Still, on the other side, we must insist that every act is a resultant from psychical conditions[1] A formal act which is not determined by its matter, is nonsense, whether you consider that act in its origin or in its outcome. And, again, if the act is not morally characterized and judged by its matter, will there in the end be a difference between the good and the bad? Whether you look at its psychical genesis or at its essential character, the act, if it is to be possible, cannot be merely formal, and it will therefore vitally depend on that which has been called non-moral.

A form independent of matter is certainly nothing, and, as certainly therefore, it cannot be morality. It can at most be offered as such, and asserted to be so, by a chance content which fills it and professes to be moral. Morality has degenerated into

---

[1] This would be denied by what is vulgarly called Free Will. That attempts to make the self or will, in abstraction from concrete conditions, the responsible source of conduct. As however, taken in that abstraction, the self or will is nothing, "Free Will" can merely mean chance. If it is not that, its advocates are at least incapable of saying what else it is; and how chance can assist us towards being responsible, they naturally shrink from discussing (see *Ethical Studies*, Essay I., and Mr. Stephen's *Science of Ethics*, pp. 282-3). Considered either theoretically or practically, "Free Will" is, in short, a mere lingering chimera. Certainly no writer, who respects himself, can be called on any longer to treat it seriously (P. 393).

self-approbation which *only* is formal, and which *therefore* is false. It has become the hollow conscience for which acts are good because they happen to be its own, or merely because somehow it happens to like them. Between the assertion and the fact there is here no genuine connection. It is empty self-will and self-assurance, which, swollen with private sentiment or chance desire, wears the mask of goodness. And hence that which professes itself moral would be the same as mere badness, if it did not differ, even for the worse, by the addition of hypocrisy.[1] For the bad, which admits not only that others but that itself is not good, has, in principle at least, condemned vain self-sufficiency and self-will. The common confession that the self in itself is worthless, has opened that self to receive worth from a good which transcends it. Morality has been driven to allow that goodness and badness do not wholly depend on ourselves, and, with this admission, it has now finally passed beyond itself. We must at last have come to the end, when it has been proclaimed a moral duty to be non-moral.

That it is a moral duty not to be moral wears the form of a paradox, but it is the expression of a principle which has been active and has shown itself throughout. Every separate aspect of the universe, if you insist on it, goes on to demand something higher than itself. And, like every other appearance, goodness implies that which, when carried out, must absorb it. Yet goodness cannot go back ; for to identify itself, once more, with the earlier stage of its development would be, once more, to be driven forward to the point we have reached. The problem can be solved only when the various stages

---

[1] We may note here that our country, the chosen land of Moral Philosophy, has the reputation abroad of being the chief home of hypocrisy and cant.

and appearances of morality are all included and
subordinated in a higher form of being. In other
words the end, sought for by morality, is above it
and is super-moral. Let us gain a general view of
the moral demands which call for satisfaction.

The first of these is the suppression of the
divorce between morality and goodness. We have
seen that every kind of human excellence, beauty,
strength, and even luck, are all undeniably good. It
is idle pretence if we assert that such gifts are not
desired, and are not also approved of. And it is a
moral instinct after all for which beauty counts as
virtue. For, if we attempt to deny this and to confine virtue to what is commonly called moral conduct, our position is untenable. We are at once
hurried forward by our admitted principle into
further denials, and virtue recedes from the world
until it ceases to be virtue. It seeks an inward
centre not vitiated by any connection with the external, or, in other words, as we have seen, it pur-
sues the unmeaning. For the excellence which
barely is inner is nothing at all. We must either
allow then that physical excellences are good, or
we must be content to find virtue not realized anywhere.[1] Hence there will be virtues more or less
outward, and less or more inward and spiritual. We
must admit kinds and degrees and different levels
of virtue. And morality must be distinguished as
a special form of the general goodness. It will be
now one excellence among others, neither including
them all, nor yet capable of a divorced and independent existence. Morality has proved unreal
unless it stands on, and vitally consists in, gifts
naturally good. And thus we have been forced to

[1] If we take such a virtue as courage, and deny its moral
goodness where it is only physical, we shall be forced in the end
to deny its goodness everywhere. We may see, again, how there
may be virtues which, in a sense, rise above mere goodness.
This from the view of morality proper is of course impossible.

acknowledge that morality is a gift; since, if the goodness of the physical virtues is denied, there is left, at last, no goodness at all. Morality, in short, finds it essential that every excellence should be good, and it is destroyed by a division between its own world and that of goodness.

It is a moral demand then that every human excellence should genuinely be good, while at the same time a high rank should be reserved for the inner life. And it is a moral demand also that the good should be victorious throughout. The defects and the contradiction in every self must be removed, and must be succeeded by perfect harmony. And, of course, all evil must be overruled and so turned into goodness. But the demand of morality has also a different side. For, if goodness as such is to remain, the contradiction cannot quite cease, since a discord, we saw, was essential to goodness. Thus, if there is to be morality, there cannot altogether be an end of evil. And, so again, the two aspects of self-assertion and of self-sacrifice will remain. They must be subordinated, and yet they must not have entirely lost their distinctive characters. Morality in brief calls for an unattainable unity of its aspects, and, in its search for this, it naturally is led beyond itself into a higher form of goodness. It ends in what we may call religion.[1]

---

[1] The origin of religion is a question which does not concern us here. Religion appears to have two roots, fear and admiration or approval. The latter need not be taken as having a high or moral sense. Wonder or curiosity seems not to be religious, unless it is in the service of these other feelings. And, of the two main roots of religion, one will be more active at one time and place, and the other at another. The feelings also will attach themselves naturally to a variety of objects. To enquire about the origin of religion as if that origin must always be one, seems fundamentally erroneous.

It concerns us more to know what religion now means among ourselves. I have come to the conclusion that it is impossible to answer this question, unless we realize that religion, in the end, has more meanings than one. Part of this variety rests no doubt

In this higher mode of consciousness I am not suggesting that a full solution is found. For religion on mere misunderstanding. That which is mainly intellectual, or mainly æsthetic, would probably be admitted in the end to fall outside religion. But we come at last, I should say, to a stubborn discrepancy. There are those who would call religious any kind of practical relation to the "other world," or to the supersensible generally. The question, for instance, as to life after death, or as to the possibility of communication with what are called "spirits," seems to some essentially religious. And they might deny that religious feeling can exist at all towards an object in "our world." Another set of minds would insist that, in order to have religion, you must have a relation of a special and particular kind. And they would add that, where you have this relation, whether towards an object of the "other world" or not, you have got religion. The question as to life after death, or as to the possibility of spirit-rapping or witchcraft, is really not in itself in the very least religious. And it is only, they would urge, because *per accidens* our feelings to the unseen are generally (not always) religious, that religion has been partly narrowed and partly extended without just cause. I consider this latter party to be wholly right, and I shall disregard from this point forward the opposing view.

What then in general is religion? I take it to be a fixed feeling of fear, resignation, admiration or approval, no matter what may be the object, provided only that this feeling reaches a certain strength, and is qualified by a certain degree of reflection. But I should add, at once, that in religion fear and approval to some extent *must* always combine. We must in religion try to please, or at least to submit our wills to, the object which is feared. That conduct towards the object is approved of, and that approbation tends again to qualify the object. On the other side in religion approval implies devotion, and devotion seems hardly possible, unless there is some fear, if only the fear of estrangement.

But in what degree must such a feeling be present, if we are to call it religion? Can the point be fixed exactly? I think we must admit that it cannot be. But it lies generally there where we feel that our proper selves, in comparison, are quite powerless or worthless. The object, over against which we find ourselves to be of no account, tends to inspire us with religion. If there are many such objects, we are polytheists. But if, in comparison with one only, all the rest have no weight, we have arrived at monotheism.

Hence any object, in regard to which we feel a supreme fear or approval, will engage our devotion, and be for us a Deity. And this object, most emphatically, in no other sense need possess

is practical, and therefore still is dominated by the idea of the Good; and in the essence of this idea is contained an unsolved contradiction. Religion is still forced to maintain unreduced aspects, which, as such, cannot be united; and it exists in short by a kind of perpetual oscillation and compromise. Let us however see the manner in which it rises above bare morality.

For religion all is the perfect expression of a supreme will,[1] and all things therefore are good. Everything imperfect and evil, the conscious bad will itself, is taken up into and subserves this absolute end. Both goodness and badness are therefore good, just as in the end falsehood and truth were each found to be true. They are good alike, but on the other hand they are not good equally. That which is evil is transmuted and, as such, is destroyed, while the good in various degrees can still preserve its own character. Goodness, like truth, we saw was supplemented rather than wholly overruled. And, in measuring degrees of goodness, we must bear in mind the double aspect of appearance, and the ultimate identity of intenseness and extent. But in religion, further, the finite self does attain its

divinity. It is a common phrase in life that one may make a God of this or that person, object, or pursuit; and in such a case our attitude, it seems to me, must be called religious. This is the case often, for example, in sexual or in parental love. But to fix the exact point at which religion begins, and where it ends, would hardly be possible.

In this chapter I am taking religion only in its highest sense. I am using it for devotion to the one perfect object which is utterly good. Incomplete forms of religion, such as the devotion to a woman or to a pursuit, can exist side by side. But in this highest sense of religion there can be but one object. And again, when religion is fully developed, this object must be good. For towards anything else, although we feared it, we should now entertain feelings of revolt, of dislike, and even of contempt. There would not any longer be that moral prostration which is implied in all religion.

[1] As to the ultimate truth of this belief, see the following chapter.

perfection, and the separation of these two aspects is superseded and overcome. The finite self is perfect, not merely when it is viewed as an essential organ of the perfect Whole, but it also realizes for itself and is aware of perfection. The belief that its evil is overruled and its good supplemented, the identity in knowledge and in desire with the one overmastering perfection, this for the finite being is self-consciousness of itself as perfect. And in the others it finds once more the same perfection realized. For where a whole is complete in finite beings, which know themselves to be elements and members of its system, this *is* the consciousness in such individuals of their own completeness. Their perfection is a gift without doubt, but there is no reality outside the giver, and the separate receiver of the gift is but a false appearance.

But, on the other hand, religion must not pass wholly beyond goodness, and it therefore still maintains the opposition required for practice. Only by doing one's best, only by the union of one's will with the Good, can one attain to perfection. In so far as this union is absent, the evil remains ; and to remain evil is to be overruled, and, as such, to perish utterly. Hence the ideal perfection of the self serves to increase its hostility towards its own imperfection and evil. The self at once struggles to be perfect, and knows at the same time that its consummation is already worked out. The moral relation survives as a subordinate but an effective aspect.

The moral duty not to be moral is, in short, the duty to be religious. Every human excellence for religion is good, since it is a manifestation of the reality of the supreme Will. Only evil, as such, is not good, since in its evil character it is absorbed ; and in that character it really is, we may say, something else. Evil assuredly contributes to the good of the whole, but it contributes something which in that whole is quite transformed from its own nature.

And while in badness itself there are, in one sense, no degrees, there are, in another sense, certainly degrees in that which is bad. In the same way religion preserves intact degrees and differences in goodness. Every individual, in so far as he is good, is perfect. But he is better, first in proportion to his contribution to existing excellence, and he is better, again, according as more intensely he identifies his will with all-perfecting goodness.

I have set out, baldly and in defective outline, the claim of religion to have removed contradiction from the Good. And we must consider now to what extent such a claim can be justified. Religion seems to have included and reduced to harmony every aspect of life. It appears to be a whole which has embraced, and which pervades, every detail. But in the end we are forced to admit that the contradiction remains. For, if the whole is still good, it is not harmonious ; and, if it has gone beyond goodness, it has carried us also beyond religion. The whole is at once actually to be good, and, at the same time, is actually to make itself good. Neither its perfect goodness, nor yet its struggle, may be degraded to an appearance. But, on the other hand, to unite these two aspects consistently is impossible. And, even if the object of religion is taken to be imperfect and finite, the contradiction will remain. For if the end desired by devotion were thoroughly accomplished, the need for devotion and, therefore, its reality would have ceased. In short, a self other than the object must, and must not, survive, a vital discrepancy to be found again in intense sexual love. Every form of the good is impelled from within to pass beyond its own essence. It is an appearance, the stability of which is maintained by oscillation, and the acceptance of which depends largely on compromise.

The central point of religion lies in what is called

faith. The whole and the individual are perfect and good for faith only. Now faith is not mere holding a general truth, which in detail is not verified; for that attitude, of course, also belongs to theory. Faith is practical, and it is, in short, a making believe; but, *because* it is practical, it is at the same time a making, none the less, as if one did *not* believe. Its maxim is, Be sure that opposition to the good is overcome, and nevertheless act as if it were there; or, Because it is *not* really there, have more courage to attack it. And such a maxim, most assuredly, is not consistent with itself; for either of its sides, if taken too seriously, is fatal to the other side. This inner discrepancy however pervades the whole field of religion. We are tempted to exemplify it, once again, by the sexual passion. A man may believe in his mistress, may feel that without that faith he could not live, and may find it natural, at the same time, unceasingly to watch her. Or, again, when he does not believe in her or perhaps even in himself, then he may desire all the more to utter, and to listen to, repeated professions. The same form of self-deception plays its part in the ceremonies of religion.

This criticism might naturally be pursued into indefinite detail, but it is sufficient for us here to have established the main principle. The religious consciousness rests on the felt unity of unreduced opposites; and either to combine these consistently, or upon the other hand to transform them is impossible for religion. And hence self-contradiction in theory, and oscillation in sentiment, is inseparable from its essence. Its dogmas must end in one-sided error, or else in senseless compromise. And, even in its practice, it is beset with two imminent dangers, and it has without clear vision to balance itself between rival abysses. Religion may dwell too intently on the discord in the world or in the self. In the former case it foregoes its perfection and peace, while, at the same time, it may none the less

forget the difference between its private will and
the Good. And, on the other side, if it emphas-
izes this latter difference, it is then threatened
with a lapse into bare morality. But again if, fly-
ing from the discord, religion keeps its thought fixed
on harmony, it tends to suffer once more. For,
finding that all is already good both in the self and
in the world, it may cease to be moral at all, and
becomes at once, therefore, irreligious. The truth
that devotion even to a finite object may lift us above
moral laws, seduces religion into false and immoral
perversions. Because, for it, all reality is, in one
sense, good alike, every action may become completely indifferent. It idly dreams its life away in
the quiet world of divine inanity, or, forced into action by chance desire, it may hallow every practice,
however corrupt, by its empty spirit of devotion.
And here we find reproduced in a direr form the
monstrous births of moral hypocrisy. But we need
not enter into the pathology of the religious consciousness. The man who has passed, however
little, behind the scenes of the religious life, must
have had his moments of revolt. He must have
been forced to doubt if the bloody source of so many
open crimes, the parent of such inward pollution can
possibly be good.

But if religion is, as we have seen, a necessity,
such a doubt may be dismissed. There would be in
the end, perhaps, no sense in the enquiry if religion
has, on the whole, done more harm than good. My
object has been to point out that, like morality, religion is not ultimate. It is a mere appearance, and
is therefore inconsistent with itself. And it is hence
liable on every side to shift beyond its own limits.
But when religion, balancing itself between extremes,
has lost its balance on either hand, it becomes irreligious. If it was a moral duty to find more than
morality in religion, it is, even more emphatically, a
religious duty still to be moral. But each of these is

a mode and an expression at a different stage of the
good; and the good, as we have found, is a self-
contradictory appearance of the Absolute.

It may be instructive to bring out the same inconsistency from another point of view. Religion
naturally implies a relation between Man and God.
Now a relation always (we have seen throughout) is
self-contradictory. It implies always two terms
which are finite and which claim independence. On
the other hand a relation is unmeaning, unless both
itself and the relateds are the adjectives of a whole.
And to find a solution of this discrepancy would be
to pass entirely beyond the relational point of view.
This general conclusion may at once be verified in
the sphere of religion.

Man is on the one hand a finite subject, who is
over against God, and merely "standing in relation."
And yet, upon the other hand, apart from God man
is merely an abstraction. And religion perceives
this truth, and it affirms that man is good and real
only through grace, or that again, attempting to be
independent, he perishes through wrath. He does
not merely "stand in relation," but is moved inly
by his opposite, and indeed, apart from that inward
working, could not stand at all. God again is a
finite object, standing above and apart from man,
and is something independent of all relation to his
will and intelligence. Hence God, if taken as a
thinking and feeling being, has a private personality.
But, sundered from those relations which qualify
him, God is inconsistent emptiness; and, qualified
by his relation to an Other, he is distracted finitude.
God is therefore taken, again, as transcending this
external relation. He wills and knows himself, and
he finds his reality and self-consciousness, in union
with man. Religion is therefore a process with
inseparable factors, each appearing on either side.
It is the unity of man and God, which, in various

stages and forms, wills and knows itself throughout.
It parts itself into opposite terms with a relation between them; but in the same breath it denies this
provisional sundering, and it asserts and feels in
either term the inward presence of the other.   And
so religion consists in a practical oscillation, and expresses itself only by the means of theoretical compromise.   It would shrink perhaps from the statement
that God loves and enjoys himself in human emotion, and it would recoil once more from the assertion
that love can be where God is not, and, striving to
hug both shores at once, it wavers bewildered.   And
sin is the hostility of a rebel against a wrathful Ruler.
And yet this whole relation too must feel and hate
itself in the sinner's heart, while the Ruler also is
torn and troubled by conflicting emotions.   But to
say that sin is a necessary element in the Divine
self-consciousness—an element, however, emerging
but to be forthwith absorbed, and never liberated as
such—this would probably appear to be either nonsense or blasphemy.   Religion prefers to put forth
statements which it feels are untenable, and to correct them at once by counter-statements which it
finds are no better.   It is then driven forwards and
back between both, like a dog which seeks to follow
two masters.   A discrepancy worth our notice is the
position of God in the universe.   We may say that
in religion God tends always to pass beyond himself.   He is necessarily led to end in the Absolute,
which for religion is not God.   God, whether a
"person" or not, is, on the one hand, a finite being
and an object to man.   On the other hand, the consummation, sought by the religious consciousness, is
the perfect unity of these terms.   And, if so, nothing
would in the end fall outside God.   But to take
God as the ceaseless oscillation and changing movement of the process, is out of the question.   On the
other side the harmony of all these discords demands,
as we have shown, the alteration of their finite char-

acter.   The unity implies a complete suppression of the relation, as such; but, with that suppression, religion and the good have altogether, as such, disappeared.   If you identify the Absolute with God, that is not the God of religion.   If again you separate them, God becomes a finite factor in the Whole. And the effort of religion is to put an end to, and break down, this relation—a relation which, none the less, it essentially presupposes.   Hence, short of the Absolute, God cannot rest, and, having reached that goal, he is lost and religion with him.   It is this difficulty which appears in the problem of the religious self-consciousness.   God must certainly be conscious of himself in religion, but such self-consciousness is most imperfect.[1]   For if the external relation

---

[1] The two extremes in the human-divine self-consciousness cannot wholly unite in one concordant self.   It is interesting to compare such expressions as—

> " I am the eye with which the Universe
>   Beholds itself and knows itself divine,"

and

> " They reckon ill who leave me out ;
>   When me they fly, I am the wings ;
>   I am the doubter and the doubt,
>   And I the hymn the Brahmin sings,"

and

> " Die Sehnsucht du, und was sie stillt,"

with

> Ne suis-je pas un faux accord
> Dans la divine symphonie,
> Grâce à la vorace Ironie
> Qui me secoue et qui me mord ?
>
> Elle est dans ma voix, la criarde !
> C'est tout mon sang, ce poison noir !
> Je suis le sinistre miroir
> Où la mégère se regarde !
>
> Je suis la plaie et le couteau !
> Je suis le soufflet et la joue !
> Je suis les membres et la roue,
> Et la victime et le bourreau !

between God and man were entirely absorbed, the separation of subject and object would, as such, have gone with it. But if again the self, which is conscious, still contains in its essence a relation between two unreduced terms, where is the unity of its selfness? In short, God, as the highest expression of the realized good, shows the contradiction which we found to be inherent in that principle. The falling apart of idea and existence is at once essential to goodness and negated by Reality. And the process, which moves within Reality, is not Reality itself. We may say that God is not God, till he has become all in all, and that a God which is all in all is not the God of religion. God is but an aspect, and that must mean but an appearance, of the Absolute.

Through the remainder of this chapter I will try to remove some misunderstandings. The first I have to notice is the old confusion as to matter of fact ; and I will here partly repeat the conclusions of our foregoing chapters. If religion is appearance, then the self and God, I shall be told, are illusions, since they will not be facts. This is the prejudice which everywhere Common Sense opposes to philosophy. Common Sense is persuaded that the first rude way, in which it interprets phenomena, is ultimate truth ; and neither reasoning, nor the ceaseless protests of its own daily experience, can shake its assurance. But we have seen that this persuasion rests on barbarous error. Certainly a man knows and experiences everywhere the ultimate Reality, and indeed is able to know and experience nothing else. But to know it or experience it, fully and as such, is a thing utterly impossible. For the whole of finite being and knowledge consists vitally in appearance, in the alienation of the two aspects of existence and content. So that, if facts are to be ultimate and real, there are no facts anywhere or at all. There will be one single fact, which is the

Absolute. But if, on the other hand, facts are to stand for actual finite events, or for things the essence of which is to be confined to a here or a now—facts are then the lowest, and the most untrue, form of appearance. And in the commonest business of our lives we rise above this low level. Hence it is facts themselves which, in this sense, should be called illusory.

In the religious consciousness, especially, we are not concerned with such facts as these. Its facts, if pure inward experiences, are surcharged with a content which is obviously incapable of confinement within a here or a now. And, in the seeming concentration within one moment of all Hell or all Heaven, the incompatibility of our "fact" with its own existence is forced on our view. The same truth holds of all external religious events. These are not religious until they have a significance which transcends their sensible finitude. And the general question is *not* whether the relation of God to man is an appearance, since there is no relation, nor any fact, which can possibly be more. The question is, where in the world of appearance is such a fact to be ranked. What, in other words, is the degree of its reality and truth?

To enter fully into such an enquiry is impossible here. If however we apply the criterion gained in the preceding chapter, we can see at once that there is nothing more real than what comes in religion. To compare facts such as these with what is given to us in outward existence, would be to trifle with the subject. The man, who demands a reality more solid than that of the religious consciousness, seeks he does not know what. Dissatisfied with the reality of man and God as he finds them there in experience, he may be invited to state intelligibly what in the end would content him. For God and man, as two sensible existences, would be degraded past recognition. We may say that the God which could exist, would most assuredly be no God. And man and God as two realities, individual and ultimate, "standing" one cannot tell where, and with a relation "between" them—this conjunction, we have seen, is self-contradictory, and is therefore appearance. It is a confused attempt to seize and hold in religion that Absolute, which, if it really were attained, would destroy religion.[1] And this attempt, by its own inconsistency, and its own failure and unrest, reveals to us once more that religion is not final and ultimate.

But, if so, what, I may be asked, is the result in practice? That, I reply at once, is not my business; and insistence on such a question would rest on a hurtful prejudice. The task of the metaphysician is to enquire into ultimate truth, and he cannot be called on to consider anything else, however important it may be. We have but little notion in England of freedom either in art or in science. Irrelevant appeals to practical results are allowed to make themselves heard. And in certain regions of art and science this sin brings its own punishment; for we fail through timidity and through a want of singleness and sincerity. That a man should treat of God and religion in order merely to understand them, and apart from the influence of some other consideration and inducement, is to many of us in part unintelligible, and in part also shocking. And hence English thought on these subjects, where it has not studied in a foreign school, is theoretically worthless. On my own mind the effect of this prejudice is personally deterrent. If to show theoretical interest in morality and religion is taken as the setting oneself up as a teacher or preacher, I would rather leave these sub-

---

[1] It leads to the dilemma, If God is, I am not, and, if I am, God is not. We have not reached a true view until the opposite of this becomes self-evident. Then without hesitation we answer that God is not himself, unless I also am, and that, if God were not, I certainly should be nothing.

jects to whoever feels that such a character suits him.
And, if I have touched on them here, it was because
I could not help it.

And, having said so much, perhaps it would be
better if I said no more. But with regard to the
practical question, since I refuse altogether to answer
it, I may perhaps safely try to point out what this
question is. It is clear that religion must have some
doctrine, however little that may be, and it is clear
again that such doctrine will not be ultimate truth.
And by many it is apparently denied that anything
less can suffice. If however we consider the sciences
we find them too in a similar position. For their
first principles, as we have seen, are in the end self-
contradictory. Their principles are but partially
true, and yet are valid, because they will work. And
why then, we may ask, are such working ideas not
enough for religion ? There are several serious
difficulties, but the main difficulty appears to be this.
In the sciences we know, for the most part, the end
which we aim at ; and, knowing this end, we are
able to test and to measure the means. But in
religion it is precisely the chief end upon which we
are not clear. And, on the basis of this confused
disagreement, a rational discussion is not possible.
We want to get some idea as to the doctrines really
requisite for religion ; and we begin without having
examined the end for which the doctrines are required,
and by which obviously, therefore, they must be
judged. From time to time this or that man finds
that a certain belief, or set of beliefs, seems to
lie next his heart. And on this at once he cries
aloud that, if these particular doctrines are not
true, all religion is at an end. And this is what
the public admires, and what it calls a defence of
religion.

But if the problem is to be, I do not say solved,
but discussed rationally at all, we must begin by an
enquiry into the essence and end of religion. And

to that enquiry, I presume, there are two things indispensable. We must get some consistent view as to the general nature of reality, goodness, and truth, and we must not shut our eyes to the historical facts of religion. We must come, first, to some conclusion about the purpose of religious truths. Do they exist for the sake of understanding, or do they subserve and are ancillary to some other object? And, if the latter is true, what precisely is this end and object, which we have to use as their criterion? If we can settle this point we can then decide that religious truths, which go beyond and which fall short of their end, possess no title to existence. If, in the second place again, we are not clear about the nature of scientific truth, can we rationally deal with any alleged collision between religion and science? We shall, in fact, be unable to say whether there is any collision or none; or again, supposing a conflict to exist, we shall be entirely at a loss how to estimate its importance. And our result so far is this. If English theologians decline to be in earnest with metaphysics, they must obviously speak on some topics, I will not say ignorantly, but at least without having made a serious attempt to gain knowledge. But to be in earnest with metaphysics is not the affair of perhaps one or two years; nor did any one ever do anything with such a subject without giving himself up to it. And, lastly, I will explain what I mean by attention to history. If religion is a practical matter, it would be absurd wholly to disregard the force of continuous occupancy and possession. But history, on the other hand, supplies teachings of a different order. If, in the past and the present, we find religion appearing to flourish in the absence of certain particular doctrines, it is not a light step to proclaim these doctrines as essential to religion. And to do this without discussion and dogmatically, and to begin one's work by some bald assumption, perhaps about the necessity of a "personal" God, is to trifle indecently with a subject which deserves some respect.

What is necessary, in short, is to begin by looking at the question disinterestedly and looking at it all round. In this way we might certainly expect to arrive at a rational discussion, but I do not feel any right to assume that we should ever arrive at more. Perhaps the separation of the accidental from the essential in religion can be accomplished only by a longer and a ruder process. It must be left, perhaps, to the blind competition of rival errors, and to the coarse struggle for existence between hostile sects. But such a conclusion, once more, should not be accepted without a serious trial. And this is all that I intend to say on the practical problem of religion.

I will end this chapter with a word of warning against a dangerous mistake. We have seen that religion is but appearance, and that it cannot be ultimate. And from this it may be concluded, perhaps, that the completion of religion is philosophy, and that in metaphysics we reach the goal in which it finds its consummation. Now, if religion essenti- ally were knowledge, this conclusion would hold. And, so far as religion involves knowledge, we are again bound to accept it. Obviously the business of metaphysics is to deal with ultimate truth, and in this respect, obviously, it must be allowed to stand higher than religion. But, on the other side, we have found that the essence of religion is not knowledge. And this certainly does not mean that its essence consists barely in feeling. Religion is rather the attempt to express the complete reality of goodness through every aspect of our being. And, so far as this goes, it is at once something more, and therefore some- thing higher, than philosophy.

Philosophy, as we shall find in our next chapter, is itself but appearance. It is but one appearance among others, and, if it rises higher in one respect, in other ways it certainly stands lower. And its weakness lies, of course, in the fact that it is barely theoretical. Philosophy may be *made* more undoubtedly, and incidentally it *is* more ; but its essence clearly must be confined to intellectual activity. It is therefore but a one-sided and inconsistent appearance of the Absolute. And, so far as philosophy is religious, to that extent we must allow that it has passed into religion, and has ceased, as such, any longer to be philosophy. I do not suggest to those who, dissatisfied with religious beliefs, may have turned seriously to metaphysics, that they will not find there what they seek. But they will not find it there, or anywhere else, unless they have brought it with them. Metaphysics has no special connection with genuine religion, and neither of these two appearances can be regarded as the perfection of the other. The completion of each is not to be found except in the Absolute.

CHAPTER XXVI.

THE ABSOLUTE AND ITS APPEARANCES.

WE have seen now that Goodness, like Truth, is a one-sided appearance. Each of these aspects, when we insist on it, transcends itself. By its own movement each develops itself beyond its own limits and is merged in a higher and all-embracing Reality. It is time that we endeavoured to close our work by explaining more fully the character of this real unity. We have certainly not attempted to do justice to the various spheres of phenomena. The account which we have given of truth and goodness is but a barren outline, and this was the case before with physical Nature, and with the problem of the soul. But to such defects we must resign ourselves. For the object of this volume is to state merely a general view about Reality, and to defend this view against more obvious and prominent objections. The full and proper defence would be a systematic account of all the regions of appearance, for it is only the completed system which in metaphysics is the genuine proof of the principle. But, unable to enter on such an undertaking, I must none the less endeavour to justify further our conclusion about the Absolute.

There is but one Reality, and its being consists in experience. In this one whole all appearances come together, and in coming together they in various degrees lose their distinctive natures. The essence of reality lies in the union and agreement of existence and content, and, on the other side, appearance consists in the discrepancy between these two aspects. And reality in the end belongs to nothing but the single Real. For take anything, no matter what it is, which is less than the Absolute, and the inner discrepancy at once proclaims that what you have taken is appearance. The alleged reality divides itself and falls apart into two jarring factors. The "what" and the "that" are plainly two sides which turn out not to be the same, and this difference inherent in every finite fact entails its disruption. As long as the content stands for something other than its own intent and meaning, as long as the existence actually is less or more than what it essentially must imply, so long we are concerned with mere appearance, and not with genuine reality. And we have found in every region that this discrepancy of aspects prevails. The internal being of everything finite depends on that which is beyond it. Hence everywhere, insisting on a so-called fact, we have found ourselves led by its inner character into something outside itself. And this self-contradiction, this unrest and ideality of all things existing is a clear proof that, though such things are, their being is but appearance.

But, upon the other hand, in the Absolute no appearance can be lost. Each one contributes and is essential to the unity of the whole. And hence we have observed (Chapter xxv.) that any one aspect, when viewed by itself, may be regarded as the end for which the others exist. Deprived of any one aspect or element the Absolute may be called worthless. And thus, while you take your stand on some one valuable factor, the others appear to you to be means which subserve its existence. Certainly your position in such an attitude is one-sided and unstable. The other factors are not external means to, but are implied in, the first, and your attitude, therefore, is but provisional and in the end untrue. It may however have served to indicate that truth which we

have here to insist on.   There is nothing in the
Absolute which is barely contingent or merely
accessory.   Every element, however subordinate,
is preserved in that relative whole in which its
character is taken up and merged.   There are main
aspects of the universe of which none can be resolved
into the rest.   Hence from this ground we cannot say of these main aspects that one is higher
in rank or better than another.   They are factors
not independent, since each of itself implies and
calls in something else to complete its defects, and
since all are over-ruled in that final whole which
perfects them.   But these factors, if not equal, are
not subordinate the one to the other, and in relation
to the Absolute they are all alike essential and
necessary.

In the present chapter, returning to the idea of
the Absolute as a whole of experience, I will from
this point of view survey briefly its main aspects.
Of the attitudes possible in experience I will try to
show that none has supremacy.   There is not one
mode to which the others belong as its adjectives,
or into which they can be resolved.   And how
these various modes can come together into a single
unity must remain unintelligible.   Reserving to the
next chapter a final discussion on the positive nature
of this Unity, I will lay stress here on another side.
The Absolute is present in, and, in a sense, it *is*
alike each of its special appearances ; though present
everywhere again in different values and degrees.
I shall attempt in passing to clear up some questions with regard to Nature, and I will end the
chapter with a brief enquiry as to the meaning of
Progress, and as to the possibility of a continuance
of personal life after death.

Everything is experience, and also experience is
one.   In the next chapter I shall once more consider if it is possible to doubt this, but for the pre-

sent I shall assume it as a truth which has held good.
Under what main aspects then, let us ask, is experience found ? We may say, speaking broadly,
that there are two great modes, perception and
thought on the one side, and will and desire on the
other side. Then there is the æsthetic attitude,
which will not fall entirely under either of these
heads ; and again there is pleasure and pain which
seem something distinct from both. Further we
have feeling, a term which we must take in two
senses. It is first the general state of the total soul
not yet at all differentiated into any of the preceding
special aspects. And again it is any particular state
so far as internally that has undistinguished unity.
Now of these psychical modes not any one is re-
solvable into the others, nor can the unity of the
Whole consist in one or another portion of them.
Each of them is incomplete and one-sided, and calls
for assistance from without. We have had to perceive this in great part already through former discussions, but I will briefly resume and in some
points supplement that evidence here. I am about
to deal with the appearances of the Absolute mainly
from their psychical side, but a full psychological
discussion is impossible, and is hardly required. I
would ask the reader, whose views in certain ways
may be divergent from mine, not to dwell on diver-
gencies except so far as they affect the main result.

(1) If we consider first of all the aspect of pleasure and pain, it is evident that this cannot be the
substance or foundation of Reality. For we cannot
regard the other elements as adjectives of, or de-
pendents on, this one ; nor again can we, in any
way or in any sense, resolve them into it. Pleasure
and pain, it is obvious, are not the one thing real.
But are they real at all, as such, and independently of
the rest ? Even this we are compelled to deny.
For pleasure and pain are antagonistic ; and when
in the Whole they have come together with a balance

of pleasure, can we be even sure that this result will be pleasure as such?[1]   There is however a far more serious objection to the reality of pleasure and pain.   For these are mere abstractions which *we* separate from the pleasant and the painful ; and to suppose that they are not connected with those states and processes, with which they are always conjoined, would be plainly irrational.   Indeed pleasure and pain, as things by themselves, would contradict their known character.   But, if so, clearly they cannot be real in themselves, and their reality and essence will in part fall beyond their own limits.   They are but appearances and one-sided adjectives of the universe, and they are real only when taken up into and merged in that totality.

(2) From mere pleasure and pain we may pass on to feeling, and I take feeling in the sense of the immediate unity of a finite psychical centre.   It means for me, first, the general condition before distinctions and relations have been developed, and where as yet neither any subject nor object exists.   And it means, in the second place, anything which is present at any stage of mental life, in so far as that is only present and simply is.[2]   In this latter sense we may say that everything actual, no matter what, must be felt ; but we do not call it feeling except so far as we take it as failing to be more.   Now, in either of these senses, is it possible to consider feeling as real, or as a consistent aspect of reality ?   We must reply in the negative.

Feeling has a content, and this content is not consistent within itself, and such a discrepancy tends to destroy and to break up the stage of feeling. The matter may be briefly put thus—the finite con-

---

[1] See above Chapter xvii. and below Chapter xxvii.

[2] Compare Chapters ix., xix., xx. and xxvii., and *Mind*, N. S. 6. I had hoped elsewhere to write something on the position to be given to Feeling in psychology.   But for the purpose of this volume I trust, on the whole, to have said enough.

tent is irreconcilable with the immediacy of its
existence.   For the finite content is necessarily
determined from the outside ; its external relations
(however negative they may desire to remain) penetrate its essence, and so carry that beyond its own
being.   And hence, since the " what " of all feeling
is discordant with its " that," it is appearance, and,
as such, it cannot be real.   This fleeting and untrue character is perpetually forced on our notice by
the hard fact of change.   And, both from within
and from without, feeling is compelled to pass off
into the relational consciousness.   It is the ground
and foundation of further developments, but it is a
foundation that bears them only by a ceaseless lapse
from itself.   Hence we could not, in any proper
sense, call these products its adjectives.   For their
life consists in the diremption of feeling's unity, and
this unity is not again restored and made good except in the Absolute.

(3) We may pass next to the perceptional or
theoretic, and again, on the other side, to the practical aspect.   Each of these differs from the two foregoing by implying distinction, and, in the first place,
a distinction between subject and object.[1]   The perceptional side has at the outset, of course, no special
existence ; for it is given at first in union with the
practical side, and is but slowly differentiated.   But
what we are concerned with here is to attempt to
apprehend its specific nature.   One or more elements are separated from the confused mass of feeling, and stand apparently by themselves and over
against this.   And the distinctive character of
such an object is that it seems simply to *be*.   If it
appeared to influence the mass which it confronts, so
as to lead that to act on it and alter it, and if such
a relation qualified its nature, the attitude would be

---

[1] This distinction, I have no doubt, is developed in time (*Mind*,
No. 47) ; but, even if we suppose it to be original, the further
conclusion is in no way affected.

practical. But the perceptional relation is supposed
to fall wholly outside the essence of the object. It
is in short disregarded, or else is dismissed as a
something accidental and irrelevant. For the reality,
as thought of or as perceived, in itself simply is. It
may be given, or again sought for, discovered or
reflected on, but all this—however much there may
be of it—is nothing to *it*. For the object only
stands in relation, and emphatically in no sense is
the relation in which it stands.

This is the vital inconsistency of the real as perception or thought. Its essence depends on qualification by a relation which it attempts to ignore.
And this one inconsistency soon exhibits itself from
two points of view. The felt background, from
which the theoretic object stands out, is supposed in
no way to contribute to its being. But, even at the
stage of perception or sensation, this hypothesis
breaks down. And, when we advance to reflective
thinking, such a position clearly is untenable. The
world can hardly stand there to be found, when its
essence appears to be inseparable from the process
of finding, and when assuredly it would not be the
whole world unless it included within itself both the
finding and the finder. But, this last perfection
once reached, the object no longer could stand in
any relation at all ; and, with this, its proper being
would be at once both completed and destroyed.
The perceptional attitude would entirely have passed
beyond itself.

We may bring out again the same contradiction
if we begin from the other side. As perceived or
thought of the reality *is*, and it is also itself. But
its self obviously, on the other hand, includes relation to others, and it is determined inwardly by
those others from which it is distinguished. Its
content therefore slides beyond its existence, its
" what " spreads out beyond its " that." It thus no
longer is, but has become something ideal in which

the Reality appears. And, since this appearance is
not identical with reality, it cannot wholly be true.
Hence it must be corrected, until finally in its
content it has ceased to be false. But, in the first
place, this correction is merely ideal. It consists in
a process throughout which content is separated
from existence. Hence, if truth were complete, it
would not be truth, because that is only appearance ;
and in the second place, while truth remains appearance, it cannot possibly be complete. The theoretic
object moves towards a consummation in which all
distinction and all ideality must be suppressed. But,
when that is reached, the theoretic attitude has been,
as such, swallowed up. It throughout on one hand
presupposes a relation, and on the other hand it
asserts an independence ; and, if these jarring aspects
are removed or are harmonized, its proper character
is gone. Hence perception and thought must either
attempt to fall back into the immediacy of feeling,
or else, confessing themselves to be one-sided and
false, they must seek completion beyond themselves
in a supplement and counterpart.

(4) With this we are naturally led to consider the
practical aspect of things. Here, as before, we must
have an object, a something distinct from, and over
against, the central mass of feeling. But in this case
the relation shows itself as essential, and is felt as
opposition. An ideal alteration of the object is
suggested, and the suggestion is not rejected by the
feeling centre ; and the process is completed by this
ideal qualification, in me, itself altering, and so itself
becoming, the object. Such is, taken roughly, the
main essence of the practical attitude, and its one-
sidedness and insufficiency are evident at once. For
it consists in the healing up of a division which it
has no power to create, and which, once healed up,
is the entire removal of the practical attitude. Will
certainly produces, not mere ideas, but actual existence. But it depends on ideality and mere appear-

ance for its starting-point and essence ; and the harmony which it makes is for ever finite, and hence incomplete and unstable. And if this were not so, and if the ideal and the existing were made one, the relation between them would have disappeared, and will, as such, must have vanished. Thus the attitude of practice, like all the rest, is not reality but is appearance.[1] And with this result we may pass onwards, leaving to a later place the consideration of certain mistakes about the will. For since the will implies and presupposes the distinction made in perception and idea, we need hardly ask if it possesses more reality than these.

(5) In the æsthetic attitude we may seem at last to have transcended the opposition of idea to existence, and to have at last surmounted and risen beyond the relational consciousness. For the æs-

---

[1] In the foregoing chapter we have already dealt with the contradictions of Goodness. For the nature of Desire and Volition see *Mind*, No. 49. Compare also No. 43, where I have said something on the meaning of Resolve. There are, indeed, instances where the idea does not properly pass into existence, and where yet we are justified in speaking of will, and not merely of resolve. Such are the cases where I will something to take place after my death, or where again, as we say, I will now to do something which I am incapable of performing. The process here is certainly incomplete, but still can be rightly called volition, because the movement of the idea towards existence has actually begun. It has started on its course, external or inward, so as already to be past recall. In the same way when the trigger is pressed, and the hammer has also perhaps fallen, a miss-fire leaves the act incomplete, but we still may be said to have fired. In mere Resolve, on the other hand, the incompatibility of the idea with any present realization of its content is recognised. And hence Resolve not aiming straight at present fact, but satisfied with an ideal filling-out of its idea, should not be called volition. The process is not only incomplete, but it also knowingly holds back and diverges from the direct road to existence. Resolve may be taken as a case of internal volition, if you consider it as the bringing about of a certain state of mind. But the production of the resolve, and not the resolve itself, is, in this case, will.

thetic attitude seems to retain the immediacy of feeling. And it has also an object with a certain character, but yet an object self-existent and not merely ideal. This aspect of the world satisfies us in a way unattainable by theory or practice, and it plainly cannot be reduced and resolved into either. However, when we consider it more narrowly, its defects become patent. It is no solution of our problems, since it fails to satisfy either the claims of reality or even its own.

That which is æsthetic may generally be defined as the self-existent emotional. It can hardly all fall properly under the two heads of the beautiful and ugly, but for my present purpose it will be convenient to regard it as doing so. And since in the Absolute ugliness, like error and evil, must be overpowered and absorbed, we may here confine our attention entirely to beauty.

Beauty is the self-existent pleasant. It is certainly not the self-existent which enjoys its own pleasure, for that, so far as one sees, need not be beautiful at all. But the beautiful must be self-existent, and its being must be independent as such. Hence it must exist as an individual and not merely in idea. Thoughts, or even thought-processes, may be beautiful, but only so if they appear, as it were, self-contained, and, in a manner, for sense. But the beautiful, once more, must be an object. It must stand in relation to my mind, and again it must possess a distinguished ideal content. We cannot say that mere feeling is beautiful, though in a com plex whole we may find at once the blended aspects of feeling and of beauty. And the beautiful, last of all, must be actually pleasant. But, if so, then once more it must be pleasant for some one.[1]

Such an union of characters is inconsistent, and

---

[1] The possibility of some margin of pleasure falling outside all finite centres, seems very slight (Chapter xxvii.). So far as that pleasure is an object, the relation is certainly essential.

we require no great space to point out its discrepancy.   Let us first abstract from the pleasantness
and from the relation to me, and let us suppose that
the beautiful exists independently.   Yet even here
we shall find it in contradiction with itself.   For the
sides of existence and of content must be concordant and at one ; but, on the other hand, because
the object is finite, such an agreement is impossible.
And thus, as was the case with truth and goodness,
there is a partial divergence of the two aspects of
extension and harmony.   The expression is imperfect, or again that which is expressed is too narrow.
And in both ways alike in the end there is want of
harmoniousness, there is an inner discrepancy and
a failure in reality.   For the content—itself in any
case always finite, and so always inconsistent with
itself—may even visibly go beyond its actual expression, and be merely ideal.   And, on the other
side, the existing expression must in various ways
and degrees fall short of reality.   For, taken at its
strongest, it after all must be finite fact.   It is
determined from the outside, and so must internally be in discord with itself.   Thus the beautiful
object, viewed as independent, is no more than
appearance.[1]

But to take beauty as an independent existence
is impossible.   For pleasure belongs to its essence,
and to suppose pleasure, or any emotion, standing
apart from some self seems out of the question.
The beautiful, therefore, will be determined by a
quality in me.   And in any case, because (as we
have seen) it is an object for perception, the relation
involved in perception must be essential to its being.
Either then, both as perceived and as emotional,
beauty will be characterized internally by what falls
outside itself; and obviously in this case it will

[1] The question of degrees in beauty, like that of degrees in
truth and goodness, would be interesting.   But it is hardly necessary for us to enter on it here.

have turned out to be appearance. Or, on the other hand, it must include within its own limits this external condition of its life. But, with that total absorption of the percipient and sentient self, the whole relation, and with it beauty as such, will have vanished.

The various aspects, brought together in the æsthetic object, have been seen to fall apart. Beauty is not really immediate, or independent, or harmonious in itself. And, attempting to satisfy these requirements, it must pass beyond its own character. Like all the other aspects this also has been shown to be appearance.

We have now surveyed the different regions of experience, and have found each to be imperfect. We certainly cannot say that the Absolute *is* any one of them. On the other hand each can be seen to be insufficient and inconsistent, because it is not also, and as well, the rest. Each aspect to a certain extent, already in fact, implies the others in its existence, and in order to become Reality would have to go on to include them wholly. And hence Reality seems contained in the totality of these its diverse provinces, and they on their side each to be a partial appearance of the universe. Let us once more briefly pass them in review.

With pleasure or pain we can perceive at once that its nature is adjectival. We certainly cannot, starting with what we know of pleasure and pain, show that this directly implies the remaining aspects of the world. We must be satisfied with the knowledge that pain and pleasure are adjectives, adjectives, so far as we see, attached to every other aspect of experience. A complete insight into the conditions of these adjectives is not attainable ; but, if we could get it, it doubtless would include every side of the universe. But, passing from pleasure and pain to Feeling, we can verify there at once the

principle of discord and development in its essence.
The sides of content and existence already strive to
diverge. And hence feeling changes not merely
through outer force but through internal defect.
The theoretical, the practical, and the æsthetic
aspect of things are attempts to work out and make
good this divergence of existence and idea. Each
must thus be regarded as a one-sided and special
growth from feeling. And feeling still remains in
the background as the unity of these differences,
a unity that cannot find its complete expression in
any or in all of them. Defect is obvious at once
in the æsthetic attitude. Beauty both attempts and
fails to arrive at immediate reality. For, even if
you take it as real apart from relation to a percipient, there is never entire accordance between its
two demands for completeness and harmony. That
which is expressed in fact remains too narrow, and
that which is wider remains imperfectly expressed.
And hence, to be entirely beautiful, the object would
have also to be completely good and wholly true.
Its idea would require to be self-contained, and so
all-embracing, and to be carried out in an existence
no less self-sufficient. But, if so, the distinctive
characters of truth and goodness and beauty would
have vanished. We reach again the same result if
we turn to the theoretical aspect of the world. Perception or theory, if it were but true, must also be
good. For the fact would have to be so taken that
it exhibited no difference from the thought. But
such a concord of idea and existence would certainly
also be goodness. And again, being individual, it
would as certainly no less be beautiful. But on the
other hand, since all these divergences would have
been absorbed, truth, beauty and goodness, as such,
would no longer exist. We arrive at the same
conclusion when we begin from the practical side.
Nothing would content us finally but the complete
union of harmony and extent. A reality that sug-

gested any idea not existing actually within its limits, would not be perfectly good. Perfect goodness would thus imply the entire and absolute presence of the ideal aspect. But this, if present, would be perfect and absolute truth. And it would be beautiful also, since it would entail the individual harmony of existence with content. But, once again, since the distinctive differences would now have disappeared, we should have gone beyond beauty or goodness or truth altogether.[1]

We have seen that the various aspects of experience imply one another, and that all point to a unity which comprehends and perfects them. And I would urge next that the unity of these aspects is unknown. By this I certainly do not mean to deny that it essentially is experience, but it is an experience of which, as such, we have no direct knowledge. We never have, or are, a state which is the perfect unity of all aspects; and we must admit that in their special natures they remain inexplicable. An explanation would be the reduction of their plurality to unity, in such a way that the relation between the unity and the variety was understood. And everywhere an explanation of this kind in the end is beyond us. If we abstract one or more of the aspects of experience, and use this known element as a ground to which the others are referred, our failure is evident. For if the rest could be developed from this ground, as really they cannot be, they with their differences can yet not be predic-

---

[1] I have not thought it necessary here to point out how in their actual existence these aspects are implicated with one another. All the other aspects are more or less the objects of, and produced by, will; and will itself, together with the rest, is an object to thought. Thought again depends on all for its material, and will on all for its ideas. And the same psychical state may be indifferently will or thought, according to the side from which you view it (p. 474). Every state again to some extent may be considered and taken as feeling.

ated of it.   But, if so, in the end the whole diversity must be attributed as adjectives to a unity
which is not known.   Thus no separate aspect can
possibly serve as an explanation of the others.   And
again, as we have found, no separate aspect is by
itself intelligible.   For each is inconsistent with
itself, and so is forced to take in others.   Hence
to explain would be possible only when the whole,
as such, was comprehended.   And such an actual
and detailed comprehension we have seen is not
possible.

Resting then on this general conclusion we might
go forward at once.   We might assume that any
reduction of the Absolute to one or two of the special
modes of experience is out of the question, and we
might forthwith attempt a final discussion of its
nature and unity.   It may however be instructive
to consider more closely a proposed reduction of
this kind.   Let us ask then if Reality can be rightly
explained as the identity of Thought and Will.   But
first we may remind ourselves of some of those points
which a full explanation must include.

In order to understand the universe we should
require to know how the special matter of sense
stands everywhere to its relations and forms, and
again how pleasure and pain are connected with
these forms and these qualities.   We should have
to comprehend further the entire essence of the
relational consciousness, and the connection between
its unity and its plurality of distinguished terms.
We should have to know why everything (or all but
everything) comes in finite centres of immediate
feeling, and how these centres with regard to one
another are not directly pervious.   Then there is
process in time with its perpetual shifting of content
from existence, a happening which seems certainly
not all included under will and thought.   The
physical world again suggests some problems.   Are
there really ideas and ends that work in Nature?

And why is it that, within us and without us, there is a knowable arrangement, an order such that existence answers to thought, and that personal identity and a communication between souls is possible ? We have, in short, on one side a diversity and finitude, and on the other side we have a unity. And, unless we know throughout the universe how these aspects stand the one to the other, the universe is not explained.

But a partial explanation, I may here be reminded, is better than none. That in the present case, I reply, would be a serious error. You take from the whole of experience some element or elements as a principle, and you admit, I presume, that in the whole there remains some aspect unexplained and outstanding. Now such an aspect belongs to the universe, and must, therefore, be predicated of a unity not contained in your elements. But, if so, your elements are at once degraded, for they become adjectives of this unknown unity. Hence the objection is not that your explanation is incomplete, but that its very principle is unsound. You have offered as ultimate what in its working proclaims itself appearance. And the partial explanation has implied in fact a false pretence of knowledge.

We may verify this result at once in the proposed reduction of the other aspects of the world to intelligence and will. Before we see anything of this in detail we may state beforehand its necessary and main defect. Suppose that every feature of the universe has been fairly brought under, and included in these two aspects, the universe still remains unexplained. For the two aspects, however much one implies and indeed *is* the other, must in some sense still be two. And unless we comprehend how their plurality, where they are diverse, stands to their unity, where they are at one, we have ended in failure. Our principles after all will not be ultimate, but will themselves be the twofold appearance of a unity left unexplained.   It may however repay us to examine further the proposed reduction.

The plausibility of this consists very largely in vagueness, and its strength lies in the uncertain sense given to will and intelligence.   We seem to know these terms so well that we run no risk in applying them, and then imperceptibly we pass into an application where their meaning is changed.   We have to explain the world, and what we find there is a process with two aspects.   There is a constant loosening of idea from fact, and a making-good once more in a new existence of this recurring discrepancy.   We find nowhere substances fixed and rigid.   They are relative wholes of ideal content, standing on a ceaselessly renewed basis of two-sided change.   Identity, permanence, and continuity, are everywhere ideal ; they are unities for ever created and destroyed by the constant flux of existence, a flux which they provoke, and which supports them and is essential to their life.   Now, looking at the universe so, we may choose to speak of thought wherever the idea becomes loose from its existence in fact ; and we may speak of will wherever this unity is once more made good.   And, with this introduction of what seems self-evident, the two main aspects of the world appear to have found an explanation.   Or we possibly might help ourselves to this result by a further vagueness.   For everything, at all events, either is, or else happens in time.   We might say then that, so far as it happens, it is produced by will, and that, so far as it is, it is an object for perception or thought.   But, passing this by without consideration, let us regard the process of the world as presenting two aspects.   Thought must then be taken as the idealizing side of this process, and will, on the other hand, must be viewed as the side which makes ideas to be real.   And let us, for the present, also suppose that will and thought are in themselves more or less self-evident.

Now it is plain, first, that such a view compels us to postulate very much more than we observe. For ideality certainly does not appear to be all produced by thought, and actual existence, as certainly, does not all appear as the effect of will. The latter is obvious whether in our own selves, or in the course of Nature, or again in any other of the selves that we know. And, with regard to ideality or the loosening of content from fact, this is everywhere the common mark of appearance. It does not seem exclusively confined to or distinctive of thinking. Thought does not seem co-extensive in general with the relational form, and it must be said to accept, as well as to create, ideal distinctions. Ideality appears, in short, often as the result of psychical changes and processes which do not seem, in the proper sense, to imply any thinking. These are difficulties, but still they may perhaps be dealt with. For, just as we could set no limits to the possible existences of souls, so we can fix no bounds to the possible working of thought and will. Our mere failure to discover them here or there, and whether within ourselves or again outside us, does not anywhere disprove their existence. And as souls to an unknown extent can have their life and world in common, so the effects of will and thought may show themselves there where the actual process is not experienced. That which comes to me as a mechanical occurrence, or again as an ideal distinction which I have never made, may none the less, also and essentially, be will and thought. And it may be experienced as such, completely or partly, outside me. My reason and my plan to other finite centres may only be chance, and their intelligible functions may strike on me as a dark necessity. But for a higher unity our blind entanglement is lucid order. The world discordant, half-completed, and accidental for each one, is in the Whole a compensated system of conspiring particulars. Everything there is the joint result of two functions which in their

working are one, and every least detail is still the
outcome of intelligence and will. Certainly such a
doctrine is a postulate, in so far as its particulars
cannot be verified. But taken in general it may be
urged also as a legitimate inference and a necessary
conclusion.

Still in the way of this conclusion, which I have
tried to set out, we find other difficulties as yet
unremoved. There is pleasure and pain, and again
the facts of feeling and of the æsthetic consciousness.
Now, if thought and will fail to explain these, and
they, along with thought and will, have to be predicated unexplained of the Unity, the Unity after
all is unknown. Feeling, in the first place, cannot
be regarded as the indifferent ground of perception
and will; for, if so, this ground itself offers a new
fact which requires explanation. Feeling therefore
must be taken as a sort of confusion, and as a nebula
which would grow distinct on closer scrutiny. And
the æsthetic attitude, perhaps, may be regarded as
the perceived equilibrium of both our functions.
It must be admitted certainly that such an attitude
if the unity alike of thought and will, remains a source
of embarrassment. For it seems hardly derivable
from both as diverse; and, taken as their unity, it,
upon the other side, certainly fails to contain or
account for either. And, if we pass from this to
pleasure and pain, we do but gain another difficulty.
For the connection of these adjectives with our two
functions seems in the end inexplicable, while, on
the other hand, I do not perceive that this connection is self-evident. We seem in fact drifting towards
the admission that there are other aspects of the
world, which must be referred as adjectives to our
identity of will and thought, while their inclusion
within will or thought remains' uncertain. But
this is virtually to allow that thought and will are
not the essence of the universe.

Let us go on to consider internal difficulties. Will and understanding are to be each self-evident, but on the other hand each evidently, apart from the other, has lost its special being. For will presupposes the distinction of idea from fact—a distinction made actual by a process, and presumably itself due to will. And thought has to start from the existence which only will can make. Hence it presupposes, and again as an existing process seems created by, will, although will on its side is dependent on thought. We must, I presume, try to meet this objection by laying stress on the aspect of unity. Our two functions really are inseparable, and it therefore is natural that one should imply and should presuppose the other. Certainly hitherto we have found everywhere that an unresting circle of this kind is the mark of appearance, but let us here be content to pass on. Will and thought everywhere then are implicated the one with the other. Will without an idea, and thought that did not depend upon will, would neither be itself. To a certain extent, then, will essentially is thought; and, just as essentially, all thought is will. Again the existence of thought is an end which will calls into being, and will is an object for the reflections and constructions of theory. They are not, then, two clear functions in unity, but each function, taken by itself, is still the identity of both. And each can hardly be itself, and not the other, as being a mere preponderance of itself; for there seems to be no portion of either which can claim to be, if unsupported and alone. Will and thought then differ only as we abstract and consider aspects onesidedly; or, to speak plainly, their diversity is barely appearance.

If however thought and will really are not different, they are no longer two elements or principles. They are not two known diversities which serve to explain the variety of the world. For, if their difference is appearance, still that very appearance

is what we have most to explain. We are not to go
outside will and thought, in order to seek our explanation; and yet, keeping within them, we seem
unable to find any. The identity of both is no
solution, unless that identity explains their difference;
for this difference is the very problem required to
be solved. We have given us a process of happening and finitude, and in this process we are able to
point out two main aspects. To explain such a
process is to say why and how it possesses and
supports this known diversity. But by the proposed
reduction to will and thought we have done little
more than give two names to two unexplained
aspects. For, ignore every other difficulty, and you
have still on your hands the main question, Why is
it that thought and will diverge or appear to diverge?
It is in this real or apparent divergence that the
actual world of finite things consists.

Or examine the question from another side. Will
and thought may be appealed to in order to explain
the given process in time, and certainly each of them
contains in its nature a temporal succession. Now
a process in time is appearance, and not, as such,
holding of the Absolute. And, if we urge that
thought and will are twin processes reciprocal and
compensating, that leaves us where we were. For,
as such, neither can be a predicate of the real unity,
and the nature of that unity, with its diversity of
appearance, is left unexplained. And to place the
whole succession in time on the side of mere perception, and to plead that will, taken by itself, is not
really a process, would hardly serve to assist us.
For if will has a content, then that content is perceptible and must imply temporal lapse, and will,
after all, surely can stand no higher than that which
it wills. And, without an ideal content, will is
nothing but a blind appeal to the unknown. It is
itself unknown, and of this unknown something we
are forced now to predicate as an adjective the un-

explained world of perception. Thus, in the end, will and thought are two names for two kinds of appearance. Neither, as such, can belong to the final Reality, and, in the end, both their unity and their diversity remains inexplicable. They may be offered as partial and as relative, but not as ultimate explanations.

But if their unity is thus unknown, should we call it *their* unity? Have they any right to arrogate to themselves the whole field of appearance? If we are to postulate thought and will where they are not observed, we should at least have an inducement. And, if after all they fail to explain our world, the inducement seems gone. Why should we strain ourselves to bring all phenomena under two heads, if, when we have forced them there, these heads, with the phenomena, remain unexplained? It would be surely better to admit that appearances are of more kinds, and have more aspects, than only two, and to allow that their unity is a mode of experience not directly accessible. And this result is confirmed when we recall some preceding difficulties. Pleasure and pain, feeling, and the æsthetic consciousness would hardly fall under any mere unity of intelligence and will; and again the relation of sensible qualities to their arrangements, the connection of matter with form, remained entirely inexplicable. In short, even if the unity of thought and will were by itself self-evident, yet the various aspects of the world can hardly be reduced to it. And, on the other side, even if this reduction were accomplished, the identity of will and thought, and their diversity, are still not understood. If finitude and process in time is reduced to their divergence, how is it they come to diverge? The reduction cannot be final, so long as the answer to such a question falls somewhere outside it.

The world cannot be explained as the appearance

of two counterpart functions, and with this result we
might be contented to pass on.   But, in any case,
such functions could not be identified with what we
know as intelligence and will ; and it may be better
perhaps for a little to dwell on this point.   We
assumed above that will and thought were by themselves self-evident.   We saw that there was a doubt
as to how much ground these two functions covered.
Still the existence of an idealizing and of a realizing
function, each independent and primary, we took for
granted.   But now, if we consider the facts given
to us in thinking and willing, we shall have to admit
that the powers required are not to be found.   For,
apart from the question of range, will and thought
are nowhere self-evident or primary.   Each in its
working depends on antecedent connections, connections which remain always in a sense external and
borrowed.   I will endeavour briefly to explain this.

Thought and will certainly contain transitions,
and these transitions were taken above as self-
evident.   They were regarded as something naturally involved in the very essence of these functions,
and we hence did not admit a further question about
their grounds.   But, if we turn to thought and will
in our experience, such an assumption is refuted.
For in actual thinking we depend upon particular
connections, and, apart from this given matter, we
should be surely unable to think.   These connections
cannot be taken all as inherent in the mere essence
of thought, for most of them at least seem to be
empirical and supplied from outside.   And I am
entirely unable to see how they can be regarded as
self-evident.   This result is confirmed when we consider the making of distinctions.   For, in the first
place, distinctions largely seem to grow up apart
from our thinking, in the proper sense ; and, next,
a distinguishing power of thought, where it exists,
appears to rest on, and to work from, prior difference.
It is thus a result due to acquired and empirical rela-

tions.[1]   The actual transitions of thinking are, in
short, not self-evident, or, to use another phrase,
they cannot be taken as immanent in thought.   Nor,
if we pass to volition, do we find its processes in any
better case; for our actions neither are self-evident
nor are they immanent in will.   Let us abstract from
the events in Nature and in our selves with which
our will seems not concerned.   Let us confine our
attention wholly to the cases where our idea seems
to make its existence in fact.   But is the transition here a thing so clear that it demands no explanation ?   An idea desired in one case remains
merely desired, in another case it turns into actual
existence.   Why then the one, we enquire, and not
also the other?   " Because in the second place,"
you may reply, " there is an action of will, and it is
this act which explains and accounts for the transition."   Now I will not answer here that it is the
transition which, on the other hand, is the act.   I
will for the moment accept the existence of your
preposterous faculty.   But I repeat the question,
why is one thing willed and not also the other ?
Is this difference self-evident, and self-luminous, and
a feature immediately revealed in the plain essence
of will ?   For, if it is not so, it is certainly also not
explained by volition.   It will be something external
to the function, and given from outside   And
thus, with will and thought alike, we must accept
this same conclusion.   There is no willing or thinking apart from the particular acts, and these particular acts, as will and thought, are clearly not self-
evident.   They involve in their essences a connection supplied from without.   And will and thought
therefore, even where without doubt they exist,
are dependent and secondary.   Nothing can be
explained in the end by a reduction to either of
these functions.

[1] On this point see *Mind*, No. 47.

This conclusion, not dependent on psychology, finds itself supported and confirmed there. For will and thought, in the sense in which we know them, clearly are not primary. They are developed from a basis which is not yet either, and which never can fully become so. Their existence is due to psychical events and ways of happening, which are not distinctive of thought or will. And this basis is never, so to speak, quite absorbed by either. They are differentiations whose peculiar characters never quite specialize all their contents. In other words will and thought throughout depend on what is not essentially either, and, without these psychical elements which remain external, their processes would cease. There is, in brief, a common substance with common laws; and of this material will and thought are one-sided applications. Far from exhausting this life, they are contained within it as subordinate functions. They are included in it as dependent and partial developments.

Fully to work out this truth would be the business of psychology, and I must content myself here with a brief notice of some leading points. Thought is a development from a ground of preceding ideality. The division of content from existence is not created but grows. The laws of Association and Blending already in themselves imply the working of ideal elements; and on these laws thought stands and derives from them its actual processes. It is the blind pressure and the struggle of changed sensations, which, working together with these laws, first begins to loosen ideal content from psychical fact. And hence we may say that thought proper is the outcome, and not the creator, of idealizing functions. I do not mean that the development of thought can be fully explained, since that would imply a clear insight into the general origin of the relational form. And I doubt if we can follow and retrace in detail the transition to this from the stage of mere feeling. But I would insist, none the less, that some distinguishing is prior to thought proper. Synthesis and analysis, each alike, begin as psychical growths; each precedes and then is specialized and organized into thinking. But, if so, thought is not ultimate. It cannot for one moment claim to be the sole parent and source of ideality.[1]

And if thought is taken as a function primary, and from the first implied in distinction and synthesis, even on this mistaken basis its dependent character is plain. For the connections and distinctions, the ideal relations, in which thought has its being—from where do they come? As particular they consist at least partly in what is special to each, and these special natures, at least partly, can be derived from no possible faculty of thinking. Thought's relations therefore still must depend on what is empirical. They are in part the result of perception and mere psychical process. Therefore (as we saw above) thought must rest on these foreign materials; and, however much we take it as primary and original, it is still not independent. For it never in any case can absorb its materials into essential functions. Its connections may be familiar and unnoticed, and its sequences may glide without a break. Nay even upon reflection we may feel convinced that our special arrangement is true system, and may be sure that somehow its connections are not based on mere conjunction. But if we ask, on the other hand, if this ideal system can come out of bare thought, or can be made to consist in it, the answer must be different. Why connections in particular are just so, and not more or less otherwise—this can be explained in the end by no faculty of thinking. And thus, if thought in its origin is not secondary, its essence remains so. In its ideal matter it is a result from mere psychical

---

[1] With the above compare, again, *Mind*, No. 47.

growth, its ideal connections in part will throughout be pre-supposed and not made by itself. And
a connection, supposed to be made, would even be
disowned as a fiction.   Hence, on any psychological view, these connections are not inherent and
essential.   But for the truer view, we have seen
above, thought altogether is developed.   It grows
from, and still it consists in, processes not dependent on itself.   And the result may be summed up
thus ; certainly all relations are ideal, and as certainly not all relations are products of thinking.[1]

If we turn to volition, psychology makes clear
that this is developed and secondary.   An idea,
barely of itself, possesses no power of passing over
into fact, nor is there any faculty whose office it is
to carry out this passage.   Or, for the sake of
argument, suppose that such a faculty exists, yet
some ideas require (as we saw) an extraneous assistance.   The faculty is no function, in short, unless
specially provoked.   But that which makes will, or
at least makes it behave as itself, is surely a condition on which the being of will is dependent.
Will, in brief, is based on associations, psychical
and physical at once, or, again, upon mere physio-
logical connections.   It pre-supposes these, and
throughout its working it also implies them, and we
are hence compelled to consider them as part of its
essence.   I am quite aware that on the nature of
will there is a great diversity of doctrine, but there
are some views which I feel justified in not considering seriously.   For any sane psychology will must
pre-suppose, and must rest on, junctions physical
and psychical, junctions which certainly are not
will.   Nor is there any stage of its growth at which
will has absorbed into a special essence these pre-

[1] How what seems a faculty of analysis can be developed I
have endeavoured to point out in the article above referred to.

A. R.   I I

supposed workings. But, if so, assuredly will cannot be taken as primary.[1]

The universe as a whole may be called intelligible. It may be known to come together in such a way as to realize, throughout and thoroughly, the complete demands of a perfect intellect. And every single element, again, in the world is intelligible, because it is taken up into and absorbed in a whole of this character.[2] But the universe is not intelligible in the sense that it can throughout be understood ; nor, starting from the mere intellect, could you anticipate its features in detail. For, in answering the demands of the intellect, the Whole supplements and makes good its characteristic defects, so that the perfected intellect, with these, has lost its own special nature. And this conclusion holds again of every other aspect of things. None of them is intelligible, as such, because, when become intelligible, they have ceased also, as such, to be. Hence no single aspect of the world can in the end be explained, nor can the world be explained as the result either of any or all of them. We have verified this truth above in the instance of thought and of will. Thought is not intelligible because its particular functions are not self-evident, and because, again, they cannot be derived from, or shown to be parts immanent in itself. And the same defect once more belongs also to will. I do not mean merely that will's special passages are not intellectual. I mean that they are not intelligible, nor by themselves luminous, nor in any sense self-evident. They are occurrences familiar more or less, but never containing each in itself its own essence and warrant. That essence,

---

[1] I have left out of the account those cases where what works is mainly Blending. Obviously the same conclusion follows here.

[2] It is intelligible also, I have remarked above in Chapter xix., in the sense of being distinguishable content.

as we have seen, remains a fact which is conditioned from without, and it therefore remains everywhere partly alien. It is futile to explain the whole as the unity of two or more factors, when none of these can by itself be taken as evident, and when the way, in which their variety is brought together, remains in detail unintelligible.

With this result it is time that we went forward, but I feel compelled, in passing, to remark on the alleged supremacy of Will. In the first place, if will is Reality, it is incumbent on us to show how appearance is related to this ground. And, on our failure, we have an unknown unity behind this relation, and will itself must take the place of a partial appearance. But, when we consider will's character, the same conclusion is in any case plain. What we know as will implies relation and a process, and an unsolved discrepancy of elements. And the same remark holds of energy or activity, or of anything else of the kind. Indeed, I have dwelt so often on this head that I must consider it disposed of. I may, however, be told perhaps that this complexity is but the appearance of will, and that will itself, the real and supreme, is something other and different. But if so, the relation of appearance to this reality is once more on our hands. And, even apart from that, such an appeal to Will-in-itself is futile. For what we know as will contains the process, and what we do not know as will has no right to the name. It may be a mere physical happening, or may imply a metaphysical Reality, and in either case we have already dealt with it so far as is required. In short, an appeal to will, either in metaphysics or in psychology, is an uncritical attempt to make play with the unknown. It is the pretence of a ground or an explanation, where the ground is not understood or the explanation discovered. And, so far as metaphysics is concerned, one can perhaps account for

such a barren self-deception. The mere intellect
has shown itself incompetent to explain all phenomena, and so naturally recourse is had to the other
side of things. And this unknown reality, called in
thus to supply the defects of mere intellect, is blindly
identified with the aspect which appears most opposed. But an unknown Reality, more than intellect,
a something which appears in will and all appearance,
and even in intellect itself—such a reality is not will
or any other partial aspect of things. We really
have appealed to the complete and all-inclusive
totality, free from one-sidedness and all defect. And
we have called this will, because in will we do *not*
find one defect of a particular kind. But such a
procedure is not rational.

An attempt may perhaps be made from another
side to defend the primacy of will. It may be urged
that all principles and axioms in the end must be
practical, and must accordingly be called the expression of will. But such an assertion would be mistaken. Axioms and principles are the expression of
diverse sides of our nature, and they most certainly
cannot all be considered as practical. In our various
attitudes, intellectual, æsthetic, and practical, there
are certain modes of experience which satisfy. In
these modes we can repose, while, again, their absence brings pain, and unrest, and desire. And we
can of course distinguish these characters and set
them up as ideals, and we can also make them our
ends and the objects of will. But such a relation to
will is, except in the moral end, not inherent in their
nature. Indeed the reply that principles are willed
because they are, would be truer than the assertion
that principles are just because they are willed.
And the possible objection that after all these things
are objects to will, has been anticipated above (p. 474).
The same line of argument obviously would prove
that the intelligence is paramount, since it reflects
on will and on every other aspect of the world.

With this hurried notice, I must dismiss finally the alleged pre-eminence of will. This must remain always a muddy refuge for the troubled in philosophy. But its claims appear plausible so long only as darkness obscures them. They are plainly absurd where they do not prefer to be merely unintelligible.

We have found that no one aspect of experience, as such, is real. None is primary, or can serve to explain the others or the whole. They are all alike appearances, all one-sided, and passing away beyond themselves. But I may be asked why, admitting this, we should call them appearances. For such a term belongs solely of right to the perceptional side of things, and the perceptional side, we agreed, was but one aspect among others. To appear, we may be told, is not possible except to a percipient, and an appearance also implies both judgment and rejection. I might certainly, on the other side, enquire whether all implied metaphors are to be pressed, and if so, how many phrases and terms would be left us. But in the case of appearance I admit at once that the objection has force. I think the term implies without doubt an aspect of perceiving and judging, and such an aspect, I quite agree, does not everywhere exist. For, even if we conclude that all phenomena pass through psychical centres, yet in those centres most assuredly all is not perception. And to assume that somehow in the Whole all phenomena are judged of, would be again indefensible. We must, in short, admit that some appearances really do not appear, and that hence a license is involved in our use of the term.

Our attitude, however, in metaphysics must be theoretical. It is our business here to measure and to judge the various aspects of things. And hence for us anything which comes short when compared with Reality, gets the name of appearance. But we

do not suggest that the thing always itself is an
appearance. We mean its character is such that it
becomes one, as soon as we judge it. And this
character, we have seen throughout our work, is
ideality. Appearance consists in the looseness of
content from existence ; and, because of this self-
estrangement, every finite aspect is called an appearance. And we have found that everywhere throughout the world such ideality prevails. Anything less
than the Whole has turned out to be not self-contained. Its being involves in its very essence a
relation to the outside, and it is thus inwardly infected
by externality. Everywhere the finite is self-transcendent, alienated from itself, and passing away from
itself towards another existence. Hence the finite
is appearance because, on the one side, it is an adjective of Reality, and because, on the other side, it is
an adjective which itself is not real. When the
term is thus defined, its employment seems certainly
harmless.

We have in this Chapter been mainly, so far, concerned with a denial. All is appearance, and no
appearance, nor any combination of these, is the same
as Reality. This is half the truth, and by itself it
is a dangerous error. We must turn at once to
correct it by adding its counterpart and supplement.
The Absolute *is* its appearances, it really is all and
every one of them. That is the other half-truth
which we have already insisted on, and which we
must urge once more here. And we may remind
ourselves at this point of a fatal mistake. If you
take appearances, singly or all together, and assert
barely that the Absolute is either one of them or all
—the position is hopeless. Having first set these
down as appearance, you now proclaim them as the
very opposite ; for that which is identified with the
Absolute is no appearance but is utter reality. But
we have seen the solution of this puzzle, and we

know the sense and meaning in which these half-truths come together into one.   The Absolute is each appearance, and is all, but it is not any one as such. And it is not all equally, but one appearance is more real than another.   In short the doctrine of degrees in reality and truth is the fundamental answer to our problem.   Everything is essential, and yet one thing is worthless in comparison with others.   Nothing is perfect, as such, and yet everything in some degree contains a vital function of Perfection.   Every attitude of experience, every sphere or level of the world, is a necessary factor in the Absolute.   Each in its own way satisfies, until compared with that which is more than itself.   Hence appearance is error, if you will, but not every error is illusion.[1] At each stage is involved the principle of that which is higher, and every stage (it is therefore true) is already inconsistent.   But on the other hand, taken for itself and measured by its own ideas, every level has truth.   It meets, we may say, its own claims, and it proves false only when tried by that which is already beyond it.   And thus the Absolute is immanent alike through every region of appearances. There are degrees and ranks, but, one and all, they are alike indispensable.

We can find no province of the world so low but the Absolute inhabits it.   Nowhere is there even a single fact so fragmentary and so poor that to the universe it does not matter.   There is truth in every idea however false, there is reality in every existence however slight; and, where we can point to reality or truth, there is the one undivided life of the Absolute.   Appearance without reality would be impossible, for what then could appear?   And reality without appearance would be nothing, for there certainly is nothing outside appearances.   But on the other hand Reality (we must repeat this) is not the

---

[1] On the difference between these see Chapter xxvii.

sum of things. It is the unity in which all things, coming together, are transmuted, in which they are changed all alike, though not changed equally. And, as we have perceived, in this unity relations of isolation and hostility are affirmed and absorbed. These also are harmonious in the Whole, though not of course harmonious as such, and while severally confined to their natures as separate. Hence it would show blindness to urge, as an objection against our view, the opposition found in ugliness and in conscious evil. The extreme of hostility implies an intenser relation, and this relation falls within the Whole and enriches its unity. The apparent discordance and distraction is overruled into harmony, and it is but the condition of fuller and more individual development. But we can hardly speak of the Absolute itself as either ugly or evil. The Absolute is indeed evil in a sense and it is ugly and false, but the sense, in which these predicates can be applied, is too forced and unnatural. Used of the Whole each predicate would be the result of an indefensible division, and each would be a fragment isolated and by itself without consistent meaning. Ugliness, evil, and error, in their several spheres, are subordinate aspects. They imply distinctions falling, in each case, within one subject province of the Absolute's kingdom ; and they involve a relation, in each case, of some struggling element to its superior, though limited, whole. Within these minor wholes the opposition draws its life from, and is overpowered by the system which supports it. The predicates evil, ugly, and false must therefore stamp whatever they qualify, as a mere subordinate aspect, an aspect belonging to the province of beauty or goodness or truth. And to assign such a position to the sovereign Absolute would be plainly absurd. You may affirm that the Absolute *has* ugliness and error and evil, since it owns the provinces in which these features are partial elements. But to assert that it *is* one of its own fragmentary and dependent details would be inadmissible.

It is only by a licence that the subject-systems, even when we regard them as wholes, can be made qualities of Reality.   It is always under correction and on sufferance that we term the universe either beautiful or moral or true.   And to venture further would be both useless and dangerous at once.

If you view the Absolute morally at all, then the Absolute is good.   It cannot be one factor contained within and overpowered by goodness.   In the same way, viewed logically or æsthetically, the Absolute can only be true or beautiful.   It is merely when you have so termed it, and while you still continue to insist on these preponderant characters, that you can introduce at all the ideas of falsehood and ugliness.   And, so introduced, their direct application to the Absolute is impossible. Thus to identify the supreme universe with a partial system may, for some end, be admissible.   But to take it as a single character within this system, and as a feature which is already overruled, and which as such is suppressed there, would, we have seen, be quite unwarranted.   Ugliness, error, and evil, all are owned by, and all essentially contribute to the wealth of the Absolute.   The Absolute, we may say in general, has no assets beyond appearances; and again, with appearances alone to its credit, the Absolute would be bankrupt.   All of these are worthless alike apart from transmutation.   But, on the other hand once more, since the amount of change is different in each case, appearances differ widely in their degrees of truth and reality.   There are predicates which, in comparison with others, are false and unreal.

To survey the field of appearances, to measure each by the idea of perfect individuality, and to arrange them in an order and in a system of reality and merit—would be the task of metaphysics.   This

task (I may repeat) is not attempted in these pages.
I have however endeavoured here, as above, to
explain and to insist on the fundamental principle.
And, passing from that, I will now proceed to remark on some points of interest.   There are certain
questions which at this stage we may hope to dispose of.

Let us turn our attention once more to Nature or
the physical world.   Are we to affirm that ideas are
forces, and that ends operate and move there?
And, again, is Nature beautiful and an object of
possible worship?   On this latter point, which I
will consider first, I find serious confusion.   Nature,
as we have seen, can be taken in various senses
(Chapter xxii.).   We may understand by it the
whole universe, or again merely the world in space,
or again we may restrict it to a very much narrower
meaning.   We may first remove everything which
in our opinion is only psychical, and the abstract
residue—the primary qualities—we may then identify with Nature.   These will be the essence, while
all the rest is accessory adjective, and, in the fullest
sense, is immaterial.   Now we have found that
Nature, so understood, has but little reality.   It is an
ideal construction required by science, and it is a
necessary working fiction.   And we may add that
reduction to a result, and to a particular instance, of
this fiction, is what is meant by a strictly physical
explanation.   But in this way there grows up a great
confusion.   For the object of natural science is the
full world in all its sensible glory, while the essence
of Nature lies in this poor fiction of primary
qualities, a fiction believed not to be idea but solid
fact.   Nature then, while unexplained, is still left in
its sensuous splendour, while Nature, if explained,
would be reduced to this paltry abstraction.   On
one side is set up the essence—the final reality—in
the shape of a bare skeleton of primary qualities;

on the other side remains the boundless profusion of life which everywhere opens endlessly before our view.   And these extremes then are confused, or are conjoined, by sheer obscurity or else by blind mental oscillation.   If explanation reduces facts to be adjectives of something which they do not qualify at all, the whole connection seems irrational, and the process robs us of the facts.   But if the primary essence after all *is* qualified, then its character is transformed.   The explanation, in reducing the concrete, will now also have enriched and have individualized the abstract, and we shall have started on our way towards philosophy and truth.   But of this latter result in the present case there can be no question.   And therefore we must end in oscillation with no attempt at an intelligent unity of view. Nature is, on the one hand, that show whose reality lies barely in primary qualities.   It is, on the other hand, that endless world of sensible life which appeals to our sympathy and extorts our wonder. It is the object loved and lived in by the poet and by the observing naturalist.   And, when we speak of Nature, we have often no idea which of these extremes, or indeed what at all, is to be understood. We in fact pass, as suits the occasion, from one extreme unconsciously to the other.

I will briefly apply this result to the question before us.   Whether Nature is beautiful and adorable will depend entirely on the sense in which Nature is taken.   If the genuine reality of Nature is bare primary qualities, then I cannot think that such a question needs serious discussion.   In a word Nature will be dead.   It could possess at the most a kind of symmetry; and again by its extent, or by its practical relation to our weaknesses or needs, it might excite in us feelings of a certain kind.   But these feelings, in the first place, would fall absolutely within ourselves.   They could not rationally be applied to, nor in the very least could they qualify Nature. And, in the second place, these feelings would in our minds hardly take the form of worship. Hence when Nature, as the object of natural science, is either asserted to be beautiful, or is set up before us as divine, we may make our answer at once. If the reality of the object is to be restricted to primary qualities, then surely no one would advocate the claims we have mentioned. If again the whole perceptible world and the glory of it is to be genuinely real, and if this splendour and this life are of the very essence of Nature, then a difficulty will arise in two directions. In the first place this claim has to get itself admitted by physical science. The psychical has to be adopted as at least co-equal in reality with matter. The relation to the organism and to the soul has to be included in the vital being of a physical object. And the first difficulty will consist in advancing to this point. Then the second difficulty will appear at once when this point has been reached. For, having gone so far, we have to justify our refusal to go further. For why is Nature to be confined to the perceptible world? If the psychical and the "subjective" is in any degree to make part of its reality, then upon what principle can you shut out the highest and most spiritual experience? Why is Nature viewed and created by the painter, the poet, and the seer, not essentially real? But in this way Nature will tend to become the total universe of both spirit and matter. And our main conclusion so far must be this. It is evidently useless to raise such questions about the object of natural science, when you have not settled in your mind what that object is, and when you supply no principle on which we can decide in what its reality consists.

But turning from this confusion, and once more approaching the question from, I trust, a more rational ground, I will try to make a brief answer. Into the special features and limits of the beautiful in

Nature I cannot enter. And I cannot discuss how far, and in what sense, the physical world is included in the true object of religion. These are special enquiries which fall without the scope of my volume. But whether Nature is beautiful or adorable at all, and whether it possesses such attributes really and in truth,—to the question, asked thus in general, we may answer, Yes. We have seen that Nature, regarded as bare matter, is a mere convenient abstraction (Chapter xxii.). The addition of secondary qualities, the included relation to a body and to a soul, in making Nature more concrete makes it thereby more real.[1] The sensible life, the warmth and colour, the odour and the tones, without these Nature is a mere intellectual fiction. The primary qualities are a construction demanded by science, but, while divorced from the secondary, they have no life as facts. Science has a Hades from which it returns to interpret the world, but the inhabitants of its Hades are merely shades. And, when the secondary qualities are added, Nature, though more real, is still incomplete. The joys and sorrows of her children, their affections and their thoughts— how are we to say that these have no part in the reality of Nature? Unless to a mind restricted by a principle the limitation would be absurd, and our main principle on the other hand insists that Nature, when more full, is more real. And this same principle will carry us on to a further conclusion. The emotions, excited by Nature in the considering soul, must at least in part be referred to, and must be taken as attributes of Nature. If there is no beauty there, and if the sense of that is to fall somewhere outside, why in the end should there be any qualities in Nature at all? And, if no emotional tone is to qualify Nature, how and on what principle are we to

---

[1] I do not think it necessary to restate any qualification required here by parts of Nature taken as not perceived. I have dealt with this sufficiently in Chapters xxii. and xxiv.

attribute to it anything else whatever ? Everything there without exception is "subjective," if we are to regard the matter so; and an emotional tone cannot, solely on this account, be excluded from Nature. And, otherwise, why should it not have reality there as a genuine quality ? For myself I must follow the same principle and can accept the fresh consequence. The Nature that we have lived in, and that we love, is really Nature. Its beauty and its terror and its majesty are no illusion, but qualify it essentially. And hence that in which at our best moments we all are forced to believe, is the literal truth.

This result however needs some qualification from another side. It is certain that everything is determined by the relations in which it stands. It is certain that, with increase of determinateness, a thing becomes more and more real. On the other hand anything, fully determined, would be the Absolute itself. There is a point where increase of reality implies passage beyond self. A thing by enlargement becomes a mere factor in the whole next above it; and, in the end, all provinces and all relative wholes cease to keep their separate characters. We must not forget this while considering the reality of Nature. By gradual increase of that reality you reach a stage at which Nature, as such, is absorbed. Or, as you reflect on Nature, your object identifies itself gradually with the universe or Absolute. And the question arises at what point, when we begin to add psychical life or to attribute spiritual attributes to Nature, we have ceased to deal with Nature in any proper sense of that term. Where do we pass from Nature, as an outlying province in the kingdom of things, to Nature as a suppressed element in a higher unity ? These enquiries are demanded by philosophy, and their result would lead to clearer conclusions about the qualities of Nature. I can do no more than

allude to them here, and the conclusion, on which
I insist, can in the main be urged independently.
Nothing is lost to the Absolute, and all appearances
have reality.   The Nature studied by the observer
and by the poet and painter, is in all its sensible
and emotional fulness a very real Nature.   It is in
most respects more real than the strict object of
physical science.   For Nature, as the world whose
real essence lies in primary qualities, has not a high
degree of reality and truth.   It is a mere abstraction made and required for a certain purpose.   And
the object of natural science may either mean this
skeleton, or it may mean the skeleton made real
by blood and flesh of secondary qualities.   Hence,
before we dwell on the feelings Nature calls for
from us, it would be better to know in what sense we
are using the term.   But the boundary of Nature
can hardly be drawn even at secondary qualities.
Or, if we draw it there, we must draw it arbitrarily,
and to suit our convenience.   Only on this ground
can psychical life be excluded from Nature, while,
regarded otherwise, the exclusion would not be
tenable.   And to deny æsthetic qualities in Nature,
or to refuse it those which inspire us with fear or
devotion, would once more surely be arbitrary.   It
would be a division introduced for a mere working theoretical purpose.   Our principle, that the
abstract is the unreal, moves us steadily upward.
It forces us first to rejection of bare primary
qualities, and it compels us in the end to credit
Nature with our higher emotions.   That process
can cease only where Nature is quite absorbed into
spirit, and at every stage of the process we find
increase in reality.

And this higher interpretation, and this eventual
transcendence of Nature lead us to the discussion
of another point which we mentioned above.   Except in finite souls and except in volition may we

suppose that Ends operate in Nature, and is ideality, in any other sense, a working force there ? How far such a point of view may be permitted in æsthetics or in the philosophy of religion, I shall not enquire. But considering the physical world as a mere system of appearances in space, are we on metaphysical grounds to urge the insufficiency of the mechanical view ? In what form (if in any) are we to advocate a philosophy of Nature ? On this difficult subject I will very briefly remark in passing.

The mechanical view plainly is absurd as a full statement of truth. Nature so regarded has not ceased at all (we may say) to be ideal, but its ideality throughout falls somewhere outside itself (Chapters xxii. and xxiii.). And that even for working purposes this view can everywhere be rigidly maintained, I am unable to assert. But upon one subject I have no doubts. Every special science must be left at liberty to follow its own methods, and, if the natural sciences reject every way of explanation which is not mechanical, that is not the affair of metaphysics. For myself, in other ways ignorant, I venture to assume that these sciences understand their own business. But where, quite beyond the scope of any special science, assertions are made, the metaphysician may protest. He may insist that abstractions are not realities, and that working fictions are never more than useful fragments of truth. And on another point also he may claim a hearing. To adopt one sole principle of valid explanation, and to urge that, if phenomena are to be explicable, they must be explained by one method—this is of course competent to any science. But it is another thing to proclaim phenomena as already explained, or as explicable, where in certain aspects or in certain provinces they clearly are not explained, and where, perhaps, not even the first beginning of an explanation has been made. In these lapses or excursions beyond its own limits

natural science has no rights. But within its boundaries I think every wise man will consider it sacred.
And this question of the operation of Ends in
Nature is one which, in my judgment, metaphysics
should leave untouched.

Is there then no positive task which is left to
metaphysics, the accomplishment of which might be
called a philosophy of Nature? I will briefly point
out the field which seems to call for occupation.
All appearances for metaphysics have degrees of
reality. We have an idea of perfection or of individuality; and, as we find that any form of existence more completely realizes this idea, we assign
to it its position in the scale of being. And in this
scale (as we have seen) the lower, as its defects are
made good, passes beyond itself into the higher.
The end, or the absolute individuality, is also the
principle. Present from the first it supplies the test
of its inferior stages, and, as these are included in
fuller wholes, the principle grows in reality. Metaphysics in short can assign a meaning to perfection
and progress. And hence, if it were to accept from
the sciences the various kinds of natural phenomena,
if it were to set out these kinds in an order of merit
and rank, if it could point out how within each
higher grade the defects of the lower are made
good, and how the principle of the lower grade is
carried out in the higher—metaphysics surely would
have contributed to the interpretation of Nature.
And, while myself totally incapable of even assist-
ing in such a work, I cannot see how or on what
ground it should be considered unscientific. It is
doubtless absurd to wear the airs of systematic
omniscience. It is worse than absurd to pour scorn
on the detail and on the narrowness of devoted
specialism. But to try to give system from time to
time to the results of the sciences, and to attempt
to arrange these on what seems a true principle
of worth, can be hardly irrational.

K K

Such a philosophy of Nature, if at least it were true to itself, could not intrude on the province of physical science. For it would, in short, abstain wholly and in every form from speculation on genesis. How the various stages of progress come to happen in time, in what order or orders they follow, and in each case from what causes, these enquiries would, as such, be no concern of philosophy. Its idea of evolution and progress in a word should not be temporal. And hence a conflict with the sciences upon any question of development or of order could not properly arise. " Higher " and " lower," terms which imply always a standard and end, would in philosophy be applied solely to designate rank. Natural science would still be free, as now, to use, or even to abuse, such terms at its pleasure, and to allow them any degree of meaning which is found convenient. Progress for philosophy would never have any temporal sense, and it could matter nothing if the word elsewhere seemed to bear little or no other. With these brief remarks I must leave a subject which deserves serious attention.

In a complete philosophy the whole world of appearance would be set out as a progress. It would show a development of principle though not a succession in time. Every sphere of experience would be measured by the absolute standard, and would be given a rank answering to its own relative merits and defects. On this scale pure Spirit would mark the extreme most removed from lifeless Nature. And, at each rising degree of this scale, we should find more of the first character with less of the second. The ideal of spirit, we may say, is directly opposite to mechanism. Spirit is a unity of the manifold in which the externality of the manifold has utterly ceased. The universal here is immanent in the parts, and its system does not lie somewhere outside and in the relations between them. It is above the relational form and has absorbed it in a higher unity, a whole in which there is no division between elements and laws. And, since this principle shows itself from the first in the inconsistencies of bare mechanism,[1] we may say that Nature at once is realized and transmuted by spirit. But each of these extremes, we must add, has no existence as fact. The sphere of dead mechanism is set apart by an act of abstraction, and in that abstraction alone it essentially consists. And, on the other hand, pure spirit is not realized except in the Absolute. It can never appear as such and with its full character in the scale of existence. Perfection and individuality belong only to that Whole in which all degrees alike are at once present and absorbed. This one Reality of existence can, as such, nowhere exist among phenomena. And it enters into, but is itself incapable of, evolution and progress.

It may repay us to discuss the truth of this last statement. Is there, in the end and on the whole, any progress in the universe? Is the Absolute better or worse at one time than at another? It is clear that we must answer in the negative, since progress and decay are alike incompatible with perfection. There is of course progress in the world, and there is also retrogression, but we cannot think that the Whole either moves on or backwards. The Absolute has no history of its own, though it contains histories without number. These, with their tale of progress or decline, are constructions starting from and based on some one given piece of finitude. They are but partial aspects in the region of temporal appearance. Their truth and reality may vary much in extent and in importance, but in the end it can never be more than relative.

---

[1] The defect and the partial supersession of mere mechanical law has been touched on in Chapters xxii. and xxiii. It would be possible to add a good deal more on this head.

And the question whether the history of a man or a world is going forwards or back, does not belong to metaphysics. For nothing perfect, nothing genuinely real, can move. The Absolute has no seasons, but all at once bears its leaves, fruit, and blossoms.[1] Like our globe it always, and it never, has summer and winter.

Such a point of view, if it disheartens us, has been misunderstood. It is only by our mistake that it collides with practical belief. If into the world of goodness, possessing its own relative truth, you will directly thrust in ideas which apply only to the Whole, the fault surely is yours. The Absolute's character, as such, cannot hold of the relative, but the relative, unshaken for all that, holds its place in the Absolute. Or again, shutting yourself up in the region of practice, will you insist upon applying its standards to the universe? We want for our practice, of course, both a happening in time and a personal finitude. We require a capacity for becoming better, and, I suppose too, for becoming worse. And if these features, as such, are to qualify the whole of things, and if they are to apply to ultimate reality, then the main conclusions of this work are naturally erroneous. But I cannot adopt others until at least I see an attempt made to set them out in a rational form. And I can not profess respect for views which seem to me in many cases insincere. If progress is to be more than relative, and is something beyond a mere partial phenomenon, then the religion professed most commonly among us has been abandoned. You cannot be a Christian if you maintain that progress is final and ultimate and the last truth about things. And I urge this consideration, of course not as an argument from my mouth, but as a way of bringing home perhaps to some persons their inconsistency. Make the moral point of view absolute, and then realize your position.

[1] This image is, I believe, borrowed from Strauss.

You have become not merely irrational, but you have also, I presume, broken with every considerable religion.   And you have been brought to this by following the merest prejudice.

Philosophy, I agree, has to justify the various sides of our life; but this is impossible, I would urge, if any side is made absolute.   Our attitudes in life give place ceaselessly the one to the other, and life is satisfied if each in its own field is allowed supremacy.   Now to deny progress of the universe surely leaves morality where it was.   A man has his self or his world, about to make an advance (he may hope) through his personal effort, or in any case (he knows well) to be made the best of.   The universe is, so far, worse through his failure; it is better, so far, through his success.   And if, not content with this, he demands to alter the universe at large, he should at least invoke neither reason nor religion nor morality.   For the improvement or decay of the universe seems nonsense, unmeaning or blasphemous.   While, on the other hand, faith in the progress or persistence of those who inhabit our planet has nothing to do with metaphysics.   And I may perhaps add that it has little more to do with morality.   Such faith can not alter our duties; and to the mood in which we approach them, the difference, which it makes, may not be wholly an advantage.   If we can be weakened by despondence, we can, no less, be hurried away by stupid enthusiasm and by pernicious cant.   But this is no place for the discussion of such matters, and we may be content here to know that we cannot attribute any progress to the Absolute.

I will end this chapter with a few remarks on a subject which lies near.   I refer to that which is commonly called the Immortality of the Soul.   This is a topic on which for several reasons I would rather keep silence, but I think that silence here might fairly be misunderstood. It is not easy, in the first place, to say exactly what a future life means. The period of personal continuance obviously need not be taken as endless. And again precisely in what sense, and how far, the survival must be personal is not easy to lay down. I shall assume here that what is meant is an existence after death which is conscious of its identity with our life here and now. And the duration of this must be taken as sufficient to remove any idea of unwilling extinction or of premature decease. Now we seem to desire continuance (if we do desire it) for a variety of reasons, and it might be interesting elsewhere to set these out and to clear away confusions.[1] I must however pass at once to the question of possibility.

There is one sense in which the immortality of souls seems impossible. We must remember that the universe is incapable of increase. And to suppose a constant supply of new souls, none of which ever perished, would clearly land us in the end in an insoluble difficulty. But it is quite unnecessary, I presume, to hold the doctrine in this sense. And, if we take the question generally, then to deny the possibility of a life after death would be quite ridiculous. There is no way of proving, first, that a body is required for a soul (Chapter xxiii.). And though a soul, when bodiless, might (for all we know) be even more subject to mortality, yet obviously here we have passed into a region of ignorance. And to say that in this region a personal

---

[1] The so-called fear of extinction seems to rest on a confusion, and I do not believe that, in a proper form, it exists at all. It is really mere shrinking from defeat and from injury and pain. For we can think of our own total surcease, but we cannot imagine it. Against our will, and perhaps unconsciously, there creeps in the idea of a reluctant and struggling self, or of a self disappointed, or wearied, or in some way discontented. And this is certainly not a self completely extinguished. There is no fear of death at all, we may say, except either incidentally or through an illusion.

continuance could not be, appears simply irrational.
And the same result holds, even if we take a body
as essential to every soul, and, even if we insist also
(as we cannot) that this body must be made of our
everyday substance.   A future life is possible even
on the ground of common crude Materialism.[1]   After
an interval, no matter how long, another nervous
system sufficiently like our own might be developed ;
and in this case memory and a personal identity
must arise.   The event may be as improbable as
you please, but I at least can find no reason for
calling it impossible.   And we may even go a step
further still.   It is conceivable that an indefinite
number of such bodies should exist, not in succession merely, but all together and all at once.   But,
if so, we might gain a personal continuance not
single but multiform, and might secure a destiny on
which it would be idle to enlarge.   In ways like the
above it is clear that a future life is possible, but,
on the other hand, such possibilities are not worth
much.

A thing is impossible absolutely when it contradicts the known nature of Reality.[2]   It is impossible
relatively when it collides with some idea which we
have found good cause to take as real.   A thing is
possible, first, as long as it is not quite meaningless.
It must contain some positive quality belonging to
the universe ; and it must not at the same time
remove this and itself by some destructive addition.
A thing is possible further, according as its meaning contains without discrepancy more and more of
what is held to be real.   We, in other words, consider anything more possible as it grows in proba-

---

[1] I have attempted to show this in an article on the Evidences
of Spiritualism, *Fortnightly Review*, December, 1885.   It may
perhaps be worth while to add here that apparently even a high
organism is possible, which apart from accidents would never die.
Apparently this could not be termed impossible in principle, at
least within our present knowledge.

[2] See, above, Chapter xxiv., and, below, Chapter xxvii.

bility.　And " Probability," we are rightly told, " is the guide of life."　We want to know, in short, not whether a thing is merely and barely possible, but how much ground we have for expecting it and not something else.

In a case like the present, we cannot, of course, hope to set out the chances, for we have to do with elements the value of which is not known.　And for probability the unknown is of different kinds. There is first the unknown utterly, which is not possible at all; and this is discounted and treated as nothing.　There is next something possible, the full nature of which is hidden, but the extent and value of which, as against some other "events," is clear. And so far all is straightforward.　But we have still to deal with the unknown in two more troublesome senses.　It may stand for a mere possibility about which we know nothing further, and for entertaining which we can find no further ground. Or again, the unknown may cover a region where we can specify no details, but which still we can judge to contain a great diversity of possible events.

We shall soon find the importance of these dry distinctions.　A bodiless soul is possible because it is not meaningless, or in any way known to be impossible.　But I fail to find any further and additional reason in its favour.　And, next, would a bodiless soul be immortal?　And, again, why after death should *we*, in particular, have any bodiless continuance?　The original slight probability of a future life seems not much increased by these considerations.　Again, if we take body to be essential —a body, that is, consisting of matter either familiar or strange — what, on this ground, is our chance of personal continuance after death?　You may here appeal to the unknown, and, where our knowledge seems nothing, you may perhaps urge, " Why not this event, just as much as its contrary and opposite ? " But the question would rest on a fallacy, and I must insist on the distinction which above we laid down. In this unknown field we certainly cannot particularize and set out the chances, but in another sense the field is not quite unknown.[1]

We cannot say that, of the combinations possible there, one half is, for all we know, favourable to a life after death. For, to judge by actual experience, the combinations seem mostly unfavourable. And, though the character of what falls outside our experience *may* be very different, yet our judgment as to this must be affected by what we do know. But, if so, while the whole variety of combinations must be taken as very large, the portion judged favourable to continued life, whether multiform or simple, must be set down as small. Such will have to be our conclusion if we deal with this unknown field. But, if we may not deal with it, the possibility of a future life is, on this ground, quite unknown ; and, if so, we have no right to consider it at all. And the general result to my mind is briefly this. When you add together the chances of a life after death— a life taken as bodiless, and again as diversely embodied—the amount is not great. The balance of hostile probability seems so large that the fraction on the other side to my mind is not considerable. And we may repeat, and may sum up our conclusion thus. If we appeal to blank ignorance, then a future life may even have no meaning, and may fail wholly to be possible. Or if we avoid this worst extreme, a future life may be but barely possible.

---

[1] The probability of an unknown event is rightly taken as one half. But, in applying this abstract truth, we must be on our guard against error. In the case of an event in time our ignorance can hardly be entire. We know, for example, that at each moment Nature produces a diversity of changed events. The abstract chance then, say of the repetition of a certain occurrence in a certain place, must be therefore much less than one half. On the other side again considerations of another kind will come in, and may raise the value indefinitely.

But a possibility, in this sense, stands unsupported face to face with an indefinite universe. And its value, so far, can hardly be called worth counting. If, on the other hand, we allow ourselves to use what knowledge we possess, and if we judge fairly of future life by all the grounds we have for judging, the result is not much modified. Among those grounds we certainly find a part which favours continuance; but, taken at its highest, that part appears to be small. Hence a future life must be taken as decidedly improbable.

But in this way, it will be objected, the question is not properly dealt with. "On the grounds you have stated," it will be urged, "future life may be improbable; but then those grounds really lie outside the main point. The positive evidence for a future life is what weighs with our minds; and this is independent of discussions as to what, in the abstract, is probable" The objection is fair, and my reply to it is plain and simple. I have ignored the positive evidence because for me it has really no value. Direct arguments to show that a future life is, not merely possible, but real, seem to me unavailing. The addition to general probability, which they make, is to my mind trifling; and, without examining these arguments in detail, I will add a few remarks.[1]

[1] The argument based on apparitions and necromancy I have discussed in the article cited above, p. 503. There, on the hypothesis that extra-human intelligences had been proved, I attempted to show that the conclusions of Spiritualism were still baseless. I had no space there to urge that the hypothesis itself is ridiculously untrue. The spiritualist appears to think that anything which is not in the usual course of things goes to prove his special conclusion. He seems not to perceive any difference between the possible and the actual. As if to open a wide field of indefinite possibilities were the same thing as the exclusion of all others but one. Against the spiritualist, open or covert, it is most important to insist that *all* the facts shall be dealt with, whether in man alone or, perhaps also, in the lower animals.

Philosophy, I repeat, has to justify all sides of our nature; and this means, I agree, that our main cravings must find satisfaction.   But that every desire of every kind must, as such, be gratified—this is quite a different demand, and it is surely irrational.   At all events it is opposed to the results of our preceding discussions.   The destiny of the finite, we saw everywhere, is to reach consummation, but never wholly as such, never quite in its own way.   And as to this desire for a future life, what is there in it so sacred?   How can its attainment be implied in the very principles of our nature?   Nay, is there in it, taken by itself, anything moral in the least or religious at all?   I desire to have no pain, but always pleasure, and to continue so indefinitely.   But the literal fulfilment of my wish is incompatible with my place in the universe.   It is irreconcileable with my own nature, and I have to be content therefore with that measure of satisfaction which my nature permits.   And am I, on this account, to proclaim philosophy insolvent, because it will not listen to demands really based on nothing?

But the demand for future life, I shall be told, is a genuine postulate, and its satisfaction is implicated in the very essence of our nature.   Now, if this means that our religion and our morality will not work without it—so much the worse, I reply, for our morality and our religion.   The remedy lies in the correction of our mistaken and immoral notions

The unbroken continuity of the phenomena is fatal to Spiritualism.   The more that abnormal human perception and action is verified, the more hopeless it becomes to get to non-human beings.   The more fully the monstrous results of modern *séances* are accepted, the more impossible it becomes, in such a far-seeing and such a silly world of demons, to find any sort of test for Spirit-Identity.   As to facts my mind is, and always has been, perfectly open.   It is the irrational conclusions of the spiritualist that I reject with disgust.   They strike me as the expression of, and the excuse for, a discreditable superstition.

about goodness. " But then," it will be exclaimed,
" this is too horrible. There really after all will be
self-sacrifice; and virtue and selfishness after all will
not be identical." But I have already explained, in
Chapter xxv., why this moving appeal finds me deaf.
" But then strict justice is not paramount." No, I
am sure that it is not so. There is a great deal in
the universe, I am sure, beyond mere morality; and
I have yet to learn that, even in the moral world,
the highest law is justice. " But, if we die, think of
the loss of all our hard-won gains." But is a thing
lost, in the first place, because *I* fail to get it or retain it? And, in the second place, what seems to
us sheer waste is, to a very large extent, the way of
the universe. We need not take on ourselves to
be anxious about that. " But without endless progress, how reach perfection?" And *with* endless
progress (if that means anything) I answer, how
reach it? Surely perfection and finitude are in
principle not compatible. If you are to be perfect,
then you, as such, must be resolved and cease; and
endless progress sounds merely like an attempt indefinitely to put off perfection.[1] And as a function
of the perfect universe, on the other hand, you are
perfect already. "But after all we must wish that
pain and sorrow should be somewhere made good."
On the whole, and in the whole, if our view is right,
this is fully the case. With the individual often I
agree it is not the case. And I wish it otherwise,
meaning by this that my inclination and duty as a
fellow-creature impels me that way, and that wishes
and actions of this sort among finite beings fulfil the
plan of the Whole. But I cannot argue, therefore,
that all is wrong if individuals suffer. There is
in life always, I admit, a note of sadness; but it
ought not to prevail, nor can we truly assert that it
does so. And the universe in its attitude towards

---

[1] The reader, who desires to follow out this point, must be
referred to Hegel's *Phänomenologie*, 449–460.

finite beings must be judged of not piecemeal but
as a system. "But, if hopes and fears are taken
away, we shall be less happy and less moral." Perhaps, and perhaps again both more moral and more
happy. The question is a large one, and I do not
intend to discuss it, but I will say so much as this.
Whoever argues that belief in a future life has, on
the whole, brought evil to humanity, has at least a
strong case. But the question here seems irrelevant. If it could indeed be urged that the essence
of a finite being is such, that it can only regulate
its conduct by keeping sight of another world and
of another life—the matter, I agree, would be
altered. But if it comes merely to this, that human
beings now are in such a condition that, if they do
not believe what is probably untrue, they must deteriorate—that to the universe, if it were the case,
would be a mere detail. It is the rule that a race
of beings so out of agreement with their environment should deteriorate, and it is well for them to
make way for another race constituted more rationally and happily. And I must leave the matter so.[1]

[1] I have said nothing about the argument based on our desire
to meet once more those whom we have loved. No one can
have been so fortunate as never to have felt the grief of parting,
or so inhuman as not to have longed for another meeting after
death. But no one, I think, can have reached a certain time
of life, without finding, more or less, that such desires are inconsistent with themselves. There are partings made by
death, and, perhaps, worse partings made by life ; and there
are partings which both life and death unite in veiling from our
eyes. And friends that have buried their quarrel in a woman's
grave, would they at the Resurrection be friends ? But, in any
case, the desire can hardly pass as a serious argument. The
revolt of modern Christianity against the austere sentence of the
Gospel (Matt. xxii. 30) is interesting enough. One feels that a
personal immortality would not be very personal, if it implied
mutilation of our affections. There are those too who would
not sit down among the angels, till they had recovered their dog.
Still this general appeal to the affections—the only appeal as to
future life which to me individually is not hollow—can hardly be
turned into a proof.

All the above arguments, and there are others, rest on assumptions negatived by the general results of this volume. It is about the truth of these assumptions, I would add, that discussion is desirable. It is idle to repeat, "I want something," unless you can show that the nature of things demands it also. And to debate this special question, apart from an enquiry into the ultimate nature of the world, is surely unprofitable.

Future life is a subject on which I had no desire to speak. I have kept silence until the subject seemed forced before me, and until in a manner I had dealt with the main problems involved in it. The conclusion arrived at seems the result to which the educated world, on the whole, is making its way. A personal continuance is possible, and it is but little more. Still, if any one can believe in it, and finds himself sustained by that belief,—after all it is possible. On the other hand it is better to be quit of both hope and fear, than to lapse back into any form of degrading superstition. And surely there are few greater responsibilities which a man can take on himself, than to have proclaimed, or even hinted, that without immortality all religion is a cheat and all morality a self-deception.

CHAPTER XXVII.

ULTIMATE DOUBTS.

It is time, however prematurely, to bring this work to an end. We may conclude it by asking how far, and in what sense, we are at liberty to treat its main results as certain. We have found that Reality is one, that it essentially is experience, and that it owns a balance of pleasure. There is nothing in the Whole beside appearance, and every fragment of appearance qualifies the Whole ; while on the other hand, so taken together, appearances, as such, cease. Nothing in the universe can be lost, nothing fails to contribute to the single Reality, but every finite diversity is also supplemented and transformed. Everything in the Absolute still is that which it is for itself. Its private character remains, and is but neutralized by complement and addition. And hence, because nothing in the end can be *merely* itself, in the end no appearance, as such, can be real. But appearances fail of reality in varying degrees ; and to assert that one on the whole is worth no more than another, is fundamentally vicious.

The fact of appearance, and of the diversity of its particular spheres, we found was inexplicable. Why there are appearances, and why appearances of such various kinds, are questions not to be answered. But in all this diversity of existence we saw nothing opposed to a complete harmony and system in the Whole. The nature of that system in detail lies beyond our knowledge, but we could discover nowhere the sign of a recalcitrant element. We could perceive nothing on which any objection to our view of Reality could rationally be founded. And so we ventured to conclude that Reality possesses— how we do not know—the general nature we have assigned to it.

"But, after all, your conclusion," I may be told, "is not proved. Suppose that we can find no objection sufficient to overthrow it, yet such an absence of disproof does not render it certain. Your result may be possible, but, with that, it has not become real. For why should Reality be not just as well something else? How in the unknown world of possibilities can we be restricted to this one?" The objection seems serious, and, in order to consider it properly, I must be allowed first to enter on some abstract considerations. I will try to confine them to what is essential here.

I. In theory you cannot indulge with consistency in an ultimate doubt. You are forced, willingly or not, at a certain point to assume infallibility. For, otherwise, how could you proceed to judge at all? The intellect, if you please, is but a miserable frag- ment of our nature; but in the intellectual world it, none the less, must remain supreme. And, if it attempts to abdicate, then its world is forthwith broken up. Hence we must answer, Outside theory take whatever attitude you may prefer, only do not sit down to a game unless you are prepared to play. But every pursuit obviously must involve some kind of governing principle. Even the extreme of theor- etical scepticism is based on some accepted idea about truth and fact. It is because you are sure as to some main feature of truth or reality, that you are compelled to doubt or to reject special truths which are offered you. But, if so, you stand on an absolute principle, and, with regard to this, you claim, tacitly or openly, to be infallible. And to start from our general fallibility, and to argue from this to the uncertainty of every possible result, is in the end irrational. For the assertion, " I am *sure* that I am everywhere fallible," contradicts itself, and would revive a familiar Greek dilemma. And if we modify the assertion, and instead of " everywhere " write " in general," then the desired conclusion will not follow. For unless, once more falsely, we assume that all truths are much the same, and that with regard to every point error is equally probable, fallibility in general need not affect a particular result.[1] In short within theory we must decline to consider the chance of a fundamental error. Our assertion of fallibility may serve as the expression of modest feeling, or again of the low estimate we may have formed of the intellect's value. But such an estimate or such a feeling must remain outside of the actual process of theory. For, admitted within, they would at once be inconsistent and irrational.

2. An asserted possibility in the next place must have some meaning. A bare word is not a possibility, nor does any one ever knowingly offer it as such. A possibility always must present us with some actual idea.

3. And this idea must not contradict itself, and so be self-destructive. So far as it is seen to be so, to that extent it must not be taken as possible. For a possibility qualifies the Real,[2] and must therefore not conflict with the known character of its subject. And it is useless to object here that all appearance is self-contradictory. That is true, but, as self-contradictory and so far as it is so, appearance is not a real or possible predicate of Reality. A predicate which contradicts itself is, as such, not possibly real. In order to be real, its particular nature must be modified and corrected. And this

---

[1] On this point compare my *Principles of Logic*, pp. 519-20.

[2] *Ibid.* p. 187. The reader should compare the treatment of Possibility above in this volume (Chapter xxiv.), and again in Mr Bosanquet's *Logic*.

process of correction, and of making good, may in
addition totally transform and entirely dissipate its
nature (Chapter xxiv.).

4. It is impossible rationally to doubt where you
have but one idea. You may doubt psychically,
given two ideas which seem two but are one. And,
even without this actual illusion, you may feel uneasy in mind and may hesitate. But doubt implies
two ideas, which in their meaning and truly are
two ; and, without these ideas, doubt has no rational
existence.[1]

5. Where you have an idea and cannot doubt,
there logically you must assert. For everything
(we have seen throughout) must qualify the Real.
And if an idea does not contradict itself, either as it
is or as taken with other things (Chapter xvi.), it is
at once true and real. Now clearly a sole possibility cannot so contradict itself ;[2] and it must therefore be affirmed. Psychical failure and confusion
may here of course stand in the way. But such
confusion and failure can in theory count for
nothing.

6. "But to reason thus," it may be objected, " is
to rest knowledge on ignorance. It is surely the
grounding of an assertion on our bare impotence."
No objection could be more mistaken, since the
very essence of our principle consists in the diame-
trical opposite. Its essence lies in the refusal to set
blank ignorance in the room of knowledge. He
who wishes to doubt, when he has not before him
two genuine ideas, he who talks of a possible which
is not based on actual knowledge about Reality—it
is he who takes his stand upon sheer incapacity.
He is the man who, admitting his emptiness, then
pretends to bring forth truth. And it is against
this monstrous pretence, this mad presumption in

---

[1] *Ibid.* p. 517.
[2] For, if it did, it would split internally, as well as pass beyond
itself externally.

the guise of modesty, that our principle protests.
But, if we seriously consider the matter, our conclusion grows plain. Surely an idea must have a
meaning; surely two ideas are required for any
rational doubt; surely to be called possible is to be
affirmed to some extent of the Real. And surely,
where you have no alternative, it is not right or
rational to take the attitude of a man who hesitates
between diverse courses.

7. I will consider next an argument for general
doubt which might be drawn from reflection on the
privative judgment.[1] In such a judgment the Reality
excludes some suggestion, but the basis of the rejection is not a positive quality in the known subject.
The basis on the contrary is an absence; and a
mere absence implies the qualification of the subject
by its psychical setting in us. Or we may say
that, while the known subject is assumed to be complete, its limitations fall outside itself and lie in our
incapacity. And it may be urged here that with
Reality this is always the case. The universe, as
we know it, in other words is complete only through
our ignorance; and hence it may be said for our
real knowledge to be incomplete always. And on
this ground, it may be added, we can decline to
assert of the universe any one possibility, even when
we are able to find no other.

I have myself raised this objection because it
contains an important truth. And its principle, if
confined to proper limits, is entirely sound. Nay,
throughout this work, I have freely used the right to
postulate everywhere an unknown supplementation
of knowledge. And how then here, it may be
urged, are we to throw over this principle? Why
should not Reality be considered always as limited
by our impotence, and as extending, therefore, in
every respect beyond the area of *our* possibilities?

---

[1] *Ibid.* pp. 112–115, 511–517. And see, above, Chapter xxiv.

But the objection at this point, it is clear, contradicts itself. The area of what is possible is here extended and limited in a breath, and a ruinous dilemma might be set up and urged in reply to the question. But it is better at once to expose the main underlying error. The knowledge of privation, like all other knowledge, in the end is positive. You cannot speak of the absent and lacking unless you assume some field and some presence elsewhere. You cannot suggest your ignorance as a reason for judging knowledge incomplete, unless you have some knowledge already of an area which that ignorance hides. Within the known extent of the Real you have various provinces, and hence what is absent from one may be sought for in another. And where in certain features the known world suggests itself as incomplete, that world has extended itself already beyond these features. Here then, naturally, we have a right to follow its extended reality with our conclusions and surmises; and in these discussions we have availed ourselves largely of that privilege. But, on the other hand, this holds only of subordinate matters, and our right exists only while we remain within the known area of the universe. It is senseless to attempt to go beyond, and to assume fields that lie outside the ultimate nature of Reality. If there were any Reality quite beyond our knowledge, we could in no sense be aware of it; and, if we were quite ignorant of it, we could hardly suggest that our ignorance conceals it. And thus, in the end, what we know and what is real must be co-extensive, and assuredly outside of this area nothing is possible. A single possibility here must, therefore, be taken as single and as real. Within this known region, and not outside, lies all the kingdom hidden by ignorance; and here is the object of all intelligent doubt, and every possibility that is not irrational.

8. With a view to gain clearness on this point, it

may repay us to consider an ideal state of things. If the known universe were a perfect system, then it could nowhere suggest its own incompleteness. Every possible suggestion would then at once take its place in the whole, a place fore-ordained and assigned to it by the remaining members of the system. And again, starting from any one element in such a whole, we could from that proceed to work out completely the total universe. And a doubt drawn from privation and based upon ignorance would here entirely disappear. Not only would the system itself have no other possibility outside, but even within its finite details the same consummation would be reached. The words " absence " and " failure " would here, in fact, have lost their proper sense. Since with every idea its full relations to all else would be visible, there would remain no region of doubt or of possibility or of ignorance.

9. This intellectual ideal, we know, is not actual fact. It does not exist in our world, and, unless that world were changed radically, its existence is not possible. It would require an alteration of the position in which the intellect stands, and a transformation of its whole connection with the remaining aspects of experience. We need not to cast about for arguments to disprove our omniscience, for at every turn through these pages our weakness has been confessed. The universe in its diversity has been seen to be inexplicable, and I will not repeat here the statement made in the preceding Chapter (p. 469). Our system throughout its detail is incomplete.

Now in an incomplete system there must be everywhere a region of ignorance. Since in the end subject and predicate will not coincide, there remains a margin of that which, except more or less and in its outline, is unknown. And here is a field for doubt and for possibility and for theoretical supplement. An incomplete system in every part is inconsistent, and so suggests something beyond. But it can nowhere suggest the precise complement which would make good each detail. And hence, both in its extent and in its unity, it for some part must remain a mere collection. We may say that, in the end, it is comprised and exhausted only through *our* incompleteness.

10. But here we must recur to the distinction which we laid down above. Even in an incomplete world, such as the world which appears in our knowledge, incompleteness and ignorance after all are partial. They do not hold good with every feature, but there are points where no legitimate idea of an Other exists. And in these points a doubt, and an enquiry into other possibles, would be senseless; for there is no available area in which possibly our ignorance could fall. And clearly within these limits (which we cannot fix before-hand) rational doubt becomes irrational assumption. Outside these, again, there may be suggestions, which we cannot say are meaningless or inconsistent with the nature of things; and yet the bare possibility of these may not be worth considering. But, once more, in other regions of the world the case will be altered. We shall find a greater or less degree of actual completeness, and, with this, a series of possibilities differing in value. I do not think that with advantage we could pursue further these preliminary discussions; and we must now address ourselves directly to the doubts which can be raised about our Absolute.

With regard to the main character of that Absolute our position is briefly this. We hold that our conclusion is certain, and that to doubt it logically is impossible. There is no other view, there is no other idea beyond the view here put forward. It is impossible rationally even to entertain the question of another possibility. Outside our main result there is nothing except the wholly unmeaning, or else something which on scrutiny is seen really not to fall outside. Thus the supposed Other will, in short, turn out to be actually the same; or it will contain elements included within our view of the Absolute, but elements dislocated and so distorted into erroneous appearance. And the dislocation itself will find a place within the limits of our system.

Our result, in brief, cannot be doubted, since it contains all possibilities. Show us an idea, we can proclaim, which seems hostile to our scheme, and we will show you an element which really is contained within it. And we will demonstrate your idea to be a self-contradictory piece of our system, an internal fragment which only through sheer blindness can fancy itself outside. We will prove that its independence and isolation are nothing in the world but a failure to perceive more than one aspect of its own nature.

And the shocked appeal to our modesty and our weakness will not trouble us. It is on this very weakness that, in a sense, we have taken our stand. We are impotent to divide the universe into the universe and something outside. We are incapable of finding another field in which to place our inability and give play to our modesty. This other area for us is mere pretentious nonsense; and on the ground of our weakness we do not feel strong enough to assume that nonsense is fact. We, in other words, protest against the senseless attempt to transcend experience. We urge that a mere doubt entertained may involve that attempt, and that in the case of our main conclusion it certainly does so. Hence in its outline that conclusion for us is certain; and let us endeavour to see how far the certainty goes.

Reality is one. It must be single, because plurality, taken as real, contradicts itself. Plurality

implies relations, and, through its relations, it unwillingly asserts always a superior unity. To suppose the universe plural is therefore to contradict
oneself and, after all, to suppose that it is one. Add
one world to another, and forthwith both worlds
have become relative, each the finite appearance of
a higher and single Reality. And plurality as
appearance (we have seen) must fall within, must
belong to, and must qualify the unity.

We have an idea of this unity which, to some
extent, is positive (Chapters xiv., xx., xxvi.). It is
true that how in detail the plurality comes together
we do not know. And it is true again that unity,
in its more proper sense, is known only as contradistinguished from plurality. Unity therefore, as an
aspect over against and defined by another aspect,
is itself but appearance. And in this sense the
Real, it is clear, cannot be properly called one. It
is possible, however, to use unity with a different
meaning.

In the first place the Real is qualified by all
plurality. It owns this diversity while itself it is
not plural. And a reality owning plurality but
above it, not defined as against it but absorbing it
together with the one-sided unity which forms its
opposite—such a reality in its outline is certainly a
positive idea.

And this outline, to some extent, is filled in by
direct experience. I will lay no stress here on that
pre-relational stage of existence (p. 459), which we
suppose to come first in the development of the
soul. I will refer to what seems plainer and less
doubtful. For take any complex psychical state in
which we make distinctions. Here we have a consciousness of plurality, and then over against this
we may attempt to gain a clear idea of unity. Now
this idea of unity, itself the result of analysis, is determined by opposition to the internal plurality of
distinctions. And hence, as one aspect over against

another aspect, this will not furnish the positive idea of unity which we seek. But, apart from and without any such explicit idea, we may be truly said to feel our whole psychical state as one. Above, or rather below, the relations which afterwards we may find, it seems to be a totality in which differences already are combined.[1] Our state seems a felt background into which we introduce distinctions, and it seems, at the same time, a whole in which the differences inhere and pre-exist. Now certainly, in so describing our state, we contradict ourselves. For the fact of a difference, when we realize and express its strict nature, implies in its essence both relation and distinction. In other words, feeling cannot be described, for it cannot without transformation be translated into thought. Again, in itself this indiscriminate totality is inconsistent and unstable. Its own tendency and nature is to pass beyond itself into the relational consciousness, into a higher stage in which it is broken up. Still, none the less, at every moment this vague state is experienced actually. And hence we cannot deny that complex wholes are felt as single experiences. For, on the one side, these states are not simple, nor again, on the other side, are they plural merely ; nor again is their unity explicit and held in relation with, and against, their plurality.

We may find this exemplified most easily in an ordinary emotional whole. That comes to us as one, yet not as simple ; while its diversity, at least in part, is not yet distinguished and broken up into relations. Such a state of mind, I may repeat, is, as such, unstable and fleeting. It is not only changeable otherwise, but, if made an object, it, as such, disappears. The emotion we attend to is, taken strictly, never precisely the same thing as the emotion which we feel. For it not only to some

---

[1] Compare here Chapter xix.

extent has been transformed by internal distinction, but it has also now itself become a factor in a new felt totality.   The emotion as an object, and, on the other side, that background to which in consciousness it is opposed, have both become subordinate elements in a new psychical whole of feeling (Chapter xix.).   Our experience is always from time to time a unity which, as such, is destroyed in becoming an object.   But one such emotional whole in its destruction gives place inevitably to another whole.   And hence what we feel, while it lasts, is felt always as one, yet not as simple nor again as broken into terms and relations.

From such an experience of unity below relations we can rise to the idea of a superior unity above them.   Thus we can attach a full and positive meaning to the statement that Reality is one.   The stubborn objector seems condemned, in any case, to affirm the following propositions.   In the first place Reality is positive, negation falling inside it.   In the second place it is qualified positively by all the plurality which it embraces and subordinates.   And yet itself, in the third place, is certainly not plural. Having gone so far I myself prefer, as the least misleading course, to assert its unity.

Beyond all doubt then it is clear that Reality is one.   It has unity, but we must go on to ask, a unity of what?   And we have already found that all we know consists wholly of experience.   Reality must be, therefore, one Experience, and to doubt this conclusion is impossible.

We can discover nothing that is not either feeling or thought or will or emotion or something else of the kind (Chapter xiv.).   We can find nothing but this, and to have an idea of anything else is plainly impossible.   For such a supposed idea is either meaningless, and so is not an idea, or else its meaning will be found tacitly to consist in experience.

The Other, which it asserts, is found on enquiry to be really no Other. It implies, against its will and unconsciously, some mode of experience; it affirms something else, if you please, but still something else of the same kind. And the form of otherness and of opposition, again, has no sense save as an internal aspect of that which it endeavours to oppose. We have, in short, in the end but one idea, and that idea is positive. And hence to deny this idea is, in effect, to assert it; and to doubt it, actually and without a delusion, is not possible.

If I attempted to labour this point, I should perhaps but obscure it. Show me your idea of an Other, not a part of experience, and I will show you at once that it is, throughout and wholly, nothing else at all. But an effort to anticipate, and to deal in advance with every form of self-delusion, would, I think, hardly enlighten us. I shall therefore assume this main principle as clearly established, and shall endeavour merely to develope it and to free it from certain obscurities.

I will recur first to the difficult subject of Solipsism. This has been discussed perhaps sufficiently in Chapter xxi., but a certain amount of repetition may be useful here. It may be objected that, if Reality is proved to be one experience, Solipsism follows. Again, if we can transcend the self at all, then we have made our way, it may be urged, to something perhaps not experience. Our main conclusion, in short, may be met not directly but through a dilemma. It may be threatened with destruction by a self-contradictory development of its own nature.

Now my answer to this dilemma is a denial of that which it assumes. It assumes, in the first place, that my self is as wide as my experience. And it assumes, in the second place, that my self is something hard and exclusive. Hence, if you are inside you are not outside at all, and, if you are

outside, you are at once in a different world. But
we have shown that these assumptions are mistaken
(Chapters xxi. and xxiii.); and, with their withdrawal,
the dilemma falls of itself.

Finite centres of feeling, while they last, are (so
far as we know) not directly pervious to one
another. But, on the one hand, a self is not the
same as such a centre of experience ; and, on the
other hand, in every centre the whole Reality is
present. Finite experience never, in any of its
forms, is shut in by a wall. It has in itself, and as
an inseparable aspect of its own nature, the all-
penetrating Reality. And there never is, and there
never was, any time when in experience the world
and self were quite identical. For, if we reach a
stage where in feeling the self and world are not
yet different, at that stage neither as yet exists.
But in our first immediate experience the whole
Reality is present. This does not mean that every
other centre of experience, as such, is included there.
It means that every centre qualifies the Whole, and
that the Whole, as a substantive, is present in each
of these its adjectives. Then from immediate experience the self emerges, and is set apart by a
distinction. The self and the world are elements,
each separated in, and each contained by experience.
And perhaps in all cases the self—and at any rate
always the soul [1]—involves and only exists through
an intellectual construction. The self is thus a construction based on, and itself transcending, immediate experience. Hence to describe all experience

---

[1] These terms must not be taken as everywhere equivalent.
There certainly is no self or soul without a centre of feeling.
But there may be centres of feeling which are not selves, and
again not souls (see below). Possibly also some selves are too
fleeting to be called souls, while almost certainly there are souls
which are not properly selves. The latter term should not be
used at all where there is in no sense a distinction of self from
not-self. And it can hardly always be used in precisely the same
sense (Chapter ix.).

as the mere adjective of a self, taken in any sense, is indefensible. And, as for transcendence,—from the very first the self is transcended by experience. Or we may in another way put this so. The self is one of the results gained by transcending the first imperfect form of experience. But experience and Reality are each the same thing when taken at full, and they cannot be transcended.

I may be allowed to repeat this. Experience in its early form, as a centre of immediate feeling, is not yet either self or not-self. It qualifies the Reality, which of course is present within it; and its own finite content indissolubly connects it with the total universe. But for itself—if it could be for itself—this finite centre would be the world. Then through its own imperfection such first experience is broken up. Its unity gives way before inner unrest and outer impact in one. And then self and Ego, on one side, are produced by this development, and, on the other side, appear other selves and the world and God. These all appear as the contents of one finite experience, and they really are genuinely and actually contained in it. They are contained in it but partially, and through a more or less inconsiderable portion of their area. Still this portion, so far as it goes, is their very being and reality; and a finite experience already *is* partially the universe. Hence there is no question here of stepping over a line from one world to another. Experience is already in both worlds, and is one thing with their being; and the question is merely to what extent this common being can be carried out, whether in practice or in knowledge. In other words the total universe, present imperfectly in finite experience, would, if completed, be merely the completion of this experience. And to speak of transcendence into another world is therefore mistaken.

For certain purposes what I experience can be

considered as the state of my self, or, again, of my
soul. It can be so considered, because in one
aspect it actually is so. But this one aspect may
be an infinitesimal fragment of its being. And never
in any case can what I experience be the *mere*
adjective of my self. My self is not the immediate,
nor again is it the ultimate, reality. Immediate
reality is an experience either containing both self
and not-self, or containing as yet neither. And
ultimate reality, on the other hand, would be the
total universe.

In a former chapter we noticed the truths contained in Solipsism. Everything, my self included,
is essential to, and is inseparable from, the Absolute.
And, again, it is only in feeling that I can directly
encounter Reality. But there is no need here to
dwell on these sides of the truth. My experience
is essential to the world, but the world is not, except
in one aspect, my experience. The world and experience are, taken at large, the same. And my
experience and its states, in a sense, actually are
the whole world ; for to this slight extent the one
Reality is actually my self. But it is less misleading
to assert, conversely, that the total world is my
experience. For it appears there, and in each
appearance its single being already is imperfectly
included.

Let us turn from an objection based · on an
irrational prejudice, and let us go on to consider a
point of some interest. Can the Absolute be said
to consist and to be made up of souls ? The
question is ambiguous, and must be discussed in
several senses. Is there—let us ask first—in the
universe any sort of matter not contained in finite
centres of experience ? It seems at first sight
natural to point at once to the relations between
these centres. But such relations, we find on reflection, have been, so far, included in the percep-

tion and thought of the centres themselves. And what the question comes to is, rather, this, Can there be matter of experience, in any form, which does not enter as an element into some finite centre ?

In view of our ignorance this question may seem unanswerable. We do not know why or how the Absolute divides itself into centres, or the way in which, so divided, it still remains one. The relation of the many experiences to the single experience, and so to one another, is, in the end, beyond us. And, if so, why should there not be elements experienced in the total, and yet not experienced within any subordinate focus? We may indeed, from the other side, confront this ignorance and this question with a doubt. Has such an unattached element, or margin of elements, any meaning at all ? Have we any right to entertain such an idea as rational ? Does not our ignorance in fact forbid us to assume the possibility of any matter experienced apart from a finite whole of feeling ? But, after consideration, I do not find that this doubt should prevail. Certainly it is only by an abstraction that I can form the idea of such unattached elements, and this abstraction, it may seem, is not legitimate. And, if the elements were taken as quite loose, if they were not still inseparable factors in a whole of experience, then the abstraction clearly would lead to an inconsistent idea. And such an idea, we have agreed, must not be regarded as possible. But, in the present case, the elements, unattached to any finite centre, are still subordinate to and integral aspects of the Whole. And, since this Whole is one experience, the position is altered. The abstraction from a finite centre does not lead visibly to self-contradiction. And hence I cannot refuse to regard its result as possible.

But this possibility, on the other side, seems to have no importance. If we take it to be fact, we

shall not find that it makes much difference to the
Whole.   And, again, for so taking it there appears
to be almost no ground.   Let us briefly consider
these two points.   That elements of experience
should be unattached would (we saw) be a serious
matter, if they were unattached altogether and
absolutely.   But since in any case all comes together and is fused in the Whole, and since this
Whole in any case is a single experience, the main
result appears to me to be quite unaffected.   The
fact that some experience-matter does not *directly*
qualify any finite centre, is a fact from which I can
draw no further conclusion.   But for holding this
fact, in the second place, there is surely no good
reason.   The number of finite centres and their
diversity is (we know) very great, and we may fairly
suppose it to extend much beyond our knowledge.
Nor do the relations, which are " between " these
centres, occasion difficulty.   Relations of course
cannot fall somewhere outside of reality ; and, if
they really were " between " the centres, we should
have to assume some matter of experience external
and additional to these.   The conclusion would
follow ; and we have seen that, rightly understood,
it is possible.   But, as things are, it seems no less
gratuitous.   There is nothing, so far as I see, to
suggest that any aspect of any relation lies outside
the experience-matter contained in finite centres.
The relations, as such, do not and cannot exist in
the Absolute.   And the question is whether that
higher experience, which contains and transforms
the relations, demands any element not experienced
somehow within the centres.   For assuming such
an element I can myself perceive no ground.   And
since, even if we assume this, the main result seems
to remain unaltered, the best course is, perhaps, to
discard it as unreal.   It is better, on the whole, to
conclude that no element of Reality falls outside
the experience of finite centres.

Are we then to assert that the Absolute consists of souls? That, in my opinion, for two reasons would be incorrect. A centre of experience, first, is not the same thing as either a soul or, again, a self. It need not contain the distinction of not-self from self; and, whether it contains that or not, in neither case is it, properly, a self. It will be either below, or else wider than and above, the distinction. And a soul. as we have seen, is always the creature of an intellectual construction. It cannot be the same thing with a mere centre of immediate experience. Nor again can we affirm that every centre implies and entails in some sense a corresponding soul. For the duration of such centres may perhaps be so momentary that no one, except to save a theory, could call them souls. Hence we cannot maintain that souls contain all the matter of experience which fills the world.

And in any case, secondly, the Absolute would not *consist* of souls. Such a phrase implies a mode of union which we can not regard as ultimate. It suggests that in the Absolute finite centres are maintained and respected, and that we may consider them, as such, to persist and to be merely ordered and arranged. But not like this (we have seen) is the final destiny and last truth of things. We have a re-arrangement not merely of things but of their internal elements. We have an all-pervasive transfusion with a re-blending of all material. And we can hardly say that the Absolute consists of finite things, when the things, as such, are there transmuted and have lost their individual natures.[1]

---

[1] For this reason Humanity, or an organism, kingdom, or society of selves, is not an ultimate idea. It implies an union too incomplete, and it ascribes reality in too high a sense to finite pieces of appearance. These two defects are, of course, in principle one. An organism or society, including every self past present and future—and we can hardly take it at less than this —is itself an idea to me obscure, if not quite inconsistent. But, in any case, its reality and truth cannot be ultimate. And, for

Reality then is one, and it is experience. It is not merely *my* experience, nor again can we say that it consists of souls or selves. And it cannot be a unity of experience and also of something beside; for the something beside, when we examine it, turns out always to be experience. We verified this above (Chapters xxii. and xxvi.) in the case of Nature. Nature, like all else, in a sense remains inexplicable. It is in the end an arrangement, a way of happening coexistent and successive, as to which at last we clearly are unable to answer the question Why. But this inability, like others, does not affect the truth of our result. Nature is an abstraction from experience, and in experience it is not co-ordinate with spirit or mind. For mind, we have seen, has a reality higher than Nature, and the essence of the physical world already implies that in which it is absorbed and transcended. Nature by itself is but an indefensible division in the whole of experience.

This total unity of experience, I have pointed out, cannot, as such, be directly verified. We know its nature, but in outline only, and not in detail. Feeling, as we have seen, supplies us with a positive idea of non-relational unity. The idea is imperfect, but is sufficient to serve as a positive basis. And we are compelled further by our principle to believe in a Whole qualified, and qualified non-relationally, by every fraction of experience. But this unity of all experiences, if itself not experience, would be meaningless. The Whole is one experience then, and such a unity higher than all relations, a unity which contains and transforms them, has positive meaning. Of the manner of its being in detail we are utterly ignorant, but of its general nature we

myself, even in Ethics I do not see how such an idea can be insisted on. The perfection of the Whole has to realise itself in and through me; and, without question, this Whole is very largely social. But I do not see my way to the assertion that, even for Ethics, it is nothing else at all (pp. 415, 431).

possess a positive though abstract knowledge. And, in attempting to deny or to doubt the result we have gained, we find ourselves once more unconsciously affirming it.

The Absolute, though known, is higher, in a sense, than our experience and knowledge ; and in this connection I will ask if it has personality. At the point we have reached such a question can be dealt with rapidly. We can answer it at once in the affirmative or negative according to its meaning. Since the Absolute has everything, it of course must possess personality. And if by personality we are to understand the highest form of finite spiritual development, then certainly in an eminent degree the Absolute is personal. For the higher (we may repeat) is always the more real. And, since in the Absolute the very lowest modes of experience are not lost, it seems even absurd to raise such a question about personality.

And this is not the sense in which the question is usually put. " Personal " is employed in effect with a restrictive meaning ; for it is used to exclude what is above, as well as below, personality. The superpersonal, in other words, is either openly or tacitly regarded as impossible. Personality is taken as the highest possible way of experience, and naturally, if so, the Absolute cannot be super-personal. This conclusion, with the assumption on which it rests, may be summarily rejected. It has been, indeed, refuted beforehand by previous discussions. If the term " personal " is to bear anything like its ordinary sense, assuredly the Absolute is not merely personal. It is not personal, because it is personal and more. It is, in a word, super-personal.

I intend here not to enquire into the possible meanings of personality. On the nature of the self and of self-consciousness I have spoken already,[1] and

---

[1] See Chapters ix. and x. Compare xxi. and xxiii.

I will merely add here that for me a person is finite
or is meaningless.   But the question raised as to the
Absolute may, I think, be more briefly disposed of.
If by calling it personal you mean only that it is
nothing but experience, that it contains all the
highest that we possibly can know and feel, and is
a unity in which the details are utterly pervaded
and embraced—then in this conclusion I am with
you.   But your employment of the term personal I
very much regret.   I regret this use mainly not
because I consider it incorrect—that between us
would matter little—but because it is misleading and
directly serves the cause of dishonesty.

For most of those who insist on what they call
" the personality of God," are intellectually dishonest.
They desire one conclusion, and, to reach it, they
argue for another   But the second, if proved, is
quite different, and serves their purpose only because they obscure it and confound it with the first.
And it is by their practical purpose that the result
may here be judged.   The Deity, which they want,
is of course finite, a person much like themselves,
with thoughts and feelings limited and mutable in the
process of time.   They desire a person in the sense of
a self, amongst and over against other selves, moved
by personal relations and feelings towards these
others—feelings and relations which are altered by
the conduct of the others.   And, for their purpose,
what is not this, is really nothing.   Now with this desire in itself I am not here concerned.   Of course for
us to ask seriously if the Absolute can be personal in
such a way, would be quite absurd.   And my business for the moment is not with truth but with intellectual honesty.

It would be honest first of all to state openly the
conclusion aimed at, and then to enquire if this conclusion can be maintained.   But what is not honest
is to suppress the point really at issue, to desire the
personality of the Deity in one sense, and then to

contend for it in another, and to do one's best to ignore the chasm which separates the two. Once give up your finite and mutable person, and you have parted with everything which, for you, makes personality important. Nor will you bridge the chasm by the sliding extension of a word. You will only make a fog, where you can cry out that you are on both sides at once. And towards increasing this fog I decline to contribute. It would be useless, in such company and in such an atmosphere, to discuss the meaning of personality—if indeed the word actually has any one meaning. For me it is sufficient to know, on one side, that the Absolute is not a finite person. Whether, on the other side, personality in some eviscerated remnant of sense can be applied to it, is a question intellectually unimportant and practically trifling.

With regard to the personality of the Absolute we must guard against two one-sided errors. The Absolute is not personal, nor is it moral, nor is it beautiful or true. And yet in these denials we may be falling into worse mistakes. For it would be far more incorrect to assert that the Absolute is either false, or ugly, or bad, or is something even beneath the application of predicates such as these. And it is better to affirm personality than to call the Absolute impersonal. But neither mistake should be necessary. The Absolute stands above, and not below, its internal distinctions. It does not eject them, but it includes them as elements in its fulness. To speak in other language, it is not the indifference but the concrete identity of all extremes. But it is better in this connection to call it super-personal.

We have seen that Reality is one, and is a single experience; and we may pass from this to consider a difficult question. Is the Absolute happy? This might mean, can pleasure, as such, be predicated of the Absolute? And, as we have seen in the preceding chapter, this is not permissible. We found that there is a balance of pleasure over and above pain, and we know from experience that in a mixed state such a balance may be pleasant. And we are sure that the Absolute possesses and enjoys somehow this balance of pleasure. But to go further seems impossible. Pleasure may conceivably be so supplemented and modified by addition, that it does not remain precisely that which we call pleasure. Its pleasantness certainly could not be lost, but it might be blended past recognition with other aspects of the Whole. The Absolute then, perhaps, strictly, does not feel pleasure. But, if so, that is only because it has something in which pleasure is included.

But at this point we are met by the doubt, with which already we have partly dealt (Chapter xiv.). Is our conclusion, after all, the right one? Is it not possible, after all, that in the Absolute there is a balance of pain, or, if not of pain, of something else which is at all events no better? On this difficult point I will state at once the result which seems true. Such a balance is possible in the lowest sense of barely possible. It does not seem to me unmeaning, nor can I find that it is self-contradictory. If we try to deny that the Absolute is one and is experience, our denial becomes unmeaning, or of itself turns round into an assertion. But I do not see that this is the case with a denial of happiness.

It is true that we can know nothing of pain and pleasure except from our experience. It is true that in that experience well-nigh everything points in one direction. There is, so far as I know, not one special fact which suggests that pain is compatible with unity and concord. And, if so, why should we not insist, "Such is the nature of pain, and hence to deny this nature is to fall into self-contradiction"? What, in short, is the other possibility which has not been included? I will endeavour to state it.

The world that we can observe is certainly not

all the universe; and we do not know how much there may be which we cannot observe. And hence everywhere an indefinite supplement from the unknown is possible. Now might there not be conditions, invisible to us, which throughout our experience modify the action of pleasure and pain? In this way what seems to be essential to pain may actually not be so. It may really come from unseen conditions which are but accidental. And so pain, after all, might be compatible with harmony and system. Against this it may be contended that pain itself, on such a hypothesis, would be neutralised, and that its painfulness also would now be gone. Again it may be urged that what is accidental on a certain scale has become essential, essential not less effectively because indirectly. But, though these contentions have force, I do not find them conclusive. The idea of a painful universe, in the end, seems to be neither quite meaningless nor yet visibly self-contradictory. And I am compelled to allow that, speaking strictly, we must call it possible.

But such a possibility, on the other side, possesses almost no value. It of course rests, so far as it goes, on positive knowledge. We know that the world's character, within certain limits, admits of indefinite supplementation. And the supplementation, here proposed, seems in accordance with this general nature of known reality. That is all it has in its favour, an abstract compliance with a general character of things; and beyond this there seems to be not one shred of particular evidence. But against it there is everything which in particular we know about the subject. And the possibility is thus left with a value too small to be estimated. We can only say that it exists, and that it is hardly worth considering further.

But we have, with this, crossed the line which separates absolute from conditional knowledge.

That Reality is one system which contains in itself
all experience, and, again, that this system itself is
experience—so far we may be said to know absolutely and unconditionally.[1] Up to this point our
judgment is infallible, and its opposite is quite impossible. The chance of error, in other words, is so
far nothing at all. But outside this boundary every
judgment is finite, and so conditional. And here
every truth, because incomplete, is more or less
erroneous. And because the amount of incompleteness remains unknown, it may conceivably go so far,
in any case, as to destroy the judgment. The opposite no longer is impossible absolutely; but, from
this point downwards, it remains but impossible relatively and subject to a condition.

Anything is absolute when all its nature is contained within itself. It is unconditional when every
condition of its being falls inside it. It is free from
chance of error when any opposite is quite inconceivable. Such characters belong to the statement
that Reality is experience and is one. For these
truths are not subordinate, but are general truths
about Reality as a whole. They do not exhaust it,
but in outline they give its essence The Real, in
other words, is more than they, but always more of
the same. There is nothing which in idea you can
add to it, that fails, when understood, to fall under
these general truths. And hence every doubt and
all chance of error become unmeaning. Error and
doubt have their place only in the subordinate and
finite region, and within the limits prescribed by the
character of the Whole. And the Other has no
meaning where any Other turns out to be none. It
is useless again to urge that an Other, though not
yet conceived, may after all prove conceivable. It
is idle to object that the impossible means no more
than what you have not yet found. For we have

---

[1] This statement will be modified lower down.

seen that privation and failure imply always an outlying field of reality; and such an outlying field
is here unmeaning. To say " you might find it "
sounds modest, but it assumes positively a sphere in
which the thing might be found. And here the
assumption contradicts itself, and with that contradiction the doubt bodily disappears.

The criterion of truth may be called inconceivability of the opposite, but it is essential to know
what we mean by such inability. Is this absolute
or relative, and to what extent is it due to privation
and mere failure? We have in fact, once more here,
to clear our ideas as to the meaning of impossibility
(Chapters xxiv. and xxvi.). Now the impossible
may either be absolute or relative, but it can never
be directly based on our impotence. For a thing is
impossible always because it contradicts positive
knowledge. Where the knowledge is relative, that
knowledge is certainly more or less conditioned by
our impotence. And hence, through that impotence,
the impossibility may be more or less weakened and
made conditional. But it never is created by or
rests upon simple failure. In the end one has to
say " I must not," not because I am unable, but
because I am prevented.

The impossible absolutely is what contradicts the
known nature of Reality. And the impossible, in
this sense, is self-contradictory. It is indeed an
attempt to deny which, in the very act, unwittingly
affirms. Since here our positive knowledge is all-
embracing, it can rest on nothing external. Outside this knowledge there is not so much as an
empty space in which our impotence could fall.
And every inability and failure already presupposes
and belongs to our known world.

The impossible relatively is what contradicts any
subordinate piece of knowledge. It cannot be, unless something which we hold for true is, as such,
given up. The impossibility here will vary in degree,

according to the strength of that knowledge with which it conflicts.   And, once more here, it does not consist in our failure and impotence.   The impossible is not rejected, in other words, because we cannot find it.   It is rejected because we find it, and find it in collision with positive knowledge.   But what is true on the other side is that our knowledge here is finite and fallible.   It has to be conditional on account of our inability and impotence.

Before I return to this last point, I will repeat the same truth from another side.   A thing is real when, and in so far as, its opposite is impossible. But in the end its opposite is impossible because, and in so far as, the thing is real.   And, according to the amount of reality which anything possesses, to that extent its opposite is inconceivable.   The more, in other words, that anything exhausts the field of possibility, the less possible becomes that which would essentially alter it.   Now, in the case of such truth as we have called absolute, the field of possibility is exhausted.   Reality is there, and the opposite of Reality is not privation but absolute nothingness.   There can be no outside, because already what is inside is everything.   But the case is altered when we come to subordinate truths.   These, being not self-subsistent, are conditioned by what is partly unknown, and certainly to that extent they are dependent on our inability.   But, on the other hand, our criterion of their truth and strength is positive.   The more they are coherent and wide— the more fully they realize the idea of system—so much the more at once are they real and true.[1] And so much the more what would subvert them becomes impossible.   The opposite is inconceivable, according and in proportion as it conflicts with positive reality.

We have seen now that some truth is certain

---

[1] Throughout this discussion the reader is supposed to be acquainted with the doctrine of Chapter xxiv.

beyond a doubt, and that the rest—all subordinate truth—is subject to error in various degrees. Any finite truth, to be made quite true, must more or less be modified; and it may require modification to such an extent that we must call it utterly transformed. Now, in Chapter xxiv., we have already shown that this account holds good, but I will once more insist on our fallibility in finite matters. And the general consideration which I would begin by urging, is this. With every finite truth there is an external world of unknown extent. Where there is such an indefinite outside, there must be an uncertain world of possible conditions. But this means that any finite truth may be conditioned so as to be made really quite otherwise. I will go on briefly to apply this.

Wherever a truth depends, as we say, upon observation, clearly in this case you cannot tell how much is left out, and what you have not observed may be, for all you know, the larger part of the matter. But, if so, your truth—it makes no difference whether it is called " particular " or " general " —may be indefinitely mistaken. The accidental may have been set down as if it were the essence ; and this error may be present to an extent which cannot be limited. You cannot prove that subject and predicate have not been conjoined by the invisible interposition of unknown factors. And there is no way in which this possibility can be excluded.

But the chance of error vanishes, we may be told, where genuine abstraction is possible. It is not present at least, for example, in the world of mathematical truth. Such an objection to our general view cannot stand. Certainly there are spheres where abstraction in a special sense is possible, and where we are able, as we may say, to proceed a priori. And for other purposes this difference, I agree, may be very important; but I am not concerned here with its importance or generally with its nature and limits.   For, as regards the point in question, the difference is wholly irrelevant.   No abstraction (whatever its origin) is in the end defensible.   For they are, none of them, quite true, and with each the amount of possible error must remain unknown.   The truth asserted is not, and cannot be, taken as real by itself.   The background is ignored because it is assumed to make no difference, and the mass of conditions, abstracted from and left out, is treated as immaterial.   The predicate, in other words, is held to belong to the subject essentially, and not because of something else which may be withdrawn or modified.   But an assumption of this kind obviously goes beyond our knowledge. Since Reality here is not exhausted, but is limited only by our failure to see more, there is a possibility everywhere of unknown conditions on which our judgment depends.   And hence, after all, we may be asserting anywhere what is but accidental.

We may put this otherwise by stating that finite truth must be conditional.   No such fact or truth is ever really self-supported and independent.   They are all conditioned, and in the end conditioned all by the unknown.   And the extent to which they are so conditioned, again is uncertain.   But this means that any finite truth or fact may to an indefinite extent be accidental appearance.   In other words, if its conditions were filled in, it, in its own proper form, might have disappeared.   It might be modified and transformed beyond that point at which it could be said, to any extent, to retain its own nature.   And however improbable in certain cases this result may be, in no case can it be called impossible absolutely.   Everything finite is because of something else.   And where the extent and nature of this " something else " cannot be ascertained, the " because " turns out to be no better than " if." There is nothing finite which is not at the mercy of unknown conditions.

Finite truth and fact, we may say, is throughout
" hypothetical." But, either with this term or with
" conditional," we have to guard against misleading
implications. There cannot (from our present point
of view) be one finite sphere which is real and
actual, or which is even considered to be so for a
certain purpose. There can be here no realm of
existence or fact, outside of which the merely supposed could fall in unreality. The Reality, on one
hand, is no finite existence ; and, on the other hand,
every predicate—no matter what—must both fall
within and must qualify Reality.[1] They are applicable, all subject to various degrees of alteration, and
as to these degrees we, in the end, may in any case
be mistaken. In any case, therefore, the alteration
may amount to unlimited transformation. This is
why the finite must be called conditional rather than
conditioned. For a thing might be conditioned, and
yet, because of its conditions, might seem to stand
unshaken and secure. But the conditions of the
finite, we have seen, are otherwise. They in any
case may be such as indefinitely to dissipate its particular nature.

Every finite truth or fact to some extent must be
unreal and false, and it is impossible in the end certainly to know of any how false it may be. We
cannot know this, because the unknown extends
illimitably, and all abstraction is precarious and at
the mercy of what is not observed. If our knowledge were a system, the case would then undoubtedly be altered. With regard to everything we
should then know the place assigned to it by the
Whole, and we could measure the exact degree of
truth and falsehood which anything possessed.
With such a system there would be no outlying
region of ignorance ; and hence of all its contents
we could have a complete and exhaustive know-

---

[1] Cp. here Chapter xxiv.

ledge.   But any system of this kind seems, most
assuredly, by its essence impossible.

There are certain truths about the Absolute, which,
for the present at least,[1] we can regard as unconditional.   In this point they can be taken to differ in
kind from all subordinate truths, for with the latter
it is a question only of more or less fallibility.   They
are all liable to a possible intellectual correction, and
the amount of this possibility cannot be certainly
known.   Our power of abstraction varies widely
with different regions of knowledge, but no finite
truth (however reached) can be considered as secure.
Error with all of them is a matter of probability, and
a matter of degree.   And those are relatively true
and strong which more nearly approach to perfection.
It is this perfection which is our measure.   Our
criterion is individuality, or the idea of complete
system ; and above, in Chapter xxiv., we have already explained its nature.   And I venture to think
that about the main principle there is no great difficulty.   Difficulty is felt more when we proceed to
apply it in detail.   We saw that the principles of
internal harmony and of widest extent in the end
are the same, for they are divergent aspects of the
one idea of concrete unity.   But for a discussion of
such points the reader must return to our former
chapter.
A thing is more real as its opposite is more inconceivable.   This is part of the truth.   But, on the
other hand, the opposite is more inconceivable, or
more impossible, *because* the thing itself is more real
and more probable and more true.   The test (I
would repeat it once more here) in its essence is positive.   The stronger, the more systematic and more
fully organised, a body of knowledge becomes, so

---

[1] For a further statement see below.

much the more impossible becomes that which in any point conflicts with it. Or, from the other side, we may resume our doctrine thus. The greater the amount of knowledge which an idea or fact would, directly or indirectly, subvert, so much the more probably is it false and impossible and inconceivable. And there may be finite truths, with which error —and I mean by error here liability to intellectual correction—is most improbable. The chance may fairly be treated as too small to be worth considering. Yet after all it exists.

Finite truths are all conditional, because they all must depend on the unknown. But this unknown— the reader must bear in mind—is merely relative. Itself is subordinate to, and is included in, our absolute knowledge; and its nature, in general, is certainly not unknown. For, if it is anything at all, it is experience, and an element in the one Experience. Our ignorance, at the mercy of which all the finite lies, is not ignorance absolute. It covers and contains more than we are able to know, but this "more" is known beforehand to be still of the self-same sort. And we must now pass from the special consideration of finite truth.[1]

[1] It is impossible here to deal fully with the question how, in case of a discrepancy, we are able to correct our knowledge. We are forced indefinitely to enlarge experience, because, as it is, being finite it cannot be harmonious. Then we find a collision between some fact or idea, on the one hand, and, on the other hand, some body of recognised truth. Now the self-contradictory cannot be true; and the question is how to rearrange it so as to make it harmonious. What is it in any given case, we have to ask, which has to be sacrificed? The conflict itself may perhaps be apparent only. A mere accident may have been taken for what is essential, and, with the correction of this mistake, the whole collision may cease. Or the fresh idea may be found to be untenable. It contains an error, and is therefore broken up and resolved; or, if that is not possible, it may be provisionally set on one side and disregarded. This last course is however feasible only if we assume that our original knowledge is so strong as to stand fast and unshaken. But the opposite of this may be the case. It may be our former knowledge which, on its side, has

It is time to re-examine a distinction which we laid down above. We found that some knowledge was absolute, and that, in contrast with this, all finite truth was but conditional. But, when we examine it more closely, this difference seems hard to maintain. For how can truth be true absolutely, if there remains a gulf between itself and reality? Now in any truth about Reality the word "about" is too significant. There remains always something outside, and other than, the predicate. And, because of this which is outside, the predicate, in the end, may be called conditional. In brief, the difference between subject and predicate, a difference essential to truth, is not accounted for.[1] It depends on something not included within the judgment itself, an element outlying and, therefore, in a sense unknown. The type and the essence, in other words, can never reach the reality. The essence realized, we may say, is too much to be truth, and, unrealized and abstract, it is assuredly too little to be real. Even absolute truth in the end seems thus to turn out erroneous.

And it must be admitted that, in the end, no possible truth is quite true. It is a partial and inadequate translation of that which it professes to give bodily. And this internal discrepancy belongs

to give way, and must be modified and over-ruled by the fresh experience. But, last of all, there is a further possibility which remains. Neither of our conflicting pieces of knowledge may be able to stand as true. Each may be true enough to satisfy and to serve, for some purposes, and at a certain level; and yet both, viewed from above, can be seen to be conflicting errors. Both must therefore be resolved to the point required, and must be re-arranged as elements in a wider whole. Separation of the accidents from the essence must here be carried on until the essence itself is more or less dissolved. I have no space to explain, or to attempt to illustrate, this general statement.

[1] The essential inconsistency of truth may, perhaps, be best stated thus. If there is any difference between *what it means* and *what it stands for*, then truth is clearly not realized. But, if there is no such difference, then truth has ceased to exist.

irremoveably to truth's proper character. Still the difference drawn between absolute and finite truth must none the less be upheld. For the former, in a word, is not *intellectually* corrigible. There is no intellectual alteration which could possibly, as general truth, bring it nearer to ultimate Reality. We have seen that any suggestion of this kind is but self-destructive, that any doubt on this point is literally senseless. Absolute truth is corrected only by passing outside the intellect. It is modified only by taking in the remaining aspects of experience. But in this passage the proper nature of truth is, of course, transformed and perishes.

Any finite truth, on the other side, remains subject to intellectual correction. It is incomplete not merely as being confined by its general nature, as truth, within one partial aspect of the Whole. It is incomplete as having within its own intellectual world a space falling outside it. There is truth, actual or possible, which is over against it, and which can stand outside it as an Other. But with absolute truth there is no intellectual outside. There is no competing predicate which could conceivably qualify its subject, and which could come in to condition and to limit its assertion. Absolute knowledge may be conditional, if you please; but its condition is not any *other* truth, whether actual or possible.

The doctrine, which I am endeavouring to state, is really simple. Truth is one aspect of experience, and is therefore made imperfect and limited by what it fails to include. So far as it is absolute, it does however give the general type and character of all that possibly can be true or real. And the universe in this general character is known completely. It is not known, and it never can be known, in all its details. It is not known, and it never, as a whole, can be known, in such a sense that knowledge would be the same as experience or reality.

A. R.   N N

For knowledge and truth—if we suppose them to possess that identity—would have been, therewith, absorbed and transmuted. But on the other hand the universe does not exist, and it cannot possibly exist, as truth or knowledge, in such a way as not to be contained and included in the truth we call absolute. For, to repeat it once more, such a possibility is self-destructive. We may perhaps say that, if *per impossibile* this could be possible, we at least could not possibly entertain the idea of it. For such an idea, in being entertained, vanishes into its opposite or into nonsense. Absolute truth is error only if you expect from it more that mere general knowledge. It is abstract,[1] and fails to supply its own subordinate details. It is one-sided, and cannot give bodily all sides of the Whole. But on the other side nothing, so far as it goes, can fall outside it. It is utterly all-inclusive and contains beforehand all that could ever be set against it. For nothing can be set against it, which does not become intellectual, and itself enter as a vassal into the kingdom of truth. Thus, even when you go beyond it, you can never advance outside it. When you take in more, you are condemned to take in more of the self-same sort. The universe, as truth, in other words preserves one character, and of that character we possess infallible knowledge.

And, if we view the matter from another side, there is no opposition between Reality and truth. Reality, to be complete, must take in and absorb this partial aspect of itself. And truth itself would

[1] It is not abstract in the way in which we have seen that all finite truth is abstract. That was precarious intellectually, since, more or less, it left other truth outside and over against it. It was thus always one piece among other pieces of the world of truth. It could be added to, intellectually, so as to be transformed. Absolute truth, on the other hand, cannot be altered by the addition of any truth. There is no possible truth which does not fall under it as one of its own details. Unless you presuppose it, in short, no other truth remains truth at all.

not be complete, until it took in and included all aspects of the universe. Thus, in passing beyond itself and in abolishing the difference between its subject and predicate, it does but carry out the demands of its proper nature. But I may perhaps hope that this conclusion has been sufficiently secured (Chapters xv., xxiv., xxvi.). To repeat—in its general character Reality is present in knowledge and truth, that absolute truth which is distinguished and brought out by metaphysics. But this general character of Reality is not Reality itself, and again it is not more than the general character even of truth and knowledge. Still, so far as there is any truth and any knowledge at all, this character is absolute. Truth is conditional, but it cannot be intellectually transcended. To fill in its conditions would be to pass into a whole beyond mere intellect.

The conclusion which we have reached, I trust, the outcome of no mere compromise, makes a claim to reconcile extremes. Whether it is to be called Realism or Idealism I do not know, and I have not cared to enquire. It neither puts ideas and thought first, nor again does it permit us to assert that any-thing else by itself is more real. Truth is the whole world in one aspect, an aspect supreme in philosophy, and yet even in philosophy conscious of its own incompleteness. So far again as our conclusion has claimed infallibility, it has come, I think, into no collision with the better kind of com-mon sense. That metaphysics should approve itself to common sense is indeed out of the question. For neither in its processes nor in its results can it ex-pect, or even hope, to be generally intelligible. But it is no light thing, except for the thoughtless, to advocate metaphysical results which, if they *were* understood by common sense, would at once be rejected. I do not mean that on subordinate points, such as the personality of the Deity or or a continu-

such a way that the system made, when understood, strikes the mind as one-sided, is enough of itself to inspire hesitation and doubt. On this head at least, our main result is, I hope, satisfactory. The absolute knowledge that we have claimed is no more than an outline. It is knowledge which seems sufficient, on one side, to secure the chief interests of our nature, and it abstains, on the other side, from pretensions which all must feel are not human. We insist that all Reality must keep a certain character. The whole of its contents must be experience, they must come together into one system, and this unity itself must be experience. It must include and must harmonize every possible fragment of appearance. Anything which in any sense can be more than and beyond what we possess, must still inevitably be more of the self-same kind. We persist in this conclusion, and we urge that, so far as it goes, it amounts to absolute knowledge. But this conclusion on the other side, I have pointed out, does not go very far. It leaves us free to admit that what we know is, after all, nothing in proportion to the world of our ignorance. We do not know what other modes of experience may exist, or, in comparison with ours, how many they may be. We do not know, except in vague outline, what the Unity is, or, at all, why it appears in our particular forms of plurality. We can even understand that such knowledge is impossible, and we have found the reason why it is so. For truth can know only, we may say, so far as itself is. And the union of all sides of our nature would not leave them, in any case, as they are. Truth, when made adequate to Reality, would be so supplemented as to have become something else—something other than truth, and something for us unattainable. We have thus left due space for the exercise of doubt and wonder. We admit the healthy scepticism for which all knowledge in a sense is vanity, which feels in its heart that science is a poor thing if measured by the wealth of the real universe. We justify the natural wonder which delights to stray beyond our daylight world, and to follow paths that lead into half-known half-unknowable regions. Our conclusion, in brief, has explained and has confirmed the irresistible impression that all is beyond us.

Everything is error, but everything is not illusion. It is error where, and in so far as, our ideas are not the same as reality. It is illusion where, and in so far as, this difference turns to a conflict in our nature. Where experience, inward or outward, clashes with our views, where there arises thus disorder confusion and pain, we may speak of illusion. It is the course of events in collision with the set of our ideas. Now error, in the sense of one-sided and partial truth, is necessary to our being. Indeed nothing else, so to speak, could be relative to our needs, nothing else could answer the purpose of truth. And, to suit the divergent aspects of our inconsistent finite lives, a variety of error in the shape of diverse partial truths is required. And, if things could be otherwise, then, so far as we see, finite life would be impossible. Therefore we must have error present always, and this presence entails some amount of illusion. Finite beings, themselves not self-consistent, have to realize their various aspects in the chance-world of temporal events. And hence ideas and existence cannot precisely correspond, while the want of this correspondence must to some extent mean illusion. There are finite souls, we must admit sadly, to whom, on the whole, life has proved a disappointment and cheat. There is perhaps no one to whom, at certain moments and in some respect, this conclusion has not come home. But that, in general and in the main, life is illusory cannot be rationally maintained. And if, in general and in the rough, our ideas are answered by events, that is all surely which, as finite beings, we have a right to expect. We must reply then, that, though illusions exist here and there, the whole is not an illusion. We are not concerned to gain an absolute experience which for us, emphatically, could be nothing. We want to know, in effect, whether the universe is concealed behind appearances, and is making a sport of us. What we find here truer and more beautiful and better and higher—are these things really so, or in reality may they be all quite otherwise? Our standard, in other words, is it a false appearance not owned by the universe? And to this, in general, we may make an unhesitating reply. There is no reality at all anywhere except in appearance, and in our appearance we can discover the main nature of reality. This nature cannot be exhausted, but it can be known in abstract. And it is, really and indeed, this general character of the very universe itself which distinguishes for us the relative worth of appearances. We make mistakes, but still we use the essential nature of the world as our own criterion of value and reality. Higher, truer, more beautiful, better and more real—these, on the whole, count in the universe as they count for us. And existence, on the whole, must correspond with our ideas. For, on the whole, higher means for us a greater amount of that one Reality, outside of which all appearance is absolutely nothing.

It costs little to find that in the end Reality is inscrutable. It is easy to perceive that any appearance, not being the Reality, in a sense is fallacious. These truths, such as they are, are within the reach of any and every man. It is a simple matter to conclude further, perhaps, that the Real sits apart, that it keeps state by itself and does not descend into phenomena. Or it is as cheap, again, to take up another side of the same error. The Reality is viewed perhaps as immanent in all its appearances, in such a way that it is, alike and equally, present in all. Everything is so worthless on one hand, so divine on the other, that nothing can be viler or can be more sublime than anything else. It is against both sides of this mistake, it is against this empty transcendence and this shallow Pantheism, that our pages may be called one sustained polemic. The positive relation of every appearance as an adjective to Reality, and the presence of Reality among its appearances in different degrees and with diverse values—this double truth we have found to be the centre of philosophy. It is because the Absolute is no sundered abstraction but has a positive character, it is because this Absolute itself is positively present in all appearance, that appearances themselves can possess true differences of value. And, apart from this foundation, in the end we are left without a solid criterion of worth or of truth or reality. This conclusion—the necessity on one side for a standard, and the impossibility of reaching it without a positive knowledge of the Absolute—I would venture to press upon any intelligent worshipper of the Unknown.

The Reality itself is nothing at all apart from appearances.[1] It is in the end nonsense to talk of realities—or of anything else—to which appearances could appear, or between which they somehow could hang as relations. Such realities (we have seen) would themselves be appearances or nothing. For there is no way of qualifying the Real except by appearances, and outside the Real there remains no space in which appearances could live. Reality

[1] For the meaning of appearance see, in particular, Chapter xxvi.

appears in its appearances, and they are its revelation; and otherwise they also could be nothing whatever. The Reality comes into knowledge, and, the more we know of anything, the more in one way is Reality present within us. The Reality is our criterion of worse and better, of ugliness and beauty, of true and false, and of real and unreal. It in brief decides between, and gives a general meaning to, higher and lower. It is because of this criterion that appearances differ in worth; and, without it, lowest and highest would, for all we know, count the same in the universe. And Reality is one Experience, self-pervading and superior to mere relations. Its character is the opposite of that fabled extreme which is barely mechanical, and it is, in the end, the sole perfect realisation of spirit. We may fairly close this work then by insisting that Reality is spiritual. There is a great saying of Hegel's, a saying too well known, and one which without some explanation I should not like to endorse. But I will end with something not very different, something perhaps more certainly the essential message of Hegel. Outside of spirit there is not, and there cannot be, any reality, and, the more that anything is spiritual, so much the more is it veritably real.

APPENDIX.

INTRODUCTION.

INSTEAD of attempting a formal reply in detail to a number of criticisms, I have thought it more likely to assist the reader if I offer first some brief explanations as to the main doctrines of my book, and then follow these by a more particular notice of certain difficulties. My selection of the points discussed is, I fear, to some extent arbitrary, but I will ask my critics not to assume, where they fail to find a recognition of their objections, that I have treated these with disrespect.

I. With regard to the arrangement of my work I offer no defence. It was not in my power to write a systematic treatise, and, that being so, I thought the way I took was as good as any other. The order of the book seemed to myself a matter of no great importance. So far as I can see, whatever way I had taken the result would have been the same, and I must doubt if any other way would have been better for most readers. From whatever point we had begun we should have found ourselves entangled in the same puzzles, and have been led to attempt the same way of escape. The arrangement of the book does not correspond to the order of my thoughts, and the same would have been true of any other arrangement which it was in my power to adopt. I might very well, for instance, have started with the self as a given unity, and have asked how far any other things are real otherwise, and how far again the self satisfies its own demands on reality. Or I might have begun with the fact of knowledge and have enquired what in the end that involves, or I could once more readily have taken my departure from the ground of volition or desire. None of these ways would to myself have been really inconvenient, and they would all have led to the same end. But to satisfy at once the individual preference of each reader was not possible, nor am I sure that in the end the reader really is helped by starting on the road which he prefers. The want of system in my book is however another matter, and this I admit and regret.

II. The actual starting-point and basis of this work is an assumption about truth and reality. I have assumed that the object of metaphysics is to find a general view which will satisfy the intellect, and I have assumed that whatever succeeds in doing this is real and true, and that whatever fails is neither. This is a doctrine which, so far as I see, can neither be proved nor questioned. The proof or the question, it seems to me, must imply the truth of the doctrine, and, if that is not assumed, both vanish. And I see no advantage in dwelling further on this point.[1]

III. But with this we come against the great problem of the relation of Thought to Reality. For if we decline (as I think wrongly) to affirm that all truth is thought, yet we certainly cannot deny this of a great deal of truth, and we can hardly deny that truth satisfies the intellect. But, if so, truth therefore, as we have seen, is real. And to hold that truth is real, not because it is true but because also it is something else, seems untenable; for, if so, the something else left outside would make incomplete and would hence falsify the truth. But then, on the other hand, can thought, however complete, be the same as reality, the same altogether, I mean, and with no difference between them? This is a question to which I could never give an affirmative reply. It is useless here to seek to prove that the real involves thought as its *sine quâ non*, for that much, when proved, does not carry the conclusion. And it is useless again to urge that thought is so inseparable from every mode of experience that in the end it may be said to cover all the ground. That is, it seems to me, once more merely the inconclusive argument from the *sine quâ non*, or else the conclusion is vitiated from another side by the undue extension of thought's meaning. Thought has now been taken, that is, to include so much more than truth in the narrow sense, that the old question as to how truth in this sense stands to reality, must break out more or less within thought itself. Nor again does it seem clear why we must term this whole 'thought,' and not 'feeling,' or 'will,' unless we can show that these really are modes of thought while thought cannot fall under them. For otherwise our conclusion seems but verbal and arbitrary; and again an argument drawn from the mere hegemony of thought could not prove the required conclusion.

But with this we are left, it appears, in a dilemma. There is a difference between on the one side truth or thought (it will be convenient now to identify these), and on the other side reality. But to assert this difference seems impossible without somehow transcending thought or bringing the difference into thought, and these phrases seem meaningless. Thus reality appears to be an Other different from truth and yet not able to be truly taken as different; and this dilemma to myself was long a main cause of perplexity and doubt. We indeed do something to solve it

---

[1] On the subject of the order of thought in my work I further refer the reader to Note A in this Appendix.

by the identification of being or reality with experience or with sentience in its widest meaning. This step I have taken without hesitation, and I will not add a further defence of it here. The most serious objection to it is raised, I think, from the side of Solipsism, and I have treated that at length. But this step by itself leaves us far from the desired solution of our dilemma; for between facts of experience and the thought of them and the truth about them the difference still remains, and the difficulty which attaches to this difference.

The solution of this dilemma offered in Chapter XV is, I believe, the only solution possible. It contains the main thesis of this work, views opposed to that thesis remaining, it seems to me, caught in and destroyed by the dilemma. And we must notice two main features in this doctrine. It contends on one side that truth or thought essentially does not satisfy its own claims, that it demands to be, and so far already is, something which completely it cannot be. Hence if thought carried out its own nature, it both would and would not have passed beyond itself and become also an Other. And in the second place this self-completion of thought, by inclusion of the aspects opposed to mere thinking, would be what we mean by reality, and by reality we can mean no more than this. The criticisms on this doctrine which I have seen, do not appear to me to rest on any serious enquiry either as to what the demands of thought really are, or what their satisfaction involves. But if to satisfy the intellect is to be true and real, such a question must be fundamental.

IV. With the solution of this problem about truth comes the whole view of Reality. Reality is above thought and above every partial aspect of being, but it includes them all. Each of these completes itself by uniting with the rest, and so makes the perfection of the whole. And this whole is experience, for anything other than experience is meaningless. Now anything that in any sense 'is,' qualifies the absolute reality and so is real. But on the other hand, because everything, to complete itself and to satisfy its own claims, must pass beyond itself, nothing in the end is real except the Absolute. Everything else is appearance; it is that the character of which goes beyond its own existence, is inconsistent with it and transcends it. And viewed intellectually appearance is error. But the remedy lies in supplementation by inclusion of that which is both outside and yet essential, and in the Absolute this remedy is perfected. There is no mere appearance or utter chance or absolute error, but all is relative. And the degree of reality is measured by the amount of supplementation required in each case, and by the extent to which the completion of anything entails its own destruction as such.[1]

V. But this Absolute, it has been objected, is a mere blank or else unintelligible. Certainly it is unintelligible if that means

---

[1] On the question of degrees of appearance see more in § VII.

that you cannot understand its detail, and that throughout its structure constantly in particular you are unable to answer the question, Why or How. And that it is not in this sense intelligible I have clearly laid down. But as to its main character we must return a different reply. We start from the diversity in unity which is given in feeling, and we develop this internally by the principle of self-completion beyond self, until we reach the idea of an all-inclusive and supra-relational experience. This idea, it seems to me, is in the abstract intelligible and positive, and so once more is the principle by which it is reached; and the criticism which takes these as mere negations rests, I think, on misunderstanding. The criticism which really desires to be effective ought, I should say, to show that my view of the starting-point is untenable, and the principle of development, together with its result, unsound, and such criticism I have not yet seen. But with regard to what is unintelligible and inexplicable we must surely distinguish. A theory may contain what is unintelligible, so long as it really contains it; and not to know how a thing can be is no disproof of our knowing that it both must be and is. The whole question is whether we have a general principle under which the details can and must fall, or whether, on the other hand, the details fall outside or are negative instances which serve to upset the principle. Now I have argued in detail that there are no facts which fall outside the principle or really are negative instances; and hence, because the principle is undeniable, the facts both must and can comply with it, and therefore they do so. And given a knowledge of 'how' in general, a mere ignorance of 'how' in detail is permissible and harmless.[1] This argument in its general character is, I presume, quite familiar even to those critics who seem to have been surprised by it; and the application of it here is, so far as I see, legitimate and necessary. And for that application I must refer to the body of the work.

VI. With regard to the unity of the Absolute we know that the Absolute must be one, because anything experienced is experienced in or as a whole, and because anything like independent plurality or external relations cannot satisfy the intellect. And it fails to satisfy the intellect because it is a self-contradiction. Again for the same reason the Absolute is one system in the very highest sense of that term, any lower sense being unreal because in the end self-contradictory. The subjects of contradiction and of external relations are further dealt with in a later part of this Appendix, Notes A and B.

---

[1] In this connection I may quote a passage from Stricker, *Bewegungsvorstellungen*, s. 35, Ein Lehrsatz wird nicht dadurch erschüttert, dass Jemand einherkommt, und uns von einer Beobachtung berichtet, die er mit Hilfe dieses Lehrsatzes nicht zu deuten vermag. Erschüttert wird ein Lehrsatz durch eine neue Beobachtung nur dann, wenn·sich zeigen lässt, dass sie ihm geradezu widerspricht.

VII. I will go on to notice an objection which has been made by several critics. It is expressed in the following extract from the *Philosophical Review*, Vol. iv. p. 235: "All phenomena are regarded as infected with the same contradiction, in that they all involve a union of the One and the Many. It is therefore impossible to apply the notion of Degrees of Truth and Reality. If all appearances are equally contradictory, all are equally incapable of aiding us to get nearer to the ultimate nature of Reality." And it is added that on this point there seems to be a consensus of opinion among my critics.

Now I think I must have failed to understand the exact nature of this point, since, as I understand it, it offers no serious difficulty. In fact this matter, I may say, is for good or for evil so old and so familiar to my mind that it did not occur to me as a difficulty at all, and so was not noticed. But suppose that in theology I say that all men before God, and measured by him, are equally sinful—does that preclude me from also holding that one is worse or better than another? And if I accept the fact of degrees in virtue, may I not believe also that virtue is one and is perfection and that you must attain to it or not? And is all this really such a hopeless puzzle? Suppose that for a certain purpose I want a stick exactly one yard long, am I wrong when I condemn both one inch and thirty-five inches, and any possible sum of inches up to thirty-six, as equally and alike coming short? Surely if you view perfection and completeness in one way, it is a case of either Yes or No, you have either reached it or not, and there either is defect or there is none. But in the imperfect, viewed otherwise, there is already more or less of a quality or character, the self-same character which, if all defect were removed, would attain to and itself would be perfection. Wherever there is a scale of degrees you may treat the steps of this as being more or less perfect, or again you may say, No they are none of them perfect, and so regarded they are equal, and there is no difference between them. That indeed is what must happen when you ask of each whether it is perfect or not.

This question of Yes or No I asked about appearances in connection with Reality, and I have in my book used language which certainly contradicts itself, unless the reader perceives that there is more than one point of view. And I assumed that the reader would perceive this, and I cannot doubt that very often he has done so, and I think that even always he might have done so, if he would but carry into metaphysics all the ideas with which he is acquainted outside, and not an arbitrary selection from them. And among the ideas to be thus treated not as true but as at least existing, I would instance specially some leading ideas of the Christian religion as to freedom, the

worth of mere morality, and the independent self-sufficiency of
finite persons and things. For myself, though I have not
hesitated to point out the falsity and immorality of some
Christian doctrines (where this seemed necessary), I cannot
approve of the widespread practice of treating them as devoid
even of existence.

But if, after all, my critics had in view not the above but
something else, and if the objection means that I do not
explain why and how there is any diversity and anything like
degree at all, I am at no loss for a reply. I answer that I
make no pretence to do this. But on the other side I have
urged again and again that a general conclusion is not upset
by a failure to explain in detail, unless that detail can be shown
to be a negative instance.

If finally the use of the phrase "mere appearance" has
caused difficulty, that has been I think already explained above.
This phrase gets its meaning by contrast with the Absolute.
When you ask about any appearance unconditionally whether
it is Reality or not, Yes or No, you are forced to reply No, and
you may express that unconditional No by using the word
'mere.' At least one of my critics would, I think, have done
well if, before instructing me as to the impossibility of any mere
appearance, he had consulted my index under the head of Error.

I must end by saying that, on this question of degrees of
appearance and reality, I have found but little to which my
critics can fairly object, unless their position is this, that of
two proper and indispensable points of view I have unduly
emphasized one. Whether I have done this or not I will not
attempt to decide, but, if this is what my critics have meant,
I cannot felicitate them on their method of saying it.

But I would once more express my regret that I was not able
to deal systematically with the various forms of appearance. If I
had done this, it would have become clear that, and how, each
form is true as well as untrue, and that there is an evolution of
truth. We should have seen that each really is based on, and is
an attempt to realize, the same principle, a principle which is not
wholly satisfied by any, and which condemns each because each
is an inadequate appearance of itself.

VIII. I must now touch briefly on a point of greater difficulty.
Why, it has been asked, have I not identified the Absolute with
the Self? Now, as I have already remarked, my whole view may
be taken as based on the self; nor again could I doubt that
a self, or a system of selves, is the highest thing that we have.
But when it is proposed to term the Absolute 'self,' I am compelled to pause. In order to reach the idea of the Absolute our
finite selves must suffer so much addition and so much subtraction that it becomes a grave question whether the result can
be covered by the name of 'self.' When you carry out the idea

of a self or of a system of selves beyond a certain point, when, that is to say, you have excluded, as such, all finitude and change and chance and mutability—have you not in fact carried your idea really beyond its proper application? I am forced to think that this is so, and I also know no reason why it should not be so. The claim of the individual, as such, to perfection I wholly reject. And the argument that, if you scruple to say 'self,' you are therefore condemned to accept something lower, seems to me thoroughly unsound. I have contended that starting from the self one can advance to a positive result beyond it, and my contention surely is not met by such a bare unreasoned assumption of its falsity. And if finally I hear, Well, you yourself admit that the Absolute is unintelligible; why then object to saying that the Absolute somehow unintelligibly is self and the self is somehow unintelligibly absolute?—that gives me no trouble. For the Absolute, though in detail unintelligible, is not so in general, and its general character comes as a consequence from a necessary principle. And against this consequence we have to set nothing but privation and ignorance. But to make the self, as such, absolute is, so far as I see, to postulate in the teeth of facts, facts which go to show that the self's character is gone when it ceases to be relative. And this postulate itself, I must insist, is no principle at all, but is a mere prejudice and misunderstanding. And the claim of this postulate, if made, should in my opinion be made openly and explicitly. But as to the use of the word 'self,' so long only as we know what we mean and do not mean by it, I am far from being irreconcilable. I am of course opposed to any attempt to set up the finite self as in any sense ultimately real, or again as real at all outside of the temporal series. And I am opposed once more to any kind of attempt to make the distinction between 'experience' and 'the experienced' more than relative. But on these and on other points I do not think that it would prove useful to enlarge further.

IX. I will now briefly touch on my attitude towards Scepticism. Most persons, I think, who have read my book intelligently, will credit me with a desire to do justice to scepticism; and indeed I might claim, perhaps, myself to be something of a sceptic. But with all my desire I, of course, may very well have failed; and it would be to me most instructive if I could see an examination of my last Chapter by some educated and intelligent sceptic. Up to the present, however, nothing of the kind has been brought to my notice; and perhaps the sceptical temper does not among us often go with addiction to metaphysics. And I venture to think this a misfortune. Intellectual scepticism certainly is not one thing with a sceptical temper, and it is (if I may repeat myself) "the result only of labour and education."

That, it seems, is not the opinion of the writer in *Mind* (N. S., No. 11), who has come forward as the true representative of the sceptics. He will, perhaps, not be surprised when I question his right to that position, and when I express my conviction of his ignorance as to what true scepticism is. His view of scepticism is, in brief, that it consists in asking, "But what do you mean?" The idea apparently has not occurred to him that to question or doubt intelligently you must first understand. If I, for instance, who know no mathematics, were to reiterate about some treatise on the calculus, "But what does it mean?" I should hardly in this way have become a sceptic mathematically. Scepticism of this kind is but a malady of childhood, and is known as one symptom of imbecility, and it surely has no claim to appear as a philosophical attitude.

If about any theory you desire to ask intelligently the question, "What does it mean?" you must be prepared, I should have thought, to enter into that theory. And attempting to enter into it you are very liable, in raising your doubts, to base yourself tacitly on some dogma which the theory in question has given its reason for rejecting. And to avoid such crude dogmatism is not given to every man who likes to call himself a sceptic. And it is given to no man, I would repeat, without labour and education.

But in the article which I have cited there is, apart from this absurd idea about scepticism, nothing we need notice. There are some mistakes and failures to comprehend of an ordinary type, coupled with some mere dogmatism of an uninteresting kind. And it is to myself a matter of regret that generally in this point I have been helped so little by my critics, and am compelled (if I may use the expression) still to do most of my scepticism for myself.[1]

X. The doctrine of this work has been condemned as failing to satisfy the claims of our nature, and has been charged with being after all no better than "Agnosticism." Now without discussing the meaning of this term—a subject in which I am not much at home—I should like to insist on what to me seems capital. According to the doctrine of this work that which is highest to us is also in and to the Universe most real, and there can be no question of its reality being somehow upset. In common-place Materialism, on the other hand, that which in the end is real is certainly not what we think highest, this latter being a secondary and, for all we know, a precarious result of the former. And again, if we embrace mere ignorance, we are in the position that, for anything we know, our highest beliefs are illusions, or at any moment may become so, and at any moment

---

[1] I may mention here that to a criticism of this work by Mr. Ward, in *Mind*, N. S., No. 9, I, perhaps hastily, replied in the next number of that journal. I should doubt if in the criticism or the reply anything calls for the reader's attention, but, if he desires to see them, I have given the reference.

may be brought to nought by something—we do not know what. And I submit that the difference between such doctrines and those of this work is really considerable.

And if I am told that generally the doctrines of this book fail to satisfy our nature's demands, I would request first a plain answer to a question which, I think, is plain. Am I to understand that somehow we are to have all that we want and have it just as we want it? For myself I should reply that such a satisfaction seems to me impossible. But I do not feel called on to criticise this demand, until I see it stated explicitly; and at present I merely press for a plain answer to my question.

And if the real question is not this, and if it concerns only the satisfaction somehow of our nature's main claims, I do not see that, as compared with other views about the world, the view of this work is inferior. I am supposing it to be compared of course only with views that aim at theoretical consistency, and not with mere practical beliefs. Practical beliefs, we know, are regulated by working efficiency. They emphasize one point here, and they suppress another point there, without much care to avoid a theoretical self-contradiction. And working beliefs of any kind, I imagine, can more or less exist under and together with any kind of theoretical doctrine. The comparison I have in view here is of another order, and would be made between doctrines each of which claimed to be a true and consistent account of the whole of things. Such a comparison I do not propose to make, since it would require much space, and, while perhaps serving little purpose otherwise, could not fail to give great offence. But there are two conditions of any fair comparison on which I would insist. In a question about the satisfaction of our nature all the aspects of that nature must first be set forth, and not a one-sided distortion of these or an arbitrary selection from them. And in the second place every side of the doctrines compared must be stated without suppression of any features that may be found inconvenient. For every view of the world, we must all agree, has its own special difficulties. Where, for instance, from a theistic or a Christian point of view a writer condemns, say, a "naturalistic" account of good and evil—would that writer, if he had a desire for fairness and truth, fail to recall the fact that his own view also has been morally condemned? Would he forget that the relation of an omniscient moral Creator to the things of his hand has given trouble intellectually, and is morally perhaps not from all sides "comfortable?" His attitude, I judge, would be otherwise, and this judgment, I submit, is that of every fair-minded man, whatever doctrines otherwise he may hold. Nothing is easier than to make a general attack on any doctrine while the alternative is ignored, and few things, I would add, are, at least in philosophy, less profitable. With this I will pass to a special treatment of some difficult problems.

A. R.   O O

Note A.   Contradiction, and the Contrary.[1]

If we are asked "What is contrary or contradictory?" (I do not find it necessary here to distinguish between these), the more we consider the more difficult we find it to answer. "A thing cannot be or do two opposites at once and in the same respect"— this reply at first sight may seem clear, but on reflection may threaten us with an unmeaning circle. For what are "opposites" except the adjectives which the thing cannot so combine? Hence we have said no more than that we in fact find predicates which in fact will not go together, and our further introduction of their "opposite" nature seems to add nothing. "Opposites will not unite, and their apparent union is mere appearance." But the mere appearance really perhaps only lies in their intrinsic opposition. And if one arrangement has made them opposite, a wider arrangement may perhaps unmake their opposition, and may include them all at once and harmoniously. Are, in short, opposites really opposite at all, or are they, after all, merely different? Let us attempt to take them in this latter character.

"A thing cannot without an internal distinction be (or do[2]) two different things, and differences cannot belong to the same thing in the same point unless in that point there is diversity. The appearance of such a union may be fact, but is for thought a contradiction." This is the thesis which to me seems to contain the truth about the contrary, and I will now try to recommend this thesis to the reader.

The thesis in the first place does not imply that the end which we seek is tautology. Thought most certainly does not demand mere sameness, which to it would be nothing. A bare tautology (Hegel has taught us this, and I wish we could all learn it) is not even so much as a poor truth or a thin truth. It is not a truth in any way, in any sense, or at all. Thought involves analysis and synthesis, and if the Law of Contradiction forbade diversity, it would forbid thinking altogether. And with this too necessary warning I will turn to the other side of the difficulty. Thought cannot do without differences, but on the other hand it cannot make them. And, as it cannot make them, so it cannot receive them merely from the outside and ready-made. Thought demands to go *proprio motu*, or, what is the same thing, with a ground and reason. Now to pass from A to B, if the ground remains external, is for thought to pass with no ground

---

[1] Reprinted with omissions from *Mind*, N.S., No 20,
[2] This addition is superfluous.

at all. But if, again, the external fact of A's and B's conjunction is offered as a reason, then that conjunction itself creates the same difficulty. For thought's analysis can respect nothing, nor is there any principle by which at a certain point it should arrest itself or be arrested. Every distinguishable aspect becomes therefore for thought a diverse element to be brought to unity. Hence thought can no more pass without a reason from A or from B to its conjunction, than before it could pass groundlessly from A to B. The transition, being offered as a mere datum, or effected as a mere fact, is not thought's own self-movement. Or in other words, because for thought no ground can be merely external, the passage is groundless. Thus A and B and their conjunction are, like atoms, pushed in from the outside by chance or fate ; and what is thought to do with them but either make or accept an arrangement which to it is wanton and without reason,—or, having no reason for anything else, attempt against reason to identify them simply?

"This is not so," I shall be told, "and the whole case is otherwise. There are certain ultimate complexes given to us as facts, and these ultimates, as they are given, thought simply takes up as principles and employs them to explain the detail of the world. And with this process thought is satisfied." To me such a doctrine is quite erroneous. For these ultimates (a) cannot make the world intelligible, and again (b) they are not given, and (c) in themselves they are self-contradictory, and not truth but appearance.

Certainly for practice we have to work with appearance and with relative untruths, and without these things the sciences of course would not exist. There is, I suppose, here no question about all this, and all this is irrelevant. The question here is whether with so much as this the intellect can be satisfied, or whether on the other hand it does not find in the end defect and self-contradiction. Consider first (a) the failure of what is called "explanation." The principles taken up are not merely in themselves not rational, but, being limited, they remain external to the facts to be explained. The diversities therefore will only *fall*, or rather must be *brought*, under the principle. They do not come out of it, nor of themselves do they bring themselves under it. The explanation therefore in the end does but conjoin aliens inexplicably. The obvious instance is the mechanical interpretation of the world. Even if here the principles were rational intrinsically, as surely they are not, they express but one portion of a complex whole. The rest therefore, even when and where it has been "brought under" the principles, is but conjoined with them externally and for no known reason. Hence in the explanation there is in the end neither self-evidence nor any "because" except that brutally things come so.

"But in any case," I may hear, "these complexes are given and do not contradict themselves," and let us take these points in their order. (*b*) The transition from *A* to *B*, the inherence of *b* and *c* as adjectives in *A*, the union of discretion and continuity in time and space—"such things are facts," it is said. "They are given to an intellect which is satisfied to accept and to employ them." They may be facts, I reply, in some sense of that word, but to say that, as such and in and by themselves, they are given is erroneous. What is given is a presented whole, a sensuous total in which these characters are found; and beyond and beside these characters there is always given something else. And to urge "but at any rate these characters are there," is surely futile. For certainly they are not, when there, as they are when you by an abstraction have taken them out. Your contention is that certain ultimate conjunctions of elements are given. And I reply that no such *bare* conjunction is or possibly can be given. For the background is present, and the background and the conjunction are, I submit, alike integral aspects of the fact. The background therefore must be taken as a condition of the conjunction's existence, and the intellect must assert the conjunction subject in this way to a condition. The conjunction is hence not bare but dependent, and it is really a connection mediated by something falling outside it. A thing, for example, with its adjectives can never be simply given. It is given integrally with a mass of other features, and when it is affirmed of Reality it is affirmed of Reality qualified by this presented background. And this Reality (to go further) is and must be qualified also by what transcends any one presentation. Hence the mere complex, alleged to be given to the intellect, is really a selection made by or accepted by that intellect. An abstraction cuts away a mass of environing particulars, and offers the residue bare, as something given and to be accepted free from supporting conditions. And for working purposes such an artifice is natural and necessary, but to offer it as ultimate fact seems to me to be monstrous. We have an intellectual product, to be logically justified, if indeed that could be possible, and most certainly we have not a genuine datum.

At this point we may lay down an important result. The intellect cannot be reduced to choose between accepting an irrational conjunction or rejecting something given. For the intellect can always accept the conjunction not as bare but as a connection, the bond of which is at present unknown. It is taken therefore as by itself appearance which is less or more false in proportion as the unknown conditions, if filled in, less or more would swamp and transform it. The intellect therefore while rejecting whatever is alien to itself, if offered as absolute, can accept the inconsistent if taken as subject to conditions.

Beside absolute truth there is relative truth, useful opinion, and validity, and to this latter world belong so-called non-rational facts.[1]

(*c*) And any mere conjunction, I go on to urge, is for thought self-contradictory. Thought, I may perhaps assume, implies analysis and synthesis and distinction in unity. Further the mere conjunction offered to thought cannot be set apart itself as something sacred, but may itself properly and indeed must become thought's object. There will be a passage therefore from one element in this conjunction to its other element or elements. And on the other hand, by its own nature, thought must hold these in unity. But, in a bare conjunction, starting with *A* thought will externally be driven to *B*, and seeking to unite these it will find no ground of union. Thought can of itself supply no internal bond by which to hold them together, nor has it any internal diversity by which to maintain them apart. It must therefore seek barely to identify them, though they are different, or somehow to unite both diversities where it has no ground of distinction and union. And this does not mean that the connection is merely unknown and may be affirmed as unknown, and also, supposing it were known, as rational. For, if so, the conjunction would at once not be bare, and it is as bare that it is offered and not as conditional. But, if on the other hand it remains bare, then thought to affirm it must unite diversities without any internal distinction, and the attempt to do this is precisely what contradiction means.

"But," I shall be told, "you misrepresent the case. What is offered is not the elements apart, nor the elements plus an external bond, but the elements together and in conjunction."

---

[1] I use "validity" much in the sense in which it was made current, I believe, by Lotze, and in which it has been said, I presume, with some truth, partly to coincide with δόξα. For my own purposes I have tried elsewhere to fix the meaning of the term, and I think it would have been better if Mr. Hobhouse, in his interesting and most instructive volume on *The Theory of Knowledge*, had remembered, when concerned with myself, that what is self-contradictory may also for me be valid. I should find it in general very difficult to reply to Mr. Hobhouse's criticisms on my views, because in so many places I have to doubt if I can have apprehended his meaning. I understand him *e.g.* to urge that a judgment must be categorically true, if its content can be shown to be "contained" in reality. But the question was, I supposed, not in the very least as to whether the content is contained in reality or not, but entirely as to *how*, being contained there, it is contained, *i.e.* whether categorically or otherwise. Again Mr. Hobhouse seems to assume that, if a complex (such as the inherence of diverse adjectives or the union of continuity and discretion) is "fact," it therefore cannot be self-contradictory for thought. But surely the view he is engaged in controverting, holds precisely that to be false here which he, as far as I have seen, without any discussion assumes to be true. So that it is better that I should admit that I must have failed to follow the argument. If Mr. Hobhouse has in general understood the main drift of the view he criticises, I have not been able for the most part to understand his criticism, and I do not doubt that I am the loser.

Yes, I reply, but the question is how thought can think what is offered. If thought in its own nature possessed a "together," a "between," and an "all at once," then in its own intrinsic passage, or at least somehow in its own way and manner, it could re-affirm the external conjunction. But if these sensible bonds of union fall outside the inner nature of thought, just as much as do the sensible terms which they outwardly conjoin—the case surely is different. Then forced to distinguish and unable to conjoin by its own proper nature, or with a reason, thought is confronted by elements that strive to come together without a way of union. The sensible conjunctions remain for thought mere other elements in the congeries, themselves failing in connection and external to others. And, on the other hand, driven to unite without internal distinction thought finds in this attempt a self-contradiction. You may exclaim against thought's failure, and in this to some degree I am with you; but the fact remains thus. Thought cannot accept tautology and yet demands unity in diversity. But your offered conjunctions on the other side are for it no connections or ways of union. They are themselves merely other external things to be connected. And so thought, knowing what it wants, refuses to accept something different, something which for it is appearance, a self-inconsistent attempt at reality and truth. It is idle from the outside to say to thought, "Well, unite but do not identify." How can thought unite except so far as in itself it has a mode of union? To unite without an internal ground of connection and distinction is to strive to bring together barely in the same point, and that is self-contradiction.

Things are not contrary because they are opposite, for things by themselves are not opposite. And things are not contrary because they are diverse, for the world as a fact holds diversity in unity. Things are self-contrary when, and just so far as, they appear as bare conjunctions, when in order to think them you would have to predicate differences without an internal ground of connection and distinction, when, in other words, you would have to unite diversities simply, and that means in the same point. This is what contradiction means, or I at least have been able to find no other meaning. For a mere "together," a bare conjunction in space or time, is for thought unsatisfactory and in the end impossible. It depends for its existence on our neglecting to reflect, or on our purposely abstaining, so far as it is concerned, from analysis and thought. But any such working arrangement, however valid, is but provisional. On the other hand, we have found that no intrinsical opposites exist, but that contraries, in a sense, are made. Hence in the end nothing is contrary nor is there any insoluble contradiction. Contradictions exist so far only as internal distinction seems impossible, only so far as diversities are attached to one unyielding point assumed, tacitly or expressly, to be incapable of internal diversity or external complement. But any such fixture is an abstraction, useful perhaps, but in the end appearance. And thus, where we find contradiction, there is something limited and untrue which invites us to transcend it.

Standing contradictions appear where the subject is narrowed artificially, and where diversity in the identity is taken as excluded. A thing cannot be at once in two places if in the "at once" there is no lapse, nor can one place have two bodies at once if both claim it in their character as extended. The soul cannot affirm and deny at a single time, unless (as some perhaps rightly hold) the self itself may be divided. And, to speak in general, the more narrowly we take the subject, and the less internal ground for diversity it contains, the more it threatens us with standing or insoluble contradictions. But, we may add, so much the more abstractedness and less truth does such a subject possess. We may instance the presence of "disparate" qualities, such as white, hard and hot, in a single thing. The "thing" is presented as one feature of an indefinite complex, and it is affirmed as predicate of a reality transcending what is given. It is hence capable in all ways of indefinite addition to its apparent character. And to deny that in the "real thing" can be an internal diversity and ground of distinction seems quite irrational. But so far as for convenience or from thoughtlessness the denial is made, and the real thing is identified with our mutilated and abstract view of the thing—so far the disparate qualities logically clash and become contradictory.[1]

The Law of Contradiction tells us that we must not simply identify the diverse, since their union involves a ground of distinction. So far as this ground is rightly or wrongly excluded, the Law forbids us to predicate diversities. Where the ground is merely not explicit or remains unknown, our assertion of any complex is provisional and contingent. It may be valid and good, but it is an incomplete appearance of the real, and its truth is relative. Yet, while it offers itself as but contingent truth and as more or less incomplete appearance, the Law of Contradiction has nothing against it. But abstracted and irrational conjunctions taken by themselves as reality and truth, in short "facts" as they are accepted by too many philosophers, the Law must condemn. And about the truth of this Law, so far as it applies, there is in my opinion no question. The question will be rather as to how far the Law applies and how far therefore it is true.

But before we conclude, there is a matter we may do well to consider. In this attempt to attribute diversity and to avoid

---

[1] Of course the real thing or the reality of the thing may turn out to be something very different from the thing as we first take it up

contradiction what in the end would satisfy the intellect supposing that it could be got? This question, I venture to think, is too often ignored. Too often a writer will criticise and condemn some view as being that which the mind cannot accept, when he apparently has never asked himself what it is that would satisfy the intellect, or even whether the intellect could endure his own implied alternative. What in the end then, let us ask, would content the intellect?

While the diversities are external to each other and to their union, ultimate satisfaction is impossible. There must, as we have seen, be an identity and in that identity a ground of distinction and connection. But that ground, if external to the elements into which the conjunction must be analyzed, becomes for the intellect a fresh element, and it itself calls for synthesis in a fresh point of unity. But hereon, because in the intellect no intrinsic connections were found, ensues the infinite process. Is there a remedy for this evil?

The remedy might lie here. If the diversities were complementary aspects of a process of connection and distinction, the process not being external to the elements or again a foreign compulsion of the intellect, but itself the intellect's own *proprius motus*, the case would be altered. Each aspect would of itself be a transition to the other aspect, a transition intrinsic and natural at once to itself and to the intellect. And the Whole would be a self-evident analysis and synthesis of the intellect itself by itself. Synthesis here has ceased to be mere synthesis and has become self-completion, and analysis, no longer mere analysis, is self-explication. And the question how or why the many are one and the one is many here loses its meaning. There is no why or how beside the self-evident process, and towards its own differences this whole is at once their how and their why, their being, substance and system, their reason, ground, and principle of diversity and unity.

Has the Law of Contradiction anything here to condemn? It seems to me it has nothing. The identity of which diversities are predicated is in no case simple. There is no point which is not itself internally the transition to its complement, and there is no unity which fails in internal diversity and ground of distinction. In short "the identity of opposites," far from conflicting with the Law of Contradiction, may claim to be the one view which satisfies its demands, the only theory which everywhere refuses to accept a standing contradiction.[1] And if all that we find were in the end such a self-evident and self-complete whole, containing in itself as constituent processes the detail of the Universe, so far as I see the intellect would receive satisfaction in full. But

---

[1] On this and other points I would refer to Mr. McTaggart's excellent work on *Hegelian Dialectic*.

for myself, unable to verify a solution of this kind, connections in the end must remain in part mere syntheses, the putting together of differences external to one another and to that which couples them. And against my intellectual world the Law of Contradiction has therefore claims nowhere satisfied in full. And since, on the other hand, the intellect insists that these demands must be and are met, I am led to hold that they are met in and by a whole beyond the mere intellect. And in the intellect itself I seem to find an inner want and defect and a demand thus to pass itself beyond itself. And against this conclusion I have not yet seen any tenable objection.

The view which to me appears to be true is briefly this. That abstract identity should satisfy the intellect, even in part, is wholly impossible. On the other hand I cannot say that to me any principle or principles of diversity in unity are self-evident. The existence of a single content (I will not call it a quality) which should be simple experience and being in one is to me not in itself impossible intrinsically. If I may speak mythologically I am not sure that, if no diversity were given, the intellect of itself could invent it or would even demand it. But, since diversity is there as a fact, any such hypothesis seems illegitimate. As a fact and given we have in feeling diversity and unity in one whole, a whole implicit and not yet broken up into terms and relations. This immediate union of the one and many is an "ultimate fact" from which we start; and to hold that feeling, because immediate, must be simple and without diversity is, in my view, a doctrine quite untenable.[1] That I myself should have been taken as committed to this doctrine is to me, I must be allowed to add, really surprising. But feeling, if an ultimate fact, is not true ultimately or real. Even of itself it is self-transcendent and transitory. And, when we try to think its unity, then, as we have seen, we end in failure. For thought in its own nature has no "together" and is forced to move by way of terms and relations, and the unity of these remains in the end external and, because external, inconsistent. But the conclusion I would recommend is no vain attempt either to accept bare identity or to relapse into a stage before thinking begins. Self-existence and self-identity are to be found, I would urge, in a whole beyond thought, a whole to which thought points and in which it is included, but which is known only in abstract character and could not be verified in its detail.

And since I have been taken to build on assumptions which I am unable to recognize, I will here repeat what it is that I have assumed. I have assumed first that truth has to satisfy the

---

[1] Feeling is certainly *not* "un-differentiated" if that means that it contains no diverse aspects. I would take the opportunity to state that this view as to feeling is so far from being novel that I owe it, certainly in the main, to Hegel's psychology.

intellect, and that what does not do this is neither true nor
real. This assumption I can defend only by showing that any
would-be objector assumes it also. And I start from the root-
idea of being or experience, which is at once positive and
ultimate. Then I certainly do not go on to assume about being
that it must be self-contained, simple or what not?—but I
proceed in another manner. I take up certain facts or truths
(call them what you please) that I find are offered me, and I
care very little what it is I take up. These facts or truths,
as they are offered, I find my intellect rejects, and I go on
to discover why it rejects them. It is because they contradict
themselves. They offer, that is, a complex of diversities conjoined in a way which does not satisfy my intellect, a way which
it feels is not its way and which it cannot repeat as its own, a way
which for it results in mere collision. For, to be satisfied, my
intellect must understand, and it cannot understand by taking
a congeries, if I may say so, in the lump. My intellect may for
certain purposes, to use an old figure, swallow mysteries unchewed, but unchewed it is unable in the end to stomach
and digest them. It has not, as some opponents of Hegel
would seem to assume, any such strange faculty of sensuous
intuition. On the contrary my intellect is discursive, and to
understand it must go from one point to another, and in the
end also must go by a movement which it feels satisfies its
nature. Thus, to understand a complex AB, I must begin
with A or B. And beginning, say, with A, if I then merely
find B, I have either lost A or I have got beside A something
else, and in neither case have I understood. For my intellect
cannot simply unite a diversity, nor has it in itself any form
or way of togetherness, and you gain nothing if beside A and
B you offer me their conjunction in fact. For to my intellect
that is no more than another external element. And "facts,"
once for all, are for my intellect not true unless they satisfy it.
And, so far as they are not true, then, as they are offered, they are
not reality.

From this I conclude that what is real must be self-contained
and self-subsistent and not qualified from the outside. For an
external qualification is a mere conjunction, and that, we have
seen, is for the intellect an attempt of diversities simply to identify
themselves, and such an attempt is what we mean by self-contradiction. Hence whatever is real must be qualified from itself,
and that means that, so far as it is real, it must be self-contained
and self-subsistent. And, since diversities exist, they must therefore somehow be true and real; and since, to be understood and
to be true and real, they must be united, hence they must be true
and real in such a way that from A or B the intellect can pass to
its further qualification without an external determination of
either. But this means that A and B are united, each from its

own nature, in a whole which is the nature of both alike. And hence it follows that in the end there is nothing real but a whole of this kind.[1]

From the other side—Why do I hold reality to be a self-contained and self-consistent individual? It is because otherwise, if I admit an external determination and a qualification by an other, I am left with a conjunction, and that for the intellect is a self-contradiction. On the other hand the real cannot be simple, because, to be understood, it must somehow be taken with and be qualified by the diversity which is a fact. The diversity therefore must fall within and be subordinate to a self-determined whole, an individual system, and any other determination is incompatible with reality. These ideas may be mistaken, but to my mind they do not seem to be obscure, nor again are they novel. But if I may judge from the way in which some critics have taken them, they must involve some great obscurity or difficulty. But, not apprehending this, I am unfortunately unable to discuss it.[2]

We have found that nothing in itself is opposite and refuses to unite. Everything again is opposite if brought together into a point which owns no internal diversity. Every bare conjunction is therefore contradictory when taken up by thought, because thought in its nature is incapable of conjunction and has no way of mere "together." On the other side no such conjunction is or possibly could be given. It is itself a mere abstraction, useful perhaps and so legitimate and so far valid, but taken otherwise to be condemned as the main root of error.

Contradiction is appearance, everywhere removable by distinction and by further supplement, and removed actually, if not in

---

[1] And hence it follows also that every "part" of this whole must be internally defective and (when thought) contradictory. For otherwise how from one to others and the rest could there be any internal passage? And without such a passage and with but an external junction or bond, could there be any system or whole at all which would satisfy the intellect, and could be taken as real or possible? I at least have given my reason for answering this question in the negative. We may even, forgetting other points of view, say of the world,

"Thus every part is full of vice,
Yet the whole mass a paradise."

[2] The Law of Identity, I may be allowed to note in this connection, is the denial that truth, if true, is alterable from the outside. For, if so, it would become either itself conjoined with its own absence, or itself conjoined with a positive other; and either alternative (to take them here as alternatives), we have seen, is self-contradictory. Hence any mere context cannot modify a truth so far as it is true. It merely adds, we must say, something more which leaves the truth itself unaffected. Truth cannot be modified, in other words, except from within. This of course opens a problem, for truth seems on the one hand to be abstract, as truth, and so incomplete, and on the other hand, if true, to be self-contained and even self-existent. For the Law of Identity the reader is further referred to the Index.

and by the mere intellect, by the whole which transcends it. On
the other hand contradiction, or rather what becomes such, as soon
as it is thought out, is everywhere necessary. Facts and views
partial and one-sided, incomplete and so incoherent—things that
offer themselves as characters of a Reality which they cannot
express, and which present in them moves them to jar with and
to pass beyond themselves—in a word *appearances* are the stuff of
which the Universe is made. If we take them in their proper
character we shall be prone neither to over-estimate nor to slight
them.

We have now seen the nature of incompatibles or contraries.
There are no native contraries, and we have found no reason to
entertain such an idea. Things are contrary when, being diverse,
they strive to be united in one point which in itself does not
admit of internal diversity. And for the intellect any bare conjunction is an attempt of this sort. The intellect has in its nature
no principle of mere togetherness, and the intellect again can
accept nothing which is alien to itself. A foreign togetherness of
elements is for the intellect, therefore, but one offered external
element the more. And, since the intellect demands a unity,
every distinguishable aspect of a "together" must be brought
into one. And if in this unity no internal connection of
diversity natural to the intellect can be found, we are left with a
diversity belonging to and conjoined in one undistinguished
point. And this is contradiction, and contradiction in the end we
found was this and nothing but this. On the other hand we
urged that bare irrational conjunctions are not given as facts.
Every perceived complex is a selection from an indefinite background, and, when judged as real, it is predicated both of this
background and of the Reality which transcends it. Hence
in this background and beyond it lies, we may believe, the
reason and the internal connection of all we take as a mere
external "together." Conjunction and contradiction in short
is but our defect, our onesidedness, and our abstraction; and
it is appearance and not Reality. But the reason we have to
assume may in detail be not accessible to our intellect.

Note B. Relation and Quality.

There are some aspects of the general problem of Relation
and Quality on which I will offer some words of explanation.
The subject is large and difficult, and deserves a far more thorough
treatment than I am able at present to bestow on it. There is
the question (i) whether qualities can exist independent of some
whole, (ii) whether they can exist independent of relations,
(iii) whether, where there are fresh relations, new qualities are
made and old ones altered, or whether again one can have a

merely external relation, and, lastly (iv), whether and in what sense, wherever there is an identity, we have a right to speak of a relation.

(i and ii) Within any felt whole—and that term includes here anything which contains an undistinguished diversity, any totality of aspects which is not broken up—the diversities qualify that whole, and are felt as making it what it is. Are these diversities to be called qualities (p. 27)? It is really perhaps a verbal question. Anything that is somewhat at all may be said to be or to have a quality. But on the other hand we may prefer to use quality specially of those diversities which are developed when wholes are analyzed into terms and relations. And, when we ask if there can be qualities without relations, this distinction becomes important. The question must be answered affirmatively if we call by the name of quality the diverse aspects of feeling. But on the other hand such diverse aspects cannot exist independently. They are not given except as contained in and as qualifying some whole, and their independence consists merely in our vicious abstraction. Nor when we pass to the relational stage does diversity cease to be the inseparable adjective of unity. For the relations themselves cannot exist except within and as the adjectives of an underlying unity. The whole that is analyzed into relations and terms can fall into the background and be obscured, but it can never be dissipated. And, if it were dissipated, then with it both terms and relations would perish. For there is no absolute "between" or "together," nor can "between" and "together" be the mere adjectives of self-existent units. Qualities in the end can have no meaning except as contained in and as dependent on some whole, and whether that whole is relational or otherwise makes no difference in this respect.

And it is not hard, perhaps, at this point to dispose of a fallacy which seems somewhat common. You may take, it is said, some terms, A, B, and C, and may place them in various relations, X, Y, and Z, and through all they remain still A, B, and C. And this, it is urged, proves that A, B, and C exist, or may exist, free from all relations or at least independently. My character, for example, may be compared with that of another man, or, having first lived to the north of him, I may then change to the south; and to neither of us need it make a difference, and therefore we both are unaffected and so independent. But an answer to this fallacy seems even obvious. What is proved is that a certain character may, as such and in respect of that character, exist indifferently in various relations. But what is not proved at all is that this character could exist independent and naked. And since the argument starts by presupposing without any enquiry the independent existence of the character and indeed rests throughout on that presupposed existence, it could in no case arrive, it seems to me, at the desired conclusion. The most that it could show would be that *some* relations are external and may make no difference to their terms. But to argue from this that *all* the relations are or even may be external, and that some qualities either do or may exist independently, seems quite illogical. Such an argument obviously could at once be met by a distinction drawn between different kinds of relations.

(iii) For myself I neither make nor accept such a distinction except as relative and subordinate. I do not admit that any relation whatever can be merely external and make no difference to its terms, and I will now proceed to discuss this important point. I will begin by first dismissing a difficult question. Qualities exist, we have seen, improperly as diverse aspects of felt wholes, and then again properly as terms which are distinguished and related. But how far are we to say that such characters as those *e.g.* of different colours are *made* by distinction, and were not of the same quality at all when mere aspects of the un-analyzed? To this question I will not attempt a reply, because I am sure that I should not do it justice. I have great sympathy with the view that such characters are so developed as to be in a sense constituted by distinction, but I cannot defend this view or identify myself with it. And for myself, and for argument's sake at least, I shall admit that a quality in feeling may already have the character, A or B, which we find when afterwards quality proper is made by distinction. In no case (to repeat) will there be a quality existing independently, but while you keep to aspects of a felt whole it will not be true that every quality depends on relation. And on the other hand between such aspects and qualities proper there may be an identity in some character A or B.

From this we are led to the question, Are qualities and in general are terms altered necessarily by the relations into which they enter? In other words are there any relations which are merely extrinsical? And by this I do not mean to ask if there can be relations outside of and independent of some whole, for that question I regard as answered in the negative. I am asking whether, within the whole and subject to that, terms can enter into further relations and not be affected by them. And this question again is not, Can A, B, and C become the terms of fresh relations, and still remain A, B, and C? For clearly a thing may be altered partly and yet retain a certain character, and one and the same character may persist unaltered though the terms that possess it are in some other ways changed. And this is a point on which in the present connection I shall have later to insist. Further our question does not ask if terms are in any sense whatever qualified by their relations. For every one, I presume, admits this in some sense, however hard that sense may be to fix. The question I am putting is whether relations can qualify terms, *A*, *B*, and *C*, from the outside merely and without in any way affecting and altering them internally. And this question I am compelled to answer negatively.

At first sight obviously such external relations seem possible and even existing. They seem given to us, we saw, in change of spatial position and again also in comparison. That you do not alter what you compare or re-arrange in space seems to Common Sense quite obvious, and that on the other side there are as obvious difficulties does not occur to Common Sense at all. And I will begin by pointing out these difficulties that stand in the way of our taking any relations as quite external. In a mental act, such for instance as comparison, there is a relation in the result, and this relation, we hear, is to make no difference to the terms. But, if so, to what does it make a difference, and what is the meaning and sense of qualifying the terms by it? If in short it is external to the terms, how can it possibly be true of them? To put the same thing otherwise, if we merely *make* the conclusion, is that conclusion a true one? But if the terms from their inner nature do not enter into the relation, then, so far as they are concerned, they seem related for no reason at all, and, so far as they are concerned, the relation seems arbitrarily made. But otherwise the terms themselves seem affected by a merely external relation. To find the truth of things by making relations about them seems indeed a very strange process, and confronted with this problem Common Sense, I presume, would take refuge in confused metaphors.

And alterations of position in space once more give rise to difficulty. Things are spatially related, first in one way, and then become related in another way, and yet in no way themselves are altered; for the relations, it is said, are but external. But I reply that, if so, I cannot understand the leaving by the terms of one set of relations and their adoption of another fresh set. The process and its result to the terms, if they contribute nothing to it, seems really irrational throughout. But, if they contribute anything, they must surely be affected internally. And by the introduction of an outer compelling agency the difficulty is not lessened. The connection of the terms with this agency, and the difference it seems to make to them, where by the hypothesis no difference can be made, seem a hopeless puzzle. In short all we reach by it is the admission that the terms and their relation do not by themselves include all the facts, and beyond that admission it is useless. And this leads to a further doubt about the sufficiency of external relations. Every sort of whole, and certainly every arrangement in space, has a qualitative aspect. In various respects the whole has a character—even its figure may here be included—which cannot be shown to consist barely in mere terms and mere relations between them. You may say that this character belongs to them, but it still is more than what they are by themselves. And if things in space by a new arrangement produce a fresh aspect of quality, of what, I would ask, are you going to predicate this quality? If the terms contribute anything whatever, then the terms are affected by their arrangement. And to predicate the new result barely of the external relations seems, to me at least, impossible. This question—as to how far by external relations fresh quality can be produced—is one which would carry us very far. I notice it here as a further difficulty which besets the thesis of mere extrinsical relation. And if in conclusion I am told that, of course, there are upon any view difficulties, I am ready to assent. But the question is whether this doctrine, offered as obvious, does not turn mere difficulties into sheer self-contradictions, and whether once more except as a relative point of view it is not as uncalled for as it is in principle false.

But the facts, it will be said, of spatial arrangement and of comparison, to mention only these, force you, whether you like it or not, to accept the view that at least some relations are outward only. Now that for working purposes we treat, and do well to treat, some relations as external merely I do not deny, and that, of course, is not the question at issue here. That question is in short whether this distinction of internal and external is absolute or is but relative, and whether in the end and in principle a mere external relation is possible and forced on us by the facts. And except as a subordinate view I submit that the latter thesis is untenable. But the discussion of this matter involves unfortunately a wide and difficult range of questions, and my treatment of it must be brief and, I fear, otherwise imperfect.

If we begin by considering the form of spatial arrangement, we seem to find at first complete real externality. All the points there are terms which may be taken indifferently in every kind of arrangement, and the relations seem indifferent and merely outward. But this statement, as soon as we reflect, must partly be modified. The terms cannot be taken truly as being that which actually they are not. And the conclusion will follow that the terms actually and in fact are related amongst themselves in every possible manner. Every space, if so, would be a whole in which the parts throughout are inter-related already in every possible position, and reciprocally so determine one another. And this, if puzzling, seems at least to follow inevitably from the premises. And from this the conclusion cannot be drawn that the terms are inwardly indifferent to their relations; for the whole internal character of the terms, it seems, goes out, on the contrary, and consists in these. And how can a being, if absolutely relative, be related *merely* externally? And if you object that the question is not about mere space, but rather about things in space, this is in fact the point to which I am desiring to direct your attention. Space by itself and its barely spatial relations and terms are all alike mere abstractions, useful no doubt but, if taken as independently real, inconsistent and false. And in a less degree the same holds, I would now urge, also of bodies in space and of their relations therein.

We have seen that a mere space of mere external relations is an inconsistent abstraction, and that, for space to exist at all, there must be an arrangement which is more than spatial. Without qualitative differences (pp. 17, 38) there are no distinctions in space at all, there is neither position nor change of position, neither shape nor bodies nor motion. And just as in this sense there are no mere spatial relations without concrete terms, so in another sense also there is nothing barely spatial. The terms and the relations between them are themselves mere abstractions from a more concrete qualitative unity. Neither the things in space nor their space, nor both together, can be taken as substantial. They are abstractions depending on a more concrete whole which they fail to express. And their apparent externality is itself a sign that we have in them appearance and not ultimate reality.

As to that apparent externality there can be no doubt. Why this thing is here and not there, what the connection is in the end between spatial position and the quality that holds it and is determined by it, remains unknown. In mechanical explanation generally the connection of the elements with the laws—even if the laws themselves were rational — remains unknown and external, and the reason why the results follow from the premises is admitted at a certain point to be left outside. Where this point is to be placed, whether at the beginning or merely when we arrive at secondary qualities, it is not necessary here to settle. But any such irrationality and externality cannot be the last truth about things. Somewhere there must be a reason why this and that appear together. And this reason and reality must reside in the whole from which terms and relations are abstractions, a whole in which their internal connection must lie, and out of which from the background appear those fresh results which never could have come from the premises. The merely external is, in short, our ignorance set up as reality, and to find it anywhere, except as an inconsistent aspect of fact, we have seen is impossible.

But it will be objected on the part of Common Sense that we must keep to the facts. The billiard-balls on a table may be in any position you please, and you and I and another may be changed respectively in place, and yet none of these things by these changes is altered in itself. And the apparent fact that by external change in space and time a thing may be affected, is,

I presume, rejected on the ground that this does not happen when you come down to the last elements of things. But an important if obvious distinction seems here overlooked. For a thing may remain unaltered if you identify it with a certain character, while taken otherwise the thing is suffering change. If, that is, you take a billiard-ball and a man in abstraction from place, they will of course—so far as this is maintained—be indifferent to changes of place. But on the other hand neither of them, if regarded so, is a thing which actually exists; each is a more or less valid abstraction. But take them as existing things and take them without mutilation, and you must regard them as determined by their places and qualified by the whole material system into which they enter. And, if you demur to this, I ask you once more of what you are going to predicate the alterations and their results. The billiard-ball, to repeat, if taken apart from its place and its position in the whole, is not an existence but a character, and that character can remain unchanged, though the existing thing is altered with its changed existence. Everything other than this identical character may be called relatively external. It may, or it may not, be in comparison unimportant, but absolutely external it cannot be. And if you urge that in any case the relation of the thing's character to its spatial existence is unintelligible, and that *how* the nature of the thing which falls outside our abstraction contributes to the whole system, and *how* that nature is different as it contributes differently, is in the end unknown—I shall not gainsay you. But I prefer to be left with ignorance and with inconsistencies and with insoluble difficulties, difficulties essential to a lower and fragmentary point of view and soluble only by the transcendence of that appearance in a fuller whole, a transcendence which in detail seems for us impossible—I prefer, I say, to be left thus rather than to embrace a worse alternative. I cannot on any terms accept as absolute fact a mere abstraction and a fixed standing inconsistency. And the case surely is made worse when one is forced to admit that, starting from this principle, one sooner or later cannot in the very least explain those results which follow in fact.

I will next consider the argument for merely external relations which has been based on Comparison. Things may be the same, it is said, but not related until you compare them, and their relations then fall quite outside and do not qualify them. Two men with red hair for example, it may be urged, are either not related at all by their sameness, or when related by it are not altered, and the relation therefore is quite external. Now if I suggest that possibly all the red-haired men in a place might be ordered to be collected and destroyed, I shall be answered, I presume, that their red hair does not affect them *directly*, and though I think this answer unsatisfactory, I will pass on. But with regard to Comparison I will begin by asking a question. It is commonly supposed that by Comparison we learn the truth about things; but now, if the relation established by comparison falls outside of the terms, in what sense, if at all, can it be said to qualify them? And of what, if not of the terms, are the truths got by comparison true? And in the end, I ask, is there any sense, and, if so, what sense in truth that is only outside and "about" things? Or, from the other side, if truth is truth can it be made by us, and can what is only made by us possibly be true? These are questions which, I venture to repeat, should be met by the upholders of mere external relations.

For myself I am convinced that no such relations exist. There is no identity or likeness possible except in a whole, and every such whole must qualify and be qualified by its terms. And, where the whole is different, the terms that qualify it and contribute to it must so far be different, and so far therefore by becoming elements in a fresh unity the terms must be altered. They are altered so far only, but still they are altered. You may take by abstraction a quality A, B, or C, and that abstract quality may throughout remain unchanged. But the terms related are more than this quality, and they will be altered. And if you reply that at any rate the term and its quality are external the one to the other, I reply, Yes, but not, as you say, external merely and absolutely. For nothing in the world is external so except for our ignorance.

We have two things felt to be the same but not identified. We compare them, and then they are related by a point of identity. And nothing, we hear, is changed but mere extrinsical relations. But against this meaningless thesis I must insist that in each case the terms are qualified by their whole, and that in the second case there is a whole which differs both logically and psychologically from the first whole; and I urge that in contributing to this change the terms are so far altered. They are altered though in respect of an abstract quality they remain the same.

Let us keep to our instance of two red-haired men, first seen with red hair but not identified in this point, and then these two men related in the judgment, 'They are the same in being red-haired.' In each case there is a whole which is qualified by and qualifies the terms, but in each case the whole is different. The men are taken first as contained in and as qualifying a perceived whole, and their redness is given in immediate unconditional unity with their other qualities and with the rest of the undivided sensible totality. But, in the second case, this sensible whole has been broken up, and the men themselves have been analyzed. They have each been split up into a connection of red-hairedness with other qualities, while the red-hairedness itself has become a subject and a point of unity connecting the diversities of each instance, diversities which are predicated of it and connected with one another under it. And the connection of the two men's diversities with this general quality, and with one another through it, I must insist is truth and is reality however imperfect and impure. But this logical synthesis is a unity different from the sensible whole, and in passing into this unity I cannot see how to deny that the terms have been altered. And to reply that, if you abstract and keep to the abstract point of red-hairedness, there is no change, is surely a complete *ignoratio elenchi*.[1]

By being red-haired the two men are related really, and their relation is not merely external. If it were so wholly it would not be true or real at all, and, so far as it seems so, to that extent it is but the appearance of something higher. The correlation of the other circumstances of and characters in the two men with the quality of red-hairedness cannot in other words possibly be bare chance. And if you could have a perfect relational knowledge of the world, you could go from the nature of red-hairedness to these other characters which qualify it, and you could from the nature of red-hairedness reconstruct all the red-haired men. In such perfect knowledge you could start internally from any one character in the Universe, and you could from that pass to the rest. You would go in each case more or less directly or indirectly, and with unimportant characters the amount of indirectness would be enormous, but no passage would be external. Such knowledge is out of our reach, and it is perhaps out of the reach of any mind that has to think relationally. But if in the Absolute knowledge is perfected, as we conclude it is, then in a higher form the end of such knowledge is actually realized, and with ignorance and chance the last show of externality has vanished. And if this seems to you monstrous, I ask you at least to examine for yourself, and to see whether a merely external truth is not more monstrous.

'But I am a red-haired man,' I shall hear, 'and I know what I am, and I am not altered in fact when I am compared with another man, and therefore the relation falls outside.' But no finite individual, I reply, can possibly know what he is, and the idea that all his reality falls within his knowledge is even ridiculous. His ignorance on the contrary of his own being, and of what that involves, may be called enormous. And if by 'what he is' he means certain qualities in abstraction from the rest, then let him say so and admit that his objection has become irrelevant. If the nature and being of a finite individual were

---

[1] No comparison, I would remark here, can possibly end in nothing. If you took two terms which had no more visibly in common than the fact that they exist or are thought, yet the comparison still has a result. You have stated the truth that existence or thought is an identity which somehow has within it these diversities, and that they somehow are connected in and qualify this unity. And I must insist that, poor as this is, it is not nothing, nor again is it the same as the mere sensuous togetherness of the terms.

complete in itself, then of course he might know himself perfectly and not know his connection with aught else. But, as he really is, to know perfectly his own nature would be, with that nature, to pass in knowledge endlessly beyond himself. For example, a red-haired man who knew himself utterly would and must, starting from within, go on to know everyone else who has red hair, and he would not know himself until he knew them. But, as things are, he does not know how or why he himself has red hair, nor how or why a different man is also the same in that point, and therefore, because he does not know the ground, the how and why, of his relation to the other man, it remains for him relatively external, contingent, and fortuitous. But there is really no mere externality except in his ignorance.

We have seen that, logically and really, all relations imply a whole to which the terms contribute and by which the terms are qualified. And I will now briefly point out that psychologically the same thing holds good. When, in the first place, I merely experience things the same in one point, or in other words merely experience the sameness of two things, and when, in the second place, I have come to perceive the point of sameness and the relation of the two things—there is in each case in my mind a psychical whole. But the whole in each case is different, and the character of the whole must depend on the elements which it contains, and must also affect them. And an element passing into a fresh whole will be altered, though it of course may remain the same from one abstract side. But I will not dwell on a point which seems fairly clear, and which, except as an illustration, is perhaps not quite relevant. Still it is well to note the fact that a merely external relation seems psychologically meaningless.

Nothing in the whole and in the end can be external, and everything less than the Universe is an abstraction from the whole, an abstraction more or less empty, and the more empty the less self-dependent. Relations and qualities are abstractions, and depend for their being always on a whole, a whole which they inadequately express, and which remains always less or more in the background. It is from this point of view that we should approach the question, How can new qualities be developed and emerge? It is a question, I would repeat, which, with regard to secondary qualities, has been made familiar to us. But the problem as to the 'limits of explanation' must for metaphysics arise long before that point is reached. Into this matter I shall not enter, but I desire to lay stress on the general principle. Where results emerge in fact, which do not follow from our premises, there is nothing here to surprise us. For behind the abstractions we have used is the concrete qualitative whole on which they depend, and hence what has come out in the result has but issued from the conditions which (purposely or otherwise) we have endeavoured to ignore and to exclude. And this should prove to us that the premises with which we worked were not true or real, but were a mutilated fragment of reality.

(iv) I will deal now with a problem connected with the foregoing. I have in this book, wherever it was convenient, spoken of identity as being a relation. And I may be asked whether and how I am able to justify this. For terms are related, it will be said, for instance when I compare them, and, it seems, not before. And my past states when recalled by identity are related to my present, but apparently otherwise not so. And my state and another man's may be more or less identical, but they seem not always to connect us. On the other hand of course we meet with the old difficulty as to my merely making the relations which I find, and any such position appears to be untenable. Hence on the one side, it seems, we must, and on the other side, it seems, we cannot say that all identity is a relation. The solution of the problem is however, in a few words, this. Identity must be taken as having a development through several stages. At a certain stage no identity is relational, while at a higher stage all is so. And because in the Absolute the highest stage is actually realized, therefore we may, where convenient, treat identity as being already a relation, when actually for us it is not one. This statement I will now proceed to explain briefly.

We have seen that as a fact sameness exists at a stage below relations. It exists as an aspect both of a diversity felt in my mind and again of a diversity taken to exist beyond my feeling. Now this aspect is not the mere adjective of independent things, and any such view I consider to be refuted. The diversity itself depends on and exists only as the adjective of a whole; and within this whole the point of sameness is a unity and a universal realized in the differences which through it are the same. But so far this unity is, we may say, immediate and not relational. And the question is why and how we can call it a relation, when it is not a relation actually for us. It would never do for us simply and without any explanation to fall back on the "potential," for that, if unexplained, is a mere attempt at compromise between 'is' and 'is not.' But if the "potential" is used for that which actually is, and which under certain conditions is not manifest, the "potential" may cease to be a phrase and may become the solution of the problem.

All relations, we have seen, are the inadequate expression of an underlying unity. The relational stage is an imperfect and incomplete development of the immediate totality. But, on the other hand, it really is a development. It is an advance and a necessary step towards that perfection which is above relations, supersedes and still includes them. Hence in the Absolute, where all is complete, we are bound to hold that every development reaches its end—whatever that end may be, and in whatever sense we are to say the thing comes to it. The goal of every progress therefore may be taken as already attained in Reality and as now present and actual. I do not mean that without exception all immediate sameness must pass through the relational consciousness. But without exception no sameness reaches its truth and final reality except in the Whole which is beyond relations and which carries out what they attempt. And in the main the way of relations is the necessary mode of progress from that which is incomplete to its perfection. All sameness then not only may but must become relational, or at least must be realized in the same end and on the same principle as would have perfected it if it had passed through relational identity. And because in the Absolute what must be is, I think that, wherever there is identity, we may speak of a relation—so long of course as we are clear about the sense in which we speak of it.

And this is how and why, in thinking, I can find the relations that I make. For what I develop is in the Absolute already complete. But this, on the other hand, does not mean that my part in the affair is irrelevant, that it makes no difference to truth and is external. To be made and to be found is on the contrary essential to the development and being of the thing, and truth in its processes and results belongs to the essence of reality. Only, here as everywhere, we must distinguish between what is internally necessary and what is contingent. It belongs to the essence of sameness that it should go on to be thought and to be thought in a certain way. But that it should be thought by you and not by me, by a man with brown hair or with red, does not belong to its essence. These features in a sense qualify it, for they are conjoined to it, and no conjunction can in the end be a mere conjunction and be barely external. But the connection here is so indirect and so little individual, it involves so much of other conditions lying in the general background, so much the introduction of which would by addition tend to transform and swamp this particular truth and fact as such—that such features are rightly called external and contingent. But contingency is of course always a matter of degree.

This leads to the question whether and how far Resemblance qualifies the real. Resemblance is the perception or feeling of a more or less unspecified partial identity; and, so far as the identity is concerned, we have therefore already dealt with it. But taking resemblance not as partial identity but as a mode in which identity may appear, how are we to say that it belongs to reality? Certainly it belongs and must belong, and about

that there is no question. The question is, in a word, about
the amount and degree of its necessity and contingency. Have
I a right, wherever I find partial sameness, to speak of resemblance, in the proper sense, as I had a right under the same
conditions to speak of a relation? As a matter of fact not all
identity appears under the form of resemblance, and can I
conclude, Somehow in the Absolute it all must, and therefore
does, possess this form, and may therefore everywhere be spoken
of as possessing it? The answer to this question is to be found,
I presume, in an enquiry into the conditions of resemblance.
What is it that is added to the experience of partial sameness
in order to make it into the experience of resemblance? Can
this addition be looked on as a development of sameness from
within, and as a necessary step to its completion, or does it on
the other hand depend on conditions which are relatively
external? How direct, in other words, is the connection between
resemblance and identity, and, in order to get the former from
the latter, what amount of other conditions would you have to
bring in, and how far in the end could you say that the resemblance came from the identity rather than from these other
conditions? If you can conclude, as for myself I certainly
cannot, that resemblance (proper) is an essential development
of sameness, then if you will also affirm the principle that in
Reality what must be is actual already—you will have a right
for certain purposes to call the same 'similar,' even where no
similarity appears. But to do this otherwise, except of course
by way of a working fiction, will surely be indefensible.[1]

With this I must end these too imperfect remarks on relation
and quality. I will take up some other points with regard to
Identity and Resemblance in the following Note.

[1] This is not an idle question but very nearly concerns a mode of thought
which, a generation or so back, was dominant amongst us, and even now
has some supporters. It was denied by this, on the one hand, that there
was any sameness in character except similarity, and it was asserted on the
other hand that except in and for an actual particular experience there was
no similarity. And yet the similarity, *e.g.* of my past and present states
of mind, was treated as a fact which did not call for any explanation.
To this point I called attention in my work on *Logic* (Book II, Part II,
Chap. i), and I adduced it as one proof among many others of superficiality
and of bankruptcy in respect of first principles. And I do not understand
why any one who is prepared to disagree with this verdict does not at least
make some attempt to face and deal with the difficulty. The ordinary device
of J. S. Mill and his school is a crude identification of possibility with fact,
of potential with actual existence, the meaning of potential existence of
course never being so much as asked. This crude unthinking identification
is, we may say, a characteristic of the school. It is all that with regard to
first principles seems to stand between it and bankruptcy, and any one who
really desires to dispute the bankruptcy cannot, I think, fairly leave unnoticed
this special question about similarity, as well as in general the relation of the
possible to the real.

Note C. Identity.

In the preceding Note we were led to consider a question about Identity, and I will here go on to deal with some others. It would of course be far better that such questions should arise and be answered each in its proper place, but except in a systematic treatise that is not possible. It may be that identity should be used only in a restricted sense, but in any case such a restriction would involve and have to be based on a comprehensive enquiry. And apart from a restriction the whole question about identity would cover the entire field of metaphysics. Wherever there is a unity of the manifold, there is an identity in diversity, and a study of the principal forms of unity in difference would not leave much outside it. And hence, because I could not treat properly the different forms of identity, I did not attempt even to set them out. Certainly I saw no advantage in cataloguing every-day distinctions, such as those between two men of the same sort, and two men in the same place or time, and again two periods of a man's one life. It did not occur to me that such distinctions could fail to be familiar or that any one could desire to be informed of them. I presupposed as a matter of course a knowledge of them, and, if I myself anywhere confused them, I have not found the place.[1] And I cannot attempt any thorough investigation of their nature or of many other problems that must arise in any serious effort to deal with identity. I will however add here some remarks which are offered to the reader for whatever they may be worth to him.

I. The first question I will ask is whether all identity is qualitative. This is closely connected with the discussion of the preceding Note, which I take here to have been read. Now the answer to our question must depend on the sense in which we use 'quality.' Any one can of course perceive that the sameness of a thing with itself at different times differs from its possession with another thing of one and the same character. And, as we have seen, if quality is restricted to that which is the term of a relation, then at any stage before distinction obviously you will have no quality. The unity of a felt whole, for example, which is certainly an identity, will as certainly not be qualitative, nor will there be qualitative sameness ever between what is felt and then later perceived. But, as we saw, the whole question is in part one of words, 'quality' being a term which is ambiguous. In its lowest meaning it applies to anything that in any sense qualifies and makes anything to be somewhat. It therefore will

[1] Cf. p. 616 (the Note on p. 313).

cover everything except the Universe taken as such. And of course to ask if in this sense relations generally, or again space or time or quantity, are or are not qualities, would be absurd. The question begins to have an interest however when we consider any attempt to set up some form of finite existence, or existence itself, as real in distinction from character in its widest sense, or an attempt in other words to discover a finite something which from some side of its being is not a 'somewhat.' And since in any something the distinction of 'that' from 'what' is not absolute but only relative, such a pursuit is in the end illusory. All appearance in the end is but content and character which qualifies the Absolute, and it is in the end the Absolute alone to which the term quality cannot be applied. Here first we find a reality which is beyond a mere 'what'; but neither here nor anywhere can we find a reality which is merely 'that.' To make reality these two aspects must be united inseparably, and indeed their separation is appearance itself. So that if the question 'Is all identity qualitative' means 'Is every sameness that of qualities proper,' we must answer it in the negative. But in any other sense our answer to the question must be affirmative. For we must repel the suggestion of a sameness which is not that of content and which consists in an identity of mere existence.

From this I pass to a kindred question, Is all identity ideal? It is so always, we must reply, in this sense that it involves the self-transcendence of that which is identical. Where there is no diversity there is no identity at all, the identity in abstraction from the diversity having lost its character. But, on the other hand, where the diversity is not of itself the same, but is only taken so or made so from the outside, once more identity has vanished. Sameness, in short, cannot be external merely; but this means that the character and being of the diverse is carried beyond and is beyond itself, and is the character of what is so beyond—and this is ideality.[1] Thus the unity of any felt whole in this sense is ideal, and the same is true emphatically of the identity in any spatial or temporal continuum. The parts there exist only so far as they are relative, determined from the outside, and themselves on the other hand passing each beyond itself and determining the character of the whole. And within each part again the parts are in the same way ideal. Nothing in fact can be more absurd than the common attempt to find the unity and continuity of the discrete in something outside the series. For if the discretes of themselves were not continuous,

---

[1] The union of aspects in each diverse aspect is, I admit, unintelligible for us in the end. But we are bound to hold that these aspects are really inseparable, and we are bound to deny that their union is external, for that is a standing contradiction.

certainly nothing else could make them so. But if of themselves
they are continuous, their continuity is ideal, and the same thing
holds *mutatis mutandis* of every kind of identity.

II. All identity then is qualitative in the sense that it all must
consist in content and character. There is no sameness of mere
existence, for mere existence is a vicious abstraction. And
everywhere identity is ideal and consists in the transcendence of
its own being by that which is identical. And in its main
principle and in its essence identity is everywhere one and the
same, though it differs as it appears in and between different
kinds of diversities. And on account of these diversities to
deny the existence of a fundamental underlying principle appears
to me to be irrational. But I would repeat that in my opinion
the variety cannot be shown as internally developed from the
principle, and even to attempt to set it out otherwise systematically is more than I can undertake. It may however perhaps
assist the reader if I add some remarks on temporal, and spatial,
and again on numerical identity, matters where there reigns,
I venture to think, a good deal of prejudice.

There is a disposition on the ground of such facts as space
and time to deny the existence of any one fundamental principle
of identity. And this disposition is hard to combat since it
usually fails to found itself upon any distinct principle. A tacit
alternative may be assumed between 'existence' and 'quality,'
and on this may rest the assertion that some sameness belongs to
mere existence, and falls therefore under a wholly alien principle.
But because not all identity is between qualities in one sense
of that term, it does not follow that any identity can fail to be
qualitative in a broader sense, and thus the whole alternative
disappears. The question in short whether one can really have
distinction without difference, or difference without diversity in
character, does not seem to have been considered.

Now we have just seen that space and time exemplify in their
characters the one principle of identity, since all their parts
are self-transcendent and are only themselves by making a whole.
And I will once more point out that, apart from distinctions
which, I presume, we must call qualitative, space and time do
not exist. In mere space or mere time there are no distinctions
nor any possibility of finding them. Without up and down, right
and left, incoming and outgoing, space and time disappear; and
it seems to me that these distinctions must be called qualitative.
And surely again time and space are real only in limited spaces
and durations. But what is it which limits and so makes a space
or a time, except that it ends here and not somewhere else, and
what does that mean except that its quality goes to a certain
point and then ceases by becoming another quality? There is
absolutely no meaning in "one time" unless it is the time of one
somewhat, and any time that is the time of one somewhat is so far

present and is one time.[1] And, if so, space and time are not alien from quality; and we have seen that their unity and identity is everywhere ideal.

I may be told, doubtless, that this is irrelevant, and I cannot say that it is not so, and I will pass rapidly to another point. I think it likely that the alleged chasm between quality and space and time may rest on the supposed absolute exclusivity of the two latter. If two things are the same or different by belonging to the same or different spaces or times, these same-nesses and differences, it will be said, are something quite apart and unique. They are not attributable to a 'what,' but merely to 'existence.' In meeting this objection I will permit myself to repeat some of the substance of Chapter xix.

Certainly the diversity of space, and again of time, has a character of its own. Certainly this character, though as we have seen it is nothing when bare, on the other hand is not merely the same with other characters and cannot be resolved into them. All this is true, but it hardly shows that the character of space or time is not a character, or that this character is not an instance of the one principle of identity in difference. And hence it is, I presume, the exclusiveness of space and time on which stress is to be laid. Now utterly exclusive the parts of space and time are admitted not to be, for, *ex hyp.*, they admit other characters and serve to differentiate them, and again one space or one time is taken to be the real identity of the other characters which it includes. Nor again can space and time be taken truly as barely external to the other qualities which they further qualify. They may remain so relatively and for our knowledge, just as in a qualitative whole the connection of qualities may remain relatively external. But a merely external qualification, we have seen, is but appearance and in the end is not rational or real (See Notes A and B).

The exclusiveness of a space or a time is to hold then, I presume, only against other times and spaces, and it is only as viewed in this one way that it is taken as absolute. Each part of space or time as against any other part is a repellent unit, and this its unity, and internal identity, is taken to lie merely in its 'existence.' But apparently here it is forgotten that the exclusive-ness depends on the whole. It is only because it is in 'this' series that the 'this' is unique, and, if so, the 'this,' as we have seen, is not merely exclusive but has a self-transcendent character. So that, if there were really but one series of space or of time, and if in this way uniqueness were absolute, I cannot perceive how that could found an objection against identity. For inside the series, even if unique, there is a unity and identity which is ideal, and

---

[1] I may refer on these points not only to this present work, but also to my *Principles of Logic*, pp. 50-55.

outside the series, if unique, there would be no exclusiveness in space or time, but simply in quality. And all this again is but hypothetical, since in space or time it is not true that there is really but one series, and any such idea is a superstition which I venture to think is refuted in this work.[1] There are many series in time and space, and the unity of all these is not temporal and spatial. And from this it follows that, so far as we know, there might be counterparts, one or more, of anything existing in space or in time, and that, considered spatially or temporally, there would be between these different things absolutely no difference at all nor any possibility of distinction. They would differ of course, and their respective series would differ, but that difference would not consist in space or time but merely in quality.[2] And with this I will end what I have to say here on the chimæra of a difference in mere 'existence.'

And obviously, as it seems to me, the objector to identity advances nothing new, when he brings forward the continuity of a thing in space or in time. The idea I presume is, as before, that in space or time we have a form of identity in difference which is in no sense an identity of character, but consists merely of 'existence,' and that a thing is qualified by being placed externally in this form. But the mere external qualification by the form, and the 'existence' of a form or of anything else which is not character, we have seen are alike indefensible; and, when the principle is refuted, it would seem useless to insist further on detail. Hence, leaving this, I will go on to consider a subsidiary mistake.

For the identity in time of an existing thing (as in this work I have mentioned) you require both temporal continuity and again sameness in the thing's proper character. And *mutatis mutandis* what is true here about temporal continuity is true also about spatial, and not to perceive this would be an error. Now whether a wholly unbroken continuity in time or space is requisite for the singleness of a thing, is a question I here pass by;[3] but some unbroken duration obviously is wanted if there is to be duration at all. And the maintenance of its character by the thing seems to me also to be essential. The character of course may change, but this change must fall outside of that which we take to be the thing's essential quality. For otherwise *ipso facto* we have a breach in continuity. And, though this matter may seem self-

---

[1] See Chapter xviii, and cf. *Mind*, N.S., No. 14. On the subject of uniqueness I would refer also to my *Principles of Logic*, Book I, Chap. ii.

[2] This holds again of my 'real' series in space or time. The foundation and differential character of that series lies, so far as I can see, in my special personal feeling, which, I presume, is qualitative. And I repeat here that, so far as we can know, there might be one or more exact duplicates of myself which would of course differ, but the differences of which would lie in some character falling outside what is observed by us.

[3] See p. 313 and the Note.

evident, I have noticed with regard to it what strikes me as at least a want of clearness.

What, let us ask, is a breach in the continuous existence of a thing? It does not lie in mere 'existence,' for that is nothing at all; and it cannot again be spatial or temporal merely, for a breach there is impossible. A time, for instance, if really broken, would not be a broken time, but would have become two series with no temporal relation, and therefore with no breach. A breach therefore is but relative, and it involves an unbroken whole in which it takes place. For a temporal breach, that is, you must have first one continuous duration. Now this duration cannot consist, we have seen, of bare time, but is one duration because it is characterized throughout by one content—let us call it A. Then within this you must have also another content —let us call it b; only b is not to qualify the whole of A, but merely a part or rather parts of it. The residue of A, qualified not by b but by some other character which is negative of b, is that part of duration which in respect of b can constitute a breach. And the point which I would emphasize is this, that apart from qualification by one and the same character b, and again partial qualification by another character hostile to b, there is simply no sense or meaning in speaking of the duration of b, rather than that of something else, or in speaking of a temporal end to or of a breach in $b's$ existence. The duration of a thing, unless the thing's quality is throughout identical, is really nonsense.

I do not know how much of the above may to the reader seem irrelevant and useless. I am doing my best to help him to meet objections to the fundamental sameness of all identity. These objections, to repeat, seem to me to rest on the superstition that, because there are diverse identities, these cannot have one underlying character, and the superstition again that there is a foreign existence outside character and with a chasm between the two. Such crude familiar divisions of common sense are surely in philosophy mere superstitions. And I would gladly argue against something better if I knew where to find it.

But, despite my fear of irrelevancy, I will add some words on 'numerical' identity and difference. I venture to think this in one way a very difficult matter. I do not mean that it is difficult in principle, and that its difficulty tends to drive one to the sameness and difference of mere 'existence,' or to distinction without difference, or to any other chimæra. If indeed we could assume blindly, as is often assumed, that the character of numerical sameness is at bottom temporal or spatial, there would be little to say beyond what has been said already.

Numerical distinction is not distinction without difference, for that once more is senseless, but it may be called distinction that abstracts from and disregards any special difference. It may be called the residual aspect of distinctness without regard for its 'what' and 'how.' Whether the underlying difference is temporal, spatial, or something else, is wholly ignored so long as it distinguishes. And, wherever I can so distinguish, I can *as a matter of fact* count, and am possessed of units. Units proper doubtless do not exist apart from the experience of quantity, and I do not mean to say that apart from quantity no distinction is possible, or again that quantity could be developed rationally from anything more simple than itself. And I have emphasized the words 'as a matter of fact' in order to leave these questions on one side, since they can be neglected provisionally. Numerical sameness, in the same way, is the persistence of any such bare distinction through diverse contexts, no matter what these contexts are. And of course it follows that, so long as and so far as sameness and difference are merely numerical, they are not spatial or temporal, nor again in any restricted sense are they qualitative.

But then ensues a problem which to me, rightly or wrongly, seems an extremely hard one. In fact my difficulty with regard to it has led me to avoid talking about numerical sameness. I have preferred rather to appear as one of those persons (I do not think that we can be many) who are not aware of or who at least practically cannot apply this familiar distinction. And my difficulty is briefly this. Without difference in character there can be no distinction, and the opposite would seem to be nonsense. But then what in the end is that difference of character which is sufficient to constitute numerical distinction? I do not mean by this, What in the end is the relation of difference to distinction? But, setting that general question here on one side, I ask, In order for distinction to exist, what kind or kinds of diversity in character must be presupposed? Or again we may put what is more or less the same question thus, What and of what sort is the minimum of diversity required for numerical difference and sameness, these being taken in the widest sense? And to this question I cannot return a satisfactory answer.

It is easy of course to reply that all distinction is at bottom temporal, or again that all is spatial, or again perhaps that all is both. And I am very far from suggesting that such views are irrational and indefensible. As long as they do not make a vicious abstraction of space and time from quality, or attempt to set up space and time as forms of 'existence' and not of character, there is nothing irrational in such views. But whether they are right or wrong, in either case to me they are useless, while they remain assertions which take no account of my difficulties. And the main difficulty to me is this. In feeling I find as a fact wholes of diversity in unity, and about some of these wholes I can discover nothing temporal or spatial. In this I may doubtless be wrong, but to me this is how the facts come. And I ask why it is impossible that a form or forms of non-temporal and non-spatial identity in difference should serve as the basis of, and should underlie, some distinction. It may be replied that without at least succession in time one would never get to have distinction at all. Yet if in fact this is so—and I do not contest it—I still doubt the conclusion. I am not sure that it follows, because without succession comes no distinction, that all distinction, when you have got it, must be in its character successive. The fact of non-temporal and non-spatial diversity in unity *seems* at least to exist. The distinctions which I can base on this diversity have, to me at least, in some cases no discoverable character of time or space. And the question is whether the temporal (or, if you will, the spatial) form, which we will take as necessary for distinction in its origin, must essentially qualify it. Is it not possible that, however first got, the form of distinction may become at least in some cases able to exist through and be based on a simpler and non-temporal scheme of diversity in unity? This strikes me as a difficult issue, and I do not pretend here to decide it, and I think it calls for a more careful enquiry than many persons seem inclined to bestow on it.[1] And this is all that I think it well to say on numerical identity.

But on the main question, to return to that, I do not end in doubt. There are various forms of identity in diversity, not logically derivable from one another, and yet all instances and developments of one underlying principle. The idea that mere 'existence' could be anything, or could make anything the same or different, seems a sheer superstition. All is not quality in the special sense of quality, but all is quality in the sense of content and character. The search for a 'that' other than a 'what' is the pursuit of a phantasm which recedes the more the more you approach it. But even this phantasm is the illusory show of a truth. For in the Absolute there is no 'what' divorced from and re-seeking its 'that,' but both these aspects are inseparable.

III. I think it right to add here some remarks on Resemblance, though on this point I have little or nothing new to say. Resemblance or Similarity or Likeness, in the strict sense of the term, I take to be the perception of the more or less unspecified

---

[1] The question, Has all distinction a temporal or spatial character? does not mean here, Have the only distinctions we can make, or the earliest distinctions we come to make, such a character in themselves *for us* and *as distinct?* This question I should answer without hesitation in the negative. The question as to which I am in doubt concerns not directly the object to which we attend, but the psychical machinery of distinction which we do not notice, but which I at least assume must be there and must in some sense qualify the object. There are some remarks on space as the one ground of distinction in *Mind*, N.S. No. 14, pp. 232-3. The case for space is, so far as I understand it, anything but strong.

identity (sameness) of two distinct things. It differs from identity in its lowest form—the identity, that is, where things are taken as the same without specific awareness of the point of sameness and distinction of that from the diversity—because it implies the distinct consciousness that the two things are two and different. It differs again from identity in a more explicit form, because it is of the essence of Resemblance that the point or points of sameness should remain at least partly undistinguished and unspecified. And further there is a special feeling which belongs to and helps to constitute the experience of similarity, a feeling which does not belong to the experience of sameness proper. On the other hand resemblance is based always on partial sameness; and without this partial sameness, which in its own undistinguishing way it perceives, there is no experience of resemblance, and without this to speak of resemblance is meaningless. And it is because of this partial identity, which is the condition of our experiencing resemblance and which resemblance asserts, that we are able within certain limits to use 'same' for 'like,' and to use 'like' for 'same.' But the specific feeling of resemblance is not itself the partial identity which it involves, and partial identity need not imply likeness proper at all.[1] But without partial identity, both as its condition and as its assertion, similarity is nothing.

From a logical point of view, therefore, resemblance is secondary, but this does not mean that its specific experience can be resolved into identity or explained by it. And it does not mean that, when by analysis you specify the point of sameness in a resemblance, the resemblance must vanish. Things are not made so simply as this. So far as you have analyzed, so far the resemblance (proper) is gone, and is succeeded so far by a perception of identity—but only so far. By the side of this new perception, and so far as that does not extend, the same experience of resemblance may still remain. And from this to argue that resemblance is not based on sameness is to my mind the strangest want of understanding. And again it is indifferent whether the experience of identity or that of resemblance is prior in time and psychologically. I am myself clear that identity in its lowest sense comes first; but the whole question is for our present purpose irrelevant. The question here is whether resemblance is or is not from a logical point of view secondary, whether it is not always based on identity, while identity need not in any sense be based on it.

I will now proceed to consider some objections that seem raised against this view, and will then go on to ask, supposing we deny it, in what position we are left. The first part of this task I shall treat very briefly for two reasons. Some of the

---

[1] See Note B.

A. R.

Q Q

objections I must regard as disposed of, and others remain to
me obscure. The metaphysical objection against the possibility
of any identity in quality may, I think, be left to itself; and
I will pass to two others which seem to rest on misunderstanding.
We are told, 'You cannot say that two things, which are like, are
the same, unless in each you are prepared to produce and to
exhibit the point of sameness.' I have answered this objection
already,[1] and will merely here repeat the main point. I want to
know whether it is denied that, before analysis takes place, there
can be any diverse aspects of things, and whether it is asserted
that analysis always makes what it brings out, or whether again
(for some reason not given) one must so believe in the power of
analysis as to hold that what it cannot bring out naked is therefore nothing at all, or whether again, for some unstated reason,
one is to accept this not as a general principle, but only where
sameness is concerned. When I know what I have to meet I
will endeavour to meet it, but otherwise I am helpless.[2] And
another objection, which I will now notice, remains also unexplained. The perception of a series of degrees, it seems
to be contended, is a fact which proves that there may be
resemblance without a basis of identity. I have tried to meet
this argument in various forms,[3] so far as I have been able to
understand them, and I will add here that I have pressed in
vain for any explanation on the cardinal point. Can you, I
would repeat, have a series of degrees which are degrees of
nothing, and otherwise have you not admitted an underlying
identity? And if I am asked, Cannot there be degrees in resemblance? I answer that of course there can be. But, if so, and
in this case, the resemblance itself is the point of identity of and
in which there are degrees, and how that is to show either that
there is no identity at all, or again that no identity underlies the
resemblance, I cannot conjecture. I admit, or rather I urge and
insist, that the perception of a series is a point as difficult as in
psychology it is both important and too often neglected. But on
the other side I insist that by denying identity you preclude
all possibility of explaining this fact, and have begun by turning
the fact into inexplicable nonsense. And no one, I would add,
can fairly be expected to answer an objection the meaning of
which is not stated.[4]

[1] See p. 348 and the Note thereto.
[2] I observe that Mr. Hobhouse appears (p. 109) to endorse this objection,
but he makes no attempt, so far as I see, to explain or justify it. And as he
also appears not to be prepared to deny that sameness always underlies resemblance, his position here and in some other points is to me quite obscure.
[3] p. 348 and Note.
[4] Whether Mr. Hobhouse is to be taken again as endorsing this objection I
am quite unable to say. The argument, on p. 112 of his book, I to my regret
have 'not been able to follow, and it would be unprofitable to criticise it in a
sense which it probably may not bear. But I have been able to find nothing

Passing from this point let us ask what is the alternative to identity. If we deny sameness in character and assert mere resemblance, with what are we left? We are left, it seems to me, in confusion, and end with sheer nonsense. How mere resemblance without identity is to qualify the terms that resemble, is a problem which is not faced, and yet unsolved it threatens ruin. The use of this mere resemblance leads us in psychology to entertain gross and useless fictions, and in logic it entails immediate and irretrievable bankruptcy. If the same in character does *not* mean the same, our inferences are destroyed and cut in sunder, and in brief the world of our knowledge is dissolved.[1]

And how is this bankruptcy veiled? How is it that those who deny sameness in character can in logic, and wherever they find it convenient, speak of terms as 'the same,' and mention 'their identity,' and talk of 'one note' and 'one colour'? The expedient used is the idea or the phrase of 'exact likeness' or 'precise similarity.' When resemblance is carried to such a point that perceptible difference ceases, then, I understand, you have *not really* got sameness or identity, but you can speak as if you had got it. And in this way the collision with language and logic is avoided or rather hidden.

What in principle is the objection to this use of 'exact likeness'? The objection is that resemblance, if and so far as you make it 'exact' by removing all internal difference, has so far ceased to be mere resemblance, and has become identity. Resemblance, we saw, demands two things that resemble, and it demands also that the exact point of resemblance shall not be distinguished. This is essential to resemblance as contradistinguished against identity, and this is why—because you do not know what the point of resemblance is and whether it may not be complex — you cannot in logic use mere resemblance as sameness. You can indeed, we also saw, while analyzing still retain your perception of resemblance, but, so far as you analyze, you so far have got something else, and, when you argue, it is not the resemblance which you use but the point of resemblance, if at least your argument is logical. But a point of resemblance is clearly an identity. And it is, we saw,

that looks like an attempt to deal with the real issue involved here. Can you have degrees which are degrees of nothing, and can you have a resemblance where there is no point of resemblance? The apparent contention that because relations of quantity and degree do not consist in bare identity, they therefore must consist in mere resemblance without any identity, I cannot comprehend. Why are we forced to accept either? But I must not attempt to criticise where I have failed to understand.

[1] The position of Mr. Hobhouse here, who appears on the one hand to deny all identity of quality or character, and yet on the other hand appears not to be willing to assert that resemblance without a basis of identity is possible, I may repeat does not seem intelligible.

the double sense of the word 'likeness,' which seems to authorize this use of likeness for sameness. Likeness may mean my specific experience of resemblance—and that of course itself is not identity—or it may mean the real partial sameness in character of two things whether to me they resemble or not. Thus 'exact likeness' can be used for the identical character which makes the point of likeness, and it need not mean the mere likeness which can be opposed to identity. And where exact likeness does *not* mean the identical character, bankruptcy at once is patent.[1]

We are warned, "You must not say that two notes are the same note, or that two peas have the same colour, for that is to prove yourself incompetent to draw an elementary distinction ; or rather you may say this with us, if with us you are clear that you do not mean it, but mean with us mere resemblance." And when we ask, Are the notes and colours then really different? we hear that 'the likeness is exact.' But with this I myself am not able to be satisfied. I want to know whether within the character of the sounds and within the character of the colours there is asserted any difference or none. And here, as I understand it, the ways divide. If you mean to deny identity, your one consistent course is surely to reply, "Of course there is a difference. I know what words mean, and when I said that it was *not* the same but *only* alike, I meant to assert an internal diversity, though I do not know exactly what that is. Plainly for me to have said in one breath, The character has no difference and yet it is not the same character, would have been suicidal." And this position, I admit, is so far self-consistent ; but it ends on all sides in intellectual ruin. But the other way, so far as I understand it, is to admit and to assert that in exact likeness there is really no difference, to admit and to assert that it involves a point of resemblance in which internally no diversity is taken to exist, and which we use logically on the understanding that divergence of character is excluded—and then, on the other side, to insist that here we still have no

---

[1] I may perhaps be allowed to illustrate the above by an imaginary dialogue. "Is that piece of work the same?" "Well, it's exactly like." "You're sure?" "Oh yes, it's identical, it's a *fac-simile.*" "H'm, it *looks* exactly like, but, as I've examined the other, I'd rather take that, though I dare say there's really no difference." The "looking exactly like," the producing the same impression, implies of course a real identity in the two things, but as I do not know what that is, I do not know if it is what I want. It is this ambiguity of 'likeness' which gave its plausibility to J. S. Mill's doctrine of reasoning from particular to particular, and it is this again which has enabled Mr. Hobhouse (pp. 280-5) to represent that Mill's doctrine, once held to be original and revolutionary, consists really in the view that you *never* do proceed direct from particular to particular, but *always* through a universal. The task that still awaits Mr. Hobhouse is the proof that, when Mill talked of Association by Similarity, he always meant nothing whatever but Redintegration through identity. But I am not persuaded after all that Mill must have been a prophet because he has at last found a disciple to build his sepulchre.

sameness but only likeness. And with this, so far as I can see, there is an end of argument. I can myself understand such an attitude only as the result of an unconscious determination to deny a doctrine from fear of its consequences.

But if we are to look at consequences—and I am ready to look at them—why should we be blind on one side? To avoid confusion between what may be called individual sameness and mere identity of character, we should of course all agree, is most desirable. But the idea that you will avoid a mistake by making an error, that you will prevent a confusion between different kinds of identity by altogether denying one kind, seems to me to be irrational. The identity that you deny will in practice come back always. It may return in a form genuine but disguised, obscured and distorted by the deceptive title of exact likeness. But on the other hand it may steal in as an illusive and disastrous error. And we need not seek far to find an instructive illustration of this. J. S. Mill may be called, I presume, the leader of those who amongst us deny identity of quality, and J. S. Mill on the other hand taught Association by Similarity. At least we must say this until it has been proved here—as elsewhere with regard to the argument from particulars—that we who criticise Mill know no more of his real meaning than in fact Mill himself did. And Association by Similarity, as taught by Mill and his school, entails (as I have proved in my *Principles of Logic*) and really asserts the coarsest mythology of individual Resurrection. And I do not think that the history of philosophy can exhibit a grosser case of this very confusion against which we who believe in identity are so specially warned. Yes, you may try to drive out nature, and nature (as the saying goes) will always come back, but it will not always come back as nature. And you may strive to banish identity of character, and identity always will return, and it will not always return in a tolerable form. The cardinal importance of the subject must be my excuse for the great length of this Note, and for my once more taking up a controversy which gives me no pleasure, but which I feel I have no right to decline.

EXPLANATORY NOTES.

Page 15. The action of one part of the body on another percipient part may of course be indirect. In this case what is perceived is not the organ itself but the effect of the organ on another thing. The eye seen by itself in a mirror is an illustration of this.

p. 18. Compare here the Note to chapter xxi.

p. 22. For the "contrary" see Note A, and for "external relations" see Note B.

Chapter iii. In this chapter I have allowed myself to speak of 'relations' where relations do not actually exist. This and some other points are explained in Note B. The reader may compare pp. 141–3.

p. 30. The Reals to which I am alluding here are Herbart's.

p. 36. By a "solid" I of course here merely mean a unit as opposed to a collection or aggregate.

p. 48. On the connection between quality and duration, cf. Note C.

p. 51. "Ideas are not what they mean." For some further discussion on this point see *Mind*, N.S. IV, p. 21 and pp. 225 foll.

p. 53. A difficulty which might have been included in this chapter, is the problem of what may be called the Relativity of Motion. Has motion any meaning whatever except as the alteration of the spatial relation of bodies? Has it the smallest meaning apart from a plurality of bodies? Can it be called, to speak strictly, the *state* either (*a*) of one single body or (*b*) of a number of bodies? On the other hand can motion be predicated of anything apart from and other than the bodies, and, if not, can we avoid predicating it of the bodies, and, if so, is it not their state, and so in some sense a state of each?

It would of course be easy to set this out antithetically in the form, Motion (*a*) is and (*b*) is not a state of body. The reader who takes the trouble to work it out will perhaps be profited.

The conclusion which would follow is that neither bodies nor their relations in space and time have, as such, reality. They are on each side an appearance and an abstraction separated from the whole. But in that whole, on the other hand, they cannot, as such, be connected intelligibly, and that whole therefore points beyond itself to a higher mode of being, in comparison with which it is but appearance.

The idea of the motion of a single body may perhaps (I am ignorant) be necessary in physics, and, if that is so, then in physics of course that idea must be rational and right. But, except as a working fiction of this kind, it strikes my mind as a typical instance of unnecessary nonsense. It is to me nonsense, because I use 'body' here to cover anything which occupies and has position in space, and because a bare or mere space (or time) which in itself has a diversity of distinct positions, seems to me quite unmeaning. And I call this nonsense unnecessary, because I have been unable to see either what is got by it, or how or why in philosophy we are driven to use it. The fact, if it is a fact, that this idea is necessary for the explanations of physics has, I would repeat, here no bearing whatever. For such a necessity could not show that the idea is really intelligible. And if, without it, the laws of motion are in their essence irrational, that does not prove, I imagine, that they become rational with it, or indeed can be made intrinsically rational at all. This, I would add, is in principle my reply to such arguments as are used by Lotze, *Metaphysik*, §§ 164, 165, and Liebmann, *Zur Analysis der Wirklichkeit*, pp. 113 foll. The whole idea, for instance, of a solitary sphere in space, to say nothing of its rotation and centrifugal force, is, considered metaphysically, I should say, a mere vicious abstraction and from the first totally inadmissible. And if without it the facts are self-contradictory, with it they still more deeply contradict themselves.

But, however that may be, I must be excused the remark that on such subjects it is perhaps not surprising that any man should come in the end to any result whatever, yet that in philosophy any man should use the idea of a single moving body, as if it were a thing self-evident and free from difficulty—this really surprises me.

Note to Chapter vi. I have left this chapter as it stood, though it would be very easy to enlarge it; but I doubt if any end would be obtained by insistence on detail. I will however in this Note call attention to one or two points.

(i) If the cause is taken as complex, there is a problem first as to the constitution of the cause itself. How are its elements united internally, and are they united intelligibly? How is it limited intelligibly so as to be distinct from the universe at

large? And, next, how does it become different in becoming
the effect, and does it do so intelligibly? And if it does *not*
become different, is there any sense in speaking of cause where
there is no change? I will return to this point lower down.

(ii) With regard to Continuity (p. 61) the point is simple, and
is of course the old difficulty urged once more. If cause is
taken as a temporal existence and has a being in time, how
can it have this unless it has some duration as itself? But, if it
has duration, then after a period it must either pass into the
effect for no reason, or else during the period it was not yet
the cause, or else the temporal existence of the cause is split
up into a series the elements of which, having no duration, do
not temporally exist, or else you must predicate of the one
cause a series of internal changes and call them its state—a course
which, we found all along, could not be rationally justified in
the sense of being made intelligible. It will of course be understood that these difficulties are merely speculative, and do not
necessarily affect the question of how the cause is to be taken in
practice.

(iii) I have really nothing to add in principle to the remark
on Identity (p. 58), but I will append some detail. It seems
to be suggested, *e.g.*, that the mere existence of a temporal thing
at one moment can be taken as the cause of its still continuing
to exist at the next moment, and that such a self-determined
Identity is intelligible in itself. To me on the contrary such an
idea is inconsistent and in the end quite meaningless, and I will
try to state the reason briefly. Identity in the first place (let me
not weary of repeating this after Hegel) apart from and not
qualified by diversity is not identity at all. So that without differences and qualification by differences this supposed thing would
not be even the same, continue or endure at all. The idea
that in time or in space there can be distinctions without any
differences is to my mind quite unmeaning, and the assertion
that anything can be successive in itself and yet merely the
same, is to me an absurdity. Again to seek to place either
the identity or the difference in mere 'existence' is, so far
as I can see, quite futile—mere existence being once more
a self-contradictory idea which ends in nonsense. This is all I
need say as to the continued identity of a thing which does
not change. But if it changes, then this thing becomes other
than it was, and you have to make, and you cannot make, its
alteration in the end intelligible. While, if you refuse to
qualify the thing by the differences of succession, you once
more contradict yourself by now removing the thing from
out of temporal existence.

In the same way we may briefly dispose of the idea that a
process may be intelligible up to a certain point, and may
therefore be taken as the cause of its own continuance in

the same character. Certainly if *per impossibile* you possibly
could have a self-contained intelligible process, that would be
the cause of its own continuance, though why it would be
so is quite another matter. But then such a process is, so far
as I can see, in principle impossible, and at all events I would
ask where it is found or how it could exist. To adduce as an
instance the motion of a single body in a straight line is to
offer that as self-contained, and in itself intelligible, which I
should have ventured to produce as perhaps the *ne plus ultra*
of external determination and internal irrationality. And I
must on this point refer to the remarks made in the Note to
p. 53.

Temporal processes certainly,· as they advance from this
extreme of mere motion in space and become more concrete,
become also more self-contained and more rational in an
increasing degree. But to say of any temporal process whatever that it is in the end self-intelligible is, so far as I can
perceive, a clear mistake. And if the succession which up to
a certain point it contains, is *not* intelligible, how could that,
if by some miracle it propagated itself, be used as a way of
making intelligible its own continuance?

It may perhaps prove instructive if we carry this discussion
somewhat further. There is, we have seen, no such thing
as a continuance without change or as a self-contained and
self-intelligible temporal process. But, it may be said, anyhow
the existence of something at a certain moment, or up to a
certain moment, is a rational ground for concluding to its
continued existence at the next moment. Now this I take
to be quite erroneous. I maintain on the contrary that no
ground could either be more irrational in itself or more wanting
in support from our ordinary practice. And first, by way of
introduction, let me dispose of any doubt based on the idea
of Possibility. The nature of our world is such that we see
every day the existence of finite things terminated. The
possible termination of any finite temporal existence is therefore suggested by the known character of things. It is an
abstract general possibility based on and motived by the known
positive character of the world, and it cannot therefore as a
possibility be rejected as meaningless. On the contrary, *so
far as it goes*, it gives some ground for the conclusion, 'This
existence will at this point be terminated.' And I will now
dismiss the general question as to mere possibility. But for
the actual continuance of a thing, so far as I see, no rational
argument can be drawn from its mere presence or its mere
continued duration in existence. To say, Because a thing is now
at one time it therefore must be at another time, or Because it
has been through one duration it therefore must be through
another duration, and to offer this argument, not as merely for

some other reason admissible, but as expressing a principle—strikes my mind as surprising. It is to me much as if a man asserted baldly, 'Because it is here now, therefore it will be there then,' and declared that no further reason either was or ought to be wanted. And that mere 'existence' should be a reason for anything seems difficult to conceive, even if we suppose (as we cannot) that mere existence is itself anything but a false, self-contradictory, and in the end meaningless abstraction.

But the true reason why we judge that anything will continue (whenever and wherever we so judge) is radically different. It is an inference based not on 'existence' but on ideal synthesis of content, and it concludes to and from an identity not of 'existence' but character. It rests in a word upon the Principle of Ideal Identity. If a thing is connected with my world now, and if I assume that my world otherwise goes on, I must apart from other reasons conclude that the thing will be there. For otherwise the synthesis of content would be both true and false. And, if in my world are certain truths of succession, then another mere context cannot make them false, and hence, apart from some reason to the contrary, the succession A-B-C must infallibly repeat itself, if there is given at any time either A or A-B. This is how through ideal identity we rationally judge and conclude to continuance, and to judge otherwise to my mind is wholly irrational. And I have ventured to dwell on this point because of the light it seems to throw on the consequences which may follow, when, rejecting the true principle of identity, we consciously or unconsciously set up in its place the chimæra of identity of mere existence.

I will add that, so far as we take the whole state of the world at any one moment as causally producing the whole state of the world at the next moment, we do so rationally only so far as we rest the succession on a connection of content, and because otherwise this connection would not be a true one, as we have taken it to be. We can only however make use of the above idea in the end on sufferance. For the state of the world would not really be self-contained, nor could the connection really in the end be intelligible. And again to take any temporal process in the Absolute as the Absolute's own process would be a fundamental error.

I will append to this Note a warning about the Principle of Ideal Identity. This principle does not of course guarantee the original truth or intelligibility of a synthesis, and it is a very serious misunderstanding to take it as used in this sense. It merely insists that any truth, because *not* existence, is therefore true everywhere *in* existence and through all changes of context. For Identity see further Notes B and C.

Note to Chapters vii *and* viii.—I have left these chapters unaltered, but I will ask the reader to remember that I am not urging that the ideas criticised are not perfectly valid and even objectively necessary. I am condemning them so far as they are taken as ultimate answers to the question, What is Reality?

p. 65. I am not saying that we may not have a sense and even a rudimentary perception of passivity without having any perception of activity in the proper sense. The question, raised on p. 97, as to the possible absence of an outside not-self in activity, applies with its answer *mutatis mutandis* to passivity also.

pp. 72–4. See Note to p. 48.

p. 79. As to what is and is not individually necessary we are fortunately under the sway of beneficent illusion. The one necessary individual means *usually* the necessity for an individual more or less of the same kind. But there is no need to enlarge on this point except in answer to some view which would base a false theoretical conclusion on an attitude, natural and necessary in practice, but involving some illusion.

p. 83. On Memory compare the passages referred to in the Index. That Memory, in the ordinary sense of the word, is a special development of Reproduction I take to be beyond doubt, and that Reproduction, in its proper sense, is Redintegration through ideal identity is to my mind certain. The nature of the psychological difference between the memory of the past on one side, and on the other side the imagination of the same or the inference (proper) thereto, is a question, I venture to think, of no more than average difficulty. It seems to me, in comparison with the problem of Reproduction in general (including the perception of a series), to be neither very hard nor very important. It is a matter however which I cannot enter on here. I have discussed the subject of Memory in *Mind*, N.S. Nos. 30 and 66.

I would add here that to assume the infallibility of Memory as an ultimate postulate, seems to me wholly superfluous, to say nothing of its bringing us (as it does) into collision with indubitable facts. There is of course a general presumption that memory is to be trusted. But our warrant for this general presumption is in the end our criterion of a harmonious system. Our world is ordered most harmoniously by taking what is remembered as being in general remembered truly, whatever that is to mean. And this secondary character of memory's validity is, I submit, the only view which can be reconciled with our actual logical practice.

Note to pp. 96–100. The view as to the perception of activity laid down in these pages has been criticised by Mr. Stout in his excellent work on Psychology, Vol. i, pp. 173–7. With regard to Mr. Stout's own account I shall not venture to comment on it here, partly because I have not yet been able to give sufficient attention to it, and partly because I do not take it to be offered as metaphysical doctrine. I shall confine myself therefore to some remarks in defence of my own position.

These pages, I must admit, were too short, and yet, if lengthened, I feared they would be too long; and it might have been better to have omitted them. But, after they have been censured, I cannot withdraw them; and I have left them, apart from a few verbal alterations, as they stood. The symbols that were perhaps misleading have, I hope, been amended. But I would ask the reader to depend less on them than on what follows in this Note.

With regard to the alleged confusion in my mind "between the fact of activity and the mere experience of being active on the one hand, and the idea or perception of activity on the other" (p. 174), I think that this confusion neither existed nor exists. I should have said on the other hand that, from first to last throughout this controversy, it was I that kept this distinction clearly in mind and strove in vain to get it recognized. This, right or wrong, is at least the view which the facts force me to take. The question, What is the content of activity as it appears to the soul at first, in distinction from it as it is for an outside observer, or for the soul later on? is exactly the question to which I failed throughout to get an intelligible reply. And if I myself in any place was blind to these distinctions—distinctions familiar even to the cursory reader of Hegel—that place has not yet been shown to me. But instead of going back on the past I will try at least to be explicit here.

(i) A man may take the view that there is an original experience of activity the content of which is complex and holds that which, when analyzed by reflection, becomes our developed idea of activity. Without of course venturing to say that this view is certainly false, I submit that we have no reason to believe it to be true.

(ii) A man may hold that we have an original experience which is not in itself complex nor has any internal diversity in its content. This experience, he may further hold, goes with (a) some or (b) all of those conditions, physical or psychical, which an outside observer would or might call an active state, and which the soul itself later would or might call so. And he may go on to maintain that this sensation or feeling (or call it what you will) is the differential condition, without the real or supposed presence of which no state, or no psychical state, would be called active at all.

Now this second doctrine is to my mind radically different from the first. Its truth or falsehood to my mind is an affair not of principle but of detail. Nay, to some extent and up to a certain point, I think it very probably is true. Why should there not be a sensation going with *e.g.* muscular contraction, or even possibly with what we may call the explosion of a psychical disposition? Why should this sensation not always colour our perception of activity (when we get it), so that without this sensation the perception would be something different, something that would fail, I will not say essentially in being what we call activity, but fail so far that we might no longer recognize it as being the same thing? This, so far as I see, may all be true to an extent which I do not discuss; and the same thing may hold good *mutatis mutandis* about passivity.

But on this comes a distinction—the distinction which Mr. Stout says that I have overlooked, and which I on the contrary claim to have preached in vain—the distinction between the psychical fact itself and what that becomes for reflection. A sensation or feeling or sense *of* activity, as we have just described it, is not, looked at in another way, an experience *of* activity at all. If you keep to it it tells you nothing, just as pleasure and pain, I should add, tell you nothing. It is a mere sensation, shut up within which you could by no reflection get the idea of activity. For that is complex, while within the sensation there is given no diversity of aspects, such as could by reflection be developed into terms and relations. And therefore this experience would differ, I presume, from an original sense of time, which I may in passing remark is neither asserted nor denied on page 206 of my book. It would differ because such a sense of time has, I understand, from the first in its content an internal diversity, while diversity is absent from the experience of activity, as we now are considering it. In short whether this experience is or is not later on a character essential to our perception and our idea of activity, it, as it comes first, is not in itself an experience of activity at all. It, as it comes first, is only so for extraneous reasons and only so for an outside observer.

This is all I think it well to say here on the head of confusion. But, before proceeding to consider the charge of inconsistency brought against me, I will venture to ask a question of the reader. Can any one tell me where I can find an experimental enquiry into the particular conditions under which in fact we feel ourselves to be active or passive? I find, for instance, Mr. Stout stating here and there as experienced facts what I for one am certainly not able to find in my experience. And if any one could direct me to an investigation of this subject, I should be grateful. I am forced at present to remain in doubt about much of the observed facts. I am led even to wonder whether we have here a difference only in the observations or in the observers also, a difference, that is, in the actual facts as they exist diversely in various subjects.

I will turn now to the special charge of inconsistency. For activity I take the presence of an idea to be necessary, and I point out then that in some cases there is not what would be commonly called an idea. But I go on to distinguish between an idea which is explicit and one which is not so. Now certainly, if by this I had meant that an idea was not actually present but was present merely somehow potentially, I should have merely covered a failure in thought by a phrase, and Mr. Stout's censure would have been just. But my meaning was on the contrary that an idea is always present actually, though an idea which many persons (in my opinion wrongly) would not call an idea. Many persons would refuse to speak of an idea unless they had something separated in its existence from a sensation, and based on an image or something else, the existence of which is distinguished from the existence of the sensation. And this separated idea I called (perhaps foolishly) an explicit idea, and I opposed it to the idea which is a mere qualification of sensation or perception — a qualification inconsistent with that sensation as existing, and yet possessed of no other psychical existence, such as that of an image or (as some perhaps may add) of a mere word. And I referred to a discussion with regard to the presence of an idea in Desire, where the same distinction was made.[1] This distinction I would remark further is in my judgment essentially required for the theory of reasoning, and indeed for a just view as to any aspect of the mind. And, not being originated by me at all, much less was it invented specially for the sake of saving any doctrine of mine about the nature of activity.

Let us take the instance, given by Mr. Stout, of a child or other young animal desiring milk. The perception, visual and otherwise, of the breast or teat suggests the sucking, but that sucking I take to qualify the perception and not to be an image apart. The breast becomes by ideal suggestion the breast sucked, while on the other hand by some failure of adjustment the breast is not sucked in fact. The perceived breast is therefore at once qualified doubly and inconsistently with itself, and the self of the animal also is qualified doubly and inconsistently. That self is both expanded by ideal success and contracted by actual failure in respect of one point, *i.e.* the sucking. And so far as the expansion, under the whole of the above conditions, becomes actual, we get the sense of activity. And there actually is an idea present here, though there is no image nor anything that could properly be called forethought.

Or take a dog who, coming to some grassy place, begins to run and feels himself to be active. Where is here the idea? It might be said that there is none, because there is no forethought nor any image. But this in my opinion would be an error, an error fatal to any sound theory of the mind. And I will

---

[1] *Mind*, No. 49, pp. 22-4. In once more referring the reader to this discussion I will ask him to delete the error "in" on p. 23, line 5.

briefly point out where the idea lies, without of course attempting to analyze fully the dog's complex state. The ground in front of the dog is a perception qualified on the one hand, not by images, but by an enlargement of its content so as to become "ground run over." It comes to the dog therefore at once as both "run over" and "not." And the "run over" is ideal, though it is not an explicit idea or a forethought or in any sense a separate image. Again the dog comes to himself as qualified by an actual running, supplemented by an ideal running over what is seen in front of him. In his soul is a triumphant process of ideal expansion passing over unbrokenly into actual fruition, the negative perception of the ground as "not run over" serving only as the vanishing condition of a sense of activity with no cloud or check of failure. This is what I meant by an idea which is not explicit, nor, except that the name is perhaps a bad one, do I see anything in it deserving censure. I should perhaps have done better to have used no name at all. But the distinction itself, I must repeat, is throughout every aspect of mind of vital importance.

But that I failed to be clear is evident, both from Mr. Stout's criticism and also from some interesting remarks by Professor Baldwin in the *Psychological Review*, Vol. i, No. 6. The relation of felt activity to desire, and the possibility of their independence and of the priority of one to the other, is to my mind a very difficult question, but I should add that to my mind it is not a very important one. I hope that both Mr. Stout and Professor Baldwin will see from the above that my failure was to some extent one merely of expression, and that our respective divergence is not as great as at first sight it might appear to be. As to the absence of felt self-activity in certain states of mind I may add that I am wholly and entirely at one with Professor Baldwin.

The above remarks are offered mainly as a defence against the charge of inconsistency, and not as a proof that the view I take of activity and of passivity is in general true. I must hope, in spite of many disappointments, to address myself at some time elsewhere to a further discussion of the perception no less of passivity than of activity. [See now *Mind*, Nos. 40, 41 and 46.]

p. 143. I have in this edition re-written pp. 141-3, since their statement was in some points wanting in clearness. The objection, indicated in the text, which would refute the plurality of reals by an argument drawn from the fact of knowledge, may be stated here briefly and in outline.

The Many not only are independent but *ex hyp.* are also known to be so ; and these two characters of the Many seem incompatible. Knowledge must somehow be a state of one or more of the Many, a state in which they are known to be plural ; for except in the Many where can we suppose that any knowledge falls? Even if relations are taken to exist somehow outside of the Many, the attempt to make knowledge fall merely in these relations leads to insoluble difficulties. And here, since the Many are taken to be the sole reality, such an attempt at escape is precluded. The knowledge therefore must fall somehow within the reals.

Now if the knowledge of each singly fell in each severally, each for itself would be the world, and there could nowhere be any knowledge of the many reals. But if, one or more, they know the others, such knowledge must qualify them necessarily, and it must qualify them reciprocally by the nature both of the known and of the knower. The knowledge in each knower—even if we abstract from what is known—seems an internal change supervening if not superinduced, and it is a change which cannot well be explained, given complete self-containedness. It involves certainly an alteration of the knower, and an alteration such as we cannot account for by any internal cause, and which therefore is an argument against, though it cannot disprove, mere self-existence. And in the second place, when we consider knowledge from the side of the known, this disproof seems complete. Knowledge apart from the known is a one-sided and inconsistent abstraction, and the assertion of a knowledge in which the known is not somehow and to some extent present and concerned, seems no knowledge at all. But such presence implies alteration and relativity in both knower and known. And it is in the end idle to strive to divide the being of the known, and to set up there a being-in-itself which remains outside and is independent of knowledge. For the being-in-itself of the known, if it were not itself experienced and known, would for the knower be nothing and could not possibly be asserted. Any knowledge which (wrongly) seems to fall outside of and to make no difference to the known, could in any case not be ultimate. It must rest on and pre-suppose a known the essence of which consists in being experienced, and which outside of knowledge is nothing. But, if so, the nature of the known must depend on the knower, just as the knower is qualified by the nature of the known. Each is relative and neither is self-contained, and otherwise knowledge, pre-supposed as a fact, is made impossible.

Suppose, in other words, that each of the Many could possess an existence merely for itself, that existence could not be known, and for the others would be nothing. But when one real becomes something for another, that makes a change in the being of each. For the relation, I presume, is an alteration of something, and there is by the hypothesis nothing else but the Many of which it could be the alteration. The knower is evidently and plainly altered; and, as to the known, if it remained unchanged, it would itself remain outside of the process, and it would not be with it that the knower would be concerned. And its existence asserted by the knower would be a self-contradiction.

Such is in outline the objection to a plurality of reals which can be based on the fact of knowledge. It would be idle to seek to anticipate attempts at a reply, or to criticise efforts made to give existence and ultimate reality to relations outside the reals. But I will venture to express my conviction that any such attempt must end in the unmeaning. And if any one seeks to turn against my own doctrine the argument which I have stated above, let me at least remind him of one great difference. For me every kind of process between the Many is a state of the Whole in and through which the Many subsist. The process of the Many, and the total being of the Many themselves, are mere aspects of the one Reality which moves and knows itself within them, and apart from which all things and their changes and every knower and every known is all absolutely nothing.

Note to pp. 155–8. I will add a few words in explanation of the position taken up in these pages, though I think the main point is fairly clear even if the result is unsatisfactory. If there is more pain than pleasure in the Universe, I at least could not call the Universe perfect. If on the other hand there is a balance of pleasure, however small, I find myself able to affirm perfection. I assume, on what I think sufficient ground, that pleasure and pain may in a mixed total state counterbalance one another, so that the whole state as a whole may be painful or pleasurable. And I insist that *mere* quantity has nothing whatever to do with perfection. The question therefore about pleasure and pain, and how far they give a quality to the Whole, may be viewed as a question about the overplus, whether of pain or pleasure. This I take to be the principle and the limit, and the criterion by which we decide against or for Optimism or Pessimism. And this is why we cannot endorse the charming creed of Dr. Pangloss, " Les malheurs particuliers font le bien général, de sorte que plus il y a de malheurs particuliers et plus tout est bien."

It is therefore most important to understand (if possible) the ultimate nature both of pleasure and pain, the conditions of both and also their effects. For I would add in passing that to suppose that anything could happen uncaused, or could have no effects at all, seems, at least to me, most absurd. But unfortunately a perfect knowledge about pain and pleasure, if attainable, is not yet attained. I am but very incompletely acquainted with the literature of the subject, but still this result, I fear, must be admitted as true. Mr. Marshall's interesting book on *Pleasure and Pain,* and the admirable chapter in Mr. Stout's *Psychology* both seem to me, the former especially, more or less to force their conclusions. And if, leaving psychology, we betake ourselves to abstract metaphysics, I do not see how we are able to draw any conclusions at all about pleasure or pain. Still, in general, though in this matter we have no proof, up to a certain point we possess, I think, a very strong probability. The compatibility of a balance of pain with general peace and rest of mind seems to me so improbable that I am inclined to give it but very little weight. But, this being granted, the question is whether it helps us to go forward. For it will be said, 'Admit that the Universe is such as not to be able to contradict itself in and for knowledge, yet why, none the less, should it not be loaded with a balance of misery and of practical unrest? Nay Hell itself, when once you have explained Hell, is for the intellect perfect, and itself is the intellect's Heaven.' But deferring for a moment the question about explanation, I make this reply. We can directly use the intellect pure, I believe, but indirectly the intellect I am sure is not pure, nor does any mere intellect exist. A merely intellectual harmony is an abstraction, and it is a legitimate abstraction, but if the harmony *were* merely intellectual it would be nothing at all. And, by an alteration in conditions which are not directly intellectual, you may thus indirectly ruin the intellectual world. Now this I take to be the case with our alleged possible surplus of pain. That surplus must, I consider, indirectly produce, and appear in the intellect as, a self-contradiction.

We can hardly suppose that in the Whole this balance of pain and unrest could go on quite unperceived, shut off from the intellect in some by-world of mere feeling or sensation. And, if it were so, the intellect itself would by this have been made imperfect. For, failing to be all-inclusive, it would have become limited from the outside and so defective, and so by consequence also internally discordant. The pain therefore must be taken to enter into the world of perception and thought; and, if so, we must assume it to show itself in some form of dislike, aversion, longing or regret, or in short as a mode of unsatisfied desire. But unsatisfied desire involves, and it must involve, an idea which at once qualifies a sensation and is discordant with it. The reader will find this explained above in the Note to pp. 96-100, as well as in *Mind*, No. 49. The apple, for instance, which you want to eat and which you cannot reach, is a presentation together with an ideal adjective logically contrary thereto ; and if you could, by a distinction in the subject of the inconsistent adjectives, remove this logical contradiction,[1] the desire so far also would be gone. Now in a total Universe which owns a balance of pain and of unsatisfied desire, I do not see that the contradiction inherent in this unsatisfied desire could possibly

[1] See Note A.

be resolved. The possibility of resolution depends (as we know) on rearrangement within the whole, and it presupposes that in the end no element of idea contrary to presentation is left outstanding. And if the Reality were *not* the complete identity of idea and existence, but had, with an outstanding element of pain, a necessary overplus of unsatisfied desire, and had so on the whole an element of outstanding idea not at one with sensation—the possibility of resolving this contradiction would seem in principle excluded. The collision could be shifted at most from point to point within the whole, but for the whole always it would remain. Hence, because a balance of pain seems to lead to unsatisfied desire, and that to logical collision, we can argue indirectly to a state at least free from pain, if not to a balance of pleasure. And I believe this conclusion to be sound.

Objections, I am well aware, will be raised from various sides, and I cannot usefully attempt to anticipate them, but on one or two points I will add a word of explanation. It will or may be objected that desire does not essentially involve an idea. Now though I am quite convinced that this objection is wrong, and though I am ready to discuss it in detail, I cannot well do so here. I will however point out that, even if conation without idea at a certain stage exists, yet in the Whole we can hardly take that to continue unperceived. And, as soon as it is perceived, I would submit that then it will imply both an idea and a contradiction. And, without dwelling further on this point, I will pass on to another. It has been objected that whatever can be explained is harmonious intellectually, and that a miserable Universe might be explained by science, and would therefore be intellectually perfect. But, I reply at once, the intellect is very far from being satisfied by a "scientific explanation," for that in the end is never consistent. In the end it connects particulars unintelligibly with an unintelligible law, and such an external connection is not a real harmony. A real intellectual harmony involves, I must insist, the perfect identity throughout of idea with existence. And if ideas of what should be, and what is not, were in the majority (as in a miserable Universe they must be), there could not then, I submit, be an intellectual harmony.

My conclusion, I am fully aware, has not been demonstrated (p. 534). The unhappiness of the world remains a possibility to be emphasized by the over-doubtful or gloomy. This possibility, so far as I see, cannot be removed except through a perfect understanding of, or, to say the least, about both pain and pleasure. If we had a complete knowledge otherwise of the world in system, such that nothing possible fell outside it, and if that complete system owned a balance of pleasure, the case would be altered. But since even then, so far as I can comprehend, this balance of pleasure remains a mere external fact, and is not and cannot be *internally* understood to qualify the system, the system would have to be in the completest sense all-inclusive and exhaustive. Any unknown conditions, such as I have admitted, on p. 535, would have to be impossible. But for myself I cannot believe that such knowledge is within our grasp; and, so far as pleasure is concerned, I have to end with a result the opposite of which I cannot call completely impossible.

p. 206. In what I have said here about the sense of Time, I am not implying that in my view it is there from the first. On the contrary I think the opposite is more probable; but I saw no use in expressing an opinion.

Chapter xviii. The main doctrines put forward in this Chapter and in Chapter iv, have been criticised incidentally by Professor Watson in the *Philosophical Review* for July and September 1895. In these articles I have to my regret often found it impossible to decide where Professor Watson is criticising myself, or some other writer, and where again he is developing something which he takes to be more or less our common property. And where he is plainly criticising myself, I cannot always discover the point of the criticism. Hence what follows must be offered as subject to some doubt.

The main doctrine to which I am committed, and which Professor Watson certainly condemns, is the regarding Time "as not an ultimate or true determination of reality but a 'mere appearance.'"[1] Professor Watson, with some other critics, has misunderstood the words 'mere appearance.'[2] The point he wishes to make, I presume, is this, that everything determines Reality in its own place and degree, and therefore everything has its truth. And I myself have also laid stress on this point. But, agreeing so far, Professor Watson and myself seem to differ as follows. Though he agrees that as a determination of Reality time is inadequate and partial and has to be corrected by something more true, Professor Watson objects to my calling it not an ultimate or true determination, and he denies that it is self-contradictory and false. Now here I have to join issue. I deny that time or anything else could possibly be inadequate, if it were not self-contradictory. And I would ask, If this or any other determination is a true and consistent one, how are we to take on ourselves to correct it? This doctrine of a merely external correction of what is not false, and this refusal to admit the internal inconsistency of lower points of view, though we have to attribute it to Professor Watson, is certainly not explained by him. I venture however to think that some explanation is required, and in the absence of it I must insist both that time is inconsistent, and that, if it were *not* so, it would also *not* be

---

[1] *Phil. Rev.* p. 489.   [2] See above pp. 557-8.

inadequate, and again that no idea can be inadequate if it is *not* more or less false. This is the main point on which Professor Watson and myself seem to differ.

In reply to detail it is hard for me to say anything where I so often fail to apprehend. As I do not hold "a pure continuous quantity" to be self-consistent, how, when time is regarded thus, am I affected? How is it relevant to urge that time "can be thought," when the question is whether it can be thought consistently, and surely not in the least whether it can be thought at all? And if it is so easy to understand that the idea of change is not really inconsistent, cannot Professor Watson formulate it for us in a way which is true and ultimate, and then explain what right he has to treat it as calling for correction? The objection—to turn to another point—raised against the doctrine of distinct time-series,[1] I am unable to follow. Why and how does this doctrine rest on the (obviously false) view of time's independent reality? Why, because time is an aspect of the one reality, must all series in time have a *temporal* unity? Why again must there be only one causal order? Where again and why am I taken as holding that "pure time" has direction? With regard to these criticisms I can only say that I find them incomprehensible.

Nor do I understand what in the end Professor Watson thinks about the ultimate truth of succession and change. The view of Reality as one self-consciousness realizing itself in many self-consciousnesses does not, so far as Professor Watson has stated it, appear to my mind to contain any answer whatever to this question. The many selves seem (we know) to themselves to be a succession of events, past, present and future. By a succession I do *not* of course mean a *mere* succession, but still I mean a succession. Well, all this birth and death, arising and perishing of individuals, is it ultimately true and real or is it not? For myself, I reply that it is not so. I reply that these successive individuals are an appearance, necessary to the Absolute, but still an appearance, self-inconsistent, mixing truth with falsehood, and—if and so far as you offer it by itself as the truth—then not the truth but a *mere* appearance. And I have answered this question as best I could, because it seemed to me a question that must be answered by any one who undertakes seriously to deal with the Absolute and the Time-process. And I do not say that Professor Watson has not answered this question at all. But, if he has answered it, I am myself unable to discover what his answer means.

On the subject of time the reader may consult with advantage a paper by Mr. Bosanquet in the *Proceedings of the Aristotelian Society*, Vol. iii, No. 2.

[1] *Phil. Rev.* p. 495.

pp. 253-4. With regard to the window-frame the possible objection which I had in my mind was the reply, 'But a frame surely is at least as real as a window-pane.' That objection, so far as I know, has not yet been made. I have however seen this urged, that, when limited transparencies are gone, we are left with empty space. But I cannot imagine why through my window should come nothing but white light, and I see nothing but blank space. Why *must* a transparent window, when I look through it, be a mere formless translucency?

p. 256. With regard to Redintegration—without wishing to commit myself to any decided view—I have assumed that to be fact which is generally taken to be so, viz., that among the members of a series there is reproduction only forwards, *i.e.* from *a* to *b* and not also from *b* to *a*. The first member in the series cannot therefore be recalled by any later member *directly*. This must be done indirectly and through the common character and the unity of the series. This character, because associated with the whole series inclusive of the end, can, given the end, recall the beginning. But in what this character and unity consists is a most difficult problem. It is a problem however which calls for treatment by any one who tries to deal systematically with the principles of psychology. It will be understood that in this Note I am speaking of mere serial reproduction, but that on the other hand I am not assuming that even reproduction forwards, from *a* to *b*, can be taken ultimately as merely direct.[1]

Chapter xxi. In Part III, Chapter iii, of Mr. Hobhouse's work on the *Theory of Knowledge*, I find an argument against "subjective idealism" which it may be well to consider briefly. The same argument would appear also suited, if not directed, to prove the reality of primary qualities taken as bare. And though this is very probably not intended, and though I find the argument in any case difficult to follow, I will criticise it, so far as I understand it, from both points of view.

The process seems to consist, as was natural, in an attempt at removal by elimination of all the conditions of a relation *A-B*, until *A-B* is left true and real by itself. And *A-B* in the present case is to be a relation of naked primary qualities, or again a relation of something apart from and independent of myself. After some assertions as to the possibility of eliminating in turn all other psychical facts but my perceptive consciousness—assertions which seem to me, as I understand them, to be wholly untenable and quite contrary to fact—the naked independence of *A-B* appears to be proved thus. Take a state of things where one term of the connection is observed, and the other is not observed. We have still here to infer the existence of the term unobserved, but an existence, *because* unobserved, free (let us say first) from all secondary qualities.

[1] Cf. *Mind*, N.S. No. 30, p. 7.

But I should have thought myself that the conclusion which follows is quite otherwise. I should have said that what was proved from the premises was not that $A-B$ exists naked, but that $A-B$, if unconditioned, is false and unreal, and ought never to have been asserted at all except as a useful working fiction. In other words the observed absence of one of the terms from its place, *i.e.* the field of observation, is not a proof that this term exists elsewhere, but is rather here a negative instance to disprove the assumed universal $A-B$, if that is taken unconditionally. Of course if you started by supposing $A-B$ to be unconditionally true, you would at the start have assumed the conclusion to be proved.

And, taken as directed against Solipsism, the argument once more is bad, as I think any argument against Solipsism must be, unless it begins by showing that the premises of Solipsism are in part erroneous. But any attempt at refutation by way of elimination seems to me even to be absurd. For in any observation to find in fact the absence of all Cœnesthesia and inner feeling of self is surely quite impossible. Nor again would the Solipsist lightly admit that his self was co-extensive merely with what at any one time is present to him. And if further the Solipsist admits that he cannot explain the course of outward experience, any more than he can explain the sequence of his inmost feelings, and that he uses all such abstract universals as your $A-B$ simply as useful fictions, how can you, by such an argument as the above, show that he contradicts himself? A failure to explain is certainly not always an inconsistency, and to prove that a view is unsatisfactory is not always to demonstrate that it is false. Mr. Hobhouse's crucial instance to prove the reality of $A-B$ apart from the self could to the Solipsist at most show a sequence that he was unable to explain.[1] How in short in this way you are to drive him out of his circle I do not see—unless of course he is obliging enough to contradict himself in advance by allowing the possibility of $A-B$ existing apart, or being real or true independently and unconditionally.

The Solipsist, while he merely maintains the essential necessity of his self to the Universe and every part of it, cannot in my opinion be refuted, and so far certainly he is right. For, except as a relative point of view, there is no apartness or independence in the Universe. It is not by crude attempts at elimination that

---

[1] The position of the Solipsist I understand to be this, that no reality or fact has any existence or meaning except the reality of his self. And when he is pressed as to an order of phenomena which he cannot explain, I do not see how *on and from his own premises* he is to be precluded from appealing to unknown conditions in his self. 'Surely,' he might reply, 'on any view no one can actually explain everything, and merely for the sake of explaining things somewhat better I decline to assert what is demonstrable nonsense.' And the only proper course is, as I have pointed out, to show that his premises are partly mistaken.

you can deal with the Solipsist, but rather (as in this chapter I have explained) by showing that the connection which he maintains, though really essential, has not the character which he assigns to it. You may hope to convince him that he himself commits the same fault as is committed by the assertor of naked primary qualities, or of things existing quite apart from myself—the fault, that is, of setting up as an independent reality a mere abstraction from experience. You refute the Solipsist, in short, by showing how experience, as he has conceived it, has been wrongly divided and onesidedly narrowed.

p. 268. On the question whether and how far psychical states are extended, see an article in *Mind*, N.S. No. 14.

p. 273. I would here request the reader's attention to the fact that, while for me "soul" and "finite centre" are not the same (p. 529), I only distinguish between them where it seems necessary.

p. 313. In the fourth line from the bottom of this page I have altered "the same. Or" into "the same, or." The full stop was, I presume, inserted by an error. In any case I have removed it, since it may lead some reader, if not careful, to take the words "we should call them the same" absolutely. This in fact I find has been done, but the meaning was not really, I think, obscure. I am in the first place not maintaining that no continuous existence at all is wanted for the individual identity of a soul or of anything else. On the contrary I have in several places asserted the opposite. I am speaking here merely of an interval and a breach in continuous existence. And I certainly am not saying that all of us would as a fact assert individual identity despite this breach or interval. I am pointing out that, whether we assert it or deny it, we are standing in each case, so far as I can see, on no defensible principle.

I am far from maintaining that my answer to the question, "What is the soul, especially during those intervals where there seems to be no consciousness," is wholly satisfactory. But willing and indeed anxious as I am to receive instruction on this matter from my critics, I cannot say that I have been able as yet to gain the smallest fresh light on it.

p. 333. Without entering here into detail, I will venture to make a remark which I cannot think quite uncalled-for. You cannot by making use of a formula, such as "psycho-physical parallelism"—or even a longer formula—absolve yourself from facing the question as to the causal succession of events in the body and the mind. When we say, for example, that the physical prick of a pin causes pain, is this assertion in any sense true or is it quite false? Is the pain not really to any extent, directly or indirectly, the effect of the prick? And, if it is not, of what else is it the effect, or can it again happen quite uncaused and itself be effectless? Clear answers to these questions are, I should say, more easily sought than found.

p. 348. On the question whether and in what sense difference depends on a relation, see Note B, and for a discussion of Resemblance, see Note C. The controversy, mentioned in the footnote to p. 348, was continued in *Mind*, N.S. Nos. 7 and 8, and I would venture to refer any reader interested in the matter to it.

p. 356. On the topic of Association holding only between universals the reader should consult Hegel, *Encyklopädie*, §§ 452–6.

pp. 363–4. The argument in these pages, the reader will observe, depends on the truth of certain doctrines. (*a*) A merely external relation has no meaning or existence, for a relation must (at least to some extent) qualify its terms. (*b*) Relations imply a unity in which they subsist, and apart from which they have no meaning or existence. (*c*) Every kind of diversity, both terms and relations alike are adjectives of one reality, which exists in them and without which they are nothing. These doctrines are taken as having been already proved both in the body of this work and in the Appendix.

From this basis we can go on to argue as follows. Everything finite, because somehow together in one whole with everything else, must, because this whole is one above the level of bare feeling, co-exist with the rest *at the very least* relationally. Hence everything must somehow, at least to some extent, be qualified from the outside. And this qualification, because *only* relational (to put it here in this way), cannot fall wholly inside the thing. Hence the finite is internally inconsistent with and contradicts itself. And whether the external qualification is merely conjoined in some unintelligible way to its inner nature, or is connected with that intrinsically—may for our present purpose be ignored. For anyhow, however it comes about, the finite as a fact will contradict itself.

From the side of the Whole the same result is manifest. For that is itself at once both any one finite and also what is beyond. And, because no 'together' can in the end be merely external, therefore the Whole within the finite carries that outside itself.

By an attempt to fall back upon mere feeling below relations nothing would be gained. For with the loss of the relations, and with the persistence of the unity, even the appearance of independence on the part of the diversity is gone. And again feeling is self-transcendent, and is perfected mainly by way of relations, and always in a Whole that both is above them and involves them (P. 583).

The way to refute the above would be, I presume, to show (*a*) that merely external relations have in the end, and as ultimate facts, a meaning and reality, and to show (*b*) that it is possible to think the togetherness of the terms and the external relations— for somehow, I suppose, they are together—without a self-contra- diction, manifest directly or through an infinite process of seeking relations between relations and terms.

p. 366, *footnote.* I may remark here that I am still persuaded that there is in the end no such thing as the mere entertainment of an idea, and that I, for example, went wrong when in my book on Logic I took this to exist. It see_m_s to be, on the contrary, the abstraction of an aspect which by itself does not exist. See *Mind*, N.S., No. 60.

p. 398, *footnote.* To the references given here add *Mind*, N.S., iv, pp. 20, 21 and pp. 225, 226.

Chapter xxiv. The doctrine of the Criterion adopted by me has in various quarters been criticised, but, so far, I venture to think, mainly without much understanding of its nature. The objections raised, for example, by Mr. Hobhouse, *Theory of Knowledge*, pp. 495-6, I cannot understand in any sense which would render them applicable. I will however in this con- nection make some statements which will be brief, if perhaps irrelevant.

(i) I have never held that the criterion is to be used apart from, instead of on, the data furnished by experience. (ii) I do not teach that, where incompatible suggestions are possible, we must or may affirm any one of them which we fail to perceive to be internally inconsistent. I hold on the contrary that we must use and arrange *all* available material (and that of course includes every available suggestion) so that the reality qualified by it all will answer, so far as is possible, to our criterion of a harmonious system. On this point I refer specially to Chapters xvi, xxiv, and xxvii, the doctrines of which, I venture to add, should not be taken as non-existent where my views are in question. (iii) I do not think that where a further alternative is possible a disjunc- tion is complete. But I have always held, and do hold, J. S. Mill's idea of the Unmeaning as a third possibility to be the merest nonsense. (iv) I do not admit but deny the assumption that, if our knowledge could be consistent, it could then be made from the outside to contradict itself. (v) And I reject the idea that, so far as our knowledge is absolute, we can rationally enter- tain the notion of its being or becoming false. Any such idea, I have tried to show, is utterly unmeaning. And on the other hand, so far as our knowledge is liable to error, it is so precisely so far as it does not answer to the criterion. (vi) Finally I would submit that the sense in which this or that writer uses such principles as those of Identity and Contradiction, and the way in which he develops them, cannot always safely be assumed *à priori* by any critic.

This is all I think it could be useful for me to say in this connection, except that I would end this Note with an expression of regret. The view adopted by Mr. Hobhouse as to the nature of the criterion has, it seems to me (I dare say quite wrongly), so very much that is common to myself, as well as also to others,[1] that I am the more sorry that I have not the advantage of his criticism on something which I could recognize as in any degree my own.

p. 407, *Footnote.* On the subject of Hedonism I would add references to the *International Journal of Ethics*, Vol. iv, pp. 384–6 and Vol. v, pp. 383–4.

pp. 458–9. We cannot, if we abstract the aspects of pleasure and pain and confine ourselves to these abstractions, discover directly within them an internal discrepancy, any more than we could do this in every abstracted sensible quality. But since these aspects are as a fact together with, first, their sensible qualities and, next, the rest of the world, and since no relation or connection of any kind can be in the end merely external, it follows that in the end the nature of pleasure or pain must somehow go beyond itself.[2]

If we take pleasure and pain, or one of them, to be not aspects of sensation but themselves special sensations, that will of course make no real difference to the argument. For in any case such sensations would be mere aspects and adjectives of their whole psychical states. I would add that, even in psychology, the above distinction seems, to me at least, to possess very little importance. The attempt again to draw a sharp distinction between discomfort and pain would (even if it could be successful) make no difference to us here.

p. 463, *Note.* The account of Will, given in *Mind*, No. 49, has been criticised by Mr. Shand in an interesting article on Attention and Will, *Mind*, N.S. No. 16. I at once recognized that my statement in the above account was defective, but in principle I have not found anything to correct. I still hold Will always to be the self-realization of an idea, but it is necessary to provide that this idea shall not in a certain sense conflict with that which

---

[1] Mr. Hobhouse seems to me (I suppose mistakenly) to adopt somehow in the end, as the criterion of truth and reality, the idea of a consistent all-inclusive system. If and so far as he does this, I naturally think he is right, but I think he would be wrong if and so far as he simply assumed this principle as ultimate. But as to what his view in the end actually is I could not venture an opinion, partly perhaps because I have been able to give but a limited time to his work.

[2] Cf. the Note on p. 363, and Notes A and B of this Appendix.

in a higher sense is identified with the self. By 'higher' I do *not* mean 'more moral,' and I am prepared to explain what I do mean by the above. I would on this point refer to an article by Mr. Stout (in *Mind*, N.S. No. 19) with which I find myself largely though not wholly in agreement. I must however hope at some future time to deal with the matter, and will here state my main result. "It is will where an idea realizes itself, provided that the idea is not formally contrary to a present resolve of the subject"—so much seems certain. But there is uncertainty about the further proviso, "Provided also that the idea is not too contrary materially-to the substance of the self." Probably, the meaning of "will" being really unfixed, there is no way of fixing it at a certain point except arbitrarily.

Since the above was written an enquiry into the nature of volition, with a discussion of many questions concerning conation, activity, agency, and attention, has appeared in *Mind*. See Nos. 40, 41, 43, 44, 46, 49, and parts of 51.

p. 513. With regard to the "familiar Greek dilemma," the attentive reader will not have failed to observe that, when I later on, p. 544, maintain that no possible truth is quite true, I have explained that this want of truth is not the same thing as intellectual falsehood or fallibility. The "sceptical" critic therefore who still desires to show that I myself have fallen into this dilemma, will, I think, do well still to ignore pp. 544-7.

A probability, I may here go on to remark, of many millions to one against the truth of some statement may be a very good and sufficient reason for our putting that, for some purpose or purposes, on one side and so treating it as nothing. But no such probability does or can justify us in asserting the statement not to be true. That is not scepticism at all, but on the contrary it is mere dogmatism. Further I would here repeat that any probability in favour of general scepticism which rests on psychological grounds, must itself be based on an assumption of knowledge with regard to those grounds. Hence if you make your sceptical conclusion universal here, you destroy your own premises. And, on the other side, if you stop short of a universal conclusion, perhaps the particular doctrine which you wish to doubt is more certain by far than even your general psychological premises. I have (p. 137) remarked on this variety of would-be scepticism, and I find that a critic in the *Psychological Review*, Vol i, No. 3, Mr. A. Hodder, has actually treated these remarks as an attempted refutation on my part of scepticism in general. It probably did not occur to him that, in thus triumphantly proving my incompetence, he was really giving the measure of his own insight into the subject. With reference to another "sceptical"

criticism by another writer I may perhaps do well to emphasize
the fact that for me that which has no meaning is most certainly
not possible. I had, I even thought, succeeded in laying this
down clearly. See for instance p. 503.

p. 520. The reader will recall here that, so far as diversity
does not imply actual relations, it involves presence as a mere
aspect in a felt totality. See pp. 141-3 and Note B.

pp. 527-8. With regard to this question of some element of
Reality falling outside of finite centres I find but little to add.
The one total experience, which is the Absolute, has, as such, a
character which, in its specific aspect of qualitative totality, must
be taken not to fall within any finite centre. But the elements.
which in their unity make and are this specific "quality," need
not, so far as I see, to the least extent fall outside of finite
centres. Such processes of and relations between centres, as
more or less are not experienced by those particular centres,
may, for all we know, quite well be experienced by others.
And it seems more probable that in some form or other they
are so experienced. This seems more probable because it
appears to involve less departure from given fact, and because
we can find no good reason for the additional departure in the
shape of any theoretical advantage in the end resulting from
it. We may conclude then that there is no element in the
process of making all harmonious within the Absolute which
does not fall within finite centres. What falls outside, and is
over and above, is not the result but the last specific character
which makes the result what it is. But even if some of the
matter (so to speak) of the Absolute fell outside of finite centres,
I cannot see myself how this could affect our main result, or
indeed what further conclusion could follow from such a
hypothesis. The reader must remember that in the Absolute
we in any case allow perfections beyond anything we can know,
so long as these fall within the Absolute's general character.
And on the above hypothesis, so far as I see, we could not
go one single step further. It could not justify us in predicating
of the Absolute any *lower* excellence, *e.g.* self-consciousness or
will or personality, *as such*, and still less some feature alien to
the Absolute's general nature. But to predicate of the Absolute,
on the other hand, the highest possible perfection, is what in any
case and already we are bound to do.

INDEX.

The reader who finds this collection of references useless, as well as faulty and incomplete, is requested to treat it as non-existent.

A. R.

PRINTED BY
WILLIAM BRENDON AND SON, LTD.
PLYMOUTH, ENGLAND

CPSIA information can be obtained
at www.ICGtesting.com
Printed in the USA
BVOW01s0459151216
470762BV00008B/145/P